Inhumanities

Inhumanities is an unprecedented account of the ways Nazi Germany manipulated and mobilized European literature, philosophy, painting, sculpture, and music in support of its ideological ends. David B. Dennis shows how, based on the belief that the Third Reich represented the culmination of Western civilization, culture became a key propaganda tool in the regime's program of national renewal and its campaign against political, national, and racial enemies. Focusing on the daily output of the *Völkischer Beobachter*, the party's official organ and the most widely circulating German newspaper of the day, he reveals how activists twisted history, biography, and aesthetics to fit Nazism's authoritarian, militaristic, and anti-Semitic world views. Ranging from National Socialist coverage of Germans such as Luther, Dürer, Goethe, Beethoven, Wagner, and Nietzsche to "great men of the Nordic West" such as Socrates, Leonardo, and Michelangelo, he reveals the true extent of the regime's ambitious attempt to reshape the "German mind."

David B. Dennis is Professor of History at Loyola University Chicago. He is the author of *Beethoven and German Politics, 1870–1989* (1996) and other works on the intersection of German culture and politics.

Inhumanities

Nazi Interpretations of Western Culture

David B. Dennis

CAMBRIDGE
UNIVERSITY PRESS

CAMBRIDGE UNIVERSITY PRESS
Cambridge, New York, Melbourne, Madrid, Cape Town,
Singapore, São Paulo, Delhi, Mexico City

Cambridge University Press
The Edinburgh Building, Cambridge CB2 8RU, UK

Published in the United States of America by Cambridge University Press, New York

www.cambridge.org
Information on this title: www.cambridge.org/9781107020498

First published 2012

Printed and bound in the United Kingdom by the MPG Books Group

A catalogue record for this publication is available from the British Library

Library of Congress Cataloging in Publication data
Dennis, David B., 1961–
Inhumanities : Nazi interpretations of western culture / David B. Dennis.
   p.   cm.
Includes bibliographical references and index.
ISBN 978-1-107-02049-8
1. Nazi propaganda – Germany.   2. Nationalsozialistische Deutsche Arbeiter-
Partei – Party work.   3. Völkischer Beobachter (Munich, Germany : 1920)
4.   Fascism and culture – Germany.   5. Germany – Civilization – 20th century.
6. Germany – History – 1918–1933.   7. Germany – History – 1933–1945.
8. Civilization, Western.   9. Press and politics – Germany – History – 20th
century.   10. World War, 1939–1945 – Propaganda.   I. Title.
DD254.D46   2012
909'.09821–dc23

2012015443

ISBN 978-1-107-02049-8 Hardback

To Mariko and Cecilia

*The worst readers are those who act like plundering soldiers:
they take a few things they can use, dirty and tangle up the
rest, and desecrate the whole.*

FRIEDRICH NIETZSCHE, Menschliches, allzumenschliches:
Ein Buch für freie Geister, *vol. 2, aph. 137*

*It is a fact of history that these ideas were embraced by many
normal men. It is important to keep in mind that the Nazis
found their greatest support among respectable, educated
people.*

GEORGE L. MOSSE, German Jews Beyond Judaism, *1*

CONTENTS

ILLUSTRATIONS

ACKNOWLEDGMENTS

It is fitting that a book about intersections between the best and worst of Western history was written through some of the most beautiful and some of the more challenging experiences that life offers. Of course, it could not be otherwise. Trying to adhere to the academic version of Beethoven's favorite maxim, "nulla dies sine linea," is the scholar's way, practiced to derive and share wonder for all that life brings. But as family, friends, and colleagues know, both joy and struggle arise on this path too. For sharing this way with me, I extend loving thanks to all my family and friends – both terms meant in the fullest sense. While reading this list of acknowledgments, please know that my gratitude for your care – manifested in so many ways – is beyond words.

At every stage of work on this project, I have had the compassionate support of my father, James M. Dennis, my brother, John Dennis, and my colleague, Robert Bucholz. Each of them has contributed pivotal advice about every aspect of the book, as well as counsel about how to manage the process through thick and thin. At a critical juncture, John Slavney proved himself a true friend in spirit and deed by closely reading and carefully editing the manuscript, adding insight, clarity, and polish to the whole. To each: my deepest thanks.

For constantly encouraging and inspiring me, on a warm personal level and as model scholars dedicated to the highest achievement in interdisciplinary research, writing, and teaching, I am profoundly grateful to Robert Wohl, Glenn Watkins, Otto Dann, and *in memoriam*, Eugen Weber and George L. Mosse.

For their ongoing comradeship and guidance in matters academic, technical, and existential, I am beholden to all my other colleagues at Loyola University Chicago, especially, but by no means limited to, Lew Erenberg, Tim Gilfoyle, Susan Hirsch, Konstantin Läufer, Brian Lavelle, Barbara Rosenwein, George Thiruvathukal, and *in memoriam*, Paul Messbarger and Joe Gagliano.

For kindnesses proving that our lives remain marvelously interdependent, no matter distances in time, space, and otherwise, I give thanks to Robert Bast, the Birschbach family, Laurie Bucholz, Jim Burnett, David Cerda, the Chiericozzi family, Richard Christian, the Conley family, George Freeman, Gloria Gonzalez, John Hall, Phyllis Hall, Harry Haskell, Stefan Hersh, Cathy Hug, the Iwano family, Peter Kazor, Hans-Georg Knopp, Dare Law, Laurel Lueders, Jim Loy, Leon Mangasarian, Peter Neagle, Duane Nelsen, Alexander Platt, Chuck Polenz, the Rock family, the Scaggs family, Stefan Sanderling, Alex Shibicky, the Siebuhr family, Jon Smoller, Nicholas Vazsonyi, my wondrous daughters, Mariko and Cecilia – to whom this book is dedicated – their mother, Amy Iwano, and, in loving memory, Claudia Dennis.

For expert help and generosity in preparing the illustrations, I am indebted to Jim Dennis, John Dennis, the staff of StudioActiv8, and Tom Capparelli at Kriegcards.com. For research services, I am appreciative of the Loyola University Chicago libraries, particularly the staffs of the Inter-Library Loan office and the Lewis Library periodicals room, as well as the Newberry Library, the Regenstein Library, the Center for Research Libraries, and the Kohler Art Library at the University of Wisconsin-Madison.

For "keeping an eye" on this project for many years, then convincing me that it was time to bring it to completion, and finally urging me to make it accessible to the widest possible audience, I express my special gratitude to Michael Watson at Cambridge University Press. Constructive recommendations by the outside readers were invaluable in helping me decide how to best organize and present this wide array of material. Professional management of the final stages of editing and production came from Chloe Howell, Sarah Roberts, and Lyn Flight.

Over the many years of work on this book, Loyola University Chicago provided leaves of absence in the spring of 2001 and the fall of 2005, a summer stipend in 2007, a course reduction in the spring of 2008, and manuscript publication assistance, which paid for half of the illustration costs. I am thankful for these forms of financial aid, as well as the NEH Summer Stipend I received in 2007.

Some of the material incorporated into this book first appeared in "Honor Your German Masters: The Use and Abuse of 'Classical' Composers in Nazi Propaganda," *Journal of Political and Military Sociology*, vol. 30(2), 2002; "The Most German of all German Operas: *Die Meistersinger* Through the Lens of the Third Reich," in Nicholas Vazsonyi (ed.), *Wagner's Meistersinger: Performance, History, Representation* (University of Rochester Press, 2003); "Nietzsche Reception as Philosopher of *Führermenschen* in the Main Nazi Newspaper," *International Journal of the Humanities*, vol. 5(7), 2007; and *Beethoven in German Politics: 1870–1989* (Yale University Press, 1996). I am obliged to these publications and presses for their permission to revisit this material here.

INTRODUCTION

As cultural and political conflicts raged in Weimar Germany, the editor-in-chief of the Nazi Party's official newspaper, the *Völkischer Beobachter* (*The Folkish Observer*), published a front-page editorial marking the 100th anniversary of Ludwig van Beethoven's death on 26 March 1927. In it, Alfred Rosenberg declared that during the present epoch of "spiritual battle," followers of Adolf Hitler could consider Beethoven's music a powerful source of inspiration. Whoever understood the spirit of the National Socialist movement especially, Rosenberg claimed, knew that "an impulse similar to that which Beethoven embodied in the highest degree lived in all its members": namely, the "desire to storm over the ruins of a crumbling world, the hope for the will to reshape the world, and the strong sense of joy that comes from overcoming passionate sorrow." When the Nazis achieved victory in Germany and across Europe, Rosenberg implied, they would enjoy "heart-warming consciousness" that "the German Beethoven towered over all the peoples of the West." They would then remember that Beethoven had passed on to National Socialists the "will of German creation." Living in the "*Eroica* of the German Volk," Nazis "wanted to make use of" this willpower.[1]

This inspirational evocation of a cultural-historical hero in the Nazi newspaper was entirely consistent with Hitler's proclamations that if the National Socialist revolution was going to have a "transformative effect," its spokesmen would have to "strive by all available means" to get the German people to "believe in its mission with conviction." Above all, the Nazi leader insisted, this required "demonstrating its cultural worthiness." At times of "weakened faith" in Germany's "highest merits," it was necessary to revive the Volk's confidence by "invoking works that remained untouched by political and economic troubles," that is, by invoking great works of Western culture in the name of his ideals.[2]

This book reveals how Hitler's party continually pursued these propaganda goals by means of its main instrument of mass media, the *Völkischer Beobachter*, which was the most widely circulating newspaper of Nazi Germany. This study analyzes how the paper's editors, staff writers, and contributors presented the history of European literature, philosophy, painting, sculpture, and music according to National Socialist beliefs. Nazi leaders regarded their movement as the culmination of Western culture, and this examination of their daily paper shows how they and their followers sought to substantiate this proposition with reference to intellectual and cultural history. Through investigation of every major cultural article published in the *Völkischer Beobachter*, it demonstrates how they wrote about German creators considered foremost (including Luther, Dürer, Goethe, Beethoven, Wagner, Nietzsche, and many others), about non-Germans sometimes deemed related in "Germanic" spirit (such as Socrates, Leonardo, Michelangelo, and Rembrandt), and about the party's anointed "enemies" (among them, Heine, Einstein, and Thomas Mann). As such, this book is the first comprehensive survey of the terms National Socialist propagandists used to appropriate the great names of European art and thought, exposing how the party linked them rhetorically to Nazi ideology and policies. Tracing precisely what *Völkischer Beobachter* writers asserted about their favorite masters and about those they despised makes clear how the party tried to convince readers that Nazism offered not just political renewal but cultural advancement, while at the same time advocating the destruction of Jews along with other perceived opponents.

Scholarship on nineteenth- and twentieth-century "German identity" consistently testifies that the fine arts played a pivotal role in the developing symbolism of the modern nation. Activists seeking to strengthen German political unity emphasized shared conceptions of beauty. Competing political movements sought to increase their respectability by demonstrating that cultural heroes – *Meister* or masters – could be aligned with their respective ideologies. Consequently, as George L. Mosse observed, German politics and high culture penetrated each other: philosophy, literature, painting, sculpture, architecture, and music all came to be perceived as symbolic of political attitudes.[3] In recent years, excellent work has been done to trace connections between the arts and politics in modern Germany. Particularly in the area of "Nazi culture," researchers have investigated how cultural leaders and organizations collaborated in the production of party and state propaganda. To great effect, scholars have concentrated on the biographies of German creators and the administrative histories of cultural institutions.[4] But scholarship on the biographical and institutional background of National Socialist cultural politics (*Kulturpolitik*) functions only as a first step toward answering the central question of this field: how were particular works of art, literature, and music interpreted and then employed as tools of Nazi politics? We must press our investigation beyond determining who was responsible for politicizing culture to learn precisely how the Nazi canon retroactively aligned specific creators with National Socialist principles.[5]

Research in this direction fits into the historiography of cultural reception, which concentrates on meanings drawn from or attached to the arts once published, exhibited, and performed. The history of cultural reception in German political circles indicates how art forms are associated with sociopolitical development: not necessarily as a direct result of creators' intentions, but often as manifested in the responses of audiences.[6] National Socialist appropriation of intellectual history is a haunting example of this process. In my book on Beethoven in German politics, for instance, I traced the history of reception accorded to that composer by political activists from 1870 to 1989.[7] There I examined how Germans across the political spectrum interpreted Beethoven's music to justify their ideas and actions, thereby transforming composer and compositions into symbols for every major party. While I discussed affiliations made from the far right to the far left, significant sections of that book were devoted to describing the ways Nazis exploited this "master" as part of their propaganda. As the example above indicates, to describe the manner by which Beethoven was "Nazified," I paid particular attention to how the *Völkischer Beobachter* promoted him. However, surveying recent literature on Nazi music policy in particular and cultural policy in general, I notice few references to the *Völkischer Beobachter* or other Nazi publications intended for the wider public. Most scholarly work concentrates on periodicals, including art, music, and literary journals, that were targeted at specialized audiences.[8] A few studies of specific topics or individuals have referred to articles from the party daily. For example, Jeffrey Herf has carefully assessed the front-page articles and headlines of the *Völkischer Beobachter* in his work on anti-Semitic propaganda during the Second World War.[9] But the Nazis' most significant publicity instrument requires nothing less than a comprehensive analysis; without it, our histories of National Socialism are incomplete.

As surveyed in a handful of studies, the *Völkischer Beobachter* was a minor bi-weekly publication before being purchased by the National Socialist German Workers Party (NSDAP) in 1920.[10] Hitler personally promoted this early undertaking, arguing that: "if a movement is to be successful in enlightening the broad masses of our people, then meetings, discussion evenings, and political instruction courses will not be adequate over time since these are only accessible to a small circle of listeners. Volkish propaganda must also totally avail itself of the use of the most potent weapon: the press."[11] Under the leadership of Max Amann and Dietrich Eckart, what Hitler later described as the party's "best weapon"[12] became a daily newspaper in February 1923. After the failed Beer Hall Putsch the paper was banned until March 1925. But once reinstated its distribution increased steadily – to 30,000 by 1929 – and a Berlin edition was launched in 1930. By the time of the war, the *Völkischer Beobachter* had become the first German newspaper with a circulation of more than 1 million. From 1923 until 1938, Alfred Rosenberg served as the editor-in-chief;[13] thereafter he was replaced by Wilhelm Weiss through 1945.[14] But whether under Rosenberg's or Weiss' leadership, the paper was always Hitler's primary publicity organ.[15] No other publication compares in significance in the history of Nazi propaganda. It was an official outlet of the party throughout its existence and ultimately had a dominant position over other newspapers.[16] As such, it was undoubtedly the most representative instrument of Nazi propaganda, including propaganda devoted to advancing Nazi cultural interpretations.[17]

In every portion of the *Völkischer Beobachter*, including its front pages (with their screaming red and black headlines), business and sports sections (the latter usually emphasizing *Kampfsport* [battle sports] such as boxing and ice hockey), even advertisements and crossword puzzles (swastika-shaped), one can learn how Nazi media presented events, policies, and ideology to the general public. But it is also possible to draw from the *Völkischer Beobachter* important details about the party's treatment of cultural matters. From its purchase by the NSDAP in 1920, the paper included a cultural section that appeared every day up to April 1945 (although under varying titles, including *Feuilleton*, *Kunst und Kultur*, and *Kultur*).[18] This section included concert, book, and exhibition reviews, articles about cultural topics of general interest, and especially pieces commemorating major anniversaries in the history of Western art and ideas – particularly the birth- and death-days (*Todestage*) of important creators and thinkers. All of these articles offer valuable information about how party ideologues presented Western intellectual and cultural history to its readers in an effort to appropriate "spiritual comrades."

In the course of my research, I examined every page of the *Völkischer Beobachter* from January 1920 through April 1945 in search of each major article it published on literature, philosophy, painting, sculpture, architecture, and music.[19] In so doing, I gathered more than 1,600 articles. After carefully examining every item for National Socialist "spins" on important creators and works, I extracted and translated all passages in which the paper's writers and editors utilized creators and masterpieces of art, literature, and music as tools of Nazi ideology. In this book, I have woven these examples into a thematic and chronological tapestry of Nazi cultural interpretations, examining how they correlated the party's doctrines with the Western tradition of humanities or *Kultur*.[20] Very little of the material investigated in this research has been addressed in German scholarship before, and even less of it has been translated into English. Therefore, I hope it will be of interest to fellow scholars, teachers, students, and anyone intrigued about how high culture can be appropriated and manipulated by a political regime.

In Part I, "Foundations of Nazi Cultural History," I address the conceptual framework of Nazi ideology that these articles promoted: namely, establishing that major figures were of German racial origin, highlighting the volkish impulses behind even high culture, emphasizing the political and nationalist significance of such works, and, most intensively, insisting that anti-Semitism was a major current in the Western cultural tradition. These core themes of the Nazi outlook were reinforced via repeated references to the greatest figures of Western culture up through the romantic age. Major figures who were regularly invoked included Luther, Dürer, Rembrandt, Shakespeare, Bach, Mozart, Schiller, Goethe, and Beethoven. In many of these sections, the culminating example was Richard Wagner. Records of Wagner reception in the *Völkischer Beobachter* confirm the composer's enormous stature in National Socialist culture: few themes were addressed in the paper without some accompanying reference to Wagner's supposedly supportive views on the matter.

Having established these thematic foundations in Part I, I then provide a mainly chronological survey of the paper's coverage of examples, allowing readers to follow the line of the Western tradition according to the Nazi point of view. Thus, Part II, "Blind to the Light," relates how the *Völkischer Beobachter* addressed the Western rationalist tradition from the Ancients to the French Revolution and its consequences, closing with discussion of the paper's promotion of romantic culture as the superior alternative to Western "civilization." Throughout its treatment of Romanticism, the paper played down any "proto-modernist" aspects of the movement, while highlighting nationalist, militarist, and racist elements. Finally, the cultural legacy most cherished by Hitler and his movement, according to the *Völkischer Beobachter*, was the romantic musical tradition – particularly the actual music dramas of Wagner.

Part III, "Modern Dilemmas," addresses how *Völkischer Beobachter* references to cultural history from the mid-nineteenth through the early twentieth century conveyed paradoxical attitudes toward modernist expression in the arts, correlating with debates that occurred within the party well into the Third Reich. On the one hand, it derided "socialist realism" and distanced itself from impressionist "superficiality." But, on the other hand, the paper identified "volkish" features in other depictions of nineteenth-century underclasses. Similarly, it identified with the "romantic" facets of some Symbolist and Expressionist creators, while rejecting others as navel-gazing nihilists. In search of "Nordic existentialism," the paper celebrated Søren Kierkegaard, but its reception of Friedrich Nietzsche wavered, ultimately implying that he just missed becoming "The Nazi Philosopher" because he did not quite grasp the seriousness of the Jewish threat. More consistently, the paper promoted volkish theorists as voices of the Nazi future. Coverage of late nineteenth-century music essentially involved determining where music could go after Wagner: committed late romantics were pitted against "French disease" and "psychopathia musikalis" manifested in modernist styles.

Part IV, "'Holy' War and Weimar 'Crisis,'" covers Nazi treatment of First World War literature and then surveys the paper's attacks against Weimar era culture and politics. Even before the *All Quiet on the Western Front* controversy broke out, the *Völkischer Beobachter* featured those it considered to be the true "Heralds of the front experience" as opposed to cowardly passivists. Part IV then surveys the *Völkischer Beobachter*'s ongoing attacks against Weimar era politics and culture. It initially demonstrates how the paper articulated its disdain for the Weimar Republic by complaining about the ways earlier cultural-historical figures (already covered in Parts I–III) were ignored or dishonored by "leftist" or "Jewish" controlled cultural authorities of the period, in commemorations, scholarship, and educational policies. The *Völkischer Beobachter* also insinuated that the great figures of the German and Western cultural past would have shared their critical attitude toward specific conditions in post-First World War Germany. Then, having claimed cultural-historical justification for their positions on contemporary issues, the paper also launched direct attacks on prominent "modernist" representatives of Weimar culture. According to the *Völkischer Beobachter*, the Weimar "crisis" manifested itself culturally in the writings of "November criminals" and "asphalt literati," such as Berthold Brecht, Alfred Döblin, and the Mann brothers. The trial of George Grosz for blasphemous caricatures was likewise grist for the paper's antimodernist mill, but its main complaints were directed against music by the likes of Schoenberg and Weill.

Finally, Part V, "Nazi 'Solutions,'" covers *Völkischer Beobachter* claims that a great change in German cultural history occurred with the Nazi "seizure of power." Like the treatment of the Weimar era material, this part opens with discussion of how the paper associated earlier "masters" with events and policies undertaken by the regime, especially in commemorative articles that claimed that it was only under Nazi leadership that these creators were finally comprehended accurately (according to the main themes of Nazi ideology) and appropriately honored (in reformed festivals, performances, and educational programs). Thereafter, Part V covers a few of the "acceptable" alternatives to Weimar decadence that the paper posited from the so-called Era of Struggle (*Kampfzeit*) through the Third Reich. Though not exhaustive, this section indicates that much effort was expended to enhance the reputation of figures now largely forgotten. With the war, of course, the theme most emphasized in *Völkischer Beobachter* cultural coverage was militarism. Part V concludes with a retrospective of how revered cultural figures of the past were scrutinized for indications that they had engaged with or contemplated conflict and combat, demonstrating in their works and biographies that they had "fighting natures" that could serve as inspiration for the German Volk at war.

I intend in this structure to provide a synthesis of thematic analysis and chronological coverage that highlights concepts that transcended individual arts and artists in the ideological symbolism of the party, while approximating the flow that the newspaper's readers would have experienced through its cultural coverage. Reviewing the constant repetition of these themes via ongoing references to the major figures of Western culture can be trying. But it was precisely by way of incessant reiteration that these "principles" were intended to appear "unshakeable" (*unerschütterlich*) and "binding" (*bindend*) to the newspaper's readers. As Hitler put it in *Mein Kampf*: "effective propaganda must be limited to a very few points and must harp on these in slogans until the last member of the public understands what you want him to understand."[21]

In an immediate sense, this book is a contribution to the study of Nazi propaganda. The *Völkischer Beobachter* often referred to itself as a "combat paper" (*Kampfblatt*) since – at least until 1933 – its cultural coverage was part of a publicity competition with other German political parties to communicate the main points of its platform and demonstrate that each was consistent with high cultural values.[22] In *Beethoven and German Politics*, I covered the specific struggle over the legacy of Beethoven, showing how every major party from far left to far fight "fought tooth and nail" to claim him, retrospectively, as a fellow traveler. In this present book, we see the National Socialist side of this struggle over rights to other "masters" of music (along with Beethoven) and to leading figures in other creative genres.[23] As a committed Nazi who produced a doctoral dissertation (subsequently published by the NSDAP press) on the function of the newspaper's cultural section up to the "seizure of power" in 1933, reading Gerhard Köhler's assessment of this journalistic "war" is worthwhile: "The cultural-critical work of the editors and staff of the *Völkischer Beobachter* was in great part determined by an attitude of battle which saw the paper as taking part in a cultural-political fight between National Socialism, Liberalism, and Marxism."[24] Editors, staff members, and freelance contributors – the last of whom, as will be discussed in the Conclusion below, made up the majority of authors[25] – all knew their assignment was to convince others to accept National Socialist outlooks.

Of course, within the imagined Nazi "community" (*Gemeinschaft*), there were diverse views about all these matters. The point is not that there was a single, monolithic formulation of Western cultural history or its various components, but that this sort of argumentation was used to justify the regime's positions and policies in this important forum.[26] In the *Völkischer Beobachter*, we study the party's publicity efforts as manifested in high-cultural discourse directed via their most prominent and widely distributed media outlet to the widest possible audience.[27] In his analysis of Nazi propaganda, David Welch insisted on the importance of studying such material: "I make no apologies for using these speeches [or in this case, articles]; they represent not simply 'official' thinking on the subject, and thus the rationalization for measures undertaken, but, equally importantly, the direct contact between the Führer and his propaganda minister and the German people." As such, "they serve as examples of propaganda in action, a living fusion of theory and practice that sheds important light on the Nazi mentality"[28] – or, more precisely, what Nazis wanted the German mentality to be.[29]

Beyond communicating the main tenets of Nazism, moreover, the cultural-historical discourse of the *Völkischer Beobachter* was also dedicated to establishing respectability for the party and especially its anti-Semitic ideology. To put it in German terms, the goal was to demonstrate that while revolutionary, the National Socialist movement and its postulates belonged within the broader tradition of *Bildung* or self-cultivation that was pivotal to national identity.[30] The paper's editors and writers clearly considered this "educational" undertaking to be crucial to the Nazi movement. As one contributor put it: "to win over to our movement spiritual leaders who think they see something distasteful in anti-Semitism, it is extremely important to present more and more evidence that great, recognized spirits shared our hatred of Jewry."[31] Within this framework, George Mosse recognized that interpretations of arts and literature were geared toward a political-educational function. As he put it, "myths and heroes were all-important in what Hitler called the 'magic influence' of mass suggestion," so "building myths and heroes was an integral part of the Nazi cultural drive."[32] This deeper goal was to make "Nazi intellectual prejudices intellectually respectable."[33]

Thus, the Nazi "combat paper" was not just a utilitarian political instrument, it also worked to lend the movement a sense of respectability. But even more was involved in this high-cultural discourse disseminated via mass media. As Jeffrey Herf has pointed out, newspaper propaganda supplied a powerful "interpretive framework" that gave readers ways to make sense of ongoing events, offering "plausible explanations for what was going on in the world."[34] This point is consistent with Mosse's insight that the appeal of nationalism as it evolved over the nineteenth century, and then Nazism in particular, was that they provided "fully furnished rooms" – or structured and organized ways of perceiving what otherwise seemed to be disorienting facets of modernization.[35] In his early analysis of cultural coverage in the *Völkischer Beobachter*, the Nazi dissertator Köhler articulated the contemporary attraction of this "quality": "the frequent use of clear standards and measures, bases for comparison and targets for achievement founded on broader ideological views of art and the world ... gave National Socialist art criticism its particular stamp." Contributors to the cultural section, he continued:

> *almost always used these measures and standards in their assessments, which resulted in the development of a communal sense of evaluation among them ... This community extended, of course, into the masses of readers of the* Völkischer Beobachter. *Because, for them the cultural-criticism of their paper constituted a public means of expressing their National Socialist art and world view, promoting their group opinion regarding the events of the art world. It was the art critics who stood by them with advice and support in the manipulative war over their opinion.*[36]

Providing masses of readers with group opinions by which they could measure and rank not just artistic achievement, but also matters pertaining to history, politics, and race was a fundamental aim of the cultural politics practiced in the *Völkischer Beobachter*.[37]

Therefore, the material presented below, while part of the propaganda efforts of the party, was not just propaganda. Taken as a whole, it represents an ongoing formulation of the essential concepts that comprised what National Socialists touted as their "world view" (*Weltanschauung*). In each of these articles, whether written by party leaders, paper editors, staff writers, or a host of occasional contributors, the *Völkischer Beobachter* cultural section held up idealized cultural-historical images to German readers so they could see how great they had been and were capable of becoming again. By worshipping German *Kultur* – or the supposed place of Germans in Western culture – in these terms, members of the so-called Volk community (*Volksgemeinschaft*) were given a renewed opportunity to worship themselves.[38] Thus, in an age of confusion and relative disorientation after their nation had suffered military defeat and economic collapse, they were presented with idealized renderings of what was best about themselves (and worth fighting for), as well as what was worst about their enemies (and worth fighting against).[39] Of course, the front page and the rest of the *Völkischer Beobachter* addressed these issues in all-important stories about politics, economics, social conditions, military developments, and in every other feature of a daily newspaper functioning as a *Kampfblatt*. The cultural section, however, presented the more idealistic reasons to pursue National Socialist aims. This was the heart, or spirit (*Geist*) of the matter: here readers could read that they and the NSDAP were part of a long-standing, beautiful tradition that was ostensibly consistent with the highest expressions of *Kultur*.[40]

Of course, the collaborative "working toward the Führer" that led to piecemeal construction of this cultural history of Nazi ideals in the *Völkischer Beobachter* inevitably implied its opposite: the identification of enemies who did not fit or conform with these ideals. George Mosse again led the way in observing the double-bladed nature of nationalistic and then Nazi formations of politicized "beauty." On the basis of whether an individual or group fitted into standards of *Kultur* so described, the individual or group – not just art and policy – would themselves be measured: "racism gave everyone a designated place in the world, defining him as a person and, through a clear distinction between 'good' and 'evil' races, explaining the puzzling modern world in which he lived. Who could ask for more?"[41] Determination of one's place in the order, therefore, was not exclusively but predominantly a question of aesthetic taste: "racial classification … was based upon aesthetic preferences that were necessarily highly subjective."[42] Publicized "mostly in newspapers and pamphlets," like the *Völkischer Beobachter*, the "Jewish stereotype which was thought to typify ugliness could not be allowed to disturb the beauty which informed national worship."[43] Thus, anti-Semitism, antimodernism, and other antipathies were predicated, to a significant degree, on cultural criticism; aesthetic versions of the arguments were not just added on to validate them. As Hitler insisted, one's relationship to *Kultur* – or that of one's "race" – was key: do you create it, imitate it, or destroy it? Again, these "measures" provided clear standards for judgment – "the value of a race could thus be measured by its *Kultur*"[44] – but they also provided premises for policies designed to eliminate those perceived and represented as obstacles to the ideal. In Eric Michaud's analysis: "whatever the physical criteria for their elimination may have been, Jews, Gypsies, 'degenerates,' and homosexuals were shut away and exterminated for the same reasons as were the strictly political opponents of Nazism: because of what all these 'Jews in spirit' might say that was *unheimlich* (unfamiliar and disturbing) to Nazism"; or, rather, to the ordered visions of the past, present, and future that Nazi *Kulturpolitik* fabricated.[45]

The writings inspected here from the pages of the *Völkischer Beobachter* are monumentally disturbing. From other perspectives on Western culture, Nazi views seem perversions. Yet they must be considered on their own terms. The aim of this book is not to enter into an argument with these long-dead voices, but to directly encounter their line of thought in order to better understand how great works of humanism can ultimately be used to validate inhumane policies. Nazis wanted to associate themselves with the finest thinkers and creators of the Western tradition. So, popular or "volkish" proclivities notwithstanding, the paper tried to make men of knowledge into Nazi heroes as well. This book tracks and analyzes that effort. Here one learns how Hitler and his followers tried to persuade Germans that their actions – in Germany, at the front, and behind it – were consistent with the trajectory of Western creativity; indeed, would lead to its pinnacle.

PART I
FOUNDATIONS OF NAZI CULTURAL HISTORY

1 THE "GERMANIC" ORIGINS OF WESTERN CULTURE

Among the most famous statements in *Mein Kampf* are those in which Hitler formulated the primary methods of Nazi propaganda. Perhaps based on the system of leading motives (*Leitmotiven*) that his creative hero, Richard Wagner, ostensibly practiced in music drama, Hitler was adamant that major principles of National Socialist ideology should be repeated relentlessly so followers would acquire a familiarity with them verging on religious certainty. In his words, the "most brilliant propaganda technique will yield no success unless one fundamental principle is borne in mind constantly and with unflagging attention. It must confine itself to a few points and repeat them over and over." The "art of propaganda," in his view, consisted of "putting a matter so clearly and forcibly before the minds of the people as to create a general conviction regarding the reality of a certain fact."[1] It was through this process of propagandizing with a hammer, as it were, that Nazism bridged the gap between theory and practice: by drilling its followers in ritualized, popular forms, ideological principles became a liturgy in action.[2]

Part I of this book will demonstrate how the *Völkischer Beobachter* repeated the main themes of Nazi culture with liturgical regularity while working to establish that these points were indeed eternal verities and ideals based on a solid foundation of truth. The newspaper claimed that Nazi ideals were fundamental components of Western intellectual and artistic tradition and insisted that important creators and works from the ancient world through the romantic period shared similar principles. The most prominent of these themes were: establishing that major figures were of German or Aryan racial origins and that their works were representative of Nordic culture; highlighting the volkish (folkish) or *volkstümlich* (popular) impulse behind even the major works of Western high culture (partly as a way of mitigating intellectual pretension); emphasizing the political and nationalist significance of great artists and their works; and, most intensively, insisting that anti-Semitism was a major current in the Western cultural tradition.

A primary axiom of National Socialist thinking was that all Western cultural innovation was the product of the German race – described alternately as German, Germanic, Aryan, or Nordic: only creators of this background could produce genuinely innovative thought and art.[3] Drawing from a German ideological tradition that had evolved over the nineteenth century,[4] Hitler endorsed this view in *Mein Kampf*:

> All human culture, all the results of art, science, and
> technology that we see before us today, are almost exclusively
> the creative product of the Aryan ... If we were to divide
> mankind into three groups, the founders of culture, the
> bearers of culture, the destroyers of culture, only the Aryan
> could be considered as the representative of the first group.[5]

Following this line, Nazi cultural operatives worked to demonstrate that great thinkers and artists were of either specifically German or generally Nordic origins or "spirit," no matter how contorted the justification. Just as it was necessary to demonstrate that one possessed such racial backgrounds to be included in the volkish *Gemeinschaft* as a whole and organizations such as the German Art Society in particular, the first prerequisite for the Germanic style was that the creators themselves be of appropriate blood.[6]

Nazis were not original in making such statements, which were central to volkish ideology from its earliest formulations. Strong, earlier articulations of such views – which may have influenced Hitler – appeared throughout Houston Stewart Chamberlain's *Foundations of the Nineteenth Century* (1899), for instance, in his section on "The Teutons as Creators of a New Culture."[7] Similar precedents for the volkish Germanicization of Western cultural history were works by Ludwig Woltmann: *The Germans and the Renaissance in Italy* (1905) (included in Hitler's personal library);[8] *The Germans in Spain* (1906); and *The Germans in France: An Investigation into the Influence of the German Race on the History and Culture of France* (1907). As his titles made clear, Woltmann claimed that the leading lights of Western humanities from Athenian Greeks to exponents of the Enlightenment were of German background. Whether their ideas or works coordinated with volkish ideology or not, the point of Woltmann's racial analysis of the Western tradition was that all creative energy came from Germanic genetic inheritance.[9] As will become apparent below, *Völkischer Beobachter* articles did not go quite as far – at least not as far back in Western cultural history – as Woltmann's cultural Aryanization project. But starting with the Renaissance era, the paper suggested similarities between the supposedly Nordic natures and ideas of past creators and the ideals of Nazi ideology. As its coverage of Western cultural history moved forward in time, the biographical agenda of the newspaper became more and more insistent that the forerunners it claimed as part of the Nazi cultural legacy were not tainted by Jewish genes.

The *Völkischer Beobachter*'s interpretation of the great artists of the Renaissance came straight from the leading editorial voice of the paper, Alfred Rosenberg. As in the opening example of this book, the so-called philosopher of the NSDAP would occasionally grace the cultural section – especially with passages from his own "masterwork," *The Myth of the Twentieth Century*. From its passages on "mysticism and deed" came material identifying the "dynamic German nature" that ostensibly underlies all Western creativity. More concerned with "action than contemplation," Rosenberg felt that above all others Meister Eckhart, Beethoven, and Goethe exemplified his murky aesthetic theory. But, echoing Woltmann, he also included Leonardo da Vinci and Michelangelo in his collection of exemplary "great men of the Nordic West."

In his view, Leonardo (1452–1519) manifested a synthesis of spirituality and practicality "fundamental to the Nordic soul" in the two facets of his creative impulse. On the one side, the artist conjured up a transcendental world, as in his holy Anna, in the eyes of his John the Baptist, and in the face of his Christ. But, simultaneously, he was an engineer, a "cool-headed technician," who devised inventions to make nature serviceable to man (Figure 1.1). Therefore, according to Rosenberg, many of Leonardo's ideas might well have originated from that "other Nordic genius," Goethe. Similar "deep, Nordic expressions"

Figure 1.1 *Völkischer Beobachter*, Leonardo da Vinci tribute page: "The Italian Faust," 30 April 1944

also formed Michelangelo's personality, said Rosenberg. In his view, works such as his Sibyls and his "world-condemning" Christ made it clear that Western religiosity did not reject life but, on the contrary, "chose creative existence as a partner" – and this was also true of

"Nordic mysticism" which "had need of its antithesis." As represented by Michelangelo's titanic figures, the "heroic soul" produced the mightiest outward achievements. In all the works of great men of the Nordic West – even those Italian-born – Rosenberg saw that the "dynamic Germanic nature" never expressed itself in flight from the world, but in struggling to overcome it.[10]

Völkischer Beobachter references to Michelangelo (1475–1564) also included a short story based on his influence on one of his apprentices – without, of course, any mention of the artist's sexual orientation[11] – and, on the 375th anniversary of his death (*Todestag*) in 1939, a tribute in verse by the well-known poet, Josef Weinheber – a strong supporter of the Austrian Nazi Party who broadcast speeches calling for *Anschluss*. Wartime articles in the winter of 1944 provided deep art historical analyses of Michelangelo's statues themselves, including an extended interpretive essay by the prominent cultural philosopher, Rudolf Kassner – a close friend of Rainer Maria Rilke.[12]

Such summaries presented Michelangelo as a Renaissance Superman (*Übermensch*). The language of power, competition, and overcoming – particularly overcoming the rational Hellenic tradition by imposing his strong passions – pervaded *Völkischer Beobachter* descriptions of his works. According to art historian Marlies Schmitz-Herzberg, Michelangelo was indubitably a man of the High Renaissance, the era that sought to learn from antiquity, adopting perfect forms of the human body from the art of the ancients. But he went beyond them, because he was not satisfied with the calm of ancient statues that followed formal laws of ideal beauty even when representing scenes full of pain. As he worked, his "all-powerful inner vision" broke forth and marked figures with his own spirit. Thus did the marble he formed – the world he created – "ravish and overwhelm" the viewer. Under his chisel, the free-standing statue of a naked man became a "symbol of power" for the state of Florence. His *David*, thought Schmitz-Herzberg, expressed the joy Michelangelo felt regarding the "power and force" of the human species. The older Michelangelo became, she went on, the more he removed himself from the goal of mere physical beauty – moving further away from the Hellenic ideal toward a more "expressionistic aesthetic." In his last representation of the *Pietà*, for instance, he countered the Greeks with figures of "visionary spirituality" embodying "eternal divinity" in stone (Figure 1.2). Likewise in painting, Schmitz-Herzberg felt, Michelangelo overcame the "increasingly bourgeois" art

Figure 1.2 Michelangelo, *Rondanini Pietà* (1564), Museo d'arte antica
in the Sforza Castle, Milan, Italy

of his contemporaries with a new idealism that allowed a "tremendous
sculptural strength" to grow in his figures, resulting in symbols of
"super-humanity" (*Übermenschentum*).[13]

In these terms, the *Völkischer Beobachter* made Michelangelo
out to have superior, "Faustian" powers, which he applied in art and
beyond. According to an article by Ludwig Pastor, a leading historian of
the Papacy who had served as Austrian minister to the Vatican, the artist
shared a "terrible character" with the political-religious leaders of his
day, especially Pope Julius II.[14] The newspaper was particularly interested in Michelangelo's reactions to the political history of Florence. One
sign of Michelangelo's political engagement discussed in the *Völkischer
Beobachter* was drawn not from his visual masterworks, but from his
poetry: a quatrain he composed in response to Giovan Battista Strozzi's
praise of the figure of *Night* for the Medici tombs.

Strozzi had written:

Night, which you see here sleeping in peace,
From this stone an Angel wrought.
Sleeping, it lives;
Just wake it up, and it will speak to thee.

And, speaking for *Night*, Michelangelo answered:

Sleep is dear to me; even better to be stone.
Who cannot see or feel is fortunate,
So long as crime and shame rule the land.
Therefore do not waken me: be quiet, and leave.

For Pastor and the *Völkischer Beobachter*, Michelangelo's dark reflection on Florence under the Medici signified an ongoing political awareness in all of his creative work: utterly bound to family and clan, his "oversensitive soul" was in anguish as Florence was losing its liberty.[15] From the Nazi perspective, Germans living in the Weimar Republic – also a time of crime and shame – could feel the same way.

Given, as we will see, that its cultural-political outlook rested on belief that a self-conscious German identity originated in the culture of the Reformation, the *Völkischer Beobachter* faced an irritating art historical difficulty: the greatest visual artist of the Protestant tradition was from the Netherlands rather than German lands. This dilemma might explain why the paper so intensively endorsed Julius Langbehn's *Rembrandt as Educator* (1890), which depicted Rembrandt van Rijn (1606–1669) as the antithesis of modern culture and as the model for Germany's "third reformation."[16] Indeed, it even recommended that every party member put books by Langbehn under the Christmas tree, since contemplating German art according to the interpretation of "The Rembrandt-German" (*Der Rembrandtdeutsche*) was a way to overcome the "weakening of the blood."[17] Besides numerous tributes to Langbehn himself (see discussion in Part IV), the *Völkischer Beobachter* laced its articles on Rembrandt with concepts drawn from Langbehn's volkish appropriation of the Dutch master. In any case, art and theater historian, Richard Biedrzynski – a regular contributor to the *Völkischer Beobachter* in the later years of the Third Reich, whose career nonetheless extended successfully into the postwar era – had no qualms about identifying Rembrandt's as an "extreme case of Nordic art."[18]

In line with Langbehn's theories about Rembrandt's Nordic nature, Biedrzynski insisted that his "violent aspiration" was to make the "invisible visible," and his methods were those of a "seer." The Nordic proclivity to "combine paradoxical extremes" manifested itself clearly in his prints: he considered darkness to be the ally of the light he wrestled from it; this was the "secret source of mastery" behind the chiaroscuro of his prints. Moreover, he was an intuitive artist, unconcerned with surface reality alone – or superficial success. His art was never calculated; seeking to surprise by representing the incalculable, he was neither careful, economical, nor conventional. Consequently, said Biedrzynski, his works never became models for academic drawing. Driven by profound emotions, his art embodied "visionary fanaticism" rather than intellectual inquiry (Figure 1.3). Especially in his later paintings, he developed a "passion for color" that was similar to the "passion for light" symbolized in prints like the *Hundertguldenblatt* (1647–1649): the master of chiaroscuro became the "fanatic of red" to the point where objects seemed to "glow in an unreal fashion." And, like all "Germanic-volkish artists," he was restless, ever-searching, never satisfied with his achievements. No stage of development became dogmatic for him: his art had no patience for "stagnation of the soul."

While these *Rembrandtdeutsche* assessments placed the artist within the framework of Nordic creativity, the *Völkischer Beobachter* sought to more precisely align him with the specifically German tradition more than Dutch art. To do so, the paper raised the issue of Rembrandt's social and financial difficulties later in life. According to Biedrzynski, Rembrandt's art "overwhelmed Holland." The reasons for the poor reception of the *Night Watch*, for instance, lay more in its "nature" than in the circumstances of its production. His art conformed to the "bourgeois dabbings" of the Dutch no more than the artist himself got along with the bourgeois society of Holland. Especially the late self-portraits did not show a man who rued his fate, but a figure with "great consciousness of the power to assert himself" through forceful art reaching depths of the soul that "contemporary compatriots could no longer understand." It was highly significant, said Biedrzynski, that, as a result, Rembrandt was appreciated "more in Germany than in the land of his birth." Seen through a broad "Germanic consciousness" – paying attention not to political divisions, but to "volkish connections" – Rembrandt's were to be

Figure 1.3 Rembrandt, *The Slaughtered Ox* (1655), Glasgow Museums and Art Galleries, Glasgow, UK

considered more than Netherlandish, or even Nordic, but among the "sacred works of Reich Art" (*Reichskunst*).[19]

Biedrzynski acknowledged that the "inner appropriation" of Rembrandt that he, Langbehn, and the *Völkischer Beobachter* undertook corresponded to the "Germanization of Shakespeare," on whom German Romantics, he said, "held a second copyright."[20] In doing so, Biedrzynski was referring to volkish claims on the Bard with reference to August Wilhelm Schlegel's German translations of Shakespeare's plays – completed in the first half of the nineteenth century by Ludwig Tieck, Tieck's daughter Dorothea, and Wolf von Baudissin. Rudolf Hofmüller, a regular contributor on the history of literature, wrote for the *Völkischer Beobachter* on Schlegel's 175th birthday that, although some details might be disputed, his German Shakespeare was a "creative achievement and cultural deed" in its own right. In fact, Hofmüller went as far as to say that everything Germans loved and admired in Shakespeare was formulated by Schlegel. Through his translation, the dramatic work of the "Germanic-Nordic tragedian" became the "secure possession" of the German nation.[21] Whether based on the original or on Schlegel's version, Nazi admiration for Shakespeare extended to including him in the Valhalla of Nordic creators. Marking a Shakespeare week in 1927, Baldur von Schirach – future head of the Hitler Youth, but then a student of *Germanistik* and Art History at the University of Munich who contributed regularly to the newspaper[22] – also referred to Shakespeare (1564–1616) as a Nordic genius who, between Dante and Goethe, stood as a "fighter for bravery and loyalty."[23]

Moving to German-born masters, and especially those of music, the *Völkischer Beobachter* dedicated itself to stipulating what made some creators more Germanic than others, and finessing cases where outside influences may have been involved. The paper worked intensively to appropriate Johann Sebastian Bach (1685–1750) into National Socialist culture. Marking the anniversary of Bach's death in 1923, the Nazi newspaper referred to this composer as the "greatest German musician of all." According to Hans Buchner, a musicologist on the *Völkischer Beobachter* staff as early as 1920 who became an editor in the cultural section while preparing collections such as the *Horst Wessel March Album: Songs of the National Socialist German Workers Party*,[24] Bach arose as if to say: "you Germans must have a great master."[25] Bach was indeed the first German master of the musical canon who members of the National Socialist *Gemeinschaft* were expected to honor. In the words of musicologist Max Neuhaus, he was the "starting point" of their great musical development.[26] Karl Grunsky, a Stuttgart music journalist who produced regular articles for the *Bayreuther Blätter* and the *Völkischer Beobachter*,[27] reminded readers that when they asked themselves who raised German music to superior repute – who furnished it with universal value – the answer "came with the sound of his illustrious name: Johann Sebastian Bach."[28] In the eyes of National Socialists like Heinrich Stahl, author of more than fifty major articles on music for the paper, "Germanness" became an "incontrovertible reality" in Bach. As a "conqueror of souls," the "aura of his being" had spread out beyond Germanic lands to have repercussions over all nations.[29] Covering a 1934 Bach Festival for the *Völkischer Beobachter*, Neuhaus attempted to identify the Germanic elements of Bach's music: powerful, but full of "mystical presentiment"; complex, and yet of great simplicity; daring, but placing everything under the "iron law of order"; full of love without sentimentality, full of hate without malice; cheerful to the point of witty comedy, yet serious and solemn; controlling forces of heaven and hell, but at home on earth; and above all, "manly, heroic – and childlike."[30] Most significant, according to the paper, was the racial link between Bach, his art, and the German Volk of the twentieth century: in their phrase, the "blood unity" between them. In Bach's personality were combined the "best hereditary powers of a healthy species" and therefore his art constituted a "culmination of racial development." The feelings that his music awoke in the hearts of Nazis, the *Völkischer Beobachter* commentary ran, resulted from the "resonance" of "Nordic-Germanic soulfulness" that they had in common.[31]

Establishing the Germanness (*Deutschtum*) of every major composer from Bach onward was a primary point on the *Völkischer Beobachter* agenda. Only the terms by which each master was drawn into the Germanic fold varied. The case of Georg Friedrich Händel (1685–1759) required extra effort not because his German origins were in dispute – as was the case for Beethoven, Liszt, and even Wagner – but because of his permanent move to London in 1712. Although Nazis could deem him a "true German composer,"[32] they had to launch a polemic against associations of his life and art with English culture. The issue of the composer's country of residence underlaid all reception of Händel in the *Völkischer Beobachter*.

The first element of the Nazi strategy to reclaim him was to constantly assert that Händel (always spelled in the *Völkischer Beobachter* with the original *Umlaut*, though he dropped it after moving to London) ever remained a consciously nationalistic artist. He was this brand of artist, according to an article marking the 175th anniversary of his death in 1934, "by disposition, instinctively, because he couldn't help it." Thus, he remained "forever and completely," even during the half-century that he spent in England, "the great Saxon."[33] Beyond remaining conscious of his German roots, Waldemar Hartmann – an art historian who studied with Georg Dehio and Josef Strzygowski – portrayed Händel for the paper as actively promulgating a Germanic outlook abroad. In Hartmann's terms, Händel served as the "earliest and most effective" champion of German music in foreign lands. If German music enjoyed the highest respect throughout the world, and particularly in English-speaking lands, this was above all thanks to Händel's "pioneering work." His "cultural-political significance" for Germany could therefore not be overestimated.[34]

To support these claims, the *Völkischer Beobachter* delved into the history of Händel's life abroad. Despite his long-term residence in England, the newspaper reported, he "never became an Englishman," which was clear from the fact that he didn't trouble himself to master any more than the barest essentials of the English language.[35] In spite of his forty-seven-year stay in London, wrote Hartmann, Händel sprinkled his English with German, French, and Italian phrases, and started using English texts for his oratorios only in the last ten years of his life. Moreover, he maintained a "fundamentally German" household: his closest company consisted of two Germans named Schmidt – a father and son who followed him from Germany and remained on the staff of his house. Throughout his stay, Hartmann held, he maintained close relations with his home town, Halle, since his mother lived there her whole life. But in the end, Hartmann decided that the question of whether the music of the "German Händel living in England" should be considered German or English seemed irrelevant. Händel, said Hartmann, did not "displace English music with a German one." Rather, he drew the musical culture of "Nordic England" into the "great German stream of Nordic creative power." Händel's music was a product of the "phenomenon of creative exchange between peoples of Nordic blood," according to Hartmann, "just as were the works of Shakespeare."[36]

In whatever way this Nordic cultural exchange was imagined to function, though, the *Völkischer Beobachter* worked intensively to wrench Händel's *Messiah* in particular from its British origins and transform it into a German nationalistic symbol. Above all, wrote Friedrich Baser, a musicologist who produced Bach studies and also work on Nietzsche's interest in composition, the *Messiah* was Händel's "most German work" – born out of "German faith and fighting spirit." With it, Baser held, Händel returned to the artistic sources of his homeland, to his memories of youth in Halle, to his experience of German chorales, cantatas, and passions during his earliest, most impressionable years. Thus, did he compose the *Messiah* out of forms which "arose from German tradition alone."[37] In the Nazi newspaper, then, the *Messiah* was a cultural product that evinced the "force and illuminating seriousness of Nordic creativity" – and had nothing to do with Britain.[38]

Similarly, for the editors of the *Völkischer Beobachter*, an immediate concern regarding the case of Wolfgang Amadeus Mozart (1756–1791) was to evaluate his "blood heritage" (*Bluterbe*). The details of their analysis reveal the depths of pedantry to which the

National Socialist "racially determined music politics" could sink. In the most extensive *Völkischer Beobachter* article on Mozart's *Bluterbe*, Uwe Lars Nobbe – otherwise the author of well-known books on First World War volunteers – argued that the main factors behind Mozart's creativity were "determined by blood." Mozart's father was born of a marriage between a grandfather from Augsburg and a grandmother from Baden, Nobbe's analysis emphasized, resulting in a "blood mixture" of "heavy Swabian style with vivacious-Allemannisch temperament." His mother, on the other hand, was of a "Salzburger-Bavarian" background. As a result, the blood heritage passed on from his mother and father led to a "uniquely harmonious balance" in Mozart himself, which determined the symmetrical nature of his creativity. Nowhere in his character, Nobbe contended, were there signs of excess: "typical Swabian peculiarities," such as stubbornness and pedantry, which were part of his father's make-up, did not show up in him. From the mother, this blood portrait ran on, Mozart received "joy for life, openmindedness, enthusiasm, depth of feeling, cheerfulness, thoroughness, pensiveness, diligence, tenacity, the power of observation, single-mindedness, a quiet, dry sense of humor, impartiality, self-assurance, self-confidence, and clarity of conception."[39] (What more could a child ask of his mother?) In other articles on Mozart's background, Nazi experts like Karl Grunsky also described the balance they perceived in his genetic make-up. He inherited from his mother "true cheerfulness," while "from the blood of his father came 'Swabian seriousness – the capacity to sense all that is wrong with the world.'"[40]

In many ways, these convoluted efforts to define the regional characteristics of a German artist mark a continued effort among the Nazis to classify individual traits that together made up German identity. Historians have justifiably concentrated on the terms by which Nazi racism defined non-Germans, but these sources remind us that they also had to work at clarifying what constituted a German, given the historical and cultural diversity of the groups they wished to subsume within that category. A further example with reference to Mozart reflects the problems they created for themselves in this process. *Völkischer Beobachter* staff music critic Erwin Bauer,[41] wrote that one often "heard it said" that "Mozart belonged to Salzburg." But this was not completely accurate, Bauer argued, his "taste for happiness, the droll amorousness of his being, his chattiness, and even that dark shadow of a philosophical way of looking at things" – all of this was "completely

Swabian." Still, Bauer allowed, those who considered "Salzburg and Mozart" as a unity "weren't all wrong."[42] So, the verdict remained out in the *Völkischer Beobachter* as to precisely what sort of German blood determined Mozart's greatness.

While divided about precisely which sort of German Mozart was, Nazi critics were united in the opinion that he was in fact a German composer. They did, however, consider it necessary to defend this point, owing to Mozart's closeness to the Italian music tradition and his reputation – promoted by Nietzsche among others – as a "European" artist. References to Mozart as the "ultimate Rococo musician," Nobbe argued in the *Völkischer Beobachter*, did not take into account that Mozart was a "heroic-demonic fighter" and a "profound source of the ultimate wisdom," which were purely German attributes. There was also a tendency, said Nobbe, to overlook the "line that runs directly from Bach to Mozart," so he reminded readers that the musical outlook of Mozart's father, Leopold, was based primarily on the "thoughts of the North German school." This aesthetic was "passed on to the *Wunderkind*" and contributed to the fact that despite his "Italianate endeavors" Mozart conceived himself as a "German musician, in the best sense of the word."[43]

Another issue that *Völkischer Beobachter* contributors felt compelled to address was the fact that Mozart often traveled outside German lands during his formative years. A number of tactics were devised to counter this supposed problem. One effort, by Hans Buchner, ran as follows. As the "most musical person of all time," the genius of Mozart flowed from two sources – an "uncommon sense of form" and "profundity" – both of which ultimately merged in his "stream of truly German artistry." Being a "German man of his times," Mozart learned to honor his "oppressed, misunderstood, and insulted" nationality.[44] According to Eduard Mayr, despite his wide travels Mozart "preserved the German inheritance of his birth – pure and unadulterated." Thus, it was "a German" who raised Italian opera to its perfect, ideal state and then "brought it to his own people."[45] Similarly, in response to a reference by the head of the Munich Mozart Society about the composer's "universal" importance, Ferdinand Moessmer retorted that Mozart's significance was universal, but that did not hinder one from perceiving him as a "decidedly *German* master." The German significance of Mozart, Moessmer's argument went, was based on his "positive attitude toward Germanness" in general – on his "deep, genuine love for his people." Understanding this required awareness of the conditions under which his personality developed. In Mozart's lifetime, "Latins suppressed the German language and the German soul altogether," and a Frenchman, Voltaire, "exercised absolute authority at the Berlin court." But in spite of this "general negation of Germanness," Moessmer argued, Mozart had a "decided attachment to his nationality." Indeed, he constantly fought to "increase German prestige."[46] The text of a lecture by Dr. Heinrich Ritter von Srbik, reproduced in the *Völkischer Beobachter*, put this thesis even more directly. During the period between the Seven Years War and the French Revolution, Mozart's life could not have remained "unaffected by national issues," especially since he constantly received impressions of political developments through his travels. Therefore, he must have been "conscious of his German nationality already as a child," and "with increasing maturity as a man and as an artist it came to a breakthrough."[47]

To back up assertions about Mozart's essentially German, ultimately patriotic, nature, *Völkischer Beobachter* writers combed his biography for supporting details. Central to this effort was information about Mozart's difficult experiences in Paris in 1778. According to Josef Stolzing, editor of the cultural section of the *Völkischer Beobachter* from 1925 to 1932 and the most prolific contributor to the cultural section of the paper through the 1930s,[48] Mozart never felt worse in his life than he did during his stay in Paris when he lost his mother. But Stolzing emphasized that it was not just personal circumstances that made him miserable in France: he developed "true hatred" for the French. Very quickly he saw through the "superficial culture," which decorated the fashionable Parisian world like a "whitewash." Statements in Mozart's letters to his father wherein he gave air to this frustration – "Here I am among loud beasts, where music is concerned; if only the cursed French language weren't so lousy for music" – were clear evidence, said Stolzing, of the composer's Francophobia.[49] Likewise, according to Victor Junk, music editor, a close associate of Hans Pfitzner, an author of books on Max Reger as well as on Mozart, Mozart's letters illuminated above all how indignant he became over the "contempt with which German art was held" in France. Moreover, it was clear that he preferred to suffer and starve rather than place his art "in the service of fashion and foreign taste": in Paris, where he felt "disdained as a German," he "prayed for the strength to hold out and do honor to himself and the whole German people."[50]

Even more so than in the case of Mozart, the NSDAP also injected race issues into Beethoven reception.[51] Indeed, dictates of racial anthropology nearly nullified the composer's value as a party hero. The Nazis almost rejected Beethoven as a symbol of their movement simply because his physical appearance disquieted theorists who contrived their race-based musicology. While portraits and observations of Beethoven (1770–1827) by his contemporaries differ tremendously, all reveal that he had few of the physical characteristics associated with Aryan stereotypes.[52] Noticing this, a handful of pseudoscientists concluded that Beethoven was of impure blood: careful analysis of his portraits, they said, led to the discovery that although his eye color may have been blue (it was not), he was short, dark-haired, and swarthy. Based on these findings, racist savants such as Hans F. K. Günther and Ludwig Ferdinand Clauss determined that Beethoven's genetic background was "mixed."[53]

Even so, although their ideology rested on the tenets of racial science, most National Socialist propagandists were not willing to accept that Beethoven had been of impure racial stock. Upholding such a position would have required discarding his music as alien, and many in the party designated Beethoven's art as a musical symbol of how the German Volk would thrive under Hitler's rule. To National Socialist cultural politicians, then, Beethoven's legend was simply too valuable to risk. The *Völkischer Beobachter* recognized its duty and therefore vouched for the composer's racial purity in a number of articles produced with the obvious intention of cleansing Beethoven of his apparent physical flaws.

One of these articles, "Portrait of His Heredity," stressed indications that Beethoven's paternal grandfather was of Germanic ancestry: in a portrait of the grandfather by Leopold Radoux, the court painter in Bonn, "we see a conspicuously Nordic head of the finest racial stamp."[54] Another article, "His Outward Appearance," performed a similar ratifying service on the composer's behalf. Here, *Völkischer Beobachter* editors excerpted from Anton Schindler's contemporary depiction of Beethoven, in which Schindler referred to the composer's stocky physique, overbearing laugh, and unruly hair. Furthermore, Schindler reported that while the tint of Beethoven's face was yellowish, "he usually lost this through his wanderings in free nature during the summertime, when he received a good tanning and his skin came to be covered with a fresh varnish of red and brown." In all probability, this excerpt from Schindler was reproduced to discount reports that Beethoven was a dark racial type, implying instead that his skin was tinted by the sun.

But Nazi propagandists used only those portions of Schindler's recollections that served their immediate purposes. In a telling annotation, following Schindler's statement that Beethoven's "forehead was high and wide, his brown eyes small," the *Völkischer Beobachter* added in parentheses the question, "blue?" In this way the paper insinuated that Schindler, Beethoven's reverent secretary, had inaccurately described his hero's eye color. Additional support was offered in the next paragraph, which opened with the revelation that Friedrich August Klöber, the sculptor who made a bust of Beethoven in 1818 and who also painted him, indicated in words and in images that Beethoven's eye color was "gray-blue."

The *Völkischer Beobachter* then denounced racial scholars who had raised questions about Beethoven's genetic purity: "Dr. Hans Günther errs decidedly when … he characterizes Beethoven as predominantly Eastern."[55] Thus did the paper try to eradicate evidence of aspects of Beethoven's appearance that failed to meet the physical standards of the racially pure Volk it fantasized. Not only by birth, but "by virtue of his whole essence," Ludwig van Beethoven was a "pureblooded German," the paper concluded: he was the "spiritual possession of all Aryan mankind."[56]

Nevertheless, diligent wardens of the so-called Aryan community were troubled by another aspect of Beethoven's family background: his father.[57] Since it was well established that Johann van Beethoven had been a severe alcoholic, some National Socialists had difficulty reconciling the life of son Ludwig with their rigid theories of inheritance. If blood and family background were the basis for acceptance in the Nazi *Gemeinschaft*, Beethoven would have to be denied on the basis of his father's record. Scholars supportive of Nazism had to come to the composer's rescue again. Ludwig Schiedermair, professor at the University of Bonn and head of the Beethovenhaus Archive, concocted a remedy for this blot on the composer's background. In a *Völkischer Beobachter* article on Beethoven's parents, he argued that it was unjust to damn Beethoven's father: persons who condemned him as a drunk simply did not understand the importance of alcohol in Rhenish culture. "If he loved gaiety and high spirits; if he frequently wanted to make the rounds; if he gladly drank wine and punch, and once in a while offered girls of his acquaintance little kisses in jest," this could be understood as part of the "Rhenish nature that he embodied in excess" – tempting persons from outside the Rhineland to engage in "erroneous moralizing." Moreover,

Schiedermair avowed, the idea that a genius could have derived from a "family swamp" was absurd: since Beethoven was a great German artist, he simply could not have come from inferior stock; therefore, the father must have been sound. Anything else would represent a contradiction of biological laws.[58]

In 1933, as Nazi theory moved closer to practice, this issue was addressed even more intensely. Fritz Lenz, physician, geneticist, and advocate of sterilization based on "artificial selection," was one of the leading promoters of the Nazi program of racial hygiene. Drawing from his textbook on the subject, *Human Selection and Racial Hygiene* (1921), Lenz used the case of Beethoven to present his views to the wide audience of the *Völkischer Beobachter*. A popular objection against racial-hygienic sterilization, he reported, was the allegation that it represented a "danger to culture." As proof, some raised the case of Johann van Beethoven, arguing that had such legislation required castration of the composer's father, the renowned son would never have been born. One such critic of eugenic measures said, according to Lenz: "I wish to mention one more man whose existence counterbalances hundreds of thousands of patients who are mentally ill: Beethoven. Imagine what a priceless treasure of German – and not just German – art would have been lost if the father of Beethoven had been sterilized for eugenic reasons!" To that, Lenz responded that no racial-hygienist had ever stated that Beethoven's father should have been sterilized. To the contrary, "the family of Beethoven stood as an example of the inheritability of high musical ability." In any case, Lenz argued, Beethoven's father was a capable musician and he apparently began drinking seriously only after Beethoven's birth. So, even if he had been sterilized for his drinking, the birth of Beethoven would not have been prevented. Thus, the case of Beethoven did not constitute for Lenz or the *Völkischer Beobachter* a sound objection to racial-hygienic sterilization; rather, those referencing Beethoven in this context did so for the purpose of fueling opposition to racial-hygiene "on emotional grounds in the minds of an uncritical public." Besides, Lenz went on, it also seemed doubtful whether the life of a single Beethoven really "counterbalanced" the unfortunate existence of hundreds of thousands of the mentally ill. It was a fact, Lenz explained, that millions of births were intentionally prevented every year. As a result, numerous highly talented humans – and quite a few geniuses – remained unborn. This was all the more reason to ensure that birth prevention primarily targeted "inferiors," since the "habitat

[*Lebensraum*] for more capable individuals" and the "probability for the birth of important spirits" would thereby be increased. Therefore, Lenz concluded, it was "not racial-hygiene, but rather, short-sighted hostility against racial-hygiene," that was a "danger for culture."[59]

Ultimately, the *Völkischer Beobachter* extolled Beethoven's works as exemplifying the greatness of Germanic art – and the German race itself. In his music the "soul of the struggle-tormented, northern German" came to expression.[60] According to Hans Buchner, its forceful spirit proved the "world-wide validity of the spiritual work and the soulful nobility that the greatest sons of the German nation were capable of." Moreover, Buchner concluded, Beethovenian spirit was not just a factor of German history: Nazis knew "what this force of the past indicated about the possibilities of the future."[61]

Franz Liszt (1811–1886) presented another challenge for the *Völkischer Beobachter* in certifying German credentials. Because Liszt had been born and raised in Hungary, controversy ensued over his ethnicity. The newspaper undertook a variety of strategies in formulating its claims on Liszt. First, its contributors assessed the region of Hungary from which he originated. According to Josef Stolzing, Liszt was born in an "almost purely German" area of Hungary.[62] Karl Grunsky went into greater detail, adding that since Liszt's home town officially belonged to Hungary, he went as a Hungarian instead of as an "*Auslandsdeutscher,*" but the region of his birth was – as local place names like Stein am Anger, Oedenburg, and Wieslburg indicate – settled by Germans, and there they "maintained their racial customs and language."[63] Second, the newspaper presented investigations into the composer's family background. According to Hans Kellermann, although Adam Liszt, the father, might have been a "Magyar," one thing was certain: Liszt's mother, Anna Maria Langer, from Krems in Upper Austria, was "definitely of German origins."[64] The vitriolic antimodernist and anti-Semitic opera critic, Paul Zschorlich, agreed that while there were "some questions" about the father's nationality, the possibility that he had some Gypsy blood in his veins "could at the most be guessed, but never proven." However, Zschorlich felt this genealogical weakness was overcome by the mother's background: the daughter of a merchant from Krems, Maria Anna Langer, had been shown "definitively to be German."[65] Going further, Karl Grunsky stressed the "obvious Germanness" of the father's side of the composer's heritage too: "the great-grandfather was Sebastian List, an officer who died in Raigendorf bei Oedenburg; that was where the grandfather Georg Adam List was born in 1755, and he became an official under Prince Esterhazy."[66] This assertion highlighted another issue that the Nazi newspaper emphasized: the spelling of the composer's name. As Stolzing put it, his father was baptized List – clearly German – though his name was "later Magyarized with the addition of a z, because he was a civil servant of Prince Esterhazy."[67] In any case, Stolzing pointed out, the mother was Viennese with the "utterly German name: Langer."[68] However, even in the pages of the *Völkischer Beobachter*, this argument based on the spelling of Liszt's name was not treated as definitive. Paul Zschorlich had to admit the "assumption that Liszt's father was a German named List who added the z to his name only once in Hungary" was "on shaky grounds." In the birth record of the composer, the name of his father was written as List, but "the name Esterhasy was also spelled without a z." It was risky, Zschorlich concluded, to base the determination of Liszt's race on the "inaccurate spelling of village officials," since "Liszt himself always wrote his name with a z."[69]

In view of this controversy, a third way the newspaper countered notions of Liszt's Hungarian roots was to insist that German was spoken exclusively in the house of his parents, and through his whole life "the master never learned the Hungarian language."[70] According to Zschorlich, the "most important fact" was that Liszt couldn't speak Hungarian: since he left home as a child, living first in Vienna and then in Paris, he "never had the opportunity to learn" it.[71] Grunsky concurred that Liszt "hardly understood a word of Hungarian: he heard only German in his parents' home and at school."[72] And Stolzing put it most strongly: "he didn't just have imperfect command of the Magyar language – he didn't understand it at all!"[73]

One reason why the issue of Liszt's origins was of such importance to the paper was the arrival of occasional reports that the Hungarian state intended to request that the city of Bayreuth allow the transfer of Liszt's remains to the land of his birth. The *Völkischer Beobachter* voiced serious opposition to this plan. Stolzing asserted that efforts at removing his bones and taking them to Hungary were "remarkable": one "couldn't raise enough objections against this," because "Franz Liszt was German by descent and by education."[74] Still, recognizing that even the combination of arguments recounted above "failed to clear up everything"[75] – that, as Karl Grunsky put it, "no final clarity over Liszt's descent can be attained"[76] – *Völkischer Beobachter* contributors had to press their objections even further.

According to Kellermann, if Liszt was called Hungarian, then this assertion was based "solely on the fact that he was born there." He spent
almost the whole second half of his life in Germany, Kellermann noted,
working for decades in Weimar as conductor, composer, and teacher –
helping the city of Schiller and Goethe to "enjoy an unexpected dose of
new blood." Moreover, what he did "for German music, above all for
Richard Wagner," could never be forgotten. Further, Cosima Wagner,
"this wonderful woman, so infinitely important for the creativity of the
Bayreuth master," was Liszt's daughter. In Zschorlich's view, the extent
to which Liszt, in his creative life, "grew into, engaged with, and felt
himself bound to German culture" was incontrovertible. No more proof
was necessary to show how strongly he "stimulated German music
creativity," so Germans could regard him "completely as their own."[77]
Finally, Karl Grunsky pulled out the ultimate weapon from the Nazi
arsenal for proving Germanic origin: the "blond, blue-eyed appearance,
the form of the body, the features of the face all left scarcely any doubt
that Franz Liszt represented the epitome of the Nordic race."[78]

Surprisingly similar efforts to ensure that a cultural figure was of
certifiably pure German origins were necessary in the case of Richard
Wagner (1813–1883). Given that, as Joseph Goebbels put it, Wagner
ranked in Nazi propaganda as the "most German of all Germans," it was
of particular importance that the *Völkischer Beobachter* put aside doubts
about his heritage. Josef Stolzing took this issue on directly. From time to
time, he wrote, the "old swindle kept arising," that "one of the greatest
German geniuses of all, Richard Wagner, had Jewish blood in his veins."
These claims were based on rumors that Wagner's mother had been the
lover of Ludwig Geyer (whom she married after her first husband, Carl
Friedrich Wagner, died) at the time when the composer was conceived.
Stolzing and the *Völkischer Beobachter* strove to "overcome this filth
and break through these lies once and for all" with a two-pronged
argument: first, by demonstrating that relations between Geyer and
Wagner's mother were innocent until they married – and that Richard
was born before this happened; then, by insisting that, in any case, Geyer
was not Jewish. As Stolzing put it, it was absolutely certain, "according
to the portraits that we have," that Geyer had a "completely German
head without the slightest indication of alien blood."[79]

Composer and music critic Hugo Rasch seconded Stolzing's
claims. "We know that Geyer was a perfectly pure Aryan." His portrait,
"similar in noblesse to that of Carl Maria von Weber," left "absolutely

no doubt." Moreover, the letters between Geyer and the wife of his deceased friend were of "such a respectful and eloquent tone" that this "fairytale could finally disappear from the table-talk of Puritan philistines and from the coffee clutches of uptight old spinsters." This "typical Jewish tall tale," Rasch insisted, had to be put to rest, though "it would have suited Jewry just fine if they could conjure away one of the greatest German geniuses of all with such a trick."[80] Freiherr von Leoprechting, an editor and writer for the cultural section of the *Völkischer Beobachter* before and immediately after the NSDAP purchased the paper,[81] also placed the blame for this issue at the feet of National Socialism's main targets. "Here and there" one heard voices suggesting that Wagner was a Jew, Leoprechting reported: though his family history was well known, this "dirty story continued to circulate." But it had been proven, Leoprechting continued, that "the actor Ludwig Geyer was no Jew and never had any Jewish blood in his family." So, like the "whole house of lies built up by Jewish wiles," this "mendacious construction would ultimately fall apart – to the shame and disgrace of Judah."[82] According to the *Völkischer Beobachter*, then, there was "only one correct answer to these accusations," and it was best stated by Wagner's son, Siegfried: "All one has to do is listen to the first three beats of the *Meistersinger* Overture to know that my father was not of Jewish descent."[83]

2 VOX VOLKISH

As we have seen, the editors of the *Völkischer Beobachter* were dedicated to validating Nazi ideology with reference to the main figures and ideas of Western creative history, thereby providing the National Socialist movement with cultural legitimacy and grounding it in a far-reaching past. However, adhering to another significant strain of volkish ideas, Nazi ideologues were simultaneously wary of identifying their movement or its supposed forefathers with any sort of intelligentsia.[1] While contributors to the paper often supported their efforts to assimilate iconic hero-artists into Nazi culture by turning to claims of German descent – real or projected – the notion of *Volkstümlichkeit* or volkishness also served to identify those creators who deserved elevation into the party's pantheon.[2]

Although he maintained a self-image as a man of *Bildung*, especially in extensive table talks where he pontificated on every conceivable political and cultural topic, Hitler denounced intellectual pretension and cultivated the public image of a man of the Volk. Above all, he prided himself in being able to bridge the gap between his presumed genius and the "smallest minds," claiming in *Mein Kampf* that "among a thousand speakers there is perhaps only a single one who can manage to speak to locksmiths and university professors at the same time, in a form which not only is suitable to the receptivity of both parties, but also influences both parties with equal effect or actually lashes them into a wild storm of applause."[3] He insisted, accordingly, that Nazi ideology be promoted in terms easily accessible to the average German, holding that, particularly in the field of propaganda, "we must never let ourselves be led by aesthetes or people who have grown blasé because the form and expression of our propaganda would soon have drawing power only for literary teas, instead of being suitable for the masses."[4] It was important, in his mind, that Nazi leadership should not appear effete, "since a nation composed of learned men who are physical weaklings, hesitant about decisions of the will, and timid pacifists, is not capable of assuring even its own existence on this earth."[5]

Goebbels, too, for all his intellectual pretension, articulated the view that all profound art had roots not in the erudite realms of Weimar culture in particular, but in the common experience of everyday Germans. In his speech opening the Reich Culture Chamber in 1933, Goebbels stated that:

> *culture is the highest expression of the productive forces of a Volk; the artist its chosen medium. It would be a mistake to believe that his sacred mission can be achieved outside the Volk; it is undertaken for the Volk, and the power that he applies comes from the Volk. If the artist once loses solid footing in the Volk, on which he must stand with hard, pithy bones against the storms of life, he opens himself to the hostility of civilization to which he will succumb sooner or later ... An art that separates itself from the Volk has no right to complain when the Volk separates itself from it.*[6]

Firmly in line with principles of *Volkstümlichkeit*, then, the *Völkischer Beobachter* consistently excoriated professional intellectuals who produced nothing but ideas for ideas' sake – or even worse, did so for money. In general, this anti-intellectual stance in Nazi ideology opposed writers and thinkers who existed as sophisticates out of touch with the more genuine lives of the rural Volk. Ultimately, this notion served as the primary prong of an attack on the "asphalt literati" of urbane Weimar culture, supposedly either under the influence of Jews, or Jews themselves. On the other hand, the paper insisted that the chosen leaders of Western and German spiritual life never lost themselves in the "arid chaos" of art for art's sake.

As we will see in Part II, the *Völkischer Beobachter* typically treated Western classical tradition with disdain. Still, not all references to Roman culture in the *Völkischer Beobachter* were negative. One article on the life of poets in Late Rome, based on material culled from a book by a "beloved author," classicist Theodore Birt, portrayed Horace in frankly positive terms: as a well-rounded, even earthy character. "Scribbling poetry was not his sole occupation," according to Birt, he was also "a farmer with all his body and soul; a man who cultivated wine with smudged hands." On his farm, he was "well grounded": most of his *Odes* were composed there in the "rural stillness of summer"; he only "tread the pavement of Rome" during the winter. To be sure, the most distinguished houses were open to him and he found Maecenas' young wife – who sang and danced in his presence – beautiful and attractive. Even so, noted the paper, "as crudely erotic as he might have pretended to be," he never went near married women: Horace "stood high above the frivolous vice that dominated his time."[7]

In so arguing, the *Völkischer Beobachter* clearly desired to present Horace as an exception among leading figures in an otherwise decadent stage of antiquity. The author of *dulce et decorum est, pro patria mori* was thereby set aside for recognition in the Nazi newspaper. Representative of the selective reporting that characterized its ideologically driven cultural reporting, the *Völkischer Beobachter* herein located evidence in Horace's biography that he spent extensive time on his farm, relished the rural quiet, dirtied his hands producing wine, and only occasionally deigned to tread the pave stones of Rome (the ancient equivalent to Berlin's asphalt). All this marked him as a cultural figure the paper could honor with one of its favorite monikers: *volkstümlich*. But, of course, attributing to the highly civilized Horace this rough-edged, Plebian reputation required that *Völkischer Beobachter* editors ignored manifold and otherwise firmly established aspects of his biography, including his close association with both Virgil and Caesar Augustus, and the impeccable sophistication of his Latin verse.

Similar strategies can be found in the paper's coverage of the Renaissance era. Besides Leonardo and Michelangelo, the *Völkischer Beobachter* made only passing reference to other major painters of the Italian Renaissance such as Titian[8] and Raphael (referring to the latter as "merely superficial"[9]) if only because the newspaper was far more occupied with trumpeting the achievements of the German Renaissance. While acknowledging that most of the northern artists had directly or indirectly "breathed the colors and techniques of the warm South," the *Völkischer Beobachter* held that they had all, like the Augsburg painter and designer of woodcuts, Hans Burgkmair (1473–1531), "nevertheless remained thoroughly German, incorporating lessons learned from the

Italians sometimes a little roughly, the way Germans speak Italian: sometimes a little uncertainly, even distorting them; but always in their own way." Masters of the German Renaissance "looked upon the external world, taking it onto themselves with strength and will, but never losing themselves to multicolored, shining superficiality." Whatever they borrowed from the south, "their core remained German, producing things that only Germans could produce."[10]

For instance, it was precisely such a "distorted, rough-hewn" quality that made Albrecht Altdorfer's art Nordic, wrote Ernst Buchner – a student of Heinrich Wölfflin, then General Director of the Bavarian State Picture Collections (*Bayerischen Staatsgemäldesammlungen*), and later participant in Nazi art seizures.[11] In Buchner's opinion, Altdorfer (c. 1480–1538) (Figure 2.1) would always be famous as the "discoverer of the German landscape." His feeling for space was "naive and elementary, far from cool, perspectively correct calculation." Seeing nature as an "exciting cosmos, radiant with light and color," the artist sensed the "secret forces of organic growth." Thus, his forest was not, as with earlier painters and all of his contemporaries, "a sum of trees," but "an organic whole"; his images captured the "mysterious weaving and rushing of the branches, leaves, and twigs."[12]

"Naive and elementary" rather than "intellectual and over-refined" like the works of Italian contemporaries, these were positive attributes within an aesthetics of volkish simplicity, realized best, according to Buchner, in the "stronger, coarse-grained language of woodcut prints which Altdorfer also mastered." His was "art for the wide Volk," to which Altdorfer was "inwardly close." Few of his contemporaries achieved the "warm, Volk tone that spoke directly to the heart" like he did. His figures almost all came from the rural world: his Virgin Mary was a "maid of the Volk" (Figure 2.2); his angels were "strapping farm boys." Occasionally, Buchner allowed, critics argued that his figures were "not beautiful enough," but it was "precisely from this strong, inner unity with unbroken, national character and pure, authentic nature, that arose the best powers of this master whose art was the purest embodiment of Bavarian folk style."[13]

This sort of rhetorical tactic, in which an artist's attention to the "deep problems" of art was distinguished from the mere technical processes associated with Italian culture, was also central to the *Völkischer Beobachter* characterization of Albrecht Dürer's art as essentially volkish. According to art historian Wilhelm Rüdiger, a staff writer who also

Figure 2.1 Albrecht Altdorfer, *Saint George in the Forest* (1510), Alte Pinakothek, Munich, Germany

worked with Baldur von Schirach to arrange exhibitions in the Third Reich,[14] if one asked what were the best known works of German art, "not just among particular sections of the populace, but among all of the Volk, hanging – in good or bad reproductions – in every house," then there were only a handful of names which "really had a volkish sound to them": among visual artists, "really only Arnold Böcklin, whose *Isle of the Dead* was everywhere, and Dürer (1471–1528), whose famous

Figure 2.2 Albrecht Altdorfer, *The Birth of the Virgin* (1525), Alte Pinakothek, Munich, Germany

paintings and wood-cuts were known by all Germans." This, it was argued, was because of the "volkish nature" of Dürer's works, which "made them ever accessible to popular audiences." The visual language of his contemporaries seemed "ancient: sometimes quaint, often strange," but Dürer's remained "widely comprehensible, more so than any other painter of his time"; it "spoke more directly and more urgently than that of Holbein, Cranach, or even Grünewald."[15]

For instance, Rüdiger asked, "what sort of thoughts lay behind an image like *Knight, Death, and the Devil*?" (Figure 2.3). While the image of an *eques christianus* – the Christian knight riding between Death and the Devil – was common in the age of the Reformation, to

Figure 2.3 Albrecht Dürer, *Knight, Death, and the Devil* (1513)

modern laymen it had become meaningless. Nevertheless, the form Dürer gave to it "still said something to moderns, because it was not born of pure intellect, but from completely different depths of the artist's soul." The work functioned, "for courageous people facing great pressures," as a "visual correlate to Luther's *A Mighty Fortress Is Our God*." In Rüdiger's opinion, *Melencolia* also had an "earthy tone: one could say that the setting is untidy" (Figure 2.4). A mature, "almost beautiful woman" sits amid things that give the impression of complete disorder, thinking without regard for her surroundings. This "peculiar atmosphere, lacking feminine care, fills the room to the brim; all activity has stopped, as if any action has become senseless." This "lugubrious mood" of *Melencolia* was no accident, according to Rüdiger, for Dürer created the image after the death of his mother. It was, therefore, a prime example of "German art wrought in pain."

Moving to Dürer's *St. Jerome in his Study* (Figure 2.5), Rüdiger also saw its representation of a common Renaissance subject as

Figure 2.4 Albrecht Dürer, *Melencolia* (1514)

"uniquely German – and homespun in a volkish way." The "old bachelor dwelling of the holy one" – with the lion stretched out in the sun and the "not so terrible" skull on the window – "reeked of warm intimacies like those of a happy family home." This "cordial tone" warmed all Dürer's representations of Biblical stories, especially scenes from the childhood of Jesus – with angels rendered as "holy scamps at play" – as well as in depictions of Christ's suffering. Dürer's God was, for Rüdiger, "no Byzantine Pantocrator, not an omnipotent and autonomous ruler before whom subjects rolled in the dust; it was, rather, *deus charitatis*, as in the magic visions of the Apocalypse: high and lofty, but not despotic." To convey such a close connection to earthly things, Dürer even gave Christ the features of his own face. Likewise, he renounced any idealization in his images of Mary, representing the baby Jesus as cared for "not by the most beautiful woman in the world, but rather by the best mother in the world." This was not degradation of the divine, but rather the "discovery or visualization of the divine in mankind." Similarly, a

Figure 2.5 Albrecht Dürer, *St. Jerome in his Study* (1514)

body such as that of the nude in *Fortuna* (1501) (Figure 2.6) was "downright ugly," and the figures in his illustrations of ancient myths were "far from classical." This "genuinely German reverence before nature" signified the legacy of the Gothic in this son of a Nürnberg goldsmith who, in his "absolute truthfulness regarding the things the earth," stood with "both feet on the soil of the Middle Ages."[16]

But Rüdiger still had to confront the fact that, for all his down-to-earth German qualities, Dürer greatly interested himself in the technical matters of proportion and perspective – indeed, that his general reputation as a Renaissance master was based on these inquiries. Getting straight to the point, Rüdiger simply dismissed such non-volkish elements of Dürer's work as "tragic mistakes." That this "most German master" initiated, with his theoretical investigations, a "neoclassical movement which was not native to lands north of the Alps, and which subsequently darkened his reputation, was – in world historical terms – his tragic fate." If he turned during his later years toward Renaissance

Figure 2.6 Albrecht Dürer, *Fortuna* (1501)

ideals that were "alien to the Volk," that was a "purely intellectual enterprise which remained foreign to his blood."[17]

Moving to the musical master of Reformation expression, the paper likewise attributed volkish directness to Bach. Every aspect of his work, Hans Buchner held, emerged out of "Germanic sensibility and perception" – "Nordic polyphony achieved its greatest heights under the tutelage of Bach." But it was not primarily the technical achievements of Bach's music that National Socialists emphasized, for musical virtuosity alone was not sufficient ground for volkish greatness. "Neither Bach, master of fugue, nor Bach, master of the art of calculated phrases" was of the greatest importance: it was "Bach, the conqueror of souls, whose themes of noble beauty, purity, and nobility of feeling stood guard over the Reich of music."[18] What made his music relevant to the popular Germanic mind, Buchner argued, was Bach's application of the "power of the volkish feeling for life to synthesize external influences and make them useful."[19]

The *Völkischer Beobachter*'s approach to Händel's music also emphasized its connections to the Volk community. For Ludwig K. Mayer – a musicologist who contributed regularly to the Nazi newspaper and would remain active after the war, publishing studies of Mozart, Richard Strauss, Pfitzner, and twentieth-century music in general – Händel's work was "the perfect expression of the heroic feeling for life." To be sure, "his genius processed inspirations from his personal ego," but at the moment when he reached for his pen, this ego "lifted itself out of the narrow confines of its individual existence and elevated itself into the comprehensive terms of the Typical." In this sense, Händel "always spoke to the community, to the *Volksgemeinschaft*." Nazis "striving to achieve a new ideal of a *Gemeinschaftsmusik* would find the model in Händel and his great orchestral works and oratorios."[20]

The *Völkischer Beobachter* likewise perceived in Mozart's music an underlying volkish quality that made it relevant to National Socialist culture, supplementing its supposedly Germanic, even patriotic, origins. What struck Nazis above all was "its singability – its melodic character," wrote Viktor Junk. For this reason it could never become obsolete, because it rested on this "primal basis of music." The simplest melodies contained the "life force of music": that's why Mozart's music "stirred even the simplest people; it was not addressed to experts in the least." Thus could a Mozart song like *Komm, lieber Mai, und mache die Bäume wieder grün* (Come, dear May, and make the trees green again) become a "*Volkslied*."[21] The Nazi effort to draw Mozart from the domain of elite culture continued with reference to *The Abduction from the Seraglio* (1782). Therein, thought Erwin Voelsing – a music critic who worked for the *Amt Rosenberg*[22] – Mozart formulated a "German song style despite the Italian *buffo* element and in spite of the apparent influence of French *opéra comique*." This volkish tendency in Mozart's art culminated in *The Magic Flute* (1791), where the "German-national thrust of the work," especially Papageno's melodies, was "dominated by the Volk tradition of the Vienna Singspiel – therefore, strongly colored by local influences."[23]

Treating Mozart's literary contemporary, Friedrich Schiller (1759–1805), Karl Berger – who had produced a two-volume biography of the poet before the First World War and contributed to the *Völkischer Beobachter* beginning in 1931[24] – bolstered a volkish view of his works as "realistic political dramas that attacked the problems of the German world under despotic rule, and called for self-sacrifice in the interest of the Volk."[25] To Berger, the poet of *The Robbers* (1781) evinced a spirit "directed on the political-social world, on the busy people of public life, and the power of a will that was ready for battle and self-sacrifice – which received wounds and suffered pains along with the groaning Volk enslaved by despots." *The Robbers* was a "devastating attack on the rotten state of the day, the errors in its world view, its political and social crimes – on the ever recurring evils committed against the individual as well as the whole Volk, arbitrarily and under the pressure of special interests." With it Schiller declared war against the "rapists of the Volk and the destroyers of justice." No German poetry did more toward "liberation from the yoke of servility and bondage" than Schiller's first drama. That the play called for "true liberation" was clear because its hero, Karl Moor, "established the rights of the many over those of the individual." Moor's plans for revenge and justice, Berger held, seemed to anticipate what would happen a decade later on the streets of Paris: the "anarchical revolution with its injustice, its errors and its fateful tragedy." In this first work, therefore, Schiller proved himself to be a "prophetic poet" who "didn't remain stuck in revolutionary ideology."[26]

For Robert Krötz – who would act as combat correspondent and war historian for the *Schutzstaffel* (SS) – the core of Schiller's dramatic works was the "relationship between individual and community." From this viewpoint, the works held a "new meaning" for Nazis. In *Wallenstein* (1799), a "creative man was depicted reaching outside the limits of the constrained individual into the social world of state order." But he never developed a "full sense of community." In the "collision between these two interests, he broke apart, for even the weakest structure of community is stronger than the individual with no bonds." That, according to Krötz, "was Schiller's point, and it was very close, indeed, proximate, to us," that is, to the ideas of Nazism.[27]

Similarly, thought Albrecht Adam, *Maria Stuart* (1800) expresses a "heroic willingness to die" and *The Maid of Orleans* (1801) "leads her Volk to liberty in the sign of a higher power." Then came *Wilhelm Tell*. Completed in the years 1803 and 1804, it appeared at an "unfortunate time," so this "Volk freedom drama" did not receive the attention it deserved, except in Prussia. Thereafter, the freedom fighters in *Wilhelm Tell* became symbols, "calling the German Volk again and again to act in the hour of national distress according to their fiery example."²⁸ Ultimately, added F. O. H. Schulz – who produced anti-Semitic literature, including a book for the Institute for the Study of the Jewish Question – the "German Volk came to recognize what it possessed in this work of divinely-willed love for the Fatherland," and *Wilhelm Tell* became a "sacred song of patriotic love, received by the German people with indescribable joy as a moral weapon against the Corsican's conquest." A half century before Fichte gave his *Speeches to the German Nation*, Schulz added, Schiller called out in *Wilhelm Tell*:

> How powerful is the drive of the Fatherland ...
> O, learn to feel which tribe you are part of!

By penning such lines, Schiller emerged as a voice of German unification and nationalism against Napoleon.²⁹ A century later, Robert Krötz contended, "anyone could read his works to understand National Socialist thoughts on the same issues."³⁰

For articulation of the volkish nature of Richard Wagner's work, the newspaper simply had to turn to Joseph Goebbels' speech on the 50th anniversary of the composer's death in 1933. After a performance at the Bayreuth Festival, Goebbels broadcast to the nation that *Die Meistersinger* was the "incarnation of *Volkstum*." In it was contained "everything that marked and filled the German soul." It was an ingenious combination of "German melancholy and romance, of German pride and German diligence, of that German humor, about which it is said that one 'laughs with one eye and cries with the other.'" It was an image of the "hearty and yea-saying German Renaissance," moving from "bitter, pure tragedy, through jubilant musical triumph, to the sonic pathos of a rousing Volksfest." Never had the "fragrance of a German night in June been so tenderly represented in music" as in its second act. Never had the "tragedy of an aging man in love – laughing despite the melancholy of renunciation – found such transfigured expression" as in Hans Sachs' *Wahn* monologue. Never had the "outcry of the Volk sounded more rousingly and thrillingly" than in the opening chords of the *Wacht auf* chorus. Wagner's art was "written for the Volk: it would give the Volk comfort in its misery and strength in its suffering; it was balm for grief- and pain-filled souls; it was healthy art in its innermost sense; it could heal people by reminding them of the original sources of their own existence." In short, Goebbels claimed, Wagner's music "towered over all other as the most German of all."³¹

3 THE WESTERN TRADITION AS POLITICAL AND PATRIOTIC

Walter Benjamin wrote, "the logical outcome of fascism is an aestheticizing of political life."[1] But as seen in the strategies of Nazi ideologues, it can be argued that the opposite was also true: that fascism as practiced also worked to politicize artistic culture. Thus, in addition to attesting that favorite figures of Western cultural history were of Germanic and definitely not of Jewish descent, and volkish rather than urbane, Nazi propagandists also countered notions of art for art's sake by promoting the view that the primary creative impulse was as much political – especially patriotic and nationalistic – as artistic.[2] Hitler contributed to the politicization of art history on numerous occasions. While acceding that "art has at all times been the expression of an ideological and religious experience," he insisted that it is "at the same time the expression of a political will."[3] For him, "all great art is national ... Great musicians, such as Beethoven, Mozart, Bach, created German music that was deeply rooted in the very core of the German spirit and the German mind ... That is equally true of German sculptors, painters, architects."[4] At the opening of the Reich Culture Chamber in 1933, Joseph Goebbels expanded on this view of the true artist as engaged in the politics of his day:

> *Revolutions are never limited to the purely political. They*
> *reach into every area of human interaction. Science and art do*
> *not remain unaffected. We understand politics in a higher*
> *sense ... Even the creator – especially he – is drawn into the*

> *vortex of revolutionary events. He only rises to his time and its tasks if he does not remain content with passively letting the revolution unfold, but when he actively intervenes in it, consciously affirms it, takes on its rhythm, and makes its goals his own. In short: if he marches not in the rearguard, but at its head.*[5]

So, another central dictum of Nazified cultural history promoted in the *Völkischer Beobachter* was that the great works of the Western tradition were politically inspired, especially in the spirit of patriotism and nationalism, as these concepts might have been relevant for any particular historical context.

For ideologues writing for the paper, the relative lack of historical information about one medieval German figure left a convenient opening to begin nationalistic mythmaking. To establish the roots of volkish literature and song, the *Völkischer Beobachter* turned to the legendary *minnesinger*, Walther von der Vogelweide (c. 1170–c. 1230). An important Germanist, Johann Georg Sprengel – author of nationalistically oriented books on the idea of the state in German poetry from the Middle Ages on, as well as numerous works calling for politically charged educational reform in postwar Germany – characterized Vogelweide as an early exponent of "German reason of state" (*Staatsgedank*). Without mentioning the dearth of reliable biographical information available about Vogelweide (a circumstance that had allowed for claims on his national origin by Austrians, Tyroleans, and Bohemians alike), Sprengel was adamant about the minnesinger's German nature and significance. According to Sprengel, Vogelweide was a "pure German lyrical poet," the "first bloom of German lyrical art which arose from the soil of chivalry." Anticipating "romantic aesthetics," Vogelweide "seized life from the inside out" and measured its true values "according to genuinely German world feeling." But rather than find significance in Vogelweide's work for its expression of personal passion, Sprengel instead celebrated Vogelweide as the first poet who "praised Germany above all else in the world." Vogelweide's love lyrics, which had revolutionized chivalric court poetry, were largely ignored. Instead, Sprengel concentrated on lines which he argued established Vogelweide's reputation as an "enthusiastic herald of Fatherlandish spirit," namely, those lyrics that were supposedly incorporated into the modern German national anthem.[6]

The *Völkischer Beobachter* did acknowledge the pastoral lyricism of Vogelweide's other songs, stating in other articles marking the 700th anniversary of Vogelweide's death in 1930 that all of *Deutschtum* should honor this "shining singer" of the Hohenstaufen era. Particularly, he should be honored, said the paper, in the Lusamgärtlein of Würzburg, where Vogelweide was buried and the "smell of the fairy tale wondrously wafts" (from a Vogelweide song text: *vom Duft des Märchens wundersam umwehten*), but also on the Wartburg, in Vienna, and Tyrol – "everywhere that the German tongue sounds" – in schools, in literary and musical circles, and in the Youth Movement, all would think of him with joy: he was, said the paper, the patron saint of poets, singers, musicians, the *Wandervögel*, bird lovers, and the month of May. Even so, the editors left no doubt that the singular achievement that earned the minnesinger a place in Walhalla, as a "great man of the German nation" whose art resonated into the German future, was to have been the "singer of the first Song of Germany" – *Deutschlandlied* – the inspiration for what would become the modern national anthem.[7]

Four years after the Vogelweide septicentennial and a few months after the Nazi Party had attained control in Germany, the *Völkischer Beobachter* again asserted that Vogelweide's medieval songs would resound in the German future as Nazis visualized it. Any past reservations about invoking Vogelweide were being laid to rest by a cultural and political regime that would forcefully heed Wagner's *Meistersinger* exhortation to "honor your German masters." Writing of the Weimar era, the poet Franz Langheinrich complained that it had seemed hopeless to speak about German song and poetry in an environment where "cold-hearted literary big-wigs" ridiculed German lyrics as "private pangs of the soul." But by the fall of 1934, in the "warm morning sun of the rebirth of the Fatherland," the German *Lied* was arising to new life. The inaugural celebrations of the Nazi government marking the "preparedness of its determined ranks" were consecrated by *Lieder* that came from "young hearts" and "old sources." After passing reference to his other works, Langheinrich then sounded the familiar refrain of the *Völkischer Beobachter*'s prize song about Vogelweide: "most importantly, the stanzas of the *Deutschlandlied* came from one of the oldest of these *Lieder*." With this, Langheinrich went on to summarize the connection between Vogelweide and the national anthem. In 1841, Langheinrich posited, Heinrich August Hoffmann von Fallersleben found Vogelweide's text in the *Liederborn* of the Middle Ages, and "called it to new life after a sleep of many centuries." Thus, it was "the great singer of the Middle Ages, the first German poet, whose tunes sounded with praise for the Reich" who penned the original text of the *Deutschlandlied*. Langheinrich did allow that Vogelweide "rose up as a splendid poetic totality": after seven centuries, his other *Minnelieder* still moved Germans in their "original freshness, naturalness, and beauty"; his "reflective and religious poetry" contained the most profound elements that his era was capable of drawing from human experience. But it was above all his "political songs and sayings, filled with a power and fighting greatness for the glory of the Reich," that remained alive in the Nazi era. Once again, Vogelweide was "most important for giving the German Volk the original text of its *Vaterlandlied*."[8]

By repeatedly emphasizing the political nature of Vogelweide's poetry in order to link it with the "reason of state" that Sprengel felt essential to medieval German literature and beyond, the paper overwhelmed his "reflective religious and love poetry." But in their intensive attribution of the words of the "Song of the Germans" (*Lied der Deutschen*[9]) to Vogelweide, contributors like Langheinrich also neglected to point out that Hoffmann von Fallersleben (1798–1874) drew only the second stanza of what became the German national anthem from Vogelweide's song, and that even this was only loosely based on the original:

> German women, German loyalty,
> German wine, and German song
> Shall continue to be held in high
> Esteem all over the world,
> And inspire us to noble deeds
> Our whole lives long.
> German women, German loyalty,
> German wine, and German song!

However one chooses to read the controversial first stanza of the *Deutschlandlied*, it was not Vogelweide who praised Germany above all else in the world, but Hoffmann von Fallersleben.[10] From a medieval perspective – be it Austrian, or Tyrolean, or Bohemian – the medieval minnesinger had praised the women, loyalty, wine, and song of his culture, but not a geographical conception of something that would become a German nation.

Chronologically, the first major cultural figure to be described by the *Völkischer Beobachter* as a Superman (*Übermensch*) was Dante Alighieri (1265–1321). As this term was drawn into Nazi usage, however, the basis for attributing Dante as such was not primarily the poet's creative work. More significant here was Dante's social and political experience in the Florence of his lifetime. Implying similarities between the instability of late medieval Florentine politics – with constant infighting between Ghibellines and Guelfs Black and White – and the complexities of Weimar republican politics, the paper argued that Dante's political stand shared features with modern conservative patriotism. As *Übermensch*, the primary source of suffering that Dante had to overcome was forced exile from his homeland. The *Völkischer Beobachter*'s mention of Dante therefore highlighted the "powerful waves of grief and homesickness" that marked his poetry as a result. Not platonic love for Beatrice, but political struggle was the main drive behind his writing. Against "forces of disorder ravaging his personal existence," Dante posited strong stabilizing institutions: fatherland, clan, family. These, according to the paper, were the "strong roots of Dante's artistic and human powers – both sad and joyful."[11]

Supporting generalizations about Dante's fatherlandish sentiments, the *Völkischer Beobachter* delineated commonalities between his political views and the right-wing German outlook. The stated goal of a 1940 article entitled "Dante and the Imperial Idea" was to extract Dante's "volkish ideas" from his experiences as a man of his time. Above all, it held, Dante "yearned for stability" by hypothesizing a new political order. The wars of his time caused in him the desire for change, but rather than reaching for weapons, he decided on a "battle of ideas." Against a medieval premise that went back to Augustine – that the Papacy represented the irrefutable power in the world under which all of humanity must be united – Dante offered up the "new idea of a state that stands above the Church." In doing so, he moved toward a modern conception of the secular state, not itself divine, but "ultimately sanctified by the spirituality of nationalism." At the time, the *Völkischer Beobachter* commented, this notion was still an essentially mystical, utopian conception. But, in retrospect, "from the volkish-nationalistic perspective," Dante had seen the future by virtue of a "correct intuition, timeless and universal." From then on his ideas penetrated "into the spirits of his time and posterity." This was Dante's Nazi significance: not as the greatest medieval poet-theologian, but as the first in a line of prophets who foretold the evolution of the volkish state. As a "powerless thinker without a following," he had to put forth these ideas in the *Divine Comedy* without acting on them. However, the paper implied, his intuitions were finally being acted upon in twentieth-century Italy and Germany.[12]

According to the *Völkischer Beobachter*, the next lighthouse beaming volkish-nationalist ideas through the Western tradition of political thought was Niccolò Machiavelli (1469–1527). The newspaper intensively analyzed Machiavelli's political catechism for elements that pertained to the modern German situation. Ruthless strategies against both external and internal enemies were held up as common between "Machiavelli and us." His words seemed to "admonish contemporary Germany," Z. L. Schember asserted: one should "use one's enemy's weapons against him," wrote Machiavelli, "surpassing him in their use toward his destruction." Above all, Schember relished Machiavelli's *Reason of State*: with one powerful tug he "pulled political science free from theology and jurisprudence," and set it forth as an independent field. Putting Machiavellian *Realpolitik* in its own terms, the *Völkischer Beobachter* contended that the state was an end in itself: "all had to be subservient to it, including morality and religion." Most intently, Schember sought justification for policies against *internal* enemies, turning to Machiavelli's *Discourses on Livy*, from which he quoted: "When it is a matter of the survival of the homeland, one cannot ask what is just or unjust, nor what is merciful or cruel, nor what is praiseworthy or ignominious; all other considerations must retreat before the resolve to save the life of the Fatherland and maintain its freedom."[13] For Nazis, wrote Schember, Machiavelli's voice was "rising once again, heavy with responsibility" like the voice of a judge making a life and death decision, on which "neither mercy nor appeal" had any influence. "Sharp and cold like a sword, this merciless message was cutting through the German heart: whoever shows himself an enemy of the Fatherland, in thought or deed … should be treated as a patricide."[14] As surveyed by Friedrich Meinecke not long before the appearance of Schember's article, whatever the tradition of Machiavellian *Staatsräson* had wrought through the ages, *Völkischer Beobachter* allusions indeed marked the beginning of an ignominious phase, free from theology and jurisprudence. Here the paper stipulated reason of state as justifying the use of hooks, wires, and guillotines in places like the prison at Plötzensee and other sites where, to be sure, neither mercy nor appeal had any influence.

Following on this ruthless view of Renaissance ideas, discussion of Martin Luther (1483–1546) in the *Völkischer Beobachter* was marked with militaristic language evident in article titles like "Luther at War against the Papacy," "The Decisive Battle," and, most telling, "Luther's Fight against the Jews." The Nazi paper described Luther as motivated first and foremost by German patriotic impulse, making him a "German Hero of Faith" whose life's work was dedicated to the "spiritual and cultural development of the German Volk."[15] Throughout its coverage, the paper followed a nationalistic line expressed by Wilhelm Frick, the Nazi Minister of the Interior, at Wittenberg on the 450th anniversary of Luther's birth in 1933: Luther had become a "global force," but only because he was "German with every fiber of his heart and every vibration of his soul: 'I was born for my Germans, I will serve them' – these were his words; this is what he meant."[16]

By concentrating on and reproducing Luther's strongest statements from "Against the Papacy in Rome,"[17] the *Völkischer Beobachter* articulated a tendency to construe Luther's message as wholly German, even to the point of distinguishing Lutheranism from the Judeo-Christian tradition. With "clarity that could not be misunderstood," wrote Adolf Hösel, Luther challenged faith in the infallibility of the Pope: he turned against the "Devil's work" of idolatry, the sale of indulgences, and other abuses by the Catholic Church. But most importantly, for Hösel, Luther's actions constituted a "call for the Nordic peoples of Europe to shake off the curse of racially foreign spirituality that had weighed upon them since the outbreak of Roman Christianity, and to follow the formation of their inner relations to God in their own way."[18]

Karl Bornhausen, a leader of the *Kampfbund für Deutsche Kultur* (Fighting League for German Culture) in Silesia and proponent of a "Church-free German Christianity," pressed *Völkischer Beobachter* Luther reception even further in the direction of a Germanic-Christian interpretation. After expressing wonder at the fact that Luther's biblical expertise meant he had been expert in Hebrew as well as other ancient languages, Bornhausen took this position to its extreme: "One could no longer say that Germans derived their faith from Palestine" because "the Lord Jesus came to Luther and spoke German with him so heartily that Luther could do nothing other than let the love and goodness of the Holy One sound in the German language and the German being." Thus was German "the language of religion," and that is why "one had to be either a German Christian or nothing." Germans therefore had to obey Luther's "harsh order – to sacrifice one's life for the Volk – as readily as they adhered to his command of love, happily giving work and service to their brethren." Moreover, they had to stand by him when he "lashed the foreign economy of gold and warned not to do harm to their souls in the pursuit of Mammon."[19]

As Bornhausen argued, defending this position meant separating Luther not just from Rome, but from the "Hebrew biblical tradition" itself, and the *Völkischer Beobachter* tried to do so, arguing in a summary of Alfred Rosenberg's views that it was "scientifically careless to call Luther merely the 'Man with the Bible.'" For Rosenberg it was clear that the "Germanic belief in God as a friend" (*Freundgottglaube*) was alive in Luther, and this belief caused him to have "scruples and blasphemous thoughts about the 'God of the Bible.'" These thoughts disappeared only when he no longer saw the Bible in opposition to his "Germanic-German religious preconceptions." As Rosenberg said "correctly," according to the paper, the "Germanic protest against oriental-Roman religious conceptions broke out in Luther." All interpretations are "determined by the blood and race of the interpreter," argued Rosenberg, and therefore Luther's interpretation of the Bible was a Germanic, not a Judeo-Christian version, toward which "Nazis could move."[20]

While navigating the differences between German Protestants who supported Hitler, *Deutsche Christen*, and proponents of Germanic Christianity, involved such theological contortions, the *Völkischer Beobachter* was utterly consistent in its handling of two themes in particular: Luther's formalization of the German language, and his vicious anti-Semitism, which will be covered below. Regarding the former, the paper described Luther's translation of the Bible as the work that provided the German Volk with the "unified German language that Luther desired."[21] In this way, then, the *Völkischer Beobachter* supported Frick's position that it was Luther who allowed Germany to "once again express the best of its thoughts, not with borrowed tones, but with the original force of the German linguistic legacy." As a result, the German language was "forever marked with the stamp of majesty" and as a result "Holy German Art grew from religious roots." Frick exhorted, "Forget not, you Volk of the Reformation, what Luther gave to you!" Germans had to be grateful to Luther as the "pathfinder for the whole life of the nation who gave them the eternal watchword which applied in the Nazi era more than ever: 'Though earth all full of devils were … the kingdom ours remaineth.'"[22]

The exemplar of all the themes that the *Völkischer Beobachter* ascribed to the masters of the German Renaissance was Albrecht Dürer. It was important for the paper, intent on demonstrating that Germany's was a "world culture," to demonstrate that northern artists had earned the respect of more famous southern greats. So the newspaper was delighted to point out Raphael's admiration for Dürer, reporting that as Raphael chanced to see a few woodcuts and engravings, he cried out: "Really, this master would outstrip us all, if he had the masterworks of art before him as we do." On Dürer's second trip to Italy, the paper also reminded, Raphael honored the German master by accepting a work from his hand and reciprocating with one of his own drawings.[23]

While acknowledging the Italian influences on Dürer's life and work, the *Völkischer Beobachter* also worked hard to prove that he nevertheless remained "thoroughly German, in style and especially spirit." To this end, the Nazi newspaper twice ran a piece of historical fiction by the novelist Franz Herwig, who specialized in adventure stories set in sixteenth- and seventeenth-century wars. For the 400th *Todestag* of Dürer, Herwig depicted the artist working in a rough studio during one of his stays in Italy. He had recently enjoyed some success, so he was feeling satisfied with "life down in Italy." But a moment later, there was a knock at the door. When he opened it he found an old soldier outside, smelly, half starving, with festering wounds, and begging for a morsel. Dürer gave the "old sod" a *scudo*, but then noticed from the accent that the man was not Italian, so he asked after his nationality. "A German," the old man answered, and Dürer responded that he too was German. "That's what I thought," said the old man, looking him over. "My God, a German! A German artist! Even here in this frivolous country!" As he accepted Dürer's invitation to sit down, the soldier sighed deeply and continued: "Good God, I'm not going to last much longer. I can't serve any more; they don't even need me; and I don't even want to anymore. But Germany – I would love to see it again. It makes no difference to wish, though. I will die in foreign lands. That's okay – serves me right! The devil's plaything, that's me! But if I could only see a little piece of the homeland, so it could say to me just one more time: 'You belong to me, here you are at home.' Then I would die happy ... Hey, I have an idea! The Master has been so kind to me, and is a German artist. I'm so dumb, and don't even know how to ask and make you understand, but maybe the Master would let me take a quick look at his paintings?" And with that, he stopped and dropped to his wounded, shaky knees.

"Naturally," the artist granted this emotional request. And once he had seen the paintings, the soldier seemed to be completely transformed. He stood straight upright, with a "blessed smile," as if he were at the top of a mountain looking out over the rooftops of his home town. "Ach Master, how you have refreshed me," the *Landsknecht* said, "I am an old cuss, but I can see what you have created there. The wops [*Welschen*] can't do that!" With that he looked the master straight in the eye and laughed. Later, when Dürer was alone again, he "felt pounding in his chest; he sat for a long time, blubbering like a little kid." Then, slowly, he began to draw the image of a farm boy in the middle of a bunch of pigs and manure, saying "I want to go home and see my father!"[24]

Thus did the *Völkischer Beobachter* use a fiction – which it recommended as reading for children – to convey major themes of its Dürer reception: though he spent a couple of years in frivolous Italy, he suffered from homesickness particularly when observing the pain of a soldier serving in the Holy Roman Imperial Army of Maximilian I, and he communicated his *Heimatsgefühl* through rustic imagery of the German Volk. Moreover, even when created abroad, his paintings were capable of filling German hearts with fond feelings for their homeland, something that the *Welschen* could never understand. According to the *Völkischer Beobachter*, this early patriotism motivated Dürer to return north despite his Italian successes, and when he was offered a more lucrative position in Venice he declined it "out of love for his *Vaterstadt*," Nürnberg. As he put it, "better to live modestly in your *Heimat* [homeland] than to become rich and famous abroad."[25] Once there, the paper reported happily that Dürer gave "lifelong evidence" that he favored the authority of the German Emperor Maximilian I and "even caricatured Jewish figures" – as in his depiction of *The Twelve Year Old Jesus in the Temple* (c. 1494–1497) (Figure 3.1) – ensuring that "his name and his art would live as long as there was German art and German culture."[26] But, according to the *Völkischer Beobachter*, overcoming or surpassing the Greco-Latin tradition in Renaissance art was the main mission accomplished by Dürer. A major art and cultural historian, Willy Pastor, put the artist's anti-Roman significance in theological terms: if the Reformation was a "renewal of German essence, a renunciation of the South as a culture that was foreign to Germans," then Dürer was a "force in this heroic development, a leading personality equal in significance to Martin Luther."[27]

Signs of Dürer's *Deutschtum* were to be found in his works as well as his biography – fictionalized or not. He was the "painter of the German

Figure 3.1 Albrecht Dürer, *The Twelve Year Old Jesus in the Temple* (c. 1494–1497), Gemäldegalerie, Dresden, Germany

soul," read a commemorative article in 1928: nowhere were "German feeling and German faith reflected so masterfully" as in his woodcuts.[28] For justification of such views, the paper turned to experts such as art historian, Hugo Kehrer, whose works were widely published into the 1970s. In 1935, Kehrer delivered what the *Völkischer Beobachter* deemed an "outstanding lecture" on the subject of Dürer's self-portraits at a National Socialist Culture Society (*Kunstring der NS-Kulturgemeinde*) meeting. His thesis was that self portraiture was more than a technical, practical affair: it was "a problem, one of the deepest in art overall – and a particularly Nordic problem at that." Thanking Kehrer for this "profound assessment," the *Völkischer Beobachter* summarized his argument. The ancient Greeks did say, "Know thyself," but realization of this precept in art had to wait for 2,000 years – that is, until Dürer captured his own

Figure 3.2 Albrecht Dürer, *Self-Portrait* (age 13) (1484)

image. There had been self-representations before his time, in "self-portraits in assistance" (*Selbstbildnis in Assistenz*) where artists depicted themselves among secondary, background figures. The autonomous self-portrait, "done for its own sake," was rare. Even the Italian Renaissance, which led to what Burckhardt called the "revelation of the personality," did not address the problem. But "the German Renaissance was different"! An artist who at the age of thirteen had the "urge to do a self-portrait, to represent himself, as did Dürer, did not do so as a mere technical exercise, but as a serious problem that he had to solve" (Figure 3.2). So, the "Nordic line of inner exploration via self-portraiture" led from Dürer to Rembrandt to Lovis Corinth: throughout, it revealed itself as a "Nordic problem that other peoples were never able to address in any measure."[29]

Shifting to that other "great Nordic creator" of the Reformation era, William Shakespeare, the paper emphasized not his psychological insights, but his "political-historical awareness." For the *Völkischer Beobachter*, the greatest plays of Shakespeare were those that, as Rudolf Hofmüller put it, "inspired drama anchored in the development of the state, in political events," especially "German landmarks in the formulation of the heroic drama of the state," including works like Goethe's *Götz von Berlichingen* and *Egmont*, and Kleist's *Prinz von Homburg* and *Die Hermannsschlacht*. Shakespeare, the "great scene shaker" (*Szenenerschütterer*), created "unequalled models for the genre of political tragedy." His historical plays were the testimonial of a poet who "weighed world events according to their political significance." His tragedies were not just dramatic historical depictions, but "illuminated the forms of existence and the stream of life of the English Volk." In his plays, "the fate and the struggle of a Volk" were brought forth with "unprecedented forcefulness." This was what struck Nazis about Shakespeare's dramas of English royal history: not subtly shaded depictions of individual characters driven by psychologically complex motivations, but rather "representation of the unfolding, in a political sense, of a chain of apparently aimless crimes and bloody tests of strength." This, stated the *Völkischer Beobachter*, was "the greatest achievement of Shakespeare's dramatic genius."[30]

The music of Bach, too, was less important to the *Völkischer Beobachter* as an expression of personal faith than as a national symbol. National Socialist implementation of Bach involved minimizing his religious significance and transforming him into a nationalistic rather than a religious cultural hero. Hans Buchner pursued this tack in the following terms. People had often referred to Bach's work as "the musical incarnation of Protestantism," wrote Buchner, but it achieved much more outside the mere context of music, managing to represent the "musical component of the culture of Friedrich II's Prussian state." It provided the "best proof in all Western musical history" of the possibility to "overcome artistic cosmopolitanism through the creed of nationalism."[31] Referring to Bach's cantatas, Wilhelm Hitzig, archivist of the Breitkopf & Härtel publishing house who edited important collections of composers' letters as well as a popular series of illustrated biographies, asserted that while the cantatas were essentially liturgical, it was "a mistake to assume that their effect was relevant only to church services." The tremendous impact of the cantatas "functioned deeply whether they were performed as part of Protestant liturgy or not."[32]

Furthermore, Buchner held that the Bach revival of the mid-nineteenth century was not primarily an artistic phenomenon, but was above all a nationalistic phenomenon. It was the German Wars of Liberation and the "victorious emergence of a volkish view of life" which brought about the return to Bach. "Nationalist that he was," wrote Buchner, the effort to revive the works of a master "so clearly German" was natural during the era of the Karlsbad decrees.[33] It was certainly not Mendelssohn's involvement with the Bach revival that interested Nazi cultural politicians. Instead, they highlighted the Bach interpretation of their preferred nineteenth-century master, Richard Wagner, which prefigured many of their favorite themes. "If you want to grasp the wonderful originality, force, and significance of the German spirit in an incomparably eloquent image," Wagner wrote and the *Völkischer Beobachter* reprinted,

> *you should look long and hard on the otherwise almost inexplicably puzzling phenomenon of the musical* Wundermann, J. S. Bach. *His story alone constitutes a history of the innermost life of the German spirit during a dreadful century in which the German Volk was completely extinguished. Suddenly there appeared this German head, though hidden under a ridiculous French wig ... Now one finally sees what a world of inconceivable greatness [Johann] Sebastian formulated ... I can do no more than direct your attention to these creations, because it is impossible to convey through any sort of comparative analysis their richness, their sublimity, and their universal significance.*[34]

According to Nazi interpreters, Bach explicitly acknowledged the value of his works for political purposes. Musicologist Josef Klingenbeck – a regular contributor to the *Völkischer Beobachter* who later became an expert on Ignaz Pleyel – cited Bach's statement that "it belongs among the political duties of a good composer to accommodate oneself to the conditions of the time, the place, and the audience." Following this dictum, Klingenbeck pointed out that Bach's famous Brandenburg concertos were "contributions to court concert music," and that he wrote many secular cantatas for ceremonial occasions. For instance, Klingenbeck recalled, he wrote the cantata *Du Friedensfürst, Herr Jesu Christ* "amid terrible wartime conditions in 1745," and "one must not forget that his *Musikalisches Opfer* owed its existence to the festive occasion of a visit by Friedrich the

Great." Klingenbeck then reminded that Bach communicated the political intentions behind this work in his dedication to this piece: "Everyone must revere and admire the glory of a monarch who demonstrates his greatness and strength ... in all the sciences of war and peace, particularly in music."[35]

We have seen how the *Völkischer Beobachter* appropriated Händel and the *Messiah* as German, not British, icons. Beside the *Messiah*, Nazi cultural politicians paid attention to works Händel produced for national festivities, including his *Birthday Ode for Queen Anne*, the *Water Music*, and *Alexander's Feast*.[36] In addition, Klingenbeck pointed out, Händel's *Dettlingers Te Deum* "sounded splendidly as a monumental work for the celebration of victory in the Battle of Dettlingen" (27 March 1743). Moreover, Händel wrote a march for the London Corps of Volunteers; the oratorio, *Judas Makkabeus* (1747), "a unique, heroic musical victory for a nation just beginning to realize its full potential"; and *Music for the Royal Fireworks*, "marking the end of the Spanish War of Succession."[37] Though limited, the coverage given to the life and music of Christoph Willibald Gluck (1714–1787) also involved an emphasis on the political. In the Nazi cultural outlook, Gluck appeared as the "great German reformer" of opera. "No genius is conceivable," ran the usual *Völkischer Beobachter* argument, "without links to the nation out of which it arises." While "there are nations and races which, on the surface, have had a more immediate natural gift for making music than did the Germans," Gluck made "the first breach in the effort to change this situation."[38] In his operas, "French and Italian grace were paired with austere rigor – a German virtue." Acknowledging that Gluck did not compose an opera with a German text, the *Völkischer Beobachter* nevertheless held that the composer was devoted to German poetry, particularly that of Goethe and Klopstock, "with whom he had personal relations and for whom he served as musical pioneer." Indeed, the paper pointed out, at the end of his life he was busy preparing music for the text of Klopstock's *Hermannsschlacht* (*Hermann's Battle*) – an icon of early nationalism, along with Kleist's work on the same theme. As proof of Gluck's "national consciousness," moreover, the *Völkischer Beobachter* repeated the following anecdote. At a concert he once heard an Italian critic loudly question whether a "*tartaruga tedesca*" (German turtle) could write great music. Gluck confronted him, saying, "With your permission, sir, I am also a 'German turtle,' and have had the honor of writing music to be performed at the opening of the Royal Opera." With this, the paper gloated, "the Italian had to eat humble pie and assure Gluck that in light of this fact he was freed of prejudice against German artists."[39]

   In an effort to prove that Joseph Haydn (1732–1809) had a powerful national consciousness, the *Völkischer Beobachter* printed under the title, "Haydn's Happy Hour," an account of the composer by Gustav Christian Rassy, also the author of a novel about Bach published for soldiers by the Central Publishing House of the NSDAP (*Zentralverlag des NSDAP*) in 1942. According to the story, Haydn pined for his *Heimat* in conversation with an English woman friend: "My life is now like a deep, golden day in autumn. I would like to be home among Germans. Yes, it first became apparent to me here in England how much I depend on my homeland, which is so great and beautiful, and yet so torn apart since there isn't even one song that belongs to all Germans. Even the hour of my greatest honor, at Oxford University, filled me with the greatest shame." After saying this, according to Rassy, Haydn sat down at his piano and began to play quietly. "Not the Hofburg with all its imperial splendor, but the countryside – German soil as he had seen it on a recent trip home – stood before him again. Measure followed measure and a shiver of emotion passed through him. This was not him, not his will, not his music: this was Germany. He lost himself in the sound that flowed over him as if from another world, and – lost to his reveries – played over and over the melody which insured his immortality," by which the *Völkischer Beobachter* meant, naturally, the tune of *God Save Emperor Franz* (*Gott erhalte Franz den Kaiser*) – and ultimately, the German national anthem.[40]

   According to Wolfgang Gottrau, who covered music on the *Völkischer Beobachter* staff starting in 1930,[41] with Haydn came "the birth of the greatest epoch of German music," whose "influences reached into the present, and whose consequences resisted all radical efforts at revolution."[42] The major musicologist Erich Valentin, editor of the *Zeitschrift für Musik* and a regular contributor to the *Völkischer Beobachter*, added that it was Haydn who "boldly formed the German symphony" on the foundations constructed by the Mannheim School and Vienna's Pre-Classical Period.[43] Specifically, Gottrau asserted, Haydn replaced the minuet – "an alien tradition imposed on the German artist" – with the German *Ländler*.[44] Moreover, with his oratorios *The Creation* and *The Seasons*, Haydn moved from "entertainment produced for a small circle of amateurs and connoisseurs limited to the court" toward "a true national theater of the Volk."[45] But for all his creative achievements as the greatest *Klassiker* of the German musical tradition, the *Völkischer Beobachter* focused attention on three particular aspects of his career: the composing of what became the German national anthem; his attitude toward German lands during visits to England; and his ostensibly patriotic death.

The music critic of the *Deutsche Zeitung*, Paul Zschorlich, wrote for the *Völkischer Beobachter* that the "powerful German national consciousness" of Haydn, which he "always worked to preserve," became clearest in the fact that "fate chose him to be the creator of the German national anthem." This was not his conscious intention when he put "the little tribute poem," *Gott erhalte Franz den Kaiser*, to music in 1796. But his "singable and warm-hearted melody" later inspired the poet Karl Wilhelm to give it a new text which "disassociated it from any individual personage and – in short – encompassed the totality of Germanness, making out of it the German Volk hymn, *Deutschland, Deutschland, über alles.*"[46] Though written years beforehand, the *Völkischer Beobachter* held up Haydn's *Volkshymne* as a "spiritual weapon against Napoleon's triumphant advance": it therefore became "his most significant work." Whenever Nazis heard it, according to the paper, they were to think of the "immortal genius whose greatest source of pride was always to be a solid German guy" (*recht deutscher Mann*).[47]

Indeed, Haydn "proved himself a patriot to his end," the *Völkischer Beobachter* held, and it supported this proposition with the following anecdote. In the middle of May 1809, as Napoleon occupied Vienna for the second time, "sadness and anger filled the heart of the seventy-seven year old composer." On 26 May, he called all his servants into his room, had himself taken to the piano, and played his "Volk hymn" three times "with an expressive force that shook everyone present." Five days later, he died.[48] Thus did the greatness of Joseph Haydn lie principally, according to Nazi propagandists, in writing the melody for the German national anthem – and in playing it as his last musical act.

Mozart, too, according to the *Völkischer Beobachter*, was driven by nationalistic impulse. In addition to his difficult experiences in France, he faced the challenge of convincing fellow Germans of the need for a national style, since high Viennese culture – the center of German music life at the time – was infected by *Welschen*, that is, the Italian music contingent. So, Mozart's "patriotic mission" – of primary interest to Nazi pamphleteers – was to replace Italian fashion with a "genuinely German" opera tradition. Strong emphasis on Mozart's few statements to this effect was designed to drive this point home in the paper. According to Karl Grunsky, conditions in Viennese theaters drew from him "a cry of distress": "Were only a single patriot aboard, then things would look different! Perhaps then this germinating National Theater would blossom – if we were to finally start to think in German, trade in German, converse in German, and even sing in German!" In another source reproduced by Grunsky, Mozart wrote: "I don't believe that Italian opera can hold out for long, and I side with the Germans. Every nation has its opera, why shouldn't we Germans have ours?"[49] Elsewhere he stated: "I would serve no monarch in the world as willingly as I do the Kaiser, but … if Germany, my beloved Germany of which I am so proud, won't take me up, then in God's name France or England will profit by another clever German – much to the shame of the German nation."[50] Thus, according to Grunsky, did Mozart's "Germanness break out completely in Vienna."[51] While the subtext of the preceding citation was Mozart's suffering in his homeland – reaching the point of despair – Viktor Junk demanded recognition of his music as "incontrovertibly German." For Junk, art had its "deepest roots" in the nationality of its creator: only its effects could be international; its essence was always national. Mozart's music "conquered the world," but it "belonged to Germans, and could only have been created by a German."[52]

Josef Stolzing likewise identified Schiller as having called for sacrifice to national causes, instead of demanding individual freedom. In his greatest plays, he argued, Schiller "symbolized Fatherlandish thinking in bright glory," exalting the heroic struggle of his people for its freedom. First, in *The Maid of Orleans* when Dunois thunders, "That nation is worthless which does not joyfully stake everything on her honor";[53] second, in *Wilhelm Tell*, when Attinghausen admonishes his nephew Rudenz as follows:

> The native bonds knit firmly to
> The Fatherland, to th' cherished, join thyself,
> Hold fast to it with thine entire heart.
> Here are the sturdy roots of all thy strength,
> There in the alien world thou stand'st alone,
> A slender weed, that every storm may snap.[54]

As a dramatist, Stolzing continued, Schiller was the "poetic herald" of the period when the German people began to reflect upon its history and "sense volkish unity after the terrible disintegration caused by the Thirty Years War." The problems he addressed in his plays – and in his historical and aesthetic writings – were "problems that the Volk had been trying to solve for a century" and, by 1930, still hadn't.[55]

The *Völkischer Beobachter* insisted that its interpretation of Schiller was consistent with a nationalistic reception of his works originating in the early patriotic movements of the nineteenth century. Karl Hans Strobl, who before becoming an NSDAP member and directing the *Reich Literature Chamber* in Vienna, was a popular Austrian author – not only of historical novels based on the lives of Friedrich Barbarossa and Bismarck, but also of fantastic stories with vampire characters – prepared an extended description of German fraternities (*Bürschenschaften*), transforming performances of Schiller's *The Robbers* into patriotic demonstrations during the Napoleonic wars.[56] The paper also made particular note of the importance that Schiller Festivals had in nineteenth-century unification efforts. As Erich Valentin put it in an article about the centennial Schiller Year of 1859: the celebrations were "political manifestations whose core was the unanimous call for a unified, Greater Germany, providing a rallying point for the betrayed nation."[57]

Efforts such as these to undermine notions of an artist as a creator of international or universal significance were also pertinent to the paper's presentation of Goethe (1749–1832). A first complaint that it lodged against the majority of Goethe interpretations was, simply, that they concentrated too much on his poetry and paid insufficient attention to his political writings and statements. According to the paper, a conspiracy culminating in the cultural directorship of the Weimar Republic was responsible for the "excessive aestheticization" of Goethe's reputation: beyond his poetry and dramas, what Goethe said about politics in his correspondence with the Grand Duke Karl August, Heinrich Luden, Johann Peter Eckermann, the Chancellor Friedrich von Müller, and Charlotte von Stein was never discussed. This alone was proof of the "falsification that the leaders of the new Germany were perpetrating against the Spirit of Weimar for their party purposes."[58] *Völkischer Beobachter* arguments were dedicated to righting this aesthetic rather than political imbalance in Goethe reception.

To establish that at heart Goethe remained a royalist supporter of hierarchical social structure, the *Völkischer Beobachter* had to confront his reputation as a promoter of supranationalist ideals of pan-European or global cooperation. The paper derided reception of Goethe in internationalist terms as a liberal-leftist ploy. In the century which had passed since his death, it wrote, Goethe had often been called a "citizen of the world." Describing him as such had "naturally been in the interest of those for whose politics it had been most useful – who had recently made cosmopolitanism a program."[59] As a result, the Spirit of Weimar – Goethe's spirit – had been presented in contrast to the Spirit of Potsdam – Friedrich the Great's spirit. But Adolf Dresler, one of Goebbels' operatives who occasionally edited the cultural section and would subsequently write a history of the *Völkischer Beobachter* as well as studies of Mussolini and the Italian press,[60] countered for the paper that Goethe "wasn't such a globalist [*Allerweltsmann*] that the Wars of Liberation didn't stir his heart, as some would have Germans believe." That he was patriotically inclined and that in Strasbourg he discovered his Germanness in contrast to a French character was well known.[61] Any criticisms he made of conditions in German lands during his lifetime were not because he renounced his nationality, but "precisely because he was a German, consciously a German."[62] Though he was known as a "world citizen," he nevertheless said in the following conversation with the historian Heinrich Luden:

> *Don't think that I am indifferent to the great ideas: Freedom, Volk, and Fatherland! No! These ideas are part of us! They are a part of our being, and no one can dismiss them! How dear Germany is to my heart! I have often experienced bitter pain at the thought of the German Volk that is so reputable on the individual level and so miserable as a whole.[63]*

Likewise, in a portrait of the "German Goethe" derived from a collection of quotes gathered by Ernst Schrumpf – whose volkish tracts on Goethe and Schiller made it into Hitler's library[64] – the *Völkischer Beobachter* held that Goethe "deeply regretted not belonging to a great, strong, respected and feared Volk for which national honor is not a dream … embattled by internationalist utopians without character."[65]

The author Hanns Johst – who originated the line, "When I hear the word culture, I release the safety catch of my revolver," and who would later head the Reich Literature Chamber – similarly rejected the "internationalist utopian view of humanity consolidated in one world city with one world postmark and one world language." For him, "global fever" with its phrases like "worldly man, world city, world exhibition, world view, world economy, and world history" devalued everything in a "voluptuous orgy of materialism, capaciousness, and superficiality." According to Johst, Goethe likewise rejected this "global drivel." The "impulsive idea of expansion and sense of mission in the German character: that was the meaning of the word 'world' when Goethe used it."[66]

As in the case of Albrecht Dürer, the *Völkischer Beobachter* also had to address the fact that Goethe had succumbed to yearnings southward: the *Drang nach Süden*. Like its story about Dürer's encounter with a decrepit imperial soldier, the paper made use of historical fiction to deal with the poet's Italian journeys. The novelist Hans Watzlik, who specialized in fictional accounts of German masters, including *The Romantic Travels of Carl Maria von Weber* (1932), *The Coronation Opera: A Mozart Novel* (1936), and *The Master of Regensburg: An Albrecht Altdorfer Novel* (1939), was a regular contributor. He produced a short story that purported to represent Goethe's true emotions while down south. The tale described a relationship between the poet and an urchin named Fausto(!) whom Goethe allowed to accompany him on a sight-seeing trip – despite the boy's rough appearance and behavior. When the boy interrupted him while he was contemplating the Italian coastline, Goethe wondered why had he taken this little barbarian along on the trip. But then a brown child's hand reached out, lifted its finger, and shyly touched the great man's arm. "Forgive me, Sir," said Fausto. "But this is my Fatherland!" This stirred the poet's soul. "The deepest longing seized him – for the gloom of Nordic mountains, for a valley closed in on itself – and before his eyes, the sea and palms and bay trees disappeared, while the rough firs of Thüringia rose up dreamily."[67] Watzlik's rendering of Goethe's yearning for his homeland was the paper's only major reference to his travels in Italy. Perhaps fictionalization such as this was the only way it could contrive to suggest that despite Goethe's well-known attraction to things southern, he nonetheless suffered from *Heimweh* when he succumbed to it.

Were he present in the Weimar era, the paper stated, Goethe could have repeated what he said to Chancellor von Müller: "A comparison of the German Volk with other peoples leads to painful feelings that I try to avoid through science and art."[68] But he also believed that "our Volk is to be perceived and protected like a storehouse of powers, out of which degenerating mankind can always replenish and refresh itself."[69] Therefore, at the time of its "deepest humiliation," Goethe had the following to say about Germany's future,[70] which he viewed "with the eyes of a prophet"[71]: "Yes, the German Volk promises a future – has a future. The fate of the Germans is not yet complete! If they had no other role than to destroy the Roman Empire and create a new world order, they would have collapsed long ago. Since they remain standing – so bravely and strongly – they must still have a great future, in my opinion."[72] According to the paper, he conveyed his support for and anticipation of a unified German nation even more precisely in other places: "because he was a German writer, he saw pure Germanness and *Grossdeutschland* [Greater Germany] as the main goals." Not an internationalist dreamer, he "definitely wished for the union of all Germans in a great state, in one Germany."[73]

As it was for Goethe, some selective political biography was necessary in the case of Beethoven. Despite the re-evaluations of his heredity discussed above, the composer's politics still remained problematic for the NSDAP. Though he could, with some reservations, be counted as a member of the German race, Beethoven had exhibited some quasi-socialist political tendencies. This fact necessitated a further process of purification, purging his image of contamination by leftist political ideology. To minimize Beethoven's enthusiasm for the French Revolution and the rise of Napoleon, National Socialists countered that although Beethoven had been exposed to French revolutionary (in their words, cosmopolitan and internationalist) ideals, he was "always a Rhinelander at heart." When it came to defending his nation against French rule, the *Völkischer Beobachter* held, Beethoven had "always sided with Germany"; and though he "temporarily suffered from revolutionary fever, his heart remained with his German *Heimat*."[74]

Substantiation of these assertions was offered in various forms (Figure 3.3). One essay in the *Völkischer Beobachter* reviewed the story of the Grätz Castle incident, when Beethoven fled the country home of Prince Lichnowsky after refusing to perform on the piano for guests, among whom were several French officers. Significantly titled "The Patriot," the Nazi version retold the legend without mentioning the standard explanation of Beethoven's anger on this occasion: that his artistic pride had been affronted. Instead, the paper implied that he had acted "on nationalistic impulse alone."[75] Beethoven "stood firm at Grätz," music historian Friedrich Baser declared, because "his patriotic feeling bristled violently against performing his art for the enemy of his Volk."[76]

Figure 3.3 *Völkischer Beobachter*, Beethoven tribute page: "On the 150th Birthday of the German Master," 20 January 1921

Another *Völkischer Beobachter* story, "The Great Pathfinder," reproduced the most jingoistic passages of Richard Wagner's 1870 essay on Beethoven's significance during the Franco-Prussian War:

> *Whilst German forces are victoriously penetrating to the center of French civilization, a feeling of shame has of a sudden risen amongst us about our dependence upon that civilization. But nothing can more inspiringly stand beside the triumphs of [German] bravery in this wonderful year … than the memory of our great Beethoven, who just a hundred years ago was born to the German Volk. In France, indeed Versailles itself, at the high seat of "insolent fashion" – whither our weapons are now penetrating – his genius has already begun the noblest conquest. So let us celebrate the great path-breaker in the wilderness of a paradise debased!*

The *Völkischer Beobachter* apparently sensed that while Germans were feeling the effects of the Versailles Treaty, Wagner's assertions complemented perfectly the depictions of Beethoven as a proto-Nazi.[77]

Finally, in articles like "The Words of Beethoven," National Socialist journalists pulled citations out of context – including Beethoven's jest that power was his morality and his angry wish that he could meet Napoleon on the battlefield – and presented them as evidence that the composer had been a "fierce enemy of the French."[78] Carefully selected stories, essays, and quotations suited Nazi use of Beethoven to fuel bitterness against the enemy to the west. The paper warned that all Germans had to fight along with the National Socialists to protect Beethoven from the French: "Woe if his spirit was ever stolen, since that would mean ultimate defeat – because his spirit was *German* spirit."[79]

Remarkably the newspaper also looked to a non-German creator for evidence that great artists were allied with Nazism in opposition to a common foe. The *Völkischer Beobachter* went to great lengths in presenting Lord Byron (1788–1824) as a sharp and consistent critic of the perfidious English. According to Claus Schrempf, author of a book on Byron and anti-urban cultural criticism during the Weimar era, Byron became an intense critic of British society – including Jewish influence there. This was the feature of his work and biography that the newspaper emphasized, especially after war commenced against Britain in 1940.

Byron "became great as a man and as a writer in his revolt against his time and contemporaries." When his early verses were "ruffled by the critics," he took revenge with a "hot-tempered pamphlet in which he exposed England's literary greats of the day as ridiculous windbags." This was the first stage of his success, according to the paper. Then he proceeded on his Mediterranean journey, which "sharpened his view of England's weaknesses." Significantly, according to Schrempf, he wrote home from Athens:

> It should be made a law that young people travel for a while, and visit the few allies that the war on the continent has left to us. Here I see and speak with Frenchmen, Italians, Germans, Danes, Greeks, Turks, Americans, etc., and without losing sight of my own Fatherland. I form for myself an opinion about foreign countries and peoples. If I see that on some points the Englishmen are right, and incidentally we are frequently wrong enough about this, I am glad. If I think, however that others can do it better, I learn something.
> I could have roamed around at home for a hundred years without learning this.

In this way, Schrempf opined, Byron discovered the "dark side of England and the English." It was not only the literary market in his homeland that seemed rotten to him: he also found British foreign policy objectionable. Likewise did he "hate the bigotry, the Mammonism, and the social injustice in England." More and more, English politics appeared to him as a system of "arrogance, hypocrisy, and lust for power," designed to "exploit and oppress the weak everywhere: at home, the lower classes; out in the world, the smaller nations." A "particularly glaring case of the English methods of robbery," which he experienced directly brought his fury to poetic expression. In Athens, Byron was a witness to the way Lord Elgin "unscrupulously looted the art treasures of Greece."[80] Elgin "snatched from the poor Greeks the most sacred thing that a Volk possesses: its national symbols." Filled with indignation about this "abomination perpetrated by his country-man," Byron composed the *Curse of Minerva* – a poem full of polemics "against the predatory Lord and against the worldwide despotism of Great Britain," of which the *Völkischer Beobachter* printed extensive selections in translation, including:

A fatal gift that turn'd your friends to stone,
And left lost Albion hated and alone …
Look last at home – ye love not to look there;
On the grim smile of comfortless despair:
Your city saddens: loud though Revel howls,
Here Famine faints, and yonder Rapine prowls …
Go, grasp the shadow of your vanish'd power;
Gloss o'er the failure of each fondest scheme;
Your strength a name, your bloated wealth a cream.

Upon Byron's return from Greece, Schrempf continued, he found "hopeless conditions." The Continental System that Napoleon established against England stifled all trade: finished goods decayed in the shops, grain prices rose, unemployment increased. While spending the winter of 1812 at Newstead Abbey, he heard shots outside. "A revolt!" Starving weavers had ganged up, stormed the factories, and smashed the mechanical looms that had rendered them jobless. The police hunted down the rebels. A new law was announced which brought in the death penalty for the machine destroyers. In reaction, "Byron's blood boiled in fury." He made inquiries, went to London, and surprised the House of Lords with a "fervent speech of accusation" against the government which tried to "repress the people driven to despair by hunger" with "bloody dragoons."

However, Schrempf related, Byron's appeal to social conscience "found no resonance in the hearts of the lords." The Loom Law was accepted and the death penalty was executed in a dozen cases, since in England "business interest came before all others." Nonetheless, Byron's revolutionary nature made him into the "fearless spokesman of all the oppressed," and he then took on the case of the "cruelly abused Irish people against the brutal despotism of the English," writing: "How is it with the upper classes in England? On the basis of what I have experienced, what I have seen and heard there – and I have lived in the highest and so-called best society – there is nothing as rotten as their way of life."

After his social fall, by which – according to Schrempf – he learned to know the "darkest side of the moral hypocrisy of his countrymen," his fight against the "prejudiced British way of thought and policy" became his life's task. Byron found his "sharpest weapons" while living in Italy. There, he became a satirical critic of English imperialism and the advocate of international law against "tyrannical hypocrisy." His poems, letters, and diaries "teemed with attacks on England and the English way," whose main features were "lying and hypocrisy." When he participated in the Carbonari uprising and had to flee to Ravenna, he wrote home to Lady Byron: "Judge for yourself how much I abhor England and its inhabitants, if I now distain returning home even when my financial interests and personal security are at stake."

Byron's masterpiece, *Don Juan*, Schrempf held, was likewise a "barrage against English national vices, English arrogance, and English prejudices." In Schrempf's view, Byron's main enemy was the ruling system in Great Britain, whether it presented itself in terms of the "cold-hearted egoism of the feudal oligarchy, or as the narrow-minded intolerance of the rich official church, or in the guise of an exclusive 'good society' that demanded inexorable rules of etiquette from the public, while allowing secret vices for itself." With "all the passion of his demonic nature," he fought against the politics of reaction in England which worked to make "all the peoples of Europe dependent on Britain."[81]

In contrasting British and German political characters, the *Völkischer Beobachter* also turned to home-grown perspectives. For the most part, the newspaper's presentation of Arthur Schopenhauer (1788–1860) highlighted statements he made about national character and political leadership, rather than his metaphysics. Interestingly, in 1929 the newspaper ran a collection of citations in which Schopenhauer voiced his typically cynical outlook on Germans and even compared the British favorably against his fellow countrymen. As a philosopher, Schopenhauer was "herald of the idealistic world view," the introduction to this collection ran, but he had a "sharp eye for material reality: judgments he made about politics testified to his incorruptible gift of observation." Who could deny, the *Völkischer Beobachter* asked, that "utterances he made about the German national character hit the nail on the head?" Extracting from Schopenhauer's *Parerga und Paralipomena*, the paper ran the following judgments about the German personality. In his opinion, the true national characteristic of the Germans was "heaviness": they characteristically "looked in the clouds for that which is lying at their feet." Getting "dizzy over words like justice, freedom, the good, they went into a kind of delirium and began to speak in insignificant, high-sounding phrases in which they artificially lined up the broadest and therefore shallowest terms, instead of confronting reality directly and looking at real things and conditions in the eye." In contrast, Schopenhauer felt the English showed great understanding in that they kept their old institutions, sites, and customs strong and holy, because "such things were not half baked in idle heads, but arose gradually from the force of circumstances and the wisdom of life – and were therefore appropriate for them as a nation."[82] But the *Völkischer Beobachter* also culled from Schopenhauer's *Parerga und Paralipomena* a statement that was much more critical of the British:

> *In his neglectfulness and complete savagery with regard to all speculative philosophy or metaphysics, the Englishman is capable of no spiritual view of nature. Therefore he knows no middle between a view of its effects as following strict, mechanical laws or as the product of the Hebrew God whom he calls his "Maker." The clerics in England have to answer for this, the most crafty of all obscurantisms. They have turned heads so that even the most experienced and enlightened has a basic system of thought that is a mixture of the crassest materialism and the fattest Jewish superstition which is as messy as a combination of vinegar and oil.*[83]

As discussed below, the *Völkischer Beobachter* made more use of Schopenhauer's anti-Semitic views in particular. Here, though, we see how careful selections from his writings were exploited to align the philosopher with the newspaper's political aims, here anti-British.

But it was not just Schopenhauer's occasionally patriotic and anti-British statements that the *Völkischer Beobachter* drew upon to associate him with Nazi politics. Karl Friedrich Weiss paraphrased Schopenhauer's philosophy in an effort to make it serve as a foundation for Nazi statism. Emphasizing elements in his writings that echoed theories of Thomas Hobbes, Weiss constructed for the paper an interpretation of Schopenhauer's philosophy as proto-typically volkish. According to Weiss, Schopenhauer's pessimistic philosophy saw man as a beast: "injustice, unfairness, harshness, even cruelty marked the way men treat each other – the opposite only occurred exceptionally." On this was based the need for state and law: "in all areas that weren't covered by rules, men demonstrated themselves inconsiderate to one another, acting on boundless egoism mixed with malice." To found a perfect state, Weiss derived from Schopenhauer, one had to start out with "an essence whose nature sacrifices personal well-being to the public weal." This was the ultimate goal: "a state founded upon national, racial, or cultural willingness to surrender individual interests to those of the whole – the

Volk." In articulating these views, Weiss asserted, Schopenhauer was the "first genuine volkish philosopher." However, during his lifetime the volkish view of the state was a mere premonition. So, according to Weiss, Schopenhauer counseled making do with an "artificial compromise between systems in which relations remained between independent wild men (anarchy) or between slaves controlled arbitrarily (despotism), because in both cases no state was present." The preferable temporary alternative was monarchism. Until a genuinely volkish system emerged, it would be "best to function under a family whose interest is identical to those of the state": this was the strength of the hereditary monarchy. Its advantage, Weiss had Schopenhauer say, lay in the fact that "if the ruler is raised so high, given so much power, wealth, security, and absolute invulnerability, there is nothing left for him to wish, to hope for, or to fear, so that in him ingrained egoism is neutralized and eliminated, and he is capable of applying justice since he no longer has his own interests but only those of the public in mind." This was the origin of the "superhuman majesty that accompanied royal dignity everywhere, and distinguished it so completely from that of a mere president."[84] Thus, according to the *Völkischer Beobachter*, Schopenhauer promoted the authority of a born leader with the baroque majesty of an absolutist monarch above any notions of republicanism – at least until that point when a genuine volkish society could develop and members would wholeheartedly subsume their egos under the reason of the state.

Among other romantic era writers the newspaper presented as important political figures, Franz Grillparzer (1791–1872) also ranked very high. Robert Hohlbaum, a well-known conservative and anti-Semitic writer who produced historical novels on Goethe and Bruckner, formulated an analysis of "the political Grillparzer." It had taken a long time, Hohlbaum observed, to "put this great one in the place he deserved." Austria only knew Grillparzer as a liberal (*Schwarz-Gelber*). Then the Wilhelmine Reich had to pass "because its borders did not cover the area of German speech, German feeling, German longing." Indeed, it was not until the Greater German Reich was erected that Grillparzer "could be recognized as a secure cultural foundation stone." So it was only Greater Nazi Germany that "discovered Grillparzer fully." For Hohlbaum, there were multiple Grillparzers: there was the Grillparzer of the ancient drama that culminated in the hero-tragedy; the Grillparzer of the colorful fairy tale in *The Dream a Life* (1834); the Grillparzer of the "sweetest, most tender, magical short stories"; and the Grillparzer who created the "most monumental, profound historical drama of the Germans." But it was the "political Grillparzer" whom Hohlbaum wanted Nazis to most appreciate, despite the fact that this manifestation of the writer was most evident in his early works. For Hohlbaum, it was important that the fifteen-year-old Grillparzer did not debut with love poetry: his first poem was a "political satire of the military and diplomatic errors of 1805." He hated political clericalism and fought it with his "purest works." The political Grillparzer was also revealed in "countless journal entries" and was best seen "in the genre in which he had no rival": the epigram. When one appreciated the "richness of jokes and word play by which he expressed his world view," it was clear, thought Hohlbaum, that Grillparzer was a "political seismograph." He sketched out these qualities in this autobiographical epigram:

> Though I once pursued liberal goals,
> Now the freedom frenzy leaves me cold.
> No longer searching extremes here and there,
> I suppose I'm almost reasonable.

The particular political positions that Hohlbaum featured in his portrait of Grillparzer were those of staunch anti-republicanism and pan-German patriotism. Having experienced the occupation of Vienna in 1809, Grillparzer "despaired of the Napoleon of Peace," complaining that Bonaparte had gone to the devil. He therefore launched a call for military resistance, and the result was a "moving homage to true soldiery." In addition, he caricatured "egocentric England" better than anyone else at that time. Moreover, Hohlbaum held, his "ingenious judgment of Metternich as an obstacle to German unity" was apparent in the trilogy of the *Golden Fleece* (1821) where the "German-Austrian Grillparzer, compared himself to a Greek fighting against the little nations of the monarchies."

Later, having experienced the revolution of 1848, Grillparzer described the results sarcastically:

> This is the true republic,
> Of equality to the point of tears.
> Here one sees no upper house,
> Just a chamber of mediocrities.

He saw that the "drive to freedom inspired the rabble more than others," and struck at the "childhood illnesses of the growing nation with jabs like the following":

> Freedom of the Press
> Is placed above all,
> Though half the land can't read,
> And the other half can't write.

Thus did the paper align the political Grillparzer with its Greater German and anti-liberal views.[85]

But of all the romantic creators that the *Völkischer Beobachter* extolled as politically motivated, Richard Wagner was its ideal. While staunchly defending its superhero's racial purity, the next order of business in Wagner reception was to confirm his credentials as a political artist. Given the composer's engagement with nineteenth-century German political culture, this was not a difficult step. However, it is remarkable how intensively the *Völkischer Beobachter* emphasized Wagner's political writings – as much as or even more so than they concentrated on his musical productivity. As musicologist Erich Valentin put it, the writings were "essential, not marginal" to understanding the composer: "as an analogous and relevant extension of his artistic works, they testified with unequivocal clarity the considerable sureness of his political perception and political will." It was a mistake to consider Wagner's artwork "isolated and inner oriented." Doing so, one "missed the real, living content they contained."[86] According to Emma von Sichart, a regular contributor to the *Völkischer Beobachter* and later known for her work on the history of theater costumes, if one familiarized oneself with his prose writings, it "seemed as though they were written expressly to address our misery and struggle" – by which she clearly meant the National Socialist struggle.[87]

What writers like von Sichart found so resonant with the National Socialist outlook were the volkish components of Wagner's politics. The newspaper reported extensively on a lecture given for the *Kampfbund für Deutsche Kultur* by Darmstadt professor Werner Kulz to this effect. According to the paper's summary of the lecture, Kulz argued that the military defeat and political revolution of 1918 had marked the "collapse of the strength of German soul." This could have been prevented "if care had been taken after 1871 for the inner enrichment of the German people, as Wagner had always endeavored to do." In Kulz's view, the composer was the "pathfinder of the German resurrection," since he "directed the Volk back to the roots of its nature found in Germanic mythology." His friendship with Count Gobineau as well as his own "thoughtful observations" led Wagner to recognize quite early "the meaning of the Germanic Volk as part of the Nordic race." Moreover, "as a consciously German person, Wagner had to turn against the evil Asiatic breed."[88]

A section inserted into the *Völkischer Beobachter* specifically for the stormtroopers of the Nazi movement, entitled *Der S. A. Mann*, expressed similar ideas. Under the title, "Richard Wagner's Battle for the Volkish Ideal," H. Sturm held that the composer felt himself "ever strengthened by his German-Germanic [*Deutsche-Germanischen*] thoughts, and constantly sought to realize this spirit." Besides Adolf Stöcker, Heinrich von Treitschke, Paul de Lagarde, and Hans von Wolzogen, who were "more comprehensively volkish" than most, it was Wagner who "fought hardest for the volkish idea with pen and word." As in the cases of its treatment of other leading figures, the *Völkischer Beobachter* regularly put together selections of Wagner quotations – presented out of context with little comment – that seemed to complement Nazi ideals. One such collection was gathered together for the paper by Fritz Stege, editor of the *Zeitschrift für Musik*, activist in the *Kampfbund für Deutsche Kultur*, and head of the Professional Society of German Music Critics in the Third Reich. Stege was also the librettist of a Nordic *Volksoper* and after the war was on the staff of the Humboldt Institute in Wiesbaden, where he wrote and promoted music especially for the accordion. All the Wagner quotations that Stege put together were obviously considered relevant to Nazi ideology, especially such lines as: "If I am German, then I must carry a Germany within me; The beautiful and noble came not into the world for sake of profit, nay, not for sake of even fame and recognition: everything done in the sense of this teaching is German; therefore is the German great; and only what is done in that spirit can lead Germany to greatness";[89] and "Only on the shoulders of this great social movement can true art lift itself from its present state of civilized barbarianism and take its post of honor. Each has a common goal, and the twain can only reach it when they recognize it jointly. This goal is the strong, fair man, to whom revolution shall give his strength, and art his beauty!"[90]

Another example of this strategy for making use of Wagner's political writings appeared in the paper on the 50th anniversary of his death under the title, "The German Prophet." After quoting the following from Wagner's writings: "the Volk is the epitome of all those men who feel a common and collective desire: to it belongs, then, all of those who recognize their individual desire as a collective desire, or find it based thereon,"[91] literary historian Hermann Seeliger broke in and asked: "Doesn't this infallible logic constitute point for point the moral legitimation of the National Socialist movement and of its wonderful leader?" Seeliger's selections were clearly aimed toward linking Wagner with the anti-leftist and authoritarian principles of the movement. He also included quotes in which Wagner directly criticized the German Socialist movement. From the composer's essay, "Art and Politics," Seeliger selected: "Can you not see that this doctrine of a mathematically equal division of property and earnings is simply an irrational attempt to solve that problem, at any rate dimly apprehended, and an attempt whose sheer impossibility itself proclaims it stillborn?"[92] Then, from an unpublished letter of 1890, Seeliger reproduced: "We have no movement but that which is decidedly social, yet in a different sense than our Marxists imagine." By offering another selection from *What is German?*, Seeliger also worked to show that Wagner understood democracy as completely un-German: "In German, 'democracy' is purely a translated term. It exists merely in the 'press'; and what this German press is, one must find out for oneself."[93] Finally, Seeliger found evidence in Wagner's writings that he would have wholeheartedly supported the leadership principle of the Nazi movement. Consider the following thoughts, Seeliger directed:

> *In the person of the king the state retains its true ideal – in the* person *of the king, not an abstract notion of royalty. From that follows … the idea that love and admiration of the Volk is directed not toward the abstract notions of royalty or even state, but the person of the king who embodies them … The Volk does not think in abstractions – one does not love and respect an idea, but real persons. The King, or Kaiser, is no more – but nothing has changed in the character of the German Volk: just as in its earliest history it demands a Führer – whether you call him Prince, Duke, or King, or whatever.*[94]

According to Walter Lange – who had written on the religious dimension of Wagner's work and would go on to concentrate on his racial constitution in works like *Richard Wagner's Family Origins* (1938) – Nazis admired the "prophetic foresight" of Wagner who "saw through the true spirit of the revolutionaries of 1848–49 with bitter disappointment" and, anticipating future developments, "turned away from liberal efforts without hope." Wagner "broke from the powers of his day with reckless abandon and severe stubbornness," Lange continued, to "bring about ideals through countless battles against stupidity and evil." Therefore, all his writings were the "worthiest weapons for the final battle that approached." Already in 1850 he had said: "Just as all our liberalism was a not very lucid mental sport, since we pursued freedom for the Volk without knowledge of that Volk itself … our eagerness to give equal rights to Jews was stimulated more by a general idea than by any real sympathy."[95] These ideas were so similar, thought Lange, that "in the speeches of young Germany" – that is, Hitler's in particular – it "seemed like one was hearing Richard Wagner speaking to the Volk in order to open its eyes to the sins being committed against the Holy Spirit of the nation." This was a sign that in the "Third Reich of Richard Wagner," the "Führer principle of genius would prevail more than ever."[96] Ludwig Schoewe concurred with all associations of Wagner and the volkish outlook, because he was "the most inexorable investigator of all volkish issues," the composer was the "strongest and most distinctive thinker of his time." Living when the "violent process of clarifying nationality according to race" commenced, he was the "first great German cultural politician – the first fighter and cultural political pioneer among all the geniuses of his nation."[97]

On the issue of Wagner's significance as a political thinker and writer, Josef Stolzing provided a powerful summary. In the composer's numerous philippics, he – "the revolutionary" – spoke out against the nineteenth century for "retreating after the wars of liberation into comfortable philistinism and self-satisfied prosperity." With the "clear-eyed perspective of a genius," he saw into the future, "recognizing the significance of the racial question and the terrible threat that Jewry was to the Volk." Wagner even sensed the World War – "with Bolshevism and the end of western culture that it threatened" – almost half a century before its outbreak. Moreover, he was "profoundly aware of the social misery of the German working class," which he mentioned "again and again" in treatises like *Art and Revolution* – where he "demanded remedies emphatically." Finally, a "genuine German culture determined by blood was his ideal." In Wagner's political writings, Stolzing concluded, one "always ran into National Socialist views: when we read them, it seems as though he divined our movement."[98]

4 THE WESTERN TRADITION AS ANTI-SEMITIC

Establishing that the greats of the tradition were Germanic, grounded in popular existence, and politically active in the service of nationalism were important goals of cultural reporting in the *Völkischer Beobachter*. But the paper gave uppermost priority to convincing its readers that anti-Semitism served as a primary motivation for the artists, writers, and composers it preferred. Clearly, this was a major component of the anti-Semitic propaganda at the core of Nazism. In Saul Friedländer's words: "the Nazi system as a whole produced an 'anti-Jewish culture,' partly rooted in historical German and European Christian anti-Semitism but also fostered by all the means at the disposal of the regime and propelled to a unique level of incandescence, with a direct impact on collective and individual behavior."[1] The role of German academics in the construction of a culture targeting "others" – especially the Jewish enemy – ostensibly arrayed in opposition against supposedly Germanic ideals has been the object of increasing scholarly attention.[2] Concentrating on major front-page stories of the *Völkischer Beobachter*, moreover, Jeffrey Herf has shown how articles in Hitler's main media instrument were "central elements in the regime's anti-Semitic campaigns and in the translation of Nazi ideology into an ongoing anti-Semitic narrative of events."[3] Here we study a synthesis of both these prongs of Nazi *Kulturpolitik*: how cultural-historical interpretations that appeared in the party's daily "combat paper" contributed to the campaign of hatred. As we have seen, one contributor stated her view of the paper's function in this process most explicitly: "to win over to our movement spiritual leaders who think they see something distasteful in anti-Semitism, it is extremely important to present more and more evidence that great, recognized spirits shared our hatred of Jewry."[4]

Hitler, naturally, was unequivocal about the need to place anti-Semitic ideology at the center of the tradition, holding that "the task of the volkish state is to see to it that a world history is finally written in which the racial question is raised to a dominant position."[5] As he related, it was primarily his supposed "discovery" that Jewish influence on art had undermined the traditions he preferred – to the point of supposedly wrecking his own chances for a career in design and architecture – that compelled him to seek out and ultimately try to destroy this perceived enemy:[6]

> *Was there any form of filth or profligacy, particularly in cultural life, without at least one Jew involved in it? If you cut even cautiously into such an abscess, you found, like a maggot in a rotting body, often dazzled by the sudden light – a kike! What had to be reckoned heavily against the Jews in my eyes was … their activity in the press, art, literature, and the theater … This was pestilence, spiritual pestilence, worse than the Black Death of olden times … When thus for the first time I recognized the Jew as the cold-hearted, shameless, and calculating director of this revolting vice traffic in the scum of the big city, a cold shudder ran down my back. But then a flame flared up within me. I no longer avoided discussion of the Jewish question; no, now I sought it … I learned to look for the Jew in all branches of cultural and artistic life and its various manifestations.*[7]

Given Hitler's self-identification as an artist, coupled with the obvious fact of his failure as such, and taken together with the anti-Semitism that grew from (as Hitler claimed) his revelation that Jews were responsible for the rot of German culture, it is likely that Hitler had a deeply personal stake in rationalizing his own convictions by promoting the belief that the great creators of the Western line shared his attitudes toward the Jewish threat. Certainly, the party newspaper, as demonstrated below, was committed to finding confirmation for this hypothesis at every opportunity.

It was in articles pertaining to high medieval culture that this fundamental component of Nazi ideology made its first forceful appearance in the *Völkischer Beobachter*'s chronology of Western humanities. The great medieval syntheses of faith and reason, most famously manifested in masterworks such as Aquinas' *Summa Theologica*, Dante's *Divine Comedy*, and high Gothic architecture did not much interest the ideologues of the paper. Rather, they limited their analysis of medieval thought to those works (often minor) that lent themselves to the paper's efforts to underscore concepts supposedly consistent with their world views – especially fear and hatred of Jews. The most "salient feature" of the culture of the Middle Ages according to the *Völkischer Beobachter* was its darkest: "God willing, we will model our treatment of the Jews on that of the Middle Ages," one contributor hoped.[8]

The focus and intensity with which Nazi ideologues applied this strategy with regard to the medieval era is apparent in a 1926 article by Franz Gerstner: "Saint Thomas Aquinas and anti-Semitism." The great theologian "clearly laid out his attitude toward the Jews" in his *Summa contra Gentiles*, Gerstner opened, and recognizing "what a danger the Jew was to Christianity," Saint Thomas "strongly warned Christians against any involvement with Semites." According to Gerstner, moreover, Aquinas (1225–1274) agreed with Nazis that it was "sheer madness to allow Jews to participate in political or religious administration, because it lies in the innermost heart of the Israelites to pursue directions that will hurt Christians." For the medieval philosopher, it was therefore "not only the social duty of the government but even a moral necessity" to eliminate officials of Jewish confession from public service and pursue "similar measures to remove them from other positions." Aquinas believed, said Gerstner, that anyone of the "naive opinion" that an "aggressive policy against this injurious race does not conform to the commandment of brotherly love" must be told that it is "precisely with regard to this commandment that they are required to defend our Volk as much as possible against damage caused by Jews." Thus did Gerstner conclude that Aquinas was a "thorough anti-Semite," and that his was a "medieval equivalent to the Nazi view."[9]

Numerous examples of anti-Jewish enmity were evoked in the pages of the *Völkischer Beobachter*. But the individual identified as the first anti-Semite, in a fully conscious, modern sense, was Martin Luther. Nowhere, it argued, was Luther's relevance and significance clearer than in his approach to the matter that was "still the fateful question of the modern world: the Jewish Question." The paper thought it necessary to emphasize what a "one-sided and unshakeable position" Luther took against Jewry: he was the only one of his time to "raise his voice against Jewry with a sharpness, a clarity, and a primal fury that stood as a model." The paper did perceive some historically determined differences between Luther's theologically based views and their "political" – here a euphemism for racial – theories: "while Nazis regarded the global danger of the Jews primarily from the political side, Luther approached it from religious insight outward, concentrating on the moral attitude of Jewry." But these nuances aside, the *Völkischer Beobachter* consistently promoted the view that Luther and the party shared the same conclusions: once Luther became "wary of the rootlessness and degeneracy of the Jewish way of life," he "no longer made a secret of his deep dislike for Jewry."[10]

The primary method the paper used to present Luther as a vehement hater of Jews was to repeatedly publish blatantly anti-Semitic portions of his writings and sermons. Adopting a strategy that would be applied throughout the paper's run, *Völkischer Beobachter* contributors scoured Luther's writings for every passage, major or minor, that contained signs of anti-Semitic sentiment. If these writings were not already well known, the *Völkischer Beobachter* would celebrate them as once lost and now rediscovered masterpieces which indicated the most important line of the author's thought. For instance, the article, "Luther's Battle against the Jews," opened with the following description by an anonymous *Völkischer Beobachter* writer: "An old, leather-bound book lies before me. It was published in 1556 in Wittenberg by Georgen Rhawen Erben and contains two long, devastating battle essays [*Kampfschriften*] by Dr. Martin Luther against the Jews. They are entitled, *Vom Schem Hamphoras* and *On the Jews and their Lies*." Both writings were primarily theological in content, the *Völkischer Beobachter* acknowledged, but their conclusions "have been largely overlooked." The paper asked, "How had that been possible?" and then provided its own answer: these writings "made the Jew uncomfortable; he considered them dangerous: so he bought them all up and condemned them to oblivion." Luther would have been shocked to learn that these "words of war" against the Jews were left out of all the collections of his works – that "no one had heard of them." The *Völkischer Beobachter* intended to right this perceived historical wrong, since "to revive memory of them had become a duty." So, the remainder of this article, and others such as "Luther on the Jews" and "Words of Luther," reviewed these "lost treasures" of German theological and intellectual history wherein Luther first described the Jews and then proposed methods for dealing with them in passages that "still have relevance, and were only being correctly understood in the Nazi era."[11]

Luther "clearly recognized the spiritual foreignness of the Jews," according to the paper, when he said they are "the malicious, stiff-necked people that would not be converted from evil to good works by preaching, reproof, or teaching." Elsewhere he called them "a lazy, idle, malignant, blasphemous, desperate people." About the "very limited capacity that Jews had for real work," Luther wrote that "the Jews force us to exist by the sweat of our brow, make money, and live the good life on the products of our labor: 'tis a pernicious race, oppressing all men by their usury." Moreover, Luther "knew about the hatred of the Jews toward everything that is German and Christian," and issued a warning to the Christian world: "Dear Christian, be advised and do not doubt that next to the devil, you have no more bitter, venomous, and vehement foe than a real Jew who earnestly seeks to be a Jew."[12]

These and many other anti-Semitic statements represented "the best of Luther," the *Völkischer Beobachter* felt, even in terms of writing style: it found Luther's "battle-friendly manner" to be "open, original, and refreshing." None of this was presented as tangential to Luther's theology and politics; in the paper Luther was presented as "an enemy of Jewishness to the core of his heart." Even in his very last sermon, Luther issued a "Warning Against the Jews," the *Völkischer Beobachter* emphasized, demanding that "authorities no longer tolerate Jews in the land, given their daily blasphemies."[13] According to the paper, it was clear that Luther was "serious about eliminating Jews from public life because he also made practical suggestions about how to handle them." On the persecution of Jews in the Middle Ages, he "commented with satisfaction that they received a good box on the snout because the Jews wanted to kill us all." Following the medieval model, Luther demanded the closure and destruction of all synagogues and Jewish schools and the prohibition of all teaching by rabbis. He said, moreover, that they should be forced to work, and if they refused to work, they should be expelled: "Let them go back to Jerusalem and there they can blaspheme, slander, murder, steal, rob, commit usury, and scoff."[14]

Above all, the *Völkischer Beobachter* insisted that the time had come to act on Luther's anti-Semitic attitudes and recommendations: "if Luther judged Jews in this way already in the sixteenth century, how much heavier did his words weigh in the modern era, when Jewry had incomparably more influence over the whole world than it did in Luther's time?" Luther's legacy was "not yet exhausted": his confessions addressed an issue that was "still the burning question of the day."[15] Readers could see in anti-Jewish laws inspired by Luther and put into place within the Holy Roman Empire in 1577 that their sixteenth-century predecessors "did not shy from applying sharp laws to the Jews when they exploited and plundered the Volk too maliciously, whereas in the so-called enlightened twentieth century, Germans were allowing themselves to be led around by the Jews like lambs to the slaughter."[16]

According to Ernst Buchner, Luther's ideas about Jews were also manifested in the art of the Reformation. In addition to pieces that represented the best of Nordic and volkish traditions, Buchner implied, Altdorfer also left behind works in tune with the darkest Nazi principles. A born painter, Altdorfer was "also good with the etching needle," and with it he captured the portico and interior of the Regensburg synagogue in two 1519 etchings (Figure 4.1). Most importantly, wrote Buchner, Altdorfer executed these etchings as "mementos of a vanishing culture" after having decreed, as a member of the Outer Council, the eviction of the Regensburger Jews from the imperial city. Blaming Jews for an economic downturn, the city had given the expellees only two days to vacate the synagogue and five days to leave the city. Altdorfer made preparatory sketches of the site in the days leading up to its destruction on 22 February 1519: "fully aware of and partly responsible for its fate." Buchner's assessment of the resulting etchings was that they "belonged to the finest and most beautiful examples of Nordic graphics, picturesque, forceful in mood, rich in tone value," and – clearly – anti-Semitic in meaning.[17]

Outside German territories, the newspaper pressed to demonstrate that the "greatest Nordic writer of all," Shakespeare, also shared Nazi attitudes toward Jews. For all his depiction of the "bloody tests of strength that made up political reality" according to the *Völkischer Beobachter*, one particular feature of Shakespeare's historical dramas interested the Nazi newspaper most. F. L. Zander wrote that in the England of Shakespeare, people were "genuine in their passions and wishes"; likewise, drama was "completely free of trendiness and almost

Figure 4.1 Albrecht Altdorfer, *Regensburg Synagogue* (1519)

always free of theoretical nonsense." Therefore, plays were "unre-strained in their expression of popular likes and dislikes: it was no sacrilege to show the criminal as a criminal, even if he seemed to be physically weak and humble, and deserving of compassion." In Zander's estimate, this was particularly true in theatrical representation of Jews. It was "self-evident" that Jews were utterly detested by the English of this era, and their writers: "first because of their being foreign; then because of their ridiculous physical appearance, their dirtiness, and their atro-cious dress; and finally because of their usuriousness." Consequently, in the drama of the day, the Jew was "always turning up as a profligate – with a certain air of the tragic – living off of immeasurable riches derived from interest." Above all, Marlowe's *Jew of Malta* and Shakespeare's *Merchant of Venice* "most powerfully conveyed the hatred of the Asiatic for all that is Aryan, and the limitless contempt of the Aryan for the racial scum of the ancient world."

After this opening, Zander culled the most potent examples of Shakespeare's treatment of the Jews and commented on their wider anti-Semitic implications. Of course, the majority came from *The Merchant of Venice*. According to Zander, Shakespeare felt that "Jewish hatred of the Aryan was fateful, not just a matter of personal disputes that come about in daily life." To demonstrate Shakespeare's recognition that Jews "felt broad, impersonal feelings of enmity for Aryans in general – based on religious, economic, and racial differences" – he cited Shylock from act I, scene 3:

> *I hate him for he is a Christian, but more for that in low simplicity he lends out money gratis and brings down the rate of usance here with us in Venice. If I can catch him once upon the hip, I will feed fat the ancient grudge I bear him. He hates our sacred nation, and he rails, even there where merchants most do congregate, on me, my bargains and my well-won thrift, which he calls interest. Cursed be my tribe, if I forgive him!*

To demonstrate Shakespeare's belief that "the Jew was busy with his hatred day and night, that his whole being was consumed by it," Zander reproduced Shylock's response to being invited to dinner by Bassanio and Antonio: "But wherefore should I go? I am not bid for love; they flatter me: But yet I'll go in hate, to feed upon the prodigal Christian" (II.5).

In return, Zander held, Shakespeare allowed his Aryan characters to answer: "Jewish hatred comes strong and hot, and is countered by the other side – to the point of real contempt." As proof, he cited Launcelot describing Shylock as devilish: "To be ruled by my conscience, I should stay with the Jew my master, who … is a kind of devil … Certainly the Jew is the very devil incarnal" (II.2). Likewise, Zander pointed out, did Solanis utter strong anti-Semitic language "on seeing the Jew rampaging" after being tricked by his daughter: "I never heard a passion so confused, so strange, outrageous, and so variable, as the dog Jew did utter in the streets" (II.8). Above all, Zander implied, Shakespeare expressed the contemporary resentment against the stereotypical Jew as usurer. In his depiction of Shylock, "the Jewish parasite resisted the social law of Nordic-natured communities that forbad usury, and even worse, disdained Christian charity that required help for comrades of the people without profit." Shylock's insistence on the arrest of Antonio stood as evidence: "Gaoler, look to him: tell not me of mercy; this is the fool that lent out money gratis: Gaoler, look to him" (III.3). Shakespeare's Jew was, in Zander's view, "a monster who would discard all of humanity in the interest of his own wealth," as suggested in his reaction to Jessica's elopement, when he claims to care more about losing a jewel she wore than his daughter herself: "I would my daughter were dead at my foot, and the jewels in her ear! would she were hearsed at my foot, and the ducats in her coffin!" (III.1).

About the character of Jessica, whose attractiveness might have been a sign that Shakespeare saw through the anti-Semitic attitudes of his day, Zander firmly assumed the mentality of the hate-filled secondary characters to be Shakespeare's own. The daughter of the Jew, he argued, "couldn't really be of Jewish breed, since she was loyal, noble, and beautiful." According to Zander, the stout Solarino said as much, "right to the Jew's face": "There is more difference between thy flesh and hers than between jet and ivory; more between your bloods than there is between red wine and Rhenish" (III.1). Moreover, Zander wrote, Launcelot was of the same opinion, saying to Jessica herself: "Marry, you may partly hope that your father got you not, that you are not the Jew's daughter" (III.5).

It was "completely hopeless to discuss Nordic justice and fairness with a Jewish foreigner," Zander held. Moreover, it was "impossible to change a Jew and dissuade him from his wicked ways, to make him kill himself, and annihilate his kind." The English writers, especially Shakespeare, he said, were perfectly aware of this, having "learned it from the 'Dark' Ages and their own Volk." It was anti-Semitic awareness that lay behind Antonio's sense of hopelessness about the possibility of reasoning with Shylock: "Think you question with the Jew: You may as well go stand upon the beach and bid the main flood bate his usual height" (IV.1). Therefore, Shakespeare would have agreed with Zander that the "only solution was elimination of the enemy: abstract discussion of justice had no role in the matter; the Volk of the Shakespearean age didn't trouble with the letter of the law; the Jew might have obtained his pound of flesh, but the monster had to be destroyed."

Not satisfied with gleaning anti-Semitic language from the play, Zander went on to offer the original publicity used to promote it as further proof that Shakespeare shared his views wholly – even in modern German racist terms. According to Zander, a theater poster of the Elizabethan era announced that the "essential element of the comedy lay in the heroic struggle of noble Aryans against the unbelievable cruelty of a monster: they are almost defeated, but in the end triumph over the hated creature." Lest readers get the impression that Shakespeare was the author of only a single anti-Semitic masterpiece, Zander then provided additional examples from other Shakespeare works that he felt also showed how much the Bard detested and hated Jews, "on account of their usurious cruelty, foreign ways, and ridiculous physique."

From *Loves Labour Lost*, he quoted:

> *Boyet: Therefore, as he is an ass, let him go. And so adieu, sweet Jude! nay, why dost thou stay?*
> *Dumain: For the latter end of his name.*
> *Biron: For the ass to the Jude; give it him: – Jud-as, away! (V.2)*

From *Henry IV, Part I*:

> *Prince Henry: Speak, sirs; how was it?*
> *Gadshill: We four set upon some dozen –*
> *Falstaff: Sixteen at least, my lord.*
> *Gadshill: And bound them.*
> *Peto: No, no, they were not bound.*
> *Falstaff: You rogue, they were bound, every man of them; or I am a Jew else, an Ebrew Jew. (II.4)*

From *Two Gentlemen of Verona*:

> *Launce: He is a stone, a very pebble stone, and has no more pity in him than a dog: a Jew would have wept to have seen our parting. (III.3)*

And again, from *Two Gentlemen of Verona*:

> *Launce: If thou wilt, go with me to the alehouse; if not, thou art an Hebrew, a Jew, and not worth the name of a Christian.*
> *Speed: Why?*

> Launce: Because thou hast not so much charity in thee as to
> go to the ale with a Christian. Wilt thou go? (II.5)[18]

For those who might not have immediately comprehended the significance of Shakespeare's work from an anti-Semitic perspective "completely free of trendiness and theoretical nonsense," contributors like
Baldur von Schirach had nothing but disdain. Reviewing a presentation
at a festival organized by the Shakespeare Association of Bochum,
Schirach reported that a Professor Gundolf of Heidelberg – "a Jew,
really [named] Gudelfinger!" – gave a lecture entitled "State and
Tragedy," which, Schirach claimed, remained incomprehensible to
even scholarly listeners because of its "un-German complexity."
Perhaps, Schirach proposed, this would be useful as a lesson for the
future, because it demonstrated that it was "simply impossible to let a
Jew speak about Shakespeare." Nazis, he went on to state, were of the
opinion that a "complete purge of foreign elements" should be the next
task of the Shakespeare Association because "it was not proper for a
German Shakespeare Association to have Jews on its list of
speakers."[19]

While the editors of the *Völkischer Beobachter* found many
ways to exploit the works of Shakespeare, none was more important
and useful than the invocation of Shakespeare's depiction of the Jew as
usurer. For propagandists, this familiar character could be readily referenced and effectively used to personify the malignant forces that the
Völkischer Beobachter felt were shaping twentieth-century European
politics. On 5 April 1923 – at the height of the Ruhr crisis – the paper
ran in the center of its front page a cartoon depicting Shylock having
stabbed the allegorical figure of Germania in the back, with the silhou-
ettes of black soldiers encroaching in the background – a reference to the
French policy of sending African troops into the area (Figure 4.2). Above
this image, the headline shouted, "The French Shylock in the Ruhr," and
an explanation of the situation followed: "The forefathers of the Jewish
banking firm, Rothschild-Frères – the true rulers of France – migrated
about 100 years ago from Frankfurt am Main to Paris. The holdings of
this house grew [to] around 20 billion during the World War, and are
estimated today at around 70 billion. Through the invasion of the Ruhr,
it hopes to increase its holdings to 100 billion." Finally, beneath the
image, the *Völkischer Beobachter* caption had the "Head of the House of

Figure 4.2 *Völkischer Beobachter* cartoon, "The French Shylock in the Ruhr Region," 5 April 1923

Rothschild" – the modern-day Shylock – saying: "The stab in the back disarmed you; now I can cut out a piece of your heart!"[20]

Beyond Shakespeare, the next great author of supposedly anti-Jewish literature featured in the *Völkischer Beobachter* was Goethe. As well as portraying him as an anti-revolutionary, pro-German militarist, it was essential to the *Völkischer Beobachter*'s interpretive agenda that Goethe's credentials as an anti-Semite be established. This required, in the words of Joachim Petzold, discrediting "fairy tales about the inner affinity of Goethe with the Jews."[21] Citing a lecture on "Goethe and the Jews" by Franz Koch – who was appointed Berlin Professor of Literature under the Nazis – the paper chided "Jewish literary historians" for showing their colors when they "stamped Goethe as a philo-Semite."[22] And after surveying writings on Goethe for the paper, Adolf Bartels – author, critic, and literary historian who produced histories of German literature that were highly influential in conservative, anti-Semitic, and volkish circles – concluded that they were "full of Jewish mistakes." "Why don't the Jews just stick to the *Talmud*?" he asked bitterly, before insisting that one must read Houston Stewart Chamberlain's 1912 *Goethe* instead.[23] Among his many other achievements, Koch wrote, Chamberlain had "worked against such a falsification of Goethe's portrait": the "legend of Goethe's philo-Semitism" was based on his high appraisal of the Bible and the fact that he graced a circle of Jewesses like Dorothea Veit, Henriette Herz, and Rahel Levin – "nothing more."[24]

Further, from the *Völkischer Beobachter*'s perspective, Goethe's appreciation of the Old Testament could simply be ascribed to its "value as a literary product and pedagogical tool," rather than to its dogmatic content. The Bible interested him as the self-representation of a "tough, sharply coined Volk" – as a representation of "Jewish national life" – because Goethe approached it as an "early practitioner of racial science." As a "typical biological thinker," he had a "premonition of race in the sense of an inescapable reality" and by observing with the eye of a natural scientist, he recognized Jews as an "extreme case of classification." Naturally, the paper held, he "perceived the Jews as a foreign body, in accordance with the Faustian notion: 'The life of mankind flows through its blood.'"[25]

These racial-scientific views supposedly formed the theoretical background for Goethe's positions against Jewish emancipation and intermarriage. In the "Goethean organic-biological world view" there was no room for these "products of Enlightenment philosophy." This position, the paper held, was proven in a letter by Goethe to Bettina von Arnim, in which he responded to a brochure against emancipation efforts, and even more clearly in a statement he made to Weimar minister, Friedrich von Müller. According to the *Völkischer Beobachter*, Goethe was in a "fervent fury" about the Jewish Law of 1823, which permitted marriage between Jew and Christian. Under the headline, "Goethe on Mixed-Marriages," the paper relished reprinting Müller's recollection of 23 September 1823: "I had scarcely entered Goethe's room when the old man poured out his passionate scorn for our new Jewish law that permits marriage between persons of both faiths ... All moral feeling in the family that was still based on religion would be undermined by such a scandalous law ... His worry about the Jews came through everywhere, despite his free-thinking."[26]

In addition to this observation by Müller, Petzold felt strongly that Nazis were in a position to emphasize numerous statements by Goethe on the Jews that "stood close to the biological world view of their era."[27] Hanns Johst agreed, stating that Goethe "recognized the need for racial purity" when he thundered: "The main thing is that the race remain pure – as pure as when Tacitus first praised it!" This wrathful line, Johst added, clarified the "strong anti-Semitic tradition that moved Goethe as a German": given this, "all opinions, perceptions, and interpretations tarnished with blood and spiritual associations of foreign races" – that is, all notions of Goethe as philo-Semite – became "irrelevant."[28]

From Goethe's *Wilhelm Meisters Wanderjahre* (1829), the *Völkischer Beobachter* repeatedly reproduced the single line: "We can suffer no Jews among us; because why should we let him partake in the advantages of the highest culture whose origins he rejects?"[29] – adding, on one occasion, that the meaning of this sentence became doubly clear if one realized the impossibility of applying a similar statement to the Greeks and their culture: there was an "inner, organic bridge from German to Greek culture," while there was "no living connection to Jewish culture."[30] Through the study of Homer, Petzold tried to show, Goethe discovered the "unmentionable mischief the Jewish race has done to us"[31] – and added that "humanity would have had a different face if it had remained with Homer and never come to know the Biblical Sodomites." Moreover, Petzold contended that another line from *Wilhelm Meister* "followed from this last remark": "The Israelite people has never been good for much, as its leaders, judges, chiefs, and prophets have been reproached a thousand times; it possesses the least virtues and the most errors of all the peoples."[32]

It was on the basis of this collection of citations, repeated at every opportunity, that the *Völkischer Beobachter* built its case that Goethe would have supported Nazi policies against Jews. The paper and its contributors seemed to realize, however, that these selections did not amount to much when compared with the mass of his lyrical works. They therefore wished to show that on the so-called Jewish Question, "the poet's verses said more than some theoretical remarks or off-the-cuff expressions."[33] In this sense, they found – in the form of one scene in a little known early work – a secret weapon that they hoped would give National Socialists victory in the competition over Goethe's political legacy. At barely thirty years of age, Petzold crowed, Goethe "gave us the following unsurpassable image of the eternal Jew," in *The Annual Fair at Plundersweilern*.[34] From this satirical drama the *Völkischer Beobachter* reproduced more than once the scene of a play-within-the-play where Old Testament figures Haman and Ahaseverus discuss the need to punish Jews for their excessive pride. Therein, Goethe's Haman denounces Jews as "knowing how to control everyone through borrowing and lending and playing an evil game with our women too." As long as there is order, Haman warns, "they don't have much to hope for: but, secretly they are lighting the fire, and before we see it the land will be in flames." Therefore, Haman continues, the king "should teach them about their obligations with a law, and if they are stubborn, then with flame and sword."[35] This is proof, the paper triumphantly exclaimed, that "our Wolfgang Goethe clearly recognized the Jewish race and portrayed it in deed, word, and writing!"[36]

Moreover, the paper continued, despite such clear evidence of the true nature of Goethe's beliefs, leaders of the Society for Defense Against anti-Semitism (*Verein zur Abwehr des Antisemitismus*), "university professors, and Rabbis with all their countless titles and doctorates," still had the audacity to state precisely the opposite: "roughly, that 'Goethe didn't have an anti-Semitic bone in his body.'" "Judah" had long recognized Goethe as "one of its most dangerous enemies" and had therefore worked tirelessly – "applying classic Talmudic tactics of perversion" – to present Goethe as an "outspoken friend of Jews throughout the world." Why? So that Germans and others wouldn't notice how a genius like Goethe "clearly assessed and condemned the Jewish race." In particular, "Judah's powerful fist of gold" insured that *The Annual Fair at Plundersweilern* had disappeared from the Goethe editions of the last fifty years, and had therefore been "utterly deleted for the Volk!" "Woe to the publisher who dared to include it in a new Goethe collection: he would be immediately destroyed – morally and financially – by Judah." That was an indication of "how far things had gone," and what readers of the Nazi paper had to dedicate themselves to undoing – in the name of the main figure of German *Bildung*: Goethe.[37]

Despite assertions about the long-standing significance of hatred toward Jews in German and Western culture, there did exist in the pages of the *Völkischer Beobachter* different opinions as to precisely when modern racial anti-Semitism was formulated. According to Robert Hohlbaum, it was not Goethe, but Franz Grillparzer who first perceived the Jewish issue in terms of race rather than religion and culture. While others took on the matter in different terms, Hohlbaum acknowledged, it was Grillparzer – even before Wagner – who first recognized that the Jewish Question was a "racial problem." As proof, Hohlbaum cited the following quatrain:

> A Christ stood at the Gates of Heaven,
> But Saint Peter wouldn't let him in,
> Because a cohort of baptized Jews,
> Were just storming their way through.[38]

What an "abyss," Hohlbaum observed, separated the Viennese from the Berlin romantics, the Friedrich Schlegels, and the Varnhagens, who "quietly married their Jewesses and let themselves be enchanted by mystic Catholicism," and Grillparzer "recognized this difference in anti-Semitic consciousness." From his journal Hohlbaum cited Grillparzer's statement that the "famous monotheism of the Jews" probably arose from the fact that they were originally "such a despised nation they could not imagine more than one divinity being interested in them." Moreover, Hohlbaum argued, Grillparzer produced perhaps the "sharpest fighting poem that was ever directed at the heart of Judaism." Targeting the Austrian critic, Moritz Saphir, personally, but also as a "representative of his race," he wrote:

> The devil wanted to create a murderer.
> So he put together some parts from different animals
> Like the wolf, fox, and jackal.
> But he forgot to add one thing: courage.

Furious, he pulled on the creature's nose and cried,
Rascal, become a Jew and write reviews!

Finally, the paper pointed to one of Grillparzer's poems, which, in its "caustic, sharp, amusing imitation of Jewish ways of speaking," was a "model of poetic description that could serve as the landmark of an age." Already in his time, "all theatrical art was subject to restless Jewish interests and the notorious 'Jewish censor' obstructed anything that wasn't kosher." So Grillparzer wrote:

They have destroyed epochs in their storm.
Nothing and no one pleases them.
They write poems and create pictures that are indescribable.
The Jews poach on German art.
And we blind pigeons are supposed to believe
That nothing can happen to the Jews.
But we will see. We will see.[39]

Like a "shrill scream of indignation from the noble breast of a German poet," the *Völkischer Beobachter* asserted, these previously unknown pearls of poetry should have been "resounding in the hearts of SA men [*Sturmabteilung*, Nazi stormtroopers] at a time when German culture and race were embarking on the final battle against the dominion of the *Untermenschen*."[40] He hadn't been well understood by contemporaries, but Grillparzer "saw and strode far ahead of his times." So, "Goethe's great warning" went for him too: "Posterity will give him completely what life has only given him in half – or not at all." Posterity – that is, Nazi Germany – Hohlbaum concluded, "owed him a great, noble debt."[41]

Alongside Grillparzer, the *Völkischer Beobachter* also published articles stipulating that his contemporary, the philosopher Schopenhauer, also deserved praise as a leading anti-Semite. Karl Grunsky sought to "lay out everything that Schopenhauer had in his heart against the Jews." The Old Testament comes off very badly in his works, said Grunsky: in particular, Schopenhauer had pointed out Abraham's "outrageous and nefarious behavior" and Jacob's "infamous roguishness." According to Grunsky, the philosopher complained strongly that the culture of this "minor people" (*Winkelvolk*) – the Jews – had served as the base of Western Christian culture instead of Indian, Greek, or Roman. His "stance against Jewish spirit," Grunsky closed, also "bound

Schopenhauer with Wagner," and therefore National Socialists should "recognize that the thinker, as far as his wisdom applied to Germany, was a genuine child of the German Volk."[42]

The Nazi paper drew further associations between Schopenhauer and anti-Semitism in an extended article on "Schopenhauer and the Jews." The author, Maria Groener, who had triggered a controversy in 1920 with the publication of a book of the same title,[43] opened a reprise of her arguments for the *Völkischer Beobachter* by stating that proving Schopenhauer to have been a fellow anti-Semite was "one of the most important tasks required of the new intellectual community [*Lehrgemeinschaft*] that Nazism needed to establish." Toward that end she reported that some letters written to the philosopher had been left out of a collection of correspondence published by the Schopenhauer Archive. She felt that on the basis of their one-sided content and some marginal notes penned by Schopenhauer, one could interpret these letters as strong indications of the philosopher's attitudes toward Jews. Based on her interpretations of these sources, Groener posited that Schopenhauer believed the Jew "as such" could not come to a natural realization of the truth at all – this was "simply impossible on the basis of his blood." The best a Jew could hope to achieve was "artificial knowledge derived from logically precise argumentation" since "intuitive cognition" – "certainty of the truth before a proof is available" – was impossible for him. "The Jew can never see into nature; in spiritual terms, his eyes are sick and they can only be operated upon by an Aryan." Without such help, Groener implied, the "completely blind Jew lives in Jewish monomania and Jewish megalomania." For him, "thought is just a way to ward off boredom"; in him, "there is no burning need or desire to search for truth." From these letters, Groener insisted, Schopenhauer's personal attitude toward Jews – "which should be a model for us all"– spoke out clearly: the Jew must be "made to feel insecure in this era when the Aryan is overcoming him spiritually" and thereby be forced to "decide whether to disappear or to serve." In conclusion, Groener wrote for the *Völkischer Beobachter*, as Germans "gradually freed themselves from Jewification" (*Verjüdung*), the "best of them would heed Schopenhauer's ideas on this subject more and more." Concepts like these would give the Volk the "strength necessary for achieving the renaissance of the Germanic [*Godisch*] and for overcoming the Judaic."

Outside Germany, to prove that the romantic Byron was not only critical of British society, but was also "the first who brought up with unsparing clarity the increasing Jewification of the English upper class and its dangerous consequences," the newspaper reproduced extended citations from his *Age of Bronze* (1823), relishing such lines as:[44]

> How rich is Britain! not indeed in mines,
> Or peace or plenty, corn or oil or wines;
> No land of Canaan, full of milk and honey,
> Nor (save in paper shekels) ready money:
> But let us not to own the truth refuse,
> Was ever Christian land so rich in Jews? ...
> All States, all things, all Sovereigns they control,
> And waft a loan from Indus to the Pole ...
> Two Jews but not Samaritans direct
> The world, with all the Spirit of their sect.

But all the examples of anti-Jewish rancor that the *Völkischer Beobachter* culled from preceding Western culture pale in comparison with those drawn from their preferred master. Undoubtedly, the aspect of Richard Wagner's political writings that seemed most consistent with the Nazi perspective was their articulation of anti-Semitic views (Figure 4.3). From its earliest days, the paper's Nazi cultural coverage emphasized Wagner's treatment of the "Jewish issue." As early as 14 November 1920, one critic, Freiherr von Leoprechting, gathered and presented extracts from Wagner's *Judaism in Music*, which the paper subsequently relied upon above anything else the composer produced.[45] Leoprechting introduced his favorite citations from the infamous article by reporting that Wagner had noticed the influence of Jews in musical life when in Paris, and thereafter "forthrightly expressed the disgust that Germans felt toward Jews as a whole," in statements such as: "The Jew – who, as everyone knows, has a God all to himself – in ordinary life strikes us primarily by his outward appearance, which, no matter to what European nationality we belong, has something disagreeably foreign to that nationality: instinctively we wish to have nothing in common with a man who looks like that."[46] Leoprechting closed his presentation of what he considered to be the composer's most important insights by insisting that the publication of Wagner's "open-hearted article" caused a "vicious campaign" against him and his music. According to Leoprechting, the difficulties he subsequently experienced in achieving his artistic aims were

Figure 4.3 *Völkischer Beobachter*, Richard Wagner tribute article: "On Germany's Renewal: Richard Wagner's Political Will," 22 May 1938

caused by Jews in response to this publication, since "Jewry already had much influence over the press at the time."[47]

Again, in 1922, Hans Buchner wrote that *Judaism in Music* was "more relevant than ever before, seeming as if it had been written yesterday, not a half-century ago" – the only difference being that in the meantime, "everything that Wagner prophesied had become true, and that which had operated secretly was now determining the future." Time had not yet passed over Wagner's anti-Semitism, Buchner continued, and was even less likely to do so now, in the 1920s. The "oppression of German art" continued even more intensely than in his day. "Cartels, trusts, and associations worked secretly for the systematic suppression of the truly German." To fight against them "with all possible means" was the only solution. Wagner had to fight alone against a system that was just coming into existence and he prevailed because of the force of his "phenomenal personality." But in the Weimar era, "that system completely dominated all of public life" – including art – so the individual was powerless against it and "only committed solidarity would guarantee success."[48]

Another survey of Wagner's letters and publications on Jews with an extensive collection of citations appeared in 1923. Reproducing the following from a letter to Countess Marie Muchanoff, which Wagner wrote to mark the New Year of 1869, the paper commented that he "recognized the extent of the danger that Jewry, which was already at that time a prevalent power, posed to the *Volkstum*":[49]

> *Just as the influence which the Jews have gained upon our mental life – as displayed in the deflection and falsification of our highest culture – is definitive, so too is the fact that this influence is no mere physiologic accident beyond dispute. Whether the downfall of our Culture can be arrested by a violent ejection of the destructive foreign element, I am unable to decide, since that would require forces with whose existence I am unacquainted.*[50]

After this, more selections from *Judaism in Music* appeared, including: "According to the present constitution of this world, the Jew in truth is already more than emancipated: he rules, and will rule, so long as money remains the power before which all our doings and our dealings lose their force."[51] Commenting on reproductions of Wagner's attacks on the "cultured Jew" and the merely "imitative" efforts of Jewish poets and musicians, who were not sufficiently rooted in German language to produce "genuine" lyric or music, the *Völkischer Beobachter* commented that "whoever had eyes to see and ears to hear" would recognize that the "terrible, dangerous Judaic influence on every field of art over the last fifty years was all the proof necessary to demonstrate the accuracy of Wagnerian, i.e., German, views."[52]

On the 50th anniversary of Wagner's death, the *Völkischer Beobachter* further underscored his anti-Semitism, stating that he had to be designated as one of the few who clearly recognized the "cultural dangers of Judaism" and, "without any consideration for his own person, steadfastly went into battle."[53] Thus, in a letter to Ludwig II in April 1866, Wagner wrote: "With Germany my artistic ideals stand or fall and my works live or die. What will follow the collapse of the German princes will be that Jewish-German horde that I once described to you in my journal." Then, the paper noted, fifteen years later, Wagner again wrote to the king complaining about a Jewish member of his personal circle: "I regard the Jewish race as the born enemy of pure humanity and everything that is noble in it; it is certain we Germans will go under before them, and perhaps I am the last German who knows how to stand up as an art-loving man against the Judaism that is already getting control of everything."

Above all, Hermann Seeliger added, Wagner found – like the Nazi leadership – "the main cause of the decline of humanity in the deterioration of the blood, in the 'decay of race' – i.e., in the mixing of noble races with lower ones." In these views, argued Seeliger, Wagner advanced the racial theories of Gobineau beyond more traditional forms of anti-Semitism, by "synthesizing eugenics and policy via thoroughgoing investigation." Wagner "treated the demon of decay, in close connection with the problem of racial degradation – in terms of a psychological assessment of the Jewish Question – that is, as it concerned the demoralizing influence of Judaism on non-Jewish peoples." Because he sensed these things, Wagner was a "German prophet: no historian or biologist had taken on the problem as energetically on German soil."[54] Therefore, the *Völkischer Beobachter* continued, Wagner was for Nazis more than an "ingenious creator of phenomenal works of art": he was simultaneously the "presentiment and the fulfillment of volkish longing, outlook, and confidence." He gave Nazis "beautiful words for their difficult path out of the harsh present to a better and purer future."[55] In his opinion, which the paper shared, "the only hope for liberation from the demon of decay was through the application of brutal force."[56] Thus did the *Völkischer Beobachter* invoke Wagner's writings as early as 1923 in order to raise decisive notions of eliminationist anti-Semitism.

5 THE ARCHENEMY INCARNATE

We have learned so far that the *Völkischer Beobachter* vigorously promoted the notion that great cultural figures in the Western tradition were of Germanic origins, politically engaged, grounded in the Volk, and, especially, anti-Semitic – going as far in this last respect as to claim that in their work and lives, these masters had indeed prefigured Hitler's goals of seeking out and combating the Jew in all branches of cultural and artistic life. In this chapter, we will hear what the paper's contributors said about significant cultural figures who were actually Jewish, and, as such, embodied the worst Nazi fears. To the *Völkischer Beobachter*, these creators represented the treacherous threat of Jews who had insinuated themselves into German culture and then worked to undermine it.[1]

One problem Nazi cultural critics faced, of course, was that the presence and influence of Jewish artists, writers, and composers in the Western tradition was indisputable. In an effort to come to terms with this fact, Nazi cultural critics resorted to tactics of racial stereotyping that echoed many of the themes of cultural anti-Semitism that predecessors such as Richard Wagner and Houston Stewart Chamberlain had percolated in the second half of the nineteenth century – as filtered through Hitler's own interpretations. And among these themes, the most useful for its ability to explain away the fact that Jews had assimilated the German tradition of *Bildung* was the assertion that, lacking their own culture, Jewish artists functioned as little more than cynical, opportunistic imitators of their supposed superiors. As Hitler explained:

*Since the Jew was never in possession of a culture of his own,
the foundations of his intellectual work were always provided
by others ... The Jewish people, despite all apparent
intellectual qualities, is without any true culture, and
especially without any culture of its own ... The Jew takes
over foreign culture, imitating or rather ruining it ... Hence
his intellect will never have a constructive effect, but will
be destructive ... Culturally he contaminates art, literature,
the theater, makes a mockery of natural feeling, overthrows
all concepts of beauty and sublimity, of the noble and the
good, and instead drags men down into the sphere of his own
base nature. Religion is ridiculed, ethics and morality
represented as outmoded, until the last props of a nation in its
struggle for existence in this world have fallen.*[2]

The *Völkischer Beobachter* vilified a number of the leading lights
of the German Jewish intellectual tradition along these lines – essentially
branding them as first imitators and ultimately as destroyers of the existing
cultural tradition.[3] In each case, the paper's contributors worked to associate the works and lives of these figures with the theory that their contributions amounted to little more than clever appropriations, utterly
lacking in the Germanic "essence" that supposedly made art meaningful.[4]

Thus, following the tradition of Wagner's personal attacks on
Felix Mendelssohn and Giacomo Meyerbeer in *Judaism in Music*, the
Völkischer Beobachter ran a book review in which the critic Lore
Reinmoeller, who would later produce a study of Nietzsche in addition
to dramas about Lou Salomé and Theodore Fontane, summarized the
basic volkish attitude toward these two composers. The book she
reviewed for the newspaper was Karl Blessinger's *Judaism and Music:
A Contribution to Cultural and Racist Politics* (1944). Blessinger, a
teacher at the Munich Academy of Music, had written a number of
attacks on music modernism before aligning himself with Nazi ideology.
In this book, as Reinmoeller explained, Blessinger surveyed "a century
and a half of ongoing attempts by Jews to corrupt the Western music
tradition, wherein Jewish composers and musicians had adopted
German music with particular eagerness, with the goal of making it
subservient to the purposes of Jewry as a whole." Through this period,
even domestic music making (*Hausmusik*) was "drawn under Jewish
control as a result of some refined chess moves." And so, ran the

argument, as soon as a new opera came out, some Jew converted the favorite numbers into "fantasies, rondos, and potpourris." Thus packaged with the subversive appeal of popular music, the "alien elements worked on a wide front to corrupt the musical sense of the public": the "fashionable phenomena of salon and operetta music had an emotional effect on the hearers, aimed at disturbing their inner equilibrium, breaking down the inner powers whether through sugar-sweet sentimentality or through an artificial passion that gave the appearance of strength that was not actually present." According to Wagner, Reinmoeller recounted, Meyerbeer (1791–1864) was "little more than a plagiarist," who "did not shrink at all from making obvious borrowings." As for the plots of Meyerbeer's operas, the "combination of unrestrained eroticism with insatiable lust for murder had to be understood as particularly consistent with the Jewish nature."[5]

In the case of Felix Mendelssohn (1809–1847), Reinmoeller complained that he had been represented in "attractive Jewish propaganda as the rescuer and savior of the whole German tradition," and was best known in this capacity for his "so-called advocacy" of Bach's *St. Matthew Passion*. But not content to let this chapter in Mendelssohn's career stand unopposed, Blessinger (and Reinmoeller in review) argued that it was actually Mendelssohn's teacher, Carl Friedrich Zelter, who "planned and wanted to lead the revival," but "he fell ill all of a sudden, and turned the direction over to Mendelssohn." Then, "as a result of omissions and rewritings, arbitrary changes to the orchestration, and a completely new instrumentation – all perpetrated by Mendelssohn – a completely false version of this great work resulted."[6]

As it concerned Mendelssohn's own compositions, Reinmoeller explained that while "the Jews had worked hard for a century to present it as outstanding," in truth closer consideration revealed that Mendelssohn had "absolutely no creative gifts of his own." He had just borrowed from his great German predecessors and "fiddled around until he produced things that weren't immediately recognizable and therefore seemed to be products of his own," drawing a substantial number of his themes from French ballet music – even, for instance, the main melody of the Overture to *A Midsummer Night's Dream* (1842).[7] Actually, the *Völkischer Beobachter* was inconsistent in its treatment of the incidental music for *A Midsummer Night's Dream*, and this confusion was representative of Nazi reception of Mendelssohn's most famous work in general.[8] In the first year of *Völkischer Beobachter* cultural coverage, the musicologist Otto Keller, on the paper's staff from the beginning,[9] reviewed a production and concluded that the music of Mendelssohn was "so pleasant and so appropriate for the character of the play that one still cannot put a better version in its place" – though he evidently felt it was desirable to do so.[10] However, by 1944 the tone had changed: Josef Klingenbeck reported enthusiastically about a performance of the ballet produced by Otto Falckenberg with "new music that was supposedly well received by the audience."[11]

Outside the music tradition, a favorite strategy in the *Völkischer Beobachter*'s coverage of leading German-Jewish intellectuals was to "use Jews' own words against themselves." The method was applied to the dissident writer of political satire, Ludwig Börne (1786–1837), in particular. Committed to principles of liberalization and ultimately associated with the Young Germany movement, Börne was characterized in the paper as a self-hating Jew whose writings inadvertently coordinated with National Socialist ideology. In one article, "Börne on the Jews," in the paper extracted from a letter to the "Jewess" Henriette Herz, Börne wrote: "There are three things that [Jews] treasure, first: money, second: money, third: money. It is typical of their humor that they translate Hamlet's monologue: Money or no money, that is the question."[12] One hears, the *Völkischer Beobachter* continued, "the same tone in his Parisian letters," wherein Börne – "whose given name was Baruch," the paper reminded – "lashed the egotistical one-sidedness with which Frankfurt Jews perceived world events from the standpoint of how they affected the stock market." For instance, he responded to a meeting between Rothschild and the Pope in the following sarcastic terms:

Now everything is going to come out as God really wanted when he created the world: a poor Jew kisses the Pope's hand. Had Rothschild offered Rome a better interest rate, so that Cardinal Kämmerling could spend another ten thousand ducats, he would have had the Pope hugging him around the neck! How much more honorable are the Rothschilds than their forefather, Judas Ischariot! He sold Christ out for a mere thirty thalers, but if he were for sale today the Rothschilds would just buy him outright. I think that's great!

Most intensively, the *Völkischer Beobachter* featured statements in which the radical Börne critiqued Jews associated with aristocratic and monarchical circles. Thus, the paper found that Börne had written the following in a "Parisian rag" about the Rothschilds:

> *It's always the same game that the Rothschilds play to enrich themselves at the cost of the country they exploit ... They have contributed the most to the undermining of freedom. Without a doubt the majority of Europeans would be in full possession of freedom if the Rothschilds [and other prominent Jewish families such as] the Ouvrards, the Aguados, the Casimir Perriers, and others didn't support absolutist monarchies with their money.*

Of course, the Nazi paper provided no context for Börne's remarks, leaving the impression that the writer's sentiments aligned perfectly – even a century later – with the paper's racial perspective on the Jewish Question.[13]

Among those in the Jewish cultural intelligentsia selected for anti-Semitic demonization in the pages of *Völkischer Beobachter*, however, none was targeted more directly or consistently than the poet, essayist, and political wit, Heinrich Heine (1797–1856). The paper's preoccupation with Heine manifested itself as early as 1920 in a lengthy attack on the writer that quoted from Wagner's most odious opus, *Judaism in Music*. Here, the paper reveled in Wagner's description of Heine as the "highly-gifted poet-Jew" who gave himself "the airs of true poesis" and thereby became "the conscience of Judaism, just as Judaism is the evil conscience of our modern Civilization."[14] Thus taking their cue from Wagner, contributors to the *Völkischer Beobachter* unleashed a torrent of venom against Heine, which continued throughout the history of the newspaper.

An issue that the Nazi cultural community found particularly irksome was the fact that Heine, like Börne, had himself baptized in an effort toward assimilation. In a reversal of the process by which the *Völkischer Beobachter* endeavored to demonstrate the German origins of creative leaders, the paper's contributors worked intensively to establish that Heine's conversion had been a "sham" and that he therefore "should not be considered a German poet in any sense." The paper took every opportunity to remind its readers that Heine was raised in the Jewish tradition and that his given name was Chaim Bückeburg. Furthermore, the paper explained, his "supposed" conversion to

Christianity was undertaken "just so that he could ridicule his new faith";[15] it was the "equivalent of one of our grandfathers spitting in the face of a usurious Jew." His attempt to "get into his hands an entry ticket to European culture" showed clearly that he was a "true blue Jew – even if it didn't work."[16] Indeed, the paper reported that Heine was "very open about how sacred his baptism was for him," writing to his "racial brother," Julius Moser, that "a baptism doesn't mean much to me; its symbolism isn't important. I am more dedicated to the maintenance of my fellow unhappy Jews. Whoever has themselves baptized out of conviction is a fool!" To this, the newspaper remarked, "That's how 'Heine the convert' felt about this sacred ritual: that it was just a means to an end."[17] The whole thing reminded one, the *Völkischer Beobachter* continued, of the statement by a "Jewish historian, Professor Graetz," who said of Heine's baptism that "he was putting on the uniform of the enemy in order to better fight him."[18]

Of course, the salient issue here was racial anti-Semitism: the circumstances of Heine's baptism provided a familiar example that could be readily cited in the effort to prove the case against the notion of assimilation in general. Of uppermost importance, then, was that the newspaper used Heine as a cultural-historical representative for all converted, or would-be converted, Jews. As the paper put it in an extensive 1930 article entitled "The Comedy of Heine's Baptism," when discussing the Heine case, "measures for quick abolishment of Jew baptism were at the forefront because this practice not only opened the gates of Christian communities to absolutely anti-Christian spirit, but beyond this – after a century of further development in anti-Semitic ideology – the policy became pure nonsense once one recognized the inseparability of Jewish religion from Jewish blood." Just as the terms "order and chaos" were forever mutually exclusive, the article went on, so "even the slightest, crazy attempts to unify them endangered – if not completely destroyed – the former," in the same way that the concepts of "Christ and Judas as well as Siegfried (Germans) and Judah (Jews) excluded one another according to natural law." The "blood of cosmic light and the blood of stifling chaos would never in all eternity make common cause," the newspaper insisted. Then, citing Matthew 19:6 – "What Heaven has put together, let no man put asunder!" – the *Völkischer Beobachter* added, "if one takes this seriously, then one should take just as seriously its inversion: 'What Heaven (Nature!) has put asunder, let no man bring together! Let no man knit or bundle!' This sacred teaching should have long ago deterred from the mischief of Jew baptism!" Here, the newspaper came to the essence of its obsession with the issue of Heine's conversion: "we want a true portrait of a particular case – the baptism of Heine – because this shameful cultural-historical picture will wake us out of our dogmatic indifference to the natural-historical nonsense of Jew baptism."[19]

But in demanding the elimination of Heine from the German cultural tradition, the *Völkischer Beobachter* confronted a significant obstacle: many of Heine's works were considered central to the romantic canon. A particular difficulty was the fact that many of his verses had been set to music, further ingraining them in the German cultural tradition. Facing this challenge, the paper and its contributors launched an onslaught on the poet's creative integrity, drawing upon the anti-Semitic strategy of denying that Jews had any creative capability – only imitative talent.

An article entitled, "Heine the Muckraker," signed by a Dr. König, admitted that people read his *Book of Songs* and "found him wonderful"; then they sang songs written to his poems by Schumann and others, and "found him heavenly." These opinions were passed from generation to generation and it was "taken almost as a crime if cooler heads were critical of some of his works." Without a doubt, König allowed, Heine "composed many beautiful poems."[20] "No one could deny that Heine's Lieder contained many beautiful verses," the newspaper acknowledged elsewhere, but "as soon as one discovered that all of these poems were spurious – all of them – then one turned away in disgust."[21]

He became a well-known poet, the paper complained, but the "greatest expert of the time," Heinrich von Treitschke, "called him a phony," and Josef Nadler – a significant literary historian who authored a number of German literature surveys – found that he was "a playful acrobat in words; one never knew when he was being serious or cynical; but above all his style was modeled on primitive song forms," that is, it was plagiarized.[22] König agreed: "those who were not seduced by him" were of the opinion "that Heine's best pieces were based on the work of others, for instance, Byronic motifs." So, contemporary German poets like Emanuel von Geibel, Friedrich Rückert, and Adelbert von Chamisso "deserved preference over him." Indeed, König added, one never read even Heine's most beautiful poems for pure pleasure, because "his satirical, Cheshire grin was always shimmering through." For instance "everyone knew" that the poem, *Thou Art Lovely as a Flower* (*Du bist wie eine Blume*), was "fabricated to ironically glorify a dirty, ugly waitress at a beer joint of the lowest sort." Supporters of Heine revered the "poet of *Die Lorelei*," König allowed, however, it was "rarely noted that *Die Lorelei* should not be considered Heine's own work, but was very similar to a poem of the same name by the German poet, Graf Heinrich von Loeben."[23] In view of all this, König concluded, "Heine resembled a swamp over which one could see from afar dancing and flickering lights: these attract the wanderer, but as he approaches, he realizes that the deceitful lights had lured him into the swamp; up close, he can see that the effect came from bubbles of stinky poison ascending and then bursting."[24]

Hermann Seeliger, a literature scholar who had written at the turn of the century about the multiplicity of Lorelei legends, echoed many of the same themes. According to Seeliger, there had developed a "cult of excessive overestimation for the poet who called himself Heinrich Heine." Celebrated historians of literature had even placed him next to Joseph Freiherr von Eichendorff, Eduard Mörike, and Nikolaus Lenau. But Seeliger intended to show how much "Fool's Gold" had been accepted as real. At base, Heine was, despite his lyrical gift, "nothing more than a journalist" (*Feuilletonist*). First, Seeliger held, Heine had "pitiful rhyming technique: it teemed not just with false rhymes, but also with cheap and trivial ones, such as *Herz-Schmerz*; *Rosen-losen*; *dunkelt-funkelt*; *Bildnis-Wildnis*." This, Seeliger acknowledged, had been taken for romantic irony, but in Heine's case it was "nothing other than the Jewish will to disrupt." In addition, Seeliger went on, his "constant coquetterie with the pains of love often rang untrue." It was deceptive because the wonderful music of Schubert, Schumann, Robert Franz, and Hugo Wolf had "made these merely fabricated feelings seem genuine."[25] But Heine was "no lyrical genius," the *Völkischer Beobachter* held, because "lyricism was soul, was tenderness, was a sympathetic resonance with the soft rhythms of innocent nature." The lyricism of "thousands of others who wrote, even poorly, out of inner need and a religious attitude toward nature" was greater than that of Heine, who was "nothing but a revolver journalist, pornographer, and joker."[26]

The term "revolver journalist" and references to Heine as the "Father of the Revolver Press"[27] were common features of *Völkischer Beobachter* reception. These were phrases commonly used to describe "*ad hominem* journalism designed to incite rancor and inflame prejudice,"[28] so it is ironic that the Nazi newspaper complained about such practices. But fundamental to its presentation of Heine were complaints about his critical statements regarding other German writers and poets. In his attack, König stated that "a great poet is always pleased about all poetic achievements, and recognizes without envy the works of other poets," but the "supposedly great Heine certainly did not meet the standard." Like a "vicious cur," he "attacked all German poets who threatened him with dangerous competition (what could be worse for a Jew?)," including the "spirited poets and heroes of freedom," Theodor Körner and Ernst Moritz Arndt. Indeed, König held, Heine "threw manure on the grave of the former" in a letter of 7 June 1822 in which Heine wrote that Körner's "liberation verses are still often recited and sung in those *gemütlich* little corners where people warm themselves with the innocent fancy that crackles in these patriotic songs ... When some Berlin woman hears a Körner poem, elation arises, she puts her hand gracefully on her bosom ... and she says, 'I am a German virgin.'"

Heine "celebrated" Arndt – who "enthused German youth for the Wars of Liberty" – similarly, König complained, when he sneered about "his scabby, shabby little work, in which he wags his tail like a dog, and, doggish as a Wendish dog, barks at the July sun!"[29] Infuriated by this sarcasm directed at one of the literary heroes of the nationalist right, König closed this portion of his Heine critique by stating that "highway robbers" were "not so despicable as the common thug, Jew Heine, since they expose themselves to danger, while Heine just took shots from a safe hiding place or had hired assassins shoot his victims with poisoned arrows." As Heine said of himself, recalled König, "his was a soul of shit."[30]

Alfred Rosenberg joined the assault, expressing venomous disdain for Heine's statements regarding other German writers. "It was no surprise that as an impudent Jewish youth," Heine tried to "knock German philosophers and writers off their pedestals." He even went after Kant, stating that "Kant's life history is not worth writing, since he had neither life nor history." In Heine's opinion, "Kant was a Philistine: a genius must have new words for new ideas – Immanuel Kant, however, was no genius." To which Rosenberg responded, "Well, at least we have the genius Heine – what a relief!"[31]

Naturally, the aspect of Heine's outlook that drew the most attention from volkish propagandists was his critical stance toward the politics of German territories in his lifetime. As Rosenberg quoted him, Heine wrote to a French correspondent, "Our enemies are in

Germany";[32] and in the *Völkischer Beobachter*, Heine's enemies rose to the bait. "How did Heine think and act politically?" one asked. He sought connections in Prussia just in order to gain a market for his journals, "but they saw right through him, for he actually hated them." He once called Prussians "a 'mixture of *Weissbier*, lies, and sand' – the same Prussians from whom he wanted financial support!" Rather than trying to help Germany unify, moreover, "he did everything he could to unnerve it."[33]

König chimed in on this theme too: "if insulting the German Fatherland and the House of Hollenzollern were patriotic deeds, then Heine was a patriot like none other."[34] Of a Prussian aristocrat, he said that he "could not even look at the black winged toad, without my stomach turning." Beyond that, König reported, Heine had "no respect for the German people as a whole." To him, the German Volk was "nothing but a great fool … carrying a tremendous whip of iron, with which it furiously strikes anyone who recommends a remedy for its great pains."[35] But his "particular targets were the German rulers." Of Friedrich Wilhelm III, Heine complained that he "induced other German princes to falsehood and breach of faith."[36] Moreover, König protested, in his poems *The Changeling* and *The New Alexander*, he "threw such filth on the princely house and person of his majesty, King Friedrich Wilhelm IV, that most of them couldn't be published at the time." Therein, for instance, Heine referred to the monarch as "a drunkard who stumbled from glass to glass, blabbing with his wagging tongue about conquering the world."[37] In addition, König went on, Heine insulted King Ludwig I of Bavaria – "just because he refused to give him a pension" – in lines describing him as a "stuttering king," an "art eunuch," and the future "patron saint" of apes and kangaroos who convert to Christianity.[38] In addition, König went on, he besmirched the black-red-gold colors of the German fraternity movement (*Burschenschaften*) as "resembling those of a monkey's bald ass."[39]

König allowed that "every once in a while Heine could express some understanding for Germany's place in world history." But "then a couple of pages later one was always confronted with something like *The Weavers*,"[40] with its threat that Germany's "shroud is on our loom."[41] After reprinting this "patriotic tirade" in full, König asked readers to "consider an 1849 poem wherein Heine insulted the troops led by the then Prince of Prussia, our unforgettable Kaiser Wilhelm I" as "bowed beneath the yoke of heartless wolves, and common dogs, and swine."[42]

Even "thoughts of a unified Germany drew sarcastic verses about the Prussian eagle" from Heine:

> Hateful bird, if you should fall
> Into my hands one day,
> I'll pluck each feather from your back
> And chop your claws away.

And he "ridiculed the prospect of an emperor" by indicating that the post should be filled by a leading liberal, Jacob Venedey, whom Heine also mocked – as a "Carnival King."[43]

In addition to the Heine sarcasm directed against German hierarchy, the *Völkischer Beobachter* found unforgivable any and all positive statements the poet made about France and the French. König was outraged that "our great compatriot" spoke of Paris as the "bouquet on the breast of Europe, the capital of the whole civilized world, a Pantheon of the living – where a new art, a new religion, a new life is being built, and the creators of a new world bustle about merrily." In contrast to Germans, the French were "great, and sense their sublime destiny."[44] In his opinion, the most terrible disaster that could come to pass would be that "the dialect of the Potsdam nobility might be heard snarling in the streets of Paris, and dirty Teutonic boots again defile the holy ground of the boulevards."[45] "Our brave troops – honorable German *Landsmänner* – would turn over in their graves," König predicted, "if they knew of such writings."[46] And, "as if that weren't enough," M. Edbach reported, Heine also came to know Karl Marx and Ludwig Börne in Paris, "and thus was a major Jewish conspiracy established," thereafter "spreading the deracinating effects of the Socialist leader farther than anyone else, and intensifying the explosive effects of French spirit as much as he could."[47]

Beyond his political positions, *Völkischer Beobachter* contributors condemned Heine for critical statements about Christianity. "What a dirty character he was," König scolded, "shamelessly deriding all that was sacred to Christians." Not wanting to imply that defending Christianity was central to National Socialist ideology, König acknowledged that Nazis were "far from determining the worth of a poet on the basis of his stance *vis-à-vis* Christianity," pointing out that Schiller, Goethe, and Lessing "were no orthodox Christians." But, he added, "they didn't use their talent as poets to pour sarcasm all over Christianity in the most frivolous and general ways: that was left to the

Jew Heine." In support, König cited Heine's *Italian Travel Sketches*, in which he "called Christianity the Gothic lie that permits only blind, groping pleasures in secret, and hastens to stick a hypocritical fig-leaf in front of every free feeling."[48] On another occasion, said König, Heine saw an image of Christ, and was inspired to write:

> Poor cousin of mine, I'm filled with woe
> Whenever I see your face.
> You hoped to save the world – you fool![49]

In particular, the paper reported, Heine said Catholicism "treated God as if he is dead, smelling of incense, as at a funeral with funeral music blaring to the point that one is constantly depressed."[50] Of Protestantism he said, "impudently," it "doesn't help any: I've tried it, sir – and the trial cost me four marks, fourteen schilling."[51] For 1,800 years, Christianity had "plagued the air for us poor." These words, König concluded, were from the "true voice of Heinrich Heine the Christian."[52]

Discussing Heine as a "communist agitator," the paper held that "the little Jewish poet revealed himself to be a first-rate communist" in his *Confessions* of 1854. There he wrote on the growing number of communists in Germany, stating that they were building an army motivated by atheism and led by great logicians. These, he felt, were the "most capable and energetic characters in Germany, indeed the only lively men in the country." The future belonged to them. All other parties and leftist representatives were "dead, dead as a doornails." It "wasn't even necessary to comment on this," said the paper: that would be "giving too much credit to this little scribbler." Furthermore, the *Völkischer Beobachter* said, Heine was "right about his friends the communists" when he said in his *Thoughts and Ideas*: "I predict to you: one winter there will be a revolution that will be more horrible than any that have yet happened; blood will run in the snow." He "spelled that out with sneering salaciousness," the paper found.[53]

However, the *Volkischer Beobachter* also attacked Heine for his statements about Judaism, marking him as a "typically hypocritical representative of his race."[54] Jewish self-assessments could "sometimes be important," the paper informed its readers, so one must read "Heine's judgment of his fellow Jews with interest," such as when he "saw the pig-sties" in which Jews in a Polish village "lived, spoke bad German, and haggled."[55] Picking and choosing from his *Pictures of Travel*, the paper added that Heine had "further ingratiating things to say about his racial brothers,"[56] such as describing Jews as a "mummy of a race, which wanders over the world wrapped in most ancient swathing bands of letters, a petrified fragment of the History of the World, a specter which gets its living by trading in bills of exchange."[57]

Thus, ironically, even statements that might have come directly from Nazi propaganda were condemned in the *Völkischer Beobachter*. There was no place in the hall of exalted German writers, the paper sarcastically noted, for "this 'poet' who honored his racial brothers with such 'excellent dithyrambs.'" Accordingly, the paper contended, no matter what Heine might have written, even lines intimating Jewish self-hatred, the "insightful German statement of Otto von Bismarck applied perfectly to him: 'The German Volk doesn't owe anything to the shabby Hebrews.'"[58]

Above all, Heine served as a cultural-historical symbol of the presumed threat of a pro-Jewish conspiracy. According to the *Völkischer Beobachter*, just when Jews were given citizenship in Germany, "the spiritual leadership of Jewry – including Baruch [Börne], Marx, and Heine – attacked the existence of the German Volk: from their secret hideaways they worked for the destruction of their hosts while they simultaneously demanded rights, love, and respect from them."[59] Heine's "restless work and propaganda" for the Society for the Culture and Science of the Jews (*Verein für Kultur und Wissenschaft der Juden*) "betrayed the fact that his suffering for humanity was really just suffering for the Jews, because his fanfares for freedom were really just fanfares for the unlimited rights of Jews."[60]

In keeping with the anti-Semitic tenet of accusing Jewish men of sexual degeneracy, the *Völkischer Beobachter* also condemned Heine and his works as immoral as well as politically suspect. For Edbach, indeed, the "two dimensions of Heine's depravity intersected, since he mixed politics with erotica." According to the paper, "one of the few university literary historians who had any guts," Josef Nadler, put it best: "Heine was the Wandering Jew and undermining morality in Germany was his only work."[61] To prove Heine an immoralist, König felt "the first evidence" was his strong language: "he constantly used terms like manure oxen, manure barrow, shit, crap, lice, bedbugs, piss pot, and shit bucket." Moreover, he "always wished upon his opponents afflictions such as invalidity, salivation, arthritis, and hemorrhoids." So his writing "read like honey on the tongue," König opined, sarcastically.[62] Even more shocking were his "impudent representations of romantic and sexual relations." Often leaving out or overlooking verses that added an element of humor or self-deprecation, König cited long portions from Heine's more daring pieces, such as *Diana*, as evidence of his "personal immorality":

> These fair limbs, of size so massive,
> Of colossal womanhood,
> Now are, in a yielding mood,
> Under my embraces passive …
> How her bosom, neck, throat charm me!
> (Higher I can scarcely see);
> Ere alone I'd with her be,
> Pray I that she may not harm me.[63]

In *Yolante and Mary*, Heine's "degeneracy became even clearer" as he described thoughts of a *menage à trois*:

> Their bosoms how fair! Their shoulders how white!
> My heart is soon trembling all over;
> They presently jump on the bed with delight,
> And hide themselves under the cover.[64]

"What was love according to Heinrich Heine?" König wondered. He felt the answer could be found in *The Evil Star*:

> What is the love by poets sung?
> A star amid a heap of dung.
> Like a poor mangy dog, when he's dying,
> Beneath all this filth it is lying.[65]

"Speaking for the paper [*Völkischer Beobachter*] and the party [Nazi]," König stated, "we call not on the highest standards, but just on the average sense of propriety." Considering such "poems written on the mattress grave, Heine seemed to have none."

König therefore considered it "shocking that Heine's love songs were given to every young girl even though they contained lines such as these," from *I Can't Forget It*:

Your body still I crave for,
Your body young and fair;
Your soul you may dig a grave for,
I've soul enough, I swear.[66]

But most disturbing to König were lines he read as "intimations of necrophilia" in the *Book of Songs*:

My own dear love, when in the tomb –
The gloomy tomb – you're sleeping.
Then I unto your side will come,
Up to you softly creeping.
I'll press you, caress you with kisses wild.[67]

"Did one really have to be an old biddy to consider such poems disgusting?" König wondered. He knew no better word for it than "bordello poetry." And "then there was Heine's prose!" Speaking for Nazis as a whole, König asserted, "We don't think that German literature has a dirtier product than *The Baths of Lucca*, wherein the poet practically dances in shit and never gets tired of brutish expressions." How could one describe such a work? "'Smut' is just too weak a word for it!"[68]

But of all Heine's works, none was the target of more hostility in the *Völkischer Beobachter* than *Germany: A Winter's Tale*.[69] In "no other place in Jewish literature," the Wagnerian Walter Bohe held, did the "true essence of Jewry reveal itself so clearly." Therein Heine "degraded the idealistic Aryan soul as much as possible while glorifying the materialistic Jewish character." This poem was "so rich in Jewish self-confessions" that the paper "felt compelled to share a few samples" on more than one occasion.[70] A summary of the passages it found most disturbing, and the commentary its contributors made about Heine's words, demonstrates how the *Völkischer Beobachter* could painstakingly address a single work passage by passage in its efforts to illuminate the ostensibly heinous attitudes and intentions of the Jewish cultural leadership.

About Cologne Cathedral, König reminded readers that Heine thought:

It will never be finished, despite the great
Outcry of owl and raven,

> Old-fashioned birds, who like to make
> A high church tower their haven.

Following "such a prophecy," he then had the Father Rhine say, "traitorously,"[71]

> For if the French come back again,
> My cheeks will blush and burn,
> I who so often prayed to God
> That they might soon return.

After the Prussian government was "reasonable enough to throw the scoundrel out of the country and censor many of his publications,"[72] Heine lived in Paris. But he returned to Germany and wrote the following:

> This is the muck of my Fatherland:
> This mud of the country road!

Traveling on, "the Protestant Heine became outraged at the sight of a crucifix" along the way:

> They've given you a dirty deal,
> Those lords of high estate.
> Who told you to speak so recklessly
> Against the church and the state? …
> You scourged the bankers, the changers of gold,
> You drove them out of the temple.
> Luckless crusader, now on the cross
> You hang as a warning example.

Bohe asked, "what would it take to get a justice system that would punish such blasphemies instead of locking up upstanding German men like Theodore Fritsch [the notorious publisher of anti-Semitic literature] for insulting *Jahwe*?" According to Bohe, "the last section meant, basically: "Jesus, this is the way it's going to go for non-Jews who dare to fight Jewish bankers and Jewish capital in the stock exchange – the same as it went for you when you dared to chase the

Jewish bankers from the temple." In other words – Bohe stated bluntly – "Heine predicted that it's going to go 'horribly' for us National Socialists, right?"

In Hamburg, where Heine "luxuriated in sensual pleasures," he "treated the Hamburg city goddess, Hammonia, as a whore – in a way that symbolized his attitude toward his non-Jewish victims" and then had her "foretell the German future in the following tasteful terms," by instructing him to look into a chamber pot.

> It is a magic pot, in which
> The magical powers brew;
> Stick in your head, and future times
> Shall be revealed to you –
> Germany's future, like waving dreams,
> Shall surge before your eyes;
> But do not shudder, if out of the mess
> Foul miasmas arise!

Then, Bohe interjected, "after giving a classically Jewish oath of silence," Heine "nonetheless went ahead and reported":

> Against my will those cursed, vile
> Aromas come to mind:
> The startling stink, that seemed to be
> Old cabbage and leather combined.
> And after this – O God! – there rose
> Such monstrous, loathsome stenches;
> It was as though the dung were swept
> From six and thirty trenches.

"Boy, he really saw the future of Germany!" Bohe commented ironically. But "at the end comes an interesting, colorful speech" where Heine "did make some predictions which had unfortunately come precariously close to coming about, owing to the activity of his racial comrades":

> I am no sheep, no shellfish, no dog;
> I play no councilor's part;
> I've stayed a wolf through all the years

With wolfish teeth and heart.
I am a wolf, and with the wolves
I'll howl my whole life through.
Yes, count on me and help yourselves;
Then God ["That should be: 'Jahwe,'" Bohe added.]
will help you too.

"Do you see, German people?" asked Bohe. "This supposedly great poet clearly outlined his goal, which was the same for all Jews: I, Heine, a Jewish wolf, see that my main task is to break down non-Jewish sheep and dogs – to undermine the dear German people!' Really neat, huh?" Bohe closed.[73] Here, then, in its reception of Heine perhaps more so than any other, did the *Völkischer Beobachter* indeed, as Saul Friedländer put it, "depict the archenemy needed by the regime, whose threatening image would culturally and historically justify any further steps, if and when decided."[74]

PART II
BLIND TO THE LIGHT

6 CLASSICISM ROMANTICIZED

National Socialist attitudes toward the Western Classical tradition were complex. As George Mosse pointed out, the main streams of German national and then Nazi aesthetics were confluences of Romanticism and Classicism, yet they always contained a strong component of classicized order, especially as manifested in design and architecture. Undoubtedly, the "loose synthesis, or co-existence" of Classicism and Romanticism in Nazi culture reflected Hitler's personal tastes.[1] His own statements confirm the importance of the classical tradition in his artistic outlook. In *Mein Kampf*, he wrote that the "ideal of Hellenic culture should be preserved for us in all its marvelous beauty … Roman history correctly conceived in extremely broad outlines is and remains the best mentor, not only for today, but probably for all time. The Hellenic ideal of culture should also remain preserved for us in its exemplary beauty."[2]

It is important to underscore, however, especially as pertaining to ancient Greek culture, that it was the visual aspects of this culture, as rendered in ancient design and architecture, that Hitler respected most, and not necessarily its intellectual content. Hitler had little use for the tradition of Western rationalism held to have originated in Ancient Greece. And so, the historical model he recommended for the German future was the culture of ancient Rome, not that of Athens.[3] In this sense, then, while relishing ancient design sensibilities for their value in symbolizing his ordered world view, Hitler remained consistent with volkish ideological rejection of rationalist and humanistic trends derived from the ancient tradition.

Part II of this book will first relate how the *Völkischer Beobachter* addressed the Western rationalist tradition from the Ancients, through the Scientific Revolution and the Enlightenment, to the French Revolution and its outcomes. In the course of such treatment, the paper generally emphasized the "Dionysian" rather than the rational side of ancient society as a reference for the romantic German culture it preferred. Surprisingly, the paper did not associate the Hitler movement with Roman imperial tradition. Instead, it equated Roman policy toward Carthage with the Versailles Treaty, and compared the Late Roman Empire with Weimar "decadence." Despite Hitler's taste for neoclassical architecture, then, the *Völkischer Beobachter*'s attention to the ancients was minimal, but consistent with volkish rejection of so-called Latin influence on Western culture. Above all, contributors to the Nazi paper conveyed disdain for the rationalist or Apollonian side of the ancient tradition.[4]

A Dionysian or anti-Socratic orientation was clear in the only major article in the *Völkischer Beobachter* to explicitly address ancient Athenian history. On 5 April 1927, the paper responded to news from contemporary Athens that a lawyer, M. Paradopoulos, had initiated an effort to reopen the trial of Socrates in the Greek legal system. Paradopoulos hoped for a reversal of the philosopher's condemnation – partly as a way of removing the stain on Greek national honor left by the injustice committed in 399 BCE. Paradopoulos' effort received international press attention when the court rejected his appeal.

The Nazi response to this judicial-historical initiative was derisive. Paradopoulos was lucky, the *Völkischer Beobachter* chirped, if he had nothing else to worry about than taking up a 2,000-year-old trial. But more than merely chiding the failure of an over-zealous Greek patriot, the newspaper revealed a deeper current of National Socialist thought when it stated emphatically that "we naturally do not share an exaggerated valuation of Socrates," and even that "with regard to the trial that ended in the death sentence for the philosopher, we agree with the position of the Athenian court." In the *Völkischer Beobachter* article that reached furthest back into Western cultural and intellectual history, then, Nazi journalists made clear their rejection of the Socratic tradition.[5]

While this was the sole article in which the paper treated ancient Greek history directly, a survey of references to Greek culture in pieces dealing with other topics reveals that Nazi disinclination toward the rational-democratic side of Athenian history was consistent. *Völkischer*

Beobachter contributors invariably dismissed the Apollonian–Socratic tradition, instead aligning themselves and their preferred cultural heroes with the emotional orientation they associated most directly with the more "romantic" works of Homer. In doing so, *Völkischer Beobachter* editors and authors pressed for a National Socialist culture infused with the "passion" and "spirituality" ultimately associated with Romanticism.

When viewed chronologically over a representative collection of references to ancient Greek history and culture, this tendency toward the Dionysian becomes clear. Thus, as discussed above with regard to Albrecht Dürer, the *Völkischer Beobachter* held that it was not until the production of Dürer's self-portraits that the Western tradition in the visual arts achieved the objective of self-awareness established by the ancients. But importantly, the paper declined to extend this association of Dürer with Socrates to encompass the philosopher's logical prescription for self-knowledge. Self-knowledge was a worthy goal, but it was knowledge that derived from intuition and insight, rather than from rigorous thought and analysis that should be sought. Accordingly, the paper presented Dürer's work as the product of "spirit, religiosity, the plumbing of soulful depths" – "not born of pure intellect." Indeed, as we have already seen, the paper bemoaned the fact that Dürer was known for contributing to the neoclassicism of Renaissance art, which remained "foreign to his blood."[6] Instead, Dürer should be seen to function, above all, as a source of the "romantic stream that would flow into the passionate psychological paintings of Böcklin, Van Gogh, and Corinth." Not the rationalistic but the Dionysian was the nature of his classicism.[7]

Another indication of *Völkischer Beobachter* resistance to neoclassical tradition was the treatment of its most important exponent: J. J. Winckelmann. On the occasion of Winckelmann's 175th *Todestag*, the paper ran a commemorative article honoring "one of the great men of eighteenth-century German letters." But the essay only summarized the relations between Winckelmann and Gotthold Ephraim Lessing, and barely treated Winckelmann's views of classicism – and even then, only in highly romantic terms.[8] Thus did the paper associate itself with an important German thinker while omitting his major ideas, if these were not consistent with its cultural outlook.

But a more complex strategy was required for dealing with Winckelmann's contemporary, Goethe. Given the poet's well-known neoclassical tendencies, convincingly casting Goethe as a figure essentially aligned with the romantic tradition represented a significant undertaking for the *Völkischer Beobachter*. One way in which contributors attempted to do so was to imply that Goethe's interest in ancient Greek culture focused primarily on the works of Homer. According to Adolf Dresler, if Goethe modeled himself on ancients, it was on "the Pre-Socratic singer above all"; indeed, "Goethe had the ambition, if not to be a German Homer, at least to be a *Homeride* – he wanted to compose an *Achilles*."[9] Further, Joachim Petzold insisted that it was through the study of Homer that Goethe had discovered what "unmentionable mischief the Jewish race had done."[10] In this way the *Völkischer Beobachter* managed to associate the main plank of National Socialist ideology with the earliest stages of Western cultural history.

But the Nazi paper could only assert that Goethe was principally aligned with the Pre-Socratic tradition – that "with him the romantic was classic and the classic was romantic"[11] – if it could maintain that Goethe was mainly interested in the Dionysian aspects of Greek culture. Even among volkish intellectuals this position was only marginally tenable. One such intellectual, and one of the premier cultural historians of the volkish bent, was Richard Benz. In 1940, Benz spoke at the Richard-Wilhelm-Gesellschaft on the theme of "Goethe and Romantic Art" and the *Völkischer Beobachter* covered the lecture. As Benz argued, no one knew better than Goethe about the "danger of losing oneself, of boundlessness, of the unending digressions of the romantic attitude of mind." In his resistance to the dangers of romantic excess, Goethe sought an "objective view of the world that would provide him a fixed hold on experience according to law-giving norms." According to Benz, Goethe found this objective view in the ancients: he recognized the classical norm as the "only valid principle and rejected anything that stood against it as heresy." Whatever was not based on antiquity seemed to him "inappropriate." This was the basis for Goethe's "hostile attitude toward Romanticism," Benz contended, and out of it arose the conflict that still permeated German emotional life: "the contrast between Classicism and Romanticism."[12]

Thus, said Benz, was Goethe aligned with the Apollonian–Socratic side of Greek culture. But the *Völkischer Beobachter* would have none of it. The paper's reviewer, Rudolf Hofmüller, dutifully praised the volkish cultural theorist, recommending that Benz's lecture be published – but only after some editing. Given the breadth of the subject, he argued, it was "impossible to explain Goethe's anti-romantic attitude in a two-hour lecture without one-sided exposure and dangerous demarcations." Above all, Hofmüller complained, Benz had placed too much weight on Goethe's leaning toward a "normalizing or standardizing art theory" – by which he clearly meant Benz's view that Goethe recognized the classical norm as the only valid principle.[13] It was this assertion that classicism offered an objective view of the world, providing law-giving norms which countered the Pre-Socratic, Dionysian emphasis preferred by the *Völkischer Beobachter*, that Hofmüller identified as "dangerous" – and it certainly was, for the Nazified version of Goethe that will emerge further below.

For the Nazi newspaper, resistance to the foreign (French, Latinate) principles of the Enlightenment was the first phase in the German struggle for liberation that would become more fully realized in the nineteenth century, with the actual Napoleonic wars and the start of the volkish battle against Jews, establishing precedent for the battles that were continuing in the modern era. Writing about Heinrich Kleist, in a review of a production of *Amphitryon*, Hofmüller lauded Kleist's version of Plautus' Roman comedy as "a more complete version than had ever been written." According to Hofmüller, Kleist's play "glorified the elevated spiritual flights of German poetry." Into it he had poured the "whole glowing stream of his feelings." While retaining the humor of the original, he had tapped into its "deeper emotional undercurrents" by focusing on the "tragic center" – the "soulful battle" for the disappointed and suffering Alkmene – in the otherwise cheerful events of Amphitryon. By doing so, he had produced a play of "true Dionysian hilarity," which operated at a deeper Pre-Socratic level than even Plautus had achieved. But more importantly, Kleist had "undone the mischief perpetrated on the subject by Molière." The French playwright, one of the leading exponents of French rationalism, had penned an *Amphitryon* for Versailles, and in Hofmüller's opinion reduced it to nothing more than "a typical divorce comedy for entertaining court society." By "tapping the Dionysian core of the saga," the German Kleist "returned the material to its profound basis, and lifted it back into the mythical." If one looked at the content and its development in detail, Hofmüller held, one could perceive the confrontation between Kleist and Molière as "deeply informative about the differences between German and French spiritual history – especially their contrasting invocations of ancient Greek legend."[14]

Even more resonant with the *Völkischer Beobachter*'s taste for the Dionysian were the works of Friedrich Hölderlin. In a tribute marking the 175th anniversary of Hölderlin's birth, playwright Friedrich Wilhelm Hymmen, the author of numerous pieces known as "blood and soil plays" (*Blut-und-Boden-Stücke*), acknowledged that Nazi readers might not initially be comfortable with the dominance and intensity of classical references in Hölderlin's poetry, since these references appeared to undermine his German romantic nature. But Hölderlin didn't need to be defended for the many antique symbols and forms which "probably gave some readers pause," Hymmen countered, because their origin lay not in an "accidental, time-bound preference, but in the depths of the writer's intentions, to the extent that one may speak of intentions." For Hölderlin, Hymmen asserted, classical invocation was "not a matter of Greek mythology or dusty allegories, but living Mythos." He struggled to bind all life with divinity again. That he chose to employ Greek images actually arose from his longing for *Volkstümlichkeit:* he wished to inspire the German Volk with that which he found in ancient Greece, namely "inner power, form, and unity." He saw the "god-like totality" of ancient Greek culture as "completely German": it was "no pale harmony – not an island of the blessed." Hölderlin knew too much of the "fertility of sorrow," in the certainty that it contained "all that is great and heavenly." Thus, while Hölderlin fled to "that time and Volk that became a second home to the best Germans of the end of the eighteenth century – to classical Greece – he did so in search of models of Dionysian spirituality and thereby helped to invent German Romanticism." Hymmen concluded that one could say about Hölderlin's love of Greece what Moeller van den Bruck once said about the most important German philosopher of the period, Hegel: "Greece was a detour on his way to Germanness."[15]

Citing ancient Greek history not as a progenitor of the Western tradition of individualism and democracy, but rather as a source of cultural historical legitimization of the state-centered communalism forwarded by the volkish movement, was an important feature in *Völkischer Beobachter* discussion of George Wilhelm Friedrich Hegel's philosophy, particularly of its political dimension. For the 100th *Todestag* of the philosopher, Max Wundt prepared the leading commemorative article. Wundt was a prolific author of popular histories of Western philosophy, a number of which are still in print. Along with his histories, Wundt also formulated his own political and cultural philosophy which was strongly marked by a volkish anti-Semitic outlook, as indicated in titles such as *The Eternal Jew: An Examination of the Meaning and Significance of Jewry* (1900), *Philosophy of*

State: A Book for Germans (1923), *The German Worldview: Foundations of Volkish Thought* (1926), and *The Roots of German Philosophy in Bloodline and Race* (1944).[16]

Wundt's summary of Hegel (1770–1831) for the *Völkischer Beobachter* highlighted the philosopher's statism, and identified it explicitly as statism of a "volkish" nature, rather than one that trended toward "democratic individualism." As Wundt put it, the great significance that antiquity had for Hegel's cultural views lay in the fact that "the ancient peoples and especially the Greeks made of themselves Volk Individuals." In ancient culture, life derived its energy from a unified source: every individual constituted a "living image of the whole content of the Volk." Further, Hegel perceived the main danger of the modern age as being the loss of this "living and unified Volk-consciousness." Every individual acted solely on the basis of his own opinion, without any understanding for the great forces of communal life. Against this isolation of the individual and the indiscipline that resulted from "manifold opinions," Hegel called forth the "Spirit of the Volk," as manifested in the "profound forces of morality and religion." In the *Völkischer Beobachter*, then, Ancient Greece was valued not for its role as the cradle of democracy, but rather for its role in inspiring "a renewal of the volkish existence driven by the inner forces of the Volk-life."[17]

Of course, the dichotomization of ancient Greek culture and history into Apollonian and Dionysian modes was not unique to Nazi culture. As expressed in the *Völkischer Beobachter*, this notion was clearly derived from ideas developed most intensively in Nietzsche's writings. According to its coverage of a lecture by Alfred Bäumler (the "Reich expert on Nietzsche," who was appointed Professor of Philosophy at the University of Berlin in recognition of his Nazified interpretations), "penetrating the quintessential point of [Nietzsche's] philosophy" required considering his earliest trains of thought, which focused on Greek philosophy and Heraclites' notion of "contrast, conflict, and eternal battle as the nature of the world." This was a common way of understanding Nietzsche, but what made Bäumler's version of this approach consistent with the Nazi world view was its omission of Nietzsche's opinion that Pre-Socratic Greek culture was a synthesis of Dionysian and Apollonian streams. This fitted the volkish view of politics as a field of contrast, conflict, and eternal battle, but it contradicted the more complex synthesis of Classicism and Romanticism at the core of Hitler's own cultural outlook.[18]

While the *Völkischer Beobachter* did not carry discussion of the Peloponnesian wars that ultimately led to the dissolution of the golden age of ancient Greek culture, it did run a telling article on the career of Alexander the Great (356–323 BCE). On 19 March 1926, the paper printed an extract from a newly published book, *Alexander the Great and His Followers*, by Fritz Geyer, an expert on Macedonian history. In this extract, Geyer asked whether Alexander was an aimless conqueror who hurried from success to success "just to insatiably add country after country to his sphere of power," or, rather, was a statesman who "knew not only how to destroy, but how to construct – one of the greats who indicated new paths for mankind."

Given the imperialistic impulses of Nazi leadership, it is interesting to consider what drew *Völkischer Beobachter* editors to the issue of Alexander's goals. According to Geyer, Alexander started his crusade with the intention of thrashing the Persian enemy and reaping revenge for all the hardship it had caused the Greeks. However, after the battle of Issos, there gradually developed a "more shining, infinitely more ambitious goal": the construction of "a global realm that would encompass all the culture nations [*Kulturnationen*] and bring peace to the world." An image of the future became ever clearer to him: Hellenic culture, which Alexander had enthusiastically adopted, "would be the band that would bind all peoples, lead to a higher civilization, and ultimately develop into world culture." Alexander fully recognized that the Semitic peoples of Anterior Asia, accustomed to slavery for centuries, were "not yet mature enough" to stand beside the Macedonians and Greeks as equals. But in the "physically fit Iranian breeds" he believed he saw an element that was "worthy of being merged" with the dominant Macedonian–Greek culture. Therefore, he tried to draw distinguished Persians, Meders, and Baktrers around himself, giving them positions of responsibility and his full confidence.

Surely, Geyer commented, Alexander must have seen that the "Eastern habits and also the national pride of the Asiatic nobility would not be easily overcome," but he did not give up hope of "gradually acclimatizing the Iranian breeds." This, Geyer held, was apparent in the training of young Persians in Macedonian combat techniques, their incorporation into the Macedonian regiments, and even in the formation of purely Persian divisions. According to Geyer, Alexander was driven in this attempt by the insight that it would be impossible to rule the enormous empire with the Macedonians and Greeks alone. Certainly, his "compatriots" (*Volksgenossen*) constituted the core of his army, and he selected most of his governors and generals from them; but in the long run the Macedonian people could not remain the sole basis of his power. Only if he won the Iranians over to "joyful cooperation" could he expect that his idea of a "global realm of unified culture and civilization" might be realized. Thus, Geyer continued, Alexander was forced to take a further step: the Persians could perceive him as their king only if he embodied their views of royal worth and royal appearance. If he remained the "Macedonian *Volkskönig*," he could not expect them to see him as anything other than the hostile conqueror. Therefore, he took on Persian court ceremony, at least partially: carrying the royal badges, and adorning himself in clothes that fused Greek and Persian customs. He even allowed himself to be honored by his Eastern subjects with traditional groveling in the dust.

However effective these tactics of interacting with the Persians were, Alexander alienated himself from the Macedonians. Geyer felt it understandable that his Macedonian nobles were "pained by this trans-formation of their king," although he "continued operating with them in comradely fashion." After his death they showed that they were not sympathetic to his "politics of amalgamation" (*Verschmelzungspolitik*). Moreover, even the army had "forebodings that its national character was threatened by the inclusion of foreign elements," and mutinied against the king in Opis, though his forces were later brought back into obedience. Only an Alexander, Geyer held, could overcome this inner opposition and gradually make his Macedonians serve plans of "international fusion" (*Völkerverschmelzung*). In any case, Alexander was firmly determined to bring about the "synthesis of peoples" even to the point of plans for transplanting whole populations from Europe to Asia and vice versa – as were indicated in the last records of the king.

The value to the editors of the *Völkischer Beobachter* in publish-ing this extended summary of Alexander's internationalist ambitions becomes clear only in Geyer's concluding remarks. In closing, Geyer raised the question of whether such a "leveling of peoples" would be advantageous for human culture. He then argued that Alexander's goal was "naively idealistic, unworkable, and ultimately detrimental to the interests of his Macedonian–Greek base." In Geyer's opinion, further development in this "utopian direction" might have led to an interpene-tration of Greek and eastern cultures, but in the end would have mainly strengthened the East. This would have led to the "disintegration of the empire and the weakening of the states involved."

That the *Völkischer Beobachter* agreed with this critical assessment of Alexander's globalist outlook – indeed, that the article ran primarily in order to convey this point – was made explicit at the very end of the column. Setting aside his own negative opinion of the ideal, Geyer finished his analysis by reiterating that Alexander hoped to unify the different peoples gradually and thereby to "establish a supranational culture in which the unique characteristics of the individual peoples would be combined into a higher unity." At this point, the voice of the *Völkischer Beobachter* literally spoke out on the matter, for the article ended with the following addition: "Something that is very doubtful. The Editors."[19]

It would be natural to assume that Nazi ideology could have found ancient historical precedent in the record of Alexander's Hellenistic *Blitzkrieg*. In addition, it is tempting to wonder whether Nazi followers might have posed Geyer's initial questions about their own leader: should they have seen in Hitler an aimless conqueror who would hurry from success to success just in order to conquer, just to insatiably add country after country to his sphere of power, or a statesman who knew not only how to destroy, but how to construct? Neither of these perceptions corresponds with the apparent aims of the *Völkischer Beobachter* editors in evoking Alexander. Instead, it seems likely that the paper resorted to ancient history for authorization of the Nazi rejection of post-First World War internationalist institutions such as the League of Nations and other humanitarian initiatives that the paper derided. While Nazi plans led toward a European, perhaps even global empire, they certainly were not directed toward a supranational culture in which the unique characteristics of the individual peoples would be combined into a higher unity. German culture as perceived in volkish terms would be the band that would bind all the conquered peoples, but it would achieve this result only to serve the interests of Germany. The Nazi Alexander and his followers would never flinch before the national principle and would never allow enslaved peoples to the east to stand beside them as equals. Foreign nationals later attracted to notions of a Fascist Europe might have done well to heed such indications of long-term Nazi objectives. Though contained in a seemingly innocuous historical reference within the cultural section of the *Völkischer Beobachter*, this was a clear warning sign – already in 1936 – of the direction that lay ahead.

Given the ruthless and self-serving imperial designs that under-lay Nazi ideology and, in the end, its foreign policy, the way the history of the Roman Empire was treated in the *Völkischer Beobachter* also comes as a counterintuitive surprise. Nazi pageantry, partly influenced by fascist culture developed by Rome-obsessed D'Annunzio and Mussolini, was encrusted with symbolic references to ancient Roman militarism and authoritarianism, manifested in countless ways – from the standards carried before each Gau in rally formations to, arguably, the *Hitler Grüss*. But references to Imperial Rome in the *Völkischer Beobachter* did not extol the most successful *Kaiserreich* as the model for a third German version. Instead, articles concentrated on weaknesses that led to the decline of the Caesars. Accordingly, the *Völkischer Beobachter* resisted the temptation to identify the Nazi movement or Reich with Roman hegemony, and instead sought to associate the decadence of the Late Empire in particular with problems they had identified in the Weimar Republic.[20] The paper even went as far as to compare the foreign policy of Weimar Germany with the fate of ancient Rome's foremost enemy and victim: Carthage.[21] In this view, Rome was held up not as a historical precedent to emulate, but as a vicious force bent on destruction of helpless – and, according to the *Völkischer Beobachter*, witless – opponents. Thus, it was not a renewed German empire that was the contemporary corollary of brutal Roman power, but rather the allied nations of France and England with their Versailles *Diktat*.

While indirect connections were drawn between Hellenic history and contemporary German affairs, it was in discussion of republican Roman military and foreign policy that the earliest explicit comparison was made in the *Völkischer Beobachter* between post-First World War Germany and the ancient past. Contributor Hans Speihmann left no doubt that Germany faced a fate similar to the liquidated civilization of Carthage if it adhered to the Versailles Treaty. Reminding readers that in 208 BCE, the Romans defeated the Carthaginians in the Second Punic War, Speihmann offered a direct comparison of the ancient Carthaginian and modern German situations: the peace that was imposed on Carthage at that time had "shocking similarities" to the Peace of Versailles. A full survey of its execution, he asserted, had "many features in common with the destiny that we are currently living through." Carthage's demise therefore served as a warning to German readers. In Speihmann's view, Livy, the Roman writer who recorded these events, remarked "very appropriately" that the victors over Hannibal were not the Romans, but the senate of Carthage and its conflicting parties: the general was undone by a senate that "showed no inner strength" and a population "split and weakened by party quarrels." To Livy's assessment, Speihmann added: "Who does not think instinctively of Germany during the last years of the war?" Thus was the Carthaginian case interpreted as an historical precedent for the "Stab in the Back" legend that permeated right-wing ideology in Weimar Germany, for the *Völkischer Beobachter* answered his rhetorical question in no uncertain terms: "Above all, the comparison between the two generals, Hannibal and Ludendorff, is unavoidable; both of them were let down by their Volk. The Editors."

The rest of Speihmann's article was devoted to justifying this comparison. First, the Carthaginians had to deliver all overseas possessions and their colonies to the Romans. Then came discussion of excessive reparations imposed upon the defeated. The Carthaginians had to pay for the whole African expedition of Scipio, plus they had to raise a war tribute of 10,000 talents payable in fifty annual installments. Like the reparations faced by the German nation, Speihmann implied, the half-century duration of these payments seemed unfathomable. On top of this, Speihmann continued, so that the Carthaginians could never again threaten the power of the Romans by naval war, they had to relinquish all war ships. But parallels between Carthaginian and German demilitarization could be made even clearer: they also had to give up all tamed elephants and agree never to tame elephants again. Therefore, Speihmann added, "the Romans saw to the elephants in the peace treaty just as the English treated U-boats: both were weapons that had caused the victors great damage."

The main point of the harsh treaty, according to Speihmann, came next. The Carthaginians had to agree not to wage war inside or outside of Africa without the special agreement of the Romans, thereby giving up their political independence. "A country which up to then had a dominant position in the cultural circles of the world parted forever from the realm of the leading states." The Romans praised the just nature of the peace: "All people," one said, "should know that Rome ends wars with the same justness with which she begins them." Here Speihmann broke in again: "The word 'justness' sticks out here. One can't help laughing because this word has been used on us Germans for years as sweetener for all the rapes being perpetrated on our Volk."

The great majority of the Carthaginian people had no notion of what this peace would mean to them, thought Speihmann: it became clear only when the first tribute was due. The money could not come from the treasury, so there was nothing to do but impose nationwide taxes. Only then did complaints rise up in the Carthage senate. In this session, Hannibal gave his "historical laugh of scorn," saying to his countrymen: "You should have cried when they took the weapons from us and burned the ships that protected us from wars! With those wounds we received the death blow. You notice the hazards of state only when they affect you individually. Only the loss of money angers you. Now you cry because you have to tax your own property." Speihmann clearly believed that the same complaints echoed in German politics of his day, and that corruption was rife in both cases.

In spite of the tribute payments, there then occurred another disturbance. Massinissa invaded the Carthaginian border lands. Carthage protested to Rome, with negative results. The Romans sent a commission to Carthage to investigate the incident. But at its head they put a man who "carried an indelible hatred for Carthage": Cato. Reporting back to the Roman senate, he ended every one of his speeches with: "I will never tire of demanding: Carthage must be destroyed!" Now the Carthaginians began to despair and set up troops in defense. But when Carthage attempted to rearm, the Romans intervened, using this as the pretext to go to war again. At this point, Speihmann commented, "the Carthage Volk showed how low it had fallen: it agreed to accept any punishment; and it sent a legation with full power to accept mercy and disgrace." The Carthaginian legation was ordered to provide 300 hostages in thirty days, and "wait for further orders from the Roman consuls." Without determining what "waiting for further orders" meant, they signed – just as, Speihmann surely meant to suggest, German Social Democrats had done in 1918.

Three hundred youths of the city were shipped to Sicily, where the enemy received them – only to send them to Roman dungeons from which they would never return. Nevertheless, in 149 BCE, 84,000 men landed on the plains of Carthage, supposedly because the apologies and hostages were not sufficient. The Carthaginians then agreed to turn over more than 200,000 arms and an additional 3,000 catapults – "that is, heavy artillery." Similar to German Liberals, Speihmann implied, "they wanted to demonstrate to all the world that they sincerely wanted to do trade and business in peace." After Carthage had been rendered completely defenseless, they received the final decision of the Roman senate: "Devastation of the city!" It was only in these last hours of life that

Carthage "demonstrated what a Volk condemned to death is capable of." The gates of the city were closed and all public buildings were razed for materials to produce new armaments. Women had their hair cut to provide webbing for new catapults. But "even now the Carthaginians trusted in their beloved 'justice': believing that the gods will not let the Roman abuse of the contract go without impunity." At this Speihmann sniffed: "as if one receives justice if one has no power!"

The ultimate results of "Carthaginian complicity" unfolded. Rome instructed Scipio to take Carthage, which "he did in no time." Romans penetrated the defenses, massacred the inhabitants, and set the city ablaze. After everything was destroyed and plundered, the Roman priests cursed the ruins: "Never shall a house or a cornfield rise here again. There where Carthage once lay, shall remain uninhabited and desolate!" And "so it remained," Speihmann concluded: "a great city never appeared in that place again, despite its important geographical location ... The Romans had applied the most effective measures in their policy of destruction."[22]

Thus, implicitly and explicitly – when necessary through interjections and asides – Speihmann and *Völkischer Beobachter* editors made it clear that there were numerous parallels between the Carthaginian and Weimar German situations: enemy demands for colonial holdings; excessive reparations; and demilitarization were part of an unbridled policy of destruction aimed not just at punishing, but at utterly eliminating the vanquished society. But even worse, efforts at fulfilling the treaty and subsequent demands in order to demonstrate to the world that the defeated sincerely wanted to do business in peace was a shameful position. Strong men like Hannibal had been stabbed in the back by cowardice and corruption and, above all, by dreamy hopes for international justice: "as if one receives justice if one has no power." The message was clear: if Germans continued to accept the terms of the Versailles Treaty, they would meet the same fate as the Carthaginians. This time, warnings from the likes of Hannibal had to be heeded.

Blind to or ignoring possible parallels between their own authoritarian and imperialistic ideology and that of Carthage's conquerors, Nazi propagandists working for the *Völkischer Beobachter* projected a critical view of Roman society as they surveyed the culture of the Empire after the Republican era. To paint the Roman Empire as corrupt the paper drew material from the work of another publication in ancient history: Theodor Trede's *Belief in Miracles in Paganism and the Early Church* (1901). From this "excellent book" the *Völkischer Beobachter* culled a number of "lively and historically accurate descriptions," which proved that while the Roman Empire had a highly developed culture, such an attribute "did not protect it against the increasing burden of the faith in miracles which approached the magical." From Trebe's text the paper reviewed a series of examples in which respected Roman writers mentioned magical and spiritualist practices in imperial culture and even expressed their own belief in them. In the *Eighth Satire of the First Book*, for instance, Horace (65–08 BCE) wrote about observing the "uncanny wonderworks" of two witches in a moonlit cemetery where he heard the "howling of souls lured by their charms." In the *Second Epistle of the Second Book*, he asked a Roman whether he was capable of "doubting wise dreamers, magic, miracles, and witches." Elsewhere, in his *Seventeenth Epode*, Horace described a woman who obtained through the night goddess, Hekate, a book full of powerful spells that would "draw the stars from the heavens." Likewise, in the *Eighth Idylle* of his Rural Poems, Virgil described a witch who could draw her lovers back to her as well as a magician who called the dead forth from their graves and even moved seeds planted in one field to another. Further, in the "Banquet of Trimalchio" by Petronius – a friend of Nero – Roman tables were entertained with tales of witches and miracles. Especially the Thessalians were famous as "miracle workers": according to Martial, magic Thessalian women were thought to be able to draw the moon from the sky and create love potions.

To what end did the *Völkischer Beobachter* recite these indications of superstition rampant even among the great lights of Roman literature? An answer can be inferred from the opening lines of the article: "We see in our age of decline how superstition and the belief in miracles bloom again. Proof lies in the rise of spiritualism, occultism, and nonsense about fortune tellers … Things were similar in the Roman Empire, as it collapsed under the Caesars."[23] Here, comparison between Roman history and contemporary affairs was again couched in negative terms: rotten with superstitions perhaps triggered by séances in search of loved ones fallen in the First World War, the decadent Weimar Republic was – from the Nazi perspective – sure to collapse just as Roman society had.

7 INTOLERANCE TOWARD ENLIGHTENMENT

We have seen in the newspaper's cultural coverage of the dynamic forces of rationalism and classicism its "Nordic" spins on the Renaissance and its emphasis on the "Germanic" tradition of the Reformation era. As *Völkischer Beobachter* treatment moved from Late Antiquity to the Scientific Revolution and the Enlightenment, little more was said about the intervening periods. However, when its coverage, perceived chronologically, reached the seventeenth and eighteenth centuries, it is not surprising that Nazi critics belittled enlightened thought and emphasized ostensible origins of romantic culture. Criticism was directed against Spinoza's "Jewish ethics," Newton as the father of modern materialism, Lessing's philo-Semitic *Nathan the Wise*, and Moses Mendelssohn as an originator of the shadowy "Jewish conspiracy." Supposedly in opposition to this, Kant's rationalization for anti-Semitism was "rediscovered."[1] Subsequently, the *Völkischer Beobachter* analyzed the French Revolution as primarily a racial conflict between Latin underclasses and the "Germanic" French nobility. In this context, Schiller appeared in the Nazi newspaper as a great German (not "international") humanist and counterrevolutionary. Goethe was claimed as "ours" by underplaying his neoclassical tastes and highlighting his elitism and patriotism. Likewise, the *Völkischer Beobachter*'s reception of Beethoven centered on the composer's reactions to the Revolution in an effort to refute assertions that he experienced a case of "revolutionary fever." Finally, the Nazi newspaper extolled Prussian reformers and early nationalists like Fichte and Herder as "Prophets of National Socialism."

Naturally, the *Völkischer Beobachter* rejected the philosophy of Baruch Spinoza (1632–1677) out of hand. "Certain Christian precepts were foreign to the Jew," the paper said; in Spinoza, "one could observe profound differences between Aryan and Semitic spiritual foundations." Apparently ignoring the status ordinarily accorded to Spinoza's major work on the topic, the paper concluded that ethics – the "touchstone and goal of all philosophical observations" in German thinking – was nothing more than a "handmaiden" in the philosophical system of the Jew, who was "tortured by arbitrarily speculative thinking." Indeed, to the paper, Spinoza was one of the "greatest Jewish thinkers," though, of course, this was not a compliment in Nazi discourse.[2] It did, on the other hand, describe Spinoza's German contemporary, Gottfried Wilhelm Leibniz (1646–1716), as a "genius of bold and outstanding spirit whose ideas found rich fulfillment."[3] But uneasiness ran through all *Völkischer Beobachter* discussion of the early modern rationalist tradition.

On the 250th anniversary of the publication of *Philosophiae Naturalis Principia Mathematica*, the paper ran an article about "Newton's Effect on Europe," by Hermann Hartmann – then a student of physical and theoretical chemistry, and later a professor at the University of Frankfurt well into the postwar era. Here Hartmann attempted what seems logically to be an impossible task: to articulate a "racially-determined" History of Science. Isaac Newton (1642–1727) was a truly giant spirit, Hartmann argued; the insights he set forth in the *Principia* constituted the "shining culmination" of the first period of "Nordic natural science." In Hartmann's opinion, two characteristics marked Newton as the model of a "purely Nordic natural scientist." First, he experienced the world with "childlike impartiality, free of prejudice," perceiving its miracles in both the largest and smallest things. Second, although he recognized the magnitude of his task – "modestly standing before it in all humility" – he did not waver: "fervid desire to seize understanding of the world drove him to achieve the impossible." Having thus identified the qualities of "Nordic science" that Newton embodied, Hartmann turned to address the nature of Newton's body of work, and he perceived a racial dimension even here. Above all, it was Newton's "ingenious intuition" to complete Copernicus' work by combining the astronomer's observations in a synthesis with those of the Italian, Galileo, that struck Hartmann as particularly "Nordic." Galileo, who, "with his long face, blond hair, and blue eyes was unmistakably a descendant of Germanic immigrants," had studied the laws of falling bodies, movement on inclined planes, and the motion of the pendulum, and his results awakened in Newton the idea that it might be possible to interpret the laws of Kepler as the logical consequence of general mechanical principles. This insight led to his formulation of the basic laws of classical mechanics.

However, as much as he admired the achievements of Newton's Nordic science, Hartmann expressed reservations about the subsequent effect that the *Principia* had on the intellectual life of Europe, positing a volkish critique that counseled against overemphasizing the importance of rationalism, preferring instead an approach grounded in romantic *Naturphilosophie*. According to Hartmann, the "representatives of rationalism" seized Newton's ideas, and tried to make them serve to explain every natural phenomenon though mechanical procedures. Because Newton influenced the most important subsequent scientists, mechanics was raised over all the other disciplines of physics, and this contributed to the "dominance of scientific materialism," even in Germany. Without a doubt, Hartmann asserted, Newton's work was one of the main reasons for the tremendous development of the natural sciences and technology that became so characteristic of European culture in the coming century. But, he warned, even Newton – the creator of those ideas himself – had recognized the "great ocean of the unknown and warned against overconfidence in this mechanizing tendency."[4]

And so, even in the *Völkischer Beobachter*'s limited discussion of seventeenth-century philosophy and science, one can perceive patterns that are repeated through the newspaper's treatment of Western rationalism in the modern era. Taken as a whole, its coverage of the Enlightenment was minimal.[5] While some discussion of the major figures of the German *Aufklärung*, including Winckelmann, Kant, and Schiller, appeared, the purpose of most of these articles was to distinguish these thinkers from the "French tendencies" of the period – especially tendencies that had led to revolution. On the other hand, *Aufklärer* of Jewish descent, such as Moses Mendelssohn, were despised as the originators of the modern Jewish-intellectual conspiracy. Above all – and this was particularly true of its reporting on the German music tradition – the *Völkischer Beobachter* sought to promote the proto-romantic elements in the works of the eighteenth-century masters it preferred.

A strong sign of the *Völkischer Beobachter*'s romantic prejudice was its almost complete lack of reference to eighteenth-century visual art. Despite Hitler's own obsession with neoclassical architecture, it is difficult to find mention even of eighteenth-century German artists,

Figure 7.1 Andreas Schlüter, *Dying Warrior* (1698–1705), Zeughaus, Berlin, Germany

let alone important French artists such as Jean-Baptiste Greuze or Jacques Louis David. For instance, in a survey of "German Masterpieces for Our Times," works of the sculptor Andreas Schlüter (1664–1714) were the only eighteenth-century pieces mentioned. For Richard Biedrzynski, Schlüter's reliefs for the Berlin Zeughaus were masterpieces of the "German courage to accept pain" (Figure 7.1). No other Volk could have produced the "Iliad of the North" that Schlüter created in his masks of dying warriors. The "will to power that lay in the mission of Prussia was here combined with the courage to accept self-sacrifice and pain – without which power would not be sincere, but only brute force."[6] Thus was the *Völkischer Beobachter*'s preference for neoclassical imagery manifested: in sentimental tribute to art produced for the king of Prussia, tinged with a Hellenistic agony that could be associated with Romanticism in general, and with the militarism of the Nazi movement in particular.

Another example epitomized the paper's tendency to either reject or romanticize the Western neoclassical tradition. As we have seen, on the 175th anniversary of J. J. Winckelmann's death, the *Völkischer Beobachter* ran a summary of the relationship between the art historian and Gotthold Ephraim Lessing. In this article, it repeated the most famous passage from Winckelmann's *Thoughts on the Imitation of Greek Works in Painting and Sculpture*: "The last and most eminent characteristic of the Greek works is a noble simplicity and sedate grandeur in gesture and expression. As the bottom of the sea lies peaceful beneath a foaming surface, a great soul lies sedate beneath the strife of passions in Greek figures."[7] But thereafter the article's author, Adalbert Bornhagen, set about contradicting the most fundamental tenets of Winckelmann's formulation by recasting the leading classicist's attitude toward the Ancients in starkly romantic terms. In Bornhagen's opinion, Winckelmann (1717–1768) transformed our understanding of the "far-away land of the Greeks" – which up to then had been little more than an area of "pedantic antiquarian scholarship" – into "a grandiose vision that magically lit up earth, people, and sky." This was the noble achievement of this "seer and herald": he was "thrilled by" the sculpture of the ancients as the "incarnation of a comprehensive theater of life."[8]

Some degree of subtlety was also required in handling the case of Voltaire (1694–1778). Given its broad distaste for Enlightenment culture, it is noteworthy that the *Völkischer Beobachter* did not reject Voltaire as a matter of course – this, in part, because of his involvement with Friedrich the Great and the emerging Prussian state of the late eighteenth century. According to an article marking Voltaire's 250th *Todestag*, a "problematic nature" like his makes it "difficult for posterity to form an opinion" of the writer. Voltaire was "a bit strange to most people," so one had to resist "forcing him into a cliché." Just as posterity had made Friedrich out to be a "Hero King" (*Heldenkönig*) by omitting the "demonic, fearsome, and bewitching" aspects of the man, Voltaire had been seen as only a "malicious, perfidious egoist." Both portraits were true, claimed the paper, but "both were also only half true." People were probably right when they "instinctively raised protective walls against inharmonious natures" like theirs: "life would really be unbearable if loud Friedrichs and Voltaires ran around all over the place; but it would be even more unbearable if there were no Friedrichs or Voltaires at all."

Still, the paper's portrait of Voltaire contained more negative than positive judgments. He was above all "the cynical scoffer, the reckless smart aleck." Reading his *Maid of Orleans* (*La Pucelle*, 1755), for instance, "one felt like one had landed in real filth." It was "impossible to express distrust of female purity more infuriatingly" than he did in this satire of the "heroic poem": Voltaire's was to Schiller's depiction of Joan of Arc what "a gutter stream is to a majestic river." But the main reason he was unpopular in Berlin, according to the *Völkischer Beobachter*, had to do with his relationship with a Jew and his financial affairs: he earned the contempt of the Prussian court when he became embroiled in a "most unpleasant controversy" with a "Jewish moneylender," and then resorted to using all the tricks of a "wily stockbroker," including the falsification of documents, in an attempt to extract himself from the controversy.

In addition, the paper took issue with Voltaire's "unconscionably hypocritical" dealings with the French Catholic Church. Cultural history had "rarely seen such a coward" as Voltaire, said the paper: he could hardly take pen in hand without writing something malicious about the Church. But "when he thought about it afterward, sweat of fear broke out on his forehead since the powerful opponent might seek revenge, so he made all his friends swear on their lives that they would not reveal him as the author." It was "shameful" to see how "he, who did so much to destroy Catholic authority, so cravenly assured the Academy that there was no better Catholic than him – only because he vainly longed for a seat in that body." Moreover, before his death – just because he was afraid of being buried in unconsecrated soil – "the sworn enemy of Catholic dogma confessed." By the same token, however, to the extent that *Völkischer Beobachter* reception of Voltaire was positive, it was mostly due to his stand against the Church: "that people today can pray to God according to their own hearts is largely thanks to Voltaire." Therefore, the paper admitted, "despite the confusing combination of so many weaknesses and so many virtues, his impact on posterity could not be overlooked."[9]

Despite some grudging acknowledgment of his rapport with Friedrich the Great and his stand against the Catholic Church, the *Völkischer Beobachter* more consistently attacked Voltaire as the embodiment of eighteenth-century French cultural dominance that Germans had to overcome in order to establish a national identity. This critical view of Voltaire was most evident in articles describing the struggles of isolated German creators who fought for space in public spheres – namely, the theaters and opera houses of German courts – "under the foreign control of French or Italians, or German toadies who emulated them."

Culminating in its coverage of Mozart, the *Völkischer Beobachter* presented the careers of eighteenth-century German dramatists like Gotthold Ephraim Lessing as constituting early skirmishes in the Wars of Liberation. Although German patriotism could not yet manifest itself in political or military action, "increasingly aware artists and writers who stood up for German style" took the first step toward establishing the cultural foundations of a nationalistic movement – and ultimately of national unity.

The case of Lessing (1729–1781) reveals how the paper promoted this agenda simply by overlooking or denying aspects of Lessing's life that did not operate to advance it. Above all, Lessing was identified as an early resistor against foreign cultural influence: for his whole life Lessing "directed his hatred against the nation that was then 'blessing' Germany with its culture and morals – France."[10] This required, first and foremost, his position as the sworn enemy of "that courtly flatterer," Voltaire, then the most prominent embodiment of French culture in Germany.[11] And so, in *Minna von Barnhelm* (1767), the paper pointed to Lessing as being the first to dare to bitterly satirize a Frenchman on stage. Indeed, this was Lessing's method of political fighting: he was conscious that he could better "awaken true patriotism and genuine national feeling" in this way – on the stage – than through open political rebellion. As the "reformer of the German stage," he freed it from the French influence that had held exclusive sway for so long. In this he achieved a "national deed."[12]

According to Albert Müller's article on "Lessing as Politician," for a Volk that was ruled by more than three hundred great and small nobles, there was "no chance for political education – no basis for thoughts of liberation or unified efforts toward a constitution." At such a time, when Germany was powerless and disdained – "a world of subjects without rights" – there was no way to develop the national feeling that would serve as "the sole basis for a healthy political operation." Conditions did not exist for open work on reform in German politics, and Lessing recognized this. So his method was not to take on things that could be addressed only through violent means – for he was a "wielder of spiritual weapons" – instead, he "expressed nationalist sentiment" far more than any of his contemporaries in literature, art, and philosophy. While few knew anything of patriotic feeling, he possessed it to the highest degree: he was disgusted by anyone who "shamed their nationality, or copied foreign morals and speech, thereby shunning their own."[13]

According to Konrad Mass, author of numerous tributes to Hitler, Lessing proved that French theater was "not compatible with German ways of thinking." His work was moved not just by "French tenderness, superficial grace, and amorousness," but by "the great and the powerful." He also resisted the unities of action, time, and space in French plays, proving that only the "unity of action" was necessary – "those of place and time only insofar as the action demanded." After 180 years, *Minna von Barnhelm* was still a model for good comedy, and still had its place on the German stage because it was the "first play of true German national content." It "breathed German life; it showed German people; it had a unifying effect through its comparison of supposed Prussian and Saxon differences; it sharply and humorously satirized the decadent French … and it placed at the center of the action – without actually putting him on stage – the deeds of the great Friedrich that so impressed the world." Above all, it avoided the frivolous comedy of contemporary farces, emphasizing German "seriousness toward life" – "without which no good comedy can function." Therefore, even if some aspects of Lessing's work contradicted "the German sensibility of today," Nazis nonetheless gave him a significant place in the development of German literature: he created the "basis for the higher art" that gave rise to greats like Goethe and Schiller. Even if he was too early for explicit discussion of German nationalism, Lessing was nevertheless "a man of German racial origins and German culture, inspired by the German courage to tell the truth, and therefore a German man, a German poet, and a German scholar."[14]

To embrace Lessing, however, the *Völkischer Beobachter* had to deal with a number of aspects of Lessing the man, and of his work, that were not compatible with National Socialist sensibilities. As a preliminary matter, Nazis had to dispel questions about his racial background. Elsewhere, the "racial expert" Eugen Dühring stated that "this Lessing was Slavo-Hebraic mixed," but others at the paper rejected this emphatically. Josef Stolzing took up the issue in his 200th birthday tribute, acknowledging that "we can provide no racial proof for Eugen Dühring's assertion: we know that Lessing came from a generation of Evangelical ministers that went back deep into the sixteenth century, and that his blue eyes and blond hair gave the impression of a predominantly Nordic racial type."[15]

Such matters aside, Lessing had also undeniably committed the cardinal sin of the Nazi world view: "though we find a number of elements in Lessing's political outlook that are sympathetic to our political views, we may not overlook one which we find repellent today: he was openly a friend of the Jews."[16] And this, the paper had to admit, affected some of Lessing's writing as well. According to Stolzing, Houston Stewart Chamberlain wrote "correctly" in his *Foundations of the Nineteenth Century* that "one does not have to have the authentic Hittite nose to be a 'Jew.'" This word, "Jew," describes, rather, "a particular way of feeling and thinking; a person can very quickly become a Jew without being an Israelite; some only need to socialize with Jews, read Jewish newspapers, and become accustomed to Jewish lifestyle, literature and art." Associations with his "Jewish bosom buddies," therefore, influenced Lessing's way of thinking: he couldn't look out at the world "without Jewish glasses on his nose." These "Jewish ways of thinking and feeling" ran through all his writings and poems, particularly in his "immeasurable over-estimation of the Old Testament and his ignorance of the true history of the Jewish people."[17]

But Stolzing provided excuses for Lessing's erroneous ways. One explanation was that he had simply been seduced by Jews intent on using him for their own purposes. Perhaps his "clear Jew-friendliness" could be explained by the fact that Lessing was "drawn into Jewish circles as a youth." Since then, the Jewish nation – "that had to work more and more intensively to glorify itself, due to increased recognition of the Aryan race as superior to Hebrew nature" – had manipulated Lessing's veneration of Judaism. Indeed, Stolzing had to admit that the hero of Lessing's masterpiece, *Nathan the Wise* (1799), was drawn in such complete and perfect human lines that "one automatically thinks: 'If only a handful of Jews were like this Nathan, then there would be no anti-Semitism.'"[18]

The paper also allowed that Lessing came too early to be fully alert to the "Jewish threat." Motivated, or rather "confused by" Enlightenment idealism, his friendship with Jews corresponded with the "world view of his time," to which "racial consciousness was foreign" and where "Jews were included in the general notion of loving mankind."[19] Contributors could explain this characteristic of Lessing that was "so strange to us" only by noting that he "placed himself on the side of all oppressed according to his attitude as a citizen of the world, and that he did not perceive the harmfulness that Jewry had for the national future of Germany."[20] The racial question that had "become authoritative for us today" lay completely outside of his field of view.[21] Ultimately, they argued that the main cause of his philo-Semitic reputation was that simply too much attention was given to *Nathan*: readers of "today's Jewish press," wrote Stolzing, saw Lessing and his works "not as they really were, but according to a highly one-sided image as the creator of the 'Jew-friendly' *Nathan the Wise* alone."[22]

Writers for the *Völkischer Beobachter* therefore explored his works for signs that he was actually anti-Semitic, emphasizing poems by Lessing which could not be "deemed Jew-friendly at all," and which also contained "remarkable contradictions regarding his position *vis-à-vis* Freemasonry." For instance, in a satirical poem against Voltaire – written when he was involved with a case against Abraham Hirsch regarding Saxon taxes – Lessing brought out the following introductory verses, that "certainly can't be called Jew-friendly":[23]

> The cleverest Hebrews in Berlin,
> For whom no fraud is too difficult,
> For whom no trick seems too wicked;
> The Jews, who excel
> in lying, conning, and cheating,
> despite the hangman and other dangers, etc.

On the basis of such evidence, the *Völkischer Beobachter* tried to reverse the traditional view of Lessing for its readers. For expert justification, they turned to "our volkish historian of literature, our party comrade, the German-to-the-Core Prof. Adolf Bartels," who "dealt with this theme exhaustively in his comprehensive work, *Lessing and the Jews*." There Bartels expressed the opinion that "if he lived among us today, Lessing would certainly be an anti-Semitic enemy of the Jews, because he would have undoubtedly resisted the lust to rule and measureless over-representation of the Jews."[24]

In these contorted revisions to the biography of Lessing one can perceive a slight effort to establish links between the volkish-Nazi outlook and eighteenth-century German cultural history. Correct in presenting the *Aufklärung* as the first stage of modern German cultural expression – with German creators pressing for independence from French and Italian prevalence in Baroque court society – the paper had to overcome the fact that the principles of the German Enlightenment included many supposedly "French" elements, such as religious tolerance and political liberalism, that ultimately pointed in the direction of revolution. And so, in addition to his attitudes toward the "Jewish

Question," the political views of an *Aufklärer* like Lessing had to be reformulated as well. Although Lessing "never called for a specific form of state, his political outlook was thoroughly republican," Müller recognized. However, Müller held that it would be a mistake to conceive Lessing "as a republican in today's sense of the word." The "concept of freedom that fired his soul" – and which may have found its ideal expression in the line of *Nathan the Wise*: "No man must must" – was "part of the spiritual atmosphere of his time." Undoubtedly, the "spirit of political rebirth was hurrying toward the French Revolution." But Lessing would not experience this outcome, and he would not have agreed with it, since he was "no revolutionary in the usual political sense." In his "deepest soul he was an enemy of violent change, searching to realize a higher ideal of humanity."[25] To support this view of Lessing, the *Völkischer Beobachter* again deferred to Adolf Bartels for the last word: "All in all, he is an important writer who staunchly promoted his Volk in every area of his activity. Even if his pugnacity, contradictoriness, and brilliance occasionally led him down the wrong paths, he was a man who sought truth above all. We Germans will always count him as one of us and never stop treasuring persons like him, even in times of stupidity and confusion" such as the Weimar era.[26]

Moses Mendelssohn (1729–1786) presented an entirely different challenge. Besides criticizing his role in seducing Lessing for Jewish propagandistic purposes, the *Völkischer Beobachter* had to confront Mendelssohn's fame as a leading exponent of the German Enlightenment. The problem, from the volkish-Nazi perspective, resided in explaining why leading figures in eighteenth-century German culture sided with forces of reform – including, significantly, religious tolerance – or were themselves Jewish. Accordingly, while the *Völkischer Beobachter* could not deny Mendelssohn's importance outright, it would instead apply every means at its disposal to undermine his reputation, including using techniques derived from Richard Wagner's attacks on Judaism in the nineteenth-century music world.

First, the paper tried to explain away Mendelssohn's celebrity as an unfortunate by-product of progressive Enlightenment thinking. In brief, it held that he was popular only because of the increasing eighteenth-century tolerance of Jews, not because his work was of any intrinsic value. "Full of surprise," wrote Heinz Henckel, "we must ask ourselves today" how it was possible that Mendelssohn was "overrated" to such a point that his contemporaries compared him with Socrates and even "had the cheek" to depict him on a medallion together with the Greek wise man. Henckel perceived a couple of reasons for this: the general tolerance of the Age of Enlightenment, "which extended to Jews in particular," and the fact that among Jews, Mendelssohn was a "singular development at the low point of their culture." So they were "more than pleased that a Jew was ready to spread the ideas of the Enlightenment among his racial comrades." His Judaism "surrounded Mendelssohn with protective walls" that prevented the penetration of any serious criticism of his work. But it wasn't just the advantage of "all-too-mild and tolerant" criticism that Mendelssohn enjoyed, but also that – "just as in the case of so many other Jewish intellectual greats after him" – he was "celebrated and artificially promoted by a Jewish clique."

Just as his grandson, the composer Felix Mendelssohn-Bartholdy, was accused by Richard Wagner of copying rather than contributing to the German music tradition, the fundamental accusation launched against Moses Mendelssohn's work was that he plagiarized its best aspects. According to Henckel, Mendelssohn's main work, *Phädon* (1767), proved how little difference there was between "eclecticism and plagiarism." While the first part was an "almost verbatim translation" of the Platonic dialogues, the second was a "colorful conglomeration of opinions" taken from a wide variety of philosophers. Mendelssohn wisely protected himself from precise source references by hedging in the introduction: "If I had been able to indicate the authors, then the names Descartes, Leibniz, Wolf, Baumgarten, Reimarus, etc., would have been often cited." Henckel contrasted this "laxity in the question of intellectual property" with the "meticulous exactitude" with which Lessing compiled his sources. Mendelssohn gave birth to no great ideas of his own, in Henckel's view: "as he put it himself, he just 'took up gratefully what he found useful in others,' with great literary skill." One could not deny, Henckel quipped, that Mendelssohn's was a "light, easily comprehended Enlightenment philosophy – a pocket-book philosophy, so to say."

But despite admitting that Mendelssohn's plagiarizing and popularizing was done skillfully – that is, with the "superficial polish and even attractiveness supposedly manifested in other Jewish extrapolations from German culture such as Felix Mendelssohn's music for the 'Nordic play,' *A Midsummer Night's Dream*" – the *Völkischer Beobachter* was not about to let Mendelssohn's status as a major exponent of eighteenth-century German culture, whether enlightened or not, go unchallenged. Despite his reputation as an *Aufklärer*, Henckel went on, his work was based on "traditional Judaic religion through and through." In Mendelssohn it was apparent above all "how the Jew held fast to the religion of his fathers." One had to bear in mind that the philosopher of the Enlightenment, who supposedly battled against the exaggerated orthodoxy of the Jews, upheld the "most unimportant and insignificant ceremonial laws" of the Jewish religion "with the same stubbornness of an orthodox Rabbi from Poland." In his translation of the *Pentateuch*, for instance, Mendelssohn "embarrassingly refrained from deviating in the least from excessive rabbinical commentary." Here he "never left a word for reason," which otherwise meant so much to him. Mendelssohn's translation of the five books of Moses was "a cultural deed from the Jewish point of view alone."[27]

"Born a Jew, always a Jew" – and for the *Völkischer Beobachter*, this meant active involvement in a conspiracy dedicated to more than just upholding Orthodox traditions within the Jewish community.[28] According to the Nazi paper, Mendelssohn's philosophy and poetry initiated the "Jewish influence on German literature."[29] Thus, "the strongest barrier between Jews and Germans was torn down and the path to assimilation – the final aim of the Western Civilization Jew – was open!" Mendelssohn's philosophy was a dead issue: it was more important to consider the "early Jewish politician and fighter," because he stood at the start of a process that would "end with their rule, if the German Volk wasn't careful." Until the rise of Nazism, a wrong evaluation of Mendelssohn had been upheld in historical and literary works – so much that it was "difficult to determine what he really was." But the *Völkischer Beobachter* was committed to clarifying things for its readers, summarizing its portrait of him as a "lightweight popular philosopher, an orthodox Jew, a pettifogging *Talmudjünger*, an enemy of Christianity, and a preparer of the path to Jewish world control."[30]

For the Nazi newspaper, resistance to the "foreign" principles of the Enlightenment was the first phase in the German struggle for freedom that would become more fully realized in the nineteenth century with the Wars of Liberation, and the even more desperate volkish struggle against a conspiracy of Jews bent on global dominance, establishing precedent for the battles that were continuing in the modern era. Remarkably, the paper enlisted the most illustrious of German illuminati, Immanuel Kant (1724–1804), in both efforts. By the 1920s Nazi conspiracy theorists were actively promoting the notion that Jewish control over German culture had become reality, at least with regard to the journalism of the Weimar

Republic; indeed, only outlets of the volkish press were seen to be free from such influence. That the *Völkischer Beobachter* could address this issue of cultural domination even in a sarcastic tone was apparent in Josef Stolzing's response to a positive review in another Munich publication – *Die Kuhhaut* – of a book by significant Kant expert, Ernst Marcus.[31] Upon citing *Die Kuhhaut*'s statement that Marcus' book provided useful clarifications of Kant's work – "bringing it into the light of day" – Stolzing objected, "What a *Geschmüse*! As if we need to see through Ernst Marcus' glasses in order to understand Kant. All that would do is allow us to see him in Jewish light!"[32] But Stolzing took this single example further, inflating its significance by offering it up as a case demonstrating the overwhelming nature of the Jewish influence in Weimar Germany in general. Thus, what Nazis had long known, namely, that the Jews had "graciously" taken administration of German culture into their "superior hands – because we dumb Germans couldn't do anything good with it – was confirmed once again in this essay."

By such references to "seeing Kant through Jewish glasses," Stolzing plainly intended to direct attention to those interpretations that omitted discussion of the thinker's anti-Semitic attitudes and statements. And so, to complement Kant's famous line – "Two things fill the mind with ever new and increasing admiration and awe the oftener and the more steadily we reflect on them: the starry heavens above and the moral law within"[33] – the *Völkischer Beobachter* featured quotes such as: "Judaism is really not a religion at all but merely a union of a number of people who, since they belonged to a particular stock, formed themselves into a commonwealth under purely political law,"[34] and "the Palestinians living among us have, for the most part, earned a not unfounded reputation for being cheaters, because of their spirit of usury since their exile."[35]

This material thus put into the record, the *Völkischer Beobachter* then dedicated itself to demonstrating that in addition to the general anti-Jewish policies advocated by the Nazis, the philosopher would have agreed with the specific Nazi position on German disarmament as stipulated by the Versailles Treaty. Günter Macketanz bemoaned, for example, the fact that in support of pacifist parties' "dogma of disarmament," Democrats had misused Kant as a "star-witness for their republican goals" by stretching out "like a banner" his postulate that "over time, standing armies should be dissolved."

Macketanz wanted to "help assess the validity" of this misusage: first, while Kant did say that a standing army should dissolve "over time," for Macketanz, this prescription could not have been meant to refer to a time span as short as Kant's lifetime or even one extending into the next century. Also, Macketanz argued, according to Kant in *Perpetual Peace* (1795),[36] the natural state of men was the state of war and as long as his Volk had "not received unqualified securities from its neighbors, it had to feel itself threatened by enemies." In such a situation one did not need to wait until a neighbor had "done active damage before being able to proceed as an enemy against him," but rather one could "compel him to yield." If one considered further that in Kant's view, strength was based on the "number of citizens capable of wielding weapons, inspired not by greed, but patriotism and education – the most dependable tools of war" it became clear that Kant would have had nothing against the implementation of compulsory military service. And such a conclusion was even more certain since it was "self-evident to him" that eternal peace was brought about and secured not through the weakening of all powers, but through their equilibrium – "via the liveliest rivalry between them." Kant was therefore useful to pacifists neither for "besmirching our old army, nor for their utopias of disarmament." If they tried to employ him nevertheless, it was "with the worst sort of smoke and mirrors."[37]

While it did pay attention to thinkers such as Lessing, Mendelssohn, and Kant, the focus of the *Völkischer Beobachter*'s coverage of eighteenth-century culture was mainly on its music. Here began its main coverage of the German music tradition, which – from its point of view – culminated in the romantic era. As implicit in the few examples of literary and art historical analysis above, *Völkischer Beobachter* music reception exaggerated the proto-romantic components of the rococo and neoclassical heritage. Throughout these sources, the paper insisted on continuity between classical masters and the nineteenth-century romantic composers whom contributors and editors clearly preferred, and among these, none more so than Richard Wagner. Accepting Wagner's own views wholeheartedly, they promulgated the claim that all paths of German musical development led to his formulation of music drama, and that this was the very summit of the German tradition. The *Völkischer Beobachter* interpretation of the classical era in German music was therefore unapologetically romantic. In its view, everything led to the Steel Romanticism that Goebbels, for one, identified as the cultural basis for uniting the *volkish Gemeinschaft* and girding it for battle against enemies both internal and external. Implicitly, then, while this outlook constituted a rejection of the ideals of the *Aufklärung*, it was nonetheless communicated in terms that were explicitly designed to salvage the masters of the period for National Socialist propaganda use.

Among those masters, none was more in need of reclamation – or indeed could be more profitably reclaimed – than Mozart, whose artistic output had been typically viewed as the acme of musical neo-classicism. Ignoring such sensible prejudices, National Socialist reception opted to present Mozart as a major innovator of Romanticism in music. Central to this argument was the assessment of Mozart as an essentially passionate rather than a cerebral composer. As Viktor Junk put it, Mozart's creations were not "reflections of a pure artistic soul," but rather were the "confessions of a suffering soul: the more thoroughly we engage ourselves with them, the more completely we give ourselves up to them, the more ridiculous seems the foolish judgment of his music as playful and full of conventional rococo flourishes." Thus, corresponding with the anti-intellectual themes of National Socialism, for Junk, it was emotion rather than process that lay at the heart of Mozart's works: sensing the "bliss of creativity" at the highest level, the act of composing provided him with his happiest moments – he himself referred to the process as his "sole joy and passion," during which "ideas came in streams." He served Nazis, therefore, in two ways: as a "prototype for the creative genius, and at the same time as a serious admonishment against our 'productive' times, reminding that music should be taken as a gift from the Godhead, not as a product of cool reflection or frantic intellectual work."[38] Clearly, Nazis also perceived in their version of Mozart a counterexample to trends in modern music they despised. Hans Buchner advised that instead of a "New Viennese Impressionistic piece by a Franz Schreker or the like," one should produce Mozart's operas and thereby commit not only a "volkish, Fatherlandish deed," but also fill an "artistic need that is today greater than ever."[39] As Junk put it, "our era, the Nazi era, which has just left behind an unfortunate period of horrible confusion in the areas of art, confesses itself with open heart to Mozart: whenever art loses its sanity, it will return to health under the sign of Mozart."[40]

For the *Völkischer Beobachter*, the most politically compelling aspect of Mozart's creative output was his contribution to the "Idea of a German National Opera." Ferdinand Moessmer saw the "birth of German opera" in Mozart's "plan for founding a National Opera in Vienna" via the "German Singspiel," *The Abduction from the Seraglio*.[41] Hans

Buchner added that the opera's score surpassed "hackneyed, worn-out applications" of forms associated with the Italian style, radiating the "fire of a lively sensitivity" such as one found nowhere among the Italians themselves, even the best of them.[42] But *The Abduction from the Seraglio* was only a start, according to Moessmer: what Mozart was not able to achieve in his *Abduction*, namely, help German opera triumph over Italian, he attained – as paradoxical as it may seem – via his "Italian" works, *The Marriage of Figaro* (1786) and *Don Giovanni* (1787). It was these operas that "violently broke from Italian influence," because with them Mozart "beat the greatest Italian masters of his time on what had been exclusively their own turf."[43]

Naturally, the *Völkischer Beobachter* had to take some care in appropriating *The Marriage of Figaro* (which it usually referred to by its German title), given its reputation as a document of eighteenth-century liberal values. Admittedly, wrote Heinrich Stahl, *Figaros Hochzeit* drew from Beaumarchais' sociocritical, revolutionary work, but "it was not in the slightest sense oriented in that direction: its concern, rather, was with mankind in general."[44] This problem so deftly solved, Nazis still had to confront the issue of Lorenzo da Ponte, Mozart's favorite librettist, who was of Jewish background. According to Stolzing, that "da Ponte was a Jew" was "unbeknownst to most people." But in all of his work and life he demonstrated himself a definite precursor of that "crummy bunch of Jews" who write too much prose and poetry – "not out of inner compulsion, but just because they know how to make a living out of it." Stolzing's basis for this assessment was the simple fact that da Ponte would work on more than one libretto at a time (as if the German Mozart wouldn't have resorted to such conduct).[45]

Beyond this, the *Völkischer Beobachter* simply criticized da Ponte's work as being substandard – the weak link in Mozart's creative process that the "German" composer had to overcome. For Buchner, his operas were great *"in spite of* inferior librettos written by a Jew." Mozart's "hired poet – the Venetian Jew – didn't always give the Salzburg genius the best of service." In his hands, the libretto of a *buffo* opera became a "very slippery slope that required the balance of a first-class dancer to traverse." But Mozart did not slip and fall on da Ponte's "shiny *Glitz.*" Instead, he ennobled the "frivolous text of Figaro by applying to it the reserve, refinement, and soulful depth of German music." Thereby did he provide the librettist "a sort of unearned renown, in the shadow of his immortal genius."[46] Ultimately, the *Völkischer*

Beobachter's simple solution to the da Ponte problem was to recommend German translations of his libretti as superior to the original. Heinrich Stahl argued that since *Figaros Hochzeit* was without a doubt a *German* opera, the effort to "harmonize its musical inspiration perfectly with a German text" was absolutely necessary. In his opinion, Georg Schünemann's adaptation – commissioned by the Ministry of Propaganda in 1941 – was "extremely solid": if one compared the old and the new texts along with a piano transcription, "one would come to the happy conclusion that very few of the listener's favorite impressions disappear while, particularly in the case of the recitatives, much of great advantage and meaning for the musical line and accent results."[47]

Written in Italian and set in Spain, *Don Giovanni* also required some nationalistic rehabilitation for use in the Third Reich. There was a tendency to misconstrue this work as "European" or "above nationality," wrote Stahl, and yet it could only have "arisen from a German nature."[48] In the pages of the *Völkischer Beobachter*, *Don Giovanni* was considered a proto-romantic work – meaning, of course, "German." In Buchner's view, Mozart "seized hold of the darker motives of human passion with firm grip and hoisted forth into the bright light of the stage a treasure of life's deepest truths." From this point it was only a short step to the romantic: "*Fidelio, Freischütz,* and *Tannhäuser* went forth on the path broken by *Don Giovanni*."[49] Indeed, *Don Giovanni*'s major significance was that it led to Wagner's music drama. "With one giant step, it crossed the threshold into the nineteenth century," and therefore must be regarded as "the upbeat to Romanticism." Without it, a large percentage of Beethoven's works, as well as those of Weber and Wagner, would have been "simply unthinkable." In this ingenious score raged "the first storm of the 'music drama,' which one Richard Wagner was destined to perfect."[50] But, as in the case of *Figaro*, Nazis were not happy with da Ponte's Italian libretto. In Friedrich Bayer's view, a good German translation was required, but for the time being one just had to remember that it was a "German opera." Of all Mozart's operas, he explained, the most attempts had been made to translate *Don Giovanni*, though the results had been weak. There just hadn't been a translator with "enough sensitivity, talent, and musicality to find the proper German words." However, "anyone could sense that the opera was no less German because of this – if they just let Mozart's chaste and pure German music work on them."[51]

About *Così Fan Tutte* (1790), the *Völkischer Beobachter* had little to say. Insinuating that it was not one of the composer's best works,

Stolzing seconded Richard Wagner's opinion that it was "too bad that Mozart had to write it quickly." He did not, however, pass up the opportunity to blame the Jew for all of *Così*'s weaknesses. Stolzing insisted that da Ponte had provided a "silly and cynically frivolous text" based on a story that "simply wasn't believable." It was "another mark of Mozart's brilliance," that he could make of this libretto something that satisfied the expectations of Emperor Joseph II.[52]

The Magic Flute was a different matter. Ignoring that they also attributed this achievement to Händel, Carl Maria von Weber, and Richard Wagner, *Völkischer Beobachter* writers commended Mozart for writing the "first truly German opera."[53] It was, according to their articles, the work with which Mozart secured a place for his operatic art on every stage in the world. With it he "fixed his place in music history," and, "as a German, gained victory over Italian opera which still dominated in his day."[54] Overnight, as if out of nowhere, Moessmer exclaimed, "German opera emerged in its most perfect form." German above all was its "tonal language" – "for all its sublimity, simple and richly sensitive; German was the *Lied* form making its first appearance in opera; German was the magically romantic impact of the music; German was the musical representation of the characters, especially Sarastro and the lovers, Tamino and Pamina." For Germany, 30 September 1791 – the day of the work's premiere in Vienna – was also "the birthday of German opera." Without *Die Zauberflöte*, "German Romanticism would be unthinkable." It was the "prerequisite for Beethoven's *Fidelio*, *Freischütz*, *Oberon* – actually, all of the operas of Weber, Lortzing, and every other romantic – just as necessary as the German *Lied*." Richard Wagner was right when he said that "Germans cannot begin to honor this work enough. Up to that point, German opera hardly existed; it was born with this work."[55]

What attracted National Socialists to The Magic Flute in particular were its popular – in their term, volkish – elements, probably best embodied in the character of Papageno. According to musicologist Franz Posch, it was not "merely an opera," but a "*Volkstuck* of the Viennese magical and mechanical theater tradition with all its popular, sentimental, and naive features – reviving the spirit of that era, particularly its typically South German aspects."[56] But *Völkischer Beobachter* reception of The Magic Flute was not wholly unproblematic. For Nazis, the trouble with The Magic Flute lay in its Masonic connotations. People were constantly trying to "make sense of the brittle layers [*spröde Gefüge*] of Schickaneder's text," Buchner complained. But "analysis of this made-for-the-occasion libretto" revealed absolutely nothing with regard to Mozart's music – the "ethos of which has neither a Masonic nor any other sort of subtext." Perhaps, Buchner offered, more people would have understood Schickaneder's text in those days than "we can today" (in 1923), since "cabalism and Freemasonry" were being "banished from politics and forced into the ghetto."[57] Continued assumptions about the Masonic content of *The Magic Flute* were, from Posch's perspective, the fault of inappropriate staging: over time, through "grandiose productions replete with an enormous array of decorations that run against the spirit of the piece and sin against its music," symbols of Freemasonry and principles of the French Revolution had been "retrospectively philosophized onto the work" – ignoring completely the grounds upon which *The Magic Flute* stood. This "extreme overestimation of the symbolism" in *The Magic Flute* had led to a "violation of the responsibility to be true to the work, to represent the living organism, and to revive its spirit."[58] Referring to a production at the Salzburg Festival in 1928, the *Völkischer Beobachter* made this point much more caustically: describing the performance as a "Jew To-Do" (*Judenrummel*), the paper reported that the "Bolshevik opera studio in Salzburg and the Jew Max Reinhardt" were using *Die Zauberflöte* as an "advertisement for world-wide Freemasonry," and were thereby "ruthlessly raping a musical masterpiece which is dear to us."[59]

The challenge of gleaning useful references from eighteenth-century intellectual and aesthetic history – a history replete with Voltaire's skepticism, Lessing's tolerance, Kant's reason, and Mozart's humanism and Freemasonry – is also apparent when one considers the following brief article. As the Weimar Republic lurched toward financial collapse in November 1930, the paper published a short citation under the title, "Montesquieu on the German Democracy?":

The advantage of a free state is that there are no favorites in it. But when that is not the case – when it is necessary to line the pockets of the friends and relatives, not of a prince, but of all those who participate in the government – all is lost. There is greater danger in the laws being evaded in a free state than in their being violated by a prince, for a prince is always the foremost citizen of his state, and has more interest in preserving it than anyone else.[60]

To this extract, the *Völkischer Beobachter* added the following comment: "Ch. de Montesquieu, from whom this statement comes, lived from 1689 to 1755. Therefore, he never experienced 'modern democracy.' But he characterized it perfectly!"[61] Leaving aside the anachronistic nature of this assertion – in this passage from *Considerations on the Causes of the Greatness of the Romans and their Decline* (1734), Montesquieu addressed ancient Rome and Carthage, not eighteenth-century politics – the commentary was symbolic of a selective, but not incorrect reading of the Enlightenment thinker as favoring monarchy over the "tyranny of the many." More strange was the *Völkischer Beobachter* emphasis on the fact that Montesquieu was of German origin,[62] which presumably justified mention of this French Enlightenment thinker in the Nazi newspaper. "Many French nobles were proud of their German ancestry, including Montesquieu – author of the important work, *The Spirit of the Laws* [1748],"[63] the paper reported. But this rather jarring declaration of Germanic cultural prowess was consistent with the paper's remarkable presentation of the French Revolution as a fundamentally racial conflict.

According to a 1927 article on "racism in the French Revolution," ancestral differences played a much greater role in social and political revolutions than indicated in historical writings that "didn't pay attention to racial questions." For instance, the English Civil War that led to the "dictatorship of Oliver Cromwell" was strongly marked by "racial differences between the Anglo-Saxon majority and the French-Norman aristocracy that had conquered it in 1066." In similar ways, the war of the Third Estate against the nobility in the French Revolution correlated with the "conflict between the Gallo-Roman majority of the French Volk and the originally mainly German class of nobles – among them, Montesquieu." Right away in the first battles of the Third Estate for equality of rights, "racial thinking was used as a weapon, especially in the writings of the Abbé Sieyès, who had such a powerful influence on the path of the French Revolution." For the paper, it was no coincidence that Sieyès was a French southerner, coming from Fréjus – an area where "Germanness was of significance during the early Middle Ages, then overwhelmed by the superior numbers of Gallo-Romans." An excellent speaker, he was a "typical Gallo-Roman Frenchman." And as such, he used "racial concepts" (*Rassengedanken*) in his political advocacy. For instance, to explain why the "nobility of the nation was foreign" in *What is the Third Estate?* Sieyès "first discussed its laziness, then its political and civil privileges."

Then he argued that the "French Volk had lived in slavery – that is, enslaved by the aristocrats." Therefore:

> *Why should it not repatriate to the Franconian forests all the families who wildly claim to descend from the race of the conquerors. And to inherit their rights of conquest? "True enough" some will say; "but conquest has upset all relationships and hereditary nobility now descends through the line of the conquerors." Well, then; we shall have to arrange for it to descend through the other line! The Third Estate will become noble again by becoming a conqueror in its own turn.*[64]

While Sieyès usually proceeded "completely ahistorically and purely rationalistically," the *Völkischer Beobachter* interjected, here he tried to "strengthen his argument for class war with reference to the racial foreignness of the nobility." Moreover, he also sought to draw a portion of the nobility over to the side of the Third Estate, stipulating that since the conquering of Gaul by the Germans "a strong mixture between them and the Gallo-Romans had taken place." So, although the numerically superior Third Estate had to be considered the "Fathers of the Nation," some nobles could be rehabilitated into the ranks of the Third Estate. Therefore, the paper argued, Sieyès' representation of the French aristocracy as a "racially foreign class of conquerors" led to the "rooting out and dissipation of the nobility from France." The "battle against everything Germanic that had commenced in the Renaissance continued in the form of hatred toward everything German." It was not until the nineteenth century that a French nobleman – Count Gobineau – "again came forth as a herald of German spirit," but he received more attention in Germany than in France. Since then, France had concerned herself with "disowning every drop of Germanic blood in its population – to allow for the immigration of Negroes and Eastern Jews."[65]

Actually, the majority of *Völkischer Beobachter* references to the French Revolution appeared in articles about German contemporaries, especially those who had been critical of developments across the Rhine. But in the case of many important figures of the period, the paper was forced to contend with biographical records indicating complex, evolving reactions to the stages of the Revolution that belied simplistic counterrevolutionary, anti-French, and pro-German mentalities. For some of the most important cultural figures of the German tradition as a whole – including Goethe, Schiller, and Beethoven – the *Völkischer Beobachter* had to compete against alternative claims by major parties across the German political spectrum.

Of primary concern were Goethe's responses to the French Revolution. Above all, the paper maintained that while he expressed curiosity about happenings in France, he perceived them as exclusively French developments that could not be successfully transferred across the Rhine. According to Adolf Dresler, unlike Schiller, Georg Forster, and others, he did not immediately jump to support the French Revolution: in his comedies, *The Citizen General* (1793) and *The Excited Ones* (1793), he mocked "Germans who would imitate the French revolt." Moreover, Dresler said, one should also remember the lines in the fourth song of *Hermann and Dorothea* (1797), in which Hermann commits himself to battle against the thieving French:

> So has my spirit declared, and deep in my innermost bosom
> Courage and longing have now been aroused to live for my
>   country,
> Yea, and to die, presenting to others a worthy example.
> If but the strength of Germany's youth were banded together
> There on the frontier, resolved that it never would yield to the
>   stranger,
> Ah, he should not on our glorious soil setting his footsteps,
> Neither consuming before our eyes the fruit of our labor,
> Ruling our men, and making his prey of our wives and our
>   daughters.[66]

Summarizing the rest of the play, Dresler felt that the "disunity and lack of common defensive will among the Germans" forced Hermann to give up on his wish to settle on the Rhine. But in the last song, when asking Dorothea to marry him – Dresler asserted – "he still says manly words about the French Revolution."[67]

> It poorly becomes the German to give to these fearful
>   excitements
> Aught of continuance, or to be this way and that way inclining.
> This is our own! Let that be our word, and let us maintain it! ...

Not with anxiety will I preserve it, and trembling enjoyment;
Rather with courage and strength. Today should the enemy
    threaten,
Or in the future, equip thee thyself and hand me my weapons.[68]

However, as we have seen, most articles on Goethe in the paper addressed not his poetry, but his political position expressed in letters and conversations, especially conversations with Johann Peter Eckermann. For example, Goethe communicated his "mocking attitude" toward supporters of a "German phase of French-style revolution" in the following quote registered by Eckermann, which was often reproduced in the *Völkischer Beobachter*:[69]

The only good thing for a nation is that which develops out of its own essence and its own needs without imitating another apishly. Because, that which is nourishing to one Volk at a particular stage of development can perhaps be poison to another. All attempts to import some sort of foreign innovation for which the need is not rooted in the heart of the nation itself are therefore foolish, and all seriously intended revolutions refrain from such blundering. If there is a genuine need for major reform in a Volk, God is with it and it succeeds.[70]

To make it clear whereof they felt Goethe spoke in this citation, the *Völkischer Beobachter* inserted parenthetically, "Western democracy! The Editors" – in case readers might not grasp his point.[71]

Another anti-French quote preferred by the paper came from a conversation between Goethe and Graf A. E. von Kozmian:

The French nation is the nation of the extremes. It does nothing in measure, least of all its hatred against its eastern neighbor. The old Rhine may be always watchful, that no Gallic blood dirties its sanctified water. In the future, I wish for us statesmen who maintain peace by holding the Germanic fist up against the Gallic cock … And the main German thing is to support such statesmen. Germans: above all be in love with yourselves![72]

But the *Völkischer Beobachter* was not satisfied with simply establishing that Goethe rejected French developments as French. Its contributors assumed the task of proving that he disagreed with every element of democratic, pacifist, and internationalist ideologies manifested in liberal and progressive parties through the Weimar era. Hanns Johst wrote: "If you want to get closer to Goethe and understand him better, you must ask after his contemporary political views." And this meant, according to Johst, recognizing that Goethe remained a resolute royalist through his whole career. He lived during the Seven Years War, the split of America from Great Britain, the French Revolution, and the whole Napoleonic era up to the downfall of the "hero" with all its ramifications. Friedrich the Great, Washington, Robespierre, Napoleon, and Metternich were all his contemporaries in "a world theater with a very bloody display." Nevertheless, in those times when – "as in ours" – political views of every shade blew in the wind, Goethe "went as a royalist!" That was just as difficult for a spiritual leader then "as it would be today," but Goethe "saw things with his own eyes." What could all of the sociological theories and philosophical inquiries in the world mean to him "whose senses never lied"? He saw the lives of the nobles and princes whom he served, and "there he saw men who were servants of their state and subjects of their people." A politics that justified itself by winning the support of a majority and thereby gave up "personal impulse and aristo-cratic independence" could not have seemed important to him. Politically speaking, Goethe was therefore "a subject." To him, Johst continued, the term "subject" was not an insult, but rather described the man who did not run away from work imposed on him by the structure of his environ-ment: he "subordinated his political activity to a leadership that he trusted like other institutions based on tradition." To him, politics was not the province of the average man, but required talent and practice. From this perspective as a subject, "Goethe the official" just did his duty. He worked "in the service of his state to the best of his wisdom and conscience," never confusing the "beautiful laws of poetic vision with the real affairs of political–scientific experience and state–political insight." Through every-thing, "he remained a loyal servant, ready to sacrifice everything for his monarch."[73] Should his duke have fallen, the paper asserted elsewhere, he would have "accompanied him as a beggar throughout German lands, declaring the shame to the German people."[74]

To support claims like Johst's, the *Völkischer Beobachter* tapped not into Goethe's works of poetry but, again, into selected portions of conversations with Eckermann and others. Thus, "freedom consists not in refusing to recognize anything above us, but in respecting something which is above us"[75] was offered as a rejection of equalitarian notions of liberty. Further, since Goethe was himself "a Minister of a German state," one collection of quotations opened, he also knew how to think as a statesman – as expressed in lines such as: "What is important is not that something is torn down, but that something is constructed";[76] "The biggest need of a state is that of a brave authority";[77] and "I cannot believe in the wisdom of majority resolutions. All that is great and clever exists only in the minority. Reason will never become popular. Passions and feelings may become popular, but reason will always be the possession of some elite."[78]

As in the case of Goethe, *Völkischer Beobachter*'s treatment of Schiller had to deal with his reactions to the French Revolution. This approach required rendering interpretations of his works as politically motivated, in the main, which allowed the paper to connect the author with its aesthetic of action rather than reflection (Figure 7.2). The paper did refer to Schiller's "unhappy youth" before 1789, but largely as a way to explain away his initially positive outlook toward developments in

Figure 7.2 *Völkischer Beobachter*, Friedrich Schiller tribute page, 10 November 1934

France. F. O. H. Schulz, author of *The Downfall of Marxism* (1933) and *Jew and Worker: A Chapter from the Tragedy of the German Volk* (1934) – both of which made it into Hitler's personal library[79] – surveyed Schiller's path to a "German conception of freedom" as follows. Because the terrible experiences of Schiller's Stuttgart youth affected him deeply, he greeted the French Revolution as a "redemption." Even so, he was far from being a "Frenchy" (*Französling*). He despised the "literary windbags" among the French writers of that time: Voltaire and his followers disgusted him. In fact, shortly before the outbreak of the revolution he had "even discovered a series of errors in his favorite, Rousseau." Nevertheless, he hoped that the "great popular uprising" (*Volksbewegung*) on the other side of the Vosges mountains would lead to a "wholesome social renewal." When, however, the first news of "mob rule" arrived and when he heard that they also wanted to drag the king and his family onto the "efficiently operating guillotine," he sat down to write a defense of the king. Without letting him know about it, though, the revolutionaries appointed Schiller as a "citizen of the Republic." When he found out, he decided to "use the whole weight of his personality" for the rescue of the royal family. But he failed to arrive before the execution, and thereupon "rejected the 'rights' given him with disgust." He then, according to Schulz, became an anti-revolutionary – shifting his emphasis on individualism to a nationalistic notion of liberty: "When the revolutionaries then started violating their own bloodless ideas and began to export their bloody praxis over the borders and to rape the people of Europe, Schiller began to go the way of the Kantian concept that the idea of freedom is connected indissolubly with the idea of the Fatherland."[80]

Angered by the excesses of the French Revolution, but above by all the rise of Napoleon and the invasion of German lands – the *Völkischer Beobachter*'s H. Krause continued elsewhere – Schiller warned his countrymen of bad times to come if they did not act. "Fierceness and deep pain filled him, and in grief he called out to his Volk that shame and terrible suffering would come down on all Germans for all time, if they were not capable of freeing themselves from Europe's Angel of Death." He looked on "with hatred" as the world was conquered by Napoleon while German princes honored him. He scorned and held in contempt those who "defamed the hereditary crown of its aristocracy, who bowed before foreign gods, who rendered treasure to Brits and finery to the Franks."[81] As a result, while other Germans ignored these realities, he called for "patriotic love and action." The thought of state unity seemed hopeless: scholars and artists escaped either into antiquity or the Middle Ages; nobody expected anything of the present. But in Schiller's *Das Lied von der Glocke* (1799) and *Wallenstein* (1799), "the German face appeared – conveying the hope that Germany would live and that an undefeatable spirit would serve as the noble vessel for a strong power." Schiller recognized that the flight of most poets into art – their aversion from the realities of political life – was impossible under these circumstances: "the moral-reasonable man and his liberating ideals could only unfold in a free Fatherland." Schiller saw that "no Volk is given freedom, but it must be demanded forcefully and fought for." Through his work on *Wallenstein, Maria Stuart* (1800), the *Maid of Orleans*, and the *Bride of Messina* (1803) this political outlook "matured to the point where he could create *Wilhelm Tell* [1804]." And it was this work – above all – that conveyed the "need to fight for national freedom."[82]

Schiller was a rationalist, Krause allowed, but as such "perceived Germans alone as having a mission to take control of world developments." Here he recognized the "essence of human history," and thence lived in the certainty that the "Volk which most believed in itself would fulfill a great world historical mission." He "gave this mission to the German people in the certainty that Germany would take the lead." Therefore, his notion of the progress of humanity was not an example of universalist Enlightenment thinking, but applied to Germans alone. He wanted the "*German* Reich of humanity, which would embody the power of the spirit over the power of the earth." He did not wish that all the peoples of the world would celebrate this humanity: "only in his own Volk did he want to awaken a life full of brotherly love and brotherly care." Therefore, he was not an apostle of universal humanism, but of German volkishness and nationalism:

> All should dedicate themselves to such work, that unity and freedom will be achieved and secured for all time, through goodness and justice among all those who speak the same language. To express this most clearly today is our holy duty to this poet who was so full of glowing love for his Volk, but whom one wants to make into an apostle for universal human fraternity.[83]

As in the cases of Goethe and Schiller, the *Völkischer Beobachter* also rejected any suggestion that Beethoven had been a supporter of modern democratic ideals, asserting instead that he recognized the need for autocratic leadership and would have seconded their call for the strong hand of a Führer. Ludwig Schiedermair stipulated for the paper that Beethoven had "no absolute hatred of aristocrats," then went on to point out that the composer had been enthralled with Napoleon's charisma and domineering tactics: what made him enthusiastic about Napoleon was that "the Corsican had with a strong hand transformed the chaos of the gruesome revolution into state order." Ultimately, Schiedermair argued, Beethoven feared chaos brought on by revolution, thus recognizing that authoritarian rule was occasionally necessary. He "did not close his mind to understanding that in special times of anarchical uprising an oligarchic aristocracy had its attractions."[84]

Thus, is it clear that the *Völkischer Beobachter* strove mightily to demonstrate that the main German creative figures who were exposed to the French Revolution ultimately remained immune to its "fever." However, in this context, the arts section of the paper did not restrict itself to extolling German creators alone as anti-revolutionary heroes. In addition, *Völkischer Beobachter* editors and contributors frequently paid homage to the German political thinkers they held as being the first to oppose the doctrines of the "French disease." In Johann Heinrich Pestalozzi, Johann Gottlieb Fichte, Johann Gottfried von Herder, Wilhelm von Humboldt, and others, it identified influential advocates for a series of reforms that were intended to strengthen Prussia for a "war of liberation." Honoring them as the first consciously volkish thinkers whose ideas would feed directly into Nazism, the paper dedicated thousands of words to acclaiming the ideas and policies of these political leaders.[85] We will not survey this facet of the paper's coverage in the same proportion it received in its own pages, but it is important to recognize the pride of place these individuals had in the history of ideas according to the *Völkischer Beobachter*.

Though admitting that his "pedagogical ideas came to him in his homeland, Switzerland," the *Völkischer Beobachter* presented Pestalozzi (1746–1827) as a "German thinker." Moreover, according to Wilhelm Westphal, it was Prussian reformers who actually put Pestalozzi's theories to practical use. Indeed, Fichte devoted the second and third of his "unforgettable" *Speeches to the German Nation* (1806–1807) to discussion of Pestalozzi's ideas, and identified Germany as "the place to implement them." Westphal asserted that "Prussia's liberation" came faster because of the "great reorganization of the Prussian-German

Volkschul system in the spirit of Pestalozzi's ideas." For Westphal, Pestalozzi's great historical contribution was that on the basis of his ideas, "Prussian masses received their basic training so that they might become material out of which the three great architects – Bismarck, Roon, and Moltke – could construct the Second Reich." Prussian school-masters who trained according to his ideas were the ones who won the wars from 1864 to 1871. According to Westphal, Pestalozzi dedicated himself to his work "with almost demonic passion, never thinking of himself, but only of people that needed help." He thus was the very model of a "truly socialist man." More than just respect, "love and admiration fill us when we think of his personality and his struggle," Westphal continued: "especially today when it is a matter of overcoming Liberal individualism, it is very attractive to consider this man."

With regard to Pestalozzi's writings, at least, what Westphal found most attractive to consider were two brief passages selected from his total output. In the first of these, Westphal drew attention to a single line devoted to matters of racial pride: "Not the ego, but the race! That is the imperative expression of the sacred voice in the self; the only nobility in human nature lies in perceiving and obeying it." Next, excerpting from an illustrated book for children, *Figuren zu meinem ABC-Buch* (1797), Westphal highlighted Pestalozzi's complaints about Jews "nest-ing" in a small town, "making themselves rich and the town poor." So, despite the acclaim accorded to Pestalozzi for his contributions to the Prussian educational system and its military successes, it was his concern about the impact of the Jews on village life that the *Völkischer Beobachter* found most compelling and worthy of excerpting.[86]

Among the other Prussian reformers, the *Völkischer Beobachter* presented Fichte (1762–1814) as one of the greatest "initiators of real volkish thinking." For the paper, Fichte's "main demand" was the "transformation of the Germans into a Volk." Aligned with this agenda, he took up political, social, moral, philosophical, and religious matters "in order to attain a thorough renewal of Volk conviction" – above all, through the control of selfish impulses "under the idea of the whole" and through the "national education of the German Volk." Fichte's challenge applied to all: "to youth, to the aged, to the high and low; to the rulers and the Volk; to the men of finance and to the thinkers – all at the same time." According to him, "our descendants will live in vain – their history will be determined by their conquerors – if we do not ensure that our spiritual life is renewed from top to bottom."[87] Moreover, the paper found value in Fichte's anti-Semitic views. For instance, it quoted the following from *Contribution to the Rectification of the Public's Judgment of the French Revolution* (1793–1794) without comment – despite the fact that the bulk of the work was a defense of French revolutionary principles:

> *In almost every nation of Europe a powerful, hostile state is spreading itself which stands in constant war against all the others and in some already presses hard on the citizens: it is the Jews. What is terrible is that I do not think ... it is aimed at building a separate state, but that this state is based on hatred toward all of humanity.*[88]

Elsewhere in the paper, Konrad Karkosch – a literature and later film expert – agreed with Fichte's call for national education as the basis for the Volk, but felt that Fichte's ideas had to be modified. Fichte "believed a little too much in the omnipotence of education," argued Karkosch, as the main "precondition for the ascendance of Germany." For the education of the youth of the Third Reich, however, said Karkosch, "inheritance studies" (*Erblehre*) and "racial science" (*Rassenforschung*) had shown how much significance "spiritual inheritance" had. Thus, a reformed educational system could no longer be based solely on educational criteria, but had to emphasize "biological character." "Racial selection" (*Auslese*), said Karkosch, would be a "necessary part of any reformed educational system." Such an approach amounted to a means for "improving the gene pool of the German Volk though broad-based race care" (*Rassenpflege*), and at the same time served as the "precondition for building healthy and appropriate character education." In a "biologically based education," the strength of the body, the strength of character, and the power of knowledge become "an organic unit." Fichte's great achievement was his contribution to "a biologically based *Bildung* – a truly Volk education – that would be perfected for the first time" under Nazism.[89]

The *Völkischer Beobachter* took a similar interest in Herder (1744–1803). Though best known as a romantic philosopher, the paper held that, like Fichte, Herder's "most important role" was that of an "initiator of volkish movement." Theodor Stiefenhofer, author of a number of patriotic German literary histories, argued that the eighteenth century had led to a "dangerous crisis": the "internationalist intellectual movement of the Enlightenment spilled out all over Europe and washed up

against German life with its icy cold breath." At the crucial point, however, Herder "took up the fight for the renewal of the old *Volksgeist*" and
tried to direct the "cultural and creative life of the nation down the eternal
path again." Sensing a coming catastrophe that threatened to "dry up the
German and European life-dream," Herder wanted to protect the human
spirit from "excess and degeneration" and bind it again to the "natural
life – to the unconscious forces of the organic which he saw endangered
by the Enlightenment." Above all, he "sharply castigated the utter disintegration of German things," writing in *From the German Museum* (1777):
"Great, strong Volk! It gave customs, laws, and inventions to Europe"
but "we poor Germans have always been determined never to remain true
to ourselves: always legislator and servant to foreign nations ... their
exhausted, bleeding, burnt-out slaves."

  With all the force given him, Stiefenhofer continued, Herder
"braced himself" against the intellectual character of his time. With
pain and annoyance, he traced how the ruling classes shifted the "original substance of Germanness toward the flat mediocrity of intellectualism" and thereby undermined national character. Recognizing that the
German essence was founded on feelings and moods, he deemed "longing" (*Sehnsucht*) to be the "greatest driving force" of the German people.
This was particularly true in the spirit of German artists: "dynamism,
passion, emotion, and faith" drove them from German Romanticism
onward. Only through the emotional application of this "strong imagination and earth-bound will" could the Volk overcome the "rationally
determined ethics of success" established by the Enlightenment.

  Thus was Herder's "revolutionary battle cry for original genius
to be understood," according to Stiefenhofer, with which he attacked the
"almost omnipotent" Enlightenment movement. Working from a "deep
fount of original ideas," he saw forces and tendencies far beyond the
average thinking of his contemporaries – like "storm clouds and lightning on the far horizon." Burning these thoughts into the hearts of the
Storm and Stress generation, Stiefenhofer concluded, Herder remained
a great name "on the rolls of German fighting, German strength, and
German faith – an inspirational, exciting symbol in the time of our
decisive volkish battle."[90]

  As for Wilhelm von Humboldt (1767–1835), as it was for so
many cultural figures the paper featured within its pages, *Völkischer
Beobachter* editors revealed a strong preference to depict Humboldt's
significance as more political than academic. To do so, rather than focus

on Humboldt's philosophical or linguistic works, or on his accomplishments as founder of Humboldt Universität in Berlin, it instead chose to reprint excerpts from letters he wrote to his wife during the Napoleonic wars, featuring strong German patriotic sentiments like the following:[91]

> *There is no country which deserves to be as independent and free as Germany, because none is called to its freedom so intently and purely through such charitable efforts. Of all nations the German has the least destructive and the most constructive power within itself, and if it wins possession of its liberty, Germany will very soon stand out in every area of education and conviction. That is why it is so gratifying to work for the Fatherland ... The love of Germany is therefore quite different than that which other nations have for their Fatherland ... It is not mere attachment to the earth, it is more longing after German spirit and feeling. [To his wife, Karoline, 8 November 1813]*

On this basis, literary historian Adolf Hösel – author of a 1928 book on Nietzsche and Richard Dehmel[92] – strongly associated Humboldt with "German views of the state." Contrary to Enlightenment notions, his view was that "no state constitution could succeed if based wholly on reason according to a pre-established plan." Where time and nature had not prepared, "constitutions could not be grafted upon men as sprigs upon trees." These and similar statements showed Humboldt to be "in opposition with the ideas of the French Revolution." Hösel felt Humboldt's essential contribution was to shift from being a "rationalistic Enlightenment thinker to ... a carrier of historical truth – i.e., not reason and individualism, but community and the laws of living events that unfold within it." Opposing Enlightenment notions, he was a proponent of the "state in great style" who saw "one great task for the future that applied directly to the present": Germany had to be "free and strong, not just so that it can defend itself against this or that neighbor, but because only an externally strong nation retains the spirit from which all benedictions flow." Thus, concluded Hösel, Humboldt's views were "completely in accord with our conception today."[93]

Similarly, the paper insisted that the Prussian statesman, Heinrich von Stein (1757–1831), was a "far from liberal," volkish thinker. With "every fiber of his being," Hanns Ebner asserted, Stein was "reverently and faithfully bound to his Volk and Fatherland." It was for this reason that he wanted to support what he considered to be the main "social foundation" of the Volk: the farming community that was "wasting itself away by following foreign ways of life." Instead of modernizing, he wanted to return to "native traditions." Therefore, only "liberal perversions," Ebner argued, could claim that Stein was "infected by the mad doctrines of 1789 and motivated by the Enlightenment concepts of liberty, equality, and fraternity."[94] The paper also presented Stein as anti-Semitic, explaining that when the Prussian Maritime Enterprise (*Preussische Seehandlung*) – a banking institution established by Friedrich II – was "gradually taken over by Jews," Stein complained about this, referring to "the cunning, perseverance … and avarice of Jewish bankers [that had] a pernicious effect in every state and is particularly detrimental to the world of bureaucrats." As part of intensive efforts to showcase the anti-Semitic record of all its heroes, the paper printed these passages in italics, editorializing that one could see here that it was "once again the Jews" who took what was originally a great undertaking such as the Preussische Seehandlung, "undercut it, transformed it into a ruinous institution, and then plundered it." Based on his response, it was apparent that Stein was "fully conscious of the danger that Jewry posed for Prussia," and of the measures necessary to deal with it.[95]

While the focus of this investigation into the culture-based propaganda of the *Völkischer Beobachter* is on its treatment of creative artists and its works, these few examples do represent the fact that in its pages, those political leaders and theorists who first confronted "the mad doctrines of 1789" were posited as the modern sources of specifically political ideals that Hitler addressed when referring to the "essential principles" that the NSDAP, in formulating its doctrine, extracted from "the general conception of the world based on the Volk idea" – and which were therefore "suited to the purpose of uniting in a common front all those who are ready to accept them as principles."[96] This second part of the book will now turn to an examination of the paper's promotion of romantic culture as the most important response to the Western rationalist tradition, especially in "steely" forms said to have emerged during the "Wars of Liberation." These political examples notwithstanding, it was in artistic responses to Napoleonic occupation of German lands that *Völkischer Beobachter* contributors perceived the origins of volkish *Kultur* which, they felt, anticipated Nazi tastes and values.

8 FORGING STEEL ROMANTICISM

The appropriation of the German romantic tradition – with its attendant rejection of Western attitudes toward reason and rationalist structure – is a well-known feature of National Socialism's cultural constitution.[1] Significantly, however, Nazis were selective in their borrowing, and resisted inclusion of certain "modernist" aspects of Romanticism that they saw as fostering luxuriation in psychological self-indulgence. Goebbels, most openly, stipulated that there were various Romanticisms and that the Nazi version was a "steely" (*stählernde*) variation with no room for the dreamier and even ironic aspects of the trend:[2]

> *Every time has its Romanticism, its poetic presentation of*
> *life – ours does as well. It is harder and crueler than the earlier*
> *version, but it is just as romantic. The Steel Romanticism*
> *of our time manifests itself in intoxicating actions and restless*
> *deeds in service of a great national goal, in a feeling of duty*
> *raised to the level of an unbreakable principle. We are*
> *all more or less romantics of a new German form.*[3]

Neither the yearning of a young Werther nor the madness of a Kapellmeister Kreisler would survive in Goebbels' romantic ideal:

> *Instead of an exhausted lassitude that capitulates to, denies,*
> *or flees from the seriousness of life, a heroic view of life steps*
> *forth and sounds out in the marching steps of brown columns,*

accompanying the farmer as he pulls the plowshare through fields, giving the worker meaning and higher purpose in its difficult struggle for existence, never leaving the unemployed in despair, and furnishing the great work of German reconstruction with an almost soldierly rhythm. It is a kind of Steel Romanticism that has made German life worth living: a Romanticism which does not try to escape and hide in the blue distance from the hardness of existence – a Romanticism which rather has the courage to confront problems and stare into their pitiless eyes without flinching. This new attitude gives Germany tempo and power for its constructive work … Only pure artistic and cultural striving, willingly and wholeheartedly filled with it, will last to conquer the future.[4]

Moving from early nationalist political thinkers and activists, and working to underscore the steelier aspects of romantic culture, the *Völkischer Beobachter* concentrated on romantic poets who directly engaged with the politics of the Napoleonic era in their lives and through their works. The newspaper placed particular emphasis on Ernst Moritz Arndt and Heinrich Kleist, both of whom it could immediately associate with early volkish and anti-French attitudes. But reverence for activist poets was merely the first step toward claiming the whole romantic tradition as the inherited legacy of Nazi culture.

H. Sturm, author of *Experiences of a Volunteer, with Particular Relevance for German Youth* (1915), a book that had encouraged the spirit of volunteerism in juvenile audiences during the First World War, set out to prove that Arndt (1769–1860) was a proto-volkish thinker. For Sturm, "although the word *völkisch* was not yet known," one had to designate Arndt the "first great volkish thinker." In expressing his love for Germany, he set forth the "volkish idea of a unified German state." Beyond this, Sturm noted that Arndt addressed the Jewish Question "to the point where he was called a barbarian and a man eater by his opponents." But such behavior was "properly volkish," Sturm held: Arndt could not imagine the German state as anything but a Christian state, and the Jews – "with their gruff way of repudiating everyone else" – remained completely outside Christendom.

Further, according to Sturm, Arndt described modern Jewry as a "degenerate Volk" and "judged correctly the Jewish danger for the

Germans." Referring to their "wheeler-dealer spirit," he recognized the threat to German morality posed by "a people compelled to follow the apostles of liberalism and cosmopolitanism." Further, "one should forbid and prevent the import of strangers into Germany," Arndt said. "The admission of foreign Jews is a disaster and a plague on our people." Based on these views, Sturm explained, Arndt's position was twofold: first, that Jews who were resident or born in Germany should be neither oppressed nor persecuted, but absorbed; second, that one should prohibit the inflow of other Jewish elements by means of the strongest legal measures available. Sturm had qualms about the first point, but he reminded that even if Arndt set up a program for assimilating the existing Jewish population, he did not underestimate the "racial significance of mixing blood." One could not forget, Sturm explained, that Jewry had not yet "assumed such monstrous forms" in Arndt's era as it had by the Nazi era. That fact, for Sturm, explained Arndt's relative optimism about assimilating Jews already living in German territories – a position "which he would certainly have adjusted in light of later developments."[5] Moreover, according to volkish writer, Theodore Stiefenhofer, Arndt could be counted not only as an anti-Semite, but also as an early *racial* thinker. In his view, Arndt often engaged in making comparisons of respective national characteristics everywhere: the "structure, growth, face, features, and gestures of human types interested him intensely." So, although written at a time when the methods of making such observations had not yet been formalized, Arndt's assembled works offered a "treasure trove" of racial observations and conclusions. This alone, Stiefenhofer held, made him "one of the greatest Volk educators of the Germans."[6] Finally, in Sturm's view, two quotes of Arndt had "particular meaning and usefulness" for those who experienced the difficult times of the late Weimar Republic. First, "Existence is not and should not be eternal war; but it involves struggle and fighting, and always will, if we don't want to go to sleep"; and second: "Whoever gives up on himself, will be given up on; the Volk that despairs of itself, will be despaired of by the world, and history will be eternally silent about it. Our Volk is within each of us – therefore, we must remain strong!"[7]

The anniversary of Arndt's 75th *Todestag* occurred in 1935, giving the paper an opportunity to revisit his legacy in light of Hitler's rise to power. According to Adolf Hösel's commemorative article, Arndt was for Nazis not just the "Poet of the Wars of Liberation" – a historical figure who defended German honor at the time of

Napoleonic foreign rule – but a "life philosopher of prophetic greatness whose works continued to be of value." Nazis had the right to claim that his "passionate and forward-looking spirit" was active among them. Reference to the "deepest content" of Arndt's thought illustrated this assertion, Hösel insisted: more than a hundred years earlier, Arndt prophetically announced the unification of Volk and state, which Nazis were "presently in the position to establish and finally perfect." His views "coordinated with ours almost exactly, when he described the Volk as a living organism and even compared the growth of a state, grounded in the laws of nature, with the organic development of a tree that drives its roots as deeply as possible into the earth so that it will reach higher and wider above." More specifically, Arndt voiced the "protest of German people against the threat of Western influences." He saw the danger that the French Revolution and its ideology held for Europe; he foresaw the calamity that sooner or later the peoples would experience under the rule of "exaggerated reason based on natural law" and the "progressive dissolution of all holy structures and orders." In Arndt's volkish opinion, it would only be possible to construct a "healthy, organically arranged state on the soil of natural growth which was stamped with the mental shape of a Volk," just as Nazis claimed to be doing.[8]

In 1938, as the *Anschluss* of Austria proceeded, the *Völkischer Beobachter* invoked Arndt's pan-German views again, this time to justify the *Grossdeutsch* option being implemented. In a series of articles on "Great Germans Discussing Greater Germany," the paper stated that for Arndt the "idea of whole Germany was a self-evident inner obligation as long as the German tongue sounded and God sang songs in heaven." He knew very well that the German character was multifaceted, and marked by various "tribes" (*Stämme*), but he did not see this as cause for political division: rather, he "decided for German wholeness."[9] Beyond unification, the paper presented Arndt as anticipating other foreign policy developments as "inevitable." According to Sturm, Arndt considered it "self-evident" that Alsace would ultimately return to the Reich, and that Belgium would be the entry point for war between Germany and France – "regardless of which side used it as such, it would not be able to remain neutral."[10]

Once the conflict resulting from such policies peaked, Stiefenhofer turned again to Arndt, but this time as an author of motivational wartime poetry. "What German does not know Arndt's blazing calls from the time of the Wars of Liberation?" Stiefenhofer asked in 1944: "Whose heart is not moved by the eternal songs, *The God Who Gave Man Iron* or *What is the German Fatherland?* – songs that continue to serve as reminders of German spirit even in our days!" In the midst of "our decisive volkish battle," said Stiefenhofer, Arndt's works sounded as a warning: "We should look great times straight in the eye; we should understand their terribleness and their glory, so that we can rise to their height and accomplish their holy will … Freedom cannot be lost as long as smithies hammer iron."[11]

But the *Völkischer Beobachter* was not done with Arndt. In March 1945, it was driven again to recycle the author's patriotic statements in a desperate effort to show that the present chaos would ultimately lead to something better – that all had "not been for naught":

> *The world lies in chaotic ruins, all elements are fighting, all forces, all spirits, these are the signs and prophecies of great acts and tremendous beginnings – have faith: they are for you! Not in vain have you seen such storms and hurricanes; not in vain have you seen such earthquakes and volcanoes of the time; not in vain has your unhappy Fatherland been flooded with their fiery ashes and bloody flows of lava. Believe! This time is your time … I will see you, my Holy Land; crowned with victory, crowned with freedom, I will hear your eagle's sounding flight; I already see you, I already hear him; even if my dust mixes with that of those who have fallen, I will see my Germania from the stars!*

And that one must continue to be willing to die for one's Volk:

> *Völker as a whole may not be willing to die, as the individual must in order to save his Volk. Völker must will themselves to live – and prove their will to life as a totality precisely through the willingness of individuals to die.*

Thus was Arndt's brand of Steel Romanticism invoked to motivate the *Volkssturm* in the last months of 1945 – or at least to justify forcing its conscripts to sacrifice themselves.

A similar strategy served the Nazi paper in its handling of Heinrich von Kleist (1777–1811), for it was not Kleist's poetry and drama that the paper deemed worthy of attention, but rather his military background and service, and then his engagement with German politics as a journalist in the Napoleonic era. For instance, a 1926 biographical summary highlighted the fact that Kleist was descended from a Prussian officer's family. Following this tradition, he joined the army and participated in the 1796 invasion of France. Having served for three years, "only gradually did he become comfortable again with the hard realities of life in his homeland." He worked in the Königsberg Diet, but gave up the life of a state official after two years. In 1807 – under French occupation – he was arrested by the French as a spy in Dresden and spent some "difficult months" in prison. Above all, this political biography emphasized, the defeat of Prussia by Napoleon "shook him to the core; he lived only for the thought that his Fatherland might be liberated."

It was in this mood that Kleist wrote his "powerful drama of liberty, *Die Hermannsschlacht* [*Hermann's Battle*, 1808], which used the war of Germanic tribes against the Romans to show his people how to shake off the foreign yolk." According to the paper, Kleist "wanted to be the national poet of the Germans"; freed in 1808, he intended to put out a patriotic weekly, *Germania* – which was, in Kleist's words, to have been the "first breath of German freedom" – but the defeat of Austria by Napoleon in 1809 foiled this plan. Instead, starting in 1810, he produced the *Berliner Abendblätter* – the first daily newspaper of the Prussian capital. In its pages he documented the "pitiful incompetence of the Prussian leaders of the day." Surrounded by "severely demoralized Berliners, some of whom had reconciled themselves to French rule, he stood up for the Fatherland, for the monarchy, and for religion," and with its "rousing, glowing style, inspired by genuine ardor," his paper outstripped liberal and democratic papers that were "groveling before the French."[12]

Remarkably, thus far in this *Völkischer Beobachter* survey of Kleist's life, there appeared no mention of his creative work other than its reference to *Hermann's Battle*. Despite the fact that by 1811, Kleist had produced a number of important poems, stories, and plays, including *Die Familie Schroffenstein* (1803); an adaptation of Molière's *Amphitryon* (1807); *Penthesiliea*, about the love of the queen of the Amazons for Achilles (1808); a one-act comedy, *The Broken Pitcher* (1808); *Michael Kohlhaas*, *The Earthquake in Chile*, and *The Marquise von O* (all published in a 1810–1811 collection), Nazi focus remained on his political journalism alone. Moreover, according to Hans Lucke, "Kleist the journalist was never a theoretician," just a "passionate political fighter" who called for the "unification of all Germanness" into a community which could "only be brought to its grave at the cost of blood that would darken the sun."[13]

Ultimately, the stridency of Kleist's strong positions led to the demise of the *Abendblätter*. But, the *Völkischer Beobachter* insinuated that other forces were working against Kleist in the background. His publisher, Julius Hitzig, betrayed him, "since he was a Jew."[14] On top of this "chicanery" were added "poisonous attacks" by the Jewish writer and "dirty bastard," Saul Ascher. In articles appearing in various papers, this "prince of darkness" "unloaded on Kleist in every possible way." Despite his heroic efforts, Kleist could only hold on to the *Berliner Abendblätter* until 11 April 1811, when "the cowardice of the officials and the conspiracy of the Jews triumphed." In despair, Kleist shot Henriette Vogel at the Wahnsee by mutual agreement, and then himself. This was cause enough, the *Völkischer Beobachter* added, for "the Jew Ascher to write a perfidious article calling Kleist a murderer." To counter him, the "German writers" Joseph Eichendorff and, later, Friedrich Hebbel produced "beautiful and respectful tributes to the unhappy poet."[15]

Thus did the main line of *Völkischer Beobachter* reception of Kleist run: primarily as a celebration of a patriotic journalist's career thwarted by traitors and Jews. Beyond this, a great amount of attention was devoted to the circumstances of Kleist's suicide. According to Otto Gervais, author of a history of women in the circles of Friedrich the Great, no one had been able to clarify the ultimate reasons for Kleist's suicide, but "it wouldn't be a mistake to suppose that ideal and real, economic and mental causes combined to prepare this demonic-mystical life for an end." The "disgraceful state of the Fatherland, the discord between state and religion, the rejection of friends, Goethe's cold-hearted and destructive judgment, his failure as a poet, and the hopelessness of his efforts to call for an uprising of the nation," all these disappointments brought him to "convert calm resolve into deed, once he found a companion for the path into the redemptive unknown."[16]

But while the paper did mention some of these other factors, it favored attributing Kleist's suicide to his depression over the state of Germany. Most strongly, Josef Stolzing held that Kleist – "one of the most noble of Germans" – took his own life in despair over the "languishing and humiliation of his Fatherland." In Stolzing's view, the effective cause of the suicide was essentially political. The hopes that Kleist harbored after the 1809 Austrian victory over Napoleon at Aspern were not realized. Austria was not in a position to stand and carry the flag alone; Prussia did not yet have the courage to pick up the fight and march against Napoleon; and "the rest of Germany slept." The uprising against the French emperor that Kleist had hoped for would only come about later, when the "flames of burning Moscow flickered over the snowy fields of Russia." Like "every genuinely great poet," Kleist was a patriot, but the Prussian army was defeated and destroyed, and he saw his people "in deepest disgrace under the chains of Corsican foreign rule." Consequently "in despair, he completed the last act of his tragic life."[17]

Stolzing was joined in his convictions about the factors that led to Kleist's suicide by Hellmut Langenbucher, an author of literary histories who served as principal of the German Publishers and Booksellers Association (*Börsenverein des Deutschen Buchhandels*) who was a regular *Völkischer Beobachter* contributor,[18] and who would later head Rosenberg's Office for the Cultivation of Literature (*Amt Schrifttungspflege*) – accomplishments that earned him the moniker in the Third Reich of the "pope of literature." Langenbucher advised that anyone unable to grasp the "sense of tragedy in the life of a poet, soldier, and German who was overflowing with flaming energy," should "just leave him alone!" In Langenbucher's opinion, Kleist sank "under the burden of demonic impatience"; an "endlessly disappointed passionate belief in his times and in his Volk." His was a "brazen will that didn't flinch in the battle for its Volk," choosing death over life in slavery. His gruesome fate was the tragedy of a "poet without a Volk": the Volk "let him starve and freeze, leaving him in a night of boundless despair." The time was not yet ripe for Kleist, Langenbucher mourned, whose works would "give poetic form" to the era *after* the great *Völkerschlacht* near Leipzig in 1813.[19]

To the extent that the *Völkischer Beobachter* did credit Kleist as a literary artist, it limited its recognition to Kleist's role as the poet of German liberation from Napoleonic control. Langheinrich called him "the great poet of Prussianness" and ultimately the "most direct dramatic genius of the German Volk," adding that there was "something of the spirit of Friedrich the Great in the fighting titan, Kleist, because they both faced disputes in their own camps while leading bitter wars against external enemies."[20] And so, it is not surprising that among Kleist's works, it was *Hermann's Battle*, Kleist's play about German tribesmen defeating Roman invaders in the Teutoburger Forest, which the *Völkischer Beobachter* treated as his main work. According to Stolzing, this drama arose at the same time that the Hapsburg Empire first stood up against "the invincible one" to hand him his first setback at Aspern. As a result, Kleist's "fiery soul had new hope," so he dedicated the "joyous poem to the glorious victory." Though *Hermann's Battle* never appeared on stage during Kleist's lifetime, Stolzing added, "when anxious cares trouble us; when we are filled with gnawing fear for the German future; when we see how the god Loge – always busy, even in our days – divides German hearts with hatred and dissention; when we have the grim need to hate, then we reach for Kleist, for his *Hermannsschlacht*!" There the hero throws himself into battle "with the fury of one of those Germanic warriors that Roman writers tell us about: naked, swinging his weapon – just a heavy club – with sinewy fists."[21]

The *Völkischer Beobachter* did make minor references to aspects of Kleist's art other than political and military significance. E. Meunier wrote that Kleist's political works alone did not determine how great a poet he was, reminding readers what "unusually tight" short stories he produced: "how well every word fit, how gripping every scene, how lucid his language!" His *Broken Pitcher* was "most beautiful proof of the great, free, and easy soul that could have lived in the poet if the troubles of the time had not made him miserable and torn him apart." Likewise *Penthesiliea*: though "scorned as a sample of excessive imagination," only a very great writer could "risk this reproach and take on such a monumental form."[22] Into it he "poured all of the pain and radiance of his soul."[23] In the words of Hans Severus Ziegler – General Director of the Weimar National Theater, later curator of the Degenerate Music exhibition, and occasional poet of *Battle Sonnets for National Socialism*[24] – Kleist was "for us" the creator of the "storm and stressers" who were engaged in the "categorical imperative of duty." He was "for us" the creator of "true human beings of flesh and blood," the "admirable poet of the two opposites of female nature, Käthchen and Penthesiliea," the "poet of romantic mood magic," and finally the "consistent psychologist and the philosophically schooled thinker" through whom the "realistic dramas of the modern were introduced." Nazis, Ziegler claimed, were interested in the complete Kleist, "not just the nationalist, political herald; not just the ardent hater of Napoleon; but also the Kleist of the romantic *Käthchens von Heilbronn*; the comedic poet of the *Amphitron* and of the *Zerbrochenen Krug*; the novelist of

Michael Kohlhaas; the "mature, tragic poet of *Prinz von Homburg*; and likewise, the incomparable letter writer."[25]

Such assessments notwithstanding, throughout its coverage the paper mainly concentrated on – and reproduced – Kleist's patriotic works, such as the notorious *Germania an ihre Kinder* (*Germania to Her Children*):

> Color all the fields, all the towns
> White with their bones
> Those which the raven and the fox disdain
> Deliver over to the fish;
> Dam up the Rhine with their corpses.[26]

the *Kriegslied der Deutschen* (*Battle Song of the Germans*), with its final stanza:

> Only the Frenchman still shows himself
> In the German Empire;
> Brothers, take up the cudgel
> So that he also retreats.[27]

and especially the *Catechism for the Germans*, with its call for blind love of Germany:

Q: You love your Fatherland, don't you, my son?
A: Yes, my father, I do.
Q: Why do you love it?
A: Because it is my Fatherland.
Q: Do you mean because God has blessed it with many fruits, because He decorated it with many beautiful works of art, because innumerable heroes, leaders, and wise men have honored it?
A: No, my father, you are tricking me …
Q: So then, why do you love Germany?
A: I already told you, my father!
Q: You already told me?
A: Because it is my Fatherland.[28]

The paper's predominant tendency thus was to demonstrate how Kleist's romantic works leaned toward real historical and political affairs. According to Uwe Lars Nobbe, there were "profound reasons" that Kleist's oeuvre "received more attention, and was considered to have more value, in the National Socialist state than ever before." It was not just its "completely Germanic style," nor Kleist's nationalistic position – "patriotic in the best sense of the word." Without rest, "he alone steered Romanticism – the most German of all German art forms – toward the goal that its other followers saw but were never able to achieve, because they had weaker aesthetic constitutions." In this spirit he would always "stand close to and resonate with the German Volk as German art had to do." That was how Kleist had "remained modern to this day," when Nazis were "presenting his dramas throughout the land for the whole German Volk." All this, Nobbe explained, only became clear with the rise of Hitler.[29]

On the 150th anniversary of his birth, Josef Stolzing drew together the core elements of the Nazi interpretation of Kleist to articulate the poet's significance in the struggle against the perceived weaknesses of the Weimar Republic. Trying to rekindle the fervent patriotism that inspired *Hermann's Battle*, Stolzing lamented that the spirit of the poet had become a "faint spark threatened with extinction under the ashes of a weak age, unaccustomed to battle." If the spirit of this great German were still alive, then "German flags waving on the Rhine would again be flying inside *Welschenland* [France], the soil of Europe would be shaking under the threatening steps of hundreds of thousands of German men committed to either victory or final defeat, and Walhalla's light-streamed gates would be opening up to receive great crowds of new members!" In honor of the German nation, Stolzing went on, "thousands and thousands of pounding hearts" were awaiting the call to the "great bloodletting which we need in order to discharge the putrid blood which accumulated itself down in the domesticated strata as a result of the emasculating trickery of a restless dwarf race and foreign parasites who dominated through the power of gold." But the call had not yet sounded: compared with Kleist's "blood-curdling verses," the national songs that Germans were singing sounded weak. That's why Nazis "wished with all their hearts that Kleist's songs of battle – written in blood – would become the common property of all Germans again." We desperately need, Stolzing counseled, to "conjure the faded shadows of the immortal poet from their peaceful grave, to immerse ourselves in his imperishable life's work!"[30]

Ziegler seconded Stolzing, deeming Kleist a national hero even though he committed suicide, and then accommodating with extensive explanations of this apparent paradox. As Ziegler pointed out, "We have no other choice today than to turn to Kleist": he had to become the "people's property" once again, Ziegler held. This was especially so since the Jewish conspiracy of the day was proclaiming, in the words of the "Jewish Bolshevist," Ernst Toller, "Hoppla we live! Let the dead rest, Germans. Celebrate progress in the sign of Judas!" In such a time, "with spirit and soul in danger, conscientious Germans had to declare that they loved and needed Heinrich von Kleist more than ever" – despite his suicide. No one could "quibble about the manner of death of a man who had so completely fulfilled his sacred mission: Didn't he write every poem and play with his blood, and thus sacrifice himself for his nation?" Whoever leaves such a legacy behind can depart with a tranquil conscience and great courage. Even if the "long lost German land" couldn't fully revive, Nazis at least wanted to recover great German poets who had faded: they would provide moral strength for the later goal. That's how Ziegler understood Kleist's line: "The poet is born to the Volk so it can find itself when it is lost."[31]

Since it was "again time to begin preparing for military conflict," Langenbucher made even more explicit the lesson Germans had to learn from Kleist: "Enough of the old, dull image of Kleist that is still taught in many German schools … It is necessary for German youth to see in him a new beginning and raise his works as a banner in their battle for a better future for the German people."[32] On the 125th anniversary of the writer's death – which National Socialist Germany marked with a Kleist Week (which Rosenberg attended personally), and the renovation of the site on the Kleiner Wannsee where he took his life[33] – Hermann Claudius, a poet who received numerous literary awards in the Third Reich for works suffused with Nazi themes, produced a tribute poem honoring Kleist as the "most German" of all his contemporaries:

> You were the heart beat, all heart –
> Most German son of all Germans!
> The force of your work
> Stormed Germany.
> But your call was too sudden.
> It shocked and scared away
> Even the best.
> And you sank away …
> But not completely!

The force of your call
Has blasted the hill.
Today the Reich greets you!
Most German son of all Germans!
And the beat of your heart
Also beats in our breasts![34]

Völkischer Beobachter reception of Arndt and Kleist comes as little surprise, since both were strongly involved with the development of German nationalist culture during the Napoleonic era. While the Nazi paper did minimize the non-political aspects of their careers and works, its emphasis on the political and even militaristic motivations behind their creations was not inconsistent with long-standing traditions of interpreting these writers.[35] However, the *Völkischer Beobachter* also demonstrated a willingness to embrace romantics who were far less politically engaged, being more interested in spiritual flight from the exigencies of the revolutionary period. Consider, for example, the case of Johann Peter Hebel (1760–1826), the author of one of the most concise depictions of naive indifference to the world (*Weltfremdheit*) to appear in German literature. *Kannitverstan* is a very short story about a simpleton who learns important life lessons precisely because, while working in Holland, Dutchmen cannot understand a word he says, and vice versa. In the hands of Hermann Eris Busse, a prolific author of both ethnological studies and romantic fiction, Johann Peter Hebel's "vernacular poetry" was linked to "the language of the Volk." The way Hebel composed poetry, Busse held, was "the way the Volk talked, acted, laughed, loved, reflected, prayed, and lived." Likewise, in his collection of verse in Alemannic dialect, *Alemannische Gedichte* (1803), Hebel used a language "similar to the original text of the *Nibelungenlied*," formulated before the development of High German. Thus, he remained close to original Volk language, composing like the "source of a spring bubbles: strongly, clearly, and refreshingly." Above all, Busse concluded, the "delicious, informative story" of *Kannitverstan* – written in a "purity of language never before achieved" – belonged in the "iron collection of world literature."[36]

Despite the clear Nazi preference for the steely side of Romanticism – coupled with the significance that the *Völkischer Beobachter* typically placed on an artist's engagement in the politics of his time – so eager were the paper's editors to appropriate romantics that they occasionally consorted with apolitical dreamers. Such was the case with the paper's treatment of that most "otherworldly" Romantic author, Jean Paul Richter (1763–1825). Gustav Christian Rassy summarized Jean Paul's life and significance for the newspaper, concluding that if one thought in terms of gardening, he could be considered a gardener who "cared less for neatly raked paths and sections carefully measured out with a compass, concentrating solely on growth and blossoming." In contrast to the mathematical order of French gardens, Rassy went on, the messiness of Jean Paul's was "entirely German": if one had a taste for quiet moments, "one could meet fairies in his."[37] And as Christian Friedrich Hebbel put it, "explaining Jean Paul is like explaining fog." But the paper still wanted to make Jean Paul out to be political. Thus, in a body of work that included such complex and irrational novels as *The Awkward Age* (1793) and *Titan* (1801–1802), it was a pair of political statements that the *Völkischer Beobachter* decided were most deserving of recognition and saw fit to publish under the subtitle *Political Creed*. First, a statement of general patriotism:

> *There are seasons of political weather: decisive points for governments which come from above. Germany is now working in one of these times ... For Germany has suffered hardest and longest, and only in Germany have the lands been plowed under for centuries by the cannon wheels of nations: now lying fallow and growing weeds, fresh bloom and full growth promise, despite foreign intentions.*[38]

Then, an expression of hope for a "national idea and savior":

> *But what wins in the end? The idea! Whether it is a love of Fatherland or sense of freedom, or honor or religious belief or the devotion to a great man who personifies freedom or a whole Fatherland and who draws the spirits of the world together with the spirit world. If such a savior were given to the state only once in a while, then it wouldn't need a standing army and its only job would be to maintain the peace.*[39]

One of the most remarkable detours the *Völkischer Beobachter* made through dreamy side of Romanticism appeared in August and

September 1923, when the paper published in serial format the complete text of E. T. A. Hoffmann's 1817 short story, *The Deserted House*. In this macabre tale, the story's protagonist, aided by a magic mirror and a mind-reading Mesmerist physician, succeeds in unraveling the mystery of the eponymous house and its shadowy inhabitants. In response, his friends praise him as one who indeed has a "bat-like sixth sense for the deep reality of inscrutable secrets surrounding us."[40] However, despite such an exception as printing Hoffmann's disorienting tale, the paper's proven strategy in dealing with romantic figures – who often failed to gracefully align with the steelier aspects of Romanticism – was to politicize and militarize their lives and works, even while concurrently acknowledging the special characteristics that were so well known to its readers. And so, when it came to Clemens Brentano (1778–1842), the *Völkischer Beobachter* acknowledged that the writer was a "highly-strung fanatic" whose "realm was in the clouds." It further made mention of his "hot-tempered temperament and southern musicality" – traits he inherited, according to the paper's genealogical theories, as the child of a "closed-minded" Italian businessman and an "open-minded, gentle German mother." But despite such acknowledgments, the paper's emphasis remained on Brentano's reactions to the political circumstances of his era. Reviewing the period from 1778 to 1842, the paper noted that Brentano's life spanned a "world crisis" which "forced Germans to confront the events of the day." As a result, even more than in the age of Schiller and Goethe, a "sense of history" became innate to the romantic generation; thus, while Herder taught Germans to recognize Nature and Volk as the highest forces of existence, Brentano and Arnim made these notions useful in daily life. Through them, the "feeling for volkishness," the appreciation of true popular culture, and consciousness of the Fatherland came to "full blossom" in songs and legends and, through practical application in the Wars of Liberation, became the "common property of all Germans."[41] Above all, the paper contended that Brentano's and Arnim's collaborative anthology, *The Boy's Magic Horn* (1805–1808) contributed to the emergence of a national consciousness, and therefore this "wonderful collection of volkish songs" amounted to a "special cultural-political achievement." Appearing under Napoleonic rule "like a multi-colored bouquet," it led the German people to "spiritual self-contemplation."[42] According to Wagner expert, Paul Bülow – who would pen a tribute to "Adolf Hitler and the Bayreuth Circle" (and then give a copy to his Führer[43]) – *The*

Boy's Magic Horn made "mental strength" a permanent feature of the Volk, which was evident at the time of its appearance and in the 1930s.[44] Such works of Brentano and his circle, the *Völkischer Beobachter* asserted, stimulated youth to "carefully study the Volk and the German past in sagas, stories, art, poetry, and other documents of German spirit" in order to contribute to the development of national historical literature.[45]

Similarly, while the *Völkischer Beobachter* acknowledged that the Brothers Grimm were co-founders of the "scientific study of German languages," the paper was much more interested in presenting evidence that at least one brother had expressed anti-Jewish views. An article on "previously unknown anti-Semitic poems" described a work that Wilhelm Karl Grimm (1786–1859) published in the *Rose Garden of German Poetry* (1831) as "a gorgeous acknowledgment of the ongoing Siegfried War against the Jewish dragon." The paper then reproduced the poem, entitled *Awake, My Germany!*:

> Germany … is a cherubic little giant,
> He can tear oak-trees out of the soil,
> Beat the backsides of Jews until they are sore,
> And bash their heads without toil …
> Awake! One day like Siegfried you will,
> Slay the Jewish dragon.
> Streaming down from the German heaven
> Germania greets your awakening.[46]

This "powerful song of the deepest love for the Fatherland and flaming holy hatred against the Jewish threat," the *Völkischer Beobachter* exclaimed, sounded as if it "first stirred a German breast today" and "not a hundred years earlier."[47] Thereby did this malicious poem earn more attention in the paper than any of the fairy tales its author collected with his brother.

Still, the tension pervading *Völkischer Beobachter* reception of Romanticism was even more palpable in its treatment of Joseph von Eichendorff (1788–1857). On the one hand, Herbert Müller, a regular contributor starting in 1926, presented him as a poet of German dreaminess, stating that there was "a unique charm to his poems: a sweet air of fantasy, a soulful magic spoke from them." The "wonderful spiritual magic" of Eichendorff's poetry consisted of "a mixture of nature and emotion, the bursting forth of delicate, sweet-smelling morning voices, the endless nostalgia-filled, lovely yearning in evening light of the countryside ... the cheery lust for spring in the world-wide wanderer, friends smitten by the beauty of the German woods."[48] It was perhaps this side of Eichendorff that the paper intended to highlight when it reproduced his most famous work, *The Memoirs of a Good-For-Nothing* (1826) – so full of elements Müller considered attractive – in serial form over ten days in April 1929.[49] But at the same time, Müller balanced this description of Eichendorff's dreaminess with more nationalistic and even militaristic monikers such as "genuinely German, *volkstümlich* poet" and "the last knight of Romanticism."[50] Similarly, Rudolf Hofmüller discussed the lyrical aspects of Eichendorff's works, but also did so under the title, "The Last Knight of Romanticism." Eichendorff, according to Hofmüller, was *volkstümlich* because he conveyed essential ideas in a "quite simple, uncomplicated but nevertheless transfiguring style that touched the deepest part of everyone." Everything flowed out of an "intimate and pure heart – out of ever-valid human experience": each of his "joyous poems" was an "intimate expression of the German spirit and the romantic experience of life." No earlier poet had captured in such "moving tones the feeling and mood, the longing and searching, the unconscious and inexpressible aspects of a soul lost to dream."

Yet Hofmüller faithfully maintained the paradox that characterized *Völkischer Beobachter* coverage of Romanticism, insisting that despite the dreamy qualities of Eichendorff's works, the poet was "realistic" in the sense of being politically and militarily active. Eichendorff deserved particular attention in 1938, said Hofmüller, because "like the whole romantic movement, the striving and effects of this fiery, manly spirit" proved that poetic creation was not an "unrealistic activity." Eichendorff dedicated himself completely to his poetry, but he did not forget about the world in which he lived: he served the state as a soldier in the Lützows Freikorps and as a councilor in the Prussian Ministry of Education. Nazis, Hofmüller concluded, who wanted to regain the "mother earth of blood-real German culture through honorable striving," had to respect and love Eichendorff as the herald of the "essential forces of the German soul."[51]

The critic Konrad Karkosch presented this dualistic view again in 1941. First, Karkosch stated that Eichendorff belonged among those writers who were "*volkstümlich* in the truest sense of the word." Above all, his "delicious" *Memoirs of a Good-For-Nothing* had become the "common property" of the whole German Volk and could no longer be imagined as separate from its cultural life. Even so, as Karkosch explained, it was essential that "his life of sentiment was really anchored and rooted in that of his people." One had only to think of his poem, *Who in Distant Lands Would Wander* (*Wer in die Fremde will wandern*) (1826) – where he spoke of the "Greater Germany that he longed for and loved while in foreign lands" – to realize that while the "quiet secret of unaffected nature" came through in his poems, Eichendorff spent his life "between the writing desk and action" – doing honorable service as an officer and an official almost to the end of his life.[52]

In the case of Wilhelm Müller (1794–1827), author of *The Fair Miller-Maid* (1820) and *The Winter Journey* (1823), both set by Schubert, the paper developed a "heroic" interpretation based on his *Songs of the Greeks* (1821). During his lifetime these were among the poet's best-known works, and they ultimately earned him the nickname, "Müller of the Greeks" (*Griechen-Müller*). As the *Völkischer Beobachter* reported, the *Lieder* not only supported the heroic Greek people, but came to symbolize the Greek cause throughout Germany in the nineteenth century. Most importantly, for the paper, "their heroic verve and flaming enthusiasm were still gripping and could provide young hearts with an education in heroic conviction." Though originally associated with liberal politics, this "power of political inspiration" made the *Songs of the Greeks* more significant to the *Völkischer Beobachter* than Müller's better known *Waldhorn* cycles, which were stories that Schubert had put to music about heartbroken, suicidal wanderers.[53]

Maybe the strangest example of the paper's efforts to reinforce the steely aspects of German Romanticism was its argument that the poems of the famously other-worldly Friedrich Hölderlin (1770–1843) were "above all political!" Horst Rüdiger, author of many books on Greek and Latin literature and editor of numerous Goethe editions, stipulated that "what his contemporaries did not understand" was first discovered by later generations: that Hölderlin's poetry was "political poetry in the purest sense of the word; that the poet was a volkish poet of the highest rank." Under the "iron boots of Napoleonic armies," his heroic fight for the "content of the German soul via poetry" remained almost unnoticed in his day. However, his songs "applied exclusively to German nature and their validity would survive as long as Germans lived."

Most volkish, according to Rüdiger, was the close link between his works and nature: Hölderlin's poetry "rested in the friendly confraternity of his Swabian homeland." Above all, he was never unfaithful to his homeland and in return the "Angel of the Fatherland" never abandoned him. He happily sang of Stuttgart and Heidelberg, "the most beautiful of the Fatherland cities"; he dedicated his festive hymns to the "great German rivers, the Neckar, the Main, the source of the Danube, and the blessed valley of the Rhine"; and he enlivened his poems with "Germanic-Antique belief in the all-soul-fullness of nature." But beyond communing with nature, Hölderlin was always "searching for the Volk capable of hearing him," ready to take up the "struggle to achieve the highest level of human accomplishment in politics, art, beauty, and spirit." He expressed this sentiment most profoundly in the *Song of the Germans* – a poem which Rüdiger ranked among the "most magnificent testimonies in the German language to a mature political and volkish consciousness."[54]

> Oh holy heart of the Volk, Oh Fatherland!
> All-tolerant, like silent Mother Earth ...
> I rested quietly on your earth as dawn arrived.
> And on your banks I saw cities bloom,
> Where hard work is done quietly in workshops,
> Where your sun gently guides artists to serious thoughts ...
> Be honored, my Fatherland,
> For ripening the fruit of the age!

But during his own time, "Hölderlin's Fatherland paid no heed to his lonely voice": though he was "the German poet who most enjoyed the pleasures of community," loneliness was his fate. The "homeless singer" suffered because his community spirit remained unfulfilled in an era of personality cults: the homeland he yearned for with every part of his soul was stolen by a "citizenry of the world" that could not be united.[55]

Hermann Burte, who received a number of awards in the Third Reich for his volkish poetry and novels, described Hölderlin as having "disappeared" a century earlier. But in Nazi Germany, he was being acknowledged as "incomparable, unequalled, the highest, the purest of all." By Hitler's time, the Volk had "matured and taken heart": it wanted to rise "to the height of Hölderlin." It had accepted his message as an "innermost truth" and had succeeded in grasping his "manly wisdom." He had been a "singer of the German future and eternity" like none other – "the singing flame around which the Volk turned." He "moved the heart of the Volk and the Volk gave him its heart in return."

Moreover, anticipating an "ideal Reich of the Germans," he glorified battle like no one else, stating that "suffering would bring about changes in one day that wouldn't otherwise happen for a century." Therefore, Burte concluded, "he is our man, we are his Volk; we recognize him as the Great Poet of the Germans."[56]

As this interpretation of Hölderlin implied, the *Völkischer Beobachter* ultimately sought to identify in romantic literature a cultural antecedent to the Führer type; indeed, a *proto-Führer* who, as viewed through the lens of history, could be seen to prefigure (and serve as the model of) the type of leader that the paper deemed was required to fulfill Germany's destiny. But for the paper's editors, the troublesome facts of Hölderlin's well-known mental instability made the writer a less than optimal choice for this purpose. A better source was Goethe.

Not surprisingly, the paper chose not to reference *The Sorrows of Young Werther* (1774) for these purposes, dismissing its main character with a single mention: "Werther's self-martyrdom was superfluous, and such activities are particularly dangerous for Germans"; instead of "endless brooding, constant evasiveness, and guilty feelings," the Nazi movement would "provide young people with a clear, clean, and honorable sense of responsibility."[57] So, avoiding Werther – along with Egmont and Torquato Tasso – the paper instead turned to the figure of Faust. On one level, the *Völkischer Beobachter* claimed Nazi affinity for the character of Faust in aesthetic terms that were tinged with racist theory: Goethe's poem was "the most powerful poetic expression of Nordic-Western spirit"[58] and Goethe's main character was the "purest embodiment of Nordic, aristocratic being." Such a man had to have "the courage to be himself, a trait from which all others flee en masse."[59] In this vein, "Hitler's Herald" himself, Georg Schott, one of the earliest to have apotheosized the Nazi leader as Germany's Führer, provided an updated analysis of Faust – representing the character as "Goethe's Ideal of a Führer."

Schott's 1932 analysis – which served as the basis for his 1940 book, *Goethe's Faust in Present Day* – concentrated on the second part of the play where, he said, two opposing political models emerged clearly. The first is the figure of the emperor, whose authority was not "acquired, but merely inherited." For Schott, the emperor's personality is not without "remarkable characteristics or nobility," but he exhibits "neither the drive to rule, independent decisiveness, nor determination." A major problem is his "indiscriminate kindness to everyone." Moreover, in tense moments, he is dependent on the questionable help of others. The second is the figure of Faust, who existed as the "unanointed representative of a new Reich." He is full of the ruling spirit, and "in giving orders finds his bliss."[60] In Schott's view, Faust was therefore "the born leader of the Volk" who had "one great ideal in mind, superior to all contingencies": "To stand on free land with free people."

According to Schott, Faust was born to rule: "he is the Führer in possession of all the gifts necessary – whose suitability to rule glows from his brow." "A great thing tempts me!" he freely admits.[61] When Mephistopheles says that his plans are driven by ambition for fame, Faust corrects him: "Fame is naught, the deed is all."[62] According to Schott, Faust had both the "worldly and active genius" necessary to achieve his lofty goals for the world – but to understand the nature of these goals, Schott explained, one had to carefully read act IV of the second part and then compare the situation described there with "that of today." Faust arrives on a cloud that has carried him over land and sea, allowing him to view the expanse and beauty of the world. He sees the ocean's ebb and flow, and when the waters recede, he notices newly emerging coastal regions. Based on this vision, he develops a plan to produce new territories, in the process putting to use "ideas that he had been struggling with day and night." To articulate the nature of these ideas, Schott reached outside Goethe's text and inserted into Faust's mouth a National Socialist slogan – based on Hans Grimm's book title: "Volk in danger! Volk without space!" ("*Volk in Not! Volk ohne Raum!*"). Once the Nazi concept of *Lebensraum* was thus interpolated into the play, the notion that "a great thing tempts" Faust became comprehensible: "a national and social idea of unbelievable dimensions grows within him": namely, "the founding of a new state, in which a free Volk will stand on free land."

Schott then quoted directly from the drama again, implying that Faust's water management project anticipated volkish dreams of more living space for modern Germans:

> I'd open room to live for millions
> Not safely, but in free resilience.
> Lush fallow then to man and cattle yields
> Swift crops and comforts from the maiden fields,
> New homesteads near the trusty buttress-face
> Walled by a bold and horny-handed race.[63]

"Do we see now, in its deepest sense, the secret message of Faust, the born leader?" Schott asked. The emperor considers it his duty to just maintain himself at the head of his Volk, but the crisis of the day demands more: "something higher, something superior – the idea that has become conscious in Faust, the born leader of the Volk." Still, Faust doesn't go into direct competition with the emperor. He doesn't question his stature: in other words, Schott pointed out, "he is not revolutionary." But the situation requires something new: "a decisive step forward has to be taken"; the "Volk must be taught about higher goals." To bring about such a decisive step forward is the job of the Führer; failing to do so "would not be a matter of modesty or virtue, but irresponsible flinching from the will of life." With this "new truth" emerge equally important notions of what the "qualifications and duties of a genuine Führer – a true politician – are." Politics and statecraft involve the "will and power to raise the depressed conditions of the Volk – to lead it beyond itself." This is, Schott believed, what Faust meant in saying, "This planet's soil grants scope for noble deeds abounding, I sense accomplishments astounding, feel strength in me for daring toil."[64]

Concluding this not so subtle association of Faust with the new Führer he awaited in 1932, Schott insisted that one must consider *Faust* from this perspective in order to grasp the "great connections" between the situation in Goethe's text and that of Germany at the end of the Weimar Republic. He closed with a direct reference to pivotal political events occurring as he wrote this interpretation: "Let the next weeks and months bring what they may: our Volk lies like a child in the womb of its mother and, when it is time, will be reborn into the world." Though cryptically, one year before the "seizure of power," Schott was expressing confidence that the Faust-Führer was coming soon – bent on obtaining more living space for Germany.[65]

9 ROMANTIC MUSIC AS "OUR GREATEST LEGACY"

The above has made clear that the *Völkischer Beobachter* worked strenuously to establish that German composers of the Baroque and Classical ages had expressed in music Germanic, volkish, patriotic, and anti-Semitic ideals that came to full realization under National Socialism. Given the general attitude that music was the "most German of the arts" – and its command integral to any worthwhile definition of *Bildung* – it was a priority for Nazi publicists to continue establishing close associations with the great composers of the nineteenth century.[1] Consistent with their proclivity toward romantic culture as a whole, music of that period – which, from their perspective, reached its zenith in Wagner's operatic body of work – was presented as the greatest jewel in the cultural legacy of the Third Reich and as the aesthetic wellspring for any music that would henceforth emerge from the Nazi experience.

Goebbels put these ideas forth in a speech opening the Reich Music Days in Düsseldorf in 1938. Pleading that "the fame of Germany as the nation of music be once again revealed and substantiated," he spoke on the development of a Nazi music tradition as a whole, to the point of specifying the fundamentally romantic features it would have to maintain: "may the principles that have since time immemorial been the source and the driving force behind our German music again be set forth and recognized." By such "principles," Goebbels clearly meant romantic notions of music as the deepest expression of spirit and emotion:

> *Music is the most sensual of the arts and for this reason
> appeals more to the heart and the emotions than to the
> intellect ... The language of musical tones is sometimes more
> effective than the language of words. For this reason, the great
> masters of the past represent the true majesty of our people
> and are deserving of reverence and respect. And as children of
> our Volk they are the true monarchs of our people by God's
> grace and are destined to receive the fame and honor of our
> nation.[2]*

The first of the romantic "monarchs" of music to whom the *Völkischer Beobachter* accorded such reverence was Franz Schubert (1797–1828), and its primary order of business was to analyze his genealogy. The paper stipulated that Schubert was "not Viennese by blood," because he stemmed on the paternal side from "Moravian farmer blood" and from Silesia on the maternal side.[3] According to musicologist Alexander Witeschnik, who would write prolifically into the postwar years, Schubert embodied the "industrious, serious character" of the Sudeten Germans who settled in the region and helped to create Vienna. Just as the "virtues of so many German *Stämme* were united in Vienna," so the same was true of Schubert: the "spiritual powers that were stored up in his ancestors for centuries" developed in him to a tremendous degree; along with the Viennese, therefore, Sudeten Germans "sensed their dear homeland in his works."[4] Even so, the paper clarified, it was the city of Vienna that "awakened the creative seeds that resided in the blood of the family," providing the environment in which his work resonated best.[5] As Witeschnik put it, "baptized in the musical font of this soil," Schubert embodied the "*Ur-Wienerisch*, the native genius, the classical incarnation of the Viennese music soul." All the "secret voices of the city entered into his life and work – the bright as well as the dark – and he became the eternal symbol of Vienna the Music City."[6] But as another contributor warned, if some described Schubert as the incarnation of the Viennese spirit in the sense of being a "merry, playful, party genius" (*Kneipgenie*), they misjudged his nature. Having originated from lower-class conditions, Schubert was never free of worries: if, after hours of exhausting work in which he "poured out the pure gold of his essence," he went out into wine country – "into merry society" – then he did so only in order to get new strength for the next day's challenges.[7]

Pressing association of the composer with Viennese culture into twentieth-century terms, Josef Stolzing contended that the Vienna of the 1920s could no longer "beget a Schubert," since it had degenerated into a stage for the "most florid Jewish operetta nonsense." Describing contemporary Vienna and how it had changed since he was there as a soldier during the First World War, Stolzing decried all the modern developments that had "covered over the composer's world." Still, and even though the postwar period with its jazz mentality "circled around," Stolzing held that, fundamentally, Germans were always "in search of Schubert." Particularly in times of "inner poverty and soulful mediocrity," his image became "doubly heavy with promise." The continued, though degenerate, popular taste for the operetta, the *Dreimäderlhaus* (1916), and kitschy films about his life were expressions of the desire to reconnect with that "long-past and distant spirituality whose image, though distorted, still conveys an indestructible sense of blessedness."[8]

Beside such intense correlation of Schubert with Old Vienna, the paper also labored fiercely to associate him with "Greater Germany," often in surprising ways. A case in point was the piece entitled "Schubert Travels to Prussia: A Tale of the Fatherland beyond Regional and Ethnic Borders," penned by Walter Persich, author of historical novels on the Baghdad railroad as well as, in 1940, *The Private Winston Churchill: Adventurer, Lord, and Criminal*. Persich's contribution was a fictional account of Schubert's travels on a concert tour – circumstances, of course, which never occurred. After visiting Prague and Dresden he goes to Berlin and there, exhausted, is tempted to give up the trip and return home. Instead, he goes for a walk and after passing through the Brandenburg Gate, sees an advertisement for performances of *Fidelio* and *The Marriage of Figaro* to be performed at the Royal Opera. With this, the sun breaks through a cloudy day, birds began to chirp, and Schubert walks back to his room "a different man than when he had passed through the gate to leave Berlin behind." He had realized that "behind all the different faces, the same German heart always beats: whether Vienna, Prague, Dresden, Berlin, it was one Fatherland – the Fatherland of the music of the greatest masters, and the Fatherland of his music."[9]

Similar sentiments can be found a speech by Friedrich List, chairman of the German Singers' League (*Deutscher Sängerbund*), which the paper covered on the 100th anniversary of Schubert's death. A century had passed, List opened, since Schubert's creativity ended in a much too early death. But contemporaries still felt the composer's spiritual strength, which "allowed German soul and German heart to flow out in song." His *Lieder* "encompassed all Germans – wherever they were scattered in the world – like a unifying band." If their hearts ever stopped responding to Schubert, "Germans would lose themselves, the German soul would cease to exist."[10] Likewise, in Hans Buchner's view, the sense of genius which "the German Volk drew from its best sons – despite distance and time, suffering and misery – radiated from the deep tragedy of Schubert's short earthly existence." None who "openly upheld their commitment to volkish style" experienced Schubert without experiencing an "indelible impression."[11] With his songs, Bavarian Cultural Minister Franz Goldenberger stated, Schubert established a "valuable monument to the German soul and mind." Both he and Wagner "drew from the German essence of their art to the dregs": after them, nothing more could be added to the music drama nor to the *Lied* – those "utterly German" art forms. Through Schubert the German people became famous as the "Volk richest in song"; through him songs sung in German were "first made truly *volkstümlich*." Even in the twentieth century, Schubert's body of work could press musical developments forward, out of the "animosity toward melody" of present-day modernism, away from the "weaknesses of atonality and jazz, upward again into a tonal world of pure soul that spoke from and to the heart."[12]

Certain that Schubert's *Müller Cycle*, for instance, stemmed from "inexhaustible sources of German Volk sentiment,"[13] the *Völkischer Beobachter* took issue with non-volkish organizations and parties whenever they associated themselves with the composer. When a bust of Schubert was erected in the Walhalla near Regensburg to mark the 100th *Todestag*, the paper condemned the ceremonies since a Jew was in charge.[14] Only "a dozen Aryans" were present at the press conference for the event, the paper complained: thus the whole thing was "directed toward nothing more than making a profit." It was a "Jewish scam, not a celebration in the spirit of Schubert."[15] Noting the numerous Schubert evenings planned for the *Todestag*, the paper fretted that cities were competing against one another to have the most, and all this was just a "Jewish plan for making some cash."[16]

More appropriate, according to the *Völkischer Beobachter*, was the performance of Schubert's songs in the interest of Nazism at events like the Greater German Festival in the party room of Munich's Bürgerbräu brewery,[17] a celebration of Hitler's birthday at the Berlin

Staats-Oper,[18] and the opening of the Reich Culture Chamber in the Berlin Philharmonic.[19] During the war, in a nationally broadcast speech announcing a Day of Music in the German Home, Baldur von Schirach remarked before a performance of Schubert's *Trout* Quintet: "Not only do we play music at home during the war, but we play music at home *because there is a war*; the man who holds the sword of the *Wehrmacht* in his strong hands, leads in the name of our poetry and song!"[20]

The paper also enthusiastically covered Schubert's contemporary, Carl Maria von Weber (1786–1826), whose works were included at the *Bürgerbräukeller* Festival,[21] in performances of the National Socialist Symphony Orchestra,[22] and at *Kampfbund für Kultur* concerts.[23] In Hans Buchner's view, Weber was one of the "most German artists of his century." As "the creator of German opera, the creator of German Romanticism" – who was active when a spirit was developing in Germany that would "culminate in the Wars of Liberation" – Weber laid the cornerstone for nineteenth-century German music as "thunder from the Battle of Leipzig still rumbled and news of victory arrived from Waterloo." The "eagle-like rise of a youthful Germany" resonated throughout his works: "horn calls, the love of hunting, the fate of soldiers, and love of the Fatherland all blossomed in a wonderful unity encompassing art, culture, feeling, and spirit." Weber's art developed amid this "strong current of volkish renewal."[24] Karl Grunsky reported that the composer dedicated himself to the "Fatherlandish movement" in 1812, producing perfect music for the *Liedertafel* – including a *Kriegslied* for the *Wache am Brandenburger Tor* that moved the commanding officer in Berlin to tears.[25] Above all, Buchner went on, Weber's aim was to give the German people "a German musical artwork" on the stage: the resulting creations proved that "an artist's engagement with the fate of his Volk was what made him a true creator, and that the Volk derived its noblest forces from its greatest sons." In the midst of the Weimar era of decline, his work served as encouragement for Nazis to "commit themselves to Volk and Fatherland."[26]

Never hesitant to render an opinion on this issue – no matter how many times – the paper pronounced that "German opera began" with Weber's *Der Freischütz* (1821) and *Oberon* (1826).[27] His commitment to the "unified opera" led the fight against the "degeneration of the German tradition," which, dominated by Italian and French opera, was "sinking beyond rescue from the weight of internationalism." Weber was therefore the originator of German romantic opera: *Freischütz* and *Euryanthe* (1823) were "steps on the way to the Parnassas of German music drama," and represented achievements that ultimately allowed Wagner to compose *Tannhäuser* and *Lohengrin*.[28] The idea of a national opera, wrote Erwin Voelsing, was Weber's: "even if German creative genius had been able to achieve an incontestable supremacy over the art of music through the influence of Haydn, Mozart, and Beethoven, the era of musical classicism had not produced truly national operas of German essence – German volkishness." Weber initiated the "promising development" of German opera by "combining native song types into a greater German national *Singspiel*." This "pathfinder" perceived the course for a "particularly Nordic-Germanic art work," which had already been marked out by Heinrich Schütz, Händel, and Mozart. But to achieve a higher unity, he "combined his Volk-bound genius with some foreign suggestions into a fruitful creative synthesis." That is what Weber meant when he said that German national opera "gladly learns from the foreign, but must be produced truly and uniquely." He recognized, moreover, that the German national opera must be a totality – "an organic, internally living thing, requiring a basis in dramatic truth." In a genuinely romantic frame of mind, then, he foresaw the *Gesamtkunstwerk* that Wagner demanded later, when he described *Euryanthe* as "a drama that works through the united cooperation of all the sister arts."[29]

In musicologist Josef Klingenbeck's opinion, *Euryanthe* was the most important transitional work in the period between Beethoven's *Fidelio* and the music drama of Wagner, especially *Lohengrin*.[30] But *Völkischer Beobachter* contributors more often highlighted *Der Freischütz*. Erwin Bauer held that *Freischütz* was "a work of the German soul," and compared with an Italian or French opera, was "more restrained in its dramatic-musical conception, and more inner oriented."[31] About *Freischütz*, Heinrich Stahl stated that despite Gluck, Mozart, and Beethoven, this is when "the hour of the birth of German opera sounded: such a unity of *Volkstum* and music had never been achieved or even imagined before, even though nationalist circles and masters had long sought to overcome unworthy foreign influences."[32]

In 1944, Edmund Pesch, who would become a prominent newspaper and journal editor after the war, reminded Nazi readers about Weber's "national significance" in an article about the exhumation and transfer of his body from Britain to Germany: "a patriotic mission which

had been led by Richard Wagner." As Pesch sadly recounted, fate over-
took Weber in London: the composer's last visit there had been "a tragic
collision of his German spirit and English shop-keeping mentality." It
was a terrible irony that the German musician "in whose melodies the
forests of the homeland sounded, who expressed the German desire for
freedom in Körner's *Sword Song* and Lützow's *Wild Hunt*, and who
captured the spirit of Waterloo in a great cantata – never suspecting that
it wasn't the freedom of his homeland but the business of England that
had triumphed in that battle – died in that foreign city." Then, although
his last letters and words were full of intense longing for the homeland,
"arrogant Albion took over the German musician's grave." To Pesch, the
interment in England mirrored British imperialism in general: while
Romanticism evolved in Germany, "London coldly calculated and
planned for world domination; the English empire expanded to include
New Zealand, Hong Kong, Nepal, and most of Burma while it continually grasped at the continent, bent on binding it in the chains of world
capitalism." A Liberalism that was "hostile to culture and dedicated to
Mammon" was exploiting the earth. However, against the background
of such developments, a "first sign of the rebellious German nature"
rising "against a world become hostile to art" occurred in 1844 when a
small group led by Richard Wagner decided to bring the ashes of Weber
"back to the Fatherland" eighteen years after his death, whereupon
Wagner gave an oration that the *Völkischer Beobachter* gladly reproduced on more than one occasion, including lines summarizing nationalistic claims to his legacy:

> *Where'er thy genius bore thee, to whatsoever distant realms*
> *of floating fancy, it stayed forever linked by a thousand*
> *tendrils to the German people's heart … Though the Briton*
> *may yield thee justice, the Frenchman admiration, yet the*
> *German alone can love thee … Who shall blame us if we*
> *wished thine ashes, too, should mingle with this earth – to*
> *form a portion of dear German soil?*[33]

Compared with its treatment of Schubert and Weber, remarkably little appeared in the *Völkischer Beobachter* about Robert
Schumann, leaving one to wonder if the composer's mental imbalance
lessened his value as a Nazi icon. Instead of his music or his formidable
body of work as a music critic, the paper preferred to occupy itself with

the damage Jews supposedly inflicted on his career. Josef Stolzing related this view of "poor Robert Schumann" as a victim of Jewish treachery by citing a passage from Wagner's *Judaism in Music*.[34] There Wagner inquired after the causes of Schumann's decline in the second half of his life, and "found the answer in Jewish influence." Addressing the "idleness that too many Germans were falling into," he wrote that "Schumann's genius sank into this passivity too, when it became a burden for him to make a stand against the restless, busy spirit of the Jews."[35] On the centennial of his death, moreover, Gustav Christian Rassy related an anecdote about an evening at Auerbach's Keller in Leipzig that seemed to confirm Wagner's assessment. It was noteworthy, wrote Rassy, when on one night the usually withdrawn Schumann came into the smoky hall and sat down with a group of teachers and students from the Leipzig conservatory. He raised his glass and everyone waited, but he didn't drink. Instead, he started a strange, fragmented monologue, which suggested that "beneath the outward appearance of courage, a long-standing pain smoldered and tormented him." Then, Schumann stood up, his head bent limply to the side "like an exhausted soldier," and continued: "The new German music found a home here thanks to one composer. I drink to Bach and Beethoven and to our master." Then Schumann put his glass down and left quietly. As the door closed behind him, a "dark-haired man with darting eyes and a clever face" said, "These Germans are weird – really weird – and sometimes rude." The man who said this was the conservatory director: Felix Mendelssohn. "We know from music history," Rassy went on, that while Schumann expressed great appreciation for Mendelssohn in his letters, "one looks in vain for even one friendly word about the creative German from this artistic Jew" – "a long-forgotten Jewish composer."[36]

As discussed above, the *Völkischer Beobachter* found in key selections from Wagner's writings and in the carefully documented circumstances of his life myriad indications that his politics, his volkish outlook – especially as manifested in anti-Semitism – and his beliefs regarding other German enemies such as the French and British, were in perfect alignment with essential features of the National Socialist program. Even Wagner's love of animals and vegetarian diet coordinated with Hitler's personal outlook as manifested in Nazi culture.[37] But however valuable such sources proved, it was Wagner's music – and, above all else, his music dramas – that existed as the ultimate treasure of the romantic culture revered in the *Völkischer Beobachter*. Taken as a whole, Wagner's creative output was considered as having "uppermost national significance." According to Otto Daube – a musicologist who sent the *Völkischer Beobachter* music reports from Karlsruhe, headed the Bayreuth German Youth Group (*Bayreuther Bundes deutscher Jugend*), and later produced books on *Fidelio* and biographies on other composers – the modern era, with its "progressive ideas of materialism, technology, and trade" had overshadowed the "last impulses of cultural sensitivity": true culture had been reduced to "superficial civilization"; the "soul of the German Volk had gone under." But the culture of Bayreuth had been spared from such progress. At the top of its Green Hill, "the Grail continued to shine over modern times." There, a German art "continued to live while modernized technicians worked away in the valleys, not in order to improve the German soul, but out of selfish motives of earning fame by destroying its culture."[38] To Herbert H. Mueller, who sent in articles on music and art from Berlin,[39] Wagner's work was an intellectual and moral force in the "battle for the German will and the German ideal": if Nazis "made his creations their own," then they wouldn't have to be anxious about the future.[40]

In addition to such general statements, the *Völkischer Beobachter* made specific references to many of Wagner's major works. In reviewing the negative reception that Wagner's *Tannhäuser* (1845) suffered in Paris, the paper maintained that what made this scandal so significant to Nazis was the "sharp line of separation" that it revealed between Germans and French. It was at this line of separation that "peaceful German efforts toward friendship with this neighboring nation had to come to an end." About *Lohengrin* (1850), according to pianist and music critic Alexander Dillman, it was forgotten that the opera was an affirmation "of the union of German tribes against a common threat which the German land so often faced in the East." With courage unheard of at the time (twenty-four years before the founding of the second German Reich, shortly before the movement of 1848, and at the height of German sectionalism [*Kleinstädterei*]), Wagner "bound the music and images of *Lohengrin* fast with fundamental German thoughts." Portraits of "Germans and German towns, religious processions, recognition of the necessity of unity, confidence that Germany would survive difficult days – all these emerged directly from the music." At the least, "the message brought with the Grail was one of German style and German essence."[41]

Particular attention was given in the *Völkischer Beobachter* to *Die Meistersinger von Nürnberg* (1868). In 1933 came the first Bayreuth Festival of the Third Reich, and it opened with a production of this opera "in the presence of the Reich Chancellor." The performance was broadcast throughout Germany and Goebbels took advantage of the occasion to make an extended radio address verifying the prominence of *Die Meistersinger* in Nazi culture. The paper printed the propaganda czar's radio address on the front page in full. "There is certainly no work in all the music literature of the German *Volk* that so closely relates to our times and our spiritual condition," Goebbels opened. "How often in recent years," he asked rhetorically, has the *Wach auf* chorus "been experienced by faithful Germans," as a tangible symbol of the "reawakening of the German Volk out of the deep political and spiritual narcosis that it entered in November 1918?" Towering over all Wagner's other music dramas as "the most German of all," *Die Meistersinger* is the "incarnation of our *Volkstum*," representing "everything that marks and fills the German soul":

> *It is an ingenious combination of German melancholy and romance, of German pride and German diligence, of that German humor, about which it is said that one "laughs with one eye and cries with the other." It is an image of the hearty and yea-saying German Renaissance, moving from bitter, pure tragedy, through jubilant musical triumph, to the sonic pathos of a rousing Volksfest.*

Goebbels continued by acclaiming the pro-Wagner spirit of the new regime: "Richard Wagner's heirs can today rest assured that the master and his work are safe and secure in the care of a government" whose leader personally visited "sites of Wagnerian creativity during the very first year of the German Revolution, paying humble homage to the greatest musical genius of all time." He concluded his *Meistersinger* address with an extended reference to the opera's finale as a manifesto of National Socialist cultural policy: "May the German people never lose this spirit of respect for the great men of the nation!" Only then would the new Reich "do justice" to the demand that Richard Wagner made via Hans Sachs in the close of "the most German of all German operas": "Therefore I say to you: honor your German masters! Then you will conjure up good spirits; even should the Holy Roman Empire dissolve in mist, for us there would yet remain holy German art!"[42]

The notoriously anti-modernist and anti-Semitic musicologist Hans Joachim Moser, responsible for the *Lexicon of Jews in Music* (1934), expressed complete agreement with Goebbels' assessment, stating that what "Haydn's and Hofmann von Fallersleben's *Deutschlandlied*" was to German *Lieder*, *Die Meistersinger* was to German musical drama: both were "representative of the German national being, as a Volk and a Reich." *Die Meistersinger* was "full of the heavy-footed sturdiness of Düreresque guild master figures, genuine German humor, and Wagnerian wisdom about life and art." All such characteristics were "drawn from German sensibility, which justified Nazi pride in possessing this work of art."[43]

However, among all references to Wagner in the *Völkischer Beobachter*, it was Josef Stolzing's treatment of the Ring Cycle that made the most direct association between Wagner's music and contemporary German affairs. In August 1923, Stolzing's article, "The World War in the *Ring of the Niebelungen*,"[44] was published over multiple issues. Here, Stolzing made the strongest assertions ever to appear in the Nazi daily about anti-Semitic stereotypes in Wagner's music dramas. Stolzing started with an understatement: though Wagner was not a politician, he "had a political outlook." Such a perspective allowed Wagner to recognize the problems which "now confront Germans in ugly forms" after their "disgraceful exit from the World War." Already in 1851, according to Stolzing, Wagner perceived "with uncannily clairvoyant foresight" the horrible war to come, and that "in the end, the war machine would fall apart from within, as happened with the mutiny of the German fleet." He had also predicted "world-wide famine, realized in 1918 and 1919." Moreover, Stolzing feared, Europe faced a worse horror breaking out in Russia, "spewing out in the form of Bolshevism": if Germany's enemies were not challenged, there would occur "a world revolution that would lead not just to the never-never land of communism, but rather into the most naked barbarism – the downfall of the Western world." All this "the Master addressed, in imagery of a twilight of the gods, four decades before Spengler!"

According to Stolzing, Wagner anticipated the tragedies of the World War in his drama and music by depicting the "fight for power" symbolized in the ring that Alberich forged out of the Rheingold. Alberich embodied the "dark spirit of Jewish Mammonism," which took its "ghastliest form" in industrial capitalism, manifested especially in the "haunting, abstract specter of the corporation – the epitome of loveless and coldhearted business interests." As the Rhine Maiden, Wellgunde, put it:

> He who from the Rheingold
> fashioned the ring
> that would confer on him immensurable might
> could win the world's wealth
> for his own.

It was in this form that Mammonism "came to rule the whole world," Stolzing held, marked by the characteristics of the "atrocious mixed-bloods" whom "the Master gave voice" through Hagen:

> My blood would taint your drink;
> it does not flow pure
> and noble like yours;
> stiff and cold,
> it is sluggish within me;
> it will not redden my cheeks.

The racial mixing elicited here was of particular concern to Stolzing: "What caused the fall of the Roman Empire? The racial mush brought about by its global politics." And, he warned, "Aryan-Germanic humanity" was threatened with the same end, because the First World War "not only cost the German race more than three million of its strongest men, but also introduced many thousand colored soldiers into Europe," resulting in the "infection and deterioration of the blood of European humanity to a shocking, unprecedented extent." With "infallible certainty," then, Wagner prefigured in Hagen the "dreadful catastrophe that would haunt European humanity in general and the German Volk in particular." Moreover, Stolzing asserted, it was possible to recognize the Germanic lines of princes in the "gods lured by the glimmer of gold and greedily extending their hands toward the Ring of world power." Indeed, even before they learned that the ring had been forged, they were already "entangled in guilt," because with the construction of Walhalla they were "directing their tentacles of power over humanity."

Furthermore, Stolzing viewed the giants Fasolt and Fafner as personifications of agriculture and modern industry. Their status as

brothers, concluded Stolzing, signified that each was essential to the
state's well-being; likewise, Fafner's murder of Fasolt signified that
industry was destroying farm life. All over, trade and capital were transforming the products of agriculture and craft into gold, thereby fulfilling
Alberich's Curse. When the Wanderer warned Fafner of the danger, the
dragon just yawned: "I occupy and possess – let me sleep." Thus did
Wagner symbolize the "cold indifference of the money economy."
Further, it was upon Wotan's realization that finance capital – "unin-
spired and uncreative" – was undermining traditional social arrangements, Stolzing believed, that the king of the gods first became aware of
the error in his "power politics":

> Yet how anxiety weighs upon me!
> Dread and fear
> fetter my mind;
> how to end it
> Erda must teach me:
> I must go down to her.

Here Stolzing drew more explicit connections between the story-
line of the drama and the history of the war, asking: "Do our thoughts
not wander involuntarily from the tragedy of Wotan to Schloss Doorn,
where Wilhelm II met his fate in dull resignation?" Neither Wotan nor
Wilhelm II, Stolzing lamented, was able to master the powers they
conjured up. Just as Wotan's rescue attempt petered out in "ineffective
contemplation," the whole of Wilhelm II's statecraft receded into "constant renunciation, into trembling hesitation." Yet, though he "made
mistake upon mistake in his foreign and domestic policies," his guilt did
not lie therein alone, for the last Hohenzollern emperor "entangled
himself in the same fate as Wotan's":

> I touched Alberich's ring:
> greedily I held his gold.
> The curse from which I fled
> still has not left me:
> I must forsake what I love,
> murder the man I cherish,
> deceive and betray someone
> who trusts me.

According to Stolzing, this "despairing confession" to Brünnhilde paralleled Wilhelm II's failure. Alberich's Curse immediately attached itself to Wilhelm II's heel when his reign commenced with the "treasonous betrayal" of Bismarck – just as Wotan had betrayed Siegmund when he left him to the Hundings. Moreover, the Kaiser also coveted gold – although not for the same greedy reasons as the "loveless enemy, who forged an inexhaustible source of power out of the Nibelungen hoards." Just as Wotan had paid the Walhalla debt, Wilhelm spent extravagantly to flaunt the "superficial glory of the German Reich" in ways that triggered the envy of England. Thus, he betrayed his own Volk, because he led it "ever further down the slippery slope of pursuing gold for its own sake": under his rule, the "Volk of heroes, poets, and thinkers was turned into a Volk of salesmen, grocers, and hagglers."

Meanwhile, only those who "gladly went to battle, spilled their blood, and lay dead, sick, or wounded on the field" really knew what they were fighting against. Out of Nibelheim, the "breeding ground" of gold production in the factories and the mines, arose the "dark army" of the Nibelungen – the "racial enemies of the German Volk" who, owing to their mixed blood, hated the "fair sons of Germany" in terms voiced by Alberich:

> On radiant peaks
> you live,
> lulled in bliss:
> the black gnome
> you despise, you eternal revelers!
> Beware!
> For when once you men
> serve my might,
> the dwarf will take his pleasure
> with your pretty women
> who scorn his wooing,
> though love does not smile upon him.

Ruler of "the Nibelungen-Judocracy and Social Democracy," Alberich and his forces threatened the gods, just as similar elements menaced the nation: "never before had such a large part of the German Volk been so racially alien that it stood against the other part as an enemy." This was the result of "Mammonism having created the

Nibelheim of advanced industry whereby a rich stream of proletarians from surrounding countries flowed in to mix with the domestic population." Because of his misgivings about this incursion on the German economy, Bismarck had established a politics of customs protection for agriculture. But under Wilhelm II, the industrialization of Germany proceeded at the "wildest tempo," leading to a "gruesome deterioration of German blood." Later, the "most devastating turn in the tragic war" resulted when the "reserves of good German blood" were exhausted and the industrial population had to serve as replacements: this was a "stark *memento mori* of the natural laws of racial purity." Indeed, these circumstances served as the background to the "heart-breaking tragedy" of the failed offensive at Reims in 1918, after which Wilhelm II gave himself over to his fate "in dumb, despairing resignation – as the *Götterdämmerung* exploded over him and the whole dynasty of German princes!"

Moving beyond "Wotan–Wilhelm," Stolzing turned to Wagner's depiction of the German peoples, who, because "there was no single German type," had to be symbolized in various Ring characters. Alberich was of a "completely foreign race," but insinuated himself by "mixing his blood" with the German woman, Kriemheld, whereby he "laid a cuckoo's egg in the noble family line of the Gibichungs" in the form of his son Hagen – signifying "infection of German blood with Jewish blood." So, the "black-haired bastard," Hunding, slayed Siegmund and the "half-breed," Hagen, assassinated the "pure-blooded" Siegfried. These internecine conflicts correlated, in Stolzing's view, with the fact that the nation's "merciless enemies, the English, were in the end just as German as we are ourselves: we must not overlook the fact that this battle for world control is a struggle between peoples of common [albeit mixed] blood, exactly as in the tetralogy."

In Siegfried, on the other hand, Stolzing perceived the real German: that "fearless, ever-loving person." Genuine *Deutschtum* was symbolized in his heroic course: as Wagner put it, "the essential German consciousness that the beautiful and noble came not into the world for sake of profit, nay, not for sake of even fame and recognition ... [but in pursuit of] the thing one does for its own sake, for the very joy of doing it."[45] Siegfried slayed the dragon, but when taking the ring and helmet, he sang:

> What use you are to me
> I don't know,

> but I took you
> from the pile of heaped gold
> because I was guided by good advice.
> So let your beauty serve
> as witness to today.

Therefore, Stolzing inferred, "utilitarian reasons were completely alien to his deeds" – just as alien as they were to the "wonderful young German academic regiments who charged and died at Dixmuide [in 1914] while singing *Deutschland über alles*." But Stolzing recognized that even the part of the German Volk that "carried itself with such incomparable heroism" was ultimately guilty of the kind of conduct that led to Siegfried's death. Directly or indirectly, all Germans were involved in the battle for the Ring, he acknowledged: "we were all more or less responsible for breaking the pact with our ideals; we were all subject to the sensual magic of the potion that Gutrune gave to the unsuspecting Siegfried." Germans were paying for their own sins, as Wagner had predicted they would: "Was Siegfried as chaste as Parsifal? Did he not betray Brünnhilde with Gutrune? In essence, didn't the forgetfulness potion symbolize Siegfried's contact with the temptations of this sinful world which draw the mother of the noble Gibichungs into adultery with Alberich?" This decadence, Stolzing concluded, triggered by insidious enemies taking advantage of the Volk's own moral weakness, had to be overcome: Germans of the twentieth century would "find the way to the shiny Grail and a better future even if, like Parsifal, they still had to wander paths of error and suffer for a long time." But they would discover the right path only if they "dedicated themselves to a regeneration of the Volk in the spirit of the Master." That spirit, of course, was embodied in Hitler and National Socialism.[46]

Austrian composer, Julius Bittner – whose own operas adhered to late-romantic, quasi-Wagnerian style – extended Stolzing's linkage of the characters and circumstances of Wagner's Ring cycle beyond the First World War and into the Weimar period. Referring in the *Völkischer Beobachter* to Ernst Krenek's jazz-inspired *Jonny Strikes Up* (1927), Bittner made apocalyptic associations between contemporary issues and Weimar-era operas. Western civilization was "going down while striking up Jonny," Bittner quipped. Fortunately, Wagner had provided an antidote: Siegfried did not "sing out of the dark depths of nighttime decadence" and Wotan did not "wallow in filth with jazz accompaniment," as Krenek's characters did. An affirmation of Wagner's idealism, Bittner insisted, was more urgent than ever. This meant making a clear distinction between the "dark blue tones of the Walhalla motif" and the "cacophonous howling of the saxophone that was more appropriate for accompanying lewd dances around a golden calf." A generation of men that seized women with bestial lust – "for whom the gender only existed for pleasure" – could never understand Tristan's longing or Isolde's love; it could never follow Parsifal's difficult course; and it turned its back on Lohengrin. The "modern barbarization process" – a "campaign of the impure against culture, operating under the cloak of a clinking and clanking pseudocivilization" – was all Alberich's work. Therefore, "those who were choking on a disgusting taste in their mouths – those who were not of this modern world – had to band together under Wagner's sign in a new brotherhood of the Grail."

"Don't you see him?" Bittner asked *Völkischer Beobachter* readers frantically: "The Antichrist with his wild bedlam in the pandemonium of big city nightclubs? Don't you hear him in the agonizing sounds of this music for cannibals that debases sacred rhythms into mechanical beats?" Mammon, "with hanging jowls and fleshy fingers, decorated with the gold of the Nibelungen hoard," was being heralded with the "hooting and howling of hundreds of thousands of saxophones screaming out around the globe in his honor." Such hysteria aside, the real threat for Bittner was technological modernism: the "dragon of materialism was arising through scientific innovation whereby mankind became impudent toward the gods." This, too, Wagner had represented, in Alberich's brother: "Professor Mime" with his "greasy kitchen" and technology that "served comfort alone, pampering and coddling the world, promoting laziness and the pursuit of luxury."

Intensifying his moralizing tone, Bittner warned, "truly I say to you, if you don't take this seriously, you're going to go down in the fall with them: now is the time to recognize and fight the enemy; fight with word and deed against the fate that is approaching." According to Bittner's volkish millenarian view, as the world fell apart those who renounced love for gold – the Alberichs, Mimes, and Hagens – would disappear in the flood rolling in, and only "pure men and women, free of Alberich's Curse," would be able to rebuild it. As such, Germans had to purify themselves and band together in the new brotherhood. This, Bittner preached, "was what Wagner symbolized in his Ring Cycle."[47]

Later, Stolzing took up the charge again, this time to draw connections between Wagner's *Siegfried* (1876) and modern politics. If one looked a little closer, Stolzing asserted, one found in the relationship between Siegfried and Mime a reflection of contemporary issues. Siegfried's foster parent, the "ugly dwarf," was an embodiment of the "haggling Jew who wanted to rise higher and higher like all the Eastern Jews crossing over the German borders." Significantly, he didn't raise the hero out of love: he did so only that Siegfried might kill the dragon Fafner and capture the Ring for him, whereupon Mime would cut off his head. Here, Stolzing contended, Wagner signified that the Jew was driven to "exploit the powerful labor forces of the Nordic race to his own advantages." But while he does so, Mime teaches his foster son – through his "whole disgusting, shoveling and shambling being" – to be an anti-Semite: "for Siegfried hates Mime!" All Mime's "hypocritical blubbering" about loving Siegfried is in vain. The son forges his own sword of victory with which he will slay the dragon in his own interests. Most significantly, Stolzing insisted, since the only one who can forge the sword of victory is he who knows no fear, Siegfried was "the embodiment of National Socialism, which alone possessed the courage to break the chains of slavery around the German people." Like Siegfried, Nazism was "forging the army of liberation." But the parties of Alberich, Mime, Hunding, and Hagen – "that is, Jewry and Jew-bastard hangers on" – were "throwing themselves with everything they had against the victory march of National Socialism." Meanwhile, "Philistines persisting in the possession of material goods" were symbolized in the dragon Fafner when he calls out angrily, "I occupy and possess, let me sleep" – just as, in Stolzing's view, the bourgeois in Munich were sleeping when "the Jew Eisner marched from the Theresienwiese with his pack of deserters and shirkers." Finally, Wotan, embodying "the state of order that has become weak with age," confronted Siegfried in order to prevent him from reviving Brünnhilde, "the German soul." He blocked Siegfried from the entrance with his spear, but when the hero's sword of victory broke the spear and the way to Brünnhilde was open, "the chains of enslavement fell from the body of the German Volk."

Shifting to *Götterdämmerung* (*Twilight of the Gods*) (1876), Stolzing continued his association of the fate of Siegfried and Brünnhilde with twentieth-century German experience. Siegfried now stood on the "sunny heights of his life": he has united with Brünnhilde – "the German Volk Soul" – and was enjoying good fortune, but too much. Like him, "German idealists lost all connection with hard reality in their exuberance after unification." Once again, Stolzing held, modern times reflected the myths: "how powerful the German Volk was before the World War – with its armaments and economic prowess!" Smarter politics could have "marked the world with, and made it subject to, German and Nordic spirit; thereby non-Nordic elements, hostile to Germany, could also have been blocked." But none of this happened: the German Volk wasted its powers in political adventures like the Kaiser's trips to Palestine and Tangiers, and military expeditions to China in response to the Boxer Rebellion – activities which constituted "nothing but short-term pseudosuccesses." But, asked Stolzing: "Did Siegfried do otherwise? What was the hero waiting for when he appeared at the court of King Gunther and Hagen asked him about the Nibelungen hoard?"

> I almost forgot the treasure,
> so poorly do I prize its possession!
> I left it to lie in a cavern
> where once a dragon guarded it.

Clearly, Siegfried did not know how to use his powers either, Stolzing observed. Moreover, yet another "genuinely German trait" appeared in Siegfried's character when he left Brünnhilde behind in search of adventure. This represented the "typical German longing for something distant": like the millions of Germans who "lose themselves in foreign lands and sink into the cultural manure of strange peoples, Siegfried lost himself in an inferior, even evil foreignness – not only breaking his marriage with Brünnhilde, but pushing her, the most majestic woman in the world, into the nuptial chamber of a degenerate and cowardly king, while himself entering into a second marriage with a whoring wench of inferior race." Siegfried left Brünnhilde and entered a world of evil and corruption whose lies and deceit would ruin him. This, Stolzing argued, was exactly like naive Germans stumbling into the First World War that others – not they – wanted to fight. And then, just as Hagen – the "Jewish-Nordic half-breed" – justified his crime as vengeance for perjury as he drove the spear through Siegfried from behind, "those very same forces who tricked Germans into war claimed, in the War Guilt clause, that we were responsible for the bloodbath!"[48]

Some have argued that National Socialism's obsession with Wagner was primarily Hitler's own, pointing out that other Nazi leaders were essentially uninterested in Wagner and that many were bored when required to sit through performances of his works.[49] This is true to a point, but there were fanatically Wagnerian Nazis other than Hitler. The *Völkischer Beobachter* consistently identified parallels between Wagner and the public image of the Nazi movement, and its frequent coverage in this vein surely strengthened such associations among its many readers. Staff writers like Josef Stolzing relentlessly sought to identify the similarities between the Nazi world view and Wagner's polemics and storylines. And these tactics did not mean just correlating opinions about general trends in European life through the late mid-nineteenth century that Wagner himself experienced, including the money economy, industrialization, nationalization, liberalism, socialism, and the supposed responsibility of European Jews for all and sundry. Rather, the newspaper insisted that Wagner presciently forecast historical events beyond his own time, including Wilhelm II's dismissal of Bismarck, competition with Great Britain, the outbreak of the First World War, the exhaustion of German forces, the involvement of African troops in the field, the conclusive defeat at the Marne, the naval mutiny, the flight of the Kaiser, the rise of Soviet communism, the popularization of aesthetic modernism, the decadence of the Weimar era, and the brutal measures required to restore the German Volk. Thus, along with Stolzing, significant German musicologists, historians, literary scholars, and composers contributed in the paper's pages to this characterization of Wagner as a prophet who left in his writings and music dramas explicit warnings of the dire events to come. But, as close investigation reveals, the *Völkischer Beobachter* did not seek to leverage every one of Wagner's operas for overt political purposes; *Lohengrin* and *Die Meistersinger von Nürnberg* plainly were used as such, but these works were seen by the paper more as celebrations of Germanness than as attacks on Jews – however much Beckmesser may appear to be stereotyped. Instead, the smoking gun proving incontrovertibly that Nazis brandished Wagner's work in its eliminationist anti-Semitic plot is found in *Völkischer Beobachter* reception of the *Ring of the Nibelungen*. It was in the tetralogy that National Socialist Wagnerians perceived the "Meister's" voice as most perfectly harmonizing with that of the "Führer."

PART III

MODERN DILEMMAS

10 REALIST PARADOX AND EXPRESSIONIST CONFUSION

Nazi discomfort with aesthetic modernism is a well-known characteristic of the party's cultural history. *Mein Kampf* and other aspects of Hitler's biography verify that disdain for cultural modernism was fundamental to his world view. "Such diseases could be seen in Germany in nearly every field of art and culture," he complained, with artists passing off "all sorts of incomprehensible and obviously crazy stuff on their amazed fellow men as a so-called inner experience." In his opinion, this trend had simply made it "permissible to dish up the hallucinations of lunatics or criminals to the healthy world." Moreover, he clearly believed that it was the job of rulers to monitor and control the "crazy stuff" of modernism, as prevention against cultural Armageddon:

> It is the business of the state, in other words, of its leaders, to prevent a people from being driven into the arms of spiritual madness. And this is where such a development would some day inevitably end. For on the day when this type of art really corresponded to the general view of things, one of the gravest transformations of humanity would have occurred: the regressive development of the human mind would have begun and the end would be scarcely conceivable.[1]

Direct attacks by NSDAP propaganda and policy on modernist tendencies were most evident in the staging of the "degenerate" art and music exhibitions of 1937 and 1938. But the vilification of "cultural bolshevism" that the party engaged in during the 1920s and 1930s was only the most immediate manifestation of the Nazi antimodernist outlook.[2] Indeed, the Nazis' antimodernist tack followed directly from a conservatism that had been concerned with non-traditional expression since the middle of the nineteenth century, perceiving it as evidence of the cultural and social decline that had been triggered by the French and Industrial revolutions. They did not, therefore, limit their criticism to contemporary forms of "degenerate" culture, but extended it backward to address art that, for them, represented the first, troubling deviations from classical and romantic aesthetics.[3] Consequently, the *Völkischer Beobachter* was replete with assessments of nineteenth-century cultural movements and creators that emerged outside the neoclassical and steel romantic trends that its ideologues idealized. But, as was true for National Socialist cultural policy as a whole, the newspaper failed to formulate an unambiguous position against all modernist tendencies. As cultural coverage in the newspaper evolved, inconsistencies and even outright contradictions undermined its supposedly monolithic antimodernist platform. Part III of this book will explore how the foundation themes of Nazi culture were associated with important cultural figures after the romantic era. But it will also address how the paper's references to cultural history from the mid-nineteenth through the early twentieth century conveyed highly paradoxical attitudes toward modernist expression in the arts, consonant with the complex debates that occurred within the party well into the Third Reich.

Such inconsistencies were already evident in the paper's presentation of the first significant post-romantic cultural movement: social realism. Leo Tolstoy (1828–1910) was a primary target of the *Völkischer Beobachter*'s criticism of nineteenth-century realist literature. It disdained the portrayal of Tolstoy as a "good old man who remained a child to the world," and portrayed him instead as a "dreamer" who wanted to make people happy "while destroying his own family." From the National Socialist perspective, Tolstoy and his works were dangerous "instigators of revolution": in its view, "Lenin was the deed that came from Tolstoy's thought." Indeed, while nothing about his outlook seemed acceptable, it was mainly the pacifist position Tolstoy assumed after his conversion that raised the ire of the newspaper. In the elderly Tolstoy, it complained, one could see the "degeneracy of the man of non-violence." National Socialists "could not make Tolstoy's pacifist thinking their own": they had to recognize that "only power impresses the powerful"; they had to "counter violence with violence, terror with terror!" The "spirit of the front soldier and the right to self-defense" were their ideals.[4]

Tolstoy's Norwegian contemporary Henrik Ibsen (1828–1906) prompted mixed views from the *Völkischer Beobachter*. Referring to him as a "Nordic writer," the paper felt that *Peer Gynt* (1867) was "hardened in storms of fantasy and polished by the sharpness of humor." But the paper voiced reservations about the increasingly naturalistic tenor of Ibsen works such as *A Doll's House* (1879), *Ghosts* (1881), and *An Enemy of the People* (1882). "World-wide Nordic Romanticism" – the style ostensibly marking *Peer Gynt* – compelled one to "follow its spell" into "completely different depths of the soul than the moderate illusions of the 'society piece.'" Admittedly, the paper allowed, his works stirred contemporary controversy. There was a time when it was considered unsuitable in Copenhagen to even discuss the plot of *A Doll's House*. This, it asserted, was important in the history of literature, but did not increase Ibsen's lasting value: the struggles and characters of his work were, in the paper's view, "simply no longer relevant." Rejecting his opposition to Victorian society, the *Völkischer Beobachter* decided that as a social critic, Ibsen was "already a thing of the past."[5]

The paper's presentation of Gerhart Hauptmann (1862–1946) revealed even more pronounced tensions. While the party typically distanced itself from leftist politics, the socialist element of National Socialism occasionally required acknowledgment. To this end, the paper noted that Hauptmann's "esteemed depiction" of the fate of the Silesian weavers' revolt in 1844, *The Weavers* (1892), was written with "some respect for the memory of the workers themselves." But the subsequent politics of the author drew critical fire. A 1932 article allowed that Hauptmann had entered into the arena of German letters "as a fighter." Indeed, "something burned in his soul back then" – a deep compassion for the suffering of "Volk comrades" in the ranks of handworkers – that had to be recognized and emphasized by the "German socialism of the future." The young Hauptmann had to be thanked for depicting the physical and spiritual suffering of these German people, and for "bravely breaking a lance for the alleviation of their distress." But this was praise enough for the paper: while Hauptmann was able to represent a rebellion of weavers with powerful accuracy, he did not succeed in marking this rebellion with the "convincing force of a potent idea," that is, it was not grounded in volkish ideology. As such, the play remained the "superficial depiction of a mere rebellion of human nature in pain that goes down in tragic defeat against brutal forces." Rooted in the "materialist age," Hauptmann had no inner connection with a "great idea" that would have allowed him to go "deeply into the creative and active life of the Volk." Trapped in the naturalistic image of mankind as the mere product of conditions and environment, he was barred from the path to "liberating solutions." Whether it was the "revolt (not revolution!)" of the weavers, the "dull end" of *Fuhrmann Henschel* (1899), or the dark sobriety of *Rose Berndt* (1903), the "redemptive outlook that is the essence of poetry, born of faith and idealism," was always missing in Hauptmann's works, according to Rudolf Erckmann, who contributed literary coverage to the *Völkischer Beobachter* as of 1932 and would become an official at Goebbels' propaganda ministry.[6]

Josef Stolzing concurred with this critical view of Hauptmann. For the Nazi critic, the content of *The Weavers* was "historical," but Hauptmann's approach "destroyed its accuracy." In large part, Stolzing argued, the Silesian weavers were themselves to blame for the emergency that led to the bloody riot, because they irrationally held on to their outdated mode of production. This was the tragedy of German handicrafts in general: such ways of life were sure to decline until craftsmen succeeded in modernizing their enterprises in order to compete with industry. The Prussian government recognized the danger that threatened the Silesian weaving mills; in fact, it offered support to the weavers in the form of credits to purchase modern machines. But the policy failed "because of the conservatism of the weavers." According to Stolzing, these aspects of the "bloody days in 1844" were lost on Hauptmann. When he toured the area in preparation for writing, he was "led by a social democrat." The result was a "provocative Marxist tone" in his work, characterized perfectly in the police order which closed the first performance in 1893: "the play doesn't just show the hard-heartedness of some individual owners, but attacks the whole social and political structure of the time." In Stolzing's view, if the piece had "stuck to confirmed facts," showing the real causes for the terrible outcome, it would not have been censored. Instead, Hauptmann created an "intentionally Marxist *Tendenzwerk*, and that's the way it was generally received." As a result, it had only a short life in production, which was really finished by the time of the First World War, said Stolzing: "even the November Revolution wasn't able to give it fresh relevance," and the fault for this lay in its "inner untruthfulness."

The Weavers was of no contemporary relevance, in Stolzing's opinion, because "nobody could deny" that conditions had "improved substantially for the majority of German workers" since the events it depicted, or that much more could have been achieved if the leaders of social democracy had not conducted themselves as "class warriors hostile to Germany," rejecting anything that might have led to further progress. Moreover, the outcome of the war brought about bitter setbacks, including the "enslavement of the German worker to international Jewish high finance – to the supranational world market."[7]

The *Völkischer Beobachter*'s assessment of Hauptmann's postwar career continued in this vein: the "Liberal-Bourgeois Age against which he had struggled assimilated him and brought about his bourgeoisification." Only men who were "inwardly rooted in their blood and Volk could pass this way without wavering," but Hauptmann was not a man to resist the temptation. Propelled down this path by his fame, "his muse moved into the realm of slogans, bourgeois superficiality, and flatness." The one-time revolutionary "landed painfully in the sphere of the bourgeois, watering down his original seriousness into shallowness." And, in the paper's view, the situation worsened significantly when he ascended to poet laureate of the Weimar "system" in 1918. Thus began the "sad time" when Hauptmann "cozied up to the ranks of the Jewish and Jew-loving spiritual elite of the November state," which raised him up on its shield very early because it "perceived Marxist elements in his works." Hauptmann continued to write, but without the strong awareness of reality of his early days, and without any sense that times had changed.[8] Because "German spirit" was very weak in him, he never had any real "social feeling." Therefore, while the "German tragedy" took place after 1918, Hauptmann himself benefited: "being a poet of fashion, profits flowed to him."[9]

Like Hauptmann, belittled as a symbol of contemporary decline in the Weimar era, the paper similarly approached the case of Heinrich Mann (1871–1950), focusing its attack on Mann's career in postwar Germany as a supporter of left-wing causes, as President of the Literature Section of the Prussian Academy of Art, and as an active opponent of the Nazi Party. But the *Völkischer Beobachter* also aimed at Mann's earlier work and social realist aesthetic. For ammunition, the newspaper relied on the volkish literary views of Adolf Bartels, often citing his *History of German Literature* (1901–1902), and other works, directly. According to Bartels, Mann's novel, *In the Land of Cockaigne* (1900), described the life of the Berlin stockbrokers and journalists – "so, basically Jewish circles" – in "grotesque caricature." Also troubling to Bartels was Mann's "eroticism," which he said became most pronounced in *Diana* (1902–1904). It was the exploration of sensuality in this trilogy, Bartels announced, that prevented him from taking Mann seriously. But most irritating to the volkish ideologue was the political satire of *The Loyal Subject* (1918), which, according to Bartels, "supposedly presented the age of Wilhelm II, but was nothing but an insolent caricature of German life."[10]

The paper's editors thought that Bartels was right to attack Mann viciously, stating that "Mann's fantasy exhausted itself on erotic themes," and that this was "probably the result of his blood, since his mother was Portuguese." Even his own brother, Thomas, the paper added, was critical of Heinrich's writings, describing some as "novels of aphrodisiacal fantasy – a catalogue of vices in which nothing is omitted." Moreover, the paper went on, by sketching irritating caricatures in the middle of the First World War he competed with "one Chaim Bückenburg (alias Heinrich Heine)" in "committing the most irresponsible acts against the Volk." From the Nazi perspective, the *Völkischer Beobachter* found it simply incomprehensible that the "November criminals" considered an author of this sort appropriate to "represent German spirituality" as literary leader at the Berlin Academy of Art.[11]

Thus did the newspaper treat significant figures in the social realist tradition as incompatible with the volkish world view. But the *Völkischer Beobachter*'s negation of realism still left room for accepting some artists who paid attention to the plight of underclasses in nineteenth-century European life. For instance, from March through August 1923, the paper ran the whole of Charles Dickens' *Oliver Twist* (1837) in serial form. Undoubtedly, Dickens' characterization of Fagin, the Jew, provided much of the motivation for reprinting the novel, as it could be interpreted as an early manifestation of racial stereotyping. Within the German tradition itself, the *Völkischer Beobachter* sought to demonstrate that authors such as Wilhelm Raabe, Theodor Storm, and Gustav Freytag could be counted in the patriotic and even anti-Semitic camp. According to Helmuth Langenbucher, it wasn't the writer's fault if Germans had not hitherto recognized Raabe's work and life as "contributing serious service to the German Volk." Seen from the Nazi point of view, however, this omission could be rectified: Langenbucher reported that Raabe (1831–1910) wrote in a school essay that "it was a thrill to be in the German Fatherland which, despite its inner strife, could become great and powerful," and that "the old spirit will again sound powerfully in German regions and the inhabitants will again be true and brave like the heroes of the *Hermannsschlacht*." Given that Raabe grew up in a time when "Germany had been tricked out of the fruits of the Wars of Liberation, Goethe was almost forgotten, Romanticism was being ridiculed, Heine and Börne were the greats of the day, and non-German elements threatened … the German Volk in public," Langenbucher considered it remarkable that the author remained "full of warm love for the soul of the Volk." In Langenbucher's opinion, Raabe "said in a straightforward, unrelenting way: 'Germany, I believe in you.'" Nazis could find encouragement, Langenbucher said, by immersing themselves in Raabe's "stream of indomitable faith in the eternal Fatherland."[12] As in the case of Dickens, Langenbucher and the *Völkischer Beobachter* were most enthusiastic about Raabe's depiction of an antagonistic Jewish character in his highly popular novel, *The Hunger Pastor* (1864), published in thirty-four editions during his lifetime. Langenbucher held that Raabe's depiction of "the racial enemy" in the figure of Moses Freudenstein was "clear and objective." Above all, Freudenstein was a stereotype of the influential Jew who was "doing so much damage to the German Volk." In the words uttered by this character, Langenbucher found "unvarnished and uncloaked expressions of the Jewish psyche," which was a "slow poison" that threatened the German Volk more than any other. Therefore, Langenbucher concluded that Raabe's work should be read by National Socialists as a "warning and reminder about the Jewish threat."[13]

The *Völkischer Beobachter* also moved to appropriate the realist works of Theodor Storm (1817–1888). In 1927, Baldur von Schirach complained that Storm was too often taught and presented "as a lightweight," while in actuality he was a patriotic German poet, especially attached to his homeland, Schleswig-Holstein. For Schirach, Storm's art "belonged to the German Volk." He supported this view of Storm as a politically inspired writer with reference to such works as *Graves in Schleswig* (1850?), which expressed "passionate love of the *Heimat*." Similarly, Schirach held, a "voice of battle" arises from the poem *Easter* (1848), "emerging from the era in which Schleswig-Holstein rose up." National Socialists loved such poems, which expressed "notions that we have synthesized," Schirach enthused, hoping that these examples sufficed to show that the image of this "great German poet" would be complete only when it included this patriotic side of his character, which had been "defaced from most German school textbooks." This misrepresentation was a great injustice: Storm was not just the creator of the *Pole Poppenspäler* (1874) or *Immensee* (1850) – a "master of portraits realized as if done in pastels" – but was also a "singer of German freedom." Had he lived to see the "days of German shame and decline" during the Weimar era, he would have "revealed himself to the new generation as a great leader."[14]

Parallel to its assessment of Storm's *Heimat* realism as patriotic was the *Völkischer Beobachter*'s treatment of Gustav Freytag (1816–1895) as a *volkstümlich* author.[15] Influenced by Charles Dickens and French realists, the paper reminded, Freytag was among the best-known German writers of his generation, especially admired for his depiction of middle-class culture in *Debit and Credit* (*Soll und Haben*, 1855), the novel that earned him an international reputation. According to the paper, however, *Debit and Credit* was a "valuable resource" above all for German nationalists. In fact, it reported, "right-wingers were putting this book in the hands of young bourgeois trainees in order to give them an idea of duty and the significance of their class." In addition, the book was useful to the Nazi cause because it depicted the difference between "German businessmen and international traders."[16] However, beyond such elements, Nazis were most interested in drawing attention to the novel's depiction of Jewish characters. Thus, the newspaper was irate when a 1926 edition of the book edited by Fritz Skowronnek seemed to eliminate passages that featured these individuals. "What in Freytag's *Debit and Credit* did you 'edit,' Dr. Skowronnek?" asked the reviewer, Albert Zimmermann: "In the second chapter of the first book, you cut out the ending. Why?" Here, according to Zimmermann, Freytag had used a "sharp pen" to show the difference between "the German Anton Wohlfahrt and the Jew Veitel Itzig." Wohlfahrt was, in the reviewer's opinion, a true German man: he wanted to raise himself up through honorable work since: "high ideals filled his soul." Veitel Itzig, to the contrary, just "made plans to swindle other characters." To Zimmermann's dismay, Skowronnek cut this "highly significant section" as being "no longer relevant in the Weimar age." Moreover, he suppressed every portion in which Freytag revealed the "hypocritical, clawing spirit" of the Jew. "Why, Doktor," Zimmermann asked, "did you cut these sections so carefully?"

These and other examples proved, in Zimmermann's eyes, that Skowronnek undertook his reductions "very systematically, in pursuit of a very certain end," namely, to "censor the anti-Semitic heart of Freytag's work." According to Zimmermann, Freytag wrote in his memoirs: "As a child of the borderland, I learned early to love my German essence in contrast to foreign peoples." The Nazi reviewer therefore believed that *Debit and Credit* was primarily intended to highlight these differences. By eliminating its depictions of the Jewish businessman, Skowronnek had convoluted the basic meaning of the whole book, thereby "abusing" an important German writer. In short, he had "consciously mutilated – *circumcised* – Freytag." "No more of this circumcised collection of German classics should hit the shelves," Zimmermann declared. "Let this warning cry, wake up all of Germany: watch out, Herr. Dr. Skowronnek!"[17]

So, *Völkischer Beobachter* contributors rejected the realism of Tolstoy, Ibsen, Hauptmann, and Heinrich Mann as irrelevant relics of the past at best, and as threatening instigators of revolution at worst. Simultaneously, in the works of Dickens, Raabe, Storm, and Freytag they applauded a realism that remained "full of warm love for the soul of the Volk," while conveying warnings and reminders about the Jewish threat. But the conflicted nature of the *Völkischer Beobachter*'s approach to realism is no more starkly realized than in its treatment of the foremost purveyor of social realism in French visual art, Gustave Courbet (1819–1877). Mirroring its reception of realist art in general, the paper perceived a dual nature in Courbet himself. On the one hand, it extolled him as the "herald and creator of a new naturalism" that "fueled the fire of common ideals that remained alight and influential in Europe's artistic disposition for a long time." But, like Goethe's Faust, two souls burned in his breast, and next to the "completely original, instinctive painter whose genius outshone all criticism" stood a "fuzzy propagandist for a new social order." Within Courbet, the supposed result was an "explosive nature" that corresponded to an inner struggle between his artistic and political sides. His "unbridled frankness, indeed recklessness, led to misunderstanding, ridicule, hostility, and quarrels: his strong personality alarmed and confused more people than it won, and did not make it easy for his friends to answer for him." But despite or perhaps because of this divided nature, the *Völkischer Beobachter* asserted that Courbet attracted the devotees of art in Germany more than anywhere else on the map. His paintings took effect there like a "revelation of everything German painters had long desired but could not yet develop," because of external circumstances in the nation's art centers. Courbet visited

Germany three times and had an "extraordinary effect," especially in Frankfurt where Viktor Mueller, Louis Eyusen, Otto Scholderer, and Hans Thoma were "strongly influenced by him." Moreover, in Munich he found a congenial friend in the young Wilhelm Leibl, to whom he felt immediately drawn: "in recognition of the young German's increasing mastery." Acknowledging his impact east of the Rhine, the *Völkischer Beobachter* then took the step of claiming that Courbet was of German origins: "German-Burgundian blood flowed in his blood – from this source emerged a beautifully grown person with a mane of black hair, velvet eyes, athletic exterior, forceful awareness, and ardent desire to create which determined his life for better or worse."[18]

About the extension of nineteenth-century positivist tendencies into the visual arts, as manifested in the Impressionist style, the *Völkischer Beobachter* was far less conflicted: it rejected Impressionism outright as a form of "French disease that would drive modernity into decrepitude." Foreign "isms" such as "flickering Impressionism and cerebral Constructivism" were "damned to hell" by the likes of Rudolf Paulsen, a widely published novelist and poet.[19] As Wilhelm Rüdiger explained, Impressionism consisted of merely registering on the canvas impressions from the retina in a "very routine process" that was "utterly lacking in content." Furthermore, flattening the picture plane constituted the "conscious dissolution and violation of nature – its conquest – because the coherence of nature was thereby dismantled and dismembered." An Impressionist picture was at best a "stenograph of nature aimed at sensation alone, purely fabricated and mathematical in character." The style was an "empty form of art" at odds with the fact that the essence of German art was its treatment of "that which lies *within*," not surface realities. Even worse, Impressionism had only one consequential representative in Germany and that was "the Jew Max Liebermann." Therefore, Rüdiger argued, Nazism was dedicated to countering its long-term effects. Volk, nature, and personality were the bases from which the art most appropriate for Nazis grew: "the opposition" denied these values, against which they posited "international standards, abstraction, and lifelessness." The artist who felt "spiritually and culturally responsible to his Volk" had to understand that the struggle was more than political, that it also involved an intellectual front. National Socialism, said Rüdiger, was the "political embodiment of one side of the battle for German culture." The enemy wanted to "destroy everything that stood and fought for the maintenance of volkish culture and German art through modernisms starting with Impressionism." But the Nazi Party would overcome the materialistic outlook with its "belief in the aristocratic worthiness of all persons, whatever their classification, whether rich or poor." Nazism, said Rüdiger, was the "political creed of a new movement of the Volk – the presupposition for a new and original German culture in response to the flattening of man, society, and nature implied in Impressionism."

More in line with German nature, Rüdiger continued, was the Expressionist tendency consistent with the "anti-modernist principle that content not form was most important to the German artist": form was only the language through which he realized his inner experience; the most important part lay behind the surface appearance of a work of art. In the finest works, therefore, "form served expression." Germans, Rüdiger held, would "never be mere artisans as long as they created art out of their being – from their soul." Their art was "personal and seldom modern" in that it was "never obsessed with the most fabulously new or the most cosmopolitan: to Germans art gave form to life and was never just an aesthetic problem." Every German artist was, in this sense, "an expressionist as opposed to a mere impressionistic stylist."[20]

The primacy accorded to the expressionist predisposition may help to explain the substantial coverage the paper devoted to the French Symbolist poet, Arthur Rimbaud (1854–1891). Numerous articles celebrated Rimbaud's life, paying particular attention to his retreat from civilization into the dark heart of Africa. "Who was Rimbaud?" the paper asked: a Frenchman, a businessman, a political intriguer, an adventurer, a gold seeker? No one had ever been sure. He was the "third star of French poetry," the paper explained, along with François Villon and Paul Verlaine. In three short years he completely revolutionized French poetry with his "incomparable, earthshaking power of expression"; he worked out a "completely new dynamic of words – a monstrous achievement!" But then not a single line more. "Most unbelievable, most brilliant," said the paper, was the fact that this was the work of a child – a boy with a "fiery spirit like Shakespeare's." His school notebooks "streamed with vitality and unprecedented artistic expression"; at ten he wrote an essay on Villon, wherein "flowed images that reminded one of Breughel." Then came *Drunken Boat* (1871), a "dream as could only be dreamed once in history." Here images of "Dantean greatness" raised him to immortality; here the "vastness of the ocean surrounded his brow in a green fire, a flaming stream." Anticipating

Nietzsche, he proclaimed the "vital, instinctive, life-consuming power of the dying Europe." He revealed the "imperative and the heroic in man," and through his existence, "Volk and fate became one with the poet." Bursting with a "demonic creative drive," he broke from the bourgeois, philistine milieu of his home town and wandered like a modern version of the medieval vagabond: first to Paris, then Brussels, London, and back. Then he "locked himself in an empty box" and wrote *A Season in Hell* (1873): "not weak, impotent, lyrical cant like that of thousands and thousands who believe themselves to have been kissed on the mouth by the muse, but works that let one hear the whole spiritual world."

After this "incredible comet-like flare-up," the paper continued, Rimbaud threw all art overboard and let his artistic nature die: at only 18 years of age. Disgusted with Europe, as "too small for the tremendous dynamism of his energy," he leapt into adventure: Foreign Legionnaire, circus employee, language tutor, shipper, and trader – until he reached the court of Meneliks II. Then, said the newspaper, he "conquered Africa with something other than fire and sword," for his colonial politics was founded on awareness of the "biological life forms and racial character-istics of the natives." For the indigenous peoples, he became "myth personified: a God-Man." Only "in this virgin land could his eminent vitalism thrive." There, he could become "the uncrowned emperor of Africa, the true image of Ibsen's Peer Gynt: the King of the World." Then, all too soon, he succumbed to illnesses and injuries and died. The poet had "long before become immortal," but even more impressive to the *Völkischer Beobachter* was the notion that "Abyssinian tribes still sang about the heroic Rimbaud, adventurer and arms dealer."[21]

Erhard Buschbeck, a Vienna dramaturge who worked with Georg Trakl, Arnold Schoenberg, and Alban Berg, similarly celebrated Rimbaud as a model for expressionist artists who turned their backs on the bourgeois world of Western civilization. According to Buschbeck, Rimbaud's life showed that "genius is often a Danae gift": his escape corresponded to nineteenth-century Germany's loss of Hölderlin, "the poetic youth who ended in mental derangement," as well as that of Kleist, the "greatest tragic talent of the Germans" who was "lost to suicide." The work Rimbaud left behind when he "broke out" to Africa, Buschbeck concluded, surrounded him in an "aura" in which the "problems of his time and those of eternity mixed in a unique way."[22]

Seemingly better suited to *Völkischer Beobachter* purposes were the Germans Stefan George and Rainer Maria Rilke, whom the paper viewed as practicing their art, like Rimbaud, in "vital, instinctive, life-consuming fashion." According to Rudolf Paulsen's tribute at the time of George's death, the poet (1868–1933) was "the lonely one, the genteel one, the nobleman of conviction," who moved in the realm of myth and stayed there – while remaining in touch with Nazis, "for he was ours." Remaining "the calmest one" who never stepped into the arena of daily struggles, he always maintained control. This "modern monkishness" made him seem lonely, but in this loneliness he "protected the dignity of the word." Still, despite this apparent distance from mundane affairs, Paulsen found inspiration for Nazi plans in George's work. Everyone who read him received a "seed that would bring forth fruit": on the "best, the most aristocratic, the proudest, and the noblest of hearts he inscribed sayings for life." German youth especially, Paulsen insisted, had to heed the command George issued in his "Three Songs" of 1921, calling for

> A young race that again measures man and thing
> With genuine standards, beautiful and serious,
> Happy in its uniqueness, proud in the face of strangers,
> Distancing itself from the reef of brazen darkness,
> From the shallow swamp of false brotherhood.

Such a generation was finally emerging with the successes of the National Socialist movement, Paulsen exclaimed, happily aware of its "Germanness in blood and spirit."[23]

In Nazi eyes, Rainer Maria Rilke (1875–1926) also proved to be an appealing subject – in substantial part because of the quality of Expressionistic detachment that characterized his work. But the accompanying inaccessibility of his writing, which was viewed as beyond the understanding of most German readers, raised questions about his volkish credentials. Rilke expert, Erwin Damian, tried to make sense of this contradiction. One could justifiably wonder what he meant to Nazis, Damian acknowledged, because he was admittedly "unknown to the majority of the Volk," and would remain so. While many knew Rilke because they carried *The Lay of the Love and Death of Cornet Christoph Rilke* (1906) in their packs, his works remained difficult for them, and in the end most Germans "really only knew his name." Nevertheless, Damian was certain, because Rilke's work was "lived" by its readers, it would continue to have influence – and "not only in university dissertations." According to Damian, Rilke's work "said something different and new and yet remained in the beautiful and proud row of classic German poetry." For readers in 1936, Rilke remained a model of German ideals: "German lyric had not reached such a level of purity anywhere since Hölderlin; he was an inspiration for every creative artist who remained faithful to the sacred message of his work."[24]

Heinz Grothe, who wrote on film and theater into the 1970s, seconded and attempted to clarify Damian's defense of Rilke – while adding a racial dimension to the paper's interpretation. Whoever really wanted to understand Rilke, Grothe argued, had to take into account that his ancestors were German farmers from Bohemia. A long ancestral chain could be traced back to the fifteenth century, but a certain "exhaustion of the blood" might have led to his being "over-refined." As a result, while Nazis could recognize the beauty of his poetry's form as "absolutely worthwhile," there existed a difference of opinion about its content. The latest generation of writers was no longer as influenced by Rilke as the previous had been, but his "service to the German language, his feeling for words, his distinct, precise way of expressing himself about the concrete and the spiritual, his struggle for knowledge – all this marked him as a passionate fighter for the word." In an era fraught with chaos, he had provided "peace, calm, and depth." Therefore, Grothe concluded, while some Nazis rejected his mysticism, "his inner greatness was a pole which many were trying to reach."[25]

In the case of the Austrian Expressionist, Hermann Bahr (1863–1934), the newspaper was also conflicted, though its primary concerns involved his public stance regarding Jews rather than his writings. Over the years, one article complained, Bahr's "interior" had changed even more than his outward appearance: there wasn't a political or artistic fashion that he hadn't followed. He switched from being the enthusiastic devotee of the anti-Semitic Georg Ritter von Schönerer to an equally enthusiastic philo-Semite; then he developed into an Old Austrian Liberal (*schwarzgelben Altösterreicher*), only to end up as a pious Catholic. Unfortunately, for the *Völkischer Beobachter*, since losing his youthful intoxication for the volkish movement, Bahr had remained "true to only one star: the Star of David." Once having "warmed himself by its golden rays" he couldn't even resist strewing the Zionist leader, Theodor Herzl, with compliments. In an article in the *Deutsche Akademiker-Zeitung*, Bahr had described Herzl as a "nationalistic fraternity member," then spoke of his "princely appearance" and how he was enchanted by him at first sight. This "didn't sound right," the *Völkischer Beobachter* objected, since at the time that Bahr had been a fraternity brother of Herzl, he was a proponent of anti-Semitic views that were then beginning to gain ground; in fact, he was "one of the most zealous fighters for these ideas." The paper did not want to assume that Bahr was "so lacking in character" that he would intentionally alter the facts "in such a drastic way." So it charitably characterized him as a "poor old man" who – unable to enjoy fond memories of his student days – instead had to "conceal, disown, even besmirch his own deeds."[26]

Another *Völkischer Beobachter* article addressed Bahr's "Jewish Ideal of Beauty," and treated the writer with similar condescension. Aging could "make one gabby," the paper explained, and such was often the case with writers in their later years who "made up for their lack of ideas with empty blithering." As a young student, Bahr – who "remade himself so often" – had been a "sharp racial anti-Semite." But in his old age he was "trying to preach about things he knew nothing about," as in an essay on race for a Munich paper. Therein he "correctly placed race over nation," stating that "one can change one's nation but not one's race" and that the "foundations of Western civilization were toppling and a new system based on race was emerging." In the same essay, however, Bahr also wrote that he had "never been more pleased than by the sight of perfectly beautiful figures," and among the most beautiful in his memory were those of Theodor Herzl and Emma Adler – wife of the socialist politician, Victor Adler. This passage raised the ire of the Nazi paper. One could see that the "meaning of race" was dawning on Hermann Bahr, but the fact that he then "made a bow to Judaism" was evidence of the "tragicomic side of his career." The paper allowed that "there were racially beautiful Jews and Jewesses," but "the aesthetic ideal of the Nordic race had to lie closer to the heart of a German than the Jewish." "Good God," the critique concluded, "when a Gojim makes such a compliment to Jews, they might even forgive him the occasional inquiry into the field of racial research – which Jews usually hate."[27]

Upon Bahr's death in 1934, Josef Stolzing chimed in with some personal memories of the writer. "How could people change their political outlook as easily as they change a dirty shirt?" he asked. Stolzing felt that this was a particularly relevant question on the first anniversary of the "seizure of power" when he saw so many "politicians of the hour who violently criticized us a year ago now strutting around with swastikas in their buttonholes." Bahr was such a case in point. Once, he had been one of the most enthusiastic followers of Schönerer; he had been a member of the Vienna University fraternity that ousted Herzl on account of his Jewish heritage; he was even ousted from school for giving a pan-German speech and enthusiastic pan-Germanic students had paraded with him as he went to the train station. Stolzing was shocked, then, when Bahr was included in a *Deutsche Zeitung* collection of leading personalities, including Émile Zola, who had spoken out against anti-Semitism. "What a peculiar change!" he exclaimed. Later on, though, Stolzing recounted, he and Bahr had lived in the same building in Munich. "Once I met him and he said, 'I have known you for years and I am happy to greet you. Believe me, the Hitler movement is the only one that can save our Volk from its suffering. We Germans must finally come together in a tight unity!'" For Stolzing, this final change in Bahr's shifting outlook sufficed to consider him "redeemed." "After all of his errors and wanderings the former *Schönerer-ianer* had finally found the way home to Adolf Hitler, and therefore we want to honor him respectfully as a poet and a man: despite everything, he was a German!"[28]

Other German writers associated with the Expressionist movement, however, could not be so readily redeemed, and were used in the *Völkischer Beobachter* chiefly for their value as reference points of turn-of-the-century decline and degeneration. Thus was the case with Franz Wedekind (1864–1918). In reference to Munich's once influential bohemian quarter and its flagship periodical, the paper asserted that the "Schwabing of Wedekind and *Simplicissimus*" were things of the past: "perhaps they had been among the most significant developments of their time, but *their* time was no longer ours." Sure, the paper admitted, even Nazis might have once considered Wedekind to be a great phenomenon of German literature: but then came the war. For the front generation of 1914, the war was an "entrance way to a new world established under storms of steel and fear of death." In that process, they found the basis for a "new morality," so they no longer needed "Wedekind the Moralist." On the other hand, those who stayed home – "like Heinrich Mann" – were still looking for a "synthesis between life and their moral system." For them, the war was just "another stirring episode; or, more to the point, a painful interruption of their 'business' – to borrow from Wedekind who openly called morality 'the best business.'" Maybe passages from "Wedekind's erotica" were revolutionary at one time, but the postwar age had gone well past such issues. Wedekind's moralism "would not be able to handle the schoolboy eroticism of the Weimar era," manifested in disturbing events such as the 1927 Krantz Affair (in which high school students committed a murder after a weekend of alcohol and sex – both straight and gay). In fact, the paper held, one could say the opposite: the author of *Spring's Awakening* (1891) would "probably have tried to justify the murder of a junior-high kid." Therefore "the new generation would not revive Wedekind": those who were trying to do so, "like Klaus Mann and his circle," were going to be left behind by world history. As represented in "the morality of the Nazi movement, the wisdom of thousands of years stood as the moral basis of mankind, against the despair of an individual who never achieved a synthesis between spirit and beauty."[29]

The *Völkischer Beobachter* likewise set aside as decadent the works of Hugo von Hofmannsthal (1874–1929). According to the newspaper's "investigations into his racial background,"[30] Hofmannsthal was the "Vienna-born, Catholic-baptized offshoot of an ennobled Jewish banking family." As such, he would probably have been forgotten immediately if he had not been the librettist for most of Richard Strauss' operas. Still, the paper allowed, it would have been superficial to simply dismiss Hofmannsthal as one of the "many Jewish writers who contaminated German literature with a strange world view." He had to be understood as one of the leaders of a literary movement that began in Vienna at about the same time as the "realism racket" in Berlin – both of which constituted "cultural mirrors of large German cities stinging from foreign infiltration and social degeneration." Since they could not be erased from German literary history, the Nazi newspaper covered the poetry and life of Hofmannsthal as "final cultural flowerings of a minor movement." In his works one could experience the "swan song of dying Vienna," though not accompanied by the "alluring, wistful beauty of a Strauss Waltz," but rather by the "sounds and instrumentation of a modern symphony – with thematic material that seemed rather strange to the German ear." In his works, the "racial decomposition process that had begun in the east-most German metropolis revealed itself." The "baptized Viennese Jew Hofmannsthal" was just one of hundreds of "ink Jews and their rotten Jew comrades" who had sneaked into contemporary German literature, "degrading it with their raw world of the senses, violating it with lewd, bestial sexuality, and reducing it to the level of pornography." For instance, in *Elektra* (1909), one of his three "falsifications of Greek tragedies," Hofmannsthal "speculated on the befouled instincts of educated big-city audiences by talking smut about a lesbian relationship between Elektra and her sister."[31]

The *Völkischer Beobachter* also attacked Vienna's Oskar Kokoschka (1886–1980) within its pages, although for the seemingly minor infraction of comparing his financial situation with that faced by Albrecht Dürer. Whoever honored the old masters would find any comparison of their difficult fates with that of Kokoschka – who was nothing but "a gifted businessman" – "hard and disgusting to swallow." Moreover, according to the paper, innumerable German talents were struggling without the basic necessities of life on account of the dismal economic situation and the "Jewish-capitalist sensationalism dominating the art market." Despite all their spiritual and physical distress they never received any recognition from the majority of their Volk comrades, because they were completely shut out of the German art market by the "Jewish vampire who favored only the pacemakers of his culturally destructive tendencies" – like Kokoschka.[32]

Among painters whom the *Völkischer Beobachter* felt it was its responsibility to defend against the modernist Jewish vampire were genre and historical painters like Anselm Feuerbach, Adolph Menzel, and Franz von Lenbach. According to the paper, Feuerbach (1829–1880) was an "unfortunate victim of the modernist conspiracy." His life was "just one long fight for artistic validity, and he perished in the struggle"; the lack of understanding he received in the German homeland "broke his idealistic artist's heart and dashed his courage to create; abandoned, he bled to death."[33] Art historian Werner Spanner extolled Menzel's (1815–1905) historical paintings as embodying Prussian culture: not only were the themes of his court and history paintings Prussian, but even more so the "cool, realistic sobriety of his works." Light and color became the subject of a whole series of paintings: sections of rooms, sun-filled windows with softly moving curtains, views of buildings, roofs, and gardens "in which a new way of seeing" was manifested for the first time. Menzel achieved these effects "alongside and to some degree in connection with" French Impressionism, the paper recognized. But the "iron discipline that this dwarfish man applied to his paintings: untiring, strict, without concession" was "most Prussian." In any case, far more important than Menzel's technical achievements was the one image that "lived on in the heart of the Volk in particular": his painting of the "great Prussian king playing the flute in a candlelit concert" (Figure 10.1).[34]

Figure 10.1 Adolph Menzel, *Flute Concert* (1852), Alte Nationalgalerie, Berlin, Germany

Franz Hofmann, a former gallery director who worked for the Propaganda Ministry and was on the committee for the disposal of degenerate art after the notorious exhibition in 1937, likewise strove to distinguish Franz von Lenbach (1836–1904) from modernist tendencies, by emphasizing "his love for Romanticism." During Lenbach's lifetime, according to Hofmann, the newly unified Germany had to deal with an artistic movement that "concentrated solely on the effects of light on the surface of things," constituting an "exercise in the materialist world view." Lenbach admirably resisted the rise of this materialism in painting. According to Hofmann, moreover, while Lenbach saw the main duty of the academies as preserving the foundations of craftsmanship established by the old masters, they were, to the contrary, producing an "artistic proletariat" that merely supplied goods for the art markets of the world: "craft was being diminished by the tremendous forces of competition." Already, then, Lenbach knew that "healthy art which resonated with volkish feeling had to be the basis for beauty in the future."[35]

Ultimately, as in the case of Menzel, the *Völkischer Beobachter* esteemed Lenbach mostly for his portraits of Prussian leaders. Above all, Lenbach's paintings of the "first men of Germany during the heroic epoch of the nineteenth century were a national treasure." Probably no painter in all of the nineteenth century had "such a feeling for power as he did": "in the sense that he stood with the leading spirits of his time, he could be compared with Titian – whom he emulated in all of his art and in his grandiose style of life." Moreover, for him "everything positive was manifested in the German, to which he belonged with body and soul, and which he publicized and glorified with all his artistic activity." Lenbach's fame was based on the fact that "his hand passed on to future generations images of innumerable important people of the nineteenth century," including Schopenhauer, Heckel, Helmholtz, Schwind, Semper, Björnson, Nansen, Defregger, Busch, Wagner, Liszt, Ludwig I, Ludwig II – and above all Moltke and Bismarck.[36] Indeed, most important to the Nazi newspaper was the fact that Lenbach was "almost the friend of Bismarck," underscoring the fact that the Iron Chancellor had visited him at his Renaissance palace and said: "I am happy to be immortalized by the brush of Lenbach in the way that I wish to be remembered" (Figure 10.2).[37]

With regard to other painters of the era, the *Völkischer Beobachter* generally promoted expressionist inwardness, setting this quality in opposition to the supposed dispassionate literalism of Realism and the positivist superficiality of Impressionism. It was in this spirit that the newspaper generally approved of the spiritual aspects of Arnold Böcklin's symbolist paintings. The first order of business was to distance Böcklin (1827–1901) from French-inspired naturalism. Unlike his contemporaries the Impressionists, the paper reported, Böcklin worked in the studio, not *en plein aire*. Since he represented nature so accurately, viewers often presumed that he used live models, but this was not the case: his "marvelous memory" recorded sights and experiences more faithfully than any sketchbook, and accordingly he required neither live scenes nor sketches to produce paintings. He had a "living supply of images," which he always carried with him "in spirit" and from which he constructed "color poems" through a process of free play – "including and omitting, reminding and inventing." His was no mere mechanical rendering of sensation. According to the *Völkischer Beobachter*, a connoisseur once contrasted Böcklin to the Frenchman, Zola, by reversing the realist author's famous line, "Art is a piece of nature, seen by a temperament," into its opposite: "Böcklin's art is a temperament, seen through a piece of nature." That, according to the paper, "hit the nail on the head." Böcklin's output thus marked the highpoint of a genre of German painting that the Romantics had

Figure 10.2 Franz von Lenbach, *Otto von Bismarck in Cuirassier's Uniform* (1890), Lenbachhaus, Munich, Germany

initiated: the "emotional landscape." One such landscape resulted during a visit to Florence, when he was gripped by longing for the North German woods ("Who hasn't experienced the same, down South?" the paper asked). There, to register his homesickness, he created the oddly "famous" *Silence in the Woods* (1896) (Figure 10.3).

According to the *Völkischer Beobachter*, researchers searched in vain for models in Homer's mythological world on which he based his centaurs and mermaids, but "a Böcklin did not need such tricks to

Figure 10.3 Arnold Böcklin, *Silence in the Woods* (1896), National Museum, Poznan, Poland

communicate what moved his soul." Elsewhere, to demonstrate that his creations could be enjoyed and understood "without classical erudition and snobbish high taste," the newspaper referenced the story behind his most famous painting. In 1880, Countess Orioli suggested that Böcklin produce an image "for dreaming." When she returned after some months, the artist presented her with the just completed painting: "You get what you asked for," he said. "It will make you so quiet that you will be startled if there is a knock on the door." Thus were the origins of the *Isle of the Dead* (1883) (Figure 10.4), which, the *Völkischer Beobachter* proudly noted, "could be found reproduced in almost every German house."[38]

"Of what did Böcklin's greatness consist?" the paper asked: what was the basis for the "unique magic that emitted from his works and draws us to them?" Expressionists were artists who "created from within, for whom impressions gathered from the external world served as material for the representation of their inner life." In contrast, Impressionists simply copied nature as they saw it. It was in this sense that Böcklin was

Figure 10.4 Arnold Böcklin, *Isle of the Dead* (1883), Alte Nationalgalerie, Berlin, Germany

an Expressionist, since "almost everything that he created was the representation of his fantasy." In form and color he produced "a world the likes of which does not and never will exist, but which nevertheless appears so quaint and familiar that we take it for true." Only a genius like Böcklin could "accomplish such a miracle" – and his creations were also miraculous because they "transfigured a tragic outlook through humor in a genuinely German way," as in his *Centaur in the Village Smithy* (1897) (Figure 10.5) – a "highly delectable painting," which the paper strongly recommended "pacifists and bigots pay particular attention to" (without further explanation) – or his *Susanna Bathing* (1888) (Figure 10.6), one of the "best loved send-ups of the Renaissance."

The *Völkischer Beobachter* was particularly complimentary about the latter painting. In its view, when they painted this Biblical scene, Titian, Veronese, Guido Reni, Rubens, Jordaens, and Frans Willem van Mieris "simply placed emphasis on a cute, feminine activity." However, Böcklin made a much more substantial statement by painting a "thick, fat Jewess allowing her neck to be pawed by an old Jew with sensual complacency, as another looks on." All three were, in the opinion of the Nazi newspaper, "perfectly rendered racial Hebrews."[39] Ostensibly, this racially informed version of the biblical story was an example of Böcklin's "genuinely German sense of humor."

Maria Groener asserted that there was a "fairy tale quality" about all of Böcklin's works: to her they depicted "legends of heroism without a trace of the genre sweetness so much in the air at that time." Here

Figure 10.5 Arnold Böcklin, *Centaur in the Village Smithy* (1897), Museum of Fine Arts, Budapest, Hungary

functioned a "romantic austerity" and a "defiant willfulness." With Böcklin everything was "stirred up," with "shrill, red strands of hair like crazy lentil sprigs on the foreheads, around red mouths, around rimmed eyes." Overall, however, there remained a calmness about his paintings – a calmness which "flowed out of the timelessness of the idea, not out of the loftiness of form or the smoothness of surface." Böcklin "did not bow to fashion; he would rather have gone hungry." Indeed, when a patron once demanded that he paint a nymph in a deep forest ravine, the artist refused to do so. To this the patron said, "Then I just won't buy the picture." So "we continue to eat beans," Böcklin replied. "How honorable was this confession!" Groener exclaimed: it showed that Böcklin – always true to his art and never aiming for effect – was a "model for the purity of German feelings." Groener attested accordingly that she and fellow Nazis were thus "obligated to present him with a laurel wreath."[40]

Strangely, the *Völkischer Beobachter* also strove to appropriate the works of the most pessimistic of turn-of-the-century artists: Edvard Munch (1863–1944). Thilo Schoder, a Weimar architect who emigrated to Norway in search of work (only to return to Germany a year later), contributed an article celebrating Munch in the highest National Socialist

Figure 10.6 Arnold Böcklin, *Susanna Bathing* (1888), Landesmuseum fuer Kunst und Kulturgeschichte, Oldenburg, Germany

terms – that is, as a "Nordic creator" – perhaps in an effort to re-establish himself by framing a racial interpretation of the Norwegian artist. According to Schoder, what Henrik Ibsen, Bjøernstjerne Bjøernson, and Knut Hamsun created in words – and what Edvard Grieg expressed in tones – Edvard Munch "immortalized" in form and color: "Nordic character, Nordic landscape, and a Nordic world view." In Munch's "Nordic-Germanic art," Schoder asserted, German creativity "reflected upon itself and liberated itself from foreign, Latinate influences." Since Munch resided primarily in Germany during his *Wanderjahren* between 1892 and 1908, Schoder presumed that he felt a spiritual connection with

German culture. While the "highest aspiration of Latins" was applying aesthetic theory, Germans demanded "intellectual and spiritual content as an essential component of art." In this sense, Schoder felt, Munch's realism was "typically" Nordic-Germanic: "sturdy, without intellectual refinement, without theoretical background, without aesthetic doctrine." He wanted people to "feel the sacred in" his works "so strongly that they would remove their hats, like in church." As expressed in his *Frieze of Life* series, which appeared at the Berlin Secession exhibition of 1902, Munch had "yearning, penetrating desire, and strong, deep religiosity" in common with the great German masters. In these portraits – which included his most famous work, *The Scream* – Munch presented "spiritual reality and psychic strength," by "reflecting on and reproducing the soul." But Schoder did not see the paintings as conveying a sense of anxiety in the modern age: Munch did not merely capture the emotions of individuals – he painted "national types." From 1905 to 1906, he lived in Weimar and a "rich harvest of beautiful pictures" characterized this period: he "enriched his palette, the heavy tones receded, and his technique became more agile." To Schoder, two allegorical paintings, *Alma Mater* and *The Researchers* (1910), were the "most prominent among the works of this phase," with both depicting at their centers a "broad and heavy" sustaining mother figure with "pure Nordic features" (Figure 10.7), seated firmly before an

Figure 10.7 Edvard Munch, a detail from *Alma Mater* (1910), Oslo University, Oslo, Norway

authentic Nordic landscape. No mention appeared in the *Völkischer Beobachter* of Munch's iconic representations of middle-class neurosis. Moreover, Schoder held, Munch's creative work was strongly influenced by Friedrich Nietzsche. Given that the philosopher sought "men of action in whom all knowledge, desire, love, and hate became a source of strength" and in whom the will to power "formed a harmonious system," he would have considered the "great Norwegian" a fulfillment of his words: "Away from the marketplace and from fame taketh place all that is great: away from the marketplace and from fame have ever dwelt the creators of new values."[41] According to Schoder, Munch studied Nietzsche's "sermons" on "Overcoming the Spirit of Heaviness" and engaged Zarathustra's "yea-saying philosophy of power, beauty, and serenity as the basis of his artistic life" (Figure 10.8).

Figure 10.8 Edvard Munch, *Friedrich Nietzsche* (1906), Munch Museum, Oslo, Norway

As a result, Munch's feeling for nature was "feverish." Born of the "noble, hot, red blood of life," it attended to "much more than outward, visual appearance." He transformed landscapes into "events of the soul – indeed, into religious confessions." His natural images "originated from the mystical thoughts of the Norwegian people, emanating elementary power and pointing beyond the objective." In particular, his coastal landscapes conveyed a "creative impression of cosmic growth, as if they had been formed by the force of Munch's constructive will." Most importantly, in Schoder's opinion, Munch investigated the "naked truth of his time" and expressed it prophetically. This was the instinctively "northern character" of his work. Therefore, Schoder closed, not only the Norwegian, but the "entire Germanic sphere of culture" owed him thanks for his life's work which stood "beyond good and evil."[42]

11 NORDIC EXISTENTIALISTS AND VOLKISH FOUNDERS

While asserting that Munch and his existentialist imagery embodied Nordic essence, the newspaper also worked to appropriate the Danish philosopher, Søren Kierkegaard (1813–1855). The impulse behind this cultural-historical mission came from the notorious racial theorist Hans F. K. Günther, whose books – including *The Ethnology of the German Volk* (1922), *The Racial Elements of European History* (1927), and *The Ethnology of the Jewish People* (1930) – were important sources of eugenic thought in National Socialism.[1] In an article on "Kierkegaard as a Prophet of Nordic Blood," Günther insisted that the Dane was a "Nordic herald of faith." As in the case of the poet Heinrich von Kleist, Günther felt that "racial as well as pathological factors interacted in Kierkegaard's soul." Despite what Günther described as Kierkegaard's "mental illness," a significant element of his constitution was the "drive to establish a Nordic form of Christianity." Above all, Kierkegaard's character bore "distinctive traits of Nordic piety." As Günther saw it, he followed a path to God that was contrary to the path followed by "those of the Near Eastern race" (including followers of the Judeo-Christian tradition as well as of Islamic mysticism). Whereas "Near Easterners *climbed up* to the spiritual, Nordic peoples – understood racially, not culturally" – or as the editors of the paper added, "not just North Germans or Scandinavians, but the tall, small-faced, high-foreheaded, blond, and blue-eyed people who were strongly present over all Germany" – "*internalized spirituality* until they became fit to match themselves with God." As thus interpreted, Kierkegaard's argument was that devotion was always a matter of the individual and his God, "not of this or that historical reality, Church order, or Church law." He demonstrated that every individual faces the "unique anguish" of his own decisions about "soulful relations with the holy."

Kierkegaard's form of piety had been termed "Christian individualism," but, as Günther explained, it was really more a "Nordic form of Christianity." It rejected all rules about church and faith and posited as many paths to God as there were individuals. Moreover, in Kierkegaard's view, suffering helped to clarify the relationship between the individual and God. In Günther's opinion, this was the only stance possible for a "Nordic herald of faith," because Nordic people were "insusceptible to suggestion, advertising, and instigation." Citing an American racial theorist, William Z. Ripley, Günther held that Nordics were marked by "bluff independence," just as non-Nordic races of Europe were "suggestible to all sorts of advertising." The less a Volk was Nordic, the more it could be influenced by "outside agitation." This attitude could never become dominant in communities that weren't comprised of "pure Nordic inhabitants." Every Western Church had been founded and operated according to Near Eastern or Oriental spirit and consequently had to impose rules and laws – "all because of racial mixing." But, "like Socrates," Nordics tended away from laws and associations between church and state, and this Nordic tendency was manifested in the individualistic religiosity of the Norwegian philosopher: on his deathbed he refused food because it was given to him by a minister. Thus did Kierkegaard represent, for Günther, the "Nordic individual 'alone with his God.'"[2]

However, the product of "Nordic introspection" that the *Völkischer Beobachter* coveted most was Nietzsche's philosophy. Indeed, the newspaper's contention that creative insight through suffering overcome was the basis for Nordic or Faustian cultural achievement peaked in its representation of Nietzsche (1844–1900). As George Mosse indicated, "perhaps the most important academic philosopher of the Third Reich, Alfred Bäumler, formulated a myth which put the famous philosopher at the service of the Nazi world view by stressing Nietzsche's heroism, his emphasis upon the power of the will, and his advocacy of an aristocratic community."[3] Later, Steven Aschheim showed in his book on the legacy of Nietzsche in German culture that "it is a matter of empirical record that he was incorporated into the Nazi pantheon of Germanic giants and that he became an integral part of National Socialist self-definition." Here, Aschheim continued, "was a German thinker with what appeared to be genuinely thematic and tonal links, who was able to provide the Nazis with a higher philosophical pedigree and a rationale for central tenets of their world view."[4]

But Aschheim also recognized that "the demonstrable thickness and ubiquity of the Nietzschean presence should not blind us to the complexities of Nietzsche's image and functions within Nazi discourse: besides unadulterated veneration, mindless blending, and ideological matchmaking, there were those who maintained distinctions, voiced qualifications, and demurred from claiming total identity."[5] In short, Aschheim's detailed assessment of the Nazified Nietzsche showed that fitting his ideas into any single world view was not a simple matter. But this was precisely the mission of the *Völkischer Beobachter*'s editors and writers: to make even complex ideas such as Nietzsche's appear to coordinate smoothly with the main tenets of Nazism. Moreover, Aschheim felt that "there is no way to accurately assess the degree to which his integration affected everyday popular attitudes."[6] While this may ultimately be true, looking at the terms with which the daily newspaper presented Nietzsche helps to explain how the party attempted to affect popular attitudes by putting his writings in the service of the National Socialist outlook.

A first difficulty the *Völkischer Beobachter* faced in accomplishing this task was the fact that the philosopher had broken with the most-German-of-all-Germans himself: Richard Wagner. A 1930 article surveyed the relationships within the triumvirate of Wagner, his second wife, Cosima, and Nietzsche without suppressing a general sense of disappointment that the philosopher ultimately turned against the *Prinzenpaar* of the Bayreuth Festival. *Siegfried* and *Tristan* had excited Nietzsche, but each year, he "distanced himself more and more from the master." In 1876 he celebrated Wagner with the essay, "Wagner in Bayreuth," so that Cosima could write: "Nietzsche's words were refreshing and uplifting." Even so, the paper recognized, this was the "last flash of a friendship that had long before gone bad." When he most wanted to follow him, Nietzsche was distressed that Wagner's *Parsifal* "bowed in devout prayer and renunciation." Moreover, in Wagner's late style, Nietzsche "saw only concessions to leading powers – to Cosima – to anyone." Disappointment intensified into blazing hatred: "as can only arise where there once was love: a real transvaluation of all values took place; everything fell apart."[7]

Here the newspaper implemented its usual method for dealing with troubling issues: look for the Jew. At the time of his break from the composer, the *Völkischer Beobachter* reported, Nietzsche was "trafficking with a private Jewish scholar," Paul Rée, who "welcomed the rootless fugitive from Wagner with open arms." By befriending Rée, Nietzsche "could not have gone further from Wagner," the paper exclaimed. It was at this point that Cosima gave up on Nietzsche: she "called him impoverished and suffering and imposed the great excommunication on him – no one in Bayreuth knew him any more."[8] Thus, to a certain degree contributors to the *Völkischer Beobachter* seemed to consider this punishment justified.

Another issue the *Völkischer Beobachter* had to resolve was Nietzsche's attitude toward nationalism. The newspaper did not check into Nietzsche's racial origins – as it did for many other Western creators – despite, or maybe because of, the fact that he occasionally claimed to be of Polish heritage. But it did have to confront indications that the philosopher rejected the nineteenth-century trend of nationalistic identity, including his own "Germanness." K. Kanetsberger wrote that there was "one important point in Nietzsche's mental attitude on which even his friends remained silent, from which they tried to distance themselves as much as possible: this is the matter of Nietzsche's attitude toward Germanness and the state." Nietzsche's nature was not asocial, Kanetsberger explained: he longed his whole life for a circle of like-minded people but never found it. This failing, Kanetsberger hypothesized, explained all that followed: "his bitterness, his injured scorn for Germany, even his rejection of the state." The Second Reich had been formed, but for the philosopher it remained "a shell without content." To him, nationalism seemed the "illness of the century" because it "attempted to hide its emptiness." In developing this point, Kanetsberger quoted Nietzsche: "Nationalism as it is understood today is a dogma that requires limitation."[9] But in offering such proof, Kanetsberger seized on the phrase, "as it is understood today," locating therein a way to limit the philosopher's views as applying only to the state of German nationalism of his own time.[10]

On this basis, then, by concluding that Nietzsche's opinions were time-bound and would have changed in light of the National Socialist movement, the *Völkischer Beobachter* sought to circumscribe statements the philosopher made which did not coordinate with Nazi ideology, and thereby minimize their relevance. Regarding the matter of nationalism, this maneuver opened the way for the newspaper to present him as a "fervent patriot and representative of Germanness." For instance, Ernst

Nickell traveled to Sils-Maria, wandered the region, and ruminated on passages Nietzsche had written there. The landscape, Nickell reflected, was "consecrated by German fate and German tragedy." Nietzsche "needed this landscape, he had to stand near the highest things and the firmament; he was *German despite everything*."[11] In fact, Kanetsberger reminded, Nietzsche did say of himself that "I am perhaps more German than the Germans of today."[12] He knew the German essence better than the "hurray patriots that Adolf Hitler also warned about." In his own words, he valued the "earnest, manly, stern, and daring German spirit."[13] He knew that "there was still bravery, particularly German bravery that is inwardly something different than the *élan* of our deplorable neighbors." Compared with the French essence in particular, he was "consistently, strongly, and happily conscious of the virtues of the German character." About those "elegant ones" – the French – he said specifically that "they have every reason to beware of German fire, or one day it may consume them together with all their dolls and idols of wax."[14] Above all, Nietzsche held that "it is German unity in the highest sense which we are striving for more passionately than for political reunification – the unity of the German spirit and life."[15] Very few others "saw things so clearly" in those days, concluded Kanetsberger.[16]

Regarding Nietzsche's attitude toward the state, Kanetsberger offered identical arguments. He admitted that "we find here, at first view, a sharp contrast with today's [National Socialist] thinking." But again, this was only a reaction against his own times. What Nietzsche understood by the term "the state" was "completely different from our idea of the state today." Nietzsche was the "last anti-political German of them all," because for him, politicization meant democratization, in which the state embodied the principle of the greatest good for the greatest number. Nietzsche hated any such tendency because he believed "general prosperity would make mankind too lazy to generate powerful energy in a great individual – in a genius." That was why Nietzsche wanted as little state as possible.[17]

To express such views, Nietzsche used "angry words" – such as when he proclaimed that culture and state "are antagonists."[18] Obviously, Kanetsberger allowed, such phrases were the complete opposite of "our views today: we know that that state is the defender of a Volk's culture, as long as it is a Volk state." But from Nietzsche's perspective, conditioned by his times, there was "nothing bad about that utterance": the "German Reich had had the misfortune to achieve its external form when there was no longer any inner content; the classical heights of German education had sunk; the song of German Romanticism sounded only from afar." At the same time, "Realism was on the rise, leading more and more toward materialism; money and business had become the gods of the age." A state as the "guardian and defender of culture; a state as the means of achieving the true goal of existence, not as a goal in itself; a state that is built on the Volk – that, Nietzsche would have accepted." On this basis, Kanetsberger had no option but to conclude that Nietzsche would have agreed with "today's [National Socialist] German idea of the state with all of his heart."[19]

Arthur Rathje, occasional novelist and author of treatises on nationalism, also felt that Nietzsche and his ideas were "Germanic despite everything." As Rathje explained, the notion of becoming was always in the foreground of Nietzsche's conception of Germanness. As he put it in *Beyond Good and Evil* (1886): "The German himself *is* not, he is *becoming*, he is 'developing.'"[20] Along with Goethe, Nietzsche understood the process of *Bildung* to be the foundation of German fate. Therefore, not despite but *because of* his position that no personality is set, no type is stable, Rathje was able to conclude for the *Völkischer Beobachter* that Nietzsche "promoted Germanness as a lifestyle of continual becoming in pursuit of cultural cultivation."[21]

Articles also strove to remove any doubt that Nietzsche would have shared the anti-democratic principles of Nazism. Establishing such a position, according to the paper, required attention because democrats and leftists had tried to appropriate the philosopher for their own propagandistic ends. Josef Stolzing explained that since 1918, Weimar era leaders had worked to "silence the herald of the Superman idea." The "victory of democracy in Germany," the "loss of national independence," and the reduction of Germans into "slaves working for international Jewish interests," had marked the end of the Nietzsche cult in Germany."[22] Under the Republic, the *Völkischer Beobachter* complained, Nietzsche was invoked far too frequently by "international-democratic literati" as a representative of their world view. But, the paper countered, whoever studied his fundamental spiritual attitude had to wonder at the audacity of those who tried to make him – the "first and sharpest of all anti-democrats" – a "witness for democracy." Nietzsche "hated and fought every form of democracy, both political and spiritual," and he said so in the "clearest possible terms." That which he called an "unleashing of idleness, weariness, and weakness" – that is,

notions that at base all men are the same – were symbolic of the democratic age that believed in the equality of men and established "the weak,
fat, and cowardly as standards for this equality." In Nietzsche's opinion,
this rule of the humble amounted to a blow against life itself: the herd
instinct – mass mentality – considered peace to have higher value than
war. But this judgment was "anti-biological"; indeed, was itself the
"spawn of decadence," he wrote in *The Will to Power* (posth. 1901).
To be sure, the paper chided, such words sounded "rough and raw to
ears in the age of Liberalism." But Nietzsche addressed "tough and
strong ones" alone. The others – "the all too many" – did not concern
him in the least. They and their weak dreams of humanity and eternal
peace "negated life itself, and threatened it with death." "Rejection of
equality, deliberate inequality, joy in struggle and war, self-
consciousness, assuming responsibility: those were the characteristics
of the aristocratic man that he preferred over the dull masses."[23]

Friedrich Würzbach, a leading Nietzsche scholar who edited a
number of the philosopher's works and founded the Munich-based
Nietzsche Society that included members such as Thomas Mann and
Hugo von Hofmannsthal, provided academic support for the *Völkischer
Beobachter*'s view of the philosopher as anti-democratic, and more
ammunition for the fight against "misuse" by Weimar democrats and
leftists. Moderns who read Nietzsche's assertion of the need "to change
people forcibly,"[24] Würzbach surmised, would gasp in moral indignation:
"Where did that leave private freedom, the sacred idol of Liberalism?"
Against the dominant liberal outlook, Würzbach argued, Nietzsche set
forth a way of thinking that "handled contemporary things harshly and
tyrannically – in the interest of the future."[25]

By featuring these and similar citations, the paper underscored
Nietzsche's anti-democratic thinking. However, to a certain extent, this
selective reading threatened to undermine another aspect of Nazi ideology. By presenting his philosophy as establishing an absolute position
against the political involvement of the common man, the newspaper
risked contradicting volkish principles that celebrated the popular
German mind and character. To diffuse this potential contradiction,
Eduard A. Mayr attempted to reconcile Nietzsche's elitist attitudes
toward the mob and right-wing perceptions of the Volk. Certainly,
Mayr asserted, Nietzsche would have agreed that Volk and mob were
not identical, although "mad prophets" occasionally mixed them up,
or, rather, "spoiled, degraded, degenerated the one into the other."

According to Nietzsche, all truly great, forward-thinking creators who worked effectively on the mysteries of mankind, had their origins in the Volk: "The actors who play heroic roles on the stage of the tremendous passion play – world history – arise from below." But, Mayr stipulated, "no great man had ever emerged from the mob; all of the greatest had come from the Volk": the mob was "social illness"; the Volk, "national health!"[26]

    Confronting the leftist drive in European life by determined application of a single will to power originating in Germany was one of the principal aims targeted by *Völkischer Beobachter* propagandistic use of Nietzsche. The newspaper perceived itself as a herald of the message that the *German Michel* had to get up from his *Stammtisch* and prepare again for battle – and invocations of Nietzsche were common in these warnings. As Mayr put it: "In the name of all conscientious front soldiers, I send the words of Nietzsche for shirkers to read carefully on their deplorable way to Philistine paradise, from which they will one day be driven out with a flaming sword."[27] Visiting Nietzsche's grave, Eduard Grunertus, author of *Zarathustra's Son: A Book for Higher Men* (1930), claimed that he heard exhortations coming from the site that Germans should steel themselves for approaching conflict:

> *Don't you hear anything? Is that not his voice speaking to us: we who fight and create!* "*I want to say something to you, my brothers in spirit! Life means fighting and suffering. Sorrow makes some weary and soft – but it strengthens the creator. Think of the fates of a Michelangelo, a Beethoven and a Friedrich the Great – then you will know how love and toughness can be strangely connected in man. Know love, but stay tough for me!*"[28]

    Beyond reports of ghostly commands, Josef Stolzing intensified the Nazi view of Nietzsche as militarist, "because one cannot conceive of sharper opposites than Friedrich Nietzsche and pacifism, Marxism, and egalitarian b.s. in general!" (Figure 11.1). What would the philosopher have said to a slogan like "No more war!"? Stolzing asked. Germans could not attain peace through work, as "beneficiaries of the November Crimes blabbed," but only through battle. True peace would be achieved only through German victory, and this was consistent with Nietzsche's views.[29] He constantly repeated that "struggle runs throughout nature – that life

Figure 11.1 *Völkischer Beobachter*, Nietzsche article: "What is Nietzsche to Us Today? He was a Fighter Against the Insanity of Democracy," 24 August 1930

itself is an outcome of war." As he had Zarathustra cry out: "Good old war sanctifies everything!"[30]

Paul Kuntze, who wrote military histories for right-wing publishers, like *Lost Blood: German Foreign Troops in 2000 Years of Germanic History* (1944) and *The History of Soldiering among the Germans* (1937), also saw Nietzsche's will to power as the essential political concept to be drawn from his philosophy, and helpfully supplemented by references to race and leadership. Moreover, Kuntze perceived comparisons between Nietzsche's "Nordic ideas" and recent German leaders. Nietzsche recommended over and over, Kuntze held, that one should not avoid obstacles, but seek them out in order to develop optimism in the fight against them. Confidence attained by overcoming adversity, according to Kuntze, corresponded to "Nordic essence." The "Poet-Philosopher of Leader-Types," Kuntze went on, demanded that "a hard, difficult education begin early in youth."[31] As models, Kuntze was certain, Nietzsche had in mind men raised according to "Kantian teachings and Nordic heritage." In considering "the greatest German leaders of all time, up to Hindenburg and Adolf Hitler," one always found that the "toughness they so often exhibited as fighters was the external shield that they carried into battle."[32]

Still, Würzbach did not believe all men were capable of attaining Nietzschean ends by applying their inner powers alone. In fact, the philosopher himself hoped that "men who could force people to accept his teachings would follow him in deed and power." So *Völkischer Beobachter* readers could live by Nietzsche's teachings either by applying their own wills to power or by accepting fates dispensed by National Socialist leaders. In this way Würzbach transformed an obstacle into an opportunity: individuals could demonstrate their will to power not only by becoming creators, but alternatively by "accepting the necessity of things, becoming a part and tool of great world events, and even making the ultimate sacrifice – the highest self-denial – for one's Volk." Reading Nietzsche's concept of will to power in these terms was most appropriate for the paper's propagandistic goals as Nazi Germany geared up for war.[33]

Beyond attempting to demonstrate that Nietzsche and National Socialism shared these essential political ideals, the *Völkischer Beobachter* also endeavored to associate his views of religion with the Nazi outlook. Contributors applauded Nietzsche's "battle against Christianity" and in doing so conveyed the strongest direct critique of Christianity to appear in the cultural section of the paper. For instance, art historian Herman Stenzel applauded Nietzsche's rejection of Christianity "for nay-saying this side of existence." Referring to him as "Germany's philosophical Führer at the turn of the century," Stenzel saw Nietzsche's significance for the Nazi era in the fact that he "laughed at the bourgeois disposition toward secure mediocrity." Driven by passionate will, he emphasized "not the already achieved, the quiet, the secure, but instead the dark and dangerous powers of instinct and drive – and, above all, the conscious battle against a Christianity that denied everything of this world."[34]

But, of course, Judaism was reliably the central religious issue treated in the pages of the *Völkischer Beobachter*. Stolzing recognized that Nietzsche had not been a committed anti-Semite, having criticized the views of Richard Wagner, his own sister, Elisabeth, and her husband, Bernhard Förster. Therefore, as was the case with regard to his ideas about German nationalism, the *Völkischer Beobachter* had to smooth out perceived inconsistencies in Nietzsche's writings and align the resulting reconciliations with Nazi views. As Stolzing put it:

> *his work contains other crass contradictions and obscurities, especially in his treatment of the Jewish Question, where he sometimes confesses himself as an anti-Semite, and then as a philo-Semite. Equally obscure is what he understood as race and nation. This may be a result of the eruptive nature of his creativity and the shortness of his life, which didn't allow him enough time to go into these issues deeply.*[35]

But Stolzing's acknowledgment that Nietzsche's views were not fully compatible with Nazi anti-Semitism was not always heeded by other contributors. Eduard Stemplinger, a prolific author of books about classical history and literature who also wrote about Wagner and Nietzsche, carefully selected passages from *Beyond Good and Evil* to indicate that Nietzsche expressed himself "extraordinarily farsightedly on the Jewish Question, if one considers the conditions of the times."[36] Further, under the title, "Nietzsche as Warner about the Jewish Danger," E. von Baer insisted that Nietzsche "concerned himself with the Jewish Question, as every clear thinking, ever sensitive Aryan-German person must." His "words about the Jews were once a warning to the German Volk, but in the 1930s they had become an indictment!" Nietzsche "recognized the danger threatening Germans in the form of a completely foreign and utterly different race, and warned us – and like so many hundreds of great, significant men who warned us before him, he warned in vain!"[37]

Nietzsche, von Baer went on, saw how the Jews were becoming ever more powerful in Germany and Europe and related this observation in "prophetic words about them." Above all, the thought that the Jews were "determining what distinguishes" – that is, that they were in charge of cultural taste – "filled him with fright." He knew that such power would "establish a foundation that would be favorable to the development of the Jewish race, Jewish culture, and Jewish spiritual life – against German essence, German nature, and German culture." Only one thing was important to him: "he saw a foreign race struggling at the cost of his own German Volk; and to Nietzsche – the man of action – it was incomprehensible that the whole German Volk wasn't arming itself with every weapon in order to save that which is most sacred, its volkish essence." Was Nietzsche an anti-Semite? von Baer asked rhetorically: "He was – he was in the most intrinsic, pure, and sacred sense of the word!"[38]

Faced with what Nazis perceived as a desperate situation in the 1930s, the *Völkischer Beobachter* put forth the view that it was finally time to act: extreme measures were required, and Nietzsche would have agreed. The notion that, at base, all differences between men are hereditary and racial, the paper stated in an article on "Nietzsche, the Prophet," was clear in the following lines from *The Will to Power*: "Spirit alone does not ennoble: much more is necessary for spirit to ennoble. What is that? Blood." Thus, even if he did occasionally treat racist fanaticism with sarcasm, the problem of decadence was, for Nietzsche, a fundamentally biological question. "Just as he perceived a race of criminals as something one cannot educate but must, rather, castrate, in the same sense was his notion of nobility racially determined in the end – he knew that ultimately the battle between the aristocratic world and the democratic world becomes a race war."[39]

The *Völkischer Beobachter* was ultimately designed to motivate action in this race war, and regularly invoked Nietzsche as a major source of inspiration in the struggle. Stolzing, Würzbach, Kanetsberger, Rosenberg, and, the most notorious Nazifier of Nietzsche, Alfred Bäumler, all worked to make him into an icon of National Socialist principles of leadership and militarism. What made Nietzsche so valuable to Nazis, Stolzing argued, was his "fearless acknowledgment" that a charismatic personality alone could lead toward redemption for the suffering millions: "Not only in Germany, but throughout Europe, National Socialists connect with Nietzsche in the shared recognition of the irreplaceable value of the great personality combined with energetic will to power. We address him as the preacher of action!"[40] Further, Würzbach wrote that Nazis constituted the first generation that could say that Nietzsche's ideas had "passed into our flesh and blood, not just into our brains and thoughts." To treat oneself harshly and tyrannically for the sake of the future of the Volk was one of the most important National Socialist requirements. "How often do we recite, in small gatherings, the words of Zarathustra: 'And if ye will not be fates and inexorable ones,

how can ye one day – conquer with me? ... For the creators are tough.'"
To Würzbach, "toughness, for the sake of the Volk" was Nietzsche's
essential message.[41]

Thus, despite some qualms, was the *Völkischer Beobachter*'s
treatment of Nietzsche ultimately aimed at identifying him as an immediate and fundamentally ruthless forerunner of the Nazi movement.
However, along with its frequent coverage of Western cultural celebri-
ties, the newspaper regularly extolled lives and writings from the turn of
the century which it found much more easy to incorporate into the party
line: namely, volkish ideologues including Julius Langbehn, Paul de
Lagarde, and Houston Stewart Chamberlain. Until the scholarship of
Fritz Stern and George Mosse brought the significance of these marginal
figures into focus, historians of National Socialism had largely overlooked the role they played as forerunners of Nazi doctrine.[42] To the
ideologues of the party newspaper, however, the importance of these
radicals and of the views they espoused was never in doubt. Indeed, the
paper's editors dedicated dozens of articles to the goal of establishing
that their works deserved a place in the Western canon. As with our
review of the Prussian reformers in Chapter 7, we will not address the
paper's coverage of these figures in the same proportion they received in
the newspaper, but some acknowledgment of the paper's view of their
place in Western cultural history is warranted.

In the words of Alfred Rosenberg, contemporary volkish leaders
often had to "defend themselves" against complaints that they had
remained silent for too long, failing to adequately press issues that they
now claimed were of utmost importance to the National Socialist
agenda: "Why are you only now coming with your demands?" the critics
complained, "Why didn't you say all that to us earlier?" In response,
Rosenberg insisted that almost all of the demands that volkish ideologues
were making after the First World War had, in fact, been made decades
earlier. But, then, decades earlier, "the whole world was reeling under the
influence of cheap slogans and liberal rhetoric," and no one had listened
to these "lonely fighters." According to Rosenberg, "among the bravest
of these early fighters for National Socialist thought" was Paul de
Lagarde (1827–1891). Already in 1921 Rosenberg predicted that "the
German future will build him a monument."[43] Similarly, Adolf Hösel
ranked Lagarde "at the pinnacle of nineteenth-century German cultural
achievement," insisting that his predictions be placed "next to the
accurate, prophetic images of the future produced by Nietzsche": both

"foresaw the ruin, but they also perceived the possibilities of a radical turnaround if, at the last hour, a heroic deed followed heroic thought." Such a turnaround did take place, Hösel felt, when Hitler attained power in 1933. In this way, thus, deed followed thought, and volkish theorists had been "blessed long after their death" by a man who stood in the "brightest light of historical life."[44]

According to Hellmuth Langenbucher, Lagarde belonged among those "rare German men" who, without regard for themselves, warned that the German Volk was "losing itself in the pleasures of life." During the "complacent times after the Franco-Prussian war," Lagarde demanded "more consciousness of the German essence" and an "inner struggle against the dangerous Reich." In his *German Writings* (1878–1881), Lagarde conveyed the "same love of the German Volk and the same genuine anger over its inner disintegration" that Julius Langbehn later expressed in the cry, "Back to Rembrandt!" Specifically, Langenbucher held, Lagarde's activities in the service of the German Volk included "studying the laws of decay" and finding that "its carriers, along with other destructive powers, were Jews and the 'grey international' of Liberalism." Seeing in Jewry a "nation within the nation," he did not hesitate to "identify the Jewish Question as a Jewish Danger – as one must." In Lagarde's words, "the Jews are, as Jews, foreigners in every European state, and as foreigners they are carriers of the plague." While acknowledging that it was "impossible to fully explain the significance of the Jewish Question" in a short newspaper article, Langenbucher thought it sufficed to say that Lagarde "did everything he could to prepare Germans to overcome Jewry, even to the point of suggesting radical measures." Moreover, he recognized that Jewry and Liberalism should not be distinguished from one another. That's why – saying "I hate the mere word Liberal" – Lagarde felt it necessary to fight energetically against the "servile, liberal slamming together of spiritual objects from foreign cultures," and blamed the lack of patriotic spirit within the "gray international, which murders and kills the personality in order to achieve 'consciousness.'" Lagarde knew that "whoever resisted Jewry and Liberalism in this way would naturally become an opponent of democracy, the parliamentary system, and their corrupt supporters," since, as he put it, "freedom and democracy match each other like fire and water."[45]

According to Lagarde, Langenbucher wrote, the one great possibility for freeing Europe from the "jaws of internationalism" lay in the maintenance of Germany as an agrarian state and, to ensure this, expansion of German control. As Lagarde expressed it: "The

Germanicization of the lands bordering on ours is a national deed. We will again be happy when we again become farmers, and we will only become farmers through the retaking of the old *Goten-und Burgundenlandes*." In response to such rhetoric, Langenbucher gushed, "Nazis stood to attention": in his *German Writings* "we see one of the most important stages in the path our Volk is following toward self-realization." The "beautiful view of Germany's future" that Lagarde provided "inspires us even today to believe more in the future than in the past, so we can say with Lagarde: 'Our days are so dark that they must promise a new sun.'"[46]

Lagarde was not the only volkish thinker to receive such treatment in the *Völkischer Beobachter*. Rudolf Paulsen wrote that right next to Nietzsche and Lagarde – "among men who, just two decades after the victorious war of 1870–71 and the establishment of the German Reich, recognized that its spiritual foundations were uncertain" – stood Julius Langbehn (1851–1907). Paulsen contended that Langbehn's *Rembrandt as Educator* (1890) was a "lonely criticism against the splintering of spiritual life at the turn of the century." In it, art played an important role as a tool of reform: "destined to add an internal realm of the soul to the external Bismarckian realm." Himself a "Low German," Langbehn expected much from Low German character, so he "emblazoned Rembrandt's name on his banner," as the aesthetic Führer for all Germans, and "later added Dürer." Moreover, Langbehn was "on the way to recognizing the importance of race and racially-based historical writing." His view that "study of the hair along with skull shape, growth, and color; in short, the external appearance of peoples" should be "the authoritative basis of all historical research" made him a predecessor of Houston Stewart Chamberlain. He also took on the Jewish Question openly, stating that the Jewish character "which sympathizes so much with Zola is completely opposed to the purely German nature of Walter von der Vogelweide, Dürer, and Mozart; that German theater has become trivial and in large part lascivious in the hands of modern Jews; and that depraved professors and Jewry have operated hand in hand in the last century, to the detriment of the German Volk." It was no wonder, Paulsen observed approvingly, that Langbehn was not popular with the Jews – was even hated by them – and that "long after his death they have continued to inundate him with wild invective and outrageous slander."[47]

Hellmuth Langenbucher added that Langbehn's call for "a German culture rooted in the soil" emerged from the realization that the

Second Reich was in cultural decline. At the core of Langbehn's thought was a "critique of the Marxist and Social-Democratic dogmas of equality," which was even more applicable in the Weimar era than in his time, and was "consistent with the direction of cultural renovation that National Socialism is fighting for."[48] In this vein, the paper insisted that thirty-one years after his death, Langbehn's unfailing sensitivity to the "threatening aspects of the German life – whether he addressed politics, culture, the arts, science, religion, or racial issues – appeared more accurate than it did in the years when his book first appeared." For Nazi ideologues, Langbehn's thought encompassed "all the great questions that were decisive for the structure of German life in their time." For instance, his judgment of the danger of the Jewish influence was "particularly sharp" and, shouting out, "Germany for Germans!" he recognized that Germans "have been, are, and will always be Aryans." As such, they had to "live, fight, and – when necessary – die for their inborn character, because life is a crisis in which one's own blood must survive against foreign blood." He knew that "at base the only thing worth spilling blood for was blood – that is, one's own blood, and in this struggle Aryan blood will survive against all others."[49] Langbehn's life and work, according to the paper, were of interest to "those who are most mature as well as youth looking for answers; to scholars as well as artists; to aristocratic women as well as simple workers – he truly spoke to all parties."[50] But for National Socialists, it held, Langbehn's work had special significance: "Jews undermined his efforts and muted the effect of his book, so National Socialists had to fulfill his plan by acting on his opinion that contemplating German art is the best way to overcome the weakening of the blood." Therefore, the *Völkischer Beobachter* exhorted "every party member to put books about Langbehn – the racial educator – under the Christmas tree."[51]

Of the "racial educators" that Nazis identified among turn-of-the-century volkish writers, however, the figure most heralded by the *Völkischer Beobachter* was Houston Stewart Chamberlain (1855–1927). Quotes from this British-born "German thinker" appeared regularly in the paper's treatment of other major cultural figures. But it also went to great lengths to include him among the ranks of great men, including – according to Georg Schott – Dante, Shakespeare, Kant, Herder, Rembrandt, Bach, Beethoven, and Wagner.[52] Indeed, among all the volkish predecessors, the *Völkischer Beobachter* identified Chamberlain as having had the greatest amount of direct influence on Hitler and his racist outlook.

Nazi homage to Chamberlain took spectacular form as early as September 1925, when the paper covered a "Great Chamberlain Festival" in Bayreuth. According to its report, along with members of the National Socialist Party, volkish groups, including *Wiking*, *Junglandbund*, *Sturmtrupp*, and *Wehrwolf*, gathered at the event and positioned themselves around the stage – "flags arrayed, confident of victory" – to form "an edifying picture!" Then, the *Völkischer Beobachter*'s own Josef Stolzing took the stage. In his address to the gathering, according to the article, he "formed in the hearts of listeners" a clear and vivid picture of Chamberlain's path of development. As a "young stormer," Chamberlain had based his ideals on the traditions of the three great cultural centers of German spirit: Potsdam, Weimar, and Bayreuth. There, he found "all virtues" united in the German Volk: "humility, respect, pride, faith, energy, the highest love, and the last wisdom." Thereby did this "Englishman develop into one of the best of Germans." Filled with "Wagner's gospel," along with the legacies of Kant, Goethe, and Schiller, Chamberlain "revived German cultural consciousness" with his "poetically true and prophetically innovative" creations. Above all, he "sang the high song of inalienable race purity" and was therefore "the father of the National Socialist idea." In his main work, *The Foundations of the Nineteenth Century* (1899), Chamberlain warned that a foreign spirit was always striving to imprison and control Germans: to "outlaw and torment the Nordic soul forever." According to Stolzing, Chamberlain was the first to recognize that: "if it did not resist, once the decomposition of its blood had begun, the Volk would die from the decomposition of its culture." But in his broad discussion of the racial question, Chamberlain had provided Germans with the weapon they needed in this "religious-cultural conflict": a "flaming, avenging, battle-ready sword." His fundamental concepts about this issue in particular were "indispensable" for the next generation: it was "through Chamberlain that National Socialist thought blazed forth." Stolzing concluded therefore that Chamberlain could be counted among "the most significant men of the time," along with Paul von Hindenburg, Erich Ludendorff, and Adolf Hitler. At the end of this apotheotic ritual, the gathering stood and shouted "Heil Chamberlain!" Then the lights in the hall went out, and on both sides of the stage "Bengali" torches flared up. Finally, worshippers honored Chamberlain in a moment of silence, with flags lowered.[53]

A year later, to mark Chamberlain's 71st birthday, Stolzing continued in tribute with an article stating that Nazis "regard it as our obligation to keep Chamberlain in our thoughts as the pioneer of a new era – that is, the coming Third Reich of National Socialist Germany." He insisted that Chamberlain's "immortal works should become common property of the German Volk far more than they have been" because "they constitute an almost inexhaustible arsenal of spiritual weapons for our battle." Under their influence, "we will break the bonds that – like a Great Wall of China – restrain millions of German Volk comrades." In Chamberlain, Stolzing saw "one of the most unique manifestations of spiritual Germany." Since Goethe, he felt "no one had a more universal command of knowledge than Chamberlain, except perhaps Schopenhauer." As such, his works belonged to "the best that the rich tradition of German writing offers: wherever good German spirit dominates, there we find his works on the bookshelf next to Goethe and Schiller – and we read his *Foundations of the Nineteenth Century* with feverish hearts, hot eyes, and quickened breath." Though born else-where, Stolzing asserted, Chamberlain "remained true to his German Fatherland," grounded on his "fixed, unshakable belief in Bayreuth." Even after the downfall of November 1918, "he never despaired of German thought, of the future, of the resurgence of the German Volk he loved so much." As he turned seventy-one, Stolzing exclaimed, "May he live to see that day! That is our birthday wish for him."[54]

But the paper invoked Chamberlain for more than his value as a source of faith in the Bayreuth past and Wagnerian ideas; it further sought to use Chamberlain as a motivational figure in the party's attack on modernism. And so, in contrast to the "present chaos in the cultural world" – with all its "modern whining about art" – Georg Schott in writing for the paper highlighted Chamberlain's view that the "elemental force of all art lies in race, that art must announce an idea, that true German art requires a German philosophy of life." Art, in his view, should not be produced for its own sake, but must "arise in the service of the Volk, must be good, creative, and uplifting, and must not be limited to mere technique."[55] Stolzing intensified this attack on twentieth-century culture by stating that "Chamberlain prophesied years ago the calamity that would come from atonal Negro music." His warnings had been justified since "what we are presently experiencing in German art is a systematic devastation of everything soulful and moral."[56] But Chamberlain's words had provided the means for resistance. Chamberlain "recognized the spirit of our century like few others, recognizing it as the age when the Antichrist would create his empire on earth." But Chamberlain "did not curse the era, because he knew that the forces of good would prevail and the realm of the Antichrist would be demolished rather than constructed."[57] As Stolzing put it, "we at the *Völkischer Beobachter* have always stressed that the works of Chamberlain belong in the spiritual toolbox of every National Socialist who wants to help win over supporters to our world view, and to deepen our principles."[58]

Chamberlain died in 1927, and Stolzing's birthday wish that he might experience Hitler's rule was not realized. Even so the paper continued to honor him after 1933. In 1934 came "the first opportunity to honor his *Todestag* in the new Germany that he foresaw." The paper toasted him as "one of our greatest and truest spiritual guides," offering as the basis for such an accolade that he "recognized the last wisdom and the last task of German nature as no one had done before; provided the most reverential interpretation of the greatness of our Volk; and worked indefatigably to educate and arouse Germans in the spirit of Luther, Goethe, and Kant." With this tribute, the paper expressed the hope that Chamberlain "will become the educator of youth wherever in Germany people are committing themselves to the inner revival and spiritual rebirth which alone will ensure the existence of Adolf Hitler's *Reich*."[59]

Most important in the "spiritual toolbox" of Nazism was, naturally, Chamberlain's "path-breaking work," *The Foundations of the Nineteenth Century*. Therein, said the *Völkischer Beobachter*, "he interpreted Germany's destiny on the basis of its history: not in a dry chronicle of the sensually perceptible or a barren philosophical discussion about the mythical and subconscious alone, but in a synthesis of both which engaged the most elemental aspects of the German nature and opened a new framework of perspectives and possibilities." The main theme of his work was a "great prophesy about the future, based on recognition that Germans – in the broadest sense of the term – would be the formulators and creators of a new world." But most significantly, "his history of philosophy, religion, and science arose from his pioneering knowledge of the different values of the races, the comparison of which established the basis for differing cultures." The greatest achievement of his *Foundations*, for the paper, was "its demonstration of these differences and, within them, the shining heights of the Aryan-Nordic race." Based on his racist theories, then, Chamberlain was the "first great spiritual Führer of Germany." And, as if that weren't enough, it was he who, "with an intuitive awareness, found and recognized Adolf Hitler as the one called to fulfill his dream of a German future," since "as early as 1921 these men established a friendship that never clouded, even in times of trouble and exterior hopelessness."[60]

Two weeks after German armies marched west in May 1940, the *Völkischer Beobachter* saw fit to make it clear that Chamberlain's theories implied the need for German domination of the European world and beyond, and consequently justified military aggression. The "*Leitmotiv* of Chamberlain's existence," according to the paper, was his belief that "the whole future of Europe, that is, the civilization of the world, lies in the hands of Germany." In his *Foundations*, Chamberlain based this conviction on the idea that "the life of the German is completely different than that of others." He alone has "enough self-confidence and sense of human dignity; he alone is at the same time the poet and the practical organizer, the thinker and the doer, the man of peace *par excellence* and the best soldier, the doubter and the only one capable of really believing." These gifts, however, obligated the German with great responsibilities: "the greater the gifts, the greater the task." Thus, "Germany's mission" was colossally difficult: "not only does it have a lot to do for itself, but as this happens it must stand up to the animosity and misunderstanding of all Europe." To fulfill its destiny, "the whole nation would have to understand this challenge and strive together as one man for its fulfillment."[61] From the *Völkischer Beobachter* perspective, therefore, war – and war fundamentally perceived as race war, both in 1914 and in 1940 – was the cornerstone of Chamberlain's volkish foundation for the future of Germany.

12 MUSIC AFTER WAGNER

At the same time it was searching for precedents in mid- to late-nineteenth century literary, artistic, philosophical, and political trends, the *Völkischer Beobachter* remained obsessed with tracing the path and progress of music after Wagner and devising ways to explain these developments in a manner that aligned this music with the Nazi program. Central to the National Socialist agenda was promoting the continued validity of the romantic tradition, while correspondingly refuting modernist developments in music. One way to oppose the influence and significance of modernism was to invoke once more the popular music of the nineteenth century – for instance, a Strauss waltz – as a defensive bulwark: "When you sit in a big city café listening to music in the Weimar Republic and then all of a sudden – after the hooting, moaning, and whining of modern jazz music – hear the soft, loving sounds of a particularly beautiful waltz, you will probably laugh and say: 'That can only be by a Viennese – a Strauss!'" Waltzes by Johann Strauss, Sr. (1804–1849), the paper insisted, had something "invincibly lively and electrifying about them": consequently, they remained popular even if the "rhythm of the day" had changed. Though struggling through a cold, hard, planned life – "surrounded by the noise of machines and the thousands of wheels passing in traffic" – modern Germans were "still moved by the lyrical nightscape of a Strauss waltz – ever reminded that a Viennese waltz is the language of our soul, the rhythm of our pulse, the flow of our blood, the throbbing of our heart."[1]

The *Völkischer Beobachter* also celebrated Johann Strauss, Jr. (1825–1899), like his father, as an icon of simpler times. According to Hans Buchner, the younger Strauss was not only the embodiment of all the musical qualities of "old Austria," but also the hero of the modern operetta, which he "saved from the influence of the Jew Offenbach." The Waltz King took his "well-deserved place and rank in the musical history of our people, which he earned with the sonic exuberance of his genuinely artistic soul – a place that chintzy intellectuals can't deny him." He didn't try to reach the highest levels of artistic expression, but here self-restraint was to be admired, not criticized: "within the limits that he set for himself, he was a master without rivals." While the paper usually condemned those who achieved success by catering to popular taste, and reserved special contempt for Jewish composers thought to have debased serious German music by rendering it in popular form, it complimented Strauss for "knowing how to find just the right tones for letting his fellow men share joy and sadness in their purest forms."[2] Staff writer Norbert Wiltsch added that wherever an Austrian went – "to Lapland or to southern Italy" – he could trigger familiar sentiments through the works of this master: "even in foreign lands one is greeted by the beautiful blue Danube – wherever Strauss is, that is Austria."[3] In support of a return to the more stable, purer sounds of the past, Siegfried Wagner addressed the "dancing youth" of Weimar Germany directly and questioned its propensity toward modern sounds: "Why not dance to Johann Strauss' music instead of Negro rhythms?" Wagner asked. Listening to jazz was justified in America, he felt, since it was something "native and original" there. But "did Germans have to dance to it – couldn't they find their own ways to dance?" "Promote Strauss' music among youth and bid farewell to Negro rhythms," Richard Wagner's son exhorted: "Italians have the tarantella, Spaniards the fandango, Bavarians the *Schuhplattler*, French the cancan, Germans the waltz – let's bring it back!"[4]

Of course, the National Socialist music agenda sought to accomplish more than supplanting jazz with waltzes. The search for thematic correlates in the German tradition of serious music also involved efforts to appropriate Johannes Brahms (1833–1897). Given the well-known rivalry between Brahms and Wagner – and especially between their respective adherents – such efforts might have posed some challenges, but the newspaper's reception of Brahms was highly positive. For the most part, the *Völkischer Beobachter* set the long-standing controversy aside and welcomed Brahms into the Walhalla of Nordic-Germanic geniuses. Hans Severus Ziegler dutifully cleared Brahms' racial profile by stipulating that he was "one of the greatest creative masters of music to emerge out of a Nordic nature." On his mother's side, Ziegler noted, Brahms "received some Mecklenburger-Obotriden blood" and this gave the "Holsteiner much of the bitterness and acerbity which remained a component of his artistic character and temper, but this just enhanced his undoubtedly Nordic essence."[5] Outwardly gruff, he was of a soft, sensitive nature and the combination made him a "German in the truest sense of the word: full of ideals, energy, and will power, but nevertheless shy in the depths of his heart." The "radiant blue eyes reflected his feelings more effectively than the most eloquent words: they often filled with the tears of love, friendship, and pain." All who knew him well, loved him, and Nazis – "in whom he continues to live through his works – must also love him: he is ours like few others!"[6]

Presenting Brahms as "the great North German symphonist" meant that the *Völkischer Beobachter* had to deal with his relocation to Vienna for most of his life, and it did so by drawing upon pan-German concepts of the nation. It was no coincidence, wrote Ludwig K. Mayer, that the North German was drawn to the optimism of the south. By moving to Vienna, he gave external expression to that ancient German longing: the *Drang nach Süden*. More than that, however, Brahms' creations symbolized a "spiritual bridge that represented Germany with all of its tribes [*Stämmen*] united – a Germany that despite its multitude of forms was always a great whole." Further, as they were finally taking steps to construct the long desired Greater German Reich, Nazis had to think of Brahms "with gratitude and reverence" as one of the genuine German masters whose "spirit contributed to a goal he desired longingly, and struggled for in his work": the "establishment of a united, comprehensive empire of German essence, which will help to heal the world."[7]

At the time of "national breakout" of 1933 in particular, Brahms "had a lot to say." Through his life and works he reminded Nazis that "all great and genuine art is begotten only from the forces of blood and soil, and that the creative artist is the spokesman of his Volk – the deepest essence of which he exposes in his works." Importantly, the newspaper felt that this was true of both Brahms and Wagner, who became opponents with respect to each other only "because of Jewish hatefulness." Recognizing that Jews were the cause of their discord was the first step toward overcoming differences that "Jewish figures" like Eduard Hanslick had created between the two camps. Nazis thus "decisively rejected such an oppositional confrontation of the two greatest musicians of the nineteenth century," and were "pleased that our Volk was the recipient of two such men." Both Wagner and Brahms would be Führer of a new German music, "strongly anchored in the Volk soul, but giving expression to the feeling and willing of our stormy times."[8] Just as Wagner's creations were "utterly German since they were formulated in the tradition of German sagas," Brahms "distinctly conveyed in his music the deep intellectual and emotional world of our people." Thus did the *Völkischer Beobachter* announce the accomplishment of a music-historical *Anschluss*: "We no longer think in terms of Brahms *or* Wagner, but of Brahms *and* Wagner."[9] In a similar vein, the paper also pronounced the end of hostilities between supporters of Bruckner and Brahms. It acknowledged that the "strong, life-affirming, and sensuous basis of Bruckner's broadly expansive German-Austrian/Southern-German tonal language contrasted intensively against that of the rough-cut North German who felt the pressure of pessimism and skepticism, ultimately seeking refuge in resignation."[10] But ultimately a synthesis was possible because the "Baroque sensual joy of the south built up into a deep sense of faith" – as found to the highest degree in Bruckner – was "just as German as the North-German acerbity of a Brahms."[11]

Further emphasizing Brahms' nationalism, Lore Reinmoeller, author of poetry, short stories, plays about Lou Salomé and Theodore Fontane, as well as of studies of Eichendorff and Nietzsche, highlighted the composer's intense interest in the military events of 1870–1871. Because he lived in Austria, "it was not granted to him" to take part in the military conflict, but his letters from those years revealed a "deep love of the Fatherland, a great sense of satisfaction over the German victory," and the wish that this victory would have "strong inner effect" on the German people: "May God grant that the Germans handle themselves as easily and beautifully as they have handled the French," Brahms wrote.[12] For the *Völkischer Beobachter*, the "great artistic fruit" of the Franco-Prussian war was Brahms' *Triumphal Song on the Victory of German Arms*, a composition he dedicated to Kaiser Wilhelm I. This work alone stood as proof that the composer was a great patriot and a "glowing admirer of the creator of Germany's unity, Bismarck."[13] But the paper naturally wanted to connect Brahms with the whole of Nazi ideology, including anti-Semitism. Hence, Reinmoeller's article included a claim that Brahms' correspondence with Joseph Joachim revealed "ever more alienation developing between the friends over the years which one can justifiably trace to the conflicted nature and excessive sensitivity of the Jewish violin virtuoso."[14]

While linking Brahms' biography with Nordic culture, pan-German politics, and even irritation with Jews, the *Völkischer Beobachter* simultaneously pursued echoes of similar themes in the substance and nature of his compositions themselves. Something "closed and tart" about his works could alienate some listeners, but whoever knew the character of the North German landscape – whoever could "visualize the wide green spaces of the coastline with its still peacefulness that triggers reflection and brooding" – would feel a close affinity for the music of Brahms.[15] According to Hans Buchner, one could only really love it if one "understood German people and the German past – and if one believes in the German future."[16] So, while contending that Brahms' music was as universal as that of Beethoven and Wagner, the paper maintained that its strengths were derived from its "native qualities," which made it "German music through and through." Brahms was "a man of the Volk," and as an artist he "never lost his intimate solidarity with the Volk soul." Indeed, even the themes of his instrumental works often came from German folk songs, or at least had a "strongly *volkstümlich* feeling to them."[17] The "most multifaceted, perfect command of natural and *volkstümlich* forms of expression – placed in the firm soil of solid handiwork – gave rise to his golden achievements."[18]

According to the paper, Brahms' "inner unity with the Volk" was particularly clear in his *Lieder* where he preferred to use simple forms, such as those used in folk songs. But volkish references could also be found in instrumental works such as the Piano Sonata in F-Minor, in whose slow movement the popular folk song, *Steh ich in finstrer Mitternacht* was "presented so magically," and the C-Minor Symphony which features the melody of another folk song, *Ich hab mich ergeben* – "a favorite idea of Brahms, who returned to it often in his chamber music."[19] In addition, the *Völkischer Beobachter* claimed that the *German Requiem* stood next to Bach's *St. Matthew Passion* and Beethoven's Ninth Symphony as "one of the sacred national musical possessions of the German Volk." In this case, however, the newspaper's justification had less to do with Brahms' ostensible *Volkstümlichkeit* than with notions of Germanic Christianity, such as those supposedly put forth by "Nordic thinkers" like Kierkegaard and Nietzsche. The combination of "genuine German feeling and Christian piety that this work speaks about can show the way to our future," the paper held.[20] In fact, no choral work would be more suitable for "motivating a new German religiosity without confessional directions and conditions." Selected from Holy Scripture but arranged by Brahms himself, it conveyed a "human belief in God that is independent of any church dogma and that could only be expressed in the musical revelations of this master with his deep, North-German artistic disposition."[21]

Still, while the newspaper implied its support for "Germanic Christianity," it managed to do so without directly attacking the Catholic tradition that was so important in Southern German territories. Thus, while applauding Brahms' "German religiosity without confessional directions and conditions" the paper simultaneously praised Anton Bruckner (1824–1896) as having been "filled with genuine, naive piety which was rooted deeply in his religion – Catholicism."[22] For the *Völkischer Beobachter*, Bruckner was above all a naive genius who embodied *Volkstümlichkeit* more than any other composer. Assessing Bruckner's origins – "since they interest us more than ever before in the age of Family-and Race-Research" – Karl Grunsky emphasized that the composer had come from a modest farming background: the son of an upper-Austrian teacher, who had lower-Austrian farmers as ancestors, and who could be proud that one of them ascended to such heights and achieved world significance.[23] Emphasizing his "kind, wonderfully deep blue eyes," Josef Stolzing considered Bruckner to be "next to Franz Liszt, the greatest German symphonist after Beethoven." This strong third-place ranking was founded largely on Bruckner's simple, volkish characteristics. According to Stolzing, "being of farming origins, the composer remained a simple man who never posed."[24] In his music, as in his character, Grunsky asserted, "genuinely *volkstümlich* features were indisputable."[25] Most intensively, *Völkischer Beobachter* contributors applauded Bruckner's "relatively limited education, his indifference to the society and culture of the rest of the world, and the natural, farmer-like, primitive nature of his background."[26] In the realm of tones, Bruckner was "a ruler graced by God," but otherwise he was a man of "touching naivety, clumsiness, and timidity."[27] As a result, this "heaven bound, unworldly [*Weltfremd*] artist was no formalist."[28] His works were not the product of "isolated artistic conception, aesthetic taste, momentary mood, or agitated feeling," but rather the "language of his soul, the confession of his world view, and the self-expression of his innermost being."[29]

Contributors provided a number of anecdotes to fill out the picture of Bruckner as a naively volkish genius, some of which involved descriptions of his drinking habits. According to Stolzing, the composer "definitely had one weakness: he loved to drink." But the National Socialist cultural critic did not seem to consider this much of a problem; indeed, in one instance, he wrote without reservation about Bruckner vomiting after drinking excessively, complete with details about the nearby devotee who kept as a memento of this brush with volkish genius a set of clothes which had been splattered by the composer.[30] Stolzing also related an occasion when Bruckner asked Richard Wagner, while drinking beers with him, to select one of two symphonies that would be dedicated to him. The Master made the choice, but Bruckner woke up simply too hung over to remember which one Wagner had chosen.[31] Another sign of Bruckner's simple nature that impressed Stolzing was the low fees he charged students: "how refreshing that for such modest prices one could get music lessons from a genius before whose immortal works the whole Aryan world looks on in respect."[32] The newspaper even compared Bruckner with the romantic character of *Kannitverstan*, who learns important lessons in Holland though he cannot understand a word of Dutch: "how remarkable it was when Master Anton – who, similar to the model created by Hebel, did not understand the outside world – climbed to the conductor's podium in order to take in the cheers of his listeners." At that moment it seemed as if he were "still the former teaching assistant and part-time church organist standing there help-lessly, done up in a ridiculous suit that looked like it was thrown together by the village tailor, bowing awkwardly, holding up his hands as if protecting himself from the public, and finally blowing a kiss to the house – like a big kid."[33]

Reinhold Freiherr von Lichtenberg, a professor at Berlin University who wrote about *The Homeland of the Aryans* (1913) and made contributions to the *Bayreuther Blätter*, reminded *Völkischer Beobachter* readers about the best known story of Bruckner's child-like enthusiasm. When Beethoven's remains were moved in 1888, Bruckner went into the church and actually picked up the skull. Scolded for doing so, he said that he was the "only one who really understood him."[34] Absolutely loyal to his favorite predecessors, Bruckner paid a price for his association with Wagner "at the hands of the Jewish press," accord-ing to Stolzing. In particular, the "music critic at the Jewish *Neue Freie Presse*," Eduard Hanslick, "attacked Bruckner along with Wagner," especially after Wagner had accused Hanslick of "hiding his Jewish origins." In Stolzing's opinion, Hanslick's criticisms of Bruckner's

Seventh Symphony proved how "Jewish criticism has been striving since time immemorial to spoil the joy that the German Volk derives from the creations of its great German masters." When Bruckner and Hanslick met, however, the composer bowed and treated the critic with respect. "We were utterly astounded," Stolzing recalled.[35]

Erwin Bauer explained the Nazi attention to Bruckner's music in terms of its "romantic naturalism": in his symphonies, "gigantic oaks rustle, powerful streams roar, and the rejoicing, but often also longing sound of the horn penetrates through everything." Bruckner's Fourth Symphony, particularly, was a "nature symphony" akin to Beethoven's Sixth. Comparing them in concert, Bauer stated, was pleasurable and worthwhile: on the one hand, a "bright, magical confession about idyllic life in the country," on the other, a "trembling soul exuding incomparable praise for the expanse and beauty of the cosmos"; the first was a "complete collection of feelings," while the second was marked by "wonderful melancholy and magnificent outbreaks of the soul."[36] But for Karl Grunsky, Bruckner's music was important mainly because it exhibited volkish naivety: a German master who stood on the shoulders of other greats, he did not "speak to us in gibberish and mishmash with Negroid grimaces, but in a language drawn from a natural source that reaches into the deepest interior of the unrefined German mind – the pure spirit of German childlikeness."[37]

As reported in the *Völkischer Beobachter*, Bruckner compositions were performed at numerous Nazi organized events, including the first concert[38] and concert tour[39] of the National Socialist Symphony Orchestra, in SS concerts,[40] at a Bruckner festival in the composer's small Austrian hometown – "a rare pleasure in the troubled times" of 1932, as Max Morold-Millenkovich, who covered cultural affairs in Vienna for the paper as early as 1920 and strongly advocated Bruckner's music, put it[41] – and at the First Greater German Bruckner Festival in 1939. Significant party officials attended the festival last mentioned, including among them Arthur Seyss-Inquart – previously *Reichsstatthalter* of the *Ostmark* (Austria) and *Reichsminister* without portfolio after May 1939 – and August Eigruber – *Gauleiter* of upper Austria, who helped to establish the concentration camp at Mauthausen.[42] As the newspaper related it, the opening festivities of the Brucknerfest were a "great cultural achievement on the part of National Socialism." There the regime announced that it would provide an annual grant toward the preparation of a complete edition of Bruckner's works and thereby "secure the life work of the master for the German nation and the whole music world beyond." This, along with a tribute to "the master" during the Regensburg Music Festival on the occasion of his "solemn entrance into Walhalla as a national hero," were touted as two "Official Acts of the German Head of State" that "clearly indicated how much cultural historical significance the Führer attributed to the works of his compatriot."[43]

Another Austrian compatriot of Hitler whose works were performed at SS concerts[44] and received attention in the *Völkischer Beobachter* was Hugo Wolf (1860–1903). The newspaper saw him as the "Wagner of Song" and as a victim of a Jewish conspiracy precisely because of his association with the Master. A circle of Wagnerians and a few individual patrons had enabled his ascent and, not disappointing, "he clearly upheld German style." But difficulties triggered by his support of Wagner made him very unpopular in Vienna: "for his whole life Wolf had the Hanslick press working against him – of course." For instance, according to the paper, "their representatives" once forced a well-known singer who wanted to introduce Wolf's *Lieder* to demur under threat of a sustained boycott by the press. Such malicious maneuvering was just another indication that Vienna, "the city that should have been the capital of the German *Ostmark*, was really the center of an Eastern-oriented cosmopolitan world!" But "nothing held back Wolf's triumphant course: his *Lieder* will be remembered with German consciousness!"[45]

One more composer whom the *Völkischer Beobachter* felt the renewed German race should appreciate more keenly was Max Reger (1873–1916). Like other favorites, the paper considered him the "spiritual son of the old world that the November Revolution and the subsequent Americanization of Weimar culture had eradicated."[46] The fact that he had done a year's military service in 1897 was important to Hans Buchner, Reger's most vocal champion in the pages of the *Völkischer Beobachter*: though Reger was perhaps not an ideal soldier in the sense of infantry regulations, he "enjoyed and was proud of his service." Moreover, before his death in 1916 he tried to enlist for the First World War, but was deemed unsuitable for active service, and Buchner was sure it "pained him deeply that he could only consecrate in art the patriotism he felt burning in his soul."[47] The *Völkischer Beobachter* cited ample evidence of Reger's patriotism, whether expressed in his letters ("I know I would die of homesickness if I ever left Germany"), or in his effort to "formulate musical tributes to the nation fighting for its existence" in "outstanding creations" like *Eine vaterländische Ouvertüre* (1914) and an unfinished *Requiem* for those fallen in battle. According to the paper, from the moment Reger was deemed unfit for service, "prophetic notions about his own destiny and that of his Fatherland stole over him." Though he believed "firmly and unshakably" in the ultimate victory of Germanness, he foresaw "a long and difficult time of suffering." Moreover, without ignoring the problems of the faulty Wilhelmine system, he "energetically rejected a social-democratic republic," which he regarded as an "unhappy and undesirable form of government for Germany." It was perhaps a blessing in disguise, the paper implied, that he didn't have to experience the collapse of the "strong, honest, brave, incorruptible Germany" he loved so fervently: "up to the last minute before he was carried off to eternal peace, Reger believed that Germany's final victory and the Third Reich would come after a long time of battle."[48]

Justifying Reger's ultimate place in the "German programs" of concerts by the *Kampfbund für Kultur*[49] and the *Orchester des Führers*,[50] Fritz Wolffhuegel emphasized that the composer was a "son of the Bavarian Forest." Like a "tall, isolated oak in a grove of trees of average height and girth," he resembled an "Old-Germanic Tree-of-Heaven, towering over the sparse modern landscape as a symbol of healthy, fruitful growth." In addition to his dedication "to the triumphant German army" – to an army "which lost a war, but was not destroyed" – the *Vaterländische Ouvertüre* was a "thunderous fanfare" about the Bavarian–Bohemian forest.[51] Above all, Buchner and the *Völkischer Beobachter* valued Reger's aesthetic traditionalism. Referring to "the modernists in charge of musical life" as "progressive philistines" – by which, the paper asserted, he meant the "motley crew" of "musicologists, writers, and critics who never gave him a chance" – Reger had written that "we simply have too many philologists in our music!"

As the "sole German master to watch over the legacy of Brahms," Reger protected an aesthetic morality that was "exclusively and in the highest sense volkish." Consequently, the "internationalist art directorate of the Weimar democracy" had no idea what to do with his works. For Buchner, proof that Reger's work was a national treasure was its "triumphal presence in the music-making of the German home." Neither "concert hall demagoguery nor the publicity campaigns of publishers" really prepared the way for the works of great musicians, but rather it was "the love of amateurs" – those "naive lovers of the art who played music for its own sake and not for a monthly wage." A master whose works had become treasures in the home life of the German family had no need for official concert advertisements. This, Buchner felt, was most true of Reger: his oeuvre was "created by and for the German home." There, his spirit would "show Germans the way toward the future, and not just in terms of music."[52] To Buchner, Reger was the "last pillar of the German music tradition," and, besides Brahms, the most significant representative of "German neoclassicism" – though without the slightest "propagandistic support or protection." The fact that he received little attention resulted from "Jewish-capitalistic art propaganda": like "dark shadows passing over a sunny valley, the treatment of his life's work presaged the coming struggle of the German Volk for its very existence." Reger was the "cornerstone for the proud edifice of a new German music," and even more, owing to his racial make-up and his spiritual orientation, he was the "cornerstone for a new culture that German youth were obliged to construct if they were going to fight for their volkish and political existence with the strength of their vital instincts."[53]

In the search for composers who had above all resisted modernist innovations ostensibly contrary to the Wagner tradition, the *Völkischer Beobachter* demonstrated noticeable support for Hans Pfitzner (1869–1949). According to the paper, Pfitzner was "the one who most faithfully defended the legacy of Richard Wagner."[54] For this service he earned the right to be called Wagner's spiritual heir. There was no need to go into particulars to justify this, the newspaper asserted: it was enough to consider his collected works. Like those of the Bayreuth Master, they were "emblematic of a glowing German consciousness that manifests itself in the struggle to protect the purity of German art – not without occasionally slipping into the realm of politics." Pfitzner's career proved that it is "only at the price of rejection and loneliness that the higher good can be achieved: that of preserving German forms and works from the fleeting stream of time and giving them lasting validity."[55]

Erwin Bauer saw Pfitzner as an "apostle of a pure form of art," because he "shunned all works that portray grumbling and discomfort," thereby "rejecting modernist fascination with the modern." In short, Pfitzner's was a spirit that "stood against the times, without concessions." Moreover, while not exactly popular, he was still a *volkstümlich* musician. What made his music "volkish to the highest degree," explained Bauer, was its being rooted in the "German musical legacy of Schumann and Weber, with the capability of representing musical thoughts in their purest, most soulful form." The essence of his achievement was not "external suggestion – the brilliance and sensuousness of refined orchestral colors – but the musical image itself, the magic of the idea that enters into the world with simplicity and plainness, like all truly great musical intuitions." It was in recognition of this, Bauer believed, that the Nazi "Strength through Joy" (*NSG Kraft durch Freude*) organization arranged concerts of Pfitzner's music: the organization wanted to direct attention to the life work of "a master who was obliged to his Volk for every note, and therefore was *volkstümlich* in the highest sense that art can be *volkstümlich*."[56]

Reviewing Pfitzner's music drama, *Das Herz* (1931), Wolfgang Gottrau wrote that the spirit of German music was embodied in Pfitzner more than in any other living man. Pfitzner served his calling with "priestly dedication" far from any "opportunism or concessions that could make external success easier." In works like *Der arme Heinrich* (1891–1893) ("modeled on Wagner"), *Die Rose vom Liebesgarten* (1897–1900) ("not performed enough, but this will change"), and especially the *Cantata of German Soul* (1921) ("lasting evidence that the true spirit of our century is German"), Pfitzner demonstrated that he "lived only for the idea of German art": neither pleasure in forms for their own sake nor technical routine inspired him; he composed "from the heart, from the foundations of the soul, out of inner need." A "conscious German and also a conscious romantic," Pfitzner proved that the essence of German creativity "is and will always be romantic." In this sense, Gottrau asserted in 1931, he was "really the most German musician of our time."[57]

While it covered many of Pfitzner's works, the *Völkischer Beobachter* devoted most space to *Palestrina* (1917). For Gottrau, the opera was a "sanctuary of German music."[58] Erich Valentin placed the work in the context of twentieth-century history, pointing out that Pfitzner composed it in 1914 and 1915, "at a time when the best sons of the Volk were at the front fighting and bleeding for the existence, future, and honor of Germany while behind their backs invisible forces were playing a secret game that would lead to a disastrous catastrophe." In the "twilight of this eventide – as bright day faded into dark clouds – out of the unexpected, out of the cacophony of voices and opinions, out of the struggle over existence or non-existence, *Palestrina* arose as a living symbol and clear embodiment of the unbending, victorious purity and strength of the German soul."[59] The "wonderful ethos" of the work, not least its "full-blooded nationalism that reaches its crowning moment in the council scene," secured its place in the repertoire – which it would maintain "as long as German spirit and German sensibility govern over our theaters!"[60] Moreover, in his representation of Palestrina it was clear that Pfitzner was "the last romantic" and that with his generation a cultural age came to an end, "leaving only a creaky bridge into our days." Thus, his work signified to Nazis the "drama of a whole artistic epoch at war with the tough realities of daily life."[61] The "dark shadows of the Decline of the West extended like a melancholy veil over it," but *Palestrina* would nevertheless "last for eons, giving witness to the true spirit of the century – especially its Germanness."[62]

But, music aside, it was Pfitzner the writer that the Nazi paper found most compelling. Produced amidst a "battle raging on many fronts," Lothar Band – a critic and choral director – found that Pfitzner's antimodernist polemical writings conveyed the responsibility to be aggressive and courageous in the fight to "maintain the purity of ideals in German art."[63] In modern times with "all their new orientations," said the paper, Pfitzner was the spiritual leader of a battle being fought to the end: "we call upon the author of the *Danger of Futurists*[64] and *The New Aesthetic of Musical Impotence*[65] whenever we bring about balancing, protective, and demanding deeds."[66] Alfred Morgenroth, a composer involved with Goebbels' Reich Music Chamber who was dedicated to promoting Pfitzner in the Third Reich, pointed out that his first "great battle essay," *Danger of Futurists*, appeared in 1917 during the First World War and "unflinchingly diagnosed cultural dangers that only a few perceived at that time." In the next few years the cultural catastrophe that he foresaw occurred, along with the national collapse. Contrary to the majority of "gullible intellectuals," Pfitzner was not for one moment persuaded that "the new slogans would lead to a real, healthy reconstruction." For him the mission was clear: "to resist [the slogans] at all costs, and to warn of their deadly dangers loudly and publicly." Thus was the creative artist and cultural educator transformed into a "cultural-political fighter – a herald of the day with full consciousness of his responsibility."[67] It was clear in his writings how much this man – "who was German to the core and loved Volk and Fatherland above all else" – suffered in the Weimar era. "All the pain over the betrayals that Germans have committed against Germany – all the anger that Germans have brought on themselves – break forth in the passionate energy of his writings." The sword Wagner laid down in 1883, Pfitzner picked up again in the "battle to maintain the purity of German art." If the German Volk really became conscious of its own essence, it would build a monument to him, marked with just three words: "He was irreproachable."[68]

In contrast to Pfitzner's irreproachable antimodernism, the *Völkischer Beobachter* derided the supposedly "nervous" art of Gustav Mahler (1860–1911). In dealing with Mahler, the paper reprised many of the themes that Wagner had directed against Mendelssohn and Meyerbeer in his article about Judaism and music. For instance, Friedrich Wilhelm Herzog – a NS-*Kulturgemeinde* functionary and one of the eighty-eight writers who had signed a proclamation of loyalty to Hitler in October 1933[69] – complained about "extravagant acclaim" for productions of Mahler who was "nothing but a well-known *reproductive* musician."[70] Otto Repp practically lifted the words for an attack on Mahler from Wagner's article, stating that he "appropriated the means and techniques, not the essence of our music because music for him is not the language of a soul, an inner need, but just a means to an end; and this end is always (even if unconscious – because it is racially-determined) the imposition of his own ego." Mahler's "musical-naturalistic bric-a-brac" embodied the "racial corruption among Jews and their unprofessional, self-centered, and fundamentally neurotic inclination to falsify sensuousness into debauchery, eroticism into frivolity, aesthetics into a cult of ugliness, abstraction into inner emptiness, and ecstasy into physical titillation." In Mahler's hands even the concept of happiness was all too often "reduced into wild triumphalism," while "suffering becomes sniveling, humor becomes derisive irony, pride becomes arrogance, pain becomes illness." Moreover, in his compositions, "love is reduced to sentimentality or lust because unconsciously this selfish ego always stands in the center of a universe in which god supposedly judges and punishes in the interests of the Jews alone."[71]

In the opinion of Hans Buchner, the emergence of Gustav Mahler marked the beginning of the "storm against German music." With "inconsiderateness consistent with his lack of talent, this Jew went into the legacy of our musical past and plundered the blooming garden of a century – without being able to replant the now rootless glories that he had picked." Consequently, the "remnants of German genius appear like erratic blocks" throughout his "nihilistic" compositions.[72] Works such as the *Songs of a Wayfarer* (1885), Buchner complained, were "typical

Mahler." In them, he revealed the "inner insecurity and uprootedness of the casually civilized Western Jew in all of his tragedy." According to Buchner, everyone could immediately recognize the "inconsistent, wishy-washy type of the [Otto] Weininger sort prevalent in the circles of Viennese Jewry – torn between his blood-ties and the foreign Volk that he both hates and longs for." However, Mahler was not one of those: "he hadn't come along that far and didn't have a hint of Weininger's honest despair." Instead, he was "fake and insidious: his only truly genuine characteristics were his irremediable melancholy, rejection of the world, and taste for triviality – from which he tried to escape artificially through narcotic stimulants that just led him deeper into his inferiority complex." Unable to "fully recognize his Jewish self-hatred," and "take his fate in his own hands" as had Weininger (who committed suicide), Mahler was a "hopeless case and, frighteningly, music like the *Songs of a Wayfarer* flowed directly out of this *psychopathia musikalis*."[73]

According to Lore Reinmoeller, although Mahler represented himself as an idealist and champion of the noblest German art, he was "recognized by Jewry in general as a promoter of Jewish goals." As such, his impact strengthened "dangerous principles" including "progress at any price (even, or above all, that of comprehensibility) and calculation of the value of a work according to size, noise, and difficulty." These notions had moved German music in the direction of dissolving the established tonal tradition and pointed toward "no more and no less than chaos in music development." Other "typically Jewish features" in Mahler's music were "the most intensely strained expression, an un-German lingering over certain states of feeling, and destruction of the melodic, singable character of themes through crass rhythmic accents." From here, Reinmoeller added, it was only a small step to "that Jewish sensibility that is known by the term *Jazz*."[74] Therefore, the *Völkischer Beobachter* held, continued programming of his works was nothing less than "the act of an all-powerful Central Bureau for the Jewification of Western Musical Taste."[75]

While on the lookout for Jewish influences on the repertoire, the newspaper also scanned for threats outside German lands. *Völkischer Beobachter* contributors were somewhat bewildered by the case of Georges Bizet (1838–1875). Some minimized the fact that his maternal grandparents were Spanish Jews, concluding that at least as far as the "latest research" indicated, Bizet was "not Jewish, and neither was Ravel."[76] But music and theater critic Friedrich Wilhelm Herzog identified Bizet as a *"Halbjude"* and analyzed his art in light of this assumption: "as one often finds particularly in Jewish half-bloods, Bizet was an outspoken eclectic and many a half-breed has failed prematurely because of this secret problem." Even in his "few stageable works," Bizet was "unable to negate the Jewish component of his blood," Herzog complained, asking readers to "consider his choice of material from Miremé's novel for his opera *Carmen* – with its pseudo-dramatic glorification of a degenerate character."[77]

Camille Saint-Saëns (1835–1921) was also outed as being of Jewish heritage, with the newspaper insinuating that "like a remarkable number of non-Aryan 'Frenchmen,'" he put a "sacred Christian 'saint' in front of his name for protection." Although he "completely misunderstood the essence of composing," moreover, this "pure chameleon" learned a lot from his betters while conspiring to sensualize music. An "aesthetic diviner," Saint-Saëns "fed off Germany so that he could later revile it according to all the rules of his 'art.'"[78] Other non-German composers were summarily condemned as derivative, whether they had Jewish ancestors or not. According to Erich Valentin, Claude Debussy's Impressionism "embodied all the same particularities that we perceive in the painting of this aesthetic direction" – not a compliment from the Nazi perspective. But Valentin added that a few years before his death Debussy (1862–1918) rejected his own ideals, returned to Bach – "the source of everything" – and tried to construct a "formally exact style referred to as neoclassical." For Valentin, this was proof that Impressionism came and went with Debussy alone and that "the consummate French composer ultimately considered German music superior."[79] In a similarly nationalistic vein, critic Alexander Dillmann argued that Giacomo Puccini (1858–1924) owed his success to the efforts of a German predecessor: "Richard Wagner first had to fight for the heart and soul of the German Volk, preparing the ears of his contemporaries, before a Puccini could walk through open doors."[80] Like "faded impressionism," moreover, Hans Buchner believed that Puccini's most famous work was obsolete – nothing more than a reminder of the decadence at the turn of the century. For him, *La Bohème* (1896) was a character study from the "forever vanished times of a sorrowful yet carefree artists' life in the Latin Quarter" – a "thin tragedy of tuberculosis that is really no longer relevant to us today." For Buchner it was not that health problems had disappeared from Western existence, but that Puccini's representation of the "psychopathic ruin of the social and physical cell system" was too consistent with notions of Western decline, and there-fore "went against the life energy" of the Nazi era. *La Bohème* was just more proof that the "Schwabing scene" and its era had been responsible for the "catastrophe of our century" and that the Bohemian way of life no longer had any sense: it had "lost its justification for existence."[81]

Whereas French and Italian musicians were derided for their interest in German music, some central, northern, and even eastern Europeans were applauded for supposedly adhering to the tendencies of "Nordic culture." Ludwig K. Mayer felt that from the very beginning, Smetana was "under the strongest possible influence of German music – particularly that of his German contemporaries."[82] According to Munich composer, Fritz Wolffhuegel, who contributed music analysis to the *Völkischer Beobachter* as of 1931,[83] in no composer was "the Nordic expressed so strongly" than in Edvard Grieg (1843–1907). He and Rikard Nordraak, another Norwegian composer, were both "enthusiastic friends of nature and glowing patriots": there was "nothing more beautiful for them than the Nordic mountains and the old Norse sagas."[84] Similarly, with regard to Modest Mussorgsky (1839–1891), Erwin Bauer concluded that because the composer was "unconditionally Russian and loved his Volk utterly," he could rightly be considered as the "Russian Pfitzner." Among Russians, only Mussorgsky employed the "primary musical idea" with the same passion as Pfitzner. Mussorgsky was the "greatest composer of the Russian Volk" – Tchaikovsky not-withstanding – "on the same grounds."[85] Regarding Jean Sibelius (1865–1957), the paper quoted Heinz Drewes as implying that his symphonic sagas were evidence that "while the Finnish Volk could be counted racially among the Finno-Ungrisch tribe," over many centuries it had "turned happily toward the German world." Their Russian rulers had never been able to Slavicize them because "being neighbors with the German Baltics, Prussia, and Pomerania was much more important."[86] Thus did the *Völkischer Beobachter*'s treatment of turn-of-the-century foreign composers either as cultural and racial ene-mies or as potentially belonging under the sway of a larger sphere of German cultural influence correlate with geopolitical perspectives that retrospectively validated the nation's involvement in the First World War.

PART IV
"HOLY" WAR AND WEIMAR "CRISIS"

13 HERALDS OF THE FRONT EXPERIENCE

Hitler's two most important early adult experiences were his exposure to urban life and modernism in Vienna after his failed application for art school and his four years of service in the First World War. Both of these phases determined his cultural and political outlook for the future. The negative outcomes of each fueled his antimodernist and anti-Semitic animus, convincing him that "there is no making pacts with Jews; there can only be the hard: either–or," and motivating him "to go into politics."[1] It goes without saying that the former triggered his hatred for modern culture and the Jewish influence supposedly responsible for it. But historians might not yet have sufficiently taken into account the extent to which Hitler's self-identity was wrapped in his record as a front soldier. While Parkinson's disease and stress took their deserved toll, resulting in the maniacal image of Hitler in his final bunker, we err in forgetting that his self-image was probably fixed at his stage as a hard-boned veteran of the trenches. Elementary to his perspective was the conviction that First World War duty was his most profound test, for which he "thanked heaven from an overflowing heart for granting me the good fortune of being permitted to live at this time."[2]

As for so many veterans whose efforts ended in defeat, Hitler was incapable of acknowledging that the German cause had been lost. In honor of his fallen comrades, the torch – or as in Nürnberg rally rituals, flags symbolizing each major offensive – had to be raised aloft in renewed efforts at retribution. Idealization and justification of the front experience, therefore, were "unshakeable" components of the Nazi culture he triggered: "Thousands of years may pass, but never will it be possible to speak of heroism without mentioning the German army and the World War. Then from the veil of the past the iron front of the gray steel helmet will emerge, unwavering and unflinching, an immortal monument."[3] In this, of course, Hitler was not alone: Nazism coordinated with right-wing appropriation of the front experience in general.[4] As manifested in the cultural section of the *Völkischer Beobachter*, it took the form of engagement with literature emerging from combat history. Even before the *All Quiet on the Western Front* controversy broke out, the paper drew attention to Walther Flex and Ernst Jünger as the true "heralds of the front experience." Then, when Erich Maria Remarque's book appeared – and soon thereafter, the Hollywood movie based on it – the paper drew every bit of publicity it could from the ensuing "battle."

Writing for the paper, Erich Limpach, a poet and writer whose aphorisms remain popular in German culture today – despite the fact that as early as 1924 he had dedicated some of his "Fatherlandish Poems" to Hitler[5] – reviewed three German war novels by Ernst Gläser (*Class of 1902*, 1928), Georg von der Vring (*Soldat Suhren*, 1928), and Ludwig Renn (*War*, 1928). Consistent with right-wing interpretations of front history, Limpach was disappointed because these were "war books, but not soldiers' books." In his opinion, the front soldier who read these books would recognize that "moles" were falsifying the war experience by depicting it – "in clever, camouflaged ways" – as having been completely negative. Limpach admitted that while all these writings realistically described the war in the field and on the home front as it was, with all its hardships and ugliness, the war's "high points," which "every true front soldier experienced," were "skillfully con-cealed." He searched these works in vain for any indication that the war wasn't just destructive, but that it also allowed soldiers to experience "imperishable things" – that it was actually a source of strength for all those who "lived it deeply." In his opinion, this absence of recognition of the ennobling aspects of war was the reason that "Judah touted these works so highly": the novels were "all designed to awaken pacifist thoughts exclusively," and thus failed both to capture the "true, deeper experience of the war," and to "provide bases for reconstruction after it."[6]

Such writing, Limpach complained, offended the "holiest feel-ings of millions of our people," as he singled out the following sarcastic passage from Ernst Gläser's *Class of 1902* as particularly offensive: "on 2 August 1914, as we looked out over the red, white, and blue front, singing patriotic songs through the festive night – including 'We Step Before God the Just to Pray' – I got drunk for the first time." Limpach considered Gläser's book to be one of the "most dangerous of Jewish constructs" in the literature about the war, affecting German youth like a "nerve-racking poison." He admitted that the book included some penetrating psychological insights, but behind the few high points "yawned the abyss of the Jewish cabal – to which nothing is holy and which drags everything great and uplifting into the gutter." There were laws against such filth and trash, Limpach reminded, but he knew that such laws would be applied correctly only when the state was in Nazi hands.[7]

According to Limpach, the most objective of these books was Renn's *War*, but in his opinion it "still lay under the shadow of tired resignation that the Jews use for their own purposes." In any case, Renn was "certainly no National Socialist." Limpach complained that he had searched in the general press for reviews of works that adequately embodied the Nazi spirit, but reviewers did not seem to be aware of the works of Ernst Jünger, Franz Schauwecker, Werner Beumelburg, Walter Flex, Ernst Röhm, or any others who succeeded in depicting the "true war" in their writings. "Reviewers couldn't or wouldn't write about them," he griped, warning German front soldiers and nationalists that these reviewers were "playing with that which you consider most holy." Limpach then exhorted readers to respond to "these enemies of our Volk – those who scorn everything heroic" by instead "buying the war books of German nationalists!" You must do so, he pleaded, because "the war was your father's; the eyes of millions of dead brothers are on you; the future of our Volk is in your hands; and because battle is your mission – your fate!"[8]

Despite such carping, the newspaper did find occasional "gratifying" indications through the Weimar era that the "spiritual effects" of the front experience – "initially abnegated by fearful bourgeois audiences" – gradually gained the attention of some in the literary world. At first, the "true bearer" of the war – the front soldier – had to stand by, helplessly shaking his head over the "inaccurate, sentimental, beer-hall patriotic *Kitsch* that flooded out even as the world conflict raged." But over time, the spirituality of the front experience finally "entered into the brains" of critics and they no longer greeted "front writers" like Ernst Jünger and Franz Schauwecker with silence. Unfortunately, however, the arguments of these "battle-hardened advocates for a new world view" were usually dismissed as "political" with a shrug of the shoulders.

Assessing a 1927 radio lecture on the First World War and poetry, the *Völkischer Beobachter* considered it a step forward when the Frenchman Henri Barbusse's "seductive" novel, *Under Fire* (1917) – the most famous of the works that represented the negative side of the war experience – was no longer deemed the "only acceptable primer on the war," as was often the case among literary "experts" who didn't seem to know anything about the works of "*German* front soldiers." The newspaper was relieved to see that some criticism included "loyal references" to Jünger, Schauwecker, and Flex, "honoring them as soldiers and men."[9]

Nevertheless, the paper found that "bourgeois readers" simply could not fathom the "terrible, unrelenting, shattering realities of combat that made front writers more philosophers than poets." It recognized that most readers put such books down "with an inconsolable feeling" because they were "not designed as adventure stories, nor to console the bourgeois heart." Rather, they were intended to awaken thoughts and feelings about the front in "like-minded" – that is, right-wing – readers who were the "only ones in a position to grasp the monumental achievements related on every page." The works of Jünger, Schauwecker, and Flex conveyed the horrors of the war in a "language born of the front." All the details of the gigantic struggle had to be laid out in this way before a great poet could arise and create the epic that would capture public opinion with "worldview shaking, spirit awakening renderings of war experiences."[10]

In the opinion of Philipp Witkop, expert in the history of German literature best known for editing collections of war letters by fallen German soldiers, the writings of Walter Flex (1887–1917) had approached the goal of a "great poetics for the world war." Witkop saw Flex as embodying the youth of the mobilization period – the young men of Langemarck – who still believed in the "omnipotence of the heart and in the hard realities of manliness." To "remain pure and yet become mature, that is the hardest art of life," Flex once said. In that spirit, he and thousands of other German youths "remained pure in the middle of the filth and gruesomeness of the World War," and "became mature before their early deaths amid blood and bodies." If hearts become heavy at the thought that so many young men died for this idealism, then the words of Ernst Wurche's last speech – as related in Flex's *Wanderer Between Two Worlds* (1916) – offered consolation: "No one has seen so much despicable behavior, cowardice, weakness, selfishness, and vanity as we have. On the other hand, no one has seen so much worthiness and silent nobility of the soul as we have."[11]

Military historian Hermann Böhme also cited a passage from a work by Flex about "knowing and loving the Fatherland," and then asked readers whether it seemed as though these words were "taken directly from a speech to the nation by our Führer – one of his flaming speeches that brings forth the deepest earth-shattering truth." Flex's vision was becoming reality in the Nazi movement and government for the reason that now, "arm in arm, the Volk was standing like a wall behind the Führer." The struggle was hard and difficult, but Flex's hope, said Böhme, was not for naught: it "inspired active hearts that were triumphing over the soul and future of the German Volk." Flex demanded the "ultimate sacrifice, the last proof, even of himself – of himself first!" In this spirit, he did his duty as a matter of course, because for him life and service to Volk and Fatherland were one and the same thing. Flex lived up to his own demands, for he gave his life for the Fatherland: "he was one of the best and purest of the Volk, and therefore he had to die – for us." Though killed at the age of thirty, what he loved most in his brief life was Germany. As he put it, "doing one's duty as a leader means serving your men before one's self: being the first to die is part of that." Or as Flex wrote in *A Grave in the East*:

> He was a defender of the fire,
> Pure and loyal to Germany.
> Now the halo of his youth glows above the bloody earth
> As a flame of sacrifice on the field of honor.

Böhme closed with a "solemn prayer" to Flex:

> *The eternal German lives in you and the other dead of the world war. That which was incomprehensible mystery before, you revealed to us as life; you drank for us from the soul-purifying source of Christianity. But, the suffering of the pure only serves us if we live for them: please keep the will to do so alive in us, dead brothers!*[12]

Undoubtedly, the First World War author whom the *Völkischer Beobachter* featured most prominently was Ernst Jünger (1895–1998). It celebrated Jünger as the "most powerful herald of the front experience" – master of a style that developed its "implacable, substantial form in the battles of the World War," and that gave "incomparable expression" to the "demonic elements" of modern, mechanistic warfare. The greatness of Jünger's works lay in the "elemental feeling" that raised them "above party cant, war memoirs, and war literature – making them documents of a German youth born amid fire and blood, in the furnace of a period whose ramifications have yet to be grasped and publicized." The young stormtrooper who earned *Pour le mérite* as one of the first trench fighters "grasped and testified to these ramifications in his writings of overwhelming seriousness and deep faith."[13] As evidence of the potency and relevance of Jünger's writing, the newspaper featured reprinted quotes like: "one shouldn't approach the war by asking what it was all for: here was manifested a greatness that extends beyond the realm of goals and ends – an immortal deed is unconditioned by and independent of its outcome."[14] Against its opponents, the paper wielded Jünger's statement that: "pacifists present devastated cities and fearful suffering as their reasons, as if it were our highest duty to avoid pain: the will that does not shirk the responsibility of sacrificing life and property when it is a question of realizing the greatness of the Volk and its ideas is strange to them."[15]

Indeed, the *Völkischer Beobachter* promoted Jünger's writings in the most direct fashion possible: by publishing an article Jünger produced in support of the Nazi movement. Appearing in the paper just six weeks before the Beer Hall Putsch in 1923, the article, entitled "Revolution and Idea," was Jünger's first work of political journalism following the publication of his memoir, *Storms of Steel* (1920), an extensive essay on war, *Combat as Inner Experience* (1922), and a short story, *Storm* (1923).[16] In it, Jünger attacked the Weimar revolution and threw support behind "genuine" revolt in the name of the "volkish" idea, dictatorship, and a new nation bound by blood.

Jünger argued that before the war, the word "revolution" had real significance for the youth of Germany. Although living in an authoritarian state, they were conscious that a government could become unacceptable to a population. They envisioned great uprisings when "force opposes compulsion – when a young idea comes to life on barricades amid drum rolls and red flags." Just one prerequisite seemed necessary: "an idea to fight for." Throughout history, great uprisings – including the Reformation, the French Revolution, or the ongoing Russian Revolution – had been marked by intellectual "storm signals" such as "a great literature produced by prophets and martyrs who suffered and bled for the idea, whether it was false or not."

But then, Jünger continued, Germans had just experienced something of their own revolution. Surrounded by overwhelming enemies, the nation "fought its last and most bitter struggle with everything it had," and this was not just a government at war: "the whole Volk was fighting for a new form in the world." In the end, however, the revolution that came about was "nothing more than a mutiny on a warship." Those who seized the rudder assumed a great responsibility, but "history proved that they were not equal to it." The reason for this, according to Jünger, was that they did not struggle for an idea, but merely acted out of greed. Since then "even the most limited minds" had recognized with regard to the "so-called Revolution of 1918" that what really stood behind the slogans "was no rebirth, but just a swarm of flies landing to gnaw on a body." "What idea was realized through this revolution?" he asked. In his view, it offered nothing new: "a few Russian strategies were copied, a few phrases from 1789 and 1848 were borrowed, a few long-rotten Marxist slogans were reheated." Whenever something new was required, the leaders failed: "right when they needed to fight for them – they found themselves without ideas." As a result, "capitalism grew stronger than ever, political oppression became boundless, and the freedoms of press and speech became jokes."

A "handful of sailors had conquered cities; deserters and adolescents had torn apart the insignia of the old state." There was only one explanation for this: "the old system had lost the ruthless will to live that is necessary in such times." Means of resistance had been at hand, but "there was no fist able to wield them." So, since 1918, Germany had "lived without any ideas other than those of labor disputes": no "clear and great goal had been established." It had just followed "a wobbly course of inner laceration and feebleness in the face of external force." Moreover, behind façades of ever-changing governments and cabinets, "piracy dominated in its most naked form": the populace had been reduced to nothing but "plunderers and plundered." Any efforts to further the "ideals of the Volk" simply died out; the forces of "materialism in its basest form" – profiteers, stock speculators, and usurers – were really in charge. Political culture was about nothing but "goods, gold, and profits" and the state "smelled of decay," because the revolution was "not a birth of new ideas, but rather a form of rot that took over a dying body."

This "infuriating spectacle" had lasted too long, Jünger complained. But in the weeks before the Nazi-led effort to march on Berlin, he was sanguine: the "true revolution had not taken place, but was still marching inexorably on" – complete with the prerequisite he felt most necessary: "its idea was the volkish idea, sharpened to as yet unknown hardness; its banner was the swastika; its form of expression was the concentration of the will in a single point – a dictatorship!" This genuine revolution and its ideas would "replace words with deeds, ink with blood, phrases with sacrifices, and pens with swords." Above all, "money would not be its driving force, but rather blood – whose mysterious streams unite the nation and which must flow rather than be enslaved." Under this coming revolution, blood would provide new values; the freedom of the whole would arise from the sacrifice of the individual; waves would crash against all boundaries; harmful influences would be eliminated. Those, Jünger closed, were "goals worth fighting on the barricades for!"[17]

Jünger's support for the Nazi Party in 1923 has confounded some scholars ever since, but his awareness of the fundamental components of its ideology – including radical racism – is incontrovertible. In return the *Völkischer Beobachter* was happy to promote his works and ideas. For instance, it reported that the *Evening Chronicle* of Manchester had quoted Lloyd George as saying: "I consider *Storms of Steel* by far the best book I have read."[18] In addition, the paper juxtaposed Jünger with the First World War author it detested the most, Erich Maria Remarque. "The poet of the World War, Ernst Jünger, is that which Remarque thinks he was: a front soldier. Let bourgeois society find its war experience in Remarque, so that the real warrior, 'the aristocrat of the Volk,' remains in the hands of Jünger."[19]

The *Völkischer Beobachter*'s response to the publication of Remarque's *All Quiet on the Western Front* in 1929 constituted one of the pivotal moments in its cultural-political campaign. Remarque's novel and the American-produced, Oscar-winning movie that followed a year later provided the Nazi paper with a timely *cause célèbre* around which it marshaled many of its critical weapons against Weimar culture and politics. The headline alone of its first article attacking the novel marked how energetically it responded to the opportunity:

All Quiet on the Western Front: *The War Book of "Society" –
"Broken in the War" – The Hopelessness of the Pacifist War
Experience – The Renunciation of a Broken Down
Generation – The True Front Experience – Erich Remarque
or Ernst Jünger?*[20]

Under this banner, the paper argued that Remarque (1898–1970) wrote his "so-called war book" for liberal bourgeois "society" alone: he and his kind were "not warriors by blood," but draftees who remained outside the real war. Representatives of the dying liberal age, they entered the fight already moribund, "without enough blood" to really experience the events. "The way the German liberal citizen was when drafted: tired, old, and sick; that's how he returned from the war: spiritually dead, crushed by the weight of the incomprehensible experience of war." These people only had one organ left – the brain – which they were trying to use to think about the war, and they were very proud when a book like Remarque's came out. Thus, the liberal *Vossische Zeitung* and the Ullstein publishing house advertised "their war book" intensively. Likewise, republican politicians and poets – Walter von Molo, Alfred Kerr, Ernst Toller, and Erich Koch-Weser among others – recommended it personally. For instance, Carl Zuckmayer wrote that it "belongs in the school desks, the reading rooms, the universities, on all radio stations, and all that is still not yet enough." In their opinion it should have been distributed to "the whole Volk – and the rest of the world!" Liberalism finally had its "global-humanist, anti-Prussian war book": the basis for "deep psychological conversations in all theaters, at all concerts, balls, society meetings, and tea parties." Remarque's dedication of the work to "a generation destroyed by the war" was highly appropriate: liberal bourgeois had to introduce its book in this way, because "they and their state died in the storms of steel of the World War." Even if they were still around, controlling things, "liberals stood helplessly before a new race that had been born under fire right next to them in the trenches, and which was now making things difficult for them to rule."[21]

Remarque had not found any reason to fight the war, the *Völkischer Beobachter* insinuated, and did not draw anything from it afterward. As the "stereotypical liberal bourgeois," Remarque was "neither courageous nor cowardly, neither strong nor weak, neither great nor small." If he had fallen, he would not have known why, but he was also puzzled as to why and for what he survived. He claimed to have been broken by the war, but the paper could not help thinking that he and his kind would have been destroyed even without the war by some force or another: by "a woman," or "fate," or "simply by life itself!"

For Remarque the war was "nothing but a great, monstrous, absurdity, and worse: a constant flow of beastliness." Two major figures in the book – the Prussian schoolmaster, Kantorek, and the Prussian junior officer, Himmelstoss – embodied these characteristics. After the former motivates his entire class to volunteer, Remarque says: "While the Kantorek types were still writing and talking, we were being wounded and killed; while they were saying that service to the state is the greatest good, we already knew that the fear of death is stronger." Later, former students take revenge on him, and Himmelstoss is similarly punished in the field. "How paltry this outlook was," the paper commented, interspersed with the "whole range of shocking war details which tender, pacifist souls always highlight": the sickening cries of wounded men and animals; a mortally wounded man, for whose boots his comrades immediately gamble; hunger; rats and lice; shell shock experienced at the first bombardment; the corrupt hospital official; the doctor who "bumbles around in the wounds"; a "blond kid with dueling scars and an abhorrent monocle"; poor Russian prisoners; a rear major who makes life difficult for soldiers on leave; and, finally, the "ever present German professor who wants to annex the whole world." A "constant flow of fuzzy generalities: that is all, really all that Remarque experienced in and retained from the war." As he put it: "shells, gas clouds, and flotillas of tanks; grinding, eroding, death; dysentery, flu, typhoid fever; choking, burning, death; graves, military hospitals, mass graves – there are no other possibilities." Indeed, for the paper, these lines "contained the whole of the pacifist war experience of the German bourgeoisie – "there were no other possibilities for Remarque and his kind."[22]

In contrast, the *Völkischer Beobachter* again quoted Jünger as stating that the war was a great deed that its survivors would always be proud of participating in, no matter what it was fought over; that the sacrifice of life and property could not be shirked when it was a question of realizing the greatness of the Volk and its ideas; and that:

> *to make sense of what from a lower level of thought may seem like nonsense and an expression of human imperfection is a holy duty we owe to the fallen, as well as to the upcoming generation that has to go on. Because, it will be left to them to finish some day what we couldn't finish: they will shoulder their legacy with pride, if the wonderful and eternal core of this era, the absolutely German, outlasts the clouds of everyday meanness.*[23]

The paper chastised *All Quiet on the Western Front* violently for contradicting the views of patriots like Jünger: "this is like a punch in the face for all true front soldiers who carry the memory of the great war like a holy legacy, because they don't feel themselves destroyed by the war – but rather purified."[24] Remarque, in pale comparison, was contaminated by pacifism – a "feather bed world view in which moralizing apes and egoistic spokesmen for 'mankind' combine comforting pity plus aggressive cowardice." Whoever contended that the "war was only the fruit of evil and peace a result of good will" did not understand the political process and the nature of the state as it had developed over thousands of years. Although "Jewish-Marxist journalists" were drunk with Remarque's spirit, this "civilian in uniform" left the problem of the war and its soldiers unresolved. "In the name of all conscious front soldiers," the *Völkischer Beobachter* sent "torch bearers of pacifism" a quote from Nietzsche, demanding that they read it carefully on their "deplorable way to Philistine paradise – from which they would one day be driven with a flaming sword."[25]

> *Now new duties beckon; and if in peace there is one thing remaining for us from that savage game of war, it is the heroic and at the same time reflective spirit which, to my surprise, like a beautiful unexpected discovery, I found fresh and vigorous in our army, full of old Germanic health. We can build on that: we may still have hope! Our German mission is not yet passed! I'm in better heart than ever … There is still courage – and German courage – between which and the élan of our poor neighbors there is an inward difference.*[26]

Another attack on Remarque took the form of an article relaying an anecdote supposedly submitted to the paper by an anonymous "German Woman" and involving the Norwegian author Sigrid Undset – creator of massive historical novels set in the Middle Ages and winner of the Nobel Prize for Literature in 1928. According to this article, at a social event, Undset mentioned that she had given a copy of *All Quiet on the Western Front* to her son for his birthday. Upon hearing this, the "German Woman" jerked impulsively and cried, "I would have never given that to my son." Undset quietly responded: "But this man was broken, and he represents things as if the whole generation was destroyed with him in the war." "Oh no, Frau Undset," the German Woman retorted:

It is not true that Germany's youth was destroyed and martyred, for then Germany would not be thriving, hard-working, and full of strength. Certainly, men were devastated and uprooted by the war, but not all of Germany; not all of Germany's youth! Thousands of young men fell, and I, Frau Undset, refuse to accept representations of their holy martyrdom for the Fatherland – for our freedom and our children – as a senseless and miserable breakdown. Without this wall of bodies that the army erected in France, the French and their colored troops would have brought death and destruction to the heart of Germany ... The pavement of the streets would have been sown with the bodies of children.

Remarque's indictment of the war, this anonymous woman believed, sprang from a "heart without courage, a soul that had fallen victim to a psychological problem." She wrote:

Had so much bitterness been felt toward the duties of war – had so much suffering in the service of the Fatherland really been the only experience of every soldier – then complete anarchy would have brought an end to the war. Then Germany would have lost the honor that its silent heroes saved, and it would not be worthwhile to be part of such a Volk. Remarque's book is the experience of an embittered man who turned against the spirit of a Volk to which he did not feel bound. It is a book without military honor, without heroism, a book without any sense of the eternal events in history.

In response, according to the anecdote, Frau Undset – "the herald of human heroism, of bravery before God and the world – looked at me, her large, grey-blue eyes glittering, and said warmly: 'You are right. You have convinced me.'"[27] Just how convinced Sigrid Undset was, however, given that she would flee Norway during Hitler's invasion in 1940, is unclear.

While the *Völkischer Beobachter* certainly found enough to complain about in the written version of *All Quiet on the Western Front*, its assault on Remarque reached a crescendo when word came that a Hollywood film was in production. This "despicable derider of the

German front soldier" had received an honor that he did not deserve: his "shock novel was going to be made into a film." The newspaper then went after the movie's producer, identifying Carl Laemmle as "a Jew who emigrated from Württemberg and is now residing in Hollywood," and complaining that he "already had a lot of experience at scolding and besmirching the German army."[28] A "full-blooded Jew" with all the "virtues" of his race, it went on, Laemmle had produced the "basest anti-German hate films" during the war, among which *The Kaiser: The Beast of Berlin*, *Mare Nostrum*, and *The Riders of the Apocalypse* were the most notorious.[29] The high point of Laemmle's "Jewish impudence" was that he had tried to market these "hate films" in Germany. The mere fact that such marketing efforts had been somewhat successful was an indictment of the "spirit" of many "supposedly German" fans of cinema. But as word of the million-dollar deal for *All Quiet on the Western Front* came out, the paper predicted that the production would be the worst of Laemmle's films: if there were a law in Germany for the protection of the Volk, then both the book and the movie would have been stopped. The paper could just imagine what sort of an "abominable, politically provocative flick" the "movie Jew" would make out of this book. If Germans had become the "coolies of the world, spat and trod upon everywhere," the cause was largely such "systematic Jewish atrocity propaganda." The newspaper found it sad that "every nigger in Harlem and every despicable Chinese coolie could have fun at the expense of the German nation, represented on the big screen as a Volk of fools, barbarians, and criminals by a movie Jew like Carl Laemmle."[30]

While scorning German Volk and army in front of the whole world, this film was going to be produced "solely for profit," since the author and producer were both basically war profiteers. Laemmle, who "couldn't pass up a chance to disgrace Germany," was denigrating the army with the backing of "asphalt literati" and "Ullstein gold." Such an attack on the German front soldier – put together by a "bunch of Jews for purely financial gain" – could only incite the anger of the Volk: patriotic Germans in Berlin and Vienna "shouldn't countenance such besmirching of two million fallen German soldiers."[31] In other films by this "anti-German Jew," officers abused their inferiors with blows to the head, and even waved whips in the faces of civilians. Simple soldiers were also insulted in these films: always depicted as unappealing and repulsive, they appeared in torn uniforms with deep-drawn faces, plundering palaces, maltreating civilians, and raping women in occupied lands.

In his movies, German soldiers "ate and drank like animals, only happy and content when they were able to kill rats." Adding insult to injury, dogs were shown tearing up German flags with the Iron Cross hung from their collars.[32]

Recognizing the potentially tremendous influence of popular film, the *Völkischer Beobachter* wanted to be clear about what the film version of *All Quiet on the Western Front* really meant. In Laemmle's version, it reported, German soldiers appeared as "horrible barbarians": some plunder French and Belgian homes; officers order floggings; another tries to rape the daughter of the home in which he is quartered; and others fire on a field hospital marked with a Red Cross flag. Regarding the last, the paper retorted that evidence only existed that allied troops had fired on field hospitals, and in these cases it was Germans who were the victims, but "the Jew Laemmle happily overturned the truth and slurred the facts." In addition, from the first to the last page, Remarque worked to depict the German front soldier as a "pitiful coward who shit in his pants as soon as the shells began to fly,"[33] and the movie followed suit by highlighting the deplorable howling and crying of volunteers under shelling, showing fear-distorted faces and accompanied by wild, vulgar speech.[34] Not surprisingly, Laemmle presented Remarque's Corporal Himmelstoss as an average German corporal, although there was "certainly not a single Himmelstoss in the entire German army." One could just imagine how the scene in which he forces two bedwetters to sleep in bunk-beds, one over the other, would be received on the big screen. This was not a joke, but a "conscious representation of the German Volk's army as contemptible."[35]

Why, the *Völkischer Beobachter* asked, was the German soldier not represented in this film with the dignity that he earned through incomparable service in the war? How did the American or English armies appear in other war films? There were scenes of horror in those, certainly, but even in the greatest danger, the American soldier was always shown "maintaining a certain calm superiority, with a smile that made him a model for the cool, courageous soldier." In contrast, the achievements of German soldiers in the World War were being "debased in the eyes of the world," and the Nazi newspaper wanted to "lodge a protest against this insult."[36] National Socialists had to lead a protest "sharp enough to have this shameful display forbidden."[37]

All of this, the newspaper reported, had given rise to a debate in the Educational Committee of the Reichstag, where the Foreign Office reported that an attempt was being made in Hollywood to "falsify the essence" of *All Quiet on the Western Front*. According to the Foreign Office, certain scenes with markedly anti-German content that had nothing to do with the original content of the book were being produced for the film. In particular, the character Himmelstoss was the "manifestation of an unfriendly attitude toward Germany." It was often the case, the report continued, that films featuring anti-German characters were marketed in Germany after certain scenes had been cut and changes to the text had been made – so they could be shown without causing scandal. This latest news from Hollywood demonstrated the need for adjustments to the film law that would better protect the nation against anti-German films. Henceforth, foreign films imported into Germany needed to be submitted to the censor in their original format.[38]

The *Völkischer Beobachter* responded to news of this report by stating that it was not surprising as: "American film production had long specialized in anti-German hate films." But, it added, the "gentlemen in Berlin" had no right to be indignant about this: it was their "spirit of national atrophy and blight that had created the conditions for such Jewish-pacifist propaganda films." Moreover, the *Völkischer Beobachter* did not believe at all in the "falsification" of Remarque that upset the Foreign Office so much. According to the paper, this "so-called war novel" did not really need to be falsified in order to be perceived as a "completely anti-soldier" work that "denigrated the moral greatness of the front fighters." The "in-Germany-born Jewish king of American film," Laemmle, had made this even clearer than the politicians in Berlin could comprehend, simply by deciding to make a Remarque movie in the first place. Still, the *Völkischer Beobachter* pointed out that the *Bayerische Staatszeitung* – identified as a "Munich asphalt-gazette published by the Jewish house Pflaum" – had reacted negatively to the Foreign Office's report. One could see here, the *Völkischer Beobachter* commented, how even the slightest effort to represent German interests was immediately sabotaged by the "Jewish press writing in German" whenever it concerned someone the "chosen people" considered great.[39]

In December 1930, Nazi demonstrations against the film reached their height and the newspaper covered these events intensively. It reported that on the evening of Sunday, 7 December, a "huge demonstration against the shameful film" playing in the Mozartsaal cinema took place on Berlin's Nollendorfplatz. In view of this "enormous demonstration," the theater directors had to realize that "it was not worth going on with this insult to every German-thinking person: hopefully every cinema owner in the land would reconsider participating in this mockery."[40] The next night, Goebbels gave a speech on Wittenbergplatz to a "crowd of thousands." He declared that the mere fact that a film which "ran down the best soldiers of all time, German front soldiers," could even be shown was a "cultural disgrace which no German and no front soldier could accept." Unfortunately, Goebbels noted, people were getting used to the fact that the German government "served its people this sort of cultural disgrace rather than bread." He then asserted that "National Socialists would not accept this indignity any longer." Finally, after commemorative words for the war's fallen and singing of the first and fourth stanzas of the *Deutschlandlied*, a parade formed and marched through the west side of the city as a sign of protest. "Even the police stayed back during the demonstration," the newspaper reported happily.[41]

The paper also covered actions taken that week by the Stahlhelm veterans' organization. As a band of German front soldiers "who were not broken by the war," Stahlhelm "sharply protested against this offense" and demanded that showing the film be forbidden throughout Germany. For them it was not a question of taste, but a matter of German honor and dignity. They were no longer waiting for the "thanks of the Fatherland" that had been promised to them, but they would resist with all their might when the "suffering and death of their comrades were scorned in sound and image under the protection of Weimar Germany's Marxist authorities." Thus, Stahlhelm's national leadership promised to "lobby for a ban on this hate film."[42]

The following week, the Prussian parliament held a vote of confidence on the SPD-led government of Prime Minister Otto Braun and Minister of the Interior Carl Severing, and the *All Quiet on the Western Front* affair was central to the proceedings. Indeed, the German National Volk Party (DNVP) representative, Ludwig Schwecht, called for the vote primarily in response to the government's mishandling of the movie. In his speech, Schwecht held that this "hate film" was a terrible insult to the German Volk. In his view the demonstrations on Nollendorfplatz had been completely justified because the real scandal had happened months earlier, with the appearance of Remarque's book in the first place. Remarque, he pointed out with disgust, had made so much money on this book that he was able to "buy the title, Freiherr von Buchwald" and to "wrongly appropriate the Iron Cross, First Class." A second genuine scandal, he said, was that the "Jew Laemmle" had made the struggle of the German Volk in the war an object of his "Jewish business interests." According to the *Völkischer Beobachter*, at this point the Marxists in the Prussian Landtag countered by shouting that "Laemmle is not a Jew – Laemmle is a German-American!" But Schwecht went on to state that Laemmle's "Jewish views" were evident in the American version of the film. For instance, during a break in the fighting a soldier states: "If we make it home, the first thing we'll do is get drunk and then we'll get women." In addition, the soldier Kaszinski shouts: "It is dirty and abominable to die for one's country!" This character was supposed to represent the "typical" German front soldier, but had the appearance of a criminal. Here Schwecht "responded to continued Marxist shouting by insisting that Kaszinski's statement had a lot in common with the words of a well-known social-democrat, Arthur Crispien, who had stated, 'I know no Fatherland called Germany,' at the USPD rally in December 1919."[43]

Although the film "insulted Germany and therefore should have been prohibited by law," Schwecht went on, the government of Braun, Severing, and the Police President of Berlin, Albert Grzesinsky, was "officially treating this Jewish fabrication with kid gloves." These politicians did not think for a moment about the "crisis of conscience" that some police officers must have been experiencing when they saw the need to censor this "shameful work that sullied their own honor," but could not. Even though it contained shameful statements like those above, Interior Minister Severing had not blocked a single scene. Schwecht closed with the threatening assertion that in the fight for and against this film, the unbridgeable gap between two world views had become clear: "modern neo-Prussian pacifism would ultimately be countered by the spirit of Friedrich the Great – and these two world views would ultimately meet in a decisive battle."[44]

The history of soldiers serving on the front lines during the First World War had gradually become a focus of German writers in the Weimar era. Yet, to the editors of the *Völkischer Beobachter*, novelists and memoirists who anguished over the horrors of the war represented the worst possible accounts of the front experience. Instead, as we have seen, the paper promoted right-wing interpretations that emphasized neoromantic views of the war as sublime and uplifting. As Robert Wohl wrote, their "organizing myth was the creative and renovating

306 / "Holy" War and Weimar "Crisis"

force of the front experience," according to which the trenches had taught "what fate is, and what man is, and what life is like." In the end, the National Socialist rise to power "signified not the victory of the war generation, as the Nazis claimed, but the victory of one part of the war generation over its opponents and the imposition of one interpretation of the war generation's experience on the population as a whole."[45] *Völkischer Beobachter* criticism of war literature – and films drawn from it – constituted a call to cultural battle in support of right-wing views of the war experience as sacred.[46]

14 WEIMAR CULTURE WARS 1: DEFENDING GERMAN SPIRIT FROM "CIRCUMCISION"

For all the energy directed at defining the merit and value of the cultural artifacts wrought from the German experience in the First World War, from the perspective of the *Völkischer Beobachter*, this conflict represented a mere skirmish in a larger clash between world views, and is most correctly seen as a continuation of the volkish reaction against modernity and modernist culture that had been going on since the second half of the nineteenth century. After the First World War, Hitler made it his personal task to give voice to those aggrieved by the cultural and technological encroachments of modernism on German life. As he put it: "theater, art, literature, cinema, press, posters, and window displays must be cleansed of all manifestations of our rotting world and placed in the service of a moral, political, and cultural idea. Public life must be freed from the stifling stench of our modern eroticism, just as it must be freed from all unmanly, prudish hypocrisy."[1] Aligned with this task, every word of *Völkischer Beobachter* cultural coverage was a shot fired in the Weimar culture wars. But it was more immediately an assault on the Republic itself – no matter what specific cultural forms were perceived as representing the era.

As we will see in Chapter 15, the paper's onslaught against Weimar politics and culture involved intense assaults on the major representatives of contemporary literature, art, and music. But in its campaign to appropriate the high German tradition for Nazism, another objective was to convince readers that opposing views were not legitimate parts of this heritage. This chapter will concentrate on how the paper insinuated that great figures of the cultural past would have shared its critical attitudes toward conditions in post-First World War Germany in particular, and also how it attempted to show that German masters were being misunderstood or defamed by leftist or "Jewish" cultural authorities who supposedly controlled the culture of Weimar Germany. This will involve revisiting *Völkischer Beobachter* coverage of figures treated in Part I, which showed how it linked them with fundamental themes of the Nazi outlook. But this section will address the more immediate, contemporary associations contributors made between cultural heroes and the Weimar context, including the paper's reporting on references to the "masters" at commemorations and rallies, whether organized by the NSDAP or other groups. The "technique" of National Socialist propaganda involved persistent reiteration; however, it was not a matter of mere repetition. *Völkischer Beobachter* invocations of creative heroes functioned at more than one symbolic level. We will experience here, as well as in Part V, how major cultural figures were interpreted with specific reference to major stages in the party's history: during its "era of struggle," after "seizing power," and at war.

As we have seen, fundamental to establishing the high cultural legitimacy of the Nazi Party was to associate it with Goethe, who was widely considered to epitomize the German tradition of cultivation or *Bildung*. However, until 1933 the *Völkischer Beobachter* had to contend with competing views of him as presaging the democratization of German society that had come about in 1918. Throughout the Weimar era the paper engaged in relentless debate with those who would associate the "minister of an absolute prince by the name of Wolfgang Goethe" with republicanism.[2] Those whom the paper perceived as so doing, such as the anonymous author of a 1922 article in the *Münchener Post*, could be accused of having a "very unpleasant crooked nose" and "circumcising" Goethe's statements.[3] In its response to this article, the *Völkischer Beobachter* argued that the opposition had overlooked Goethe's statement that he "couldn't stand by indifferently if someone contemplated bringing about *artificially* in Germany scenes similar to those which took place in France as a result of great necessity."[4] The *Münchener Post* had suppressed this statement because despite all its "Cabbalistic analysis" the paper could not argue away the fact that the German revolution had been achieved in "artificial fashion." In view of this "undeniable fact" – that the German revolution was led by "Jews and other foreign races" – the *Münchener Post* scribblers should have read a couple more lines in Goethe's conversations with Eckermann, counseled the *Völkischer Beobachter*, and had they done so they would have been shocked when Goethe opined that the "only good thing for a nation is that which develops out of its *own* essence and its own need, without aping after another ... All attempts to import some sort of foreign innovation ['Western democracy!' the *Völkischer Beobachter* editors added], for which the need is not rooted in the heart of the nation itself, are therefore foolish." In this dialogue with Eckermann, said the Nazi paper, Goethe had anticipated the "only correct judgment of the 1918–19 revolution." In conclusion, the *Völkischer Beobachter* found it interesting that the *Münchener Post* had borrowed material from "somewhere other than the Talmud at all," but invoking Goethe as a "witness for the Weimar system" was "laughable"[5]

The paper lodged complaints about Weimar republican Goethe reception from 1922 on, arguing that "pacifists, Jews, democrats and republicans" had been working intensively since the end of the World War to "stamp Germany's greatest poet as one of their own," and put him to use for their propagandist purposes. "Jews knew how to appropriate foreign names and ideals to cover their internationalist plots," and they were concentrating particularly on misappropriating Goethe's thoughts about "world citizenry" for their goals. But the *Völkischer Beobachter* wanted to "let him speak for himself: he, who lived in a time when Germany was nothing more than a geographical notion; he, whom one so readily associated with the Weimar coalition; he, whom one so often pitted against the Spirit of Potsdam." About the "new Spirit of Weimar," the paper felt certain, he would have said to party hacks: "You resemble that spirit, not I."[6]

Elaborating on this theme, the *Völkischer Beobachter* asked its readers what Goethe would say to a Volk that was submitting to the conditions that had been "extorted by Versailles 'treaty'"? Goethe's answer, the paper decided, could be found in his poem, *Neither This Nor That*: "If you make yourself into a whipping boy, don't blame anyone else when things don't go well!"[7] It then asked, what would the "old Spirit of Weimar" say about Germany's new domestic policies? Goethe's answer could be located in his letter to Friedrich von Müller:[8] "It is not just by tearing down, but by constructing something, that mankind feels pure joy."[9]

The paper's editors considered Goethe's genius ready-made for addressing a variety of modern issues that they found vexing. As the paper reported, Goethe viewed "world reformers" with sarcasm, stating, according to Houston Stewart Chamberlain, that "the world is becoming a big hospital, with everyone nursing each other." Further, with regard to the significance of technology for the culture of Europe and the world, he recognized the value of railways, steam engines, and telegraphs, but "also perceived their dangers"; he described the progress of his day as a "two-edged sword since the tempo of the modern age and the unbridled development of the machine age raised a sense of danger in him." Likewise, he argued that "technology combined with tastelessness was the worst enemy of art"[10] – a line to which the paper added the parenthetical exclamation: "Film!"[11]

As these examples suggest, *Völkischer Beobachter* critics felt certain that Goethe would have shared their dismay about Weimar culture: "We are far from living in a Goethean time," the paper lamented, "and we are no longer Goethean types." It was instead an age of cheap operettas and "mega-movies." Indeed, the mega-movie it had in mind, a 1926 adaptation of *Faust*, was so inadequate that it required people like "the vain Gerhart Hauptmann, supposedly Germany's greatest poet," to write an introduction: "something that no one should really need, but from which many were learning all they knew about Goethe's work."[12] In contrast to such vulgarity, the paper cited Goethe: "a play must be symbolic – that is, every scene has to be significant and point toward something even more important."[13] On such authority – however tenuously derived – the paper was convinced that Goethe would have agreed that there had to be "an end to depictions of big city nightlife, skirt-chasing, madness, and suicides," which belonged out where there is "wailing and gnashing of teeth," not in the "temple of German art."[14]

Völkischer Beobachter criticism of Weimar-era Goethe reception climaxed in 1932 on the 100th anniversary of the poet's death. Wasting no time, the paper commenced its attack on 1 January of that year, railing against the "crass and materialistic ways Jewish concerns like the *Berliner Tageblatt*" were preparing to commemorate *Goethe-Jahr 1932*. The phrase, "Goethe dead a hundred years," the *Völkischer Beobachter* admonished, should have put people in a terrible mood rather than a celebratory one. But commemorations such as this had become merely a "form of business" for the Mosse publishing house, and they promised little more than "loud noise coming from empty hearts, and in large part, empty heads." To grasp the gravity of the occasion, one needed to understand that it was the life of Goethe's works that seemed to be coming to an end; Goethe's death in the physical sense had nothing to do with the spiritual force of his creations. The death of his works, on the other hand, would mean "immeasurable spiritual impoverishment" for the German people, and had to be avoided.

If his spirit were really still alive, Germans would "abhor the tastelessness that surrounded them everywhere"; they would "not find pleasure in the vulgar market of vain literati." But "for most, Goethe *was* dead!" He was done-in by the "Americanization of a weakened race; the superficiality of a mindless generation; the pedantry of schoolmarmish teachers; the sound of scholars who just liked to hear themselves talk; the chatter of swaggering, pampered Jews; the misunderstanding of non-critical minds." The fact that a "stale Goethe cult" had arisen after the war in seminars on German literature, marked by a "cryptic form of discourse understandable only to the initiated," could not obscure the fact that his creations were not enough "a part of the lives of his fellow Volk members" so that one could refer to him as being alive. To the contrary, the Olympian of the Germans was "too often insulted" in Weimar society.[15]

In this context, then, said the *Völkischer Beobachter*, the 100th anniversary of Goethe's death had come in an era when "innumerable Volk comrades were simply not able to fulfill their cultural duties." Even *Faust* meant nothing to those whom "hunger stared in the eyes, consumed by horrible suffering." National Socialists knew that making Goethe's work the "common property of the Volk spirit" was a prerequisite for realizing truly uplifting cultural goals. But Nazis were not going to cooperate with the coarse politicization of the *Goethe-Jahr*, the paper claimed: "Brown Shirts would not do an impertinent dance around the official jubilee altar, constructed by Minister of Art Edwin Redslob and watched over by the high priests of the Weimar system." Instead, Nazis would fight for their "own Goethe."[16]

Looking ahead toward what could be expected in a Third Reich, the *Völkischer Beobachter* assumed that a Nazi era would consider the 1932 celebrations – arranged by "representatives of a decrepit and dying system" – as a curiosity at best. Unfortunately, it observed, even in Thüringen where a fanatically nationalist government ruled, there was no chance for a "strongly volkish" memorial: even there authorities would "kowtow to foreign, Jewish, pacifist, and Bolshevik speakers." And, indeed, it was no surprise to the Nazi paper that the centerpiece of the week was a lecture series entitled "Goethe and the World," since such a theme symbolized the "general nature of the commemorative events": there was nothing to expect but the "usual cant about Goethe, the cosmopolitan path-breaker, the good European, the lodge brother, and the apostle of humanism."[17]

The paper admitted that Goethe could be seen in this light, recognizing (without a trace of irony) that it was "not hard to find proof for anything in the 150 volumes he produced; one could simply compile a list of all the Goethe statements that fit one's contemporary purposes." But without respect for true volkish values, such an exercise would result only in "collecting all the lines that were perishable." And such a collection of material, the paper pointed out, did not furnish the reason that Goethe had remained famous for a century, that "the Volunteers of 1914 marched to Langemarck with *Faust* in their packs, that we [Nazis] hold the legacy of Weimar dear to our hearts!" In his *Myth of the Twentieth Century*, Alfred Rosenberg said that Goethe "portrayed in *Faust* the essence of all Germans, the eternal aspect that remained the basis of their common soul no matter what new shapes it took: Goethe was therefore the guardian and protector of the National Socialist order." So, on the anniversary of his birthday, "Nazis alone could consider him as the guardian and protector of their ways." Casting Goethe in such a role did not require agreeing with rumors that the party wanted to make him into a National Socialist; indeed, as Rosenberg explained, Nazis rejected the "Jewish-Liberal tendency to project the party-political present onto the past," even though "it wouldn't have taken too much effort to do so." Instead, Nazi claims on Goethe's legacy would be based "on what *was*," not on "what could be." It was "demonstrably true that Goethe was an outspoken German according to his inner nature; that he avowed Germanness; that his creations proved the powerful value Germanness had for all times; and that he did not stand far away from the reasonable socialism of Nazism." Treating him thus was to emphasize the "still-living, *enabling* elements of Goethe and at the same time counter moribund negatives that had been cultivated" by the other parties. Any slogan other than "Goethe, the German," the *Völkischer Beobachter* said, was irrelevant at a time when the "volkish essence" was on the line. After an incomparable collapse, the German Volk had the right to expect emphasis on such volkishness from those who represented the Volk's spiritual interests. The Nazi paper therefore rejected any Goethe commemorations that included as participants

"Thomas Mann, Walter von Molo, Gerhart Hauptmann, or any French and Polish scholars," because "none of them could begin to convey his volkish significance."[18]

Of the main speakers at the Goethe celebrations in 1932, it was Thomas Mann whom the *Völkischer Beobachter* attacked most viciously. Hans Severus Ziegler reported on Mann's commemorative address with unrestrained *ad hominem* nastiness. At the outset he stated that the paper could hardly be expected to deal with Mann objectively, given the tactlessness with which the "non-political politician" had attacked the Nazi movement – "about which he understood so little, since, as a so-called European, with Portuguese blood, he could never grasp concepts such as race and volkishness." Ziegler then griped about the "black intelligentsia-glasses" Mann wore when he came to the lectern at the official Reich commemoration in Weimar. Ziegler actually had little to say about the lecture itself, except to note that Mann was "tasteless enough to mix his Goethe themes together with a mediocre critique of contemporary political events." This did not come as a surprise to Ziegler, but he complained that after half an hour, the "ice-cold intellectual's monotonous, mannered way of speaking" was so difficult to follow that it "bored the audience to the point where many tried to leave before it was over."[19]

Hanns Johst also lashed out at Mann, pointing out that in arranging the commemorations the first step should have been to eliminate any individuals who had "thinned out their world view" by espousing liberalism and renouncing their Germanness. "Where did Mann and his kind find the gall to speak about Goethe?" Johst asked.[20] But the *Völkischer Beobachter* berated Mann most in an anonymous article that brought up his attacks on the "awakening National Socialist Germany." These anti-Nazi views, the paper held, targeted Goethe as much as they did the movement. The wise man of Weimar had never doubted for an instant that the German Volk would once again have its day of glory. So Mann should have said the same things about Goethe that he said about Nazis, since they "clearly thought in Goethean ways." The very things he said about National Socialists – that they were of an "orgiastic, radically anti-humane, frenzied dynamic character"[21] – applied to the "great one" too. To attack Nazis, the argument went, was to attack Goethe. Thus, despite his reputation as a "perfect" Goethe interpreter, this example alone showed Mann to be "incompetent and full of nonsense." "How *could* Mann understand Goethe?" the paper asked: "the two simply did not square." On the one side, Mann was a "pacifist weakling" who, trapped in the antiquated mind-set of the pre-Goethe Enlightenment, said he hoped to "eliminate war and a false and laughable sense of heroism" through "rational relations." On the other side, Goethe created heroic Egmont, with his slogan: "And to save those who are most dear to you, be ready to follow my example, and to fall with joy."[22] Mann was the admirer of the "grand Bolshevik experiment in the East"; Goethe, the "volkish-rooted" poet who wrote "Only that which comes from its own core is good for a nation, not imitating others." Mann was the "philo-Semite married to a Jew" who celebrated them as a "tough old race of quality," while he branded the volkish efforts of those with German blood as "fake and unjust," "slavish," "half-educated," and "barbaric"; Goethe, the "great conscious one," who abstained from all "sympathy with Jews and Jew-comrades," who had "no patience for Jewish professors, artists, poets, scientists, politicians, officers, judges, bureaucrats, literati, or journalists"; in short, the paper put it bluntly, who "wanted to forbid Jews any portion of German culture." Thus said, no more examples were necessary, the *Völkischer Beobachter* determined, to demonstrate where "narrow-mindedness lay, and where noble expression ruled."[23]

Elsewhere, Josef Stolzing summarized the paper's position with regard to the Goethe Year commemorations as a whole. Those responsible for this "Goethe action" were the Social-Democrats, the Center Party, and others who approved of the system – in close collaboration with a "few outsiders." To Stolzing this group of organizers looked more like an "emergency committee formed against National Socialism" than a united Volk. This was apparent in a communiqué that stated that "the name Goethe signifies a message of peace to the German Volk." This, Stolzing chided, seemed to be a promise that by whispering a "magic formula of peace," all suffering would pass. Worse, from the Nazi perspective, the authors of the communiqué used Goethe to justify the "muddled leadership" of the Weimar Republic – despite the crisis that it faced in 1932 – implying, Stolzing held, that all the average German needed was for "the Center Party that once supported the throne, Marxism with its class warfare, and the other parties that answered to the Jews" to come together in a "liberating accord" that would uphold "the fulfillment policy and the politics of emergency decree." "Thus would the Spirit of Weimar triumph?" Stolzing asked ironically: was this cooperative spirit sparked by nothing more than notions of "Goethe

the Pacifist"? "Poor Johann Wolfgang!" Stolzing finished: "One hundred years after your death you are, for the majority of the Volk, the poet and thinker of little more than a tearful politics of whining. Sir, it is a tragedy!"[24]

Besides complaining about opposing invocations in 1932, the *Völkischer Beobachter* also promoted its own view of Goethe as an inspirational figure for the Nazi movement during that crucial phase of their *Kampfzeit*. Hanns Johst explicitly justified National Socialist seizure of Goethe's most famous passages for propaganda purposes. Though a century had passed since Goethe's death, Johst's rationalization began, the struggle over the German nation and its form was not yet over: to the contrary, the extremes were more radical and fanatical than ever. Under these crisis conditions, National Socialists celebrated Goethe as the man who lived according to the maxim he loved most: "To be a man means to be a fighter." Even more importantly, just as he freely "translated the Old Testament into his beloved German, rejuvenating it according to his will," Nazis were justified in appropriating the gospel of his poetry, in "seizing his words for ourselves and freshening them with our storm signals!!"[25] With this, Johst reproduced the most famous passage of *Faust* :

> 'Tis written: In the beginning was the Word!
> Here now I'm balked! Who'll put me in accord?
> It is impossible, the Word so high to prize,
> I must translate it otherwise
> If I am rightly by the Spirit taught.
> 'Tis written: In the beginning was the Thought! ...
> Is it then Thought that works, creative, hour by hour?
> Thus should it stand: In the beginning was the Power!
> Yet even while I write this word, I falter,
> For something warns me, this too I shall alter.
> The Spirit's helping me! I see now what I need
> And write assured: In the beginning was the Deed![26]

Undoubtedly, Johst's intention was to associate Faust's emphasis on "power" and "deed" with the ideology of force and action that Nazis countered against "rational" support for the Weimar republican system. In his claims about "Goethe and Us" – drawn for the *Völkischer Beobachter* from *The Myth of the Twentieth Century* – Alfred Rosenberg concurred that Goethe represented the essence of Nazism in the character of Faust: "the eternal, which, after every recasting of our soul, is inherent in the new form." As a result, Goethe had become the "guardian and the preserver of our disposition."[27]

But it was not in just such esoteric terms that the *Völkischer Beobachter* aligned Goethe with Nazi political plans. In an article entitled "Goethe and Austria" – based on a lecture by the Berlin professor, Franz Koch – the paper directly associated Goethe with issues of pan-Germanism, arguing that his "spirit" united Germany with Austria and the Sudetenland. According to Koch, Goethe was very aware of the problems confronted by pan-Germanists to the east: the difficulties of amalgamating peoples so different as the Czechs and the Germans under one crown were clear to him. Therefore, his spirit was a unifying medium between the "Land of Goethe" and Austria. Koch acknowledged that this spiritual unity between northern, southern, and eastern (Sudeten) lands did not exist in his lifetime. But since then, "they had become one – precisely in the spirit of Goethe." Schiller said it was "the spirit that builds the body." If so, Germans had reason to hope: it was time, Koch implied, to make that spiritual unity into a physical one. In the *Völkischer Beobachter*, therefore, Goethe provided a cultural basis for Hitler's primary foreign policy aims.[28]

Schiller presented a similar cause for the paper to rally behind. Just as it criticized interpretations of Goethe in the democratic era, the Nazi paper perceived in Weimar culture a conspiracy of humanist Schiller reception at best, and indifference at worst. Responding to an article in the Social-Democratic newspaper, *Vorwärts*, the *Völkischer Beobachter* held that leftists were "torturing Schiller on the rack" since the "frozen Marxist brain" simply could not grasp the meaning of his immortal poems. The *Völkischer Beobachter* was particularly angered by the *Vorwärts* observation that young people in Germany were no longer paying much attention to classics by Schiller just because they were works "of another age." These were the "fatuous observations" of a "pathetic, dried up, schoolmarmish soul." Despite their revolutionary fuss, Marxists were really the "most annoying Philistines imaginable: such soulless people ground away at everything great, beautiful, and German without realizing how ridiculous they looked."[29] They hoped to "forcefully impose the ideas of humanity, humanism, and democratic freedom on youth" through *Don Carlos* and Schiller's other works, wrote Hans Severus Ziegler. But there was no reason to fear: young people would "easily perceive the difference" between what Schiller wanted and what the "glorious democracy with its Jewish world view" offered.[30]

Even in a "sad age of decline" in German theater, Josef Stolzing chimed in – "bolshevized and infiltrated by the culture of perversity and sub-humanity" – the works of Schiller not only remained relevant, but were among the most performed works of all. His spirit therefore "survived unbroken" even in a time when one could hear insolence like: "We know no Fatherland called Germany." But could the German Volk love a Fatherland that was "such a picture of misery, thanks to the decay of the bourgeois world and the subversive work of Marxism in the democracy"? The problems that Schiller addressed could be solved only through "the intense spiritual persistence of the German Volk: a resolution that could and would only be achieved by National Socialism." Schiller's world view would "only be firmly established in the Third Reich"; its "dome cemented with blood and tears from the history of German suffering."[31]

The *Völkischer Beobachter* also complained about conditions under the Weimar republican government by hypothesizing about the nature of Beethoven's relationship to it. In the "age of Germany's greatest need and greatest disgrace," he was "a comforter for the exhausted and a god for the faithful." He stood as a "gigantic monument" showing "the way to the future – away from all the weak 'achievements' of a miserable, intellectual time."[32] For instance, the paper was enthusiastic about a 1920 concert at Munich's Wilhelmsgymnasium for Beethoven's 150th birthday. The school chorus sang *Hymne an die Nacht* and *Das Blümchen Wunderhold*; the orchestra played the first and third movements of the First Symphony; and students performed the Quintet in E-Flat Major. All this engagement between Beethoven and young people was good, the report indicated, but "the joy of the occasion was not unclouded." The sounds of the quintet had hardly faded when a "Professor Joachimsin (correction: Joachimsohn)" took the podium: "a Jew was going to present a speech to commemorate the memory of Beethoven – the greatest German composer!" The newspaper found it unbelievable that the "German administration of a German school" would allow such a "discordant note." They must have known how "wretched" it sounded when, "of all people, a Jew speaks about the disgraceful peace of Versailles and our broken down Fatherland, when his racial comrades were the very ones whose crimes were responsible for all the misfortune." According to the paper, Joachimsin "regurgitated with his disgusting castrato voice what various leftist rags had been slamming together for the commemoration." The celebration was ruined by this "miserable figure yapping about Beethoven's piety" and struggling to give the students a portrait of his titanic greatness. To Nazi ears it just didn't sound good when "a Jew spoke of German spiritual greatness, German longing, German hope, and German struggle." They wanted "German words about Germans," and in the future would demand of German school administrations a "finer feeling for Aryan character than was shown by unleashing this alien on the audience."[33]

Similarly, the *Völkischer Beobachter* included a vicious attack on a production of *Fidelio* led by Otto Klemperer, whom the paper referred to as "The Chief Music Jew" (*der Obermusikjude*). According to Josef Stolzing, the "Music Jew had not yet been born who could project himself into what was for him a completely foreign art: Beethoven's world of feeling." That was why Klemperer had to rehearse "so infinitely much." In this production, Stolzing wrote, the conductor had made perhaps the "greatest assassination attempt ever committed against the divinely beautiful music of Beethoven." In keeping with his Jewish sentiments, he had "chopped, minced, ripped, and torn it to bits."[34]

Above all, the *Völkischer Beobachter* complained about the international commemorations of Beethoven's 100th *Todestag* in 1927, which it referred to as "global hypocrisy." Everyone would breathe easier when the "global hype" over Beethoven came to an end. The lonely one had been the victim of "fairground huckstering" that would certainly have darkened his brow. It was to be expected, said the paper, that a democratic publication in Berlin would refer to the creator of the *Eroica* as a "spokesman for democracy." But it was shocking that former enemies in the World War also made their own claims. Emile Vanderwelde, the Belgian Foreign Minister, referred to Beethoven's *Missa Solemnis* in a lecture to the German people about peace: "to the German people from whom this disgusting Marxist preacher of peace, and crony of Wilson has taken the air, light, and space necessary for life!" Moreover, Charles G. Dawes, "bank robber and Vice-President of the United States" whose "humanitarian" appraisal estimated that 15,000 Germans over sixty years of age would have to commit suicide in 1926, made himself out to be "happy and proud to unite with Germany and other nations in honoring the Shakespeare of Music."

"What a cheap comparison!" the *Völkischer Beobachter* groused: Dawes had not celebrated Beethoven – he had "violated him!"[35]

Nazis vented their disgust for reception of Beethoven in 1927 by deriding Weimar culture in general. Visual artist and art critic Julius Nitsche reported for the *Völkischer Beobachter* that he had initially been enthusiastic about the *Todestag* events after attending a concert in Munich. But then, he and a friend traveled to Leipzig to partake in the festivities there. Bemoaning the noise and confusion that inundated the city's modern streets, the two found a café, read the newspapers, and noticed that each contained articles commemorating the composer. "Beethoven was everywhere," Nitsche reported. Every newspaper, domestic and foreign, carried appreciations of him. He wondered when the memory of an artist had ever been celebrated in such a way: "every political party and every sort of confession counted him as one of their own; all of them were fighting tooth and nail to demonstrate that he belonged exclusively to their circle of life." To what extremes, he asked, could this appropriation lead? Moments later he found his answer: the Leipzig newspaper announced that *Jonny spielt auf* – Ernst Krenek's *Zeitoper* highlighting jazz rhythms and a leading man in blackface – was opening that evening. For Nitsche this was a sign of how degenerate life had become in the *System-Zeit*. It was so bad that people were capable of performing a "nigger operetta" on the day of Beethoven's death. Weimar culture placed "next to the purest, the dirtiest; next to the deepest, the most shallow; beside the most spiritual, the most lacking in spirit; and next to that of eternal content, the most ephemeral." Even on the day for honoring the creator of the *Missa Solemnis* and the Ninth Symphony, people were willing to perform a show headlining a "devilish Negro who lured the hearts of all women and girls." It was, in his opinion, a "thoroughly confused time."[36]

But nothing convinced *Völkischer Beobachter* contributors that the "era of systems" was "confused" more than efforts to erect monuments to the man they considered the most irritating figure in German cultural history: Heinrich Heine. Indeed, the paper's vehemence against Heine memorials exceeded that triggered by *All Quiet on the Western Front*. Reporting on plans to celebrate Heine in Düsseldorf, it commented that "supposedly German" Jews were at it again, beating the drums for a monument – forgetting that they had tried this before the war, but that "national character stopped them then."[37] The paper also reminded its readers that when Franz Liszt had been asked for his opinion of a monument to Heine, everyone was surprised when he expressed approval. But then Liszt added: "Yes, but make it out of shit."[38] The paper also reprinted an extended excerpt from a letter that Houston Stewart Chamberlain had written against the Düsseldorf plans in 1906. "It would really be a monument to infamy. God protect not only the German Reich, but that holy totality ... that we mean when we respectfully use the term 'Germanness' from such a shameful thing."[39]

As if Liszt's and Chamberlain's views were not strong enough, the *Völkischer Beobachter* heaped more and more spiteful arguments against honoring Heine. When a memorial to Heine was completed in Hamburg in 1926, the paper remarked that Hamburg now had a "Jewish monument to Heine and Damascus," a sign that the new age had commenced – "one in which *Alljuda* ruled!" The fact that "the mob" was listening to his voice was a clear sign that the "new age" had begun. But the *Völkischer Beobachter* would continue to resist: "the voice of Heine is not ours – we wish him and the other Jewish fighters a place on the Nile, not on the Rhine."[40] Incensed, the paper also ran the following "poem" sent in by one of its "dearest supporters":

> To think that we Germans should give a monument to
>   a Galician Jew, and on the Rhine to boot!
> Have we completely forgotten how this impudent,
>   presumptuous punk dragged the forefathers of our Emperor
>   through excrement – and how he lied?
> Phooey, let us turn our back on such a disgrace, and have
>   the courage to say: He is not of our blood!
> Don't you see what they are aiming to do? Germans have to
>   see through this Jewish card-trick, or else we're going to
>   be the suckers.[41]

Alfred Rosenberg likewise stepped into the anti-Heine fray to complain about the convictions of the so-called "national bourgeoisie," whose members may have read something of the writer's "sea virgins and moon ghosts" at the age of puberty, but who knew nothing about the true Heine. That was why the Center, German Democratic, and Social-Democratic parties had made it possible to erect a monument to "one of the greatest freaks of German history – a French-Jewish spy." Rosenberg expected National Socialists of the Rhine area to protect the honor of German culture by making it clear to the city of Düsseldorf that only one form of monument was possible for Heine, "the one that Franz Liszt already suggested: out of shit!"[42] Following Rosenberg's lead, the paper intensified its attack on those who supported or merely remained indifferent to the matter. That cultural leaders in Düsseldorf were fighting for Heine was proof that a Jewish conspiracy had stunted their volkish instincts and feelings. "Cultural Bolshevism" was obviously rampant in that city. "Listen Rhinelanders," the paper closed, "Do German Volk comrades really want to raise a monument to a man who abused and betrayed his nation in the scurviest of ways?"[43] For their part, Nazis would not have anything to do with this "communist agitator" – this "polluter of our most sacred things" – or his "friends."[44]

But as much as the *Völkischer Beobachter* chided Rhinelanders for dropping their guard, it considered other figures far more responsible for the heinous situation. In the paper's opinion, "Judah" had been particularly busy in the "Harry Heine case," trying to drag the most perfidious of all "Jewish-German" poets into the Walhalla of German spirituality. How could this happen in Germany? Through "societies" like the *Heine-Gesellschaft* and people like Thomas Mann: the "asphalt-literatus who ran in Freemason and Jewish circles in Paris; who called for censoring movies that could damage relations between peoples; who had a novelette published in France that contained perverse representations of incest, insulted the German Volk, and debased Christianity; and who called the World War a 'criminal misuse of all powers.'" Indeed, Mann was in the first row of those who advocated honoring Heine because – like him – "he had no command of the German language." Just look at the "3,712 grammatical mistakes in his *Buddenbrooks*," the *Völkischer Beobachter* recommended. The paper concluded, however, that no matter how much these "prominents" tried, all the "cheap Heine baloney" would come to nothing. Thanks to the efforts of Nazi-favored literary scholars like Adolf Bartels and Josef Nadler, Germans would ultimately see through all the efforts of these gentlemen as nothing more than "humbug about Heine."[45] In any case, no matter what they did in the Weimar Republic, "the Third Reich would make sure that these Heine-Monuments of Shame disappeared as quickly as possible."[46]

Among all cultural figures, however, even those it considered to be its archenemies, the paper was most concerned about how the life and works of Wagner were treated in the Weimar era. Throughout its Wagner reception, the *Völkischer Beobachter* stipulated that "Bayreuth thinking" should be the basis for educating the German populace and especially its youth about the principles and plans of the Nazi movement. There was "no other path for the German Volk to follow than Parsifal's: did they, like him, have the strength and will to move forward, to withstand temptations, and to sacrifice themselves for the holiest purity and freedom of the Volk?"[47] Otto Daube, chairman of the Bayreuth Alliance of German Youth, stated that the goal of the "Wagner movement" was to lead young Germans to the "ideas of Bayreuth and thereby form a new Bayreuth generation" – deeply immersed in the work of Richard Wagner – that would "consciously resist degeneration." Another group, the Richard Wagner Society in Berlin, was devoted to countering the "modern, materialistic spirit of the metropolis" with a more "inner-oriented, ideal community."[48] In the same vein, Margarethe Strauss, member of the Richard Wagner Association of German Women and author of a book on "Wagner's Germanness," contributed an article about establishing a Wagner foundation that would send university students in every field on study trips to Bayreuth. There they would be "exposed to Germanness which would strengthen and deepen their feelings for the Fatherland." Listening to the festivals, their "German feelings would flare up" and they would be filled with pride that they were German.[49]

However, the paper consistently held that any such efforts were held back by a conspiracy that had commenced during Wagner's lifetime and was at its worst in the Weimar era. Under headlines like "New Jewish Agitations against Wagner," it claimed that the German press was trying to "curse" Wagner's work: "well-armed troops" under a "unified, goal-oriented leadership" were striving to destroy Wagner's German world view. In response, the *Völkischer Beobachter* issued a "wake-up call."[50] Referring to the Weimar period as a "tragic chapter of German cultural history," the paper maintained that Jews were working wherever possible to depict Wagner's personality to the world unsympathetically. Here "naked materialism stood against naked idealism": the Jews "could not stand" the only immortal German spirit who was of a self-consciously volkish orientation; who often went to battle with them before the whole world; and who, in the course of this struggle, repeatedly and ruthlessly tore the mask of "humanitarianism" from their faces. Even more shocking was the Weimar era phenomenon of "quite a few blood-native Germans" who gawked upon the Bayreuth Master through "hateful Jewish lenses," and then disseminated this caricature throughout the Volk as "historical" or "authentic."[51] According to Paul

Schwers, editor of the *Allgemeine Musikzeitung* and one of the best-known music writers of the period, the first signs of "sullenness toward Wagner" had appeared just before the war when radicals took up the cry, "Away from Wagner," and endeavored to reduce the number of Wagner performances or eliminate them altogether.[52] Acts such as these by Germans themselves were signs of "intellectual carelessness" and a "lack of racial instinct" that had to be exposed whenever they occurred, the paper cautioned.[53]

But the supposed racial enemies of Wagnerism were of even greater concern to the newspaper. The "Talmudic hatred" that Jews directed against Wagner's world view and lifework would end only when, as Heinrich Mann wrote in the *Berliner Tageblatt* at the turn of the year 1918/19, "heroic Wagnerian figures were finally driven off of German stages." Wagner had once prophesied that his son Siegfried would have a hard time carrying his name onward, and the *Völkischer Beobachter* believed that those difficulties were the fault of "foreign-blooded elements," whose every thought and action was dedicated to "demolishing the Bayreuth cultural circle and the German Volk – or at least to falsifying them as much as possible."[54] All of this was part of an effort to reduce Wagner's significance in order to make way for "the incompetent." The "Jewish press," under the control of music educator and Prussian Minister of Culture Leo Kestenberg, had declared a "culture war" against Wagner and these attacks were "representative of genuine Semitic hatred and showed how foreign Judaism was to German sensibility."[55]

Even when members of the "race" allegedly dedicated to his eradication honored Wagner with academic attention, or by attending or producing performances, the paper found reason to attack. In August 1923, it complained that too many "foreign visitors" were marring productions of *Die Meistersinger* in Munich and proposed that foreigners should not be allowed to enter the theater during the two months of the festival. No one, it held, "except perhaps hopelessly stupid Marxists," could deny that such a tactic was a matter of national interest since "practically nothing was left to Germans but their holy art."[56] According to Josef Stolzing, this issue even affected performances at Bayreuth: if one watched the flood of humanity on the Festival Hill "with a critical eye for race," one could get the impression that "the Nordic predominated," but there were still too many foreigners around. Among the first cultural duties of National Socialist Germany, he said, would be not only to restrict performances of *Parsifal* to Bayreuth again, but to "give the Bayreuth Festival back to the German Volk – henceforth its sole public!"[57]

Even more infuriating to the *Völkischer Beobachter* were events at which "Germany's racial enemies" were directly involved with productions and performances. Simply because some of the speakers were Jewish, the paper described a Wagner evening as a "travesty": "the creator of the *Meistersinger* would have considered this festive mess to be nothing other than a desecration of his lovely work."[58] Angered over a "condensed" version of *Die Walküre* led by Otto Klemperer, they compared it with "Jewish circumcision," since the innovative conductor was Jewish. Only the "complete lack of respect among Jews" for the German cultural legacy could bring about such a crime against one of the immortal works of the Bayreuth Master. Thus it was good, the paper opined, that a coalition of Wagner groups (including the Academic Richard Wagner Society, Bayreuth Alliance of Germany, and the German Richard Wagner Society) issued a statement condemning the production at the Kroll Opera. These groups considered such performances a "sin against the spirit of Wagner and a distortion of his lifework" that operated to "instill false impressions" in German youth. The coalition condemned such "defamation of the memory of Richard Wagner" and asserted that such productions constituted the "rape of a work of art."[59]

On another occasion when "Jewish conductors" – this time, Erich Kleiber (who was not Jewish) and Leo Blech – performed at Bayreuth, the *Völkischer Beobachter* complained that this was confirmation that "Judah" was working with every possible means to "destroy the last surviving and influential sites of German culture."[60] Subsequently, Hans Severus Ziegler denigrated non-traditional staging of Wagner's operas as part of the conspiracy, rejecting a production of *Götterdämmerung* designed by Maximilian Moris as one of many "Jewish attempts" to destroy the Bayreuth Festival and bury the Wagner tradition – all led by the "Jewish press" in Vienna and Berlin. Ziegler was particularly angered by the depiction of the Valkyries' aerie: it was "a set for Hottentots with no sign of the Rhine, no Romanticism, and no warmth – just savage, childish, Asiatic primitivism." It would have been more appropriate, Ziegler felt, "to read a Dada poem" in front of it than sing Wagner's music. Ziegler ended his tirade with a call for all German Wagner organizations to protect the master, and through legal means if necessary: as long as Jewry dominated the art and music world with its money, Germans were "condemned to suffer such arbitrary acts against their tradition."[61] Even when the paper grudgingly admitted that a singer of Jewish background had done a good job of singing Wotan, it added that this exception was "a funny little joke of world history" that might lead one to believe that "even a Jew can learn something – but only momentarily."[62]

Concerned by 1927 statistics showing that more Verdi was being performed in German opera houses than Wagner, the paper worried that Wagner was losing his appeal to the public. In its continuing effort to "protect" him, the *Völkischer Beobachter* insisted that the problem was due to the fact that Weimar era productions were "much worse than before the war." Why did Wagner even provide stage directions, if no one would follow them? According to the paper, the Nazi Party had plans for rectifying the situation: through drastic measures. National Socialism would present masterpieces in productions of the highest caliber, and "eliminate all those who had systematically worked to pollute the immortal works of the Germans which – given their souls – they could never understand themselves."[63]

In addition to defending Wagner against his enemies, the *Völkischer Beobachter* frequently reported about how Nazis incorporated his music into their rituals and liturgy. In 1922, when the party was still developing its cultural pageantry in the beer halls of Munich, the paper announced that Hitler would speak at a meeting at the *Bürgerbräukeller*. Prior to the speech, bandleader Jacob Peuppus, who was famous for leading Bavarian military bands on tours throughout the world, led an ensemble in performances of the *Gralsritter-Marsch* from *Parsifal*, the Prelude to *Der fliegende Holländer*, the *Chor der Friedensboten* from *Rienzi*, and *Wotans Abschied und Feuerzauber* from *Die Walküre*. Another early example of Nazi incorporation of Wagner's music into its rallies and propaganda events took place at a Greater German Festival, which the *Völkischer Beobachter* promoted on 1 April 1922. Before Hitler delivered a speech on Bismarck, an orchestra performed the Prelude to *Rienzi*, along with the *Steuermannslied und Matrosenchor* from *The Flying Dutchman*.[64] Then, in 1932, the NSDAP founded a party orchestra, the National Socialist Symphony Orchestra. Its first concert, as covered in the paper, featured the prelude to Wagner's *Meistersinger*.[65] On its opening tour of five Bavarian towns under director, Franz Adam, it performed a program that included the Overture to

Tannhäuser. According to the *Völkischer Beobachter*, at these concerts one could really perceive "how great the effect of noble music is on simple Volk comrades who otherwise had little opportunity to enjoy art." The "artistic and – not least – the propagandistic success of first concert tour was powerful because anyone could see here that the movement was in great measure a cultural movement – indeed, the main cultural movement of the German Volk." It was above all National Socialism that would "fill the hearts of Volk comrades with love of German art and German character."[66] Committed to promoting the party orchestra, the *Völkischer Beobachter* encouraged readers to attend a subsequent Richard Wagner Morning Celebration, which was considered an important part of the Nazi campaign strategy in 1932. In the middle of the "gigantic electoral battle for Reichs presidency of the German Volk," it invited readers to this event because the party "included the Muses on its chariot" – because for Nazis, German music was not merely a form of entertainment, but daily bread for the soul: "Come and eat, Germans, that you might be strong in battle!"[67]

This was the "meaning behind all the performances" of the National Socialist Symphony Orchestra – the "significance of their concert tours through all of Germany." In the Nazi movement, Germans were to "find the harmonies of German spirit, the edification of the German masters, the spiritual unity of Germanness!" That was why "German Volk comrades" needed to go to the Morning Celebration and listen to heroic themes from *Siegfried*, *Lohengrin*, and *Tristan*. These works would resonate with what they were all "sensing at this time of the election – the joy of victory and a feeling of spring." In this spirit Nazis would "rise and shine at the *Morgenfeier!*"[68] After the event, naturally, the paper ran a rave review of the performance: "Comrade Kapellmeister Franz Adam has achieved what seemed to be completely impossible: selling out the Zirkus for a musical *Morgenfeier* in a time of vicious anger and hatred." His "courage and strength has succeeded in creating a National Socialist weapon that has achieved a great and noble victory over anti-cultural and anti-German tendencies in music."[69] In addition to touting such triumphs, the paper devoted significant coverage to events put on by the *Kampfbund für deutsche Kultur*. Its programs, which often included music by Wagner, were described as being "as German as you can possibly imagine." Such Nazi–Wagnerian events were "important steps on the path to a genuine German culture," because they showed that Germans had the right to "construct their culture on a thousand-year-old foundation, right in between Bolshevism and reaction."[70]

Bayreuth itself also occupied the paper's editors: the status and nature of the festival was a central concern of Nazi cultural politics. From the earliest phases of the movement, the *Völkischer Beobachter* championed the festival as an institution that required state support in the face of the conspiracy of racial and political enemies that were purportedly working to undermine it by economic and editorial means. When the festival was revived after the First World War, the paper ran a celebratory article by Otto Daube noting that despite all outward signs that "belief" had declined, the revival of the festival indicated that the German Volk had nevertheless preserved its inner faith: "Bayreuth lived on as the expression of German Art, German Sprit, and German Soul – and all Germany should be like Bayreuth!" As Wagner had hoped when the modern Reich was first unified, Nazis wanted – at a time when the Volk was splintering – to reawaken a feeling of German community in Bayreuth: "One Volk, One Will, One Deed!" The town, Daube thought, should have been be designated "The Custodial City of German Style."[71]

Herbert Mueller agreed that Bayreuth was succeeding in functioning as a refuge of cultural conservatism, but still worried that it was under threat. Wagner had seen the problems implicit in modernity, and built Bayreuth to resist them. But everything that he feared and fought was troubling postwar Germany: "the dike was broken; the waters were rising; the revived Bayreuth could still collapse." If that happened, German culture and art would decline "without the slightest hope for support or salvation." But, for now at least, Mueller consoled the paper's readers, Bayreuth still stood as "the revelation of German Spirit before the world and God!" – every festival year was a "fresh victory."[72]

In 1927, on the 50th anniversary of its founding, Emma von Sichart stated that without the Bayreuth Festival, the "spiritual life of Germany would be inconceivable." After the global conflagrations of the First World War, and as the fight to defend the German spirit raged on, the importance of Bayreuth was "clearer than ever." All that had been constructed in German lands "from within," could find a "secure center" and a "fixed star" there. Wagner's lifework contained a "Christian-German world outlook" that made all "selfish fighting over split hairs" unnecessary. Bayreuth had become a more important symbol than ever: out of the shock and confusion of the Weimar era, Germans were finally learning to understand the powerful tragedy of the Ring. Central, for von Sichart, was the "curse of gold-lust": it possessed even the most noble, so that even Siegfried, the "innocent-guilty one," could become its victim – just as do Fasolt, Fafner, Mime, Gunther, and Wotan – until finally, "the love of a woman releases the world from its curse and returns the gold to the Rhine maidens and pure element of water." With its festival, Bayreuth was the "gathering point for all those who wanted to fight to overcome the concerns of daily life and the forces of greed."[73]

Indeed, the paper considered the Bayreuth Festival the most important bulwark against modernization in German society and culture. According to Mueller, the troubles of the modern world could not be made right merely through "ocean crossings and world records." In the age of technology, something more was necessary: "above all, festivals in Bayreuth!" But Bayreuth was always threatened by those who wanted to advance "intellectual decline, de-Germanicization, and internationalization." The festival was the last hold-out for a "pure German art policy," promoting the spiritual world of Richard Wagner as the starting point for German regeneration and renaissance. It would be the "midwife to a rebirth" of the German Volk out of the spirit of the great master. With Charles Lindbergh's 1927 transatlantic flight, the mayor of Berlin, Gustav Böss, said that Germans must learn from Americans in order that German culture might regain its place in the world. The *Völkischer Beobachter* disagreed. Modern, international spirit would never be able to save Germany: "the source of health flowed from the Green Hill of Bayreuth alone."[74] In his report from the festival of that year, Josef Stolzing echoed these antimodernist, anti-technological themes, complaining in particular about the increased presence of automobiles in Bayreuth: "horses and wagons had lost access to the streets, even there!" But, in his opinion, the festival itself had not changed. More strongly than ever, since the ill-fated exit from the First World War and national collapse, the idea of the Bayreuth Festival had proved itself a "necessity of life": one of the "strongest symbols of German cultural conscience." For Nazis the Festspielhaus was the "temple of the German soul" – its "greatest cultural expression."[75]

Paul Pretzsche, editor of the *Official Bayreuth Festival Guide* (as well as the correspondence between Cosima Wagner and H. S. Chamberlain, and the letters of Chamberlain to Kaiser Wilhelm II), had to admit that Wagner and Bayreuth were increasingly ignored in modern times. A Channel swimmer, a world champion boxer, or some other world record breaker had more popularity than the masters of culture. Bayreuth was "surrounded by a wall of enmity and – even worse – indifference." Yet it lived: for "it was built from inside-out." The festival was "a fortress of refuge and defiance." Wagner had taken his stand in a small town in the heart of Germany, certainly aware that inwardness and big city are opposites: "out there, diversion; in here, assembling great cultural experiences, around which daily life should revolve."[76] Moreover, added Paul Schwers, Bayreuth had done more for German foreign interests since the war – more toward "influencing the mentality of enemies to its advantage" – than a dozen mediocre career diplomats could ever have done. Foreign countries envied this temple of art, so Germans "had to combat all threats to bury it under hostile criticism and apathy."[77] In these terms, the paper dug in defensive positions – symbolically on the "green hill" of Wagner's Bayreuth – against the cultural appropriation and social erosion that it feared from the Weimar regime and its policies. But, the *Völkischer Beobachter* did not merely hold out in this fortress of defiance: at the same time, it launched a *Blitzkrieg* against the "asphalt culture" Nazis so detested.

15 WEIMAR CULTURE WARS 2: COMBATING "DEGENERACY"

In rising to its vociferous "defense of Bayreuth," the *Völkischer Beobachter* strongly communicated Nazi enmity toward Weimar culture and politics via critiques of what it saw as the Republic's inability to fully understand or properly honor the greats of German tradition. But in its role as a "combat paper" in the culture wars between modernists and antimodernists that raged in Germany in 1918, it also devoted plenty of space and energy to directly attacking leading figures of "Weimar culture." As Alan Steinweis articulated:

> *although artistic modernism had made important inroads in Germany before 1918, it was during the Weimar Republic that it emerged in its full force in literature, painting and sculpture, architecture, music, and theater. Many of the artistic innovations attracted the wrath of cultural conservatives spanning the right side of the political spectrum. They condemned artistic modernism as overly cerebral and international. It did not conform to their notion of authentic "Germanness."*[1]

Creativity derided as "degenerate" was vilified as an antipode to the idealized *Kultur* that could provide a sense of order to the German present and future.[2]

Primary targets of Nazi aggression were the writers it dismissed as "asphalt literati," including Stefan Zweig, Max Brod, Maximilian Harden, Alfred Döblin, and Bertoldt Brecht. Zweig (1881–1942) presented an easy target, since he was Jewish and had not served at the front during the First World War. For those who "suffered endlessly in the field," the paper contended, it was enough to know that Zweig spent the war in Switzerland; this fact alone invalidated any morals offered by "the Jew Zweig" because "the great humanitarian lesson of the World War was that of standing at the sides of German brothers under storms of steel."[3] The paper also went after "the Prague Jew" Max Brod (1884–1968), not for his involvement with Franz Kafka, but rather for his own novel, *Stefan Rott or The Decisive Year* (1931), complaining that the book's publisher had touted it as "a *Bildungsroman* in the finest style, filled with passion, longing and insight," and that the Center Party "handed laurels" to the "Jew Brod." The *Völkischer Beobachter* countered that the novel was nothing but "a base Jewish gibe at the German race and at German decency," and wondered why no one had called for its censorship under laws against smut and filth. Then, as if dutifully rising to its own call, the *Völkischer Beobachter* announced that it was therefore pressing for a battle against such "Jewish poisoners of German culture" and would not rest until they had "disappeared."[4]

The newspaper was likewise infuriated when Walter von Molo (1880–1958) – whom it described as a "busy colleague" of the Mosse-owned *Berliner Tageblatt* ("Why do Germans really buy this rag, which is really just a Jewish family affair?"[5]) and a "member of the Central Association of German Citizens of Jewish Faith" – dared to call the overturning of Jewish gravestones a "childish, bestial crime" compared with which all others seem "minor and forgivable." This sort of statement, the paper held, obscured a litany of Jewish scandals.[6] Elsewhere, the *Völkischer Beobachter* maligned writer Maximilian Harden (1861–1927) as one of the "biggest parasites of all the Jewish journalists," who caused "immeasurable damage through the great influence he exercised via his desperately degenerate style, particularly in circles of the bourgeois intelligentsia."[7]

Perhaps the most flagrant *Asphaltliterat*, in the paper's view, was Alfred Döblin (1878–1957): the creator of a "totally flat land" in contemporary literature, which was most notably manifested in his "Bolshevik play," *Marriage* (1930) and in his "low-life novel," *Berlin Alexanderplatz* (1929). In these works, said the paper, Döblin intended nothing less than to bring about a "decline in the level of *Bildung*."[8] Even among such degenerate works, the paper reserved special criticism for *The Threepenny Opera* (1928), the iconic Weimar-era "beggar's opera" by Berthold Brecht

(1898–1956) and Kurt Weill (1900–1950) with its most enduringly famous ballad of *Mack the Knife*. The *Völkischer Beobachter* simply labeled it the "craziest thing that Weimar society produced." This "so-called opera stank with the contents of common sexual relations," said the paper, pointing out especially the story of Spelunkenjenny, Mackie's former girlfriend: "a whore through and through." The paper also noted that this "English smut" had first been translated into German by a "Mrs.(!) Elisabeth Hauptmann," then arranged by the "excessively famous literatus, Bert Brecht," who "made it even more swinish" – and that the music was written by "the Jew Kurt Weill: for jazz orchestra, of course."[9]

The *Völkischer Beobachter* had already attacked Weill for *The Czar Has His Picture Taken* (premiered 18 February 1928), in which he and the dramatist, Georg Kaiser, "blabbered nonsense which resulted in a Jewification of the audience: every third person sitting in hall was a racial comrade of the two collaborators – and even a number of Germans contributed to the applause of this infuriating Asiatic horde."[10] Still the paper considered the opening of *The Threepenny Opera* in August of the same year as even worse: "one of the most corrosive moments of the era, it was a thoroughly Jewish event." The "Jewish poet," Brecht, "dug up an old English piece, put it on like an old hat, and decorated it a bit"; then "the Jew Kurt Weill added some more or less terrible music." That's how a 300-year-old play became *The Threepenny Opera*, "designed for a predominantly Jewish audience."[11] "Frantically modernist and full of musical half-measures," Weill's was not the "noble ruler" that opera music should be, but the "submissive servant who only responds to the action out of embarrassment, hostile to every sign of healthiness, waiting on every desolate dissonance."[12] Jews "had it too easy producing such slop: this inferior racial stuff was playing week after week while German writers hoped and waited in vain for productions of their works."[13] The bourgeoisie of Germany should not have remained quiet about this, the paper complained: "press and public had to demonstrate" against such content.[14]

Rarely exercising restraint in wielding its adjectives in the superlative, the *Völkischer Beobachter* saw fit to declare that, at least among the *Asphaltliterat*, "Heinrich Mann was the worst." As seen in Part III, the paper first condemned Mann for his prewar realism, especially his novel *The Loyal Subject*, which it considered "in many ways the most Jewish works of all modern literature."[15] From that point, however, Mann's involvement in politics provided even more opportunities for Nazi outrage. According to the paper, Mann's political activity "paralleled his literary work in every sense." During the First World War he was closely affiliated with a pacifist journal, *White Papers*, that Rene Schickele published in Switzerland to further the purpose of preparing for a "European community" – an effort that met with such success that most of the editions were proscribed by the German censor. Thus, it was no surprise when Mann later expressed his support for establishing conscientious objector status in Germany: "that was heroism according to him." Thereafter, the paper contended, no one welcomed the "treachery of the November parties" as enthusiastically as "The Bard of 9 November." Already in December 1918, he spoke on the "significance and idea of the revolution"; then in January 1919 he "formulated slogans" for the Reich Office for Economic Demobilization; and at the memorial to Kurt Eisner, he "naturally showed himself to be a passionate philo-Semite." In short: "he was a November criminal from head to toe – and a pan-European *par excellence*." His 1919 statement in the *Berliner Tageblatt* – that after the revolution the "Wagnerian heroic types had left the stage" – perfectly expressed his "pan-European-pacifistic-philo-Semitic positions."

Hand in hand with his anti-volkish engagement, Mann "glorified Germany's bitterest enemy," France, with words such as "prewar France was the land in which moral seriousness ruled, whereas prewar Germany was Hell – where vainglory, arrogance, lies, self-delusion, avarice, and injustice were the order of the day." Repeated trips to Paris crowned his other "Novemberish deeds." Moreover, he condemned the Spirit of 1914 as a "spirit of conquest" and, faithful to dreams of *entente*, considered Jacques Rivière's notion that "the occupation of the Ruhr was a slightly rude but very clear invitation to Germany to work together with France" as "surprising but not paradoxical." Indeed, the *Völkischer Beobachter* found it "very paradoxical" that Mann expressed this opinion when he was at the head of the Prussian Writers Academy, but it was "not as monstrous as his statement that the poverty and suffering of the German people were not the result of the insane costs of reparations."

The paper complained that Mann apparently "had a bleeding heart for everyone in the world except German patriots." Whenever the Red Cross needed a signature, Mann was ready to "serve communist sub-humans." If a "Jewish traitor" was condemned to seven years in jail by the Hungarian government, he – along with the Jews Albert Einstein, Theodor Wolff, Ludwig Fulda, Arthur Schnitzler, Hugo von Hofmannsthal, Stephan Zweig, Felix Salten, Franz Werfel, and Max Reinhardt – would "let loose with earth-shaking screams of fury" in the *Berliner Tageblatt*, the *Vossische Zeitung*, and the *Frankfurter Zeitung*. If a committee was formed "to protect traitors, there he would be, on the Executive Committee – next to Einstein, Georg Bernhard, Dr. Feilchenfeld, Dr. Goldschmitt, Dr. Lion Feuchtwanger, Dr. Sally Friedländer, Dr. Gumbel, Dr. Kerr, Dr. Lasker, Emil Ludwig Cohn, Paul Schlesinger, Dr. Wolffstein, Arnold Zweig, Toller, and Tucholsky."

As was supposedly clear from the names of his associates, Mann's philo-Semitism was "unsurpassed," even to the point, according to the paper, that he contributed "classic lines" to Zionist publications. In one instance, for example, Mann wrote that "racial anti-Semitism has not perceived the origins and mechanism of the new society." In response, the *Völkischer Beobachter* said that this "wise prophet" should have just kept his mouth shut: in fact, things had developed differently precisely because "racist anti-Semitism *only too clearly* perceived the origins and mechanism of the new society, i.e., that of Ruth Fischer, Paul Cassirer, Mosse, Ullstein, and the great banks and stock exchanges." "Philo-Semitic democracy" was going to be spiritually exhausted, so this "big fat Writers' President could just go away and give his speeches in synagogues." The extent to which this "poet" was indebted to the Weimar political system, said the paper, was clear in the "festive" reception he enjoyed from Berlin's Academy of the Arts on his sixtieth birthday. "Ruling Marxism" thereby confirmed that this "November intellectual" was a pathfinder and herald of its views. In contrast, the "decisive energies" of a New Germany would be applied differently – "to something that should have been done a long time ago: the elimination of *literati* like Heinrich Mann from official spiritual life altogether."[16] Again, specific measures were clearly in mind among the cultural ideologues of the *Völkischer Beobachter*.

But, of course, Heinrich was not the only member of the Mann family who raised the ire of contributors to the Nazi paper, to the point of wishing him gone. Thomas Mann received much criticism from attackers who were infuriated by his increasing support of Weimar republicanism. Although Mann's shift from the conservative, pro-Wilhelmine views he had expressed in *Reflections of a Non-Political Man* (1918) marked the real gap between the Nobel laureate and Nazi ideologues, Josef Stolzing condemned his body of work outright. As a novelist, Stolzing wrote, Mann could only be considered a "second-rate talent." *Buddenbrooks* (1901), Stolzing was certain, had been "vastly overestimated by critics." Frankly, it suffered from the worst weakness a novel can have: "it is boring." Very few people, Stolzing felt, would ever read this novel more than once, and nothing that Mann had written since then reached even the level of this first work. He "never possessed a powerful, creative imagination"; his talent was for nothing but "gluing bits and pieces together"; none of his works involved inventing an exciting fable or organizing strong characters in language "glowing in spirit, humor, and color." Along with Gerhart Hauptmann, he was "condemned to serve in the funeral escort for a cultural epoch that had come to its end, and he had died with it – mummified in literary history." At best Mann's writing would be an obscure subject for dissertations by graduate students in German literature. Nevertheless, Stolzing acknowledged that all of Germany took note when he produced *Reflections of an Non-Political Man* during the war – "when the luck of the battle was still smiling on Germany," when Germans were "still certain of victory." According to Stolzing, people *thought* Thomas Mann was patriotic: "he allied himself with his Volk as it was fighting for its life!" But it didn't end that way: "old Germany crumbled under the hands of the November criminals and became a republic." Thereafter, Mann's *Reflections* came to haunt him, blocking his way down the "*via triumphalis* of the November democracy." So "he had to do a bit of re-writing in the democratic spirit," "retouching" all those passages that conveyed an aristocratic view of life during the war. That was how he made his move into the camp of the November republicans: through "touch-ups" of the *Reflections of a Non-Political Man* – and the writer himself – to make them "fit in better with the new times." In view of this, Stolzing wondered if "someone like Mann was really worthy of a Nobel Prize."[17]

The *Völkischer Beobachter* never forgave Mann for his postwar transformation, complaining that whenever the "Black-Red Democracy" required, he showed up to enthusiastically celebrate the Weimar system and attack the young volkish movement. But the paper recalled that "there had been a time when Mann thought completely differently." In his wartime "reflections" from behind the front, he had "defended the national cause very effectively": his faith that victory for the Kaiser's Germany was necessary led him to viciously condemn "rootless civilization-literati" and "fragile popular-democratic ideas." To support this point, the paper reproduced a series of passages from *Reflections* and invited readers to compare the Mann of "yesterday and today." Mann wrote, for instance: "let Europe's peace rest on the fact that the best educated, the most just, most sincerely freedom-loving nation is also the most powerful, dominant one – [let it rest] on the power of the German Reich, which cannot be touched by any machinations."[18] Further: "to be a conservatively disposed German does not mean wanting to preserve everything that exists, but wanting to keep Germany German – nothing more."[19] Indeed, while many quotes on the "uselessness of democratic ideas" could be found throughout the *Reflections*, the *Völkischer Beobachter* editorialized, even the few passages the paper reproduced would suffice to show that Mann's outlook had changed abruptly between 1917 and 1922. He had become a "close friend" of the very system of German democracy that he had sharply condemned for its ineffectiveness and un-German nature. From the Nazi perspective, he "lacked the instinct and spiritual power" to recognize that the "democratic fraternity" he associated with in the Weimar era was identical to his earlier portrait of "pseudodemocracy." As a result, he had invalidated his reputation outside democratic circles.[20]

Besides his postwar republicanism, the paper lambasted the "trendy, Euro-cosmopolitan" Mann for a writing style that was just "too complicated to follow." As Stolzing put it, because Mann incorporated all sorts of foreign terms and neologisms instead of "writing German," his style could be compared with the look of a "shaved poodle wearing a red sweater."[21] Another Nazi voice described him as the author of "society pieces about decadence and rot," whose "inside-out sentences" caused everyone trouble.[22] And neither did the *Völkischer Beobachter* hesitate to attack Mann's reputation among volkish-disposed Germans with its sharpest weapon: anti-Semitic insinuation. Reporting that "the Munich-based fiction writer" received the 1929 Nobel Prize for Literature, Stolzing stated first that Mann's mother was Portuguese, and that the writer therefore "stemmed from an expressly mixed race with a strong admixture of Jewish blood," and second, that he was married to a "half Jewess, born Pringsheim."[23]

Elaborating on Stolzing's innuendo for the paper was volkish-oriented professor, Arno Schmieder – widely published in philology, literary history, and linguistics, and editor of a "Nordic dictionary." Schmieder wrote that though he could not be counted among his most enthusiastic fans, he had appreciated Mann as a writer and had never previously been concerned about his racial origins. But when he learned of Mann's opinions about the "German movement," Schmieder realized that "whoever thinks that way cannot be a German." Then he read the following in Adolf Bartels' book, *Jewish Origins and the Study of Literature* (1925):

> *The Manns themselves contest their Jewish origins. They*
> *want to be descended from an old Lübeck merchant family.*
> *But Heinrich and Thomas had a Creole mother. I must*
> *confess that I still believe that they have some Jewish blood,*
> *probably via Portugal … But even if the Mann family doesn't*
> *have a single drop of Jewish blood, he is married to the*
> *daughter of Pringsheim, a Jewish Professor of Mathematics in*
> *Munich. Like those of his brother Heinrich, his creations*
> *don't seem fully German to me.*

Since he shared Bartels' judgment of Mann's "spiritual nature," Schmieder felt he had no reason to doubt these statements about the writer's origins. In his opinion, this was neither a matter of "suspicion" nor "degradation": it was simply necessary to rebuff Mann's views of the nationalist movement as "un-German."[24]

Other contributors to the paper scanned Mann's works for evidence of his Semitism or at least philo-Semitism. One article argued obscurely that Mann demonstrated his "spiritual attraction to Judaism" in his novel *The Magic Mountain* (1924). There, the *Völkischer Beobachter* claimed, he glorified the "gruesome torture of animals" involved in slaughter according to Jewish dietary laws while ridiculing the Christian methods.[25] The newspaper reproduced the troublesome passage where Leo Naphta remembers watching his father perform the act.[26] Then the *Völkischer Beobachter* scolded Mann for misrepresenting the Jewish ritual as "a sacred procedure." By doing so, the author was clearly trying to court the favor of Jewry at a time when, "happily," strong efforts were being made to forbid the procedure.[27]

More obviously representing Mann's philo-Semitism was the novelist's treatment of the Old Testament topic of Joseph and his brothers. In 1928, the *Völkischer Beobachter* took note of comments Mann made in a "Berlin Jewish rag" in which he described his forthcoming novel as a mere "page turner."[28] The *Völkischer Beobachter* "resisted adding anything to this self-criticism," but choice of subject piqued the paper's interest. It dutifully reviewed Biblical references to Joseph's "blessed activities" as the Egyptian Pharaoh's governor and concluded that the "pious" hero had done little more than buy up surpluses of Egyptian grain in a period of abundance, only to sell them at "usurious prices" later. He had thereby proven himself – in grand style – to be "the first Jewish grain speculator!" It was amusing, the *Völkischer Beobachter* found, that the

Old Testament described one of the "most enormous examples of grain usury" in history so dryly and naively, with not a word of indignation directed toward the man who caused and was the main beneficiary of the increase in grain prices. This proved that "Jews regarded such speculations as a natural right of Jewry, no matter how terrible the consequences were for other people concerned." For the Nazi paper, "comparisons with the present" should have been obvious to all its readers. *Joseph and his Brothers* would not appear until 1933, but the *Völkischer Beobachter* "couldn't wait" to see how Mann's "page-turner" would depict his Jewish hero.[29]

Before that, though, Mann had given the paper more Semitic grist when he traveled to Palestine to do research for the novel in 1930. Before returning, he granted an interview to the weekly journal of the German Zionist movement, the *Jüdische Rundschau*, offering his impressions of Palestine. The *Völkischer Beobachter* pounced on the story. Mann said that what he saw in Palestine was wonderful: "everything was progressive; the Jews were doing beautiful work." Those in Tel-Aviv, he felt, were "somehow different than the Jews in all other cities of the world; they seemed free, happy, alert, and strongly intellectual," so he believed in their future there. But he warned that they had to proceed carefully, because Arabs "had been in the land for over a thousand years, also believed in their historical connection with it, and likewise had well-founded rights to it." Jews and Arabs had the opportunity to live next to each other in Palestine and to commonly dedicate themselves to the development of the land. Still, in the end, he was in favor of Zionism and compared many of its goals and ideals with the romantic movement of Germany in the nineteenth century, since "both had roots in the desire for self-liberation." The *Völkischer Beobachter* observed that one could see in this report how Mann had "fallen head over heels in love with Jews." When he compared Zionism with Romanticism, he proved how "completely he had distanced himself from German essence." That said, the paper added, it "was a shame so few Jews felt the need for spiritual freedom" that Mann attributed to the Zionists. In the opinion of the Nazi daily in 1930, a mass emigration of the Jews to Palestine in search of "spiritual liberty" would have been an optimal solution for the "Jewish Question."[30]

Besides his position on that issue, the *Völkischer Beobachter* took Mann to task for a number of statements, publications, and actions it found irritating. In 1928, a writer for the *Berliner Nachtausgabe* attacked him for making remarks about German nationalism that could have arisen only from a "deep lack of awareness or an equally profound maliciousness," and therefore deserved the "sharpest response." The self-described "nationalist youth" of the *Nachtausgabe* then accused Mann of "kowtowing before Paris; using slimy and worn out clichés; soiling himself with excrement in his tailor-made suits; and bowing before the occupiers of the Rhineland in order to increase his book sales." Surprisingly, the *Völkischer Beobachter* acknowledged that Mann deserved to defend himself against such accusations. But, in his published response, Mann wrote: "With just a few other Germans, my name is celebrated world-wide. How do they dare refuse satisfaction for the author of the *Reflections of a Non-Political Man*?" For the *Völkischer Beobachter* this was going too far: it "did indeed dare," because it was distasteful to read such a "sumptuous self-assessment." While Mann's present-day fame was undeniable, time would determine its duration. As a comparison, it suggested that in his era, a Schikaneder could say that Mozart had "impaired his magnificent play, *The Magic Flute*, with poor music – but history had clearly proven otherwise."

Still, the newspaper found more to flay in what it called "this caper of injured self-estimation." It considered even more "galling and worthless" the following passage in Mann's retort:

> *Nationalism is tied together in Germany with lack of talent; it is incapable of spirit, it cannot write, it cannot fascinate in any higher sense, it is simple barbarianism. A curse – a metaphysical censure – floats over it; it is a sin against the German spirit which cannot be forgiven; the writer who falls into it, declines inexorably. For instance, Wagner's ethnic arrogance was his posthumous ruin.*

In return, the *Völkischer Beobachter* asserted that even if one assumed Mann was only referring to the bibliography of the last decades, then he was ignorant of the work of people such as Heinrich von Treitschke, Paul de Lagarde, Julius Langbehn, Detlev von Liliencron, Bogislav von Selchow, H. S. Chamberlain, and Dietrich Eckart, among others. If so, such ignorance would mark "significant deficiencies" in the education of "Professor Thomas Mann." On the other hand, if he knew about these works and still stated such things, then "*he* was the malicious liar and slanderer."[31]

In 1928, Mann made a statement which irritated the *Völkischer Beobachter* even more – and triggered recurring commentary in its pages. In April of that year, the *Bremen* – a Junkers W33-type aircraft – made the first transatlantic flight from east to west with pilot Hermann Köhl and the plane's owner, Baron Günther von Hünefeld, aboard.[32] Thereafter, the fliers were fêted throughout Germany. As they visited Munich, Mann expressed in a *Süddeutsche Zeitung* article some disdain for the popular adulation afforded the aviators: "I write [to] you on the day when our good, but misled city honors two flying simpletons [*Fliegertröpfe*] who have swept the nationalists off their feet." The *Völkischer Beobachter* shot back that one had to congratulate Captain Köhl and Baron von Hünefeld for the fact that the author was "filled with an instinctive dislike for them." That he insulted the aviators by calling them simpletons was characteristic of a man who felt himself "sort of very German."[33] Later the paper ran indignant interviews with pilots in training at an airfield near Munich. Major Hailer, head of the *Süddeutschen Lufthansa*, responded that Mann had insulted not just Köhl and von Hünefeld, but "all those who had flown for the Fatherland" in the First World War. From his perspective, Mann "couldn't be much of a writer if he didn't understand the importance of transatlantic flights."[34] By speaking with "toxic spite" about the welcome that the people of Munich had given to the great German fliers as a "nationalistic handstand," he demonstrated that "market-oriented literati" like him had "absolutely no sense of the moral value of true achievement."[35]

In 1930, Mann gave a speech with the title, "An Appeal to Reason," and Nazis were dismayed that it was subsequently published, could be seen in the windows of bookstores, and received lots of advertising – including "extensive attention" in the journal of the Central Association of German Citizens of Jewish Faith. Therein appeared the following passages on the rise of irrational nationalism, which the *Völkischer Beobachter* reproduced:

> *There was proclaimed a new mental attitude for all mankind, which should have nothing to do with bourgeois principles such as freedom, justice, culture, optimism, faith in progress ... Mind, quite simply the intellectual, it put under a taboo as destructive of life, while it set up for homage as the true inwardness of life, the Mother-Chthonic, the darkness of the soul, the holy procreative underworld. Much of this*

> *nature-religion, by its very essence inclining to the orgiastic*
> *and to bacchic excess, has gone into the nationalism of our*
> *day, making of it something quite different from the*
> *nationalism of the nineteenth century, with its bourgeois,*
> *strongly cosmopolitan and humanitarian cast. It is*
> *distinguished in its character as a nature-cult, precisely by its*
> *absolute unrestraint, its orgiastic, radically anti-humane,*
> *frenzied dynamic character.*[36]

"What could one say about this gibberish?" the *Völkischer Beobachter* asked. Content aside, it wondered how anyone could understand the "monstrous verbiage" of this "world famous writer." Thousands of copies of Mann's "wise words" were being distributed through the world: "to think that all of humanity – educated and uneducated alike – was supposed to listen to them!" Was "stunned humanity just supposed to be befuddled by it?" The paper hypothesized that if the average German really did comprehend the speech, he would have "let loose with his fists" and booksellers would have thrown peddlers of Mann's speech out of the door. "What did the association of *Jewish Faith* like about this statement?" Most likely, the paper hypothesized, its message that "the Nazi movement was a relapse into a barbaric cult of nature from which Judaism had carefully saved humanity." It was time to resist, the *Völkischer Beobachter* declared, when this "pseudo-German writer" appealed to reason though he showed no sign of "German reason" at all.[37]

Nazis were further infuriated when Mann "showed up in Paris" to give speeches on *rapprochement*. According to the *Völkischer Beobachter*, he had been invited by Freemasons and Jews who celebrated him as a "great European" and a "sincere Republican." Clearly, such estimations were "well deserved" because he was "singing hymns to German democracy and telling astounded Parisians that the Volk was developing an atmosphere where things like freedom, spirituality, and culture were being granted for the first time – and that the result would be a politics of peace between Germany and France."[38] In Paris, his name stood "against anti-Semitism and German nationalism," on the one hand, and for "every form of cultural-Bolshevik harassment," on the other.[39] Gradually the paper came to associate Mann with the threat of communism itself. In 1931, as Nazi–KPD competition intensified, it contended that he had recently discovered a "new love," and it was far from "non-political."

In a recent "so-called" German speech, Mann had referred to the "spiritual friendliness" of Marxist cultural policies. By thus expressing his "respectful devotion to Bolshevism," this "exponent of a long rotten liberal-bourgeois epoch" had found his home: Mann symbolized the "capitulation of a powerless world that had long ago submitted to psycho-analytical dissection – and was now submitting to Bolshevism." If he could say this, then Mann certainly sympathized with the "revolutionary pogroms of Bolshevik criminals."[40] Richard von Schaukal, a nationalistic Austrian poet and essayist who was a regular correspondent with Mann until the latter broke off the exchange, agreed that Mann's "only passionate conviction" was that a policy of "Marxism here, Marxism there" would bring about the deliverance of the German people.[41]

The height of *Völkischer Beobachter* harassment occurred after Mann left Germany and began his series of wartime anti-Nazi broadcasts. In response, the newspaper ran an open letter – signed with the pseudonym, "Lanzelot" – which sought to summarize Nazi frustration toward Mann's evolving treachery. Mann's new audiences Lanzelot complained, did not know about all the changes his political character had gone through, so it would not be difficult for him to distance himself from Germany. In the narrow-minded Anglo-Saxon world, the "fine airs of aestheticism" that he always knew how to put on would earn him the reputation as a "Saint of the European Spirit." Over there they would "suck the honey from his lips – though in Germany he was always just: Thomas Mann."

Lanzelot admitted that it had taken some time for Germans to recognize the decadence that lay behind his "calls to humanity," the conceit behind his "phony dialogues with the greats of German spirit," and, finally, how media praise harmonized with his book sales ("what they called 'business' in his newly chosen homeland"). At first, "tears rose even in the eyes of East Prussian Junkers when he swore to the conservatism of his Hanseatic homeland." For members of the religious Center, he produced passages that "could be set to music for congregational singing." Then, Liberals listened with emotion to his "cosmopolitan siren-songs" for the November Republic: "whenever there was something rotten in that former state, he applied his magic." After that, though, things fell apart for this "political chameleon": imagining himself secure, Mann "tripped up" by attacking the nationalistic youth of Germany in an interview with a French journal, using this as an opportunity to market himself in France where they were very happy to hear German patriots scolded by a "prominent intellectual."

But what Mann was saying over the American airwaves in 1940 was even worse. The "clouds of incense in which Mann always floated had obscured his vision," and out of "spiritless animosity" he refused to devote "even a thought – let alone his heart – to the revolutionary battle of National Socialism." Unbeknown to him, the German Volk he tried to mentor had passed him by. But "he wouldn't have been Thomas Mann" had he been able to resist "waving his tail before a new idol: Franklin Roosevelt." The American president surely loved being praised as a "modern mass leader" by this "seasoned salesman in the market of vanity." Nonetheless, the result of Mann's whole life was nothing but "empty thought formed in frozen splendor." He had spent his career "dancing on the ice of politics – slipping around the corner of history." Now all he could do was "spit over the fence" at the Germany he had left.[42]

Another major figure the *Völkischer Beobachter* rejected as out of touch with reality was Albert Einstein (1879–1955). In a 1923 article, the paper announced that it was going to spell out the "unadorned truth" about the developer of the "so-called theory" of relativity. Unfortunately, from the Nazi perspective, newspapers and journals had spread word of his "great achievement" throughout the world, even though they "hardly understand it at all." Einstein was more a media sensation than a scientific researcher, and his theory – despite the high praise accorded it – provided nothing of any value: the only thing new about it was the mathematical form in which it "expressed its futility." Einstein's way of "using the mathematical arts to do physical science was comparable to a surgeon interested only in style, without care for whether his patients live or die."

Despite these problems, Einstein's friends and followers constantly praised his teachings as the most wonderful discoveries of all time. Even physics journals "glorified him to the point where they wouldn't publish any criticism of his theory." This, the *Völkischer Beobachter* lamented, was typical of the direction physics was taking: researchers were not interested in experimentation, or dealing with reality at all, but only in working with "mathematical meditations." Theories, the newspaper argued, were useful only as long as they were based on experimental realities. But unfortunately they were increasingly considered decisive in and of themselves: theorists like Einstein were presumed to be making major contributions, while experimental researchers – for all their careful work and sharp wit – were perceived as nothing but "handymen." According to the Nazi critique, the history of natural sciences showed that the opposite was true: it was the experimenter who really followed the natural course of events, while mathematics was merely a tool. It was therefore strange that Einstein's course of research had become established and validated in Germany. In response, the paper held that it was "necessary to preserve a homeland for the German spirit that strove for truth and clear insight," by refusing any further advancement of this "arid, ghostly anti-spirit" that had "nothing to do with true scientific research."[43]

As would become increasingly clear, the *Völkischer Beobachter* attitude toward Einstein had less to do with his scientific work than with his engagement in the social and political issues of the day. Indeed, by 1923 the paper concluded that the battle over the Theory of Relativity had ended because "its hollowness had already been sufficiently perceived." As for physics, "Mr. Einstein was free to quietly retire." Still, under the title, "Einstein as Jew," the paper believed it necessary to set the record straight "once and for all" because "a sort of Einstein cult had arisen, bordering on a religious fervor." The "Jewish press" was presenting him as a role model, and even others were saying that Einstein deserved admiration. In order to "tame some of this foolishness," the *Völkischer Beobachter* wanted to "lay out a few facts." First, it reminded readers that in 1914, "ninety-three scholars had stood up against campaigns of destruction and lies launched by Germany's enemies – which was a natural step in a time of national awakening." However, along with Professor Georg Nicolai, also in physics at the University of Berlin, Einstein took the "meritorious act" of issuing a pacifist statement against the actions of the "ninety-three." In addition, Einstein and Nicolai formed an organization – the New Fatherland League – with other "traitorous pacifists" like Hellmut von Gerlach and Maximillian Harden. The organization was dedicated, the *Völkischer Beobachter* explained, to proving Germany's responsibility for the war, increasing the nation's burden in the form of disarmament, and "senselessly acting as informants to the French authorities by telling them that our disarmament policies were merely deceptions, thereby giving them fresh justifications for their sanctions."

Beyond this, Einstein undertook "Zionist fund-raising tours" of the United States to gather funds for a university in Palestine. On these trips, the paper claimed, he was taken from city to city in motorcades, "though owners of Ford automobiles were prevented from participating because the maker of these cars, Henry Ford, was an anti-Semite." Then, while American Jews stood in tight ranks behind him, "ready for battle,"

Einstein gave speeches in which he "abused the Germany that gave him shelter and support." The *Völkischer Beobachter* saw hypocrisy in all Einstein's appearances: when he was "among his kind," he presented himself as a Zionist Jew; but when it was useful, he acted as the representative and personification of German scholarship: "first Zionist Jew, then international Jew, then German, then back to Swiss."

In this vein, the *Völkischer Beobachter* contended that the "summit" of Einstein's achievements was a trip he made to France. There he took a tour of the former front to directly observe the destruction wrought in the war (caused, according to the *Völkischer Beobachter*, mainly by British guns that German troops resisted gloriously). Einstein had himself photographed at particularly "interesting" spots, such as the monument to Joan of Arc, the ruins of Reims Cathedral, a German bunker, and a destroyed village. In addition he said to the French: "All German students, all students from around the world, must come here to see how horrible the war was." Here the *Völkischer Beobachter* interjected that Einstein should have said that "Jews must visit because during the war they mainly remained behind the lines and didn't see any of this." It also suggested that Jews should do this because, "as everyone knows, the insidious baiting and greed of their financial overlords fomented the war."

In any case, the paper condemned the whole undertaking as a farce: "What could Einstein – who was 'a Jew and only a Jew,' as he said himself – really feel in front of a destroyed cathedral anyway?" The blood of every former front soldier had to boil when the "great goals for which they placed their lives on the line for years" were being "cannibalized, dragged through filth, and used against the nation in true Jewish fashion by a foreigner like Einstein who enjoyed all the advantages available to him in Germany, just as he did during the war." The paper could explain this "mean-spirited behavior" only by taking into account Einstein's "racial heritage" – a heritage that Einstein himself described in a letter to the Central Association of German Citizens of Jewish Faith, supposedly stating that he was "a Jew and nothing but a Jew," that he "had nothing to do with Germanness," and that "his relations with Eastern Jews were more important to him than any connections with Germany."[44] In light of all this, the *Völkischer Beobachter* was shocked by the stupidity of non-Jewish German scholars who were placing him in the first rank of German science just because of the "superficial gloss" of his "so-called theory and a few other card tricks." "Let Mr. Einstein finally go to Palestine, or

Pepperland for that matter," it concluded, "we're sick of spending our tax money on people who behave like this at our universities."[45]

Turning to the visual arts, the *Völkischer Beobachter* was inclined to treat the leading artists of the inter-war era as fixated on distortion, intent on undermining order and security, and overly inspired by shadowy race-based influences. For instance, while the paper was surprisingly respectful of Pablo Picasso (1881–1973), especially in his early stages, it seemed content to assess his work as merely symptomatic of anxious modernity. As an eighteen year old, it related, he still painted in Spain, the country of orthodoxy – with all "its heaviness and deep sentimentality symbolized in funeral processions." He then moved to Paris and at first things did not go well there, so depression drove him to paint the *Absinthe Drinker* (1901), "an image of the deepest despair, approaching nihilism." He then shifted to group portraits – "from the I to the We" – in *The Tragedy* (1903), with figures worn by hunger and poverty. Thereafter, came works reminiscent of "Negro statuary." But he was "Roman – a Latin – so the great classical tradition boiled in his blood," and in 1906 his work "gradually built to an explosion" with *A Boy with a Horse* (Figure 15.1).

However this neoclassical phase arose right next to paintings of pronounced cubism, such as *The Violin* (1912), where "large, heavy shadows threatened to devour shapes against which he battled." What lay behind this stage of Picasso's art, the *Völkischer Beobachter* explained, was the "urge to resist a calmer outlook through acts of violence." It had been the means by which barbarian peoples were introduced to the rich symbolic world of Rome. "Forms pressed themselves forward urgently, while human figures were represented as objects: paradox dominated throughout." The tragedy of the new era was that no one knew how to resolve paradox any more: "mankind was no longer in control of itself; all were living broken lives." Picasso was a leader in developing such a perspective: he "illuminated the issues of modern painting and contemporary mentality, sharply outlining the follies of racial, blood strangers." The paper acknowledged that he was a man of great talent and many of his well-known paintings were in private German collections. But their "inconsistencies" were a troubling sign. Some were strongly cubist, some neoclassical, and this variety was not by design: it was "reflective of humans seized by the fear of death, with torn personalities, suffering from anxiety – all due to the mixing of blood and races."[46]

The Bauhaus and its affiliated architects and artists prompted a different response from the *Völkischer Beobachter*. Its critique of Bauhaus

Figure 15.1 Pablo Picasso, *A Boy with a Horse* (1906), Museum of Modern Art, New York, USA

architecture amounted to a straightforward attack against its "insistence on the most modern, economical construction, standardization of buildings in all details, rational use of space," and "a number of other slogans with American color." As the paper put it, the quintessence of Bauhaus modernism in workers' housing was "economy taken to the extreme, with unlimited priority given to function." Without considering that these methods were good only for larger, more extensive projects, Bauhaus designers built homes out of concrete and steel, reducing construction time by "plowing through the site" with the most modern techniques. The

Sachlichkeit of these buildings spoke for itself: according to Bauhaus logic, if one wanted to build something functional and economical, "aesthetics had to come second."[47]

Less neatly articulated was the paper's treatment of the Bauhaus' most prominent visual artist, Wassily Kandinsky (1866–1944). For instance, in an article regarding a 1932 exhibition of Kandinsky's drawings, instead of taking on the works of the Russian painter directly, it chose to merely deride another paper's positive review. "These rectangles of paper," the positive review ran, "convey distant memories of things observed – in half moons, rotating suns, squares, boxed-in bodies, a considerable treasure of graphic wisdom is preserved." In response, the *Völkischer Beobachter* noted that Kandinsky's works instead instinctively recalled and evoked one's schooldays and very "dim memories" of the Pythagorean Theorem or the Golden Section. Whatever such memories Kandinsky was "skimming up with his graphic wisdom could only be explained by a psychoanalyst, say by Freud." About a work described as a "mysteriously arresting puzzle" with a "right angle consisting of five-times-four quadrants in broad lines in the upper left corner, and a small rectangle of three-times-three quadrants in lighter strokes in the lower right," the paper claimed that it could easily provide the solution: "Twenty large quadrants plus nine small ones equaled twenty-nine cash registers in a Jewish warehouse! Right?" And against the warning that cynics might say a child could create such simple forms, the *Völkischer Beobachter* posited its belief that normal children had healthier and more reasonable things to draw: the whole thing was "Cabbalistic vinegar," a "witches' multiplication table" resting on "Hebraic topsoil."[48]

Comparable with the literary controversy over *All Quiet on the Western Front*, the major Nazi *cause célèbre* in the visual arts was the trial of George Grosz (1893–1959). In 1928, Grosz was found guilty on a charge of blasphemy for the content of a series of sixteen drawings entitled *Background*. An appellate judge later reversed the conviction on grounds that the works were targeted at the military rather than at Christianity. As the controversy dragged out, the *Völkischer Beobachter* set upon both Grosz and the judge. It complained that the appellate judge, *Landgerichtsdirektor* Siegert, deeply injured public religious sentiment with his ruling. It did not require "full juridical training" to recognize Grosz's intention to disparage Christian symbols and the person of the Christ; the acquittal ridiculed Christianity and "opened the way for any dirty slugs" to mock Christ and the faith. The courts should have instead

die Ausschüttung des heiligen Geistes

Figure 15.2 George Grosz, *The Outpouring of the Holy Spirit* (1927)

been working to "protect popular religious feeling from injury by such painters."[49]

Among the drawings in the series, the paper singled out as particularly odious the drawing entitled *The Outpouring of the Holy Spirit* (1927) (Figure 15.2) in which a minister holds the Bible while vomiting grenades, cannons, and rifles. When the case came to court again in 1930, the paper ran a detailed description of the proceedings. In response to questioning by the judge, according to the *Völkischer Beobachter*, Grosz admitted that he had not been acquainted with the war "directly, physically, [or] in person," that he was a member of the Communist Party, and that he was against the war. Through the series of drawings, Grosz said that he "wanted to confront the clergymen who supported the war." The court then addressed one of the drawings, *Maulhalten, weiterdienen* (1928), which depicted Jesus on the cross and wearing half-length military boots. In defending the work, Grosz gave the following explanation:

> *If Christ were to have come back to earth he would have had no choice but to go into the trenches. Then he would have been equipped with a rifle and a gas mask just as I drew him, and one would have said to him just as to any other soldier, "shut your trap and keep moving!"* [Maulhalten, weiterdienen]*, just as I have written under my drawing.*[50]

For the *Völkischer Beobachter*, there was no doubt that Grosz and his "disgraceful images" were guilty of "besmirching Christ on the Cross"[51] (Figure 15.3).

 With its outlook so strongly rooted in the romantic German music tradition, however, what the *Völkischer Beobachter* found most detestable in Weimar culture was the cultivation of musical modernism, the whole of which it referred to as, "at best, the farcical imitation of a carnival barker selling a tent full of musical freaks,"[52] and, at worst, "Jewish terror in music."[53] The newspaper stood firm in its rejection of works by "Jews and assorted foreigners" like Weill, Milhaud, Janáček, and Stravinsky,[54] or by Germans like Paul Hindemith who supposedly associated with "international, Jewish circles."[55] And, predictably, it applauded "brave acts of resistance" against the influx of modernism, such as when a lone Nazi (*Hakenkreuzler*) stood up and shouted "phooey" at a concert of Schoenberg, Hindemith, Stravinsky, and Bartók.[56]

 The "musical foreigner" whom the *Völkischer Beobachter* derided most was Igor Stravinsky (1882–1971). While an early attack identified him as a "spiritual Polack,"[57] Fritz Stege described Stravinsky as a "Russian composer with half-Asiatic instincts hidden under the cover of French civilization," who simply knew how to manipulate open-minded German concert-goers as "objects of speculation." Not a year passed, according to Stege, when Stravinsky didn't travel around in Germany "acting as his own propaganda chief and advertising for his wretched, shameful works." The worst of all was that his "barren music of noise without any real ideas, full of hysterical orchestral outbreaks and strongly carnevalesque or jazz sections," found an enthusiastic public among Germans.[58] Herbert Gerigk – editor of the *Lexicon of Jews in Music* and editor-in-chief of *Die Musik* as it was thoroughly Nazified – wondered at the fact that Stravinsky's music to the *Rite of Spring* was able to move

Figure 15.3 *Völkischer Beobachter*, Grosz article and cartoon: Siegert: "Were you personally in the war?" George Grosz: "No!" *Shut Your Trap and Keep Moving!*, 12 June 1930

people so strongly: its popularity was clearly a "massive overestimation of Stravinsky's art – the substance of which was really weak."[59]

Of all the manifestations of musical modernism in the Weimar era, however, the event which received the most attention in the *Völkischer Beobachter* was the 1927 opening of Ernst Krenek's operetta, *Jonny Strikes Up* (*Jonny spielt auf*), which featured as its lead character a black American jazz violinist (played in blackface) working in the streets of Paris.[60] Together with the controversy surrounding *All Quiet on the Western Front* in literature and film, and the George Grosz blasphemy trial in the visual arts, the *Völkischer Beobachter* commotion over Krenek's *Zeitoper* completed a triptych of overwrought Nazi criticism of Weimar culture. In its criticism of the operetta, the paper found an opportunity to voice every major element of its vendetta against postwar German society and politics as a whole.

Writing for the paper, F. A. Hauptmann, a leader of National Socialist cultural initiatives in Leipzig who was on the *Völkischer Beobachter* staff after 1925,[61] reported that he was ashamed that the premiere took place at the Stadttheater of his home town "in the heart of Germany." Immediately resorting to a racist take on the event, Hauptmann wrote that, "even if he didn't look it," the composer Krenek (1900–1991) could be counted as Jewish "since he married the daughter of the Jew Gustav Mahler and studied with the Jew Franz Schreker." Moreover, while all of Krenek's music was "soft and effeminate" and therefore "typically Jewish," *Jonny spielt auf* – in which "a black hero seduced white women and stole valuable violins" – was most troubling. Full of jazz rhythms, it was really a jazz opera and its "deep meaning" was simply that "life is just a game: we'll dance and stumble through it, then let ourselves be finished off by Jonny the Nigger."[62] The newspaper even ran on its front page excerpts from the libretto that angered Nazis in particular. Here, Jonny praises the "Jew god," Jehovah. Then, Jonny claims that he would conquer the world, including Europe, by taking advantage of the popularity of dancing to jazz music. Finally, the scene in which he seduces the white female lead, Yvonne.[63] "Worthless and unworthy of German theater, the show did nothing but aggravate the shameless conditions of the day." For Hauptmann it seemed unnecessary to point out how this opera symbolized issues such as the "annihilation of Aryans by niggers" and the "mastery of foreign races over German culture."[64]

When the work was produced in Dresden, the *Völkischer Beobachter* decried it as a "monstrous invention of insanity," which proved that the "Jewish theater and press industry" had "stolen healthy sentiment" from the German soul: "performing noise instead of music was boring; jazzified dancing was abominable."[65] By December, the "battle against Jonny" spread to the newspaper's home in Bavaria, and it wondered what the state government was going to do about this "so-called opera that was really an apotheosis of nigger-ness" and was symbolic of the "black scandal on the Rhine" (in reference to the French occupation of the Rhineland, which was supported by African troops). Was the Bavarian state ready to "ban this piece of junk in the interest of fighting smut and filth?"[66] According to Hans Buchner, supporters of Jonny and his jazz opera were the enemies of classical and romantic opera music. Bourgeois taste had collapsed after the catastrophe of the First World War: there was no more creative strength, no more cultural leadership, and no more will to resist the new trends. This was all leading to the "bolshevization of life forms and content," the "rise of negro culture," and (however improbably) to "systematic anarchy." Theater, music, journalism, film: all were affected. Bolshevik conditions would give rise to a "mass man," not a Volk. Popular music had influenced opera before, but Krenek not only incorporated jazz, he also employed an abrasive modernist style. For Buchner, *Jonny* was "no opera – not even a jazz opera." A "mirror of the times reflecting the postwar world precisely, it was destined to failure."[67] For the paper, the popularity of Krenek was a sign of weakness (not, in this case, *Volkstümlichkeit*): "geniuses were understood only by their equals; those the public honored were just pseudogeniuses." To pursue an idea without concern for making money was "truly German"; seeking financial success was "typically Jewish." The reception of Wagner and Krenek marked this difference: "Wagner had to work for his acclaim while Krenek had it easy."[68]

In January 1928, as the *Völkischer Beobachter* was pleased to report, the show's opening at the Vienna Staatsoper was met with protesters who ignited stink bombs and spread slag powder around the entrance.[69] But it was disappointed that police officers had been stationed around the theater, to arrest hecklers against this "Jewish disgrace."[70] Krenek, the paper said, acted as if he was inspired by the "deeply religious" Bach chorale, *Jesus, meine Zuversicht*, but he "made it into a foxtrot" and then wrote an opera in which "the black race is depicted as triumphing over whites."[71] Despite Alfred Rosenberg's advocacy for legal measures against the "nigger-jazz-opera," Jonny was "still striking up the band."[72] Blacks were "raping German girls and women along the Rhine" while people were roaring approval of this "negro culture" – and whoever stood up against it was beaten and arrested by the police who "protected the aristocracy of November Germany." While poor proletarians looked on, the "chosen people" would drive up to the event in their Citroëns, Chryslers, and Chevrolets: "fat, overfed Asiatics with slim, blond German girls by their sides because they bought them with money." If anyone resisted the production by throwing out their right arm and shouting, *Heil Hitler! Heil Deutschland!* – "the lonely cry of tormented hearts, the cry of German fighters" – police harassed them. If Germany was ever to arise again, the whole Weimar "system" would have to be "completely rooted out, along with all its leaders."[73]

354 / "Holy" War and Weimar "Crisis"

Wilhelm Weiss, the former Imperial Army officer who replaced Alfred Rosenberg as editor-in-chief of the *Völkischer Beobachter* in 1928, occasionally contributed to the art section before and after assuming editorship of the paper.[74] He added to the *Jonny* harangue as well. There were people out there, he wrote, who saw this "negro in knickerbockers" – with his "primitive prurience and exotic vitality" – as the fulfillment of a modernist ideal for humanity, and did so "in recognition of their own sterility and resignation to the downfall of Europe." Did this mark the decline and fall of Western civilization? No, Weiss wrote, just the decline and fall of a period that had "confused nigger kitsch with the rhythm of life: *that* world could just go to hell – even with police protection!"[75]

The fact that German authorities allowed performances of *Jonny spielt auf* to continue was a constant source of irritation to the *Völkischer Beobachter*. "Jonny steals a violin, then rapes a white woman, so German citizens of German spirit who see this as undermining popular morality await a ban from an all-Christian [Centrist] government," and yet the government does nothing, the paper complained. Instead, police protected theater entrances – "*ad majorem gloriam* Jonnys" – while a "bastardized" Volk "that had lost all feeling for its race roared approval inside." Nazis whistled and roared, "phooey, phooey!," but the cops intervened "in the name of free speech and order."[76] Baldur von Schirach wrote an article describing his own experience of being arrested for yelling "phooey" at a performance of the opera.[77] Once Munich had a beautiful opera house, von Schirach recalled, but along came Jonny, a "poisonous half-ape right out of the Jewish bazaar of artsy trash."[78] Still, the authorities did nothing to stop this "mockery of Germans" and – even worse – the "Marxist Jews at the top" were denouncing National Socialists for fighting against it. The paper demanded that this "nigger scandal" be driven out of Munich at least – and, indeed, failure to do so would be an indication of the Bavarian government's total ineptitude.[79] Later, when news came that Chancellor Wilhelm Marx of the largely Catholic Center Party had attended a performance in Berlin, the *Völkischer Beobachter* used Jonny as a catalyst for attacking the political situation on the national level. The supposed defenders of Christian morality were protecting and enjoying Jonny: a sign that "the Center was working together with the Marxists."[80]

Ultimately, the "scandal" spread beyond German borders. Ironically, the *Völkischer Beobachter* found itself in agreement with the

Parisian press, which was also critical of the opera. It interpreted this alignment as proof that there were still "somewhat healthy racial elements" among Parisians who, despite the "colored French army," rejected the "niggerization of Western humanity as much as we Germans."[81] About the show's opening in New York, the paper claimed that because Americans feared demonstrations, producers cast Jonny as a white man, thus mitigating the issue.[82] Still, Jonny was playing on all opera stages, not just German ones, and this demonstrated that "niggerness [was] being glorified throughout the world, wherever it was inhabited by whites." That the "white race" – and here the paper stipulated that it was using the word "only to describe skin color" – tolerated this jazz opera was clear justification for Oswald Spengler's pessimism regarding the culture of the West. In Germany and abroad it was not the Volk but "masses of Jews," those with "Jewish family ties," and "upstarts completely without national character" who dominated the theater public that delighted in Jonny.[83] In the end, the newspaper could explain successes of *Jonny Strikes Up*, *The Threepenny Opera*, and similar productions that "glorified subhumanity" only by pointing out the existence of audiences with "shockingly limited national consciousness." In Germany, a conspiratorial Weimar culture had brought this about: through the modern media, "Marxists had gassed the brains of the public to a horrific degree."[84]

But for all the attention they devoted to Krenek's *Zeitoper*, even more infuriating to Nazi critics was what Arnold Schoenberg (1874–1951) conceived as polytonality. Already in 1920, Hans Buchner reported on the growing presence of the Second Vienna School in German programs, referring to Schoenberg as the "pathbreaker of absolute polyphony, the modern compositional technique that had been inaugurated by another Jewish composer: Gustav Mahler." Buchner complained that this stylistic direction, already part of the "strongly Semitic" artistic life in Austria, was gaining a solid foothold in Germany.[85] A few months later he added that this "philo-Semitic movement" presumed Schoenberg had discovered the Philosopher's Stone, which provided "aesthetic formulas for all manifestations and possibilities of modern music." Especially after the collapse of the Second Reich, such developments "constituted a significant threat to volkish consciousness and weakened hope for the future." But all its apparent successes, Buchner insisted, were really just "propaganda perpetrated by a goal-oriented press whose cultural criticism shied neither from concealed nor open demagoguery, though the conservative opposition never stooped to such methods." Buchner warned that it would take years of hard work to re-establish the worldwide reputation of German music, based on music judged according to "deeds and accomplishments rather the philo-Semitic modernism of supply and demand."[86] Two years later, another contributor chimed in to describe Schoenberg as a "prophet who had wandered in from Jerusalem; the herald of the modern era; an apostle for whom nothing sacred could be trivialized enough; a philosopher and thinker without a head; a lemonade and sugar manufacturer who did a little painting on the side." The *Völkischer Beobachter* asked: "Could anyone take such a man seriously?"[87] Buchner, for one, could. He subsequently intensified his rhetoric in the paper by arguing that Schoenberg's "Jewish-Viennese clique" was committing "musical exorcisms and rapes that were beyond the pale."[88]

Despite assertions that Schoenberg and his followers would "amount to nothing in music history,"[89] the newspaper was obliged to report in 1926 that the Accademia di Santa Cecilia in Rome was making the "founder of so-called atonal music – the Viennese Jew" an honorary member. This came as a shock to the *Völkischer Beobachter*, which found it remarkable that such a traditional institution would take into its ranks the founder of "music-bolshevism" – the leader of "Jewish-international fashion" – just when Italian nationalistic sentiment was at its strongest under Mussolini. The paper had to assume that all this was the work of the wife of the former Italian envoy to Vienna, Luca Orsini-Baroni, "who was a Jew." Accepting the "commander-in-chief of atonal noisemakers in Germany" as a member in the home of *bel canto* might have been seen as a hilarious joke, the paper said, "if Jews weren't behind it, as always."[90] Still, the paper was confident that while the reputation of a "true German like Händel" would live on for another 200 years, it was doubtful that anyone would ever say or hear anything about Schoenberg in the year 2128.[91]

Meanwhile, on 24 February 1933, a month after the Nazi "seizure of power," Schoenberg was still around to give a lecture at the Society for New Music and the *Völkischer Beobachter* reacted predictably. Any "healthy thinking person," it commented, considers as simply repulsive Schoenberg's "sickly and convulsive" efforts – "to be taken seriously; to impress his audience with witticisms of typical Jewish dialectics; to cover over the inner hollowness and instability of his ideas with a flood of words." But for Nazis, "the spiritual movement breaking through at that very moment gave them reason to hope that music would not remain under his destructive influence much longer."[92] Indeed, five years later, the paper felt it could look back on musical modernism as a distasteful thing of the past. It was clear, in retrospect, that these forces arose out of a state of crisis, but pointed in directions that could only lead to "error, degeneration, and corruption." Perhaps other peoples and races thought and felt in terms of dissonant tones, but to Germans they were "alien." Atonality was the "bogeyman" of those days: the "Jew Schoenberg made it into a principle, and the destruction of form naturally followed." This style was "undoubtedly degenerate, because it broke from the foundations appropriate to German musical taste." Indeed, Schoenberg's own compositions provided the best evidence of the futility of his theory: combining many elements that "seemed fascinating in postwar years dominated by a mood of doom, they ended in nothing but chaotic nihilism."[93] In the face of Schoenberg's modernist art of "doom" and "nihilism," ostensibly so emblematic of the Weimar era as a whole, the *Völkischer Beobachter* insisted that a great change in German cultural history was occurring with the rise of Adolf Hitler and the Nazi Party.

PART V
NAZI "SOLUTIONS"

16 "HONOR YOUR GERMAN MASTERS"

This book has shown how Nazi ideologues worked to demonstrate that their ideals were rooted in the Western cultural past. Establishing legitimacy based on tradition through invocation of the ideas and creations of historical "masters" was, as George Mosse argued, intended to make men "feel at home in this world by providing them with a reality other than that of daily life in an industrializing society" – with "a world where 'everything was in its appointed place'; a world where one was 'at home.'" In every form of artistic representation and with regard to every topic, Nazi culture addressed the "desire for permanence and fixed reference points in a changing world."[1]

Hitler was adamant about the need to preserve such reference points across every facet of his nationalized culture. From the earliest stages of his career, he had dedicated himself to applying whatever measures were required to prevent the further denigration by modern society of German cultural heritage:

> The saddest thing about the state of our whole culture of the prewar period was ... the hatred with which the memory of the greater past was besmirched and effaced. In nearly all fields of art, especially in the theater and literature, we began around the turn of the century to produce less that was new and significant, but to disparage the best of the old work and represent it as inferior and surpassed ... And from this effort to remove the past from the eyes of the present, the evil intent of the apostles of the future could clearly and distinctly be seen.[2]

Hitler thus sought to nullify the defining characteristics of modernism – its rejection of the received cultural hierarchies and traditions – by casting modernism and its apostles as an essentially destructive force that had utterly failed to produce work of any lasting value. The expression of such an impulse had no potential. The basis for a culture of the future must be grounded in a stable cultural tradition rather than in its denunciation. Hitler thus averred that "every true renaissance of humanity can start with an easy mind from the good achievements of past generations; in fact, can often make them truly appreciated for the first time."[3]

And indeed, as contributors to the *Völkischer Beobachter*'s cultural section would frequently contend, it was the "renaissance of humanity" made possible by the ascendancy of the Third Reich that would for the first time make Germans truly appreciate the cultural achievements of the past. We will see below how the paper's cultural critics covered some of the figures they accepted as creators of a new Nazi cultural tradition. But their underlying goal in all such coverage was to demonstrate that it was only through National Socialist interpretations, policies, and commemorations that the Western tradition came to full consciousness in German minds. So, we return now to the paper's coverage of historical masters as "honored" in National Socialist as opposed to "Weimar" fashion, both before and after Hitler took power, in ways that synchronized with the party's immediate leadership, policies, and views instead of just deriding others.[4]

According to the *Völkischer Beobachter*, for example, until the Nazi "seizure of power" in 1933 and the coinciding 450th anniversary of Luther's birth, the anti-Jewish component of Luther's legacy had been ignored because a "liberal" or "objective" form of Protestantism had dominated. In particular, until Nazi rule had commenced, none of the professional Luther scholars considered it important to look into his attitude toward the "Jewish Question." This oversight, said the paper, was typical of all "so-called objective" research that "passed over the issues essential to national survival."[5] But such a state of affairs would change in the Nazi era: as it was in Luther's day, a "deep longing for true renewal" was now coursing through the German Church; "under the sign of national revolution, the inner life of Germany is going to be transformed by the will of a German reformer."[6] In the words of Wilhelm Frick, the Volk was being "awakened from its torpor, shaken out of indifference to start a new life, and called by God to renewed action – just as during the great transformation of the sixteenth century."[7]

Voices of the "new" Protestant Church, "intent on renewal according to old German principles," were given full sway in the *Völkischer Beobachter*. Bavarian *Landesbischof*, Ludwig Müller, head of the *Deutsche Christen*, held that change would occur within the German Evangelical Church that could be understood only with reference to the "background of the recent German uprising and revolution." In his view, the Nazi movement, "born of faith, confidence, loyalty, and obedience," had a "strong spiritual component." In the Third Reich, church and state would be tightly bound together because, according to Müller, the Protestant Church had the mission of "underpinning the new order from within."[8] Karl Bornhausen also felt that increased statism would heighten Protestant faith, since the "German Evangelium" of Luther was manifested in "obedience, service, and sacrifice." Germans could not exist without ideals of both freedom and duty, inspiring them to "freely choose to give hand and heart, love and life to their country."

In addition, Bornhausen believed that a state-bound, Nazified Protestantism would complement the heightened spiritualism of the new regime. To him, singing the hymn, *A Mighty Fortress is Our God*, at the church services of the SA constituted a "complete expression of the renewed German will to life." Bornhausen looked to the Nazi era for a greater sense of national and religious unity, finding it striking that in National Socialist Germany, Luther was "enthusiastically greeted and understood as a German Führer by both Protestants and Catholics." As the Volk experienced its "breakthrough to genuine unity," it had to acknowledge the thanks it owed to Luther. With Nazi rule it would become clearer that "one could learn the fundamental terms of the National Socialist view of life from him." It had taken 400 years for German souls to mature: a century earlier Luther's German language had blossomed in Herder, Goethe, Schiller, and Schleiermacher; but then "a storm broke over the field and destroyed much." Nevertheless, with the rise of Hitler, "Germans were again striding toward the harvest."[9] Wilhelm Farnhorst, director of the *Evangelischer Bund*, sounded the same theme of national and religious unification through contemplation of Luther: "National Socialism – a world view born of the Volk; and Protestantism – a faith born of the Volk, belonged together inseparably." As National Socialism united Germany politically, Protestantism would "do the same in religion."[10]

August Jager, who lead a major campaign against resistant pastors, made the paper's most direct connections between the Reformation and Nazism, showing little restraint in equating their two leading figures. It was no accident, he was sure, that the 450th return of Luther's birthday was taking place when the German Volk was reawakening and experiencing its own rebirth. Luther and Hitler were "co-workers" for the salvation of the German Volk: what Luther began in religion, "Hitler was going to finish in blood."[11] Both were "leaders who came to the Germans in times of crisis." Before 1933, Germans lacked the self-discipline and strong belief of a Luther who "overcame all devils, like a mighty fortress."[12] But then Luther began to re-emerge as a "German hero who went his own way with incomparable personal courage, standing up to anything with never-failing bravery" – the "first great political and spiritual Führer of German society; the proto-type for the new one who was on the way."[13] In Luther came a leader whose "strength of will, intelligence, commitment to truth, courage, and obstinacy could not be equaled."[14] Identifying him as a courageous superhero, Bornhausen actually broke into verse full of medieval imagery of knights in shining armor, avowing Luther's "German mission" with joy:

> He swung his sword
> High over the dragon of the day.
> With fiery tongue
> He impressed his Word on eternity.
> He broke his bread with the poor.
> He aided the weak.
> Father, have pity on the Volk,
> Allow Germany to rise from the dead![15]

"Luther's Dream is Our Goal," headlined an article wherein the *Völkischer Beobachter* emphatically asserted that Nazi history flowed from Luther to Hitler. At a time when the suffering Volk had longed for a word from God, Luther became the "word leader," "showing the direction and providing the solution." Luther's significance lay in his "*Führertum*": his love for the Volk gave him "almost superhuman strength to defy the whole world, the Emperor, and the Pope." He headed a spiritual movement that could only be compared with the "great experience of the Nazi Revolution." It was not Luther's fault that the "great start toward self-consciousness in the Volk," a goal for which Nazis were still struggling, had faded out in the eighteenth century. Only the Prussian state took the message of the "political Luther" as its own and began to unify the nation, though even Bismarck could not fully form it. But Hitler had inherited Luther's legacy: it was clear that "the Nazi era and task were tied to Luther's deed."[16]

On at least one occasion, such intensive co-identification of the two Führers made it difficult to determine which one the *Völkischer Beobachter* was honoring. For instance, the following commemorative poem appeared at the center of a page covering Luther Day in 1933.

> Here speaks a man,
> Who loves his Volk's honor
> With all of his heart.
> Here speaks a man –
> There tremble interests
> Worried only about their business, wealth, and pleasure.
> Here speaks a man,
> Who must lead his German brothers
> out of unprecedented suffering …
> Here speaks a man,
> Who, strong, fighting intensely,
> Can even carry the truth to the enemy.
> Here speaks a man –
> There they err,
> Bound in a circle of fainting by a pact of shame.
> Here speaks a man,
> Who knows about the power of spirit
> With every fiber of his soul …
> Here speaks a man –
> While international organizations
> Fearfully cower and shrink before free acts.
> Here speaks a man,
> Who boldly arises
> And can triumphantly shout: I dare to do so![17]

Any confusion readers might have experienced trying to determine which man was speaking and daring in these verses must have been satisfactory to the *Völkischer Beobachter* staff.

Nazis also highlighted the powerful sense of faith conveyed in Bach's art as central to his contemporary value to the Third Reich: "Today is again a time for the great cantor of the Thomaskirche: the present is once more a time of great transition. We will not be strong enough [to master it] without faith, and no one has given clearer musical expression to faith than Bach."[18] An emotional rather than "technical" approach to Bach's work was fundamental to National Socialist music aesthetics. According to Hans Buchner, the new Germany had to honor and care for Bach's lifework: only thus could it derive the strength necessary in the struggle "to achieve the great ideal of volkish art."[19] Karl Grunsky agreed that Bach's music was the exemplary model from which one could "apprehend the collective effect of the Nordic legacy."[20]

Moreover, the *Völkischer Beobachter* insisted that Bach's music deserved renewed relevance in the context of twentieth-century German political development. For Buchner, the "fighting spirit and high religious idealism" of the choral cantatas, *The Lord God is a Sun and Shield* and *A Mighty Fortress is Our God*, could conjure for the new era the "national strength of the time when Friedrich the Great stood in the field against a world of enemies." As a symbol of Prussia "struggling and conquering in the spirit of Luther, as well as an emergent volkish Germany," Bach's art had "prophesied the fate of the Fatherland in its present, most severe volkish struggle." By performing such works, present-day musicians could provide the energy necessary to "reconstruct the nation in the spirit of Bach and his time."[21]

Thus did the *Völkischer Beobachter* deem Bach's music a legitimate instrument for propaganda use, noting with approval performances of his Double Violin Concerto on the occasion of Hitler's birthday in 1933,[22] and a number of festivals marked by commentary from Nazi leaders. The most prominent of these was the festival arranged in 1935 to honor the combined birthdays of Bach, Händel, and Schütz: the 250th of the first two and the 350th of the latter. For this celebration of the "Three Old Masters of Music," Goebbels spoke as President of the Reich Culture Chamber at the Berlin Philharmonic, flanked by party banners. In his speech, he touched upon his paradoxical goals of upholding the German music tradition while initiating new music for the Third Reich. He acknowledged that it was impossible to return to styles determined by the conditions of past centuries, but Germans had to work every day to "refresh the forces out of which the great masters created" while simultaneously laying the foundations for "every sort of artistic renaissance and for every sort of musical development." The Three Old Masters, said Goebbels, were German "not only because they shared the blood of the German Volk," but even more because they struggled their whole lives to "master the best forces of Germanness." Their forms had expired, but their spirits lived on; "external conditions changed, but the essence of Germanness remained constant as long as the German Volk lived – and it was the duty of every generation of Germans to ensure its immortality."[23]

Along with works by Bach, Händel's music was also a regular component of concerts sponsored by the party as early as 1922.[24] But the high point of Händel reception in the Nazi era was the festival for the Three Old Masters mentioned above. Seizing upon Händel's ties to Britain, the *Völkischer Beobachter* also used this prewar event to articulate a policy of improving German–British relations – on grounds of racial affinity. Too often, wrote art historian Waldemar Hartmann, the bond based on a "common world view" could be torn apart by "the insanity of fratricidal feuds." Nevertheless, despite all discord, that the "bond of blood had triumphed through centuries" was perceptible in the examples of Shakespeare and Händel: "just as the towering greatness of the former was first recognized in Germany, so did the creativity of the latter receive its earliest acknowledgment in his host country." According to Hartmann, the commemorations of Händel's 250th birthday were particularly suited to strengthen thoughts of "Nordic cultural unity." Awareness of this was strong not only in the National Socialist Third Reich, but also in British circles, he was certain.[25] But by 1936, when the Reich Music Chamber staged the oratorio *Deborah* (1733), in a production combining nine Berlin choruses into a choir consisting of 1,300 singers, *Völkischer Beobachter* comments made explicit a much more aggressive political interpretation of Händel's work. It claimed that the text of *Deborah* contained sections that could have been written explicitly for the present day, namely: "Give to our Volk a Führer whose name is full of victorious renown and honor, whose arm is strengthened with new power, and who will slay the enemy which oppresses us."[26]

Nazi cultural operatives likewise considered Mozart's music a powerful tool for the party and state on the rise. Hans Buchner insisted that it constituted a "political symbol and source of hope": just as in the acts of a great politician or military leader, "expression of volkish fate" in the works of Mozart was what made them "invaluable to Nazis and their time."[27] Tapping into the "fateful qualities of Mozart's legacy" meant performing and interpreting his creations at party events or at least politicizing more ordinary concerts and commemorations. In 1939, a new school for music was established within the Mozarteum in Salzburg. The inauguration – marked by a performance of Mozart's *Jupiter* Symphony – was attended by many Nazi Party and government officials, including *Reichsminister* Bernhard Rust, Salzburg *Gauleiter* Friedrich Rainer, and officers of the *Wehrmacht*. Statements from a podium decorated with flags of the Third Reich linked the life and art of Mozart with the regime. Rust spoke of the legacy of Mozart as "the most important component in an educational system aiming at a true and all-encompassing Volk music culture." The head of the new school, conductor Clemens Krauss, promised, "with all respect for the works of Mozart," to lead the institution "in the spirit of the great artist and educator, Adolf Hitler." This said, the *Völkischer Beobachter*'s Josef Klingenbeck reported, the "cultural-political ceremony" closed with a *Heil-Gruss* to the Führer and the national anthem.[28]

Similarly, on the 125th anniversary of Schiller's death, the *Völkischer Beobachter* insisted that his writings were of particular value to National Socialists – rather than their opponents. "Two proud watchwords of the heroic spirit of this German poet continued to sound from his tomb; two battle cries, glowing with the most splendid faith in the German Volk; two statements that Nazis needed to hammer into their hearts and minds, to make belief in their lives happier and more hopeful even during difficult times." The first was that "Every Volk has its day in history, but the day of the Germans will come at the autumn of all time." The other was that: "The German day will arise when the circle of time closes." These lines, the *Völkischer Beobachter* claimed, proved to Nazis that Schiller was theirs: "like him they saw a political Reich lying in ruins, but also like him, they knew that another Reich, the Reich of the German spirit, remained alive and unconquerable." In the "stillness of their souls they were preserving the most noble and eternal possessions," as he had demanded. In the Weimar era of "external bondage and distress," Nazis held on to them tightly, because they knew that "these alone would raise them above the world of violence and link the great Volk together: German speech, German culture, German faith, German morals, and German blood would bind all Germans of the world into a unified whole."[29]

Schiller therefore provided inspiration for Nazi plans to overcome national crisis and decline by any means necessary, including violence. According to the *Völkischer Beobachter*, "the path would be long and hard" and would require that they "fight with the sword." Just as the Netherlands and Switzerland once had to fight for their freedom, "armed struggle was the only way out of slavery" for Germans. In that hour, "after eternal law and justice had broken down," Schiller would lead the way with his words that "heralded action as the last recourse." *Wilhelm Tell*, especially, could spur Germans to unite as a Volk and take up arms:

> The burden grows unbearable – he reaches
> With hopeful courage up unto the heavens
> And seizes hither his eternal rights ...
> The primal state of nature reappears,
> Where man stands opposite his fellow man –
> As last resort, when not another means
> Is of avail, the sword is given him.[30]

Motivated by Schiller's "poetic creations which constituted a call for freedom, the last barriers between German tribes would be eliminated and all of Germany would be united in a single will" when "millions of lips repeated sacred oaths" that their "singer and prophet" had put forth in *Wilhelm Tell*:

> We will become a single land of brothers,
> Nor shall we part in danger and distress.
> We will be free, just as our fathers were,
> And sooner die, than live in slavery.
> We will rely upon the highest God
> And we shall never fear the might of men.[31]

And in *The Maid of Orleans*:

> Then will come the hour that begins a new era.
> The way that we must pass is narrow and steep.
> Many will falter, but the rest of us must go on.[32]

"Straight out of Schiller's mouth," the *Völkischer Beobachter* trumpeted, these lines exhorted Nazis to "manly action for the freedom and honor of the Fatherland." Attinghausen's orders to the Swiss as they armed themselves to throw off their oppressors carried the same message: "Therefore hold fast together – fast and always."[33] As it armed for the coming of a new German Reich, the NSDAP insisted "Schiller's name would lead them there: the great poet himself would be the Führer leading them in this fight."[34]

Hans Fabricius, who would go on to write an official history of the National Socialist movement, set about articulating more specifically why Germans could see Schiller as "Hitler's Comrade in Arms." Promoting a book he wrote on the subject,[35] he explained his position at length for the *Völkischer Beobachter*. The great Goethe deserved all honor, Fabricius opened, but in his opinion Schiller seemed to "shine as a more appropriate spiritual leader in stormy times." The Volk had to learn to understand this poet "in a new way." Some might have considered it "vulgar" of him to claim Schiller for National Socialism, but Schiller's dramas were all "political songs." One just had to understand politics in the "great and sacred sense" that National Socialism did. "Educated people" may have been able to prove that passages in Schiller's poetry, prose, and letters were not compatible with Nazism, but that did not matter to Fabricius. He knew that at first he would be understood only by those who were "already National Socialist and knew the Nazi outlook from the ground up." But he hoped to help others "learn to understand National Socialism for the first time through Schiller." On the basis of "inner experience," he was certain the spirit that spoke from Schiller's dramas was the "same that inhabited all true National Socialists."

The great figures of the German past, Fabricius went on, "spoke only to those Germans who were awake; they remained mute to those who were asleep." For those who were personally experiencing the "National Socialist awakening," life itself had a new face: "for the first time their lives were filled with profound meaning, and a thousand things and appearances that until then seemed foreign, indifferent, and dead, assumed completely new, lively significance." Moreover, the awakened German also experienced "a renewal of the forgotten Schiller." For Fabricius it was not an exaggeration to say that Germans had forgotten him. In the past, they had been aware of the meaning he had for the Volk. For instance, when he died there were intentions to erect a national monument in his honor. But the "bitter hardships of the Napoleonic wars defeated this plan." Then followed a century in which the "poison of liberal and materialist errors" ate away at the German soul: esteem for Schiller fell; the sense of his greatness died out. The more that "dark powers" weakened the "moral seriousness" of the Volk, the less it understood Schiller's poetry. The German ideals and war aims that he heralded no longer resonated in its "dead soul"; the "enflamed enthusiasm" of his words became "incomprehensible and irrelevant to modern Germans"; the "fiery herald of German will" was slandered as a poet of "pretty phrases." There was no doubt that the "powers which had been poisoning them did all they could – partly in open, partly in secret – to turn the Volk in disgust against this fighter." They saw in him a powerful opponent whose ideas threatened them unremittingly, thinking: "We need to smother the Schiller spirit, or falsify it."

Fabricius insisted that there had been no lack of attempts to make people believe that Schiller, particularly during a period of youthful irresponsibility, had pursued "Volk-destructive goals shared by modern humanitarians." The "so-called republicans" evoked *Fiesco* (1783), "masonic world-citizens" called on *Don Carlos* (1787), and Communists treated *Räuber Moor* (1782) as their own. Unfortunately, "one could make the ignorant masses believe anything," since the capitalist system shut them out from the pleasures of German cultural heritage. Superficial Philistines who "had editions of Schiller gilded and placed in the bookshelf without reading them" could be easily convinced. The problem, Fabricius argued, was that "certain nationalistic phrases" in Schiller's plays were already commonly known among Germans. So "the humanitarians" implied that Schiller regressed in his later works: "over time he sank from realist to ideologue, from republican to servant of princes, from world-citizen to nationalist, from revolutionary to philistine defender of the status quo." To sustain these "fables," they then had to make sure that no one would ever actually read his works. School masters "picked and chewed" the poems so much that they became unappealing to students. Beyond this, they spread the opinion that his "elevated kitsch" was appropriate only for immature youth. Schiller was no longer considered readable: after one's schooldays, a civilized European "could only think of him with a knowing chuckle."

For Fabricius, press coverage of Schiller's 170th birthday made it clear that this "systematic rendering of Schiller as contemptible" had been effectively applied to simple-minded Germans. One "particularly good, patriotic, German paper" had published a tribute that culminated with the assertion that the plays of the greatest German dramatist had become "completely worthless." The author described Schiller's characters as "superficial theater figures" and the Wallenstein Trilogy as "mere theatrical action." Thus did this "bourgeois-national" paper reveal the "groggy state of things": thanks to the "poisonous enemies of the Volk, Germany had forgotten its Schiller." But Fabricius could confirm with pride that the National Socialist press still understood the significance that Schiller's works had for Germany's "future fight." "National Socialists were Schiller's Awakeners: they would awaken those who were sleeping so they could hear their poet again. The sooner this was achieved, the sooner they would be able to shift their attention and finish off the Volk's enemies."[36]

Well after the new Reich was established, the *Völkischer Beobachter* continued to complain about the supposed misinterpretations of Schiller as a Humanist that had predominated before National Socialism had "reawakened the volkish Führer within him." But things had changed, Robert Krötz reported in November 1934, especially for the youth of the nation. By the Weimar era, there had been little trace of Schiller except for "lectures of secondary school teachers that went over the heads of their audiences, and a monument in Weimar that was really dominated by Goethe." Schiller was forgotten because "to the point of nonsense, he became an idol of individualists." But, contrary to such liberal interpretations, Schiller's ideas emphasized volkish and nationalist values that had "no room for cosmopolitanism and teary-eyed humanitarian sentimentality." This fact, Krötz said, constituted Schiller's significance to the newest Nazi generation: this generation was not going to fulfill the role that a "senile bourgeoisie" had in mind for them – that of an arrogant youth that lacked seriousness – but rather it would be a cohort that "perceived in history the sources of insight and knowledge; believed in its time; and recognized what was necessary: good, hard work."[37]

For all Schiller's presumed insight into the future struggle, the *Völkischer Beobachter* still saw Goethe as having "looked forward" with the most "prophetic eyes."[38] At the time of its deepest humiliation, Goethe had the acuity to say: "Yes, the German Volk promises a future – has a future. The fate of the Germans is not yet complete!"[39] So, as the regime moved to put such thoughts into action, *Völkischer Beobachter* allusions to Goethe as a supporter of "bringing more Germans home into the Reich" became increasingly flagrant. On 31 March 1938, just two-and-a-half weeks after the German army crossed the Austrian border, it ran a series of articles detailing what "great Germans" had to say about a "Greater Germany." Here the paper worked hardest to dismiss Goethe's reputation as a "world citizen" and to employ his words to justify the *Anschluss*. Because he was a German writer he saw "pure Germanness and *Grossdeutschland* as the great goals," saying to Eckermann: "Above all, may Germany be one in love! And may it always be one against the foreign foe! ... May there be no more talk about 'inland' and 'outland' among the German states!"[40] Goethe was not a man of political fantasy, the paper concluded, but he "definitely wished for the union of all Germans in a great state – in one Germany."[41]

While Third Reich reception of Goethe associated him strongly with expansionist policies, party interpretations of Beethoven revealed an effort to associate the composer and his music with the very identity of the Nazi movement itself. As we saw at the opening of this book, in his own contribution to *Völkischer Beobachter* apotheoses of Beethoven, Alfred Rosenberg reminded all Germans that no memorial day could "release more profound powers" in German life than could one honoring the death of the composer. It was a remarkable feeling, Rosenberg said, to realize that during a period when the "whole crazy world was pointing its bayonets at Germany," all nations and cities that still claimed to be cultured continued to revere one of the "all-time greats of that very same German Volk." Hundreds of millions still acknowledged his greatness – even in places like Paris and Warsaw – and thus paid homage to German culture, though sometimes "through grinding teeth." Among the "great manifestations of the Germanic West," the self-styled Nazi philosopher went on, two human types stood out. The first, embodied by Leonardo, Descartes, Kant, Leibniz, and Goethe, approached the secrets of life by "surrounding them like a fortress and trying to conquer it from all sides with a universal strategy." The other "Germanic-Western type," personified by Michelangelo, Rembrandt, Schopenhauer, and Wagner, preferred to pursue the secrets of existence with "double the energy, but from only one side: they wanted to destroy the fortress and reveal its inner contents by frontal assault."

Beethoven belonged to the second type, said Rosenberg, since he "grabbed fate by the throat." Consequently, his "demonic nature" (*Dämonie*) was more relevant in eras of "mythical-political struggle like the present" than in times of "contemplative-peaceful existence." In the present epoch, old values were disintegrating and new ones were being born, and this required a "one-sided, impulsive strategy" like the composer's. Naturally, he added, participants in the National Socialist movement would derive the most from this store of strength. "Whoever had a notion of what sort of nature operated in their movement knew that an impulse similar to that which Beethoven embodied in the highest degree lived in all of them": the "desire to storm over the ruins of a crumbling world, the hope for the will to reshape the world, the strong sense of joy that comes from overcoming passionate sorrow." When Nazis triumphed in Germany and throughout Europe, Rosenberg implied, they would recognize that Beethoven had passed on to them the ability and the will of German creation: "living in the *Eroica* of the German Volk," Nazis "wanted to make use of it."[42]

In a review of performances of the Ninth Symphony by the orchestra of the *Kampfbund für Deutsche Kultur* on 29 and 30 January 1933 – the eve of the Nazi "seizure of power" – the *Völkischer Beobachter* did make use of Beethoven's music by claiming that the event signified that the transition to "a superior Germany" had already begun. What made these two evenings so overwhelming, it held, was "a sense of communal spirit that melded the listeners together." If the choral finale were less challenging, "the whole audience would have joined in singing the Hymn to Joy: *Freude, schöner Götterfunken!*" The resonance between podium and hall was the same as the "circulation of common blood pulsing in their veins": the whole event was "a delicious foretaste of the Third Reich!"[43]

Notably, the Ninth Symphony was not initially favored in Nazi culture: some Nazis considered it suspect because the idea of all men becoming brothers did not sit well with party ideology.[44] When hearing the *Hymn to Joy* during the Weimar era, a *Völkischer Beobachter* reviewer reminded, the "contradiction between ideal and real" verified that humanity was "not yet worthy of its prophecies." But, of course, once the processes of Nazi "coordination" were under way, supporters considered Hitler's Germany much closer to manifesting the dream of the Ninth than the Republic had been: in 1935 the paper could claim that the German Volk again stood united – "Schiller's and Beethoven's high ideal of humanity was starting to be fulfilled; the band of joy was again wrapping itself around the nation."[45]

Whatever the fate of the Ninth Symphony in particular, Beethoven's music was reported in the *Völkischer Beobachter* as accompanying many events in the life of the Third Reich, including celebrations of Hitler's birthday[46] and the inauguration of the Reich Culture Chamber.[47] At the opening ceremonies of the 1936 Olympics in Berlin, the paper reported that as the Olympic flame was ignited, a choir – "forming a large white space against the dark gray masses opposite the section where Hitler and party dignitaries sat" – sang from Beethoven's *Opferlied* while "banners were lowered and young girls of the honor guard stepped forward to attach a wreath to each."[48] Beyond German borders, Nazis saw fit to exploit Beethoven's music as a foreign propaganda instrument. In September 1937, the Reich Culture Chamber arranged a Celebration of Germanism in Paris, coordinating it with the World Exhibition where the French film community acclaimed Leni Riefenstahl's film *Triumph of the Will*.[49] The nine-day German Exhibition climaxed with a concert of Beethoven's Ninth Symphony by the Berlin Philharmonic under Wilhelm Furtwängler's baton. As the performance commenced, French dignitaries watched their hosts rise to give the Hitler salute while the *Deutschlandlied* and the *Horst Wessel Lied* were played as preludes to Beethoven's symphony. Back in Germany, the *Völkischer Beobachter* heralded the event as a significant foreign propaganda victory. Anti-Semitic theater and literature historian, Herbert A. Frenzel, reported that the concert had been sold out and had caused a traffic jam because the crowd was so large. It had been, Frenzel was sure, the "most powerful and successful cultural event" to happen in Paris since the First World War. Realization that German art and German artists had achieved this great victory over French culture filled Frenzel with pride and joy: "the evening had been an important page in the history of German–French relations."[50]

Despite this ostensibly diplomatic use of Beethoven's music, when Nazi Germany marched, Beethoven's music accompanied: two weeks after the *Anschluss*, *Fidelio* was performed in Vienna, with Field Marshal Hermann Göring in attendance. Reviewing the show, the *Völkischer Beobachter* linked Beethoven's opera to the consolidation of *Grossdeutschland* by proclaiming that *Fidelio* was a prophecy of the escape of this southern portion of the German nation from "incarceration by international powers"; following the libretto one could "relive the individual phases and the final victory of the National Socialist revolution in Austria." According to this review, the Vienna production was an "uplifting festival of liberation – a religious service thanking the Creator for bestowing the Führer's genius on this poor, small, tormented people."[51]

Most conveniently for the Nazis, the 50th anniversary of Wagner's death coincided with their accession to power in 1933, and thus was the process of *Gleichschaltung* (that is, shifting German society and culture into gear) greased with references to the "master." In fact, on the morning after the fateful 30 January, the *Völkischer Beobachter* ran an article entitled "The Great Hatred: Marxist Agitation in the Wagner Year." Because "Nordic beauty, willfulness, honesty, and clear-sightedness" were horrors to them, "Jewish-Marxist journalists had outdone themselves in spreading hatred, lies, and unsurpassable infamy in their ongoing effort to alienate the Master of Bayreuth from the German Volk." In this manner they had hoped to "poison and falsify the inner engagement with the great man to which every new generation had an incontestable right." Foes of Wagner and enemies of Bayreuth thinking had "stupidly rejected" that which was "morally enlivening and spiritually restorative," because they expected no advantages from the rebirth of Germany. But the paper was certain that the "Jewish-Marxist conspiracy" would fail now that it was confronted with the "infallible instinct of a volkish generation" – and a government bent on imposing its views by all possible means, including physical elimination of said agitators.[52]

Once the NSDAP had control, it promoted the most direct association of Wagner with the new regime. On 21 March 1933, ceremonies for the Day of Potsdam peaked in a performance of *Die Meistersinger* at Berlin's Staatsoper. Having attended a torch-light parade of stormtroopers, war veterans, and students along Unter den Linden, Hitler and the rest of his government arrived for the third act of the opera.[53] The *Völkischer Beobachter* reviewer – Hugo Rasch, a composer and music critic who lead the Nazi attack against jazz – covered this event rhapsodically. Whoever witnessed how, during the third act, the Volk of Nürnberg "instinctively turned toward the Führer," sitting in the royal seats with all his helpers, and then how the eternally beautiful *Wacht auf, es nahet gen den Tag* emerged from the choir "to touch each and every heart," knew that "the moment of Germany's transformation had arrived." A worthier conclusion to the Day of Potsdam was inconceivable. At the end of Hans Sachs' final address, when everything in the hall had "risen to an exalted state, with everyone transfixed in deep emotion" – just before a "tremendous ovation" – it was clear that this audience was constituted much differently than in previous years, Rasch wrote. This was a "scene of German worthiness, unforgettable for one who had never lost his feeling for the German *Gemeinschaft*, even during the last few decades of confusion." German women, dressed tastefully, "not decorated with jewels or erotic makeup," and serious men in formal or dress brown uniforms were all "bound by an inner feeling of togetherness and a sense of being among one's own that built invisible bridges allowing everyone to be friendly with each other." The spirit of a "great community of fate – always present in even the least meeting of Nazi stormtroopers – lived just as much here, despite the apparent differences." Warm words of thanks rose from troubled hearts toward "the savior who sat above, following the opera with a unique light in his eyes and penetrating comprehension of the performance." Plus, those who looked out of the window during the intermission saw endless columns of the torch-light parade running along the Unter den Linden – "once forbidden to Nazis" – with an immense crowd of people waiting for the opera to end, hoping to get a glimpse of the "swordbearer of the new Germany." All these, for Rasch, were "unforgettable, historical events."[54]

Also unforgettable, for those with a taste for "steel romanticism," was a concert honoring Wagner and attended by Hitler that took place later in the year at Ludwig II's Wagner-inspired castle, Neuschwanstein, which the *Völkischer Beobachter* referred to as "The Bavarian Wartburg." After a detailed description of the castle and its surroundings, the paper described Hitler as sitting next to heavy torches, bending over to listen – "his eyes bright, his face serious." Around him, his loyal followers were likewise transported by the music and words of "German fate, woe, and fidelity." Then Hitler made his exit, pausing dramatically before the SA and SS men lining his path with Nazi banners.[55] Elsewhere, an even more important association of Wagner's music with the development of Nazi cultural policy occurred at the inaugural ceremony of the Reich Culture Chamber in the Berliner Philharmonic. Immediately after Goebbels' inaugural speech, amid "stormy applause" for the Reich Minister, the *Wacht auf* chorus sounded. The *Völkischer Beobachter* described the moment as a "hopeful awakening" with, "as Dr. Goebbels so perfectly put it, music for marching into the shining future of German culture."[56]

But the event at which Hitler himself most publicly expressed his personal engagement with Wagner occurred during the second year of the Third Reich. Just days after assuming the position of Reich Chancellor, Hitler had promised to erect a monument to Wagner in

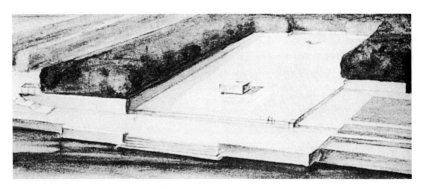

Figure 16.1 Detail from the official postcard of the foundation-stone laying for the national Richard Wagner monument in Leipzig, 6 March 1934

Leipzig, the city of the composer's birth. After a competition among German artists, the sculptor Emil Hipp from Stuttgart was awarded the commission. Conforming to traditional notions about German nationalist sacred sites, Hipp's plans called for a memorial amid a grove of oaks. The altar would be fashioned of a massive piece of marble with relief carvings communicating the fundamental motifs of Wagnerian creativity: myth, fate, love, and redemption. On 6 March 1934, Hitler dedicated Hipp's foundation stone for this never completed monument, stating that "a new German generation, chastened by decades of error and educated by sorrow without limits, was trying to find its way to its own great master" (Figure 16.1). This new generation would no longer have anything in common with that foregone "unthinkable time," because now "the wishes of one of the greatest sons of our Volk had been placed on the agenda – not only symbolically but in actuality." Already in the second year of national revival, Hitler acclaimed, this generation had found its way to Leipzig to place "the deepest thanks of the nation at the feet of its great son." Hitler then laid the cornerstone of the monument to Wagner, sanctifying it as a "testament of solemn promises to live up to the wish and will of the master, to continue maintaining his everlasting works in ever-lively beauty, and to draw coming generations of our Volk into the miraculous world of this mighty tone poet." Given that he was obviously invoking, even imitating, the poet and *Meistersinger* Hans Sachs on this occasion, it should come as no surprise that the foundation stone bore the words: "Honor your German Masters!" (*Ehrt eure deutschen Meister!*),[57] in reference not only to Wagner, but to National Socialist culture as a whole.

Three years later, and just twelve days after *Kristalnacht*, the paper ran an article on "The Musical Kremlin." Therein Otto Repp took up the assault on "Jewish music culture" on the basis of its mis-apprehension of Wagner. Appearing so soon after open violence against Germany's Jewish community, the article amounted to a cultural-historical justification for the onslaught. While many Jews idolized Wagner, Repp admitted, they did not comprehend him in terms of the "deeply tragic or redeeming aspects of his tonal world." It was only in connection with "the production, the theatrical pose, the grand gesture" that Jews could appreciate the composer's works. In this sense they perceived Wagner's dramatic style as a reflection of Jewish character, a tendency that was apparent when one heard "young Jews imitating" individual passages of Wagner in "an affected way." Their "racial corruption" and their "unprofessional, self-centered, and fundamentally neurotic" inclinations "falsified sensuousness and eroticism into debauchery and frivolity, aesthetics into a cult of ugliness, abstraction into inner emptiness, ecstasy into physical titillation." In them, the concept of happiness accessible to all mankind was "reduced into wild triumphalism – suffering became sniveling; humor became derisive irony; pride became arrogance; pain became illness; love became sentimentality or lust." To blame, as Gustav Mahler's "musical-naturalistic bric-a-brac" demonstrated, was their ego, which "always stood unconsciously in the center of a universe in which God judges and punishes in the interests of the Jews alone."[58]

Of course, Wagner and Bayreuth were indivisible. According to Friedrich W. Herzog, rescuing Bayreuth was the new regime's first major cultural-political accomplishment and posterity would "recognize the momentousness of this historical act." Motivated by a respect for Wagner that grew out of the "deepest inner unity" with Bayreuth, Hitler dedicated himself to elevating the work of the master "out of the mire of daily discourse." Declared a "national treasure of the German Volk" and thereby protected, it was no longer possible to "misuse the work of Wagner as the cover or backdrop for self-aggrandizing or biased propaganda," as had been "common practice" before 1933. In the Third Reich, Wagner would always be understood exclusively as one of the "greatest early fighters for volkish renewal, allowing for no further leftist interpretations."[59] Hugo Rasch reported on the first Bayreuth Festival to take place after Hitler came to power in similarly ecstatic terms: "that he who saved Germany from dying at the last minute was present at the opening, gave it particular significance." Hitler's appearance was a "wonderful symbol that Germany lived on and Wagner's work lived on." Had the Führer "not been given unto Germany, there would have no longer been a Bayreuth: without him, chaos." Everyone needed to be conscious that the Festspielhaus might have been torn down, Rasch insisted, "perhaps transformed into a communist-parliamentary talk shop, maybe worse." Germans tended to forget problems as soon as things got better again. But especially at this site of consecration and introspection, they had to "acknowledge their enormous debt to the Führer."[60]

Right up to the beginning of the war, this close correlation between the Führer and Bayreuth remained constant in the *Völkischer Beobachter*. On Hitler's birthday in 1939, Heinrich Stahl reproduced a series of extracts from *Mein Kampf*, and went on to say that these "fundamental remarks by the Führer on the organic connection between world view, culture, art, and state leadership – known in the soul of every National Socialist – made clear that Adolf Hitler's battle and Richard Wagner's battle were world-historically united." Whenever the Führer discussed the spiritual world of the master, Stahl asserted, the result was "a brilliant elective affinity." Whoever had the good fortune of being in the Festspielhaus on the Green Hill and witnessing the Führer "regenerating his powers through intense absorption in an artistic production," would never lose faith in the fact that "art could seriously and effectively lead men on the path of fate." Since the seizure of power, "a new Bayreuth had risen according to Adolf Hitler's will: not even his tremendous responsibilities could stop him from giving his whole soul over to the work of the master and thinking about the further development of Bayreuth."[61]

Beginning in the summer of 1939, the most intense manifestation of National Socialist policy toward Bayreuth took the form of visits to the festival by German workers, and the *Völkischer Beobachter* paid particular attention to these events. The paper recognized that while Bayreuth signified a high point of German cultural life, it had not previously meant much to the German worker, because access to performances had been affordable only to an "especially wealthy circle." But "following the will of the Reich leadership," the "Strength through Joy" organization was functioning to make Wagner's treasures available to the German worker. In 1939 alone it enabled 7,000 laborers from all over the "Greater German Reich" to take part in the festival: statistics from a single region (*Gau*) included 250 white-collar workers, 220 industrial workers, 80 typists, 20 nurses, 15 craftsmen, 15 housewives, 9 students, 7 autobahn workers, 4 kindergarten teachers, and 1 farmer. But participation at the festival was in no sense a gift: participants had to earn the experience of Wagner's operas on the Festival Hill, which had become "a holy volkish site." Special lecture series were held for the "lucky ones," led by qualified experts who emphasized that understanding of the operas came "not from knowledge, but from feeling."[62]

Mention of Wagner in association with German foreign affairs was another way the *Völkischer Beobachter* correlated Wagner's life and works with Hitler's outlook and policies. In accordance with Axis diplomacy, the Nazi paper found it significant that Wagner "always enjoyed universal admiration in Italy." Such cross-cultural affection was evident, for instance, in certain pages of Gabriele d'Annunzio's *The Flame of Life* (1900), which depicted Wagner's illness and death in Venice, as well as in "the great reception given to Wagner operas that were produced annually in the capital city." The newspaper also noted a three-column article in the *Tribuna* (Rome) on the occasion of a performance of *Die Walküre*. Therein, the *Völkischer Beobachter* happily reported that music critic and composer, Alberto Gasco, expressed the great love that Italians had for Wagner: "The Valkyries have returned to make Romans happy again," Gasco had written.[63] Hellmut Ludwig, a music writer who would go on to produce works on folk song (with an emphasis on yodeling) after the war, reiterated the tight cultural connections between Fascist Italy and Nazi Germany. Since the German Volk had become so closely allied with the Italian nation, there was no more reason to disagree or compete over the virtues of Wagner and Verdi. Indeed, cooperation between Hitler and Mussolini "set the conditions for collaborative undertakings" such as an Italian Festival in Munich. There was no more competition, Ludwig held – "no more, German music drama here, Italian opera there!" Instead, there existed only "the wish to enrich each other through common understanding." Great Italian and German masters could appear next to each other on equal terms on concert programs in both Germany and Italy, Ludwig concluded. Indeed, any perception of differences between them would be minimized if German audiences heard and saw Italian operas "in productions appropriate to their original spirit."[64]

Expansionist aspects of Nazism were also apparent in the paper's prewar Wagner discourse. Within months of the *Anschluss*, the

Völkischer Beobachter reviewed the start of the Salzburg Festival, noting that Nazi luminaries, including Goebbels, were in attendance. Holding forth on the event's pan-Germanic implications, Hans Antropp concluded that the fact that the festival opened with *Die Meistersinger von Nürnberg* was "a program, a promise, and a symbol in one." It was a program because it "expressed sublimely" the main purpose of a German music festival: "presenting art as communal experience expected to eliminate prejudices based on wealth, class, and education." It was a promise because whoever heard this version of "Honor your German Masters!" would never forget the "sense of hope for the future that was filling overflowing hearts." Finally, it was a symbol because these cheerful tones indicated how the "newly German Salzburg Festival would proceed henceforth."[65] Clearly, such an interpretation – along with other renewed Third Reich assimilations of the "masters" – were also to be seen as constituting a program, promise, and symbol that together would lay the groundwork for the evolution of a newly Nazified German culture.

17 THE NAZI "RENAISSANCE"

It is likely that Hitler did believe that by "starting with an easy mind from the good achievements of past generations" his revolution would bring about a "renaissance of humanity." Having established a bulwark against the erosion of tradition, he asserted that he was "convinced that, after a few years under National Socialist leadership of the state and nation, Germans will produce much more and greater work in the cultural domain than has been accomplished during the recent decades of the Jewish regime."[1] Seen from the perspective of Nazism as a cultural movement – as much as a political one – the task of bringing about such a renaissance might have been regarded as its highest measure of success. That Goebbels subscribed to this view is revealed in his remarks at the inauguration of the Reich Cultural Chamber: "no reproach struck us so deeply in the past," Goebbels said, "than the assertion that National Socialism is a form of spiritual barbarism and is certain to lead ultimately to the destruction of the cultural life of our Volk." But contrary to this assertion, he insisted, "it is *we* who have freed the creative powers of the German nation again, that they may develop unhindered and generate rich fruits on the tree of a renewed national character." Under Nazi leadership, a "new national art of Germany will enjoy the respect of the world," and will thereby "provide evidence that the Great German Awakening was not purely political, but was a cultural one as well."[2]

What shape this new national art would take, however, was not apparent. While Nazi critics were unified in their opinions about the deviant nature and gross inadequacies of Modernism, they were less confident about what specifically they would have replace it. In essence, they ran against the fundamental contradiction implicit in constructing a "communal sense of evaluation" rooted in the cultural past: contemporary artists were expected to advance the tradition of *Kultur*, but the "standards and measures" for future German creativity were thoroughly grounded in the works of dead masters. So even these critics found few living creators capable of living up to Nazism's history-bound "bases for comparison and targets for achievement."[3] Goebbels eventually came to recognize that the fruits of Nazi culture were not as rich as he had hoped, acknowledging that "you cannot manufacture an artist." Likewise, Göring admitted that "it is always easier over time to make a decent National Socialist out of an artist than to make a great artist out of a minor party member."[4] Yet even in the face of such a dreary state of affairs, left to bootstrap a renaissance from their copy desks, Nazi cultural critics trudged on, promoting an array of artists and artworks of little lasting merit – many of whom were at the end of their careers, and even their lives, when they were propped up as models for a Nazi cultural future. To answer the problems of musical modernism, the paper supported composers who seemed to uphold principles of Wagnerian romanticism, though none seemed to truly deserve the mantle of the Bayreuth "master" himself. In its literary coverage, much effort was expended to enhance the reputation of writers whose works are now largely forgotten. In art, besides little-knowns, Arno Breker received positive attention for his representations of martial ideals. The focus of this study is on the party's manipulation of the standing Western tradition, not on the productivity of less than significant Nazi favorites, and it must therefore leave aside conjecture as to why cultural output in and around the movement was so slim, besides reminding that many ingenious artists, composers, and writers ultimately left the country as political or racial exiles, and that – as the majority of this book demonstrates – the thrust of National Socialist *Kulturpolitik* was always toward idealizations of the past, and therefore inherently moribund. Still, some attention to their stillborn renaissance is necessary as a record of how the newspaper did attempt to give it life.

With regard to music, the *Völkischer Beobachter*'s priority was always to defend the grand tradition, but after that – particularly after Wagner – the task of demarcating the proper scope and direction of serious music remained unresolved. The paper's disorientation was especially palpable in its coverage of the pre-eminent German composer of the era, Richard Strauss (1864–1949). In its earliest days, the newspaper had reviewed the Munich premiere of Strauss' *Die Frau ohne Schatten* (1918) negatively, referring to the composer as being "in the waning years of his life, a product of his era like no other, and therefore representative of a generation suffering from profound intellectual and moral paralysis."[5] To the *Völkischer Beobachter*, Strauss' *Elektra* (1909) had "marked the end point of neoromantic music drama,"[6] and *Ariadne auf Naxos* (1912) had been "incomprehensible."[7]

But much of the paper's enmity against Richard Strauss originated with Alfred Rosenberg himself. In February 1926, the editor engaged in a particularly vicious attack that explained Strauss' inadequacies on the basis of the insinuation that the composer may have been half Jewish. "Regarding the question as to whether Richard Strauss has Jewish blood in his veins or not, there are indications that make it very doubtful that he is of pure German origin," Rosenberg opened. His mother was born into the Pschorr family; but his father "really must have been a Jew." As proof of this, Rosenberg had no evidence except the "striking" fact that as a member of the orchestra of the National Theater, the elder Strauss had been the "main agitator" against a performance of Richard Wagner's *Meistersinger* in 1868. But apart from that, Rosenberg went on, "everything that Richard Strauss has created betrays the fact that he is a halfblood." Perhaps with the exceptions of *Death and Transfiguration* (1889), which he created when suffering from a lung condition and "felt very close to death," and *Don Juan* (1889), where he "worked off a strong case of erotic sensuality," all the rest of his compositions were just "head games – ingenious mathematical arrangements of notes." Nowhere, Rosenberg held, did his music "pulse with the heartbeat of real sensation or fervent life experience."

Throughout his artistic career, moreover, there was no "consistent progress," as in the case of all great German artists, but just a "strange process of bouncing around" as Strauss followed the fashion of the day. As a young man, "like almost all German composers at the end of the century, he modeled himself on the genius of the Bayreuth Master," as is demonstrated in his opera, *Guntram* (1894). Rosenberg could not reproach him for that, but with his next opera it became clear that he was "just a slave to the spirit of the times." One-act operas became fashionable, so he followed suit with *Die Feuersnot* (1901). Then arose the Nietzsche cult, "to which we owe" Strauss' *Also Sprach Zarathustra* (1896). Soon afterwards, Oscar Wilde created a sensation with *Salome* (1905) and Strauss "shrewdly" composed it for the opera stage, taking advantage of the "perverse" poem's "drawing power." The success that Hugo von Hofmannsthal had with his "modernizations" of Greek dramas subsequently motivated him to set *Elektra* to music – where he "exhausted all the possibilities of external sound effects." But then, all of a sudden, the "music world" called for a "return to the simplicity of Mozart's orchestral language," so Strauss "churned out" *Rosenkavalier* (1911) and *Ariadne auf Naxos*.

In addition to Strauss' fad-driven creative inconsistency, though, Rosenberg found another sign of the "Jewish component in his blood": he was an excellent businessman, which was "not compatible with true German artistry." He was so wealthy, Rosenberg complained, that he could build a villa in Garmisch as well as a palace in the most expensive neighborhood of Vienna. Another indication of his business sense was the way he manipulated copyright laws between German and French publishers. On top of that, Rosenberg pointed out that the "Jew press" had produced "gigantic advertisements" for works like *Schlagobers* (1924) and *Intermezzo* (1924). Finally, the fact that his son Franz had married the daughter of a Jewish banker "completed perfectly the picture of Strauss' character as that of a half-blood."

"Race," Rosenberg concluded, was the "key to world history," and it also provided a way to "judge the creations of artistically gifted people." Strauss was undoubtedly gifted, Rosenberg concluded, but he lacked the "rootedness in a racially sound national character necessary for greatness." Like Ermanno Wolf-Farrari, Franz Schreker, and Erich Korngold, Strauss was representative of "that international type of composer" whose "most characteristic musical expression is that of raceless artistic inspiration."[8]

Following Rosenberg's line, the Hugo Wolf expert, Heinrich Werner, criticized the 1926 publication of correspondence between Strauss and Hofmannsthal. Werner found it "tasteless" to publish these letters during their lifetime. The only basis for doing so was the egotism and greed of the two correspondents. It was the worst form of self-aggrandizement for Strauss and Hofmannsthal to think that their letters were so interesting: they seemed to be placing themselves on the same level as Schiller and Goethe, and Werner damned such a comparison as "blasphemous." They were probably exploiting their names "to earn some change" and that sort of attitude would mark the death of true artistry: "artists should create, not market themselves," Werner insisted.[9]

When Strauss' *Die ägyptische Helena* opened in 1928, the *Völkischer Beobachter* again fired off harsh criticism: the work was too easily recognizable as another "clever gimmick of Strauss the first-class businessman." Despite its success, time would tell how long it would last: audience members who could not follow a libretto would have absolutely no idea what was going on, since it had no real plot.[10] In the view of the paper, all Strauss did was "run after the spirit of the time," composing whatever was in fashion. After the "Oskar Wilde-ish" *Salome*, came the "even more perverse works" with Hofmannsthal: *Elektra* (1909) and *Der Rosenkavalier. Le Bourgeois gentilhomme* (1912) was an example of "coddling French theater by bringing the comedies of Molière back onto the German stages, in view of Wilhelm II's efforts to reconcile with France." Thereafter, he produced *Die Frau ohne Schatten*, with "blurry mysticism that fit well with the rise of occultism," and after the war, *Die ägyptische Helena*, which "betrayed the aging process that was already taking effect in the creator."[11]

However, in 1933, the paper's tone changed abruptly, following Goebbels' move to appoint Strauss as president of the Reich Music Chamber. In August the *Völkischer Beobachter* referred to the composer as one of the "truest servants to great works of art."[12] With the appointment came rewards such as the chance to conduct his *Festliches Präludium* (1913) for Goebbels and Hitler at the opening of the Reich Culture Chamber in November 1933.[13] In March 1934, the paper covered the composer's 70th birthday celebration at the Berlin Philharmonic, and quoted from Strauss' remarks on the occasion: "Ten years ago was a tough time of inner disintegration and collapse, but now that Adolf Hitler has achieved the unification of the whole German Volk, we are again striving upward; he has established the conditions for a new zenith of German art."[14] In his coverage of the celebration, Max Neuhaus took the opportunity to reveal the paper's fundamentally revised assessment of the composer's artistic merit. Known as a rebel in his earlier days, Strauss "boldly carried new thoughts and forms" beyond those of Richard Wagner, and did so with "positive, not destructive effect." His style of composing was "new and surprising, to be sure, especially for those who, out of a need for comfort, closed their spirits off from reform." But the revolutionary aspect of the young Strauss was "nothing other than the expression of inner independence, without which artistic value is inconceivable." Like every ingenious creative personality, Strauss was the manifestation of an "organic process of development that operated according to inherent laws of life." His first music drama, *Guntram*, followed Wagner's technique so closely that it had to be seen as "imitative and rather empty, without its own vigor." But as part of this process, he discovered a unique, personal mode of artistic expression while simultaneously maintaining a "gruff refusal of modern currents," and this gave his creations great worth. Neither the criticism nor the resistance of "certain international circles" knocked him off his path. Despite everything that some might have held against him, his "essence was true and German." Above all, his support of Hitler's leadership over German art was "clear, unambiguous, and emotional," and it was "in the same spirit" that Neuhaus and the paper sent him "heartfelt birthday wishes."[15]

Not all *Völkischer Beobachter* writers were completely on board, however. Herbert Gerigk was critical of *Daphne* (1938), complaining that it required a "humanistic education" to comprehend: "if you didn't understand the background of the allegory, you wouldn't be able to follow the dense words and thoughts of the song, even in the best of productions." As such, it failed to resonate with the "fundamental intellectual demands" of the new era. In this opera, Gerigk predicted, Strauss' opponents would "again find what they had contested in the past." Gerigk was somewhat more positive about *Peace Day* (1936), calling it a "significant highpoint" in Strauss' work that "spoke to Nazis directly." But he still felt that Strauss was "unaccustomed to managing" the work's heroic content.[16]

Gerigk's concerns notwithstanding, the Third Reich gave Strauss full honors on his 75th birthday in 1939, with ceremonies and concerts in Berlin, Vienna, and Bad Reichenhall.[17] According to *Völkischer Beobachter* coverage, Hitler attended a performance of *Peace Day*[18] and Goebbels hosted a tribute breakfast, thanking Strauss in the name of the Führer: "In a busy life of struggle, you have helped to uphold the global prestige of German music, often defending it against a hostile world. Today you stand as the highest representative of our German music."[19] Heinrich Stahl then elaborated upon the official pronouncements in an article on the composer's "cheerful life" wherein the critic attempted to disassociate Strauss from the modern tendencies that he had most certainly followed. A "miracle" had taken place in the case of Strauss, Stahl asserted: over time the "revolutionary" had become the "classicist." This was not due to any changes in the composer, Stahl argued, but rather was the result of the fact that his contemporaries had finally recognized that what first appeared to be provocative in his works was really the result of "organic development." Nothing could have redeemed Strauss more effectively than the corrupt Weimar era with its "technological music making" and "empty note jumbling," which were "just signs of its political orientation and world view." Through it all, Strauss held unwaveringly to "thoroughly trained form, to tonal structure, to *volkstümlich* melody full of feeling," and indeed, it would have been impossible for him to "suppress his German heart and joyous Bavarian love of life." Phenomenally gifted in instrumental and vocal technique, he used these gifts "to sing life's praises": thereby he transcended "pitifully impotent weaklings who were without feeling, and came to reign over the realm of tones." Strauss' "radiant, meditative, intoxicating oeuvre" was a self-contained tonal language that carried out bold innovations with reference to an inner system that conformed to the "holy order of pure form and tonality established by the Classicists and Romantics." So, Strauss did not become a "pace-setter of the destructive elements," but on the contrary, he became their "victorious adversary" who heralded a "refined joy of life made possible by ingenious talent grounded in the southern German world of sounds, melodies, and dance rhythms."[20]

And so it went. In 1942, Friedrich Bayer wrote that for decades Germans had known what they possessed in this "living music classic," but they "did not always want to admit it." During the "hopeless postwar years of spiritual, cultural, and artistic aberration and confusion," the "scourge of International-Jewish atonality punished November Germany for its lack of instinct." At that time, the "shining star" of Strauss' music seemed pale compared with the "shrill light of newer comets." The master's "healthy, natural, straightforward music" was considered conventional and clichéd, while "artificial composition methods and contrived tonal systems were proclaimed superior." So, since he rejected the extravagances of these "modernists," they had to fight the master – "driven by feelings of inferiority."[21] This underestimation of Strauss, the *Völkischer Beobachter* made clear, had ended with the rise of Nazi political culture: on his 80th birthday in 1944, Strauss continued to be promoted in the paper as "a musician of world significance." Ironically, these accolades came even as his son and Jewish daughter-in-law were threatened with arrest by the Gestapo.[22]

The *Völkischer Beobachter* was less conflicted about Strauss' contemporary, Siegfried Wagner (1869–1930), through his life and after his death amid the Nazi *Kampzeit*. More so than any other artist, the newspaper worked to will Siegfried Wagner into the constellation of German masters, and to defend the quality and significance of his output, though it was apparent he was far from his father's equal. It insisted, for instance, that a single work by Siegfried – such as his *Commandment of the Stars* (1908) – was more significant than "any three operas of Puccini." Criticism of the son's music, furthermore, was not based on the artistic merit of the works, but rather was part of the conspiracy against Richard Wagner and the Bayreuth world as a whole.[23]

Herbert H. Mueller argued that by exploring the world of German fairy tales and "evading current fashions," the *volkstümlich* operas of Wagner the younger "provided something for the whole German Volk," and in doing so extended the stylistic tradition initiated by Carl Maria von Weber.[24] About his comedy, *Blame It All on a Little Hat* (1915), the paper observed that Siegfried knew how to "cloak his creations in genuinely German forms," which expressed the victory of a pure heart over sorrow in "plain but convincing ways." In his tonal language, he avoided obtrusive ornamentation and through simple instrumentation created a "beautiful fairytale orchestral world of depth and serenity."[25] Emma von Sichart likewise reminded readers that Wagner was a person "for whom all of Germany should have been thankful."[26] On the composer's 60th birthday, Herbert Mueller produced a lengthy discussion of Wagner as "the tone poet of the German Volk."[27] On the opening of his *Sacred Linden Tree* (1927), the paper exclaimed, "This is German!" and went on to explain that the "real and pure art of such truly German masters like Siegfried Wagner" could save the Volk from its decline. It could recover if it aligned itself with powerful spirits like his instead of "staggering along with semi-religious mania after every will-o'-the-wisp and false prophet." Thank heavens, the paper declared, that "good forces" like Siegfried Wagner were still at work: remaining "inaccessible to all foreign influences," he was "striving simply and faithfully for the rebirth of the German soul." All Germans had to "nurture his *Sacred Linden*, that it might grow strong and delightful out of the ignominy and trouble of the times, like a New Germany operating in cheerful harmony with its Volk."[28]

However, implicit in all of these efforts to extol Siegfried as a German master – to prove that he was more than a composer of "fairytale operas"[29] – was a sense that the cause was lost and the effort futile. Assessing the list of new operas produced in 1932, the *Völkischer*

Beobachter was furious that there were so many "skirt shows, negro operas, and Jewish musicals," but nothing by the likes of Julius Bittner, Hans Pfitzner, Engelbert Humperdinck, or Siegfried Wagner. Their "worthy works" were being forgotten and the paper could only hope for a "more *German* opera schedule" in the future.[30] After Siegfried's death in 1930, Josef Stolzing wrote that the composer's life had been "difficult," partly because of his mild personality – especially compared with his father's – but also because of anti-Bayreuth forces that had worked against him. Siegfried "fulfilled his artistic mission as a faithful guard over the Bayreuth legacy," said Stolzing, but he was "not granted fulfillment of his calling as a creative composer." This was not his fault, but rather was a circumstance of his times, which "rejected and destroyed German culture." He was condemned to live in a period of transition when foreign influences "penetrated deeply into the Volk and alienated it from itself." Siegfried's mission as the composer of truly German works could "only be completed in posterity – if the treasures of his creative forces were finally recognized by the race that the Third Reich of Greater National Socialist Germany would engender."[31]

The *Völkischer Beobachter* was not as supportive of another Bavarian composer: Carl Orff (1895–1982). Reviewing the premiere of *Carmina Burana* (1937), Herbert Gerigk complained that the piece was "marred by a series of problems," the foremost of which was the fact that the song texts were in "monkish Latin and thirteenth-century German." As a consequence, "no one could understand a word." Whoever listens to a song wants to follow the words, Gerigk felt, otherwise one could "just use Chinese or simply sing arbitrary vowels." Such incomprehensibility "blocked the way for his work to have any *volkstümlich* effect." In addition, Orff's music style was "lapidary": he "just placed melodies next to each other; his only means of formal development were repetition and rhythmic association; and the melodies frequently reminded one of children's songs." Moreover, Gerigk continued, despite the "intentional primitiveness," there were places where "sophisticated" cultural forms unmistakably sprouted forth: "sometimes one heard a wholly elementary sound language, at other places a jazz mood." In the end, whether *Carmina Burana* marked the starting point toward a new musical direction was "a matter of cultural politics and world view." And although hard to follow, the texts "did breathe joy of life, celebrating spring, drinking, and the bad habits of priests (already in the thirteenth century!)." But more "practical testing" was necessary, Gerigk concluded, to see if this work "would have any effect on naive audiences – on the Volk."[32]

Less challenging for Volk listeners, the paper supposed, were works of Paul Graener (1872–1944), including his orchestral suite, *Die Flöte von Sanssouci* (1930), and his opera, *Friedemann Bach* (1931). Even before he became head of the composers' section of the Reich Music Chamber, the paper wrote positively about Graener as a "German Music Romantic." Ludwig K. Mayer stipulated that Graener never followed fashions – those "inartistic shortcuts to success" – so it took him longer than his contemporaries to achieve recognition. But here was a case where good things came to those who waited: Graener created "only out of his own nature, which matured with Nordic slowness – making it particularly stable." His personal development could be seen as an example for the life of the entire Volk in the contemporary era. In this sense Graener was "up to date" in the deepest and best way: in him "the Nazi revolution had a music master who was bound to the inner essence of the Volk and its soulful experiences."[33] Once Graener assumed his official position in the regime, he spoke on the "duties of the German composer" in ways that resonated with *Völkischer Beobachter* views. "Creating new music for national festivities presents tasks of the most beautiful sorts for both serious and cheerful muses," Graener speechified: "The Third Reich needs solemn music of cultish character for rallies, large-scale choruses and songs for communal singing, songs about the life of the Volk, songs which represented Germans themselves, songs celebrating the wonderful German landscape, songs about craftsmanship, and finally music based on old folk songs."[34]

Max von Schillings (1868–1933) was another composer whom the Nazi paper held up as tragically underrated. Musicologist and committed party member Erich Roeder extolled the composer's "remarkable war record." According to Roeder, "though the forty-six year old was over the age of service in 1914, he enlisted with his seventeen-year-old son and both volunteers marched at the head of German troops in Ludendorff's advance in Liège, for which Schillings received the Iron Cross." But in 1925 the Social-Democratic Minister of Education and Culture, Carl Becker, supposedly brought about the composer's removal from the directorship of the State Opera in Berlin: "there was no longer a place for Schillings in Germany," and the composer had to go abroad. Celebrated in Spain, Italy, and America as a great conductor of Wagner, he became a "herald of German art." It was only with the "National Socialist Revolution" in 1933 that he finally received the honor he deserved: "under the Führer," the paper noted, "Schillings received full reparations." But it was only a few months later that Schillings died, and, with his death, Nazis were "obliged to care for his legacy faithfully," as "remuneration for all he did and suffered for them."[35] As L. Biagioni put it, this German artist never recovered from the "dismissal without notice" he received from the Socialist government, and "when the National Socialist movement exerted itself for the master, it was too late to make up for the injustice."[36] Heinz Steguweit likewise counted Schillings among those who "knew how to serve their nation's eternal art, but as a result became a battle victim: worn down, ground up, and grown bitter." Having passed away just as the Volk arose, he was "one of the lonely ones who symbolized Schopenhauer's observation that solitude is the lot of all outstanding spirits."[37]

The *Völkischer Beobachter* faced similar challenges in locating, defining, and establishing evidence for a renaissance in National Socialist literature. Indeed, many of the writers it most energetically promoted, many of whom – even during the run of the paper – were already dead, are now largely forgotten. Those whose names remain recognizable are limited to the Norwegian, Knut Hamsun (1859–1952), whom the paper identified as "a Nordic classicist";[38] and the ever popular Karl May (1842–1912), whom the paper celebrated retrospectively. School teacher and *Völkischer Beobachter* contributor starting in 1927,[39] Karl Muth-Klingenbrunn was happy to report in reference to May that, "alongside the Hitler movement, Old Shatterhand was enjoying a triumphant resurrection." May had "gone to the happy hunting grounds in the sky, but death which took away his silver revolver, his bear-knife, and his inexhaustible pen apparently didn't have any power over him." He lived on in the "spotlight of a renaissance." Even so, some "pseudo-psychological interpreters" had been complaining about May's renewed popularity: "experts" were testifying about inaccuracies and weaknesses in his novels; there were attempts to remove him from school libraries. So Muth-Klingenbrunn thought "a few things had to be said in the Hitler paper: in this literary war, the Nazis were going to break a lance for May's revival."

According to Muth-Klingenbrunn, May's opponents considered him guilty of the "terrible crime" of using poetic license in his travel and adventure descriptions, thereby "undermining German youth's healthy sense of reality, diverting it from its obligations, and goading it toward fantasy and adventurousness." In Muth-Klingenbrunn's opinion German youth had never suffered from exposure to the writer, at least not "normal, healthy, average kids." He reminisced that in his own Gymnasium days, he and his schoolmates were all enthusiastic Karl May readers, except for a couple of "super-achieving teacher's pets." But "no one ran off to the ravines of the Balkans or to Kentucky after reading Karl May; no one was held back a grade on account of Karl May; no minds were damaged from reading Karl May."

"Was his generation less physically or morally trained in school than the present one? Were they less capable spiritually and psychologically? Were they less normal than contemporary youth?" Muth-Klingenbrunn did not think so: back then there was "rarely a schoolboy suicide or sex crimes among youth, just as there weren't any sports crazes or movie houses." That's when May was a "truly inexhaustible source of youthful, joyous experience." Like "bees draw honey from flowers," Muth-Klingenbrunn said his school buddies derived plans for battles, lists of hunting paths, methods for crossing streams, ways to climb trees, swimming lessons, and instructions for building fires and forts from May's stories. Nevertheless, when they were not playing, they all sat in class, "refreshed, well-mannered, and submitting in a disciplined way to every thought that the teachers kindly but strictly demanded of them." Whoever understood something about education, Muth-Klingenbrunn felt, had to conclude that there was "something in Karl May for every normal, healthy, and uncorrupted boy – a pedagogically welcome, healthy antidote to the mind-numbing, confusing, and tempting impressions of the oft-praised 'culture' of speed, technology, movies, and sport – the culture of the complex and the politicized, with its endless feminine sentimentality that was undermining the coming generation." To put it succinctly, Muth-Klingenbrunn declared: "Nazis were for Karl May!"[40]

Besides sentimentalizing the tales of Old Shatterhand and Winnetou, the *Völkischer Beobachter* promoted a handful of writers, including former Austrian submarine officer Franz Wolfram Scherer (1862–1932),[41] who wrote "romantic" and "historical" novels in Salzburg, and Ernst Friedrich – running his anti-Semitic novel *The Jewish Girl from Sosnowitz* (1920) in series.[42] Another recently deceased author whose works the paper often published in serial form was Ludwig Thoma (1867–1921).[43] Hellmuth Langenbucher accorded to Thoma a solidly "volkish *Weltanschauung*," though he died too young to see the "results of his postwar efforts to rebuild the Volk politically and spiritually." He wrote political and social satire, but after a time with *Simplizissimus*, "refused to become a second Heine" – writing that "while their grandfathers fell for the sarcastic *bonmots* of a Heine, his contemporaries were too serious for this sort of thing." His critique of authorities was a "nationalist opposition," not motivated by hatred and cynicism, but by the love of Volk and *Heimat*. Moreover, Thoma's works were "rooted in farming soil": he rediscovered what a Dürer and a Riemenschneider had already delighted in. The title of his first work, *Agricola* (1897), Langenbucher said, could have been placed at the head of all his work – if one translated the Latin as "German farmers." While Thoma had depicted the downfall of farming life in his stories, he "did so out of his love for it and his concern for the German soil." Nazis could thus read these books as a warning, for Thoma showed that it was "only through the maintenance of the German farmer that the German race could be maintained."

The lack of response that Thoma's work received from the "self-satisfied Volk of his day" temporarily drove him into the arms of "Jewish literati and sterile Bohemia." As a result, he briefly "sailed the waters of democracy and pacifism." But his roots were in the soil of the homeland, so it did not take long for the "powerful core of his arch-German essence to break the chains of mendacious Europeanism." In 1908, he wrote of the "occasional need for war"; during the Morocco Crisis of 1911, he was "critical of French saber-rattling"; and with the outbreak of war in August 1914, "his love for the German Volk was enflamed." As a result, he ultimately turned his back on democracy and pacifism and returned to the position that "a farmer's hut is preferable to the Reichstag building." In this spirit, he "sang" the poem, *1 August 1914*:

> Take up arms! Thunder through woods!
> Crash over fields, weapons at hand!
> To protect the Fatherland!
> The Volk springs forth, stretching its limbs.
> Have no fear – come what may! ...
> Hurrah to Germania, the mother of us all!

Later, Britain's entry into the First World War elicited from Thoma the following *Song of England*:

> Are we worried now? No!
> We don't choose our enemies.
> We can't choose our lot.
> We must be Germans.
> Always looking forward!
> Though a weak friend betrays us,
> Good sense and actions
> Will determine our fate.

Thus, said Langenbucher, did "Thoma the German" find himself again, and after the war he knew his place in the fight for the German Volk. Disturbed by the political chaos that resulted, he declared his blood "hot for Germany and full of hatred for the French and socialists." Fighting every obstacle in the way of German reconstruction with the "sharp weapons at his disposal," he even struck against the *Simplizissimus* to which he had once contributed, referring to it as nothing but a "puppet theater." In 1921, death "ripped him from his work for German farmers, the German homeland, the German Volk, the German essence, and German greatness." But Langenbucher wanted to invoke the last two stanzas of Thoma's *Englandlied* "whenever the German Volk suffered great inner distress":

> Take courage.
> Even those who hate us understand
> That the best of humanity will go down with us.
> Once more the world will admire
> How German power passes the test of danger.

These lines, Langenbucher was certain, would serve Nazis as "a source of strength and consolation" as the "battle for the German Volk heated up again."[44]

The *Völkischer Beobachter* also accorded attention to some living writers who were directly involved with the movement. Though it failed to report on Joseph Goebbels' best known work, *Michael* (1929),[45] the paper did cover a production of his play in verse, *The Wanderer*.[46] Dietrich Eckart, a very early supporter of Hitler and the NSDAP, earned direct tributes by Alfred Rosenberg, discussions of his relationship with the Führer, and references to him as the "Poet of the German Revolution."[47] The paper also reproduced works such as a poem in which Eckart suggested that Cain had been "The First Anti-Semite!"

> The first man who recognized the Jew,
> The first man who became so angry,
> That he struck down the sneaky bastard,
> Was Cain.
> Do you recognize the "pious" fraud?
> Despite some reluctance,
> Jehovah himself had to say:
> "Whoever kills Cain,
> Will stink to high heaven."[48]

The paper threw its support behind Hanns Johst (1890–1978) even before Johst completed his homage to a Nazi "martyr," *Albert Schlageter*,[49] and became president of the Reich Chamber for Literature. Johst stood out as one of the "rare positive developments among young dramatists of the day, belonging among the few who were seriously committed to a new content for life." Truly a German poet, said the *Völkischer Beobachter*, Johst was a "great hope" in an epoch when literature was "dominated by Jewish foreigners." While, naturally, the paper admired Johst's direct tributes to Hitler and Himmler,[50] it was also particularly enthusiastic about Johst's 1927 play, *Thomas Paine*, in which the author of *The Rights of Man* is portrayed as "the spiritual leader of the American independence movement."[51] Unlikely as it may seem, Johst convinced the *Völkischer Beobachter* that Paine could be associated with the fate of Nazism: "both leader and threat, he was full of passion, longing, humility, and excessive courage; the tears of Thomas Paine, as well as the tears over Thomas Paine, were tears about the Volk – about their personal triumphs and failures – and they could sing his praise as having led a great and wonderful life!"[52]

Besides regularly citing his "expert" volkish interpretations of the German literary tradition, the newspaper also extolled Adolf Bartels' creative efforts, telling its readers "everyone should buy his books because he can't live on honors alone." As a poet during "decadent times," it found, Bartels "protected the homeland, the Volk, the healthy German character, and the rights of the great." He awoke German consciousness to resist against the "devil of stupidity" – the "spirit of fraud in every area of life." Still, his main intellectual contribution was his "incomparable service to literary history and aesthetic criticism." There, he "always worked from German *Volkstum* out: always assessing creators and works on the basis of their meaning for Volk and Fatherland." Bartels stood alone, said Karl Berger, because he was the first to arrange literary history "according to race and blood" without reducing the professional value of his work. He followed the path that he knew was correct, undeterred by favoritism or hatred, despite the resistance of all the leading powers of the day. An early fighter for volkish ideals, he was an "inexhaustible awakener, herald, and giver of warnings." A figure who remained "rooted in German soil," despite the changes of styles and trends, he was a "pathfinder for the powerful new movement of freedom and revival." He could do it

> *because he remained bound to the true nature of the Volk;
> because he remained linked to all the good spirits of the
> past and present; because even in times of trouble, under
> almost hopeless conditions, he remained true to the principle:
> "Don't despair: work"; and because he never stopped
> believing in the indestructible power of the indigenous Volk
> and its final victory over flashy and boastful evils.*

Saluting him, the paper hoped that Bartels would "see his life's work completed, as well as the full outcome of the Hitler movement."[53] Given that Bartels lived until March 1945, one might say that the paper's hope was realized.

In the visual arts, the *Völkischer Beobachter* also tried to shine a spotlight on a number of artists it considered to be underappreciated, such as Hans Thoma (1839–1924), in whose works "one could clearly see how blood and soil were manifested in art as race,"[54] and the "world famous Bavarian artist," Max Slevogt (1868–1932).[55] Aside from these perhaps more dubious luminaries, the paper heavily invested in the premier monumental Nazi sculptor of the day, Arno Breker (1900–1991), whose academic nudes were seen to embody the Nazi heroic ideal. Wilhelm Rüdiger went as far as to claim that Breker's figures were "superior to the sculpture of the ancient Greeks during the period of Pericles" from which, he acknowledged, they derived. In the modern age, Rüdiger concluded, there had no longer been any "expression of intimate empathy for the innermost of humanity." It was just a time of "sculptural game-playing." But then "went forth a great summons to Arno Breker: the new era issued a command to his art; his rich, self-fulfilling capabilities were directed toward a goal – a high, magnificent task: to create the ideal plastic image of the young, strong, combative, and resolute people of the new era." The first of these new creations extolled by the paper were the "athletic figures" of the *Decathalete* and the *Goddess of Victory*, sited at the *Reichssportfeld* in preparation for the 1936 Olympics. In them, "form became taut: everything that was previously blurry became resilient and metallically clear." Then, "for the Führer's monumental Berlin architecture, torsos of figures extended sinuously from relief areas" while, "next to new, festive buildings, Breker's heraldic and summoning youth grew far beyond life size – gigantic." Though the stride and stance of these figures were similar to the eternal models of the Greeks, Rüdiger explained, their gestures and expressions "belonged to the Nazi era exclusively." For they did not have the "smiling, dreamy self-consciousness" of the Attic sculpture of Pericles' period. Their "imperious traits and gestures expressed the wisdom, deeds, goals, and self-confidence of those called to higher duties." With torch in hand and sword in outstretched arm, these young heroes stood as "living emblems" of the "Nazi Party and the German Armed Forces in the Court of Honor of the new Reich Chancellery" (Figure 17.1). In them, the highest Greek virtues – "fitness and beauty" – were newly united and embodied.[56]

Werner Rittich, an art and architecture historian who promoted Nazi aesthetics in publications such as *Art in the German Reich* (*Die Kunst im Deutschen Reich*), a journal edited by Alfred Rosenberg and Albert Speer, also bragged about the star Nazi sculptor, claiming that Breker was appreciated not only in Germany, but also in occupied Paris where the Nazis staged an exhibition of his work in 1944. His effusive review insisted that the Breker show in Paris was a "convincing sign that significant cultural developments had occurred in the Third Reich and were celebrated not just inside but outside German borders." Rittich claimed that audiences looked with particular interest at Breker's "strength-based accomplishments" and recognized that here "something new in the world of plastic art had grown out of the German present – while also indicating its future." All his works demonstrated that he was a creator able to "symbolize heroic stature": Breker "epitomized the monumental creator." All of his figures, reliefs, portraits, and animal sculptures represented "the unity of inner bearing

Figure 17.1 Arno Breker, *The Army* (1939)

and outer form, the inner dignity of humanity based on strict discipline, and a connection between a proud past and the future." A large portion of these works had been commissioned by Albert Speer, in the architect's capacity as General Construction Inspector for Berlin. Regarding Breker's sculptures, Reich Minister Speer wrote in the exhibition guide that the "creative genius that manifested itself in Breker would further develop as Germans unwaveringly followed the will of the Führer under difficult circumstances and thereby fulfilled their duties as they worked toward victorious completion of the war." In view of the situations at the front and at home, Speer held, Breker's "powerful but at the same time internally dignified sculptures would provide the inner strength to pursue a triumphant conclusion of the war." One could therefore expect, Rittich and the *Völkischer Beobachter* maintained, that the works of Breker would have a "strengthening effect on the inner life of Germans both at the front and home throughout the decisive days ahead."[57] These expectations, expressed late in the conflict, serve as indications that even to the Nazi leadership it was clear that the promised artistic renewal of the regime had not fully arrived, and could be realized only after military success, which was perceived as the first necessary step in the cultural project of the Third Reich.

18 *KULTUR* AT WAR

The *Völkischer Beobachter* did not, of course, limit itself to presenting examples of contemporary art like Arno Breker's rigid athletes as means of "strengthening the inner life of Germans" before and during the Second World War. Indeed, Nazi propagandists enlisted the whole of the Western cultural tradition, as perceived in National Socialist terms, to serve in their belligerent cause. Just when German armies were invading Poland, Joseph Goebbels addressed an annual joint meeting of the Reich Cultural Chamber (*Reichskulturkammer*) and the "Strength through Joy" organization on 27 November 1939, with a speech on "Cultural Life in the War" that made the cultural dimension of the conflict, as envisioned by the Nazi leadership, clear. Continued cultural activity for the German Volk was "one of the most important preconditions" for guaranteeing the "steadfastness and perseverance of the whole nation" during its "battle of destiny" (*Schicksalskampf*). "What," Goebbels asked "could be more suitable for lifting up the spirit and refreshing the soul of the Volk" – raising "our soldiers, and our workers" to a heightened state of optimism – "than art?" Nazis, he went on, had "never reserved art for peacetime alone: for us, the notion that when the call to arms sounds, the muses go silent, has no validity." To the contrary, "we have always held the position that it is precisely in such a moment" that the muses "need to deploy their powers." Because, "the more trying the times, the more people require inner enlivenment and encouragement through art," and this, Goebbels contended, was "a part of the German Volk character more so than that of any other people."

The forces that had gathered at this meeting of Third Reich cultural organizations during the earliest stage of the fighting, Goebbels declared, wanted to "demonstrate before all the world that art is no mere peacetime amusement, but a sharp spiritual weapon for war." Under Hitler's leadership, the Nazis had placed this "spiritual weapon into the hand of our Volk" to wield as the "German nation was lining up to battle for its very existence." Thus armed, the arch-propagandist closed, "we Germans are not only protecting our living space [*Lebensraum*], our daily bread, and our machines against hostile plutocratic powers; we are also protecting our German culture and with it the great blessings that it can bestow on the whole Volk." Bound together by "faith in the Führer" and confidence about "our great national future," Germans were already "a Volk." Now they wanted "to be a World Volk" (*Weltvolk*); and that was going to be achieved through military conquest partly in the interest of advancing German *Kultur*.[1]

Knowing of the utter devastation it wreaked, we reject the National Socialist promotion of the war as leading to a future of German cultural advancement.[2] Still, we must recognize that Nazi propaganda did not present the war as an end in itself, but as a means toward re-establishing Germany as *Kulturnation* – revived in the aesthetic forms suggested by the *Völkischer Beobachter* cultural section, among other propaganda sources.[3] In this endeavor, they failed. The final result was instead the reduction of their country to a state of ruin far more hideous than those Albert Speer had projected in plans for the structures he and his master imagined[4] – not after a thousand years, but after just twelve years of terror and six years of carnage. Ultimately, the culmination of "Nazi culture" was the war itself; indeed, this was its hollow "master-piece." Nevertheless, to see how the party commanded a "wartime mobilization of the humanities" aimed at creating a "new spiritual order"[5] we must study how the Nazi newspaper advanced the proposition that the greatest Western cultural figures and their works could be associated with the conflict – as it approached, as it raged, and as it ended. This material will show how the thematic trajectory of the *Völkischer Beobachter*'s cultural section closely followed the war experience from the first stages of the war, through the Stalingrad debacle, to the final days of the regime. Even then, as the "new Reich" crumbled about them, the paper's editors continued to devote space to articles that laid claim – ultimately an empty one – to National Socialist cultural hegemony.

Long before the commencement of hostilities the paper had sought out signs that creative heroes had "fighting" (*kämpferisch*) natures. When stipulating that major artists, writers, and musicians had been patriotic and nationalistic, according to their historical circumstances, the implication had always been that they were willing to fight for those causes. The paper found, for instance, that the case of Albrecht Dürer afforded lessons that were suitable for a culture preparing for war. Concluding that his "reputation as one of the masters of proportion and perspective" amounted to just "one aspect of his career," the *Völkischer Beobachter* was deeply interested in his life in a "violent age of constant warfare" and the fact that he "spent much energy on martial themes and even military technology." Aligning Dürer with the military values of National Socialism on this basis was a major concern of the newspaper. For instance, from Wilhelm Rüdiger's perspective, it was troubling that the 400th anniversary of Dürer's death was celebrated "without sufficient reference to his outspoken insistence on representing the profession of soldiering and the life of the soldier."[6]

The *Völkischer Beobachter* committed itself to setting this record straight. Consistent with the notion of a Nordic artist as "active," Fritz Wiedermann insisted that martial culture was closer to him than one might assume: he lived in a war-torn era that "resounded with calls to battle." Moreover, his "best friend," Colonel Wilibald Perkheimer, who had led a Nürnberg troop against the Swiss in 1499, visited him regularly and constantly exchanged letters with him when away fighting with his troops. So the "themes of war" were familiar to Dürer. Given such circumstances, wrote Wiedermann, Dürer's images strongly reflected the soldier's life. In particular, two "siege pictures" depicted military details "with great accuracy": his drawing of the siege of Hohenasperg, along with his "great woodcut" representing the siege of another fortress provided "such exacting detail that they could function as a textbook of strategic perspective" (Figure 18.1). In addition, his woodcut series, *The Triumphal Arch* (1515) (Figure 18.2), depicted soldiers' "manner of camping and their form of attack."

Nazis should be grateful to the artist, Wiedermann wrote, for an abundance of renderings of soldiers which recorded their features with such "historical precision."[7] Further, in many drawings Dürer depicted "the splendor of uniforms and the pomp of velvet and silk – his

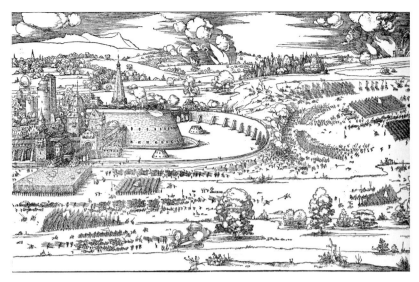

Figure 18.1 Albrecht Dürer, *Siege of a Fortress* (1527)

Figure 18.2 Albrecht Dürer, *The Meeting of Maximilian I and Henry VIII* (from the *Triumphal Arch of Maximilian*) (1515)

Figure 18.3 Albrecht Dürer, *Death and the Landesknecht* (1510)

Landsknecht was a model of the dashing soldier" (Figure 18.3). Likewise he recorded "happy camp life with its robust pranks and carousing; even drinking and dice throwing were not absent from his images." Only one who had "gone deeply into the character of a mercenary, or feels a bit of soldiering in his own heart, could have captured these particulars."[8]

Moreover, he portrayed infantry and horsemen on the march and in combat: "striding along with waving flags, conquering city gates, and storming forts." His pictures of *Saint George* (1501–1504) (Figure 18.4), along with *Knight, Death, and the Devil* (1513) – "the most beautiful monument to knighthood ever created" – revealed how very much a "sense of the warrior and the understanding of soldierly virtues were a part of him."

Figure 18.4 Albrecht Dürer, *St. George on Horseback* (1508)

What boldness of thought, what nobility of spirit shines out of the faces of both warriors! Where does a more defiant bravery and proud awareness of victory find expression than here? Whoever wished to inquire into the worthiness of German soldiers of all times, from the early stages of this history to the most recent past, could obtain exhaustive information from both of these prints.[9]

Despite such accomplishments, the *Völkischer Beobachter* maintained that Dürer was "not merely a depicter of soldiers": he was also an ingenious "theoretician of fortress and urban architecture," though this side of his career was little known. He wrote four textbooks about the construction of fortifications, including *Underweysung der Messung mit dem Zirckel und Richtscheyt* (1525) and *Etliche Underricht zu Befestigung der Stett, Schloß und Flecken* (1527). With "astounding capability," he calculated the ballistic performance of artillery, developed attack and defense theories, and measured proper amounts of rations and munitions. In short, he "handled the difficult problems of fortified warfare like an old soldier and field commander."

According to the newspaper, even Friedrich the Great studied Dürer's stratagems: "the great Prussian king drew from his ideas about the construction of independent works in front of the line of defense." This was "clear confirmation of their relevance." Still, his teachings on fortifications were almost completely unknown to moderns; so the paper felt it necessary to honor these forgotten "stepchildren." Everyone, so it seemed, owed Dürer a debt of gratitude. Craftsmen looked to him as "one of their own," as did painters and artists. Front soldiers wanted to celebrate him too, "because of his love for their profession." But they wanted to honor him in their own way, by stressing his identification with the soldierly life, "so easily forgotten in modern times." For them, Dürer had earned the "honorable title of a soldier," in addition to his reputation as a great artist. Nazi readers could therefore learn from him that "soldierly caliber is not based on the uniform alone, but must be proven by spirit and energy," and that "a soldier is comprised of a brave heart and a clear mind." To this effect, the paper reminded, Dürer himself wrote: "In order to defend such a fortification the following are necessary: good weapons, sufficient supplies, and above all, staunch and manly people who are good with their weapons. No fortification will hold without all of these."[10]

That the *Völkischer Beobachter* continually held up Dürer's works to inspire "staunch and manly activity" was further apparent in a later article that presented the artist and fellow painter and printmaker Lukas Cranach as "wrestling experts." It explained that the first printed "book about wrestling" appeared around 1500, but in 1512 – "at the height of German wrestling in the Reformation era" – Dürer published his own: "one of the greatest artists of all time also produced a wrestling book," the paper exclaimed. In this treatise, wrestling holds and moves were "captured lovingly" in images that indicated the "high level of technical skill in the old-German wrestling style" (Figure 18.5). Even the most modern schools "could not come up with better grips."[11]

Nazis also found Friedrich Schiller useful for articulating that which was going to be expected of young German men in particular. That Nazi culture co-opted the poet to prepare young men for death in battle was clear in the *Völkischer Beobachter*'s coverage of Weimar events celebrating the 175th anniversary of Schiller's birth in 1934.

Figure 18.5 Albrecht Dürer, wrestling illustrations from *Ring- und Fechtbuch* (1512)

From all over Thüringen, the paper reported, "young people gathered in Weimar to represent all of German youth" to honor "their Schiller – the young Schiller." In accompaniment to performances of *Wilhelm Tell* and *Maria Stuart*, Fritz Wächtler – involved with Nazi educational policy in various positions – spoke at the Goethe–Schiller monument. There he compared Schiller's words, "Who life would win, he must dare to die!"[12] with Adolf Hitler's cry, "You are nothing, your Volk is everything!" These, the newspaper commented, were "bright slogans" for young Germans.[13] As "youth affected by fate," the latest generation supposedly "loved Schiller instinctively" as a "tough man of will" who, in a "constant fight with the suffering that beset him, developed a willingness to die and indifference to death to the highest levels."[14] Schiller commemoration had thus been transformed into a ritual celebrating death by means of self-sacrifice to the state.

Of course, bellicose Nazi propaganda also targeted Schiller's famous friend and collaborator. Establishing that Goethe shared the opinion that the goal of a united Germany should be pursued by any means necessary, not excluding military force, meant directly opposing what National Socialists called a "pacifist tradition of interpretation." The *Völkischer Beobachter* rose to the challenge aggressively. Already in 1922 the paper had observed that an "ungovernable generation of poets and writers luxuriated in using Goethe quotes for defending their power-less pacifism."[15] But, Adolf Dresler countered, stamping Goethe as a "spiritual hero of the pacifist world view" was wholly erroneous. The poet had the ambition, Dresler insisted, if not to become a "German Homer," at least to be "Homeric": in fact, he wanted to compose an *Achilles*. He didn't get past the first song, but it included the following verses, which "certainly couldn't be called pacifist":

> Wisdom has its virtues;
> Faithfulness, duty, and all-embracing love have them as well;
> But none is so universally honored,
> As bravery that, instead of wilting before death,
> Boldly calls forth violence in battle.

Those were certainly different words, Dresler sniped, than the phrases "crammed into his mouth by those who were calling themselves Goethe admirers under the Republic – in an effort to gloss over their wimpiness."[16]

In 1930, the paper claimed that Goethe "called to Nazis" in the "true spirit of old Weimar," particularly in lines like "Germany stand united against the foreign enemy!" and "Stand armed together, and no one is your match!" Such words provided evidence that Goethe would have concurred with Nazi plans for militarizing German society and education. In the same spirit, he wrote in *Elective Affinities* (1809) that "men should wear uniforms from their youth on, because they must learn to work together, to lose themselves, to work in groups, and to work for the whole." Though a savant, the *Völkischer Beobachter*'s Goethe was "no shirker" and therefore regretted not having served: "Had the Wars of Liberation occurred when I was a twenty-year-old, I certainly wouldn't have been left behind."[17]

Notions of Schopenhauer's philosophy as one of aggressive action rather than "quietistic pessimism" were also given substantial attention in the *Völkischer Beobachter*, though not without some controversy. Alfred Bäumler – the main Nazi Nietzschean – held that there was a "Germanic strain in Schopenhauer's pessimism" since "Germanic thinking would never be optimistic in the sense of a humanitarian illusion: it would always be realistic and look life right in the eyes," and Schopenhauer's "readiness to do battle with the dark side of existence" was consistent with this. But Bäumler also warned against the "dangerous quietism" to which Schopenhauer's thought could lead: the "wish for absolute peace – for redemption – was nihilistic." Above all, Schopenhauer's "aesthetic quietism" could lead directly to "political fatalism." So, when Nazis looked to Schopenhauer, Bäumler concluded, they did so "in honor of his fearless courage, in admiration of his spirit, and in profound gratitude for what he did as a master of German prose." At the same time, however, they "clearly sensed the distance that separated them from his century": the German of the Nazi era stood "far from every quietistic philosophy because he felt himself a member of a generation which was again confident in its power to master its historical destiny."[18]

Countering such qualifications about Schopenhauer's utility to the German military cause, Stuttgart journalist Karl Grunsky acknowledged that according to Schopenhauer, "this is the worst of all conceivable worlds, kept in motion by the blind will, the endless striving, and the mental power of men simply in order to cast light on their own worthlessness." Readers did not have to share this view, but Grunsky believed that it did "bring features of suffering and evil into bright consciousness and thereby strengthened the sense of the tragic." Moreover, what Schopenhauer "demanded of human behavior" was a "noble goal that could inspire enthusiasm" among Nazis. One could correlate the "ancient Indian moods" that Schopenhauer loved with "German notions of heroism" that the thinker also praised: "if Schopenhauer's goal was to remove the guilt of existence, then Nazis could undertake to do this in a fighting rather than a passive manner."[19] Josef Stolzing also felt that Schopenhauer's ideas could influence the "rebirth of the Volk through National Socialism: to live meant to fight, and only thus did Nazis understand the heroic resistance to fate, the defiance of death, that was so characteristic of Germans." In the end, Stolzing pressed, the philosophy of Schopenhauer "was to be understood in these terms."[20]

A confirmed enemy of France, according to Nazi interpretations, Beethoven likewise appeared in prewar *Völkischer Beobachter* propaganda as a fighter (*Kämpfer*). For instance, Ludwig Schiedermair compiled for the newspaper a collection of anecdotes and quotations that purported to establish Beethoven's status as a "fighter of great willpower."[21] Nazis also reiterated a legend regarding Bismarck's feelings about the *Appassionata Sonata* – "If I heard this music often, I would always be very brave" – to imply that Beethoven's music should serve as an inspiration to all Germans to be brave in political and military situations.[22] The paper repeated the anecdote in 1929,[23] and again in 1935, with the following commentary: "to the Iron Chancellor, Beethoven's music was the sonic symbol of human heroism; after listening to this heroic, passionate music he felt that the highest virtues of the warrior had been manifested."[24]

Toward the same end, Josef Stolzing recast a First World War anecdote about Beethoven's grand-nephew. The article, "Landsturmmann Beethoven: A Wartime Memory," related the story of a German officer who trained the ill-fated grandson of Karl, and concluded with the following sentimental embellishment: "Dismissing my squad, I squeezed Beethoven's hand with particularly heartfelt feelings. Tears rolled down his cheeks. Half a year later he was no longer among the living. He died in a garrison hospital of blood poisoning caused by a leg wound that he had neglected. The sad end of *Landsturmmann* Beethoven: the last descendant of the creator of the Ninth!"[25] Implicit in this report is the notion that Beethoven would have fought in the First World War like his distant relation, and could therefore be considered a symbolic flag-bearer in future battles.

As those offensives commenced, the militaristic tone of the paper's cultural section escalated. In 1938, just days after German troops had marched into Czechoslovakia, the *Völkischer Beobachter* covered concerts by Gustav Havemann's "Orchestra of the Führer" performed in the Sudetenland towns of Rumburg und Schoenlinde. Crowds greeted them, the paper reported, cheering and shouting, "We thank our Führer." Then, at the performances, the "dramatic expression" of Beethoven's Third *Leonore* Overture "arose from the opening tones to the triumphant joy of the rescue" – all of which seemed "compellingly immediate" under the circumstances. Finally, according to the review, the "moving tonal language" of the Fifth Symphony "awakened in the souls of the deeply moved listeners a feeling for the philosophical credo of the master, which was particularly significant in view of the great national events of the last few days: 'Through suffering to joy!'"²⁶ *Völkischer Beobachter* reception of the Ninth Symphony took on even stronger wartime connotations when Heinrich Stahl argued, soon after the invasion of Poland in 1939, that Beethoven had intended his "fire-drunken call" for fraternal unity to be "a sign that he had indignantly turned away from the conqueror Napoleon." After thus conflating the history of the Ninth (premiered almost a decade after Napoleon's defeat) with Beethoven's Third Symphony, Stahl finished by stating that "as readers were recognizing more than ever in the present fight for the Volk," realization of this hope for a unified Europe would only come after "final German victory."²⁷

Upon Hitler's attack to the west in 1940, the *Völkischer Beobachter* drew from the history of the Hundred Years War between France and England for cultural-historical ammunition. Reporting from the front less than a week after French capitulation, it published a report submitted from the town of Reims, beginning with a description of the town's cathedral and its statue of the great heroine, Joan of Arc. The point of the article was not to provide readers back home with a travelogue from the front, rather, as it surveyed the conquered territory, the paper was depicting German troops and their leader as sensitive defenders of the medieval art historical past. It was only because the Reims cathedral had been "hermetically sealed by order of Hitler himself, to protect it from war damage," the *Völkischer Beobachter* insisted, that such descriptions were still possible. The Führer was committed to protecting the Gothic legacy of the Western tradition, and, indeed, even the conquered French should have been grateful for this.

However, there was more propagandistic potential in this reference to Reims under German occupation. While alluding to Joan of Arc's role in uniting the French in 1429, the *Völkischer Beobachter* addressed the immediate political and military situation. The British had just fled the field of battle from Dunkirk, and the Battle of Britain was about to begin. In light of the situation, the *Völkischer Beobachter* exhorted Frenchmen to join the German effort against Churchill's perfidious Albion, via reference to St. Joan's memory. Would not the "change of history that the German sword had brought about," the paper asked, finally teach the French "that just as in the times of the virgin [of Orleans] depicted in the high nave of the old cathedral of Reims, no one could be a friend to selfish England; that Europe could not return to peace and quiet

Figure 18.6 Rembrandt, *The Concord of the State* (1640–1641), Museum Boijmans van Beuningen, Rotterdam, the Netherlands

and to blessed work until England was forced to its knees?" If the French did not soon come to the realization that they "had to turn away from this treacherous friend and his lying democratic-plutocratic ideals, not even the virgin [warrior] would be able to help them any more."[28]

The *Völkischer Beobachter* found another source of purported justification for German moves to the west in Rembrandt's work. Richard Biedrzynski reported that volkish writer Gustav Steinbömer had discussed Rembrandt's sketch for *The Concord of the State* (Figure 18.6) in his *Politische Kulturlehre* (1933). According to Steinbömer, the work was usually taken as a political allegory celebrating "victory against a foreign enemy through the unified effort of Dutch provinces, cities, and guilds." But he felt otherwise, and Biedrzynski endorsed Steinbömer's new position. Dated 1640 or 1641, eight years before the Peace of Westphalia through which Holland became independent, the presence of the crown and empty throne in this image was "particularly noteworthy." By their inclusion, Rembrandt seemed to have been "calling out for an affiliation of Holland with the German

Reich," as if the throne was meant to be assumed by German imperial authority rather than by the Dutch.[29] As Simon Schama points out, "the overcomplicated density of the allegory makes it very difficult to decipher *The Concord of the State*,"[30] but as Nazi-led forces occupied Holland, the *Völkischer Beobachter* was prone to imply that Rembrandt would have approved of the situation.

In July 1940, as Alsace was being "reconnected to the Reich," Friedrich W. Herzog took the opportunity to reflect on Goethe reception in Strasbourg. Arguing that the French had "misappropriated Goethe" before the war, Herzog related his memories of the Goethe Year in 1932 when there had been an exhibition in the contested city that addressed the poet's relations with Alsace, accompanied by lectures from leading French literature professors. One such professor, Herzog recalled, a friend of former Prime Minister, Raymond Poincaré, had "made the Nazi movement out as a gainsayer of Goethe." Only through a return to Goethe's "conservatism," the French speaker had argued, would Germany restore peace. Such a view of "Goethe's conservatism," Herzog wrote, was a misuse of the poet for French propaganda, since it implied that Goethe would have wanted the region to remain under "Gallic patronage." In contrast, Herzog pointed out that another festival had taken place at the same time in nearby Sesenheim. Dedicated to Goethe and Frederike Brion – whom the poet had wooed in that town – this celebration had been a "true Volksfest": the "Sesenheimer sang Goethean folk songs and raised a glass to the well-being of the greatest writer of all times." Memories of this event reminded Herzog in 1940 that "even during the decades of their division from the Fatherland, the Alsatians never gave up on their connection with the great homeland." But their ordeal had ended with the invasion of France, Herzog could conclude: "Strasbourg, where the writer developed himself into an independent spirituality and greatness, and Sesenheim, where he discovered his heart, were again German land."[31]

In spite of their military successes up to that point, Germans soon received a preview of the air onslaught that would come. The *Völkischer Beobachter* reported on 18 August 1940 that "English fliers in great number" had attacked the "Gau-capital Weimar" along with other places in Thüringia. "Criminally," the paper noted, the British had tried to drop bombs on the clearly marked Red Cross station in the Belvedere Allee, but the real source of outrage for the paper was located in the attack on German culture. They "didn't even shrink from" bombarding Goethe's *Gartenhaus im Park*, the paper reported – a place "before which the whole world bowed in respect." The bombs struck in a vicinity of 23–30 meters around the house, where many unexploded charges with time fuses were later found. It was a miracle, then, that the building had not sustained more damage than it had. "With the moon shining brightly, the ground could be seen precisely and the Gartenhaus could have been clearly recognized, so there is no doubt that this wicked deed was a conscious act." In their march to the west, "German troops accepted strategic difficulties in order to spare culturally and artistically valuable buildings," the paper insisted. Driven by their "destructive frenzy," however, British fliers "did nothing to avoid attacking a place that was holy to all the world, where one of the greatest writers and thinkers produced works of incomparable greatness." Britain had thereby shown that all its preaching about fighting a "war for culture in the light of truth" was nothing but hypocrisy.[32]

The cultural section of the *Völkischer Beobachter* did its part to punish the hypocritical "Brits" with a 1941 article entitled "Händel's Martyrdom in England." Along with minimizing Händel's connections to Britain, this article was designed to associate the composer with contemporary Germans who had been living in foreign lands but were now, during the present conflict, making their way "back to the Fatherland." Friedrich Baser exclaimed that "along with the millions now returning to the Reich, there is one that we do not want to forget – one who, after a heroic half-century long battle at his lost outpost of German culture, fell." In every aspect of his work, life, and "struggle," according to Baser, he was a true German, despite the difficulties of his circumstances. Sadly, he could "only greet the *Friederizianische* dawn" (that is, the rise of Friedrich II) from a great distance. But in 1941 it was finally time to counter myths about Händel's second home of choice. In brief, Baser insisted that it would be more accurate to call it his "state" of choice, because "never has an artist of such brilliant, indisputable greatness had to fight his whole life against so much premeditated evil as Händel did in London, to the point of despair."[33]

Given its proclivity toward the German music tradition, it is no surprise that the *Völkischer Beobachter* also referred often to Mozart, Beethoven, and Wagner in the war years. Indeed, one of the best wartime opportunities for cultural politicians of the Third Reich to exploit Mozart came with the 150th anniversary of the composer's death in 1941. A *Völkischer Beobachter* summary of commemorations devised for the Mozart Year announced that "everything had been arranged according to the will of the Reich Minister for Propaganda, Dr. Goebbels." Concerts, ceremonies, and especially radio broadcasts were organized throughout Germany. As the paper noted, this celebration "crossed national borders even during wartime" with, as it boasted, "almost every European nation heeding the call to pay homage to the genius of one of the greatest men in the realm of music." Commemorations in allied regions interested the *Völkischer Beobachter* especially: as a "nice gesture of close cultural solidarity," it emphasized, Fascist Italy organized a series of Mozart productions at La Scala in Milan.[34] The *Völkischer Beobachter* also took the opportunity during the Mozart Year to discuss the composer's "mission" with regard to the shifting relations between Austria (*Ostmark*) and northeastern territories (*der deutsche Nordostraumes*) in connection with opera productions under way for the new *Reichsgautheater* in Posen. For the paper, such productions clearly symbolized policies of occupation rather than cooperation: in Mozart, "linked by blood to the Donau countryside," one could perceive "Nordic national powers merging with the grace and warmth of the South." Moreover, the paper argued that the "national awakening" he initiated led to "uncontested world dominance by Germany in matters of music," insinuating that Mozart's musical achievements somehow justified Germany's move for dominance in other areas.[35]

On Hitler's birthday in 1941, the paper announced that the Führer himself would mark the Mozart sesquicentennial by sponsoring a new complete edition of his music, to be completed at the Mozarteum's Central Institute for Mozart Research. Moreover, the 1941 *Todestag* also marked the centennial of the Mozarteum itself, and this occasion gave Reich Education Minister, Bernhard Rust, and his comrades another reason to gather at the site. In his speech for the event, Rust observed that the recent years of political and military upheaval had intensified recognition that "heydays of music did not occur in focused, creative periods exclusively," since the most important inspirational basis for musical creativity was the "natural talent of the Volk itself, which was always present"[36] – even in times of war, evidently. In May 1941, the *Völkischer Beobachter* reported on an exhibition of Mozart documents at Munich's Stadtmuseum, along with further commemorative events that were arranged in Austria and especially Vienna. Baldur von Schirach – by then *Reichsleiter* and *Reichsstaathalter* in

Vienna – announced an array of events comprising Vienna's Mozart Week, which, again, had been organized "under the patronage of Reich Minister Goebbels." Among the events announced were productions of Mozart's major operas, an academic congress, an exhibition in the National Library, the laying of a wreath at the Albertinaplatz monument, and a concluding performance of the *Requiem* by the Vienna Philharmonic Orchestra.[37] All the Austrian ceremonies were represented in the *Völkischer Beobachter* as signs of Greater German culture: with the "homecoming of the *Ostmark* to the German Reich," it contended, "a wide gap had been closed and all traces of the divided past would soon disappear." The name of Mozart, which had previously been used as a "mere advertisement for the Salzburg Festival," once again "shone with pure, unadulterated brilliance – for a fully unified nation."[38]

As for the Salzburg Festival itself, special wartime significance was attached to it in 1941. This edition of the festival was "unlike any other," the paper stated, because it was intended primarily for members of the *Wehrmacht*: "to provide the heroes of the world-historical struggle with some rest and edification." According to reports, when Goebbels – accompanied by *Gauleiter* Friedrich Rainer, *Regierungspräsident* Albert Reitter, and the *General Intendant* of the Salzburg Festival, Heinz Drewes – placed a wreath in the room where the master had been born, the streets were "strongly marked by the presence of uniforms." The *Völkischer Beobachter* found that these rituals triggered thoughts and moods that one could barely express: "Mozart, Salzburg; a war amid the peace of a great tradition; the peace of eternal artistry amid a war of world-wide transition: but they united everyone who was doing their duty both in the field and at home into a profound community."[39]

On Mozart's death day proper, 5 December 1941, Goebbels attended the main commemorative ceremony at the Vienna Staatsoper. To open, the Vienna Philharmonic Orchestra performed the overture to *La Clemenza di Tito*, and then Goebbels gave a speech that the *Völkischer Beobachter* published in full under the title, "The German Soldier is also Protecting Mozart's Music." Goebbels recognized that one might wonder whether an official function marking Mozart's *Todestag* was appropriate, in light of the "brutal events of the day." But he responded in the affirmative, for Mozart's music "belonged among all those things which German soldiers were defending against assault." Mozart's music still "ruled" in theaters and concert halls, and served as a symbol for the spiritual and cultural creativity of the Volk. More strongly than any other works of art, past or present, Mozart's music had "passed into the possession of the widest masses of the Volk." Therefore, there was no contradiction between "the world of sound in which he lived and worked, and the hard and threatening world Germans were experiencing – the chaos of which they wanted to transform into discipline and order." Like scarcely any other artist, Mozart fulfilled the greatest mission of art: "to raise the spirits of a tormented humanity and remove it to a better world." Goebbels closed by underscoring Mozart's volkish qualities: his importance was not confined to the fact that he was master of perfect musical form, only for privileged classes and art music experts to enjoy, on the contrary, "many of his arias had become possessions of the Volk; volkish spirit thrived in all of his music; he was a Volk artist in the truest sense of the word."[40]

On the day after this ceremony, another ritual in Vienna brought Nazi luminaries out again. In front of St. Stephan's Cathedral, representatives from eighteen nations gathered with the *Grossdeutsch* leadership to lay another wreath. As reported in the *Völkischer Beobachter*, "by order of the Führer and Commander-in-Chief of the Wehrmacht," the *Reichsstaathalter* of Vienna, *Reichsleiter* Baldur von Schirach, presented an olive wreath at the foot of a catafalque and memorial flame, "expressing the reverence that the German Volk had for Mozart." Göring, Goebbels, von Ribbentrop, and von Schirach together laid the wreath while the sound of all the church bells in Vienna vibrated over the city "in praise of a national immortal." Then, while Viennese gathered under "national flags" on the Stephansplatz, fanfares from *Die Zauberflöte* sounded. Thus, said the paper, "did the Volk greet Mozart." The Mozart Week of 1941, its report concluded, "once again proved the timeless significance of Mozart's work, even in the middle of war."[41]

In Salzburg at the same time, the local *Gauleiter*, Gustav Scheel, made clear the international significance of Mozart's legacy, at least from the Nazi perspective. Scheel's address, also delivered in concert with the city's church bells, first reminded listeners that the Führer had explained how important it was to preserve the memory of Mozart, as both a model and a source of inspiration. Mozart should be celebrated not only as a musician of European-wide validity, but also as a reminder that Germany, "then fighting a battle for Europe, had to take up a leading and organizing role in the cultural world." In the "great struggle for the preservation of Europe and for the preservation of European culture," this day would be marked in a quiet and profound way that "nevertheless strengthened the resolve for battle, since Mozart reminded them of the values of life and culture for which they were fighting."[42]

The following January, while looking back on the Mozart Year of 1941, Heinz Drewes summarized the "universality of Mozart's artistic personality," and its significance for a fascist Europe. In a statement the *Völkischer Beobachter* then printed, the head of the Mozarteum asserted that the composer was loved across all cultural boundaries because of his "exemplary command of form and the sweetness of his superabundant sources of invention." He embodied "unique grace, spiritual intimacy, controlled precision, and powerful tenderness – all characteristics which envious enemies commonly denied were part of the German constitution." During the Mozart commemorations in the Third Reich, the "self-contained spiritual-musical unity of the New Europe was coming to light for the first time, under the sign of Mozart."[43]

Alongside Mozart's, linkage of Goethe's name with German expansionism also reached a crescendo in the summer of 1941. Less than a week before the commencement of Operation Barbarossa, the annual Reich Cultural Convention (*Reichskulturtagung*) of the Hitler Youth took place in Weimar. The centerpiece of the convention was a speech in the German National Theater by Rainer Schlösser, editor for the *Völkischer Beobachter* cultural section after 1932,[44] by then acting as head of the Theater Division of the Ministry for Popular Enlightenment and Propaganda, and the paper summarized his address. To the audience that day, many of whom were undoubtedly fated to participate in the invasion of Russia, Schlösser first acknowledged that the time of Goethe and Schiller had been marked by the decline of Prussia and the break-down of the Holy Roman Empire. However, he maintained that the works of these writers had the "inherent power to overcome their time and space" and "carry the volkish message of the age forward, constituting a challenge to the future by filling hearts and minds with the glory of a revived Reich." Weimar was therefore not only a place of meditation, Schlösser contended, but was just as much "a thundering smithy where both the plowshare and the sword of the German spirit were forged." No one should accept that Goethe was "just something printed on paper so it can get dusty on the bookshelf." Nor was the idea of Goethe captured in the "schematizing notions of classical author and Olympian." Not only as a writer, but also as a minister, jurist, naturalist, theater manager, and educational artist, Goethe "took action." Above all, he nurtured in himself the "idea of the pan-German space as a united concept: he understood German culture, history, landscape, and people as part of the whole Germany, comprising all the areas that had been returned to the Reich by the Führer." In conclusion, Schlösser stressed to his young audience that unification of the "greater German space determined by blood and soil" could be achieved only by those who "felt the famous soldierly struggles of the German past as well as the might and effect of the German spirit as a call to the deed of political unification." Thus, the educational policies "symbolized by Potsdam and Weimar" were to build in young Nazis the awareness that "wherever Greater Germany marched, German culture – that is, in great part, Goethe – also marched."[45]

The Romantic poet, Heinrich von Kleist, was also counted among the marching ranks at this stage in the fighting. "Who answered the Napoleonic incursion into Germany more directly than he?" the paper asked. "Who felt deeper the difficult destiny of the Fatherland than he?" Kleist's works, *Hermann's Battle* and *The Prince of Homburg*, above all, "symbolized the German essence as it had passed through good and bad times." More importantly, they expressed the German "soldierly nature." He was born a hundred years too early, but history had shown that Kleist was right: he was "consumed with the wish that his Volk would march at the head of nations."[46] Thus, it was mainly an image of Kleist at the head of battle formations that the paper invoked during wartime.

Throughout the war, the party continued its tradition of marking Hitler's birthday with broadcasts of Beethoven's music and on 19 April 1942, just after Hitler personally assumed direct command of forces in the east, Goebbels arranged a special celebration. Its culmination was a performance of the Ninth Symphony, and in his accompanying speech Goebbels dictated what he expected listeners to draw from the event, and the *Völkischer Beobachter* reprinted his statement:

If ever the German nation felt itself united in one thought and one will, then it is in the thought of serving and obeying [Hitler]. The sounds of the most heroic music of titans that ever flowed from a Faustian German heart should raise this realization to a serious and devotional height. When, at the end of our celebration, the voices and instruments strike the tremendous closing chord of the Ninth Symphony, when the exhilarating chorale sounds joy and carries a feeling for the greatness of

these times into each and every German cabin, when
[Beethoven's] hymn resounds over all distant countries where
German regiments stand guard, then we want everyone,
whether man, woman, child, soldier, farmer, worker, or civil
servant, to be equally aware of the seriousness of the hour and
to experience the tremendous happiness of being able to
witness and take part in this, the greatest historical epoch of our
Volk.[47]

However, as it had profitably done in service of so much of its cultural coverage, when seeking sources to exemplify the alignment between artistic creation and the Nazi war effort, the paper placed its strongest emphasis on Hitler's favorite, Richard Wagner. For instance, in November 1940, the expansionist subtext that some Nazis perceived in the last act of *Die Meistersinger* was brought into the light in *Völkischer Beobachter* coverage of a performance in Strasbourg – the heart of newly reclaimed Alsace-Lorraine. According to Erwin Bauer, the first *Meistersinger* production in "liberated Alsace moved the heart as powerfully as the experience of a storm." In the immediate political atmosphere, the stage seemed to Bauer "as if transformed into a scene representing recent events," especially when the singer playing Hans Sachs "delivered the powerful warning of his closing address with stirring emotional effect, while turning directly toward the Alsatian audience." This was, for Bauer, a moment that "allowed everyone to relive in their deepest hearts what had taken place in the last few months, and a reminder that they had every right to celebrate at that hour." The "overwhelming jubilance" of Wagner's chorus seemed an expression of "unbounded joy in response to these developments." In the eyes of the Nazi observer, the Alsatian listeners "took part in this finale as if they were themselves the Volk of the *Festwiese*, giving thanks for all these feelings of happiness to a German master who had become a symbol of the richest and most worthy aspects of German existence."[48]

In addition to associating Wagner with anti-French revanchism, the wartime paper emphasized the composer's general distaste for the English. Erich Lauer, an active composer in the Nazi era who produced a *Farmers Cantata* and a *German Suite* for chamber orchestra, reproduced for the *Völkischer Beobachter* quotes from letters Wagner had written from London, wherein he expressed complete boredom with the cultural scene of the English capital. "I have nothing to do," he wrote to Otto

Wesendonck: "true art is something utterly foreign to them." To Liszt, he wrote extended passages articulating how uncomfortable he was in the English world. First, in an undated letter (c. March 1855): "My whole existence here is a perfect anomaly. I am in a strange element and in a thoroughly false position ... Blackguardism, obstinacy, and religiously nursed stupidity are here protected with iron walls; only a blackguard and a Jew can succeed here."[49] And again, on 16 May 1855:

> *I live here like one of the lost souls in hell. I never thought that I could sink again so low. The misery I feel in having to live in these disgusting surroundings is beyond description, and I now realize that it was a sin, a crime, to accept this invitation to London ... Through this hell my study of Dante, to which I could not settle down before, has accompanied me. I have passed through his Inferno, and am now at the gate of Purgatory.[50]*

Such remarks, Lauer said, gave Germans "a key to much that seemed backward, incomprehensible, and inconceivable in the people on the other side of the Channel." The most remarkable thing, he felt, was that the "stick-in-the-mud British world acted as if it wanted to oversee the young modern world." Readers could be thankful, Lauer wrote, that already in the middle of the last century, Wagner had provided such "poignant testimony" about the English.[51]

The most useful Wagnerian resource the *Völkischer Beobachter* could put into service in its anti-British propaganda was his short story, *A Pilgrimage to Beethoven*. Written in 1840 for the *Gazette Musicale* in Paris, Wagner portrayed a young man – much like himself at the time – who journeys to visit the master in Vienna. Along the way, the hero is regularly thwarted by a rich Englishman who has the same plan. Whoever reads the short story, wrote Willibert Dringenberg, would "grasp why the Brits had established a blockade against Wagner's work" at the beginning of the war. The "Brit" in the story was an "English snob" who was in every sense "the opposite of cultured and civilized." For Dringenberg, there could not be a better representation of the "mechanical nature of the English soul," especially when contrasted against the "humility and modesty of the German musician." In the end, as Dringenberg explains, the Englishman never manages to meet Beethoven because the "will to culture" was not what drove him, "as it did the young German." Instead, the Brit was merely motivated by "the lack of respect typical of a cultured dandy." Like this character, Dringenberg extrapolated, the contemporary English were driven by an "excessive need for gathering, for grasping – an instinctive lust for possession, be it gold, Greek reliefs, or Egyptian mummies; fruitful land, desert, or ocean; colored servants, French *poilus*, or neutral ships." His "spiritual illness – his spleen – was the desire to own everything: it knew no boundaries, and also no aesthetic style," and "it was from this spleen that English impertinence, pretentiousness, bossiness, haughtiness, restraint, and coerciveness developed." Wagner "intuitively observed these foundations of the English soul," wrote Dringenberg, and "deliberately represented the English plutocrat as the opponent of the cultured German individual." Let the English hate Wagner, Dringenberg closed, for "their hatred added to his renown, and to German pride."[52]

Later, in the summer of 1941, just eight days after German forces invaded the Soviet Union, the *Völkischer Beobachter* shifted its attention from Wagner's battle against Britain to associations it could make between his music dramas and the new front. According to Heinrich Stahl, his *Götterdämmerung*, the last of the Ring Cycle, could be interpreted as presaging the positive outcome of the Barbarossa campaign: "the stormy tempo and powerful events of the conflict were bringing the German Volk closer than ever to recognition of the deepest meanings of the Ring – of the connections between great art and the Volkish war of liberation." In the Ring Cycle, Wagner "shaped the inevitable historical progression of an old, rotten world toward self-immolation into a gigantic cultural symbol: the fall of the Walhalla gods wasn't a catastrophe, but a great process of purification – relieving the world of enormous guilt."[53] Stahl could not have known that he was inadvertently portending the *Nazidämmerung* – an act of sacrifice that would ultimately lead to the fall of the national gods, including Hitler and Wagner, and payment for enormous crimes against humanity.

The most extreme use of Wagner culture for the propagandistic aims of Nazi Germany at war was manifested in the series of wartime festivals at Bayreuth. As Frederic Spotts has written:

> Hitler's determination to keep the country's opera houses and theaters open was meant to demonstrate the Third Reich's undiminished dedication to culture. But in the case of Bayreuth, Hitler had a very special reason: at last he would be

> *able to indulge his passion for having others – indeed, now*
> *tens of thousands of others – attend Wagner's operas.*
> *Beginning with the 1940 season, Hitler instituted what were*
> *called War Festivals, open no longer to the public but to*
> *persons known as "Führer guests." Such guests were*
> *members of the military and workers in war industries who,*
> *as a reward for their patriotic service, were to be taken to*
> *Bayreuth with all their expenses paid.*[54]

Throughout the war, the *Völkischer Beobachter* dedicated intensive coverage to these bizarre manifestations of Nazi cultural politics. On 21 July 1940, the newspaper reported gleefully that 1,350 soldiers and armament workers arrived in Bayreuth, and Winifred Wagner – along with leading officials of the party and *Wehrmacht* – came to the train station to welcome them.[55] Among the attendees were nurses, officers, workers, and sailors. According to the report, one could "read on their faces the profound joy they felt in receiving the Führer's gift allowing them an unparalleled experience of Richard Wagner's works." One felt different at these wartime festivals, the paper reflected, "as if new born!" Soldiers and workers were "voraciously and thoughtfully taking in the great thoughts of poetry and music that encompassed all of humanity, with deeply moving awareness, and often revelations that struck them like lightning." In the paper's view, this "great National Socialist deed" would result in clear cultural effects, increasing the common experience of high art across the whole Reich.[56]

Most importantly, from the point of view of the newspaper, Hitler himself "shared the excitement" of the *Götterdämmerung* performance with his "soldierly workers at the front and in the armaments industry." That everyone was filled with a feeling of "infinite gratitude for the wonderful gift" could be heard in the "unceasing jubilation" that sounded from the city center to the Festival hill as Hitler went down the boulevard under the decorative banners which read "Führer: You are Germany!" Then in the hall itself, as he entered and took his place next to Winifred, "young and old Volk comrades who had been found worthy could wonder at the unmistakable fact that art does not have to retreat in the face of hard military necessities and political affairs." In the intermissions, the Führer greeted guests "in friendly fashion," while groups of local children "ceaselessly called to him in delicious rhyming chants" such as "Dear Führer, look on out, out of the big Festival House!"

(*Lieber Führer, schau heraus, aus dem grossen Festspielhaus!*) How "immeasurably great," the *Völkischer Beobachter* boasted, was the "inner healing and strengthening afforded by this event!" In it, the "artistic, national, and social mission of Richard Wagner – his cultural message as a whole – seemed to be completely fulfilled!"[57]

A year later, three weeks into Operation Barbarossa, the festival went on, and *Völkischer Beobachter* rhetoric about its wartime significance intensified. Indeed, as the stakes of the conflict increased, so did the paper's forcefulness about associating Wagner's art with Hitler's militaristic nationalism. According to Friedrich Herzog, art too was a "battlefield of hardship and immortality": the true poet was, in Wagner's words, a prophet "enabled by the deepest, most soulful sympathy with a great commonality striving for the same ends." With the new offensive, Herzog stated, the German Volk was "experiencing a sense of unity that found unique expression in love for the Führer": Hitler had "opened the way for the Bayreuth idea of Richard Wagner into the Volk." By making a gift of the Festival to the front soldiers and armaments industry workers, Hitler had "fulfilled the bequest of the Bayreuth Master, whose thoughts and creations were always directed toward the Volk, not a particular class."

Houston Stewart Chamberlain, Herzog continued, once said that the Festspielhaus in Bayreuth was "a battle sign – a standard – around which those who remained true would gather, armed for war," and this "prophecy" was being realized at the wartime festival. What was the *Ring of the Nibelungen*, Herzog asked, except a "powerful sermon against Mammonism – a fearsome drama about the curse of gold?" In the original sketch of *Young Siegfried*, the dwarf Mime – who forged the Ring on the order of Alberich – wore a red cap on his bare skull and his craftiness and treachery "knew no bounds." Therefore, when the young Siegfried slays the cowardly dwarf, "who could not see the parallels with the events of the attack on the sneaky Reds in Russia?" Whoever had experienced the Ring in Bayreuth would immediately understand why the Führer "took on the issue of Bayreuth personally and raised it to a national symbol." Indeed, it was "in this spirit [that Herzog] greeted the 1941 Festival Summer for German Workers and Soldiers" – and, by implication, the Russian invasion – with Wagner's words: "Begin!" (*Fanget an!*).[58] Complementing Herzog's greetings was a description of the soldiers and workers arriving in Bayreuth prepared by Hermann Killer, author of works on Mozart's operas and the composer, Albert Lortzing: "Here artistic experience became one of general education" and, therefore, was a "social act in which the whole Volk participated." The event, thought Killer, was "also a side of the war that marked the wide gap between the opponents: for Germans, it was a clear confirmation that final victory was certain."[59]

A week later, directly beneath photos of fighting at the Eastern front, the Nazi newspaper published an extended statement about the significance of continuing cultural life, especially the Bayreuth Festival, as the war raged on. That "such an abundant series" of cultural events like the Festival Week in Bayreuth, the Great German Art Exhibit in Munich, and the Salzburg Art Summer were being "arranged and experienced in the middle of the war was a sign of the Volk's irrepressible will to life and the feeling of longing that war had given Germans to return to their most characteristic national values via art." The Volk therefore could be "prouder than they had ever been before." It was clear that it was only with the "dramatic progress of most recent German history under Adolf Hitler, and only with the war, that they had really opened their eyes and hearts again for their old German myths." Only thereby had they once again developed a "sense for Siegfried, a sense for Wotan, a sense for Richard Wagner's magical world – only then had they become real Germans." That is why, said the paper, it was easier than ever before to speak with visitors at the Festival in Bayreuth about the works of Wagner. They all had "more sensitive ears than before," because their own "tremendous experiences had drawn them closer to the greatness of his creations." When out of the "uncanny quiet of the great space," in which you could not even hear a pin drop, the "redeeming sounds rose up the pillars and the walls fell away in a sensation of dreaming, it seemed like Germans had been standing there for a thousand years as a race that – like Siegfried – knew no fear because they wielded Nothung, the sword they forged themselves on the anvil of world envy and the darkest enmity." To provide soldiers and workers with this "unforgettable pleasure" was an achievement that could have occurred only in one place in the world, in "Adolf Hitler's Reich." The "Jews over in the lands of [English] plutocracy and [Soviet] Bolshevism could stuff their mouths more than Germans could, but they were such miserable clods that even with all the gold in the world, they could not create the slightest bit of culture." Germany's "artistic operation" (*künstlerisches Einsatz*) was an "act of war" (*Kriegstat*) – "like all the creative deeds of the nation, it was a foundation stone for victory." From this spectacle the

Führer guests at the Festival "learned to know Greater Germany: the Germany that not only fought for its existence and its global validity with weapons, but which, as in earlier centuries and millennia, was called forth to spread its cultural heritage across borders and stand as a model for other peoples."[60]

To mark the 1942 festival, Herzog continued to rant about the "Jewish and leftist cabal" which had spoiled things for Wagner during the Weimar era, and which German forces were supposedly in the process of eradicating once and for all through the war in Russia. The "beneficiaries of the November Revolution of 1918" had been united in their rejection and derision of Bayreuth thought. For them, Bayreuth was just a seat of reaction. But those "gentlemen" had no idea that it had developed into a "bulwark of nationalistic thinking," for otherwise they would have applied even heavier measures against Bayreuth and Haus Wahnfried. But the extent of the corruption of public opinion in the Weimar era was clear in the readiness with which the newspapers of the Social Democrats and Democrats had "lapped up the slime of the Muscovite Bolsheviks" after the "Jewish culture tsar," Anatoly Lunacharsky – the first Soviet People's Commissar of Enlightenment, responsible for culture and education – had "certified Wagner's *Siegfried* for the Marxists." Correcting this interpretation, Herzog countered that Nazi German life and cultural views were "worlds apart from these Bolshevik cultural ideals," and "no bridge of understanding could span the gap." With the "seizure of power, the Führer had placed Bayreuth under the protection of the Reich and thereby established the preconditions for a process of restoration that did not suffer from material concerns," and this was ultimately to the benefit of Wagner's works. For Wagner, Bayreuth was not a "center of modern cultural luxury," but rather a "site for the Volk whom he called forth to join him in indispensable efforts." From the very beginning, the Volk was included in his work; his characters "demanded public, Volk-binding effect." It was in this sense that Wagner's work "connected with the National Socialist world view."[61]

The newspaper also reported in 1942, that the leader of the Nazi Teachers' League and *Gauleiter* of Bayreuth, Fritz Wächtler (destined to be executed by the SS for "defeatism" in 1945), organized a music education forum on "Richard Wagner and German Schools." On the occasion, Wächtler issued a "call to all teachers in Greater Germany" to "honor the total personality of Wagner as an ingenious artist of German character, as a fighter for great political ideas, as a political prophet of German rebirth, as a herald of a German way of life, and as spokesman for a German world view; in short, as one of the Volk's most powerful sources of strength." In the first three years of war, Wächtler continued, Germans had experienced the "greatness and significance of the Bayreuth effect" as it had influenced the German Volk while it was fighting its "hardest and most decisive battles of fate." Tens of thousands of German soldiers and comrades from the armaments industries had come to experience the War Festivals as Führer guests. From this they had derived "proud new love for Germany, heightened enthusiasm, and strengthened powers for the battle they were fighting to protect the German nation and German culture." The Bayreuth War Festivals thus had done more than provide symbolic value, they had "carried the work of Richard Wagner to the Volk." That said, Wächtler concluded, the festivals were not an end in themselves, but the "start of a great cultural-political mission." Germans stood at the start of a "new operation," under orders the Führer gave to the whole nation in his cultural speech at the Nuremburg Rally of 1933: "only a few god-given individuals in history had perceived the goal of really creating something new and imperishable; it was the job of the nation to educate people to honor such greats sufficiently, because they were manifestations of a Volk's highest values."[62]

In 1943, when the Festival choir had to be strengthened, because its ranks were diluted by the war effort, with voices from the Hitler Youth, the League of German Girls, and the SS Standarte Wiking, the tone of the *Völkischer Beobachter* remained resolute, but discussion of soldiers and workers at the festival began to emphasize themes of "holding out" rather than of triumph. To the astonishment of the rest of the world, wrote Erwin Völsing, despite the "harshest exertions of war, because of its unwavering confidence in victory, the Volk was still capable of deep introspection in reverence to German geniuses" like Wagner, who supplied "unconquerable power to overcome the sorrows and sacrifices required by its battle of fate." Even press conference statements by the head of the German Labor Front (*Deutsche Arbeitsfront*, DAF), Robert Ley, implied that the German nation was facing overwhelming forces: "These one-of-a-kind War Festivals revitalized a sacred belief in the Fatherland and the inflexible will to promote the life of our Volk, while criminal and barbaric enemies ventured to destroy the most venerable cultural monuments and even peaceful residential areas of many German cities in an unprecedented policy of cultural annihilation."[63]

As the harsher imagery in these 1943 statements from Bayreuth evince, references to the German tradition, musical and otherwise, continued to appear in the *Völkischer Beobachter* as the tide turned, but in increasingly grave tones. Among the most poignant of these ran on 31 January 1943, during the last stage of the battle for Stalingrad, under the title, "The Musician of God." Simultaneous with the capitulation of von Paulus' Sixth Army, Günther M. Greif-Bayer, who had just finished writing a "tour guide" for occupied Prague, asserted that Mozart's music found its greatest resonance in the German populace, conveying an "artistic experience which lifted it out of the horrors of daily life into light and blessed heights."[64] One wonders if statements like these, ostensibly intended to provide solace to those who had lost loved ones on the Eastern front, had any redeeming effect at all, since the only subsequent mention of the surrender at Stalingrad to appear in the *Völkischer Beobachter* was a brief announcement from Goebbels that, as a memorial gesture, theaters and concert halls would be closed between 4 February and 6 February.[65]

By April 1943, the pre-established view of Schiller's work as "poetry of the willingness to die" was even more explicitly manifested in the pages of the *Völkischer Beobachter*. Supposedly speaking for German soldiers, who were then increasingly on the defensive at the Eastern front and in North Africa, the paper held that the "Volk of unified brothers" that Schiller had foreseen – indeed, the Volk that the "glow of his hot heart belonged to" – thought of him as one of the "noblest heroes of the patriotic freedom to which he devoted his last forces: faithful unto death."[66] Similarly, the paper increasingly emphasized Rembrandt's late portraits as representing individuals overcoming tremendous personal suffering, as Germans had to do in wartime. In June 1943, Ludwig Thoma wrote about Rembrandt's "late difficulties," and his "Nordic effort" to overcome them: "Now, as everything fell down, as everything was smashed to pieces, the greatest came forth. Tossed about by the force of fate at the heights and the depths of human experience, Rembrandt finally changed directions ... going where no one before or after him ever tread, groping toward that highest realm which only the greatest thinkers have approached."[67]

Allusions to Goethe in the *Völkischer Beobachter* likewise shifted toward an emphasis on his experience of the rigors of battle and the impact of war on the civilian population. Presenting at the New Year a "Goethe for 1944," Heinz Steguweit, a cultural-political critic and regional leader of the Reich Chamber for Literature in Gau Köln-Aachen, reminded readers that even Goethe's "beautiful poetry was written in violent times," and that it had to be understood in this way under the present conditions. Surely, earlier times were more carefree and easy than the present, but readers had to admit that "in peaceful days they thought less about issues of fate." Before the war, they often made the mistake of thinking that dealing with everyday annoyances consti-tuted a struggle for existence. Similarly, many may have taken up the writings of "the great German" under the mistaken assumption that the times of Goethe were perfectly idyllic. But this was inaccurate. Whoever took the trouble to look through the years in which he lived and worked, Steguweit asserted, would come to the "astonishing realization" that Goethe's days were also "full of difficulty and concern." Steguweit then summarized the challenges which the German nations faced in Goethe's lifetime: the Seven Years War "moved hearts until the Peace of Hubertusburg," and in the Napoleonic epoch "the Volk had to prove itself through struggle, because it had no other way out." The battle near Jena was lost, the "Schillschen officers fell to Wesel on the Rhine under the shells of foreign guns," the "sun of Austerlitz did not seem to set for the Corsican." For German unity, moreover, things stood worse than ever, because "many princes of the land formed a union in favor of the oppressor." That, "my readers," said Steguweit, was Goethe's time. It was a bitter one for the nation, and in fact their ancestors had "plenty of reason not to be as hopeful as Germans were in 1944." But by reflecting on the circumstances that Goethe faced during his lifetime, the article continued, Germans could draw a sense of confidence, if not comfort: "The Battle of Leipzig did arrive on 18 October 1813, the spring of 1814 followed, the Emperor of Europe had to resign, and the once anxious regions of Germany resounded with cries of victory through all the streets and mountains." Even more, Field Marshal Blücher was – strangely, it may have seemed in 1944 – "called to London with his king, where the now so perfidious Brits wanted to embrace him as the conqueror of the tyrant." Germans of the present day had to hold onto these memories, Steguweit maintained, and "remain proud, brave, and confident in them" because it was not only the "faith of the Volk" during Goethe's time that related to 1944, but also "the poet who illuminated such a difficult age with his songs, gave it a soul, and therefore continued to light the way to the goal." Accordingly, Steguweit concluded that Nazis should not think that Goethe's verses could be sung only during idyllic days. In 1944, he felt, they had to recognize and appreciate the greatness of the battles they were fighting, "since no one fights without the deeper knowledge of the holiness of the liberation to come."[68] Viewing Goethe's wartime experiences and verses in the present-day light of the trials of 1944 was, in the pages of the *Völkischer Beobachter*, a means of maintaining faith in the cause.

Renaissance art was also linked with the increasingly difficult German war effort when Richard Biedrzynski glorified Leonardo da Vinci in the spring of 1944 as "The Italian Faust" – in largely militaristic terms. According to Biedrzynski, Leonardo was the most universal person of the Renaissance, with a "boundless dissatisfaction" that gave him a Faustian character. While his paintings approached the spiritual – or mystical – as in the *Mona Lisa*, which "posed and solved at the same time the mysterious puzzle of feminine existence," it was the practical side of Leonardo "the inventor" that Biedrzynski celebrated in the wartime newspaper. To Nazis, he was more than a creator of "a few, fragmentary and legendary works that were fading away because of his own mistakes." Especially amid the Second World War it was Leonardo's struggles with the political and military forces of the Italian Renaissance that resonated most strongly in the pages of the *Völkischer Beobachter*. Similar, perhaps, to scientists who worked in underground facilities like Peenemünde, Leonardo "placed his practical knowledge into the hands of the strong-willed political leaders of his day" and wrestled with some of the same issues of scientific ethics. When Leonardo recommended himself to the duke of Milan, he promised the tyrant – "like all the restless natures of the Renaissance, gifted and cold-blooded, cruel and brilliant in one" – a variety of weapons and tools of war, including pontoons, bombs, underground trenches, tanks, mortars, stone catapults, rolling mines, rockets, and gas launchers. Later, Leonardo repeated his offer to Cesare Borgia, promising parachutes, airplanes, and underwater boats with which one could "break open ships below the waterline."

Leonardo's designs represented innovations that anticipated the "most ruthless possibilities of technology in its most destructive consequences," Biedrzynski pointed out, while at the same time acknowledging that Leonardo had doubts about making the technology available to a war lord running amok. Indeed, when Borgia revealed that he wanted to devastate Venice, "filling the lagoons with the ruins of ships and St. Mark's Place with corpses," Leonardo hid his inventions from him. To prevent an "all-too-horrible crime" he answered Borgia's demands by stating that "God has reserved the air for himself, the angels, and the birds." But despite such reservations, it was the "magical mechanical devices and magnificent constructions, especially the bestial madness of his war machines," that Biedrzynski offered as proof that Leonardo's nature was essentially "Faustian," exhibiting a will to knowledge and power, where "restless research" contributed to the mechanization of warfare even at the price of relinquishing the more spiritual attributes of this proto-typical man of the Renaissance.

In light of Biedrzynski's references to Leonardo's qualms about the potential for all-too-horrible crime under Borgia's leadership, the final section of his article might suggest that as the modern German war experience worsened, the *Völkischer Beobachter*'s cultural critic also had some doubts about following a cold-blooded, cruel tyrant to the end. He concluded with discussion of Leonardo's drawings of *A Deluge* (Figure 18.7), and admitted that these late visions of Leonardo had

Figure 18.7 Leonardo da Vinci, *A Deluge* (c. 1515), Royal Library, Windsor, UK

been tragic: in these "flood images," the artist sketched "enormous natural disasters with raging waters, bursting rocks, fire-breathing mountains, and furious storms." But, as if recoiling from his own vision of the abyss, Biedrzynski recovered his wartime propagandistic line by insisting that therein the artist-scientist "did not just recall the threatening and the frantic mood of medieval dances of death, but anticipated the dramatic force of the Shakespeare who wrote *Lear*, as well as the Nordic violence of Rembrandt."[69] According to the *Völkischer Beobachter*, then, when opposed with bestial madness, the Faustian soul – including Leonardo da Vinci's – would always answer with force and violence.

As shown extensively above, the *Völkischer Beobachter* worked intensively to highlight the more aggressive – "steely" – components of romantic-era German culture. The urge to militarize the Western cultural tradition also involved reading wartime significance into visual arts produced during the period. Even relatively minor works such as a couple of paintings by Philipp Otto Runge (1777–1810) were closely analyzed for indications of their value to the war propaganda effort. In April 1944, the newspaper argued that two such works, *The Hülsenbeck Children* (1805–1806) and *The Artist's Parents* (1806), "deserved increased attention in an art-sociological sense." In them, the *Völkischer Beobachter* stated, "indications of their politically and intellectually exciting times were palpable." The "pathos" expressed in these images was the "historical subsoil of the revolutionary era, Napoleonic imperialism, and the German Wars of Liberation." The people of that time "stood under the excessive pressure of forces that rose up from the historical-elementary," and they responded to it with the "gigantic works of disproportionate form."

In the portrait of Runge's parents, done in 1806 (Figure 18.8) – "Prussia's year of fate" – Runge's father "stood as a figure in which a restrained will expressed itself with almost excessive seriousness; a man who could stand up against Napoleon like Kleist's Michael Kohlhaas or [German war hero] Joachim Nettelbeck."[70] Viewing it, the paper held, "one saw monumentality, one felt greatness, one sensed superior will; one knew that a hardness had entered into this world which raised the bourgeois to the heroic – powerful punches of the will pounded inwardly, but externally everything remained restrained in busy, active waiting; one knew that force was being gathered to meet great demands."

Figure 18.8 Philipp Otto Runge, *The Artist's Parents* (1806), Kunsthalle, Hamburg, Germany

However, the *Völkischer Beobachter* believed, one "entered into the future" only with the children's portrait (Figure 18.9). Rarely had children been painted in this form, which "touched upon greatness." Both of the older children were modeled on the "marble tectonics of a pillar and were plump with inner force." From the "cords of the whip that the boy lifts like a commander's crop," the "air is torn as if by the bark of an order." Doesn't one get the feeling, the paper asked, that this "unchildish children's game expressed the same warlike spirit under which the generations of the Wars of Liberation grew up?" Yes, "one catches oneself thinking of a painted symbol, an intentional exorcism: in Autumn 1806 the Prussian army – even then the military core of Germany – had broken down before Napoleon. That is when the picture

Figure 18.9 Philipp Otto Runge, *The Hülsenbeck Children* (1805–1806), Kunsthalle, Hamburg, Germany

was painted: can't one almost hear it calling to the future" as Kleist had when he wrote:

> To arms! To Arms! …
> With the spear, with the rod
> Down into the valley of battle![71]

Thus did a "confessional picture" come into being, in which the "tone of that time was captured and passed on for future generations" – especially the present one, now enduring "total war."[72]

Upon the invasion of "Fortress Europa" by allied forces through Normandy, Richard Biedrzynski returned *Völkischer Beobachter* attention to Rembrandt's self-portraits, this time as early manifestations of themes later conveyed in Beethoven's *Eroica*, another symbol of holding out against the forces of fate. For Rembrandt, said Biedrzynski, the

Figure 18.10 Rembrandt, *Self-Portrait as Zeuxis* (c. 1662), Wallraf-Richartz-Museum, Cologne, Germany

mature works of old age became a matter of "self-defense." In the "portrait of a grinning old man" he at last revealed himself as a cynic about his misfortune, as one who defied the world – as "Nordic" (Figure 18.10). Were Germans feeling the same way as the war turned against them? In the words of art historian, Wilhelm Pinder, who was deeply involved in the wartime looting of art by Nazi authorities, who remained loyal to the regime through the German surrender, and died soon after being imprisoned as a collaborator, Biedrzynski found his answer: in this self-image the "masks of the tragic and merry muses were melted into one; the figure grins out with the mocking bow of a sad clown, ghostly and captivating, overwhelming us with sadness and at the same time with a laugh that would infect us if we did not sense the hidden tears in the throat." There, Rembrandt's grimace became "a symbol of Nordic defiance, as if all the contradictoriness of being had been combined in one single ball that he flings into our face."[73]

Figure 18.11 Rembrandt, *The Night Watch* (1642), Rijksmuseum, Amsterdam, the Netherlands

A few weeks later, for the 275th anniversary of the artist's death in October 1944, Biedrzynski reiterated his view that Rembrandt paintings constituted the "*Eroica* of a life that overcomes all of the disappointments, injustices, and faithlessness of the world: the deeper it wants to force him to the floor, the more immovably calm he becomes." The passion of his "bourgeois collapse only lifted him to the throne of his artistic singularity – of an invulnerable wisdom that stands above all coincidences of fate." Above all, *The Night Watch* (1642) (Figure 18.11) symbolized the "same tragic turning point in his life" that Hamlet represented in the biography of Shakespeare. Like Hamlet, according to Biedrzynski, Rembrandt went "the way of tragic passion" in this painting, a process that made his subsequent pictures the "elevated monologues of an afflicted soul." As a "silent, inexhaustible, earnest, and practical worker, he stares at us from the Nordic self-portraits" of the last period "with a sharp, inexorable gaze that looks through all the vanities of the world."[74] Thus did the *Völkischer Beobachter* present

Figure 18.12 Francisco Goya, *Street Battle at the Puerto del Sol, 2 May 1808* (1814), Museo del Prado, Madrid, Spain

Rembrandt as a fellow sufferer when the bonfire of Nazi vanities began to burn.

At this stage of the war *Völkischer Beobachter* space also went, somewhat strangely, to discussing the works of another non-German: Francisco Goya (1746–1828). In November 1944, a Freiherr von Merck provided extensive analysis of Goya as a "profoundly political, anti-French, artist of war." Von Merck recommended that anyone in search of a "level-headed perspective on the experience of war" look to Goya, who expressed in paint the same perception on the European situation as did his contemporary Goethe when he wrote: "Unless you master this – this dying and becoming – you are but a dreary guest on the dark earth."[75] Nothing, said von Merck, could say more about war than Goya's *Street Battle at the Puerto del Sol, 2 May 1808* (Figure 18.12). Therein, Napoleonic grenadiers attack and, caught in the fire of their weapons, Spanish insurgents sink to the ground with "gaping wounds, raging contortions, and defiant faces." Out of their lips comes "the defiant *Espana!* they screamed against their French executioners" – which, von Merck added, "sounded from Franco's infantry once again

Figure 18.13 Francisco Goya, *The Third of May* (1814), Museo del Prado, Madrid, Spain

as it threw itself against the international brigades of Bolshevism just a few years ago." Freemasonry and "feeble bourgeois dealings" with the French revolutionaries had led to the abdication of the Spanish king before Napoleon at Bayonne. On 2 May 1808, however, the citizens of Madrid rose up and died in resistance "against their subjugation, against the blind delivery of Spain to the French neighbor, and against the subversive, revolutionary teachings of 1789" – while Goya, in the attic of his house on the Puerta del Sol, painted the bloody street battle taking place below him.

Then, on 3 May 1808, he crept to the execution place on the French front line and captured the executions on canvas (Figure 18.13). It was as if, suggested von Merck, Goya wanted to "hang both of these gruesome, realistic paintings as mementos over the abdicated king's bed in the royal comfort of his Bayonne palace." For the Nazi writing in late 1944, Goya's masterpiece was a powerful example of how paintings from the past could remain current, how they continued to "speak to us in our days." The Spaniards of 1808 had reacted against the delivery of their land to foreign imperialism "just as peoples had recently done

Figure 18.14 Francisco Goya, "This is Worse," from *Disasters of War* (1810–1815)

when their governments, directly or indirectly, gave their countries up to Bolshevism." The people of a nation "instinctively recognize," better than their "pacifist politicians," that it is impossible to negotiate with aggressive imperialists. There was a "fascinating lesson to be learned" by comparing the reactions against Napoleon's "imperially draped export-liberalism" with the reactions to Stalin's "bourgeois cashiered export-communism of today."

King Charles IV was representative of "collaborators who mis-inform simple, faithful citizens," telling them that "it would be better to give up something in order not to lose everything." Were these not the same phrases, von Merck asked, "used by politicians of the present with respect to Bolshevism and its accomplices?" Such figures should have heeded Goya's powerful language before 1944, said von Merck, and should have been guided by the "masculine-European perceptions" of his paintings. His series of prints, *Disasters of the War* (Figure 18.14), were "impressive reproductions of the Iberian War against Napoleon" and remained "uncannily timely" in 1944. Goya's terrible dreams resembled the "nightmares that today haunt every human being on our continent with the thought of the victory of Bolshevism."

Figure 18.15 Francisco Goya, *The Family of Charles IV* (1800), Museo del Prado, Madrid, Spain

Moreover, von Merck went on, Goya's portrait of Charles IV and his family (Figure 18.15), with its "shocking assembly of dumb and malicious heads," was a "prophetic call for overcoming decadence in the spirit of 2 May 1808." In 1944, this "monumental painting of weaklings" had the effect of honoring, by contrast, "the strong ones who are worthy of reigning and fighting." Goya had lived at a turning point for the modern world, and modern Germans were experiencing another "decisive one." Referring to Hitler and his generals, von Merck was certain that "our leadership will never throw itself down before the storming eastern colossus in a cowardly way; it will never go toward Bayonne." A portrait of "our leadership would show hard, decisive soldier-like faces and would be an absolute counterpart to Goya's giant painting in the Prado: so we know with certainty that the future will be ours!" For the present, though, in the "dark autumn" of 1944, Europe was in "frightful pain" and had to "defend itself with blood once again." With its "feelings and values lying in rubble and ruins, along with cathedrals and other symbols of its culture," it could not afford to be sentimental. It was necessary to "bring Europe's psychological and physical life into correspondence with the harsh reality of its struggle." To do so, it could look to Goya's paintings for inspiration, since "war was the father of all things for Goya." In closing, von Merck nihilistically concluded that the Second World War had to "become the father of Europe, or Europe will no longer be," and "Goya will forever be talking to human beings who no longer understand him."[76]

By February of 1945, with Hitler in his bunker and the Europe of his plans ceasing to be, the *Völkischer Beobachter* resorted to reproducing, in serial format, Friedrich Schiller's description of the battle of Lutzen from Part III of his *History of the Thirty Years War*. Undoubtedly, Schiller's description of the battle and its effects – including passages such as the following – resonated with conditions in Germany and the rest of Europe at the time:

> *A murderous conflict ensued. The nearness of the enemy left no room for firearms, the fury of the attack left no time for loading; man was matched to man, the useless musket was exchanged for the sword and pike, and science gave way to desperation. Overpowered by numbers, the wearied Swedes at last retired beyond the trenches; and the captured battery was again lost in the retreat. A thousand mangled bodies already strewed the plain, and as yet not a single step of ground had been won ... The entire plain from Lutzen to the Canal was strewed with the wounded, the dying, and the dead ... History says nothing of prisoners; a further proof of the animosity of the combatants, who neither gave nor took quarter.*[77]

It is reasonable to wonder whether, in publishing such passages, the paper was somehow commenting on the ongoing experiences of those engaged in the final struggle. But such a possible interpretation of the editor's motives fails to mitigate the plain fact that in the pages of the Nazi newspaper, "The Poet of Freedom" had been made over into a chronicler of death.

The paper likewise implied parallels between Goethe's experiences in war and the fate of Nazi Germany, when on 2 March 1945 it published a lengthy article under the title "Goethe's War Experiences" in which W. B. von Pechmann, author of military literature such as *U-Boat*

Operations and their Success (1918), reviewed Goethe's observations during the latter stages of the siege of Mainz in 1793. "Every hour was pregnant with problems," Goethe reported:

> *One worried constantly for one's revered monarch and for*
> *one's dearest friends, forgetting to think of one's own safety.*
> *Drawn by the wild danger as by the eyes of a rattlesnake, one*
> *rushed into fatal positions, riding through and by the*
> *trenches, letting the Haubitz grenades fly by the head,*
> *shattering ruins all around: some of the wounded wanted to*
> *be put out of their misery, and you would not have wished life*
> *for some of those who were dead.*

Escaping these horrors, von Pechmann continued, Goethe got away to a blasted castle above the ruins and craters, from which he saw the city "with spires shot up, roofs with holes in them, smoking fires – a shocking sight!" Later, von Pechmann reviewed, Goethe looked on the fortress of Mainz which "aroused the most pitiable impression in him." He reported plundering, high walls threatening to collapse, towers wavering: so much that had been constructed through the centuries crashing "into rubble and ruins." His soul was "confused as to whether this devastation was more painful and sadder than it would have been if the city had been burned down by chance." That the *Völkischer Beobachter* presented this extended collection of Goethe's wartime observations in March 1945 could suggest that it intended some high-cultural solace for its readers, since the poet had undergone ordeals and witnessed sights similar to those that Germans were experiencing in the streets of shattered towns at the end of Hitler's war. But the last statement of von Pechmann's article eliminated the possibility of such an interpretation: Goethe's observations, he wrote, "led him to perceive the heroic acts of war – the soldier's role – in the light of honorable, brave and self-sacrificing manliness."[78] Thus, *Völkischer Beobachter* reception associated Goethe with the wartime propaganda theme of holding out (*Durchhaltung*) right to the bitter end.

On 14 March 1945, with Soviet troops approaching Berlin and a "Volk storm" (*Volksturm*) of barely trained conscripts preparing a futile defense, the *Völkischer Beobachter* cultural section ran a lengthy article on the "Courage to Accept Pain: German Masterworks for Our Times" – a title requiring no further comment. Therein, the "voice" of "Nazi

Figure 18.16 Matthias Grünewald, Isenheim altarpiece (c. 1510–1516), Unterlinden Museum, Colmar, France

culture" made its own last stand, still making claims for its place in the Western tradition, even – or especially – *in extremis*. On behalf of the paper and the party, Richard Biedrzynski held that above all the German "courage to accept pain" was the theme that best symbolized the nation's cultural superiority. To be sure, Leonardo and Michelangelo had not left pain out of their creations, and inclusion of signs of suffering is partly what made their art Faustian – even "Nordic." But because masters of the Renaissance from German lands proper "extended the tradition of Gothic emotionality," northern artists had to be considered even greater "painters of pain." "What Volk other than [Matthias] Grünewald's could produce the Isenheim altar?" he asked (Figure 18.16). The "deep expression of German Renaissance art" included the most "powerful representations of the suffering soul" – and this was what marked *Kultur* to the painful present. Germans experiencing the brunt of modern war shared the experience of profound suffering that ran through their tradition from the medieval era on: "Doesn't [Grünewald's] German

Pietà, born in pain and based on Gothic depictions of a mother's pain after the death of her son, also belong to us?" Whoever stands before the altar, Biedrzynski insisted, had to admit what "strong and passionate expression the German is capable of, full of shocking and fearless greatness, when he has to look at the world full of cruelty." Grünewald's (c. 1470–1528) images, "tremendous in their revolutionary piety, unmistakably German, with the force of ancient spells, say that even in dismaying times and in a bewildered mood, our art always has the force to deal with extremes and thereby to conquer."

Biedrzynski then posited that the whole romantic generation was "indescribably fearless and willing to accept its fate." Philipp Otto Runge's *Parents* was a visual manifestation of a culture that demanded "self-sacrifice" above all. Like romantic poets Novalis and Kleist, Runge "longed for an early death" while painting "orgiastic, fairytale like poem-pictures." But he was also the creator of "an image in which we see all of the terrible violence of the coming Wars of Liberation." The portrait of his parents was "not only the confession of an energetic, sincere, laconic North German middle-class character," but also "expressed the iron will and grim virtue that would come forth under the pressure of an inexorable and violent epoch, and would break the subjugator of Germany, Napoleon." As if "poured from iron," Runge's figures "walk before us in a cloak forged of destiny that lies upon them like military dress." A sculptor rather than a painter "seems to have intended for these people a metallic form, which signifies at the same time the clarity of their character and the armored will of [German] resistance."

In addition to Runge, Biedrzynski included the sculptor Andreas Schlüter among the "important political visual artists" of martyrdom in the name of national defense. "Would another Volk," he asked, "have ever managed this 'Iliad of the North' which Schlüter created in his masks of dying warriors in the Berlin Zeughaus?" For Biedrzynski, each of these masks indicated "an instant when those who are falling in battle are between life and death" – "the last face before crossing over the border to darkness." In them, the "will to power that underlay the mission of Prussia" found expression, along with the "courage to accept self-sacrifice and pain, without which power would not be sincere, but only brute force." Schlüter "shared the same sincerity" that Kleist had, "without flinching before the truth of life that includes death." Because of its "readiness to self-sacrifice, the young nation will be rewarded with the capability to endure everything." Biedrzynski concluded – as time ran out for the Third Reich – that the "examined ego always frees itself in this way and discovers the indestructible values that make it firm and even-tempered." Here "that zone is crossed, where unhappiness and cruel fate run out and shift into expectation," as Hölderlin expressed when he wrote that "a new bliss rises to the heart to hold out against and endure grief."

Therefore, Biedrzynski went on, along with such images, Germans could also "think of Friedrich Hölderlin" under the present circumstances. Lines like "he who stands on his misery, stands higher" conveyed an attitude of extreme manliness, which was "far from either cold-hearted indifference or importunate sniveling." These words did not just provide comfort in the "trouble and distress of our own situation." They expressed real heroism given only to those who become stronger on the "test bench of destiny" – able to have a "creative relationship with the pain that meets them." The German Volk always had this attitude "whenever its essential values were put to the test: never is great gain possible without great renunciation; never is profundity achieved without the troubles and concerns of doubt." "Today," Germans were learning to understand the works of the masters who "shrugged off their own pain" in order to identify and articulate the exciting destiny of their time. Such artists became "masters of fate" not by remaining distant observers, but as highly sensitive witnesses. "Softly and delicately, but also unconditionally and invulnerably," they experienced the words of the seventeenth-century German mystic, Jakob Böhme: "The steed that carries us fastest toward perfection is named suffering." Hölderlin's whole generation was of this type: romantic self-sacrifice was "indescribably fearless." Here "unhappiness and unsparing fate broke out into the hope" Hölderlin expressed that "the life-song of the world" might "sound anew."[79] Thus did Biedrzynski and the *Völkischer Beobachter* continue to project Nazified ideals of a German cultural past into the future, even as young boys and old men were being driven to stem the final assault against Hitler's rule.

And yet, ten days later, the *Völkischer Beobachter* once again leaned on Hölderlin, arguably the dreamiest of all German romantics, as inspiration for an imagined storm of steel capable of holding out against the inevitable. On 24 March 1945, Friedrich Wilhelm Hymmen wrote for the paper that "only in years of trouble" did Hölderlin move closer to Germans, so they had just "recently become mature enough" to fully understand and recognize him as one of them: "What a development in the soul of our Volk!" Hölderlin knew much of the "fertility of sorrow – certain that it contained all that is great and heavenly." He also knew "how doubtful is that which man calls happiness." In *Hyperion* he wrote, "Happiness! It is as if I had pap and lukewarm water in my mouth when they talk to me of happiness. So vapid and so irredeemable is all for which you slaves give up your laurel wreaths, your immortality!" In the same novel, Hölderlin writes: "Who stands on his misery, stands higher" and "Life nourishes itself on sorrow." In these lines "we meet the manly Hölderlin – what a misunderstanding to regard him as weak!" For "all the delicacy of his style, it is yet so radiant; in every word one senses the power and certainty that we all desire and need today." The comfort he provides "does not put one to sleep, but drives forward," as in his statements that "the more unfathomably one suffers, just as unfathomably powerful one becomes" and that "who suffers the most, is the most right." These lines referred not only to individuals, said Hymmen, but to the whole Volk: "we feel ourselves called" by phrases like "Just war brings the soul to life" and "Breaking chains is what gives mankind its youth." For, as Hölderlin put it, a "Volk where spirit and greatness produce no more spirit and greatness ... has no more rights." Thus did Hölderlin warn Germans, even before the outbreak of the Wars of Liberation: "By the flag alone no one should recognize our future Volk; it must become rejuvenated in every sense, it must be entirely different; full of seriousness in desire and cheerfulness in work! Nothing, even the smallest things, the most mundane, without spirit and the gods!" Few, Hymmen concluded, have the poetic courage that Hölderlin demanded, but "that is what we ask of poetry today" – when all other Nazi defenses had fallen – "for inner armor."[80]

But for all the "last stand" bombast of the Nazi paper, it would be a mistake to think that the end really came without any "importunate sniveling," as Biedrzynski would have had it. Over the last year of the war, as flaws in Hitler's military "genius" had become more apparent, attempts to reinforce this "inner armor" had also involved invoking the philosopher most traditionally associated with the will to overcome pain. To a great degree, the *Völkischer Beobachter*'s late references to Friedrich Nietzsche epitomized the latter stages of National Socialist cultural evocation. As the newspaper had covered it, at a 1944 event marking Nietzsche's 100th birthday, Alfred Rosenberg had given a speech associating Nietzsche directly with twentieth-century warfare. The "German spirit" that inspired Nietzsche, Rosenberg stated, "awakened from the darkness of betrayal in 1918 – to everyone's surprise – in the spirit of the Nazi Party." Therein "a new idea of life" came to light: "a will to live that was not content with studying and learning, but which formed into a political power against all enemy forces." As it took "world-historical form," there followed "a reaction by all those who saw this power as an attack on their own incomplete existence"; that is, by those "who understood that with the emergence of a true-to-life aristocratic- and yet Volk-community came danger for the big profits of the gold-kings and their accomplices." The Second World War was the result.

The National Socialist movement, Rosenberg continued, "stood as a unified whole against the rest of the world, just as Nietzsche stood as an individual against the violent forces of his time." The impact of the "whole world of despicable financiers and their henchmen, the passion whipped up by millions of envious Bolsheviks, the destructive work driven by the rage of the Jewish underworld, this all appeared shortly before the enormous purifying wave from the heart of Europe began to flow." Now, "the National Socialist pan-German Empire stood as a block of will of 90 million in the middle of this enormous struggle, serving in full conscious-ness the necessity of a great life – the necessity of a European destiny." In wartime, Rosenberg continued, "National Socialists were experiencing the effects of the forces that had become a dangerous, destructive power in the nineteenth century and continued to threaten Europe" in the form of a "great outbreak of the most dreadful illness." In the midst of this struggle, Rosenberg concluded, "Nietzsche stands with us, and we greet him as a close relative in the formulation of a broad-minded world view; as a brother in the battle for the rebirth of a great German spirituality; as a herald of a European unity; and as a promoter of creative life in our ancient, yet – through a great revolution – rejuvenating continent."[81]

At the same time, Alfred Bäumler had written in the paper that, in 1944, the Volk which had produced Nietzsche "was the only one that saw the greatest of all dangers threatening mankind." Those who were fighting against Germany were "reviling the great thinker." But in this hour, Nazis "remembered the man who wrestled a new, pure image of man out of confusion and degradation." He "foresaw and loved the idea we are protecting – that of the man whose innermost seed is bravery, the mother of all virtues; the man who believes: 'That which does not kill us, makes us stronger.'"[82]

Less than six months later, however, in March 1945, Bäumler spoke at Berlin University on the theme of "Nietzsche's Will to Power"

Figure 18.17 Max Klinger, sketch for Nietzsche sculpture (1902)

while the battle that was supposed to have made Germans stronger was pulverizing the country around him. Under these circumstances, he changed his tone significantly. No longer did he emphasize military bravery as the essence of Nietzsche's ideology, indeed, in a last-minute recanting of his wartime interpretation, he criticized the image of Nietzsche as a "hardened Nordic fighter." Bäumler started his reversal by discussing a 1902 sculpture by Max Klinger (1857–1920) (Figure 18.17), which, he felt, represented the great philosopher as "a single, clenched will." Though the bust was "indubitably a masterpiece," Bäumler thought that this external characterization had placed the teaching of Nietzsche in a "completely wrong light." The interpretation of Nietzsche "as a powerful, violent man was utterly incorrect." When writing *Will to Power*, Nietzsche considered other titles for the book. Among the potential titles, the "Innocence of Becoming" came closest to the essence of his teaching, Bäumler newly concluded. "Innocence of becoming had for Nietzsche the same meaning as will to power," and this indicated how Nietzsche's infamous concept "actually contrasted with the common notion of power." The "battle for truth had to be included in the notion of the battle for power which, carried out on the level of the individual, was a spiritual and mental one, not a physical one." The bust by Klinger represented "the fighter who defended himself to the end – a man of violence, but also of noble heroism." What was missing, though, was "the prophetic look of the thinker who fathomed the nature of things, recognized it as an enormous, dynamic struggle," and saw that the main battle was "against the soulless quantitative notion of materialistic thinking for the ethical hierarchy of existence." So, in the end, Bäumler – the Nietzschean of Nazism – perceived the German battle to apply its will to power as nothing more than an innocent process of becoming a spiritual being in a chaotic universe.[83] Nietzsche reception in the *Völkischer Beobachter*, along with its interpretation of the Western tradition as a whole, therefore followed the thematic trajectory of Nazi ideology to its ruin – ending not with a bang, but a whimper.[84]

CONCLUSION

In September 1937, after a summer in which the Nazi regime formalized its anti-modernist art policy with the dual "Degenerate" and "Great German" art exhibits in Munich, the party held its annual rally in Nürnberg. By then the polished apotheosis of Nazi ritual, the 1937 Nürnberg rally was marked by what many still consider to have been the most "sublime" spectacle born of Nazi culture: the so-called "cathedral of light" (Figure C.1). Albert Speer designed the effect by surrounding the massive Zeppelin Field with 152 anti-aircraft searchlights, training them first vertically and then on a converging spot high over the site.[1] From beneath this "dome of light" (*Lichtdom*), as ranks of party members gazed upward, they were presented with a massive representation of the ordered environment promised by the Nazi "world view."

During their visit to the rally, attendees could also purchase mementos of their heightened Nazi experience in the form of bric-a-brac familiar to anyone who attends a modern mass event. Among the items for sale was a postcard designed to capture the idealized totality of the rally experience (Figure C.2). The postcard featured a glowing image of Nürnberg's Imperial Castle (*Kaiserburg*), built and rebuilt for the Holy Roman Emperors between the eleventh and sixteenth centuries, that loomed over the city's center. Sprouting prominently from one of the castle's towers is the flag of National Socialism. Superimposed over the castle and dominating the composition is a monumental Nazi eagle derived from German national symbolism and now clutching a bright swastika wreathed in laurels. In the background is a stylized representation of the vertical pattern formed by the beams of the *Lichtdom* searchlights that pierced the night sky.

Figure C.1 "Cathedral of light," Nürnberg rally 1937

In manifold ways, the elements of imagery that together make up the composition of this 1937 Nürnberg rally postcard correspond to the themes that emerge from the material in this book. As is the case for all of the articles published in the cultural section of the *Völkischer Beobachter*, the rally postcard was mass-produced for a broad audience of common party members and Germans in general, and not particularly for leading officials or representatives of the cultural elite. In addition, the use of the Kaiserburg image – and more specifically the Nazi flag planted on its tower – paralleled National Socialist appropriation of the German and Western European cultural tradition as a whole. Above all else, the massive, stylized eagle and classically encircled swastika conveyed the forceful sense of security, clarity, and mission that Nazis sought to derive from their carefully structured interpretations of the past. Moreover, the perfectly straight lines of the luminous dome of light mirrored the relative clarity of perspective afforded by the rigorously repeated themes of Nazi ideology that the paper assiduously promoted.

The prevailing message of this postcard and of the cultural reporting of the *Völkischer Beobachter* was that despite what we know to be the villainous outcome of Hitler's rule, and perceive to be the fallacies of its cultural policies, their originators considered the party's views and practices fully justified. To completely grasp the enormity of the Nazi

Figure C.2 1937 Nürnberg rally postcard

experience and learn the lessons it holds, we must resist the urge to refuse
to acknowledge, despite our shock or disgust, that "anyone could believe
all this" and recognize that the purveyors of Nazism firmly – or, in their
word, unshakably – thought that they were bringing about political
revolution, cultural achievement, and spiritual order.

For neither the producers nor consumers of this material would any of the main concepts or themes of Nazified cultural history have seemed shocking or even particularly new. Leading scholars have proven that the fundamental pillars of Nazi *Kulturpolitik* were grounded in pre-existing and increasingly popular strains of German intellectual history that went back at least to the mid-nineteenth century. Undeniable, too, is the fact that Nazi exploitation of the Western tradition did not require fabrication of mistruths regarding the writers, artists, and composers that its propagandists exploited. Though the accounts constructed in post-1945 universities of liberalized Western nations generally disregard such facts, indications can be found in the records of literary, music, and art history that artists could share the authoritarian, militaristic, and intolerant ideas of their respective times.

As is the case with any political or cultural movement or regime, the *Völkischer Beobachter* articulation of history was manufactured through a process of selection and omission, and of emphasis and diminution, that aligned with their perspectives and prejudices, and this was a process that rarely required or involved outright dishonesty. Given their adherence to the concepts set forth by Hitler and his immediate operatives, the individual contributors to the *Völkischer Beobachter* sought to add detail and nuance to the cultural historical record that correlated their favorites with party ideals. Coming from many directions, occupations, and fields, this complex endeavor constituted a cultural-historical version of what Ian Kershaw has described as the phenomenon of "working toward the Führer." In the daily pages of the *Völkischer Beobachter*, the process entailed seeking out ways to coordinate creators' biographies and critical interpretations with the shared opinions of the movement.[2]

Pieced together in this way, from the ground up, incrementally, rather than imposed from above, the resulting version of Western cultural history as presented in the *Völkischer Beobachter* was incomplete and sometimes inconsistent. For instance, it is surprising that the paper paid so little attention to Imperial Rome since it could so ably have served as a classical model for authoritarian order and military prowess. Unexpected, too, is the dearth of references to the "Dark" or Middle Ages that were relished by some volkish thinkers as the counter-Latinate origins of "Germanic" society and art. Classical and medieval material received attention, but *Völkischer Beobachter* cultural coverage began in earnest with the Renaissance and Reformation eras where contributors perceived the most explicit roots of Germanic and anti-Semitic thought.

Another notable break in trajectory occurs in the paper's coverage of the seventeenth and early eighteenth centuries of the Baroque which – if one discounts coverage of the composers Gluck, Händel, and Bach – received far less attention than one would expect in light of Hitler's personal interest in the architecture of the era. In addition, certain grating inconsistencies stand out, for example, some contributors wrote positively about Socrates, whereas others generally negated the importance of his rationalism.[3]

This said, it is possible that some minor gaps may be ascribed to the researcher rather than the paper's editors. I believe I have assessed all the main articles that the paper published on these matters. But it is possible that in the process of reviewing every page of a daily newspaper over a twenty-five-year run, mostly on microfilm, I may have missed some relevant content.[4] Within these allowances, though, I think we can attribute most of the discrepancies represented in the excerpts highlighted in this survey to the producers of the paper and to their mode of production. And given such lack of cohesion, we should probably remain cautious about judging the larger line of interpretation in the newspaper as reflecting grand schemes or intricate debates among Nazi cultural politicians. Some trends, however, are clear and deserve further comment. First, is the paper's tremendous emphasis on music; second, is the paper's lack of reference to women.

Of the articles I gathered and studied, 1,009 were dedicated to the subject of music and its composers. Overall, an average of forty articles per year were devoted to "classical" music issues, while only an average of about fourteen each year dealt with the "masters" of all the other arts. Noteworthy, too, is the discrepancy between the highest number of articles devoted to leading figures in letters and arts – Goethe (59), Nietzsche (20), Schiller (20), Dürer (18), Heine (16), Thomas Mann (16), and Luther (13) – and those about musicians – Wagner (243), Beethoven (116), Mozart (107), Bruckner (47), Bach (43), and Schubert (35). It is clear that – especially with regard to the romantic period – the German music tradition was indeed the cultural legacy that the Nazi cultural operatives most wanted to claim as "theirs." Throughout the pages of the *Völkischer Beobachter*, music was unquestionably deemed "the most German of arts." Moreover, it is also striking that while Bach, Mozart, and Beethoven were important components in National Socialist propaganda, Richard Wagner received by far the most attention from the paper.

That Wagner was the central historical figure in the musical and cultural views of the Nazis is apparent. The most intriguing, because controversial, aspect of this practice was the way the Nazis referred to Wagner's anti-Semitism within the context of their own. Based on the discourse of the *Völkischer Beobachter*, it is clear that Wagner's writings about Jews and, to a more limited extent, his music dramas themselves, were essential sources of anti-Semitic thought and attitudes to which the paper constantly referred. The veneration for Wagner expressed in the newspaper belies arguments that it was Hitler alone among the Nazis who worshipped him, and shows that *Völkischer Beobachter* contributors in general derived a sense of historical and cultural legitimacy by consistently demonstrating that the "greatest of German masters" apparently held opinions about Jews and other "national enemies" that were consistent with their own.

Within its music coverage, moreover, by far the majority of articles in the *Völkischer Beobachter* addressed the lives and works of composers no longer living; in other words, the "German masters." Of the twenty composers most featured, only seven were still alive when articles were written about them. While Nazi propagandists were interested in the issues of new music (or more to the point, in resisting compositional developments best represented by the second Viennese school and in establishing "music for the Third Reich" derived, roughly, from romantic models), this subject was less important to *Völkischer Beobachter* contributors than associating their movement and their government with historical figures of the German tradition.

Even less represented in the *Völkischer Beobachter* than modern composers, however, were women creators. When women were mentioned in this context, moreover, it was almost exclusively in one role: that of mother. This was, of course, in keeping with the overall status of women in National Socialist ideology. In a 1935 speech to the National Socialist Women's Congress, Hitler made clear the principles behind the party program of Children, Church, and Kitchen (*Kinder, Kirche, Küche* or "KKK"), stating that "the woman has her own battlefield. With every child she brings to the world, she fights her battle for the nation. The man stands up for the Volk, exactly as the woman stands up for the family."[5] A year later, Rudolf Hess followed suit when he proclaimed that:

We want women in whose life and work the characteristically feminine is preserved. Women we can love. We grant the rest

*of the world the ideal type of woman that it desires, but the
rest of the world should kindly grant us the woman who is
most suitable for us. She is a woman who, above all, is able to
be a mother ... She becomes a mother not merely because the
state wants it, or because her husband wants it, but because
she is proud to bring healthy children into the world, and to
bring them up for the nation. In this way she too plays her
part in the preservation of the life of her Volk.[6]*

Nothing in the *Völkischer Beobachter*'s treatment of women in the arts
contradicted these demands. The most common references to female
imagery in the major articles of the paper's cultural section were to
allegories such as "Mother Germany" or "Mother Earth." These included
discussion of Edvard Munch's *Alma Mater* as bearing the "typical features of a Thüringian farm wife," Hölderlin's poems as reviving the
"Mother Earth of blood-real German culture," and Ludwig Thoma's
"Hurrah to Mother Germania, the mother of us all." Other mother
images discussed in the paper were those of the Virgin Mary: in Dürer's
paintings, a portrayal of the "best mother in the world"; and in
Grünewald's alter, a Gothic emblem of a "mother's pain after the death
of her son."

Regarding the impact of women on the history of arts, the only
contributions acknowledged by the paper were to the racial and genetic
inheritance of male artists, along with efforts to nurture them. Mozart's
mother gave the composer a "Salzburger-Bavarian blood-inheritance"
and, happily, "joy for life, open-mindedness, enthusiasm, depth of feeling, cheerfulness, thoroughness, pensiveness, diligence, tenacity, the
power of observation, single-mindedness, a quiet, dry sense of humor,
impartiality, self-assurance, self-confidence, and clarity of conception."
Liszt's mother rooted him in German, not Hungarian origins. While
countering his father's alcoholism, in genetic terms, Johanna van
Beethoven also tended the kitchen and was ultimately the composer's
"best friend." Hölderlin's Swabian homeland also featured the "ever-
loving care of his mother." From his mother, Brahms received blood that
gave him "much of the bitterness and acerbity which remained a component of his artistic character and temper" and "enhanced his undoubtedly Nordic essence." On the downside, at least one mother had a
negative genetic effect: the fact that Heinrich and Thomas Mann's
mother was Portuguese, and therefore "stemmed from a particularly

mixed race with a strong admixture of Jewish blood," perhaps contributed to the problems the paper had with her sons.

Beside mothers and mother images, the paper mentioned only a few other female figures, including Shakespeare's Jessica who "couldn't really be of Jewish breed, since she was loyal, noble, and beautiful"; Wagner's Fricka and Brunnhilde, the supposed victims of Heinrich Heine's "depravity"; Cosima Wagner; and the "German Woman" who denounced *All Quiet on the Western Front* as a "book without military honor, without heroism." Alongside the last two, the woman who received the best Nazi press in the cultural context was the wife of Max Reger, whose memoir was reviewed as "a book not only for music lovers, but a special sort of book about the role of women," because it "symbolized loving woman as a spiritually and emotionally related life-comrade of an artist who functions in higher spheres: clearing the way for him, standing by him, helping and comforting him, giving him strength and joy in the process of creation, and faithfully administering his affairs even after his death." In addition to the obvious ideological reasons that these were the main images of women in the cultural coverage of the Nazi newspaper, another clear explanation lies in the fact that only 4 percent of the writers who contributed the articles studied here were women. These, and the other 96 percent, indubitably ascribed to the "KKK"- oriented practices of the party, as well as to the rest of its founding principles.

Turning to the majority of *Völkischer Beobachter* contributors, it is worthwhile to consider, as much as feasible, the backgrounds of those who formulated the paper's cultural coverage. While my focus has been on the discourse itself, I have attempted to identify the authors whenever possible. Of the articles cited in the text, 50 percent were written by one or another of 159 authors whom I have managed to track down. The other half were written by either anonymous authors (32 percent) or by authors whom I have not been able to place (18 percent). Of the authors I have identified, only 11 percent were editors-in-chief, editors, or staff writers.[7] Therefore, 89 percent of the identified authors were "occasional contributors," who supplied articles with regularity that varied from a single piece to dozens over the run of the paper.[8] If we assume that almost all of the articles written by either anonymous or unidentified authors can also be placed in this category, we may then conclude that over 90 percent of the articles reviewed here were written by such "occasional contributors." From the total of those identified, 12 percent were journalists or critics who also wrote for other newspapers, and among those, 60 percent were music critics. Sixteen percent of the total were creative writers or poets, and, among those, over 25 percent were authors of "historical fiction" in addition to their work for the *Völkischer Beobachter*. Eight percent of the total had reputations as "volkish thinkers" or "racial experts," while verifiable Nazi Party officials and functionaries also made up 8 percent of the whole. Active composers and visual artists constituted 4 percent of the contributors and, finally, 9 percent must be categorized as having "other" occupations.

The most significant indication of these statistics is that the largest percentage of identified contributors (41 percent) to the *Völkischer Beobachter* cultural section were "academics," traceable as having been notable professors or at least as having been affiliated with some academic institution. Among those, 40 percent were musicologists or music historians; 28 percent were in literary studies or the history of literature; 15 percent were art historians; 12 percent were historians; and 5 percent were in departments of philosophy. Statistically, then, my research confirms what has been a disturbing revelation in all areas of German cultural history: that many scholars actively collaborated in the politicization, nationalization, and Nazification of the arts.[9] Such collusion was especially true among musicologists, music historians, and music critics. But the same dynamic operated in contributions from leading art historians, literary experts, historians, and professors of philosophy – a number of whom would continue their careers in East or West German academia. However, the number of presently identified writers is at least matched by that of authors without further record, or who contributed anonymously. One can only surmise that many of these contributors were freelance writers or journalists who submitted copy that somehow "worked toward the Führer" and thereby earned them a place in the Nazi newspaper, for whatever remuneration – financial or otherwise – it afforded. It is also possible that some articles were the result of collaboration, and thus not individually attributed to authors otherwise credited and accounted for here, and that some of these contributors simply chose not to be listed as author for particular articles.[10]

Left, then, is the most important, though ultimately unanswerable, question regarding this material: what effect did the cultural-historical coverage of the *Völkischer Beobachter* have on its contemporary readers? In studying the reception of art, literature, and music, we have moved beyond analyzing the intentions of their creators to determine how the works were perceived and attributed with meaning by audience members. Investigating records of interpretations that made it to print, in academic publications, and – here – in the popular press, is one step in this endeavor. From newspaper tributes, we can learn what academics, journalists, and party activists believed to be the lessons of great works, usually in accord with their ideological principles and propagandistic goals.

It is apparent that those who provided these interpretations of Western culture did not conceive them as just "reflective" of Nazi ideology or instrumental tools of Nazi politics, but as core components of Nazi thought. They did not consider major cultural figures and works as simply justifying or validating their opinions, but rather as the very sources of them. From their perspective, National Socialist *Kulturpolitik* was not a cynical manipulation or abuse of cultural history, but a more accurate, genuine, authentic reading that the center-left missed because *it* was ideologically prejudiced by the Enlightenment.[11] It is, therefore, a mistake to think that the authors of these articles did not sincerely believe that their interpretations were correct. If we do so, we lose the possibility of fully apprehending why they and many of their readers were persuaded that Nazi policies and actions were consistent with the values and ideals of the Western tradition – in other words, as Claudia Koonz has shown so well, why their conscience was clear.[12]

All the *Völkischer Beobachter* commemorations of cultural heroes had this motivating function. In Hitler's words, through such reminders of the Volk's creative and spiritual valor, "the general sense of self-confidence was increased, as well as the capacities of individuals."[13] The paper's constant recitation of Richard Wagner's exhortation to remember past creative leaders – "Honor your German Masters!" – was indeed about the present and future, not memory alone.[14] "By honoring this eternal national genius," Hitler proclaimed, "we call the creative force of the past forth into the present."[15] Respectful homage to cultural masters was inspiration for what the New Germany would be; as Baldur von Schirach declared: "the perfect artists Michelangelo and Rembrandt, and Beethoven and Goethe, do not represent an appeal to return to the past, but show us the future that is ours and to which we belong."[16] That is what the *Völkischer Beobachter* tributes essentially achieved: they indicated a German destiny that would manifest ideals based on the past, while, simultaneously, they categorized others as obstacles to that future – thereby labeling them as evil and marking them for destruction.

There is little evidence, unfortunately, indicating how readers responded to such assertions. The readership of the newspaper was wide and varied. We can assume that it included committed party members and officials, but also general readers who looked at it out of curiosity or just to obtain political, cultural, economic, and sports news. How specific articles that appeared in the cultural section would have impacted this range of readers remains an open question about which we can only posit some hypotheses. Returning to the image of the "Cathedral of Light" at the Nürnberg rally, the prevailing appeal of the paper's cultural-historical line must have been its repetition of a consistent set of themes that indeed promoted "group opinion regarding the events of the world" with "clear standards and measures, bases for comparison and targets for achievement." Again, as Hitler ordered in *Mein Kampf*, Nazi propaganda was to "confine itself to a few points and repeat them over and over" until it "created a general conviction regarding the reality of a certain fact." Exploring these arguments, or at least experiencing the strength of language used in these repeated concepts, helps us to understand – or, rather, feel – how those ideas could have provided readers with a sense of order and clarity in confusing times.

After being exposed to a few hundred pages of them, even a modern reader can become numb to their insinuations on the basis of increasing familiarity alone: "Of course, so-and-so was an Aryan, a nationalist, an anti-Semite, and a militarist – they all were, weren't they?" Frankly, it may not be so important whether contemporaries read the articles carefully or not. Scanning the titles each morning, full of phrases like "The Nordic Art of Albrecht Altdorfer," "Shakespeare and the Jews," "Luther's Battle against the Jews," "Goethe and the Jews," "Goethe's Ideal of the Führer," "Beethoven and Racial Hygiene," "The Murderers of Music: Jewish Desecration of Beethoven and Wagner," "Heinrich Heine as Communist Agitator," "Nietzsche as Warner Against the Jewish Danger," "Judah's Battle against Bayreuth," "Richard Wagner's Fight for the Volkish Idea," "The Military Ethos of German Genius," or "Jewish Terror in Music," would have had effects similar to modern advertising slogans, which was the primary goal of Hitler's "war propaganda" from the start. Whether most regular readers understood or even read the high-cultural justifications that followed or not, they could derive from the daily appearance of these messages in the newspaper assurance that these notions were obvious, proven, and historically substantiated.

The point of investigating these arguments now is not to address their validity – do we need further proof that Hitler's ideology was "wrong"? – but to recognize that, however they were received, these terms provided the semblance of cultural, historical, and academic legitimacy for Nazi cruelty. By relentlessly working to establish that the Western tradition consisted of oppositions between acceptable elements and enemy forces the *Völkischer Beobachter* strove to accustom readers to the idea that if Germany were ever to rise again, the whole Weimar "system" would have to be "completely rooted out, along with all its leaders." Or, that the "decisive energies" of a New Germany would be applied to "something that should have been done a long time ago: the elimination of literati like Heinrich Mann from official spiritual life altogether." Or, that the Nazi Party was pressing for a battle against "Jewish poisoners of German culture" and would not rest until they had "disappeared." In this sense, cultural history as propaganda condemned all those who fell outside its standards and measures.

The Nazi formulation of a Western tradition of inhumanity toward national, political, social, cultural, and especially racial enemies surely contributed to the transformation of some ordinary Germans into murderers. Through insistence on these prejudices over the course of a quarter of a century in sophisticated, high-cultural rhetoric – alongside more popular forms – it is utterly possible that many Germans would have become convinced that "creative deeds" of the "national genius" designed to "spread its cultural heritage across borders and stand as a model for other peoples" included Nazi-led "artistic operations" (*künstlerisches Einsätze*), "acts of war" (*Kriegstaten*), and even the vicious "special operations" (*Sondereinsätze*) they carried out to the end.

NOTES

Introduction

1. Alfred Rosenberg, "Beethoven," *Völkischer Beobachter*, 26 March 1927.
2. Adolf Hitler, Speech, *Bei der Kulturtagung des Reichsparteitages*, 11 September 1935.
3. Fritz Stern's *The Politics of Cultural Despair: A Study in the Rise of the Germanic Ideology* (Berkeley, CA: University of California Press, 1961) and George L. Mosse's *The Nationalization of the Masses: Political Symbolism and Mass Movements in Germany from the Napoleonic Wars through the Third Reich* (New York: Howard Fertig, 1975) paved the way for the now prevalent emphasis on interdisciplinary approaches to German arts and politics. General expositions of "German cultural studies" include Rob Burns (ed.), *German Cultural Studies: An Introduction* (Oxford University Press, 1995) and Scott Denham, Irene Kacandes, and Jonathan Petropoulos (eds.), *A User's Guide to German Cultural Studies* (Ann Arbor, MI: University of Michigan Press, 1997).
4. See Anson Rabinbach and Wolfgang Bialas (eds.), *Nazi Germany and the Humanities* (Oxford: Oneworld, 2007); Jonathan Huener and Francis R. Nicosia (eds.), *The Arts in Nazi Germany: Continuity, Conformity, Change* (New York: Berghahn Books, 2006); Celia Applegate, *Bach in Berlin: Nation and Culture in Mendelssohn's Revival of the St. Matthew Passion* (Ithaca, NY: Cornell University Press, 2005); Michael H. Kater and Albrecht Riethmüller, *Music and Nazism: Art Under Tyranny, 1933–1945* (Laaber: Laaber-Verlag, 2003); Richard A. Etlin (ed.), *Art, Culture, and Media under the Third Reich* (University of Chicago Press, 2002); Celia Applegate and Pamela M. Potter (eds.), *Music and German National Identity* (University of Chicago Press, 2002); Jonathan Petropoulos, *The Faustian Bargain: The Art World in Nazi Germany* (Oxford University Press, 2000); Pamela M. Potter, *Most German of the Arts: Musicology and Society from the Weimar Republic to the End of Hitler's Reich* (New Haven, CT: Yale University Press, 1998); Michael H. Kater, *The Twisted Muse: Musicians and their Music in the Third Reich* (Oxford University Press, 1997); Jonathan Petropoulos, *Art as Politics in the Third Reich* (Chapel Hill, NC:

University of North Carolina Press, 1996); Glenn R. Cuomo (ed.), *National Socialist Cultural Policy* (New York: St. Martin's Press, 1995); Alan Steinweis, *Art, Ideology, and Economics in Nazi Germany: The Reich Chambers of Music, Theater, and the Visual Arts* (Chapel Hill, NC: University of North Carolina Press, 1993); Erik Levi, *Music in the Third Reich* (New York: St. Martin's Press, 1994); Bryan Randolph Gilliam, *Music and Performance during the Weimar Republic* (Cambridge University Press, 1994); Michael Meyer, *The Politics of Music in the Third Reich* (New York: Peter Lang, 1991); Brandon Taylor and Wilfried van der Will, *The Nazification of Art: Art, Design, Music, Architecture, and Film in the Third Reich* (Winchester: Winchester Press, Winchester School of Art, 1990); Hanns-Werner Heister and Hans-Günter Klein (eds.), *Musik und Musikpolitik im faschistischen Deutschland* (Frankfurt am Main: Fischer Taschenbuch, 1984); Joseph Wulf, *Musik im Dritten Reich: Eine Dokumentation* (Frankfurt am Mein: Ullstein, 1983); and Fred K. Prieberg, *Musik im NS-Staat* (Frankfurt am Main: Fischer Taschenbuch, 1982).

5. Recent assessments of literature on the roles academic and artistic elites played in the Nazi exploitation of the humanities have noted the prominence of biographical and institutional histories, rather than analysis of the "Nazi canon" itself. Georg Bollenbeck has written, for instance, that "the role of academic elites before and after 1933, or the continuity and discontinuity in 'transitional eras,' has been analyzed from three perspectives to date: a biographical one focused on perpetrators and victims, one oriented towards institutional history and focused on the disciplines and their networks, and one oriented towards the history of research and focused on topics, themes, and methods": Georg Bollenbeck, "The Humanities in Germany after 1933: Semantic Transformations and the Nazification of the Disciplines," in Rabinbach and Bialas (eds.), *Nazi Germany and the Humanities*, 3. None of these "perspectives," even the third, has involved extensive analysis of precisely what they wrote about artists, composers, writers, and their specific works. See also Richard S. Levy's review of Alan E. Steinweis' *Art, Ideology, and Economics in Nazi Germany*. While extolling the excellent value of the book as an institutional history, he reminds "that the reader will learn little here about Nazi canons of taste or just what made 'decadent' art decadent to Hitler. Instead, a rigorous combing of the archives, judicious use of statistics, and tellingly chosen anecdotes reveal the regime's governance of the arts, its methods, purposes, and consequences" (*German Studies Review*, 18(1), 1995, 176–177).

6. Scholarship on the reception of major cultural figures has increased in recent years, but few studies have focused on the politicization that has been so important in German culture. For some representative examples, see: Friederike von Schwerin-High, *Shakespeare, Reception and Translation: Germany and Japan* (New York: Continuum, 2004); Wulf Köpke, *The Critical Reception of Alfred Döblin's Major Novels* (Rochester, NY: Camden House, 2003); Alice Freifeld, *East Europe reads Nietzsche* (New York: Columbia

University Press, 1998); Daniel J. Farrelly, *Goethe in East Germany, 1949–1989: Toward a History of Goethe Reception in the GDR* (Rochester, NY: Camden House, 1998); Robert Owen Goebel, *Eichendorff's Scholarly Reception: A Survey* (Rochester, NY: Camden House, 1993); Mark H. Gelber, *The Jewish Reception of Heinrich Heine* (Tübingen: M. Niemeyer, 1992); Howard Gaskill and Karin McPherson, *Neue Ansichten: The Reception of Romanticism in the Literature of the GDR* (Amsterdam: Rodopi, 1990); Sigrid Bauschinger, *Nietzsche Heute: die Rezeption seines Werks nach 1968* (Bern: Francke Verlag, 1988); and Alan Marshall, *The German Naturalists and Gerhart Hauptmann: Reception and Influence* (New York: Peter Lang, 1982).

7. David B. Dennis, *Beethoven in German Politics, 1870–1989* (New Haven, CT: Yale University Press, 1996).

8. Very little literature has been dedicated to studying the *Völkischer Beobachter*: Detlef Mühlberger, *Hitler's Voice: The Völkischer Beobachter, 1920–1933* (New York: Peter Lang, 2004), which is for the most part a useful collection of articles extracted from the paper; and Roland Layton, "*Völkischer Beobachter*, 1925–33. A Study of the Nazi Party Newspaper in the Kampfzeit" (Ph.D. dissertation, University of Virginia, 1965), are the only general assessments. As Mühlberger stated, "The relatively limited published material on the *Völkischer Beobachter* and the lack of a content analysis of the paper is astonishing given [its] undoubted importance" (18). About cultural criticism in the paper, even less has appeared: a dissertation by a committed Nazi, Gerhard Koehler, "Kunstanschauung und Kunstkritik in der nationalsozialistischen Presse: Die Kritik im Feuilleton des *Völkischen Beobachters* 1920–1932" (Ph.D. dissertation, Ludwig-Maximilians-Universität, Munich, Zentralverlag der NSDAP, 1937) and an Art History masters thesis by Barbara L. Bao, "The Development of the German National Socialist Point of View on Art and Art Criticism as Seen in the *Völkischer Beobachter*, 1920–1927" (M.A. thesis: Arizona State University, 1985). Rao covered general statements in the *Völkischer Beobachter* about Nazi policy toward the visual arts and art criticism, but she did not address articles that closely analyzed individual artists and their works.

9. Jeffrey Herf, *The Jewish Enemy: Nazi Propaganda during World War II and the Holocaust* (Cambridge, MA: Harvard University Press, 2006), 8. Herf makes over forty direct references to important articles that appeared between 1933 and 1945 in the *Völkischer Beobachter* and, along with other propaganda sources, "presented World War II and the intent to exterminate European Jewry as components of a war of defense against an act of aggression launched, escalated, and then carried to a victorious conclusion by an immensely powerful international conspiracy," 10.

10. See Layton, "*Völkischer Beobachter*, 1925–33," 17–29. As Layton reported: "It is not surprising to learn that the offices of the *Völkischer Beobachter* were the very center of the movement in this period (1920–1923). Hanfstaengel said

that Hitler's daily habits in the early twenties were to breakfast and then to go to the *Völkischer Beobachter*'s quarters, where he would talk with visitors. Hence Hanfstaengel considered the *Völkischer Beobachter*'s offices the best place to try to keep track of developments … According to a stenographer, 'The *Völkischer Beobachter*'s editorial rooms were always scenes of frenetic activity. She describes the place as 'full of confusion: phones ringing, editors dictating, visitors, the hum of voices …' Officers from an army station down the street spent their time in the staff rooms, gossiping and playing with their weapons. The journalists could hardly work for the interruptions" (88).

11. Adolf Hitler, "Ist die Errichtung einer die breiten Massen erfassenden Völkischen Zeitung eine nationale Notwendigkeit?," *Völkischer Beobachter*, 27 and 30 January 1921, as cited in Mühlberger, *Hitler's Voice*, 21.

12. Adolf Hitler, "Onward to a New Struggle," *Völkischer Beobachter*, 22 May 1928, as cited in Mühlberger, *Hitler's Voice*, 20 n. 27.

13. As described by Herf, "Rosenberg, known as one of the leading anti-Semitic ideologues in the Nazi party, became its editor. He remained in that position until 1938. His pseudoscholarly 1930 work, *Der Mythos des 20. Jahrhunderts*, conveyed a mélange of racist, anti-Semitic, and mystical ideas. Under his leadership, the *Völkischer Beobachter*'s circulation grew to 330,000 by 1933. It exceeded 1 million by 1940 and sold about 1.7 million copies a day in 1944": Herf, *The Jewish Enemy*, 26. See also Layton, "*Völkischer Beobachter*, 1925–33," 57–69 and Mühlberger, *Hitler's Voice*, 30 n. 24.

14. Weiss, who lost a leg in the First World War, joined the paper in 1927, and replaced Rosenberg in 1933. He "remained editor of the *Völkischer Beobachter* until it ceased publication in April 1945. In that capacity, he dutifully and consistently transformed the daily press directives into bold red and black headlines and front-page stories that were central elements in the regime's anti-Semitic campaigns and in the translation of Nazi ideology into an ongoing anti-Semitic narrative of events": Herf, *The Jewish Enemy*, 26. See also Layton, "*Völkischer Beobachter*, 1925–33," 70.

15. As Barbara Rao put it: "even though Rosenberg was editor-in-chief of the *Völkischer Beobachter* … it must be seen as Hitler's direct wire to his followers and would-be followers": Rao, "Art and Art Criticism as Seen in the *Völkischer Beobachter*," 37.

16. The *Nationalsozialistische Monatshefte* first appeared in 1930; *Der Angriff* was established in 1933; and *Der Schwarze Korps* was first published in 1935. Some might ask whether Goebbels' *Der Angriff* was comparable in significance. But its circulation was limited to Berlin, while the *Völkischer Beobachter* had national distribution. In addition, the *Völkischer Beobachter* provided more extensive coverage of cultural matters than the more specifically political journalism of *Der Angriff*. Layton stated that "as the official party organ, the *Völkischer Beobachter* was the authoritative source of news and views; editors of other Nazi

papers were specifically instructed to regard the *Völkischer Beobachter*'s position on current issues as binding": Layton, "*Völkischer Beobachter*, 1925–33," 142. When considering papers subsequently taken over by the party, one might inquire about tensions between previous editorial policies and policies promulgated under Nazi direction, but in the case of the *Völkischer Beobachter* there is little doubt that one encounters a consistent, undiluted ideological line. Strict measures used to regulate the press, including the Editors Law implemented after 1933, were not necessary to keep the *Völkischer Beobachter* under control. See Oron Hale, *The Captive Press in the Third Reich* (Princeton University Press, 1964), 168–170. Herf stipulates that, at least from 1937 through 1945, much of its front-page content "conveyed the core propaganda themes emanating from [Reich press chief, Otto] Dietrich's press conferences": Herf, *The Jewish Enemy*, 26. But it is clear that control was complete from 1920 on. See also David Welch, "Nazi Film Policy: Control, Ideology, and Propaganda," in Cuomo (ed.), *National Socialist Cultural Policy*, 26–27; and Jeffrey Herf, "The 'Jewish War': Goebbels and the Antisemitic Campaigns of the Nazi Propaganda Ministry," *Holocaust and Genocide Studies* 19(1), 2005, 51.

17. In Herf's words, "It was a paper by and for Nazi believers and for anyone who wanted to know what the regime's official policy was": Herf, *The Jewish Enemy*, 26.

18. Layton observed that "the *Kulturteil* is far more important in the German newspaper than it is in the newspapers of other lands. Devoting much space to cultural articles, the *Völkischer Beobachter* was no exception … Its cultural offerings dealt with art, literature, music, films, drama, religion, history, education, and other fields. Almost always the cultural articles were heavily colored by the Nazi *Weltanschauung*": Layton, "*Völkischer Beobachter*, 1925–33," 227–228.

19. By major articles, I mean feature articles that assessed a work or creator in some depth, not just reviews unless these treated subjects in a unique way or addressed performances associated with landmarks such as birth or death anniversaries or other pivotal events in German history.

20. Their focus was not on Western "civilization," but on the tradition of *Kultur* as identified in German society (and in Western European eras and regions some claimed as Germanic) from the Romantic period forward. The evolution of this distinction preceded its most famous delineations by Thomas Mann, for instance, that: "German tradition is culture, soul, freedom, art, and not civilization, society, voting rights and literature": Thomas Mann, *Reflections of a Nonpolitical Man*, trans. Walter D. Morris (New York: Frederick Ungar, 1983), 17. Herf described this distinction as it became prevalent by the Nazi era as follows: "The core juxtaposition of their nationalism was that of *Kultur* and *Zivilisation*. On one side stood the *Volk* as a community of blood, race, and cultural tradition. On the other side was the menace of *Amerikanismus*, liberalism, commerce, materialism, parliament and political parties, and the

Weimar Republic. Nationalism served as a secular religion that promised an alternative to a world suffering from an excess of capitalist and communist rationalization. German nationalists elevated Germany's geographical position between East and West into a cultural–political identity as well. The *Kulturnation* would escape the dilemmas of an increasingly soulless modernity": Jeffrey Herf, *Reactionary Modernism: Technology, Culture, and Politics in Weimar and the Third Reich* (Cambridge University Press, 1984), 35. Richard Wolin likewise underscores their rejection of "civilization": "Their withering critique of modernity, their indictment of the purportedly 'Western' ideas of reason, liberalism, individualism, and so forth – in sum, of a decadent and moribund bourgeois Zivilisation (forced unwillingly upon Germany by the victorious allies) – helped undermine the credibility of Germany's fledgling democracy during the late 1920s and early 1930s." See Richard Wolin, *The Seduction of Unreason: The Intellectual Romance with Fascism from Nietzsche to Postmodernism* (Princeton University Press, 2004), 154. See also George L. Mosse, *The Crisis of German Ideology* (New York: Grosset & Dunlap, 1964), 6, 68–69, 94–96, among many other discussions of this issue.

21. Hitler, *Mein Kampf*, trans. Ralph Manheim (Boston, MA: Houghton Mifflin, 1971), 179–181.

22. As Taylor and van der Will put it, the paper was part of "a continuous ideological war" which "had to be waged in order to produce if not a mass consensus then at least broad assent for the public actions of the regime": Taylor and van der Will, *The Nazification of Art*, 23.

23. National Socialist efforts to appropriate the Western cultural tradition did not function in a vacuum, as numerous *Völkischer Beobachter* references to opinions of the "opposition" suggest. At early stages in this project, I compared *Völkischer Beobachter* interpretations of classical music with those that appeared in the main publications of political competitors including *Vorwärts*, the *Sozialistische Monatshefte*, the *Rothe Fahne*, and similar foreign publications, such as French newspapers and music journals, as well as other Nazi publications, such as *Der Angriff* and the *Nationalsozialistische Monatshefte*. However, covering interpretations of literature, art, and other genres in addition to music required focusing on one party and source. Subsequent scholarship should be devoted to showing how the papers of the other major parties competed over the Western tradition in this way.

24. Köhler, "Kunstanschauung und Kunstkritik," 29.

25. See the Conclusion for discussion of the range of contributors to the *Völkischer Beobachter*'s cultural coverage, as well as their motivations (to the extent that we can estimate them).

26. For discussion of the fact that while "no single version of 'Nazi ideology' ever became hegemonic in the Third Reich," certain common themes were prevalent to the point of having "quasi-liturgical status," and therefore "fulfilled the

functions we associate with ideology," see Rabinbach and Bialas (eds.), *Nazi Germany and the Humanities*, xv–xviii. See also Etlin (ed.), *Art, Culture, and Media under the Third Reich*, xviii; and Claudia Koonz, *The Nazi Conscience* (Cambridge, MA: Belknap Press, 2003), 2.

27. As Rao stated it: "Art criticism in the *Völkischer Beobachter*, a boulevard paper aimed at the masses," was "ideological criticism in that it promoted the moral and political ideas of the National Socialists. The last of these classifications probably fits the writings on art in the *Völkischer Beobachter* best": Rao, "Art and Art Criticism as Seen in the *Völkischer Beobachter*," 116.

28. David Welch, *The Third Reich: Politics and Propaganda* (London: Routledge, 2002), 6. See also Alan E. Steinweis, "Nazi Historical Scholarship and the 'Jewish Question,'" in Rabinbach and Bialas (eds.), *Nazi Germany and the Humanities*, 399; and Koonz, *The Nazi Conscience*, 12.

29. See Taylor and van der Will, *The Nazification of Art*, 15; Suzanne Marchand, "Nazism, Orientalism and Humanism," in Rabinbach and Bialas (eds.), *Nazi Germany and the Humanities*, 269; and Etlin (ed.), *Art, Culture, and Media under the Third Reich*, 22–24 for more on the manipulation of the humanities for political purposes. Steinweis identifies three levels of anti-Semitic propaganda in particular: "First, crass forms in the *Stürmer* newspaper, the film, *Jud Süss*, and innumerable speeches by Nazi leaders. These were targeted at the lesser educated masses of Germans. A notch above the low-brow propaganda was a middle-brow discourse designed to secure social and intellectual respectability for anti-Semitism in the German educated middle class. This genre usually took the form of nonfiction books aimed at a general readership and political cultural periodicals such as the *National Socialist Monatshefte* and *Black Corps*. Textbooks designed for classroom use in primary and secondary schools might also be included in this category. Anti-Jewish scholarship constituted the top tier of Nazi anti-Semitism, although books and articles published by scholars attracted limited readership. The findings of German academics were reported fairly widely in the German press, thus creating a kind of trickle-down effect of scientific legitimation for Nazi ideology and policy": Alan E. Steinweis, "Nazi Historical Scholarship and the 'Jewish Question,'" in Rabinbach and Bialas (eds.), *Nazi Germany and the Humanities*, 399. It is a combination of the second and third "levels" that we are exploring here.

30. See Walter Horace Bruford, *The German Tradition of Self-Cultivation: Bildung from Humboldt to Thomas Mann* (Cambridge University Press, 1975) and George L. Mosse, *German Jews Beyond Judaism* (Bloomington, IN: Indiana University Press, 1985), 1–17.

31. Maria Groener, "Schopenhauer und die Juden," *Völkischer Beobachter*, 10 June 1928.

32. George L. Mosse, *Nazi Culture* (New York: Grosset & Dunlap, 1966), 96.

33. Taylor and van der Will, *The Nazification of Art*, 166. As Richard Wolin put it, cultural politics "of this nature, conferred an invaluable measure of legitimacy upon the regime in the eyes of Germany's educated elite (the proverbial *Bildungsbürgertum*) ..." (Wolin, *The Seduction of Unreason*, 91).

34. Herf, "The 'Jewish War,'" 53–54.

35. See Mosse, *Nationalization of the Masses*, 23.

36. Köhler, "Kunstanschauung und Kunstkritik," 256–257.

37. In Koonz's words, "Nazism fulfilled the functions we associate with ideology. It supplied answers to life's imponderables, provided meaning in the face of contingency, and explained the way the world works. It also defined good and evil, condemning self-interest as immoral and enshrining altruism as virtuous. Binding ethnic comrades to their ancestors and descendants, Nazi ideals embedded the individual within the collective well-being of the nation": Koonz, *The Nazi Conscience*, 2.

38. As Mosse put it, the "new politics" culminating in Nazism sought to "guide and formalize" processes by which "the people worshipped themselves": Mosse, *Nationalization of the Masses*, 2.

39. As Eric Michaud has written, National Socialist attention to culture was intended "to present the broken Volk with an image of its 'eternal *Geist*' and to hold up to it a mirror capable of restoring to it the strength to love itself": Eric Michaud, *The Cult of Art in Nazi Germany*, trans. Janet Lloyd (Stanford University Press, 2004), 29. While largely based on concepts initiated by George Mosse, whom he might have acknowledged more extensively, Michaud has articulated the function of the Nazi "cult of art" very strongly.

40. While I do reference the paper's coverage of some lesser known figures, including those deemed early "volkish" leaders and some contemporary creators whom the paper promoted as potentially carrying forth the ideal tradition, I concentrate mainly on *Völkischer Beobachter* treatment of individuals and works that are widely recognizable as icons of the Western tradition. The vast majority of the paper's cultural coverage – especially the main commemorative articles – centered on them, in keeping with the goal of deriving from the past a positive model for the German future. For the same reasons, this book does not extensively discuss film or jazz, which were emerging as major trends contemporary to Nazism. Similarly, amid the construction of this cultural-historical "ideal," the ban on art criticism imposed by Goebbels in November 1936 is not particularly relevant. This policy did not impact the material in my book, because it is for the most part not art criticism, but art history or art invocation in the broader ideological sense discussed here. Except when targeted against leftist enemies and others who did not share the above views, there was little "criticism" or "debate" in these feature articles. The same goes for differences that existed between Goebbels and Rosenberg, or others, over particular artists, movements, or works. The most important revelation of my

findings is the ways in which most of the Western tradition, claimed as German, was used in these ways. There are some anomalies and contradictions, as well as omissions (discussed in the Conclusion), but these were the general lines by which an idealized past was used to propagandize for an idealized future.

41. George L. Mosse, *Toward the Final Solution: A History of European Racism* (New York: H. Fertig, 1978), xxvii.
42. Mosse, *Toward the Final Solution*, 18.
43. Mosse, *Nationalization of the Masses*, 198.
44. Michaud, *The Cult of Art in Nazi Germany*, 76.
45. Michaud, *The Cult of Art in Nazi Germany*, 24–25.

1 The "Germanic" Origins of Western Culture

1. Adolf Hitler, *Mein Kampf*, 180, 185.
2. Saul Friedländer made this point powerfully: "A first glance reveals that this language is one of accumulation, repetition, and redundancy: a massive use of synonyms, an excess of similar epithets, a play of images sent back, in turn, from one to the other in echoes without end. This is not the linear language of interconnected argument nor of step-by-step demonstration; this is, under a less immediate but no less systematic and no less effective form, the circular language of invocation, which tirelessly turns on itself and creates a kind of hypnosis by repetition, like a word that is chanted in certain prayers, a dance that persists in the same rhythm unto frenzy, a call of the tom-tom, or, quite simply, the heavy music of parades, the muffled stomping of marching legions ... One knows how the sight of ten thousand banners rising all at once overcame the spectators at Nürnberg, how the serried ranks of a hundred thousand men massed on the meeting grounds overwhelmed them – though in incomprehensible ways. In an attenuated form, it is the same for the type of language we are examining": Saul Friedländer, *Reflections of Nazism: An Essay on Kitsch and Death*, trans. Thomas Weyr (New York: Harper & Row, 1984), 50–52.
3. "As the genuine, as the solely pure race of peoples, the Germans, it was claimed, represented all that was creative since the inception of time ... In essence, the German Volk was like a tree growing from particularly profound roots: it could not inherit anything; it was the sole repository of all creativity and any genius that had ever existed": Mosse, *German Jews Beyond Judaism*, 69.
4. See Stern, *The Politics of Cultural Despair*, passim, and Mosse, *The Crisis of German Ideology*, passim.
5. Hitler, *Mein Kampf*, 290.
6. Joan L. Clinefelter, *Artists for the Reich: Culture and Race From Weimar to Nazi Germany* (New York: Berg, 2005), 35.

7. Houston Stewart Chamberlain, *Foundations of the Nineteenth Century*, trans. John Lees (London: John Lane, [1899] 1911), 187–233.

8. Phillipp Gassert and Daniel S. Mattern (eds.), *The Hitler Library: A Bibliography* (Westport, CT: Greenwood Press, 2001), 325.

9. A later manifestation of these views was the procession in Munich on the Day of German Art in 1937, where floats symbolizing the German tradition included representations of the Roman, Gothic, Renaissance, Baroque, Classical, and Romantic ages. See Michaud, *The Cult of Art in Nazi Germany*, 106.

10. Alfred Rosenberg, "Sinn und Tat: Goethes germanische Wesenheit," *Völkischer Beobachter*, 22 March 1932.

11. Otto Fraas, "Michelangelos Haupt," *Völkischer Beobachter*, 27 November 1931.

12. Rudolf Kassner, "Michelangelos Sibyllen und Propheten," *Völkischer Beobachter*, 14 January 1944.

13. Marlies Schmitz-Hertzberg, "Einsame Grösse: Betrachtungen über Michelangelos Leben und Werk," *Völkischer Beobachter*, 16 February 1944.

14. Ludwig von Pastor, "Michelangelos Flucht aus Rom," *Völkischer Beobachter*, 9 July 1927.

15. Johanna Artzen-Schmitz, "Der Meister der italienischen Hochrenaissance: Ein Lebensbild Michelangelos," *Völkischer Beobachter*, 9 April 1931.

16. Stern, *The Politics of Cultural Despair*, 117.

17. Christian Wilhelm Mack, "Der Rembrandtdeutsche," *Völkischer Beobachter*, 12 December 1926.

18. Richard Biedrzynski, "Rembrandt und das Reich: Notizen zu einer niederländischen Reise," *Völkischer Beobachter*, 17 December 1942.

19. Biedrzynski, "Rembrandt und das Reich."

20. Richard Biedrzynski, "Eroica eines Lebens: Zum 275. Todestag Rembrandts," *Völkischer Beobachter*, 4 October 1944.

21. Rudolf Hofmüller, "Ein Weltmann der Literatur: Zum 175. Geburtstag von August Wilhelm von Schlegel," *Völkischer Beobachter*, 6 September 1942.

22. For more on von Schirach's early involvement with the party's *Kulturpolitik*, see Michaud, *The Cult of Art in Nazi Germany*, especially 95 ff.

23. Baldur von Schirach, "Deutsche Shakespeare-Woche," *Völkischer Beobachter*, 28 June 1927. For more on Nazi Shakespeare reception, see Rodney Symington, *The Nazi Appropriation of Shakespeare: Cultural Politics in the Third Reich* (Lewiston, NY: Edwin Mellen Press, 2005). For more on Schirach himself, see Michaud, *Cult of Art in Nazi Germany*, 30–33, 95–101.

24. Köhler, "Kunstanschauung und Kunstkritik," 25. See also Hans Buchner, *Horst Wessel-Marschalbum: Lieder der Nationalsozialistischen Deutschen Arbeiterpartei, Vaterlands- und Soldatenlieder und Märsche aus alter und neuer Zeit* (Munich: F. Eher, 1933).

25. Hans Buchner, "Joh. Sebastian Bach," *Völkischer Beobachter*, 29 June 1923. See also David B. Dennis, "*Honor Your German Masters*: The Use and Abuse of

'Classical' Composers in Nazi Propaganda," *Journal of Political and Military Sociology*, 30, 2002, 273–295.

26. Max Neuhaus, "Johann-Sebastian-Bach-Feier: Erster Tag," *Völkischer Beobachter*, 13 April 1934.

27. See Köhler, "Kunstanschauung und Kunstkritik," 26.

28. Karl Grunsky, "Weg zu Johann Sebastian Bach," *Völkischer Beobachter*, 21 March 1935.

29. Heinrich Stahl, "Der Meister," *Völkischer Beobachter*, 21 March 1935.

30. Neuhaus, "Johann-Sebastian-Bach-Feier: Erster Tag."

31. "Bach-Abend des Kampfbundes für Deutsche Kultur," *Völkischer Beobachter*, 17 November 1933.

32. "Das Problem der neuzeitlichen Händel-Aufführung," *Völkischer Beobachter*, 9 July 1927. See also Pamela Potter, "The Twentieth Century and Beyond: The Politicization of Handel and his Oratorios in the Weimar Republic, the Third Reich, and the Early Years of the German Democratic Republic," *The Musical Quarterly*, 85(2), 2001, 311 and Dennis, "*Honor Your German Masters*: The Use and Abuse of 'Classical' Composers in Nazi Propaganda."

33. Ludwig K. Mayer, "Georg Friedrich Händel: Zu seinem 175. Todestage," *Völkischer Beobachter*, 14 April 1934.

34. Waldemar Hartmann, "Georg Friedrich Händel und England: Ein Beitrag zur Geschichte nordischer Kulturverbundenheit," *Völkischer Beobachter*, 22 January 1935.

35. Mayer, "Georg Friedrich Händel: Zu seinem 175. Todestage."

36. Hartmann, "Georg Friedrich Händel und England: Ein Beitrag zur Geschichte nordischer Kulturverbundenheit."

37. Friedrich Baser, "Händels Martyrium in London," *Völkischer Beobachter*, 17 May 1941.

38. Hartmann, "Georg Friedrich Händel und England: Ein Beitrag zur Geschichte nordischer Kulturverbundenheit."

39. Uwe Lars Nobbe, "Mozarts Bluterbe," *Völkischer Beobachter*, 19 October 1941. On Nazi interpretations of Mozart, see also Dennis, "*Honor Your German Masters*: The Use and Abuse of 'Classical' Composers in Nazi Propaganda" and Erik Levi, *Mozart and the Nazis: How the Third Reich Abused a Cultural Icon* (New Haven, CT: Yale University Press, 2010).

40. Karl Grunsky, "Mozart der Deutsche: Zu seinem 150. Todestag," *Völkischer Beobachter*, 6 December 1941.

41. Köhler, "Kunstanschauung und Kunstkritik," 26.

42. Erwin Bauer, "Salzburger Schneurlregen mit Musik," *Völkischer Beobachter*, 27 April 1941.

43. Nobbe, "Mozarts Bluterbe."

44. Hans Buchner, "Zum Münchner Mozartfest," *Völkischer Beobachter*, 24 May 1923.

45. Eduard A. Mayr, "Vom Genius der Musik: Rhythmus und Harmonie in Freiheit des Geistes," *Völkischer Beobachter*, 27 January 1931.

46. Ferdinand Moessmer, "Die Geburt der deutschen Oper," *Völkischer Beobachter*, 14 October 1934.

47. "Eröffnung des Mozartkongresses," *Völkischer Beobachter*, 3 December 1941.

48. See Köhler, "Kunstanschauung und Kunstkritik," 23–29. Stolzing published under several variations on his name, including Josef Stolzing-Cerny and "S–g."

49. Josef Stolzing, "Mozart und die Franzosen," *Völkischer Beobachter*, 20 December 1927.

50. Viktor Junk, "Genie des Schaffens," *Völkischer Beobachter*, 29 November 1941.

51. For more on Beethoven reception, see Dennis, *Beethoven in German Politics* and David B. Dennis, "Beethoven at Large: Reception in Literature, the Arts, Philosophy, and Politics," in Glenn Stanley (ed.), *Cambridge Companion to Beethoven* (Cambridge University Press, 2000), 292–305.

52. See Alessandra Comini, *The Changing Image of Beethoven: A Study in Mythmaking* (New York: Rizzoli, 1987) for detailed discussion of the iconography of Beethoven reception in the visual arts.

53. Hans F. K. Günther, *Rasse und Stil* (Munich: J. F. Lehmann, 1926), 30; Ludwig Ferdinand Clauss, *Rasse und Seele* (Munich: J. F. Lehmann, 1926), 60. See further discussion of these sources in Heribert Schröder, "Beethoven im Dritten Reich: Eine Materialsammlung," in Helmut Loos (ed.), *Beethoven und die Nachwelt: Materialien zur Wirkungsgeschichte Beethovens* (Bonn: Beethovenhaus, 1986), 205.

54. "Sein Erbbild," *Völkischer Beobachter*, 26 March 1927.

55. "Erscheinungsbild Beethovens," *Völkischer Beobachter*, 26 March 1927.

56. "Beethoven und die österreich. Landschaft," *Völkischer Beobachter*, 29 March 1927.

57. Heribert Schröder also perceived this aspect of Nazi Beethoven reception: "A further 'problem' within the family van Beethoven was the character of the father … 'Gray misery tainted the house daily,' because he 'drank excessively, spent the small amount of household money, and beat the children indiscriminately'" (*Beethoven im Dritten Reich*, 203).

58. Ludwig Schiedermair, "Beethovens Eltern," *Völkischer Beobachter*, 23 January 1926.

59. Fritz Lenz, "Beethoven und die Rassenhygiene in Rasse, Volk und Staat: Rassenhygienisches Beiblatt zum Folge 4," *Völkischer Beobachter*, 17 August 1933.

60. "Beethoven und die österreich. Landschaft."

61. Hans Buchner, "Zum Beethoven-Jubilaeum," *Völkischer Beobachter*, 9 December 1920.

62. Josef Stolzing, "Franz Liszt. Zu seinem 40. Todestag," *Völkischer Beobachter*, 31 July 1926.

63. Karl Grunsky, "Zum 50. Todestag Franz Liszts," *Völkischer Beobachter*, 31 July 1936.

64. Hans Kellermann, "Franz Liszt – ein deutscher Meister!," *Völkischer Beobachter*, 11 December 1934.

65. Paul Zschorlich, "Deutsche Komponisten aus dem Burgenland," *Völkischer Beobachter*, 8 January 1936.

66. Grunsky, "Zum 50. Todestag Franz Liszts."

67. Stolzing, "Franz Liszt. Zu seinem 40. Todestag."

68. Josef Stolzing, "Ein deutscher Komponist," *Völkischer Beobachter*, 7 December 1934.

69. Zschorlich, "Deutsche Komponisten aus dem Burgenland."

70. Kellermann, "Franz Liszt – ein deutscher Meister!"

71. Zschorlich, "Deutsche Komponisten aus dem Burgenland."

72. Grunsky, "Zum 50. Todestag Franz Liszts."

73. Stolzing, "Ein deutscher Komponist."

74. Stolzing, "Ein deutscher Komponist."

75. Kellermann, "Franz Liszt – ein deutscher Meister!"

76. Grunsky, "Zum 50. Todestag Franz Liszts."

77. Zschorlich, "Deutsche Komponisten aus dem Burgenland."

78. Grunsky, "Zum 50. Todestag Franz Liszts."

79. Josef Stolzing, "Der alte Schwindel von Richard Wagners Blutbeimischung," *Völkischer Beobachter*, 12 December 1929. For my own assessments of some of the mass of literature on the issues of Wagner and Nazism, see David B. Dennis, "Review Essay on Recent Literature about Music and German Politics," *German Studies Review*, October 1997, 429–432; David B. Dennis, "Crying 'Wolf'? A Review Essay on Recent Wagner Literature," *German Studies Review*, February 2001, 145–158; and David B. Dennis, "The Most German of all German Operas: *Die Meistersinger* Through the Lens of the Third Reich," in Nicholas Vazsonyi (ed.), *Wagner's Meistersinger: Performance, History, Representation* (University of Rochester Press, 2003), 98–119.

80. Hugo Rasch, "Bayreuther Festspiele 1933: Genie am Werk," *Völkischer Beobachter*, 29 July 1933.

81. Köhler, "Kunstanschauung und Kunstkritik," 23.

82. F. von Leoprechting, "Richard Wagner: Das Judentum in der Musik," *Völkischer Beobachter*, 14 November 1920.

83. Miss., "Alljudas Kampf gegen Richard Wagner," *Völkischer Beobachter*, 29 December 1927.

2 Vox Volkish

1. As Mosse said about his collection of "Nazi culture": "Throughout the extracts in this book there run not only the themes of race and Volk, but also the drive for

rootedness in the Volk. Intellectualism was decried, for the Volk is one and culture must not separate itself from these roots": Mosse, *Nazi Culture*, xxix. Fritz Stern put this paradoxical position as follows: "They were in truth anti-intellectual intellectuals": Stern, *Politics of Cultural Despair*, 276. Eric Michaud addresses the issue as follows: "One of the bases of the Nazi theory of art was indeed that the uniqueness of the artist faded away in the face of the racial community. It was a basis in harmony with the NSDAP principle according to which 'the general interest takes precedence over individual interests.' The god who inhabited an 'inspired' artist in his work could not be a personal god but must be the national-volkish genius": Michaud, *The Cult of Art in Nazi Germany*, 133.

2. Scholars of German history still grapple with the full meaning of Volk or volkishness. Koonz posits that "The expansive term *Volk* held out an egalitarian and ecumenical promise to members of a so-called community of fate": Koonz, *The Nazi Conscience*, 9–10. Frank Trommler observed that: "no term was more indispensable to Nazi cultural politics than that of Volk. It provided the glue for that vague, unifying, and race-based projection of belonging. Yet, upon closer look, it also exposed a dual perspective on society: on the one hand, it accommodated all classes and temperaments inside and outside of national borders, and was applied as a label of inclusion; on the other, based on exclusion, it signaled agency of an authentic and especially active segment of the population": Frank Trommler, "A Command Performance? The Many Faces of Literature under Nazism," in Huehner and Nicosia (eds.), *The Arts in Nazi Germany*, 118.

3. Hitler, *Mein Kampf*, 341–342.

4. Hitler, *Mein Kampf*, 185.

5. Hitler, *Mein Kampf*, 408.

6. Joseph Goebbels, "Die deutsche Kultur vor neuen Aufgaben," Berlin, Grosser Saal der Philharmonie, Eröffnung der Reichskulturkammer, 15 November 1933, in *Goebbels-Reden, Band 1: 1932–1939*, ed. Helmut Heiber (Düsseldorf: Droste Verlag, 1971), 134–135.

7. Theodore Birt, "Dichterleben im alten Rom," *Völkischer Beobachter*, 14 August 1926.

8. "Tizians Malweise," *Völkischer Beobachter*, 29 August 1926.

9. Biedrzynski, "Rembrandt und das Reich: Notizen zu einer niederländischen Reise."

10. H. P., "Ein Maler der deutschen Renaissance," *Völkischer Beobachter*, 9 April 1931.

11. See Jonathan Petropoulos, "The Art World in Nazi Germany: Choices, Rationalization, and Justice," in Huener and Nicosia (eds.), *The Arts in Nazi Germany*, 135–163.

12. Ernst Buchner, "Die nordische Kunst Albrecht Altdorfers," *Völkischer Beobachter*, 13 February 1938.
13. Buchner, "Die nordische Kunst Albrecht Altdorfers."
14. Petropoulos, *Art as Politics in the Third Reich*, 222 and Köhler, "Kunstanschauung und Kunstkritik," 26.
15. Wilhelm Rüdiger, "Die Kunst Albrecht Dürers," *Völkischer Beobachter*, 7 April 1928.
16. W. Rüdiger, "Die Kunst Albrecht Dürers."
17. W. Rüdiger, "Die Kunst Albrecht Dürers."
18. "Münchener Bachfest 1935: 1. Abend," *Völkischer Beobachter*, 6 April 1935.
19. Buchner, "Joh. Sebastian Bach."
20. Mayer, "Georg Friedrich Händel: Zu seinem 175. Todestage." See Dennis, "*Honor Your German Masters*: The Use and Abuse of 'Classical' Composers in Nazi Propaganda."
21. Junk, "Genie des Schaffens."
22. The *Amt Rosenberg* was Alfred Rosenberg's "party office for ideological supervision," as described in Petropoulos, *The Faustian Bargain*, 113.
23. Erwin Voelsing, "Die Idee einer Nationaloper," *Völkischer Beobachter*, 26 February 1945.
24. Köhler, "Kunstanschauung und Kunstkritik," 27.
25. Karl Berger, "Die Uraufführung von Schillers *Räubern* vor 150 Jahren," *Völkischer Beobachter*, 13 January 1932.
26. Berger, "Die Uraufführung von Schillers *Räubern* vor 150 Jahren." For some discussion of Schiller reception in the Third Reich, see Wulf Koepke, "The Reception of Schiller in the Twentieth Century," in Steven D. Martinson (ed.), *A Companion to the Works of Friedrich Schiller* (Rochester, NY: Camden House, 2005), 276–279 and John London, *Theatre under the Nazis* (Manchester University Press, 2000), 26–38.
27. Robert Krötz, "Wir Jungen und Schiller: Zu seinem 175. Geburtstag," *Völkischer Beobachter*, 18 November 1934.
28. Albrecht Adam, "Das Faustische und das Heroische: Ein Gespräch vor 140 Jahren und der Freundschaftsbund zwischen Goethe und Schiller," *Völkischer Beobachter*, 20 July 1934.
29. F. O. H. Schulz, "Schillers Weg zur deutschen Freiheit," *Völkischer Beobachter*, 11 April 1943.
30. Krötz, "Wir Jungen und Schiller: Zu seinem 175. Geburtstag."
31. "Richard Wagner und das Kunstempfinden unserer Zeit: Rundfunkrede von Reichsminister Dr. Goebbels," *Völkischer Beobachter*, 8 August 1933. For more on Nazi views of *Die Meistersinger*, see Dennis, "The Most German of all German Operas."

3 The Western Tradition as Political and Patriotic

1. Walter Benjamin, *The Work of Art in the Age of Its Technological Reproducibility* (Cambridge, MA: Harvard University Press, 2008), 41.

2. Once again, this emphasis on art for state's or party's sake had earlier roots in German cultural discourse: "The artistic and the political had fused German nationalism. Having defined itself as truly-creative, the artistic became political. Artistic creativity for the German nationalist movement was not merely an expression of man's inner nature, but helped also to give form to the shapeless mass through symbols and public festivals ... Politics and life must penetrate each other, and this means that all forms of life become politicized. Literature, art, architecture, and even our environment are seen as symbolic of political attitudes": Mosse, *Nationalization of the Masses*, 15, 215. More recently, Huener and Nicosia have written that "Hitler and his followers came to understand German culture and the role of the arts primarily in political terms. Specifically, they believed that it was the responsibility of the party and the state to rescue German culture": Huener and Nicosia (eds.), *The Arts in Nazi Germany*, 2.

3. Adolf Hitler, Nürnberg Speech, 11 September 1935, reported in *Deutsche Allgemeine Zeitung*, 13 September 1955, cited in Peter Adam, *Art of the Third Reich* (New York: Harry N. Abrams, 1992), 9.

4. Adolf Hitler, Nürnberg Speech, January 1923, cited in Frederic Spotts, *Hitler and the Power of Aesthetics* (New York: Overlook Press, 2003), 17.

5. Goebbels, "Die deutsche Kultur vor neuen Aufgaben," Berlin, Grosser Saal der Philharmonie, Eröffunung der Reichskulturkammer, 15 November 1933, in *Goebbels-Reden, Band 1: 1932–1939*, 132. See Steinweis, *Art, Ideology, and Economics in Nazi Germany*, 22, for more on Goebbels' rejection of the "liberal notion" of art for art's sake.

6. Johann Sprengel, "Herr Walther von der Vogelweide," *Völkischer Beobachter*, 17 April 1930.

7. "Lusamrosen auf das Grab Herrn Walthers von der Vogelweide," *Völkischer Beobachter*, 17 April 1930.

8. Franz Langheinrich, "Herr Walther von der Vogelweide," *Völkischer Beobachter*, 21 October 1934.

9. The *Deutschlandlied* is also referred to as the *Lied der Deutschen*.

10. For discussion of Nazi attitudes toward von Fallersleben's *Lied der Deutschen*, see Jost Hermand, "On the History of the *Deutschlandlied*," in Applegate and Potter (eds.), *Music and German National Identity*, 251–268.

11. Artzen-Schmitz, "Der Meister der italienischen Hochrenaissance: Ein Lebensbild Michelangelos."

12. W. P. S., "Dante und die imperiale Idee," *Völkischer Beobachter*, 19 December 1940. For more on Nazi interpretations of Dante, see Richard H. Lansing and

Teodolinda Barolini (eds.), *The Dante Encyclopedia* (New York: Garland, 2000), 435.

13. Niccolò Machiavelli, *Discourses on Livy*, Book III, ch. 41.

14. Z. L. Schember, "Macchiavelli, der Katechet der Könige und Wir," *Völkischer Beobachter*, 30 May 1926.

15. "Dr. Martin Luther, ein deutscher Glaubensheld," *Völkischer Beobachter*, 11 November 1930. Though a full-length analysis of Luther reception in Nazi culture has not been produced, Susannah Heschel, *The Aryan Jesus: Christian Theologians and the Bible in Nazi Germany* (Princeton University Press, 2008) is important.

16. "Luthers Persönlichkeit ist eine Weltmacht geworden," *Völkischer Beobachter*, 12 September 1933.

17. "Lutherworte," *Völkischer Beobachter*, 11 October 1926. "It is now 24 years since the first Reichstag under Emperor Charles was held at Worms, at which I personally stood before the Emperor and the whole Empire. At that Reichstag all the Estates of the Empire desired that his imperial majesty work with the Pope to create and hold a common, free, Christian Council [i.e., to reform the Church] in German lands, or a national council [i.e., one that would reform the church in Germany even if it wasn't binding outside it], which the dear Emperor would have diligently done, except that the Pope wanted none of it; thus for 24 years these three words have been continually cried out: free, Christian, Council in German lands. These three words free, Christian and German are to the Pope and the Romanists nothing other than poison, death, and the devil and hell: he cannot bear to see or hear them: nothing will come of it, that is certain" (*Wider das Papsttum in Rom 1545*, IV, 124. Translation by Robert Bast).

18. Adolf Hösel, "Luther im Kampf gegen das Papstum," *Völkischer Beobachter*, 25 February 1937.

19. Karl Bornhausen, "Martin Luthers deutsche Sendung," *Völkischer Beobachter*, 1 November 1933.

20. "Rosenberg und Martin Luther," *Völkischer Beobachter*, 13 February 1938.

21. "Dr. Martin Luther, ein deutscher Glaubensheld."

22. "Luthers Persönlichkeit ist eine Weltmacht geworden." Translation from Martin Luther, *Ein' feste Burg ist unser Gott*, in *The Hymns of Martin Luther* (New York: Charles Scribner, 1883), 53.

23. "Aus Dürers Leben," *Völkischer Beobachter*, 13 April 1928.

24. Franz Herwig, "Albrecht Dürer in Venedig," *Völkischer Beobachter*, 28 June 1925.

25. "Aus Dürers Leben."

26. F. Sch., "Das Leben Albrecht Dürers," *Völkischer Beobachter*, 7 April 1928.

27. Willy Pastor, "Dürers Ende," *Völkischer Beobachter*, 20 August 1927.

28. Fritz Wiedermann, "Albrecht Dürers Bedeutung als Festungs-Baumeister," *Völkischer Beobachter*, 7 April 1928.

29. drh., "Dürer als Schöpfer des Selbstbildnisses," *Völkischer Beobachter*, 15 March 1935.
30. Rudolf Hofmüller, "Das politische Drama Shakespeares," *Völkischer Beobachter*, 21 December 1936.
31. Buchner, "Joh. Sebastian Bach."
32. Wilhelm Hitzig, "200 Bachkantaten im Rundfunk," *Völkischer Beobachter*, 8 December 1937.
33. Buchner, "Joh. Sebastian Bach."
34. Richard Wagner, "Was ist Deutsch?," cited in Karl Grunsky, "Ob er schön gewesen …" *Völkischer Beobachter*, 21 March 1935.
35. Josef Klingenbeck, "Musik von Heldentum und Seelengrösse," *Völkischer Beobachter*, 14 July 1939.
36. Klingenbeck, "Musik von Heldentum und Seelengrösse."
37. Klingenbeck, "Musik von Heldentum und Seelengrösse."
38. Wolfgang Gottrau, "Vom Wesen deutscher Musik," *Völkischer Beobachter*, 27 September 1931.
39. Karl Grunsky, "Der deutsche Opernreformator: Zu Glücks 150. Todestag," *Völkischer Beobachter*, 14 November 1937.
40. Gustav Christian Rassy, "Die glückliche Stunde Joseph Haydns," *Völkischer Beobachter*, 21 August 1938. See also Dennis, "*Honor Your German Master*: The Use and Abuse of 'Classical' Composers in Nazi Propaganda."
41. Köhler, "Kunstanschauung und Kunstkritik," 26.
42. Wolfgang Gottrau, "200 Jahre Joseph Haydn," *Völkischer Beobachter*, 31 March 1932.
43. Erich Valentin, "Die ewig klingende Weise: Musik – der tiefste und mächtigste Ausdrück deutschen Lebensgefühls," *Völkischer Beobachter*, 10 April 1938.
44. Gottrau, "Vom Wesen deutscher Musik."
45. Klingenbeck, "Musik von Heldentum und Seelengrösse."
46. Zschorlich, "Deutsche Komponisten aus dem Burgenland." For discussion of Nazi attitudes toward von Fallersleben's *Lied der Deutschen* which became, combined with Haydn's music, the *Deutschlandlied*, see Jost Hermand, "On the History of the *Deutschlandlied*," in Applegate and Potter (eds.), *Music and German National Identity*, 251–268.
47. Ludwig K. Mayer, "Ein rechter deutscher Mann: Zum 125. Todestage Joseph Haydns," *Völkischer Beobachter*, 31 May 1934.
48. Zschorlich, "Deutsche Komponisten aus dem Burgenland."
49. Grunsky, "Mozart der Deutsche: Zu seinem 150. Todestag."
50. Moessmer, "Die Geburt der deutschen Oper."
51. Grunsky, "Mozart der Deutsche: Zu seinem 150. Todestag."
52. Junk, "Genie des Schaffens."
53. Friedrich Schiller, *Die Jungfrau von Orleans*, act I, scene 5.

54. Friedrich Schiller, *Wilhelm Tell*, trans. William F. Wertz, Jr. (Washington, DC: The Schiller Institute, 1988).

55. Josef Stolzing, "Schillers Sendung als Dramatiker: Noch heute harren seine Probleme der Lösung durch das deutsche Volk," *Völkischer Beobachter*, 8 May 1930.

56. Karl Hans Strobl, "'Die Räuber' und die Studenten von Jena: Eine Schiller-Erinnerung zu seinem 175. Geburtstag," *Völkischer Beobachter*, 10 November 1934.

57. Erich Valentin, "'Ans werk, ans Werk für das Vaterland!': Das Schiller-Jahr 1859: Eine Kundgebung der verrattenen Nation," *Völkischer Beobachter*, 8 April 1938.

58. "Was hat Goethe dem heutigen Deutschland zu sagen: Zu Goethes Todestag," *Völkischer Beobachter*, 23 March 1930.

59. "'Höchstes hast du vollbracht, mein Volk': Grosse Deutsche über Grossdeutschland: Johann Wolfgang von Goethe," *Völkischer Beobachter*, 31 March 1938.

60. Adolf Dresler, *Geschichte des Völkischen Beobachters und des Zentralverlages der NSDAP* (Munich: Franz Eher Nachf., 1937) and Gassert and Mattern (eds.), *The Hitler Library*, 351, 482. See also Köhler, "Kunstanschauung und Kunstkritik," 26.

61. Adolf Dresler, "Goethe und der nationale Gedanke," *Völkischer Beobachter*, 28 August 1925.

62. "'Höchstes hast du vollbracht, mein Volk': Grosse Deutsche über Grossdeutschland: Johann Wolfgang von Goethe."

63. "Der deutsche Goethe," *Völkischer Beobachter*, 4 March 1931. Citation from *Conversations with Luden*, 13 December 1813.

64. Gassert and Mattern (eds.), *The Hitler Library*, 267.

65. "Der deutsche Goethe."

66. Hanns Johst, "Aufblick zu Goethe," *Völkischer Beobachter*, 22 March 1932.

67. Hans Watzlik, "Goethe im Südland," *Völkischer Beobachter*, 8 June 1940.

68. "Was hat Goethe dem heutigen Deutschland zu sagen: Zu Goethes Todestag."

69. "Was hat Goethe dem heutigen Deutschland zu sagen: Zu Goethes Todestag."

70. H., "Goethe: das Orakel seiner und unserer Zeit," *Völkischer Beobachter*, 27 January 1932.

71. "Was hat Goethe dem heutigen Deutschland zu sagen: Zu Goethes Todestag."

72. H., "Goethe: das Orakel seiner und unserer Zeit." Citation from *Conversations with Luden*, 13 December 1813.

73. "'Höchstes hast du vollbracht, mein Volk': Grosse Deutsche über Grossdeutschland: Johann Wolfgang von Goethe." Citation from *Conversations of Goethe, Recorded by His Friend Johann Peter Eckermann*, Thursday, 2 October 1828, 287.

74. Ludwig Schiedermair, "Beethoven und die Politik," *Völkischer Beobachter*, 26 March 1927.

75. "Der Patriot," *Völkischer Beobachter*, 26 March 1927.

76. Friedrich Baser, "Beethoven spielt nicht vor Franzosen," *Völkischer Beobachter*, 31 March 1937.

77. Richard Wagner, "Der Große Bahnbrecher" (a selection from Wagner, *Beethoven* [1870]), *Völkischer Beobachter*, 26 March 1927.

78. "Wörter Beethovens," *Völkischer Beobachter*, 26 March 1927.

79. Brunnhilde Wastl, "Ludwig van Beethoven: Zu seinem hundertsten Todestag," *Deutsche Arbeiterpresse: Nationalsozialistisches Wochenblatt* (Vienna), 26 March 1927. Emphasis original.

80. It was ironic, of course, that the newspaper complained about looting art works in 1944, at the same time that its government was undertaking the most extreme policy of art seizure in history. See Petropoulos, *Art as Politics in the Third Reich*, passim.

81. Schrempf, "Prophetischer Byron: Zu seinem 120. Todestag."

82. "Arthur Schopenhauers Urteile über die Deutschen," *Völkischer Beobachter*, 18 July 1929.

83. Cited in "Schopenhauer über die Engländer," *Völkischer Beobachter*, 5 June 1942.

84. K. Fr. Weiss, "Schopenhauers Staatslehre: Eine Paraphrase zu seinem Todestag am 21. September 1860," *Völkischer Beobachter*, 23 September 1923.

85. Robert Hohlbaum, "Der politische Grillparzer," *Völkischer Beobachter*, 24 April 1944. Nazi views of Grillparzer are addressed in Ian Frank Roe, *Franz Grillparzer: A Century of Criticism* (Rochester, NY: Camden House, 1995).

86. Erich Valentin, "Richard Wagner und seine Zeit," *Völkischer Beobachter*, 31 March 1937.

87. Emma von Sichart, "Der Genius von Bayreuth. Zum Geburtstage Richard Wagners am 22. Mai 1813," *Völkischer Beobachter*, 23 May 1928.

88. "Richard-Wagner-Abend im Kampfbund für deutsche Kultur," *Völkischer Beobachter*, 1 February 1931.

89. Richard Wagner, *What is German?*, in *Richard Wagner's Prose Works*, vol. 4, trans. William Ashton Ellis (1895), 163 (Wagner's *Prose Works* are available online from the Richard Wagner Library http://users.belgacom.net/ wagnerlibrary).

90. Richard Wagner, *Art and Revolution*, in *Richard Wagner's Prose Works*, vol. 1, trans. William Ashton Ellis (1895), 56.

91. Richard Wagner, *The Art-Work of the Future*, in *Richard Wagner's Prose Works*, vol. 1, trans. William Ashton Ellis (1895), 75.

92. Richard Wagner, *German Art and German Policy*, in *Richard Wagner's Prose Works*, vol. 4, trans. William Ashton Ellis (1895), 139.

93. Wagner, *What is German?*

94. Hermann Seeliger, "Der deutsche Seher," *Völkischer Beobachter,*
    12 February 1933.
95. Richard Wagner, *Judaism in Music,* in *Richard Wagner's Prose Works,* vol. 3,
    trans. William Ashton Ellis (1895), 80.
96. Walter Lange, "Bayreuth – ein sinnvoller Wahlspruch," *Völkischer Beobachter,*
    16 June 1934.
97. Ludwig Schoewe, "Der Kämpfer Richard Wagner," *Völkischer Beobachter,*
    15 February 1938.
98. Josef Stolzing, "Der grosse Deutsche: Richard Wagner," *Völkischer Beobachter,*
    17 April 1939.

4 The Western Tradition as anti-Semitic

1. Saul Friedländer, *The Years of Extermination: Nazi Germany and the Jews,*
   1939–1945 (New York: HarperCollins, 2007), xix–xx, 189.
2. Reviewing Alan Steinweis' major work on this issue, Wendy Lower summarized
   the point: "German scholars – particularly racial theorists, social scientists, and
   theologians – provided the Third Reich with academic legitimacy and knowledge,
   and in some cases contributed directly to the radicalization of anti-Jewish policies.
   The Nazi nadir in German scholarship will not come as a surprise to readers
   familiar with the pioneering postwar studies of Max Weinreich and George
   Mosse, but the specific manner in which scholars manipulated their findings and
   the various forces that eroded the standards and integrity of scholarship are
   significant details that Steinweis uncovers and analyzes. His exploration of Nazi-
   era research on Jewish history and Judaism yields new insights about the
   perversion of scholarship by politics and ideology": Wendy Lower, review of
   Studying the Jew: Scholarly anti-Semitism in Nazi Germany by Alan E. Steinweis,
   in *Holocaust and Genocide Studies,* 22(3), 2008, 1.
3. Herf, *The Jewish Enemy,* 27.
4. Groener, "Schopenhauer und die Juden."
5. Hitler, *Mein Kampf,* 421.
6. Herf's analysis of anti-Semitic propaganda establishes that these ultimate aims
   were and are incontrovertible: "Though the evidence presented here cannot
   resolve the issue of what most Germans believed, it does demonstrate, in greater
   detail than previously, the extent to which Hitler and his associates *told* the
   German population on numerous occasions that his government was following
   a policy of exterminating and annihilating Europe's Jews. If a person could
   understand German, read a major newspaper, listen to the radio news with some
   regularity, and view the ubiquitous Nazi political wall newspapers, he or she
   would know this basic fact. That person would know of the German
   government's insistence that current events could be understood only in
   reference to the power of international Jewry and that the Jews were conspiring

to destroy the Nazi regime and murder the German people. The existing
evidence plausibly suggests that a fanatical but not meager minority embedded
both in the Nazi party and in its front organizations believed this message to be
the truth, and that its members disseminated it to a society in which milder
forms of anti-Semitism had become commonplace": Herf, *The Jewish Enemy*,
14–15 (emphasis in original).

7. Hitler, *Mein Kampf*, 56–59.

8. "Die Nürnberger Dürertage," *Völkischer Beobachter*, 13 April 1928.

9. Franz Gerstner, "Der hl. Thomas v. Aquin und der anti-Semitismus,"
Völkischer Beobachter, 8 May 1926. For some discussion of Aquinas in Nazi-
era theology, see Robert Anthony Krieg, *Catholic Theologians in Nazi
Germany* (New York: Continuum, 2004), 47–48.

10. "Luther und die Judenfrage," *Völkischer Beobachter*, 18 November 1933.

11. "Luthers Kampf gegen die Juden," *Völkischer Beobachter*, 31 March 1931.

12. Cited in "Luther und die Judenfrage." Translation by Martin H. Bertram, in
Franklin Sherman (ed.), *Luther's Works, vol. 47: The Christian in Society IV*
(Philadelphia, PA: Fortress Press, 1971).

13. "Luther und die Judenfrage."

14. "Luther und die Judenfrage."

15. "Luther und die Judenfrage."

16. "Judengesetze in der Reformationszeit," *Völkischer Beobachter*, 27 June 1926.

17. Buchner, "Die nordische Kunst Albrecht Altdorfers."

18. F. L. Zander, "Shakespeare und die Juden," *Völkischer Beobachter*,
23 August 1927.

19. Schirach, "Deutsche Shakespeare-Woche."

20. "Der franzoesische Shylock im Ruhrgebiet," *Völkischer Beobachter*,
5 April 1923.

21. Joachim Petzold, "Goethe und die Juden: Eine aktuelle Betrachtung zur
Ausstellung 'Der ewige Jude,'" *Völkischer Beobachter*, 9 November 1937.

22. "Goethe und die Juden," *Völkischer Beobachter*, 20 January 1938.

23. Adolf Bartels, "Die Goethe-Biographien," *Völkischer Beobachter*,
5 January 1932.

24. "Goethe und die Juden."

25. "Goethe und die Juden."

26. "Goethe über die Mischehen," *Völkischer Beobachter*, 6 February 1926. Also
cited in Petzold, "Goethe und die Juden."

27. Petzold, "Goethe und die Juden."

28. Johst, "Aufblick zu Goethe."

29. Johann Wolfgang von Goethe, *Wilhelm Meisters Wanderjahre*, Book 3. Cited in
E. Ginier, "Goethe und die Juden," *Völkischer Beobachter*, 20 August 1927;
"Goethe, Frankfurt, Mosse," *Völkischer Beobachter*, 28 January 1932; and
Petzold, "Goethe und die Juden."

30. Petzold, "Goethe und die Juden."

31. Petzold, "Goethe und die Juden." Quote from Johann Wolfgang von Goethe to K. A. Böttiger (June 1794).

32. Petzold, "Goethe und die Juden." Quote from *Wilhelm Meister*, Book 2, ch. 2.

33. Petzold, "Goethe und die Juden."

34. Petzold, "Goethe und die Juden."

35. Cited in Ginier, "Goethe und die Juden." Also cited in Petzold, "Goethe und die Juden."

36. Ginier, "Goethe und die Juden."

37. Ginier, "Goethe und die Juden."

38. Franz Grillparzer, "Ein Christ steht an der Himmelspforte," in *Sämtliche Werke: Ausgewählte Briefe, Gespräche, Berichte*, eds. Peter Frank and Karl Pörnbacher (Munich: Hanser, 1960–1965), 574.

39. "Auf ünbekannte anti-Semitische Gedichte von Franz Grillparzer und Wilhelm Karl Grimm," *Völkischer Beobachter*, 17 April 1931.

40. "Auf ünbekannte anti-Semitische Gedichte von Franz Grillparzer und Wilhelm Karl Grimm."

41. Hohlbaum, "Der politische Grillparzer."

42. Karl Grunsky, "Ein urwüchsiger deutscher Denker: Zum 75. Todestage Arthur Schopenhauers, " *Völkischer Beobachter*, 21 September 1935.

43. See Andreas Hansert, *Schopenhauer im 20. Jahrhundert: Geschichte der Schopenhauer Gesellschaft* (Vienna: Böhlau, 2010), 53–54.

44. Schrempf, "Prophetischer Byron: Zu seinem 120. Todestag." See Sheila A. Spector, *Byron and the Jews* (Detroit, MI: Wayne State University Press, 2010), 125–126 for how Byron was interpreted, to the contrary, as an "icon of Jewish pride" in Britain.

45. For the full text, see Wagner, *Judaism in Music*.

46. Wagner, *Judaism in Music*, 82.

47. Leoprechting, "Richard Wagner: Das Judentum in der Musik."

48. Hans Buchner, "Richard Wagner und das Judentum in der Musik," *Völkischer Beobachter*, 19 April 1922.

49. "Richard Wagner über 'Das Judentum in der Musik,'" *Völkischer Beobachter*, 20 June 1923.

50. Wagner, *Some Explanations Concerning Judaism in Music*, in *Richard Wagner's Prose Works*, vol. 3, trans. William Ashton Ellis (1895), 121.

51. Wagner, *Judaism in Music*, 81.

52. "Richard Wagner über 'Das Judentum in der Musik.'"

53. "Der Dichter und Politiker," *Völkischer Beobachter*, 12 February 1933.

54. Seeliger, "Der deutsche Seher."

55. "Der Dichter und Politiker."

56. "Richard Wagner über 'Das Judentum in der Musik.'"

5 The Archenemy Incarnate

1. "Here was the real, tangible enemy of the Germanic faith; not a vague entity, but an actual historical people whose philosophy was inimical to German life. The supposedly fossilized Judaism was linked with materialism and thus to modernity. Correspondingly, to oppose the Jews meant to struggle against the champions of the materialistic world view as well as against the evils of modern society. The Jew, the incarnation of dishonesty, ruthless in his quest for power, egoism exemplified, was contrasted with the genial German, who longed for an end to the dissonances of modern, urban life": Mosse, *German Jews Beyond Judaism*, 69.

2. Hitler, *Mein Kampf*, 300–326.

3. "Nazism thus set up an extremely conventional opposition between the two poles of the sacred: on the one hand, the exhibitions of 'degenerate art' encompassed all that Nazism believed to stem from the forces of death and destruction; on the other hand, the Great Exhibitions of German Art brought together all the positive powers that were supposed to ensure the continuity of the German-Nordic Kultur. This fantasy of a possible clear-cut division between the pure and the impure naturally enough created for the Nazi authorities as many problems pertaining to art objects as to 'human material'": Michaud, *The Cult of Art in Nazi Germany*, 153.

4. "Jews, the Nazis argued, would always think and act like Jews, no matter how much they might take on the external characteristics of Germans. According to this logic, Jews could never really pursue an authentically Germanic culture, but only contaminate that culture with their own innately Jewish sensibility. An important responsibility of a Nazi government would be to purge Jews and their cultural production from German society": Alan E. Steinweis, "Anti-Semitism and the Arts in Nazi Ideology and Policy," in Huener and Nicosia (eds.), *The Arts in Nazi Germany*, 17.

5. Lore Reinmoeller, "Judentum und Musik: Zu einem Buche von Karl Blessinger," *Völkischer Beobachter*, 2 September 1944.

6. Reinmoeller, "Judentum und Musik: Zu einem Buche von Karl Blessinger." See Applegate, *Bach in Berlin: Nation and Culture in Mendelssohn's Revival of the St. Matthew Passion* for the full story.

7. Reinmoeller, "Judentum und Musik: Zu einem Buche von Karl Blessinger."

8. For background on the complicated reception of Mendelssohn's music for *A Midsummer Night's Dream* in the Third Reich, see Kater, *The Twisted Muse*, 77, 86, 192 and Michael H. Kater, *Composers of the Nazi Era: Eight Portraits* (Oxford University Press, 2000), 112–113, 125–142.

9. Köhler, "Kunstanschauung und Kunstkritik," 25.

10. Otto Keller, "Schauspiele und Musik: Ein Sommernachtstraum," *Völkischer Beobachter*, 4 July 1920.

11. Josef Klingenbeck, "25mal Sommernachtstraum," *Völkischer Beobachter*, 16 March 1941.
12. Ludwig Börne, letter to Henriette Herz, 28 January 1832.
13. Dr., "Börne über die Juden," *Völkischer Beobachter*, 16 January 1926.
14. Leoprechting, "Richard Wagner: Das Judentum in der Musik." Citation from Wagner, *Judaism in Music*, 100.
15. M. Edbach, "Entwurf eines Denkmals für Heine," *Völkischer Beobachter*, 13 November 1931.
16. "Das Heinrich Heine-Denkmal in Hamburg," *Völkischer Beobachter*, 23 October 1926.
17. "Heine über die Juden," *Völkischer Beobachter*, 13 November 1931.
18. Dr. König, "Heinrich Heine, der Schmutzfink im deutschen Dichterwald," *Völkischer Beobachter*, 12–19 January 1929.
19. "Die Taufkomödie Heinrich Heines," *Völkischer Beobachter*, 11–13 March 1930.
20. König, "Heinrich Heine, der Schmutzfink im deutschen Dichterwald."
21. "Ein Brief über Heinrich Heine," *Völkischer Beobachter*, 24 September 1927.
22. Edbach, "Entwurf eines Denkmals für Heine."
23. A number of Romantic poets produced versions of the Lorelei legend, among them were Brentano, Eichendorff, Vogt, Schreiber, Heine, and von Loeben. See Ignace Feuerlicht, "Heine's Lorelei: Legend, Literature, Life," *The German Quarterly*, 53(1), 1980, 82–94.
24. König, "Heinrich Heine, der Schmutzfink im deutschen Dichterwald."
25. Hermann Seeliger, "Schmock oder Dichter?," *Völkischer Beobachter*, 21 September 1930.
26. "Ein Brief über Heinrich Heine."
27. König, "Heinrich Heine, der Schmutzfink im deutschen Dichterwald."
28. Oren J. Hale, "Nationalism in Press, Films, and Radio," *Annals of the American Academy of Political and Social Science*, 175, 1934.
29. Heinrich Heine, "Die Vorrede zu den Französischen Zuständen; Geschrieben, zu Paris, den 18. Oktober 1832," from *The Works of Heinrich Heine, vol. VII: French Affairs: Letters from Paris*, trans. Charles Godfrey Leland (London: Heinemann, 1893), 21.
30. König, "Heinrich Heine, der Schmutzfink im deutschen Dichterwald."
31. Alfred Rosenberg, "Der Fall Heine," *Völkischer Beobachter*, 16 September 1928.
32. Heinrich Heine, letter to J. J. Dubochet. Cited in Rosenberg, "Der Fall Heine."
33. Edbach, "Entwurf eines Denkmals für Heine."
34. König, "Heinrich Heine, der Schmutzfink im deutschen Dichterwald." Citation from Heine, "Die Vorrede zu den Französischen Zuständen."
35. König, "Heinrich Heine, der Schmutzfink im deutschen Dichterwald."
36. Citation from Heine, "Die Vorrede zu den Französischen Zuständen," 24.

37. Heinrich Heine, *Der Neue Alexander, Part III.*

38. Heinrich Heine, *Lobgesänge auf König Ludwig II.*

39. König, "Heinrich Heine, der Schmutzfink im deutschen Dichterwald."

40. König, "Heinrich Heine, der Schmutzfink im deutschen Dichterwald."

41. Heinrich Heine, "The Weavers," in *Heinrich Heine, Poetry and Prose*, eds. Jost Hermand and Robert C. Holub, trans. Aaron Kramer (New York: Continuum, 1982), 53.

42. Heine, "In October," in *Heinrich Heine, Poetry and Prose*, 81. NB: They left out the last two lines:

> *Poet, be still; your anguish grows*
> *You are so sick … it were wiser not to speak.*

43. König, "Heinrich Heine, der Schmutzfink im deutschen Dichterwald."

44. König, "Heinrich Heine, der Schmutzfink im deutschen Dichterwald." Quote from Heine, *Französische Zustände, Artikel III*, in *The Works of Heinrich Heine, vol. VII: French Affairs: Letters from Paris*, 95.

45. Quote from Heine, *Französische Zustände, Artikel III.*

46. König, "Heinrich Heine, der Schmutzfink im deutschen Dichterwald."

47. Edbach, "Entwurf eines Denkmals für Heine."

48. Heine, *The Baths of Lucca*, in *The Works of Heinrich Heine*, vol. 3, trans. Charles Godfrey Leland (London: Heinemann, 1891), 168.

49. König, "Heinrich Heine, der Schmutzfink im deutschen Dichterwald."

50. Heinrich Heine, *Latest Poems and Thoughts*, in *The Life, Work, and Opinions of Heinrich Heine*, ed. and trans. William Stigand (London: Longmans, Green, 1875), 193.

51. Heinrich Heine, *Pictures of Travel*, trans. Charles Godfrey Leland (Philadelphia, PA: Weik, 1856), 329.

52. König, "Heinrich Heine, der Schmutzfink im deutschen Dichterwald."

53. "Heinrich Heine als Kommunistenagitator," *Völkischer Beobachter*, 13 November 1931.

54. "Das Heinrich Heine-Denkmal in Hamburg."

55. "Heine über die Juden."

56. "Heine über die Juden."

57. Heine, *Pictures of Travel.*

58. "Heine über die Juden."

59. Edbach, "Entwurf eines Denkmals für Heine."

60. "Das Heinrich Heine-Denkmal in Hamburg."

61. Edbach, "Entwurf eines Denkmals für Heine."

62. König, "Heinrich Heine, der Schmutzfink im deutschen Dichterwald."

63. Heinrich Heine, *Diana*, in *The Poems of Heine: Complete*, trans. Edgar Alfred Bowring (London: Bell & Daldy, 1866), 112.

64. König, "Heinrich Heine, der Schmutzfink im deutschen Dichterwald."

65. Heinrich Heine, *The Evil Star*, in *The Poems of Heine: Complete*, 142.
66. Heinrich Heine, *Ich kann es nicht vergessen*, in *Poems of Heinrich Heine*, trans. Louis Untermeyer (New York: Henry Holt, 1917), 64.
67. Heinrich Heine, *Mein süßes Lieb, wenn du im Grab*, in *Heine's Book of Songs*, trans. Charles Godfrey Leland (New York: F. W. Christern, 1864), 84.
68. König, "Heinrich Heine, der Schmutzfink im deutschen Dichterwald."
69. Translations of Heinrich Heine, *Germany: A Winter's Tale*, are all from Hermand and Holub (eds.), *Heinrich Heine, Poetry and Prose*, 231–287.
70. Walter Bohe, "Heinrich Heine: *Deutschland, ein Wintermärchen*," *Völkischer Beobachter*, 14 March 1928.
71. König, "Heinrich Heine, der Schmutzfink im deutschen Dichterwald."
72. Bohe, "Heinrich Heine: *Deutschland, ein Wintermärchen*."
73. Bohe, "Heinrich Heine: *Deutschland, ein Wintermärchen*."
74. Friedländer, *The Years of Extermination*, 189.

6 Classicism Romanticized

1. Mosse, *Nationalization of the Masses*, 34–35.
2. Hitler, *Mein Kampf*, 423.
3. "Hitler admired the architecture of classical Greece. But even when he invoked the common ground of Hellenism and Germans, the Athenian example was never as crucial as Rome to his program for architecture and governance": Marchand, "Nazism, Orientalism and Humanism," 308.
4. "The formula called for the subordination of science, mechanization, modernization, and a new ethics to a religious racial goal": Mosse, *German Jews Beyond Judaism*, 97. For more on the general Nazi approach to the ancients, including their interpretations of Plato and Alexander the Great, see Wolin, *The Seduction of Unreason*, 108–113.
5. "Um des Sokrates Schatten: Griechische Prozesssucht," *Völkischer Beobachter*, 5 April 1927.
6. W. Rüdiger, "Die Kunst Albrecht Dürers."
7. drh., "Dürer als Schöpfer des Selbstbildnisses."
8. Adalbert Bornhagen, "Winckelmann und Lessing: Zum 175. Todestage Johann Joachim Winckelmanns," *Völkischer Beobachter*, 9 June 1943. On Winckelmann see Mosse, *Nationalization of the Masses*, ch. 2; Michaud, *Cult of Art in Nazi Germany*, 138–140, and Wolin, *Seduction of Unreason*, 105–106.
9. Dresler, "Goethe und der nationale Gedanke."
10. Petzold, "Goethe und die Juden: Eine aktülle Betrachtung zur Ausstellung 'Der ewige Jude.'"
11. Ricarda Huch, "Der Mensch Goethe," *Völkischer Beobachter*, 9 April 1944.

12. Rudolf Hofmüller, "Goethe und die Romantik," *Völkischer Beobachter*, 7 March 1940.
13. Hofmüller, "Goethe und die Romantik."
14. Rudolf Hofmüller, "Vollendeter *Amphitryon*," *Völkischer Beobachter*, 17 July 1939.
15. Friedrich Wilhelm Hymmen, "Zurufe eines Unsterblichen: Zum 175. Geburtstag Friedrich Hölderlins," *Völkischer Beobachter*, 24 March 1945.
16. There is little doubt why Wundt's books were among those owned by Adolf Hitler. See Gassert and Mattern (eds.), *The Hitler Library*, 326.
17. Max Wundt, "Zu Hegels Gedächtnis," *Völkischer Beobachter*, 14 November 1931. On Hegel and Nazism in general, see Jon Bartley Stewart, *The Hegel Myths and Legends* (Evanston, IL: Northwestern University Press, 1996), 85–124 and Hans D. Sluga, *Heidegger's Crisis: Philosophy and Politics in Nazi Germany* (Cambridge, MA: Harvard University Press, 1995) *passim*.
18. Hans Gatettner, "Eine Nietzsche-Revision: Zu einem Vortrag Prof. Bäumlers," *Völkischer Beobachter*, 20 March 1945.
19. Fritz Geyer, "Alexander der Grosse als Staatsmann," *Völkischer Beobachter*, 19 March 1926.
20. See Marchand, "Nazism, Orientalism and Humanism," 326, for some discussion of this.
21. Other views of this issue were voiced in Nazi circles: see Marchand, "Nazism, Orientalism and Humanism," 324.
22. Hans Speihmann, "Karthagos Untergang," *Völkischer Beobachter*, 23 July 1927. For some discussion of National Socialist references to ancient Carthage, see Ben Kiernan, *Blood and Soil: A World History of Genocide and Extermination from Sparta to Darfur* (New Haven, CT: Yale University Press, 2009), 420.
23. "Wunder und Aberglaube im römischen Weltreich," *Völkischer Beobachter*, 17 August 1927.

7 Intolerance toward Enlightenment

1. As Fritz Stern put it, "they appropriated something from every intellectual tradition of modern Germany, except one. They consistently warred against the ideas of the Enlightenment and of the French Revolution – the so-called ideas of 1789 and hence they were most powerfully influenced by the men who shared this hostility, to wit, the romantics, the cultural nationalists of the late eighteenth century, and the more aggressive nationalists ... of the Napoleonic period. They illustrated what Nietzsche called 'the hostility of the Germans to the Enlightenment'": Stern, *Politics of Cultural Despair*, 277. Discussing fascism in general, Richard Wolin is adamant about the significance of this point: "For one of fascism's avowed goals was to put an end to the Enlightenment-derived

nineteenth-century world view: the predominance of science, reason, democracy, socialism, individualism, and the like. As Goebbels pithily observed a few months after Hitler's rise to power, 'The year 1789 is hereby erased from history' ... They elected to combat the values of the French Revolution with revolutionary means: violence, war, and total mobilization. Thereby, they ushered in an alternative vision of modernity, one that was meant to supersede the standpoint of the philosophies and the political champions of 1789": Wolin, *Seduction of Unreason*, 3.

2. "Spinoza," *Völkischer Beobachter*, 25 September 1927.

3. Klara Trost, "Leibniz und sein Haus: Eine Erinnerung," *Völkischer Beobachter*, 14 June 1944.

4. Hermann Hartmann, "Newtons Wirkung auf Europa," *Völkischer Beobachter*, 17 September 1937.

5. "Through the ideology which we have discussed, this unfortunate nation came to repudiate a European heritage which was still active elsewhere: that of the rationalism of the Enlightenment and the social radicalism of the French Revolution. Moreover, this repudiation was intimately connected with a general opposition to modernity which withdrew into itself": Mosse, *German Jews Beyond Judaism*, 316.

6. Richard Biedrzynski, "Der Mut zum Schmerz: Deutsche Meisterwerke für unsere Zeit," *Völkischer Beobachter*, 14 March 1945.

7. Translation by Henry Fuseli.

8. Bornhagen, "Winckelmann und Lessing: Zum 175. Todestage Johann Joachim Winckelmanns."

9. Sethe, "Ein Mensch mit seinem Widerspruch: Zum 250. Todestag Voltaires," *Völkischer Beobachter*, 21 November 1944.

10. Albert Müller, "Lessing als Politiker," *Völkischer Beobachter*, 15 February 1931.

11. Konrad Mass, "Der Dichter der *Minna von Barnheim*: Ein Wort der Erinnerung zum 150. Todestage G. E. Lessings," *Völkischer Beobachter*, 15 February 1931.

12. Müller, "Lessing als Politiker."

13. Müller, "Lessing als Politiker."

14. Mass, "Der Dichter der *Minna von Barnheim*: Ein Wort der Erinnerung zum 150. Todestage G. E. Lessings."

15. Josef Stolzing, "Gotthold Ephraim Lessing: Zu seinem 200. Geburtstag," *Völkischer Beobachter*, 22 January 1929.

16. Müller, "Lessing als Politiker."

17. Stolzing, "Gotthold Ephraim Lessing: Zu seinem 200. Geburtstag."

18. Stolzing, "Gotthold Ephraim Lessing: Zu seinem 200. Geburtstag."

19. Mass, "Der Dichter der *Minna von Barnheim*: Ein Wort der Erinnerung zum 150. Todestage G. E. Lessings."

20. Müller, "Lessing als Politiker."

21. Mass, "Der Dichter der *Minna von Barnheim*: Ein Wort der Erinnerung zum 150. Todestage G. E. Lessings."

22. Stolzing, "Gotthold Ephraim Lessing: Zu seinem 200. Geburtstag."

23. Stolzing, "Gotthold Ephraim Lessing: Zu seinem 200. Geburtstag."

24. Müller, "Lessing als Politiker."

25. Müller, "Lessing als Politiker."

26. Mass, "Der Dichter der *Minna von Barnheim*: Ein Wort der Erinnerung zum 150. Todestage G. E. Lessings."

27. Heinz Henckel, "Der wahre Moses Mendelssohn: Zu seinem 200. Geburtstag," *Völkischer Beobachter*, 5 September 1929.

28. Henckel, "Der wahre Moses Mendelssohn: Zu seinem 200. Geburtstag,"

29. Mass, "Der Dichter der *Minna von Barnheim*: Ein Wort der Erinnerung zum 150. Todestage G. E. Lessings."

30. Henckel, "Der wahre Moses Mendelssohn: Zu seinem 200. Geburtstag."

31. Ernst Marcus, *Aus den Tiefen des Erkennens: Kants Lehre von der Apperzeption (dem Selbstbewusstsein), der Kategorialverbindung und den Verstandesgrundsätzen in neuer verständlicher Darstellung* (Munich: E. Reunhardt, 1925).

32. Josef Stolzing, "Immanuel Kant in der *Sonnenhelle*," *Völkischer Beobachter*, 7 September 1926.

33. "Immanuel Kant," *Völkischer Beobachter*, 13 February 1923.

34. "Immanuel Kant." Citation from Immanuel Kant, *Die Religion in den Grenzen der bloßen Vernunft*, in Immanuel Kant, *Religion within the Limits of Reason Alone, Book Three: The Victory of the Good over the Evil Principle, and the Founding of a Kingdom of God on Earth*, trans. Theodore M. Greene and Hoyt H. Hudson (Chicago, IL: Open Court, 1934), 116.

35. "Immanuel Kant." Citation from Immanuel Kant, *Anthropologie in pragmatischer Hinsicht* (Königsberg, 1798).

36. Immanuel Kant, *Zum ewigen Frieden: Ein philosophischer Entwurf* (1795).

37. Günter Macketanz, "Kant und die Abrüstung," *Völkischer Beobachter*, 7 January 1922.

38. Junk, "Genie des Schaffens."

39. Buchner, "Zum Münchner Mozartfest."

40. Junk, "Genie des Schaffens."

41. Moessmer, "Die Geburt der deutschen Oper."

42. Hans Buchner, "Münchener Mozart-Festspiele: Die Entführung aus dem Serail," *Völkischer Beobachter*, 9 August 1929.

43. Moessmer, "Die Geburt der deutschen Oper."

44. Heinrich Stahl, "Operntext und Zeitgeschichte," *Völkischer Beobachter*, 25 December 1942.

45. Josef Stolzing, "Don Giovanni," *Völkischer Beobachter*, 17 August 1929.

46. Hans Buchner, "Festspiele im Münchener Residenztheater. 'Die Hochzeit des Figaro,'" *Völkischer Beobachter*, 1 August 1928.

47. Heinrich Stahl, "'Figaros Hochzeit' neu inszeniert," *Völkischer Beobachter*, 29 April 1940.

48. Heinrich Stahl, "Geniale Männer über das Genie Mozart: 150 Jahre Don Giovanni," *Völkischer Beobachter*, 29 October 1937.

49. Hans Buchner, "Don Giovanni," *Völkischer Beobachter*, 6 August 1927.

50. "Festspiele im Residenztheater: Don Giovanni," *Völkischer Beobachter*, 17 August 1928.

51. Friedrich Bayer, "Don Giovanni in Salzburg," *Völkischer Beobachter*, 27 July 1938.

52. Josef Stolzing, "Cosi fan tutte," *Völkischer Beobachter*, 12 June 1928.

53. Moessmer, "Die Geburt der deutschen Oper."

54. G. A., "Die Zauberflöte," *Völkischer Beobachter*, 31 December 1929.

55. Moessmer, "Die Geburt der deutschen Oper."

56. Franz Posch, "Salzburger Theater- und Musiksommer 1943," *Völkischer Beobachter*, 29 August 1943.

57. Hans Buchner, "Münchener Festspiele: Die Zauberflöte," *Völkischer Beobachter*, 26 August 1923.

58. Posch, "Salzburger Theater- und Musiksommer 1943."

59. T. H. L., "Die Salzburger Festspiele ein Judenrummel," *Völkischer Beobachter*, 6 September 1928.

60. Charles Louis Montesquieu, *Considerations on the Causes of the Greatness of the Romans and their Decline*, trans. David Lowenthal (New York: Cornell University Press, 1965), 44.

61. "Montesquieu über die deutsche Demokratie?," *Völkischer Beobachter*, 9 November 1930. Translation from Montesquieu, *Considerations on the Causes of the Greatness of the Romans and their Decline*, ch. 4.

62. See Albert Sorel, *Montesquieu*, trans. Melville Best Anderson and Edward Playfair Anderson (Chicago, IL: A. C. McClurg, 1888), 157.

63. "Der Rassegedanke in der französische Revolution," *Völkischer Beobachter*, 18 June 1927.

64. Emmanuel Joseph Sieyès, *What is the Third Estate?*, trans. M. Blondel (London: Pall Mall Press, 1963), 58–59.

65. "Der Rassegedanke in der französische Revolution."

66. J. W. von Goethe, *Hermann and Dorothea*, in *The Harvard Classics*, vol. XIX, Pt. 4. trans. Ellen Frothingham (New York: P. F. Collier, 1909), 14.

67. Dresler, "Goethe und der nationale Gedanke."

68. Goethe, *Hermann and Dorothea*, 14.

69. For instance, "Die Münchener Post und der Geheimrat Goethe," *Völkischer Beobachter*, 6 September 1922 and "'Höchstes hast du vollbracht, mein Volk': Grosse Deutsche über Grossdeutschland: Johann Wolfgang von Goethe."

70. *Conversations of Goethe, Recorded by His Friend Johann Peter Eckermann* Sunday, 4 January 1824, 53.

71. "Die Münchener Post und der Geheimrat Goethe."

72. Cited in "Was hat Goethe dem heutigen Deutschland zu sagen: Zu Goethes Todestag."

73. Johst, "Aufblick zu Goethe."

74. "Der deutsche Goethe."

75. "Goethe spricht," *Völkischer Beobachter*, 22 March 1932. Citation from *Conversations of Goethe, Recorded by His Friend Johann Peter Eckermann* Thursday evening, 18 January 1827, 164.

76. *Conversations of Goethe, Recorded by His Friend Johann Peter Eckermann* Thursday, 24 February 1825. Cited in "'Höchstes hast du vollbracht, mein Volk': Grosse Deutsche über Grossdeutschland: Johann Wolfgang von Goethe."

77. Goethe, *Wilhelm Meisters Wanderjahre*. Cited in "'Höchstes hast du vollbracht, mein Volk': Grosse Deutsche über Grossdeutschland: Johann Wolfgang von Goethe."

78. Cited in "Was hat Goethe dem heutigen Deutschland zu sagen: Zu Goethes Todestag." Original source unknown.

79. Gassert and Mattern (eds.), *The Hitler Library*, 269.

80. Schulz, "Schillers Weg zur deutschen Freiheit."

81. From an unfinished poem under the title *Deutsche Größe* (1797), cited in H. Krause, "Schiller, ein Führer zum Neuen Reich," *Völkischer Beobachter*, 8 May 1930.

82. Schulz, "Schillers Weg zur deutschen Freiheit."

83. Krause, "Schiller, ein Führer zum Neuen Reich."

84. Schiedermair, "Beethoven und die Politik."

85. "To be sure, the curious notions analyzed in this book and the bizarre scholars who advocated them would have remained in well-deserved obscurity had Adolf Hitler not given volkish thought pride of place in National Socialism. Yet Hitler would never have succeeded in demonstrating the political effectiveness of the volkish world view had this perception of reality not already been shared by a great many Germans": Mosse, *German Jews Beyond Judaism*, v.

86. "Pestalozzi über die Juden," *Völkischer Beobachter*, 17 March 1927. Citation from Johann Heinrich Pestalozzi, *Die 142 Fabeln d. Schriftfiguren zum ABC-Buch* (Scyffarth, 1901), 99.

87. "Fichte redet zur deutschen Nation," *Völkischer Beobachter*, 19 May 1937. For more on the National Socialist implications of Fichte, see Hans D. Sluga, *Heidegger's Crisis: Philosophy and Politics in Nazi Germany* (Cambridge, MA: Harvard University Press, 1995), 29–53.

88. Cited in "Johann Gottlieb Fichte über das Judentum," *Völkischer Beobachter*, 12 June 1926.

89. Konrad Karkosch, "'Die Errettung Deutschlands,'" *Völkischer Beobachter*, 19 May 1937.
90. Theodor Stiefenhofer, "Die Entdeckung des Volkstums: Zum 200. Geburtstag von Johann Gottfried Herder," *Völkischer Beobachter*, 19 August 1944. See discussion of Herder and Nazi ideology in Sonia Sikka, *Herder on Humanity and Cultural Difference: Enlightened Relativism* (Cambridge University Press, 2011), 126–149.
91. "Wilhelm von Humboldt über die Deutschen," *Völkischer Beobachter*, 13 August 1929.
92. Adolf Hösel, *Dehmel und Nietzsche* (Munich: E. Huber, 1928).
93. Adolf Hösel, "Staatsmann und Philosoph: Zum 100. Todestag Wilhelm von Humboldts," *Völkischer Beobachter*, 8 April 1935.
94. Hanns Ebner, "Zum 100. Todestag des Freiherr vom Stein," *Völkischer Beobachter*, 27 June 1931.
95. "Freiherr vom Stein und die Judenbanken," *Völkischer Beobachter*, 29 May 1927.
96. Hitler, *Mein Kampf*, 385.

8 Forging Steel Romanticism

1. "In essence it was an ideology which stood opposed to the progress and modernization that transformed nineteenth-century Europe. It used and amplified Romanticism to provide an alternative to modernity, to the developing industrial and urban civilization which seemed to rob man of his individual, creative self while cutting him loose from a social order that was seemingly exhausted and lacking vitality": Mosse, *German Jews Beyond Judaism*, 1.
2. "Nazism banished everything alien to itself, just as its 'steely Romanticism' eliminated all Romantic irony": Michaud, *The Cult of Art in Nazi Germany*, 111. See also Herf, *Reactionary Modernism*, 195–197.
3. Joseph Goebbels, Speech in Heidelberg Stadthalle, 9 July 1943, in *Goebbels-Reden, Band 2: 1939–1945*, ed. Helmut Heiber (Düsseldorf: Droste Verlag, 1971), 253.
4. Joseph Goebbels, "Die deutsche Kultur vor neuen Aufgaben," Berlin, Grosser Saal der Philharmonie, Eröffunung der Reichskulturkammer, 15 November 1933, in *Goebbels-Reden, Band 1: 1932–1939*, 137.
5. H. Sturm, "Ernst Moritz Arndt: Zu seinem 71. Todestag," *Völkischer Beobachter*, 29 January 1931. Sturm started contributing to the *Völkischer Beobachter* in this year (Köhler, "Kunstanschauung und Kunstkritik," 27).
6. Theodor Stiefenhofer, "Trommler deutscher Freiheit: Zum 175. Geburtstag von Ernst Moritz Arndt," *Völkischer Beobachter*, 26 December 1944.
7. Stiefenhofer, "Trommler deutscher Freiheit: Zum 175. Geburtstag von Ernst Moritz Arndt."

8. Adolf Hösel, "Für die Einheit von Volk und Staat: Zum 75. Todestag des deutschen Herolds Ernst Moritz Arndt," *Völkischer Beobachter*, 29 January 1935.

9. "'Das ganze Deutschland muss es sein': Grosse Deutsche über Grossdeutschland: Ernst Moritz Arndt," *Völkischer Beobachter*, 8 April 1938.

10. Sturm, "Ernst Moritz Arndt: Zu seinem 71. Todestag."

11. Stiefenhofer, "Trommler deutscher Freiheit: Zum 175. Geburtstag von Ernst Moritz Arndt."

12. Dr., "Heinrich von Kleist: Zu seinem Todestag am 21. November 1811," *Völkischer Beobachter*, 21 November 1926.

13. Hans Lucke, "Der erste Atemzug der deutschen Freiheit," *Völkischer Beobachter*, 20 November 1936.

14. Lucke, "Der erste Atemzug der deutschen Freiheit."

15. Dr., "Heinrich von Kleist: Zu seinem Todestag am 21. November 1811."

16. Otto M. Gervais, "Grab am Wannsee," *Völkischer Beobachter*, 20 November 1936.

17. Josef Stolzing, "Dem Dichter der *Hermannschlacht*," *Völkischer Beobachter*, 15 October 1927.

18. Köhler, "Kunstanschauung und Kunstkritik," 27.

19. Hellmuth Langenbucher, "Heinrich von Kleist," *Völkischer Beobachter*, 22 November 1931.

20. Franz Langheinrich, "Zehn Jahre schöpferischen Lebens," *Völkischer Beobachter*, 20 November 1936.

21. Stolzing, "Dem Dichter der *Hermannschlacht*." For further discussion of National Socialist appropriations of Kleist's *Hermannschlacht*, see Heinrich von Kleist, *The Battle of Herrmann: A Drama*, trans. Rachel MagShamhrain (Würzburg: Königshausen & Neumann, 2008), xxv–xxviii.

22. E. Meunier, "Heinrich von Kleist: Zu seinem 130. Todestag," *Völkischer Beobachter*, 21 November 1941.

23. Langheinrich, "Zehn Jahre schöpferischen Lebens."

24. Gassert and Mattern (eds.), *The Hitler Library*, 327. According to Köhler, Ziegler contributed to the *Völkischer Beobachter* regularly, with an emphasis on the Weimar cultural scene: Köhler, "Kunstanschauung und Kunstkritik," 27.

25. Hans Severus Ziegler, "Heinrich von Kleist," *Völkischer Beobachter*, 20 October 1927.

26. Reproduced in Stolzing, "Dem Dichter der *Hermannschlacht*." Translation from Rohan D. O. Butler, *The Roots of National Socialism, 1783–1933* (London: Faber & Faber, 1941), 52.

27. Heinrich von Kleist, "Kriegslied der Deutschen," in *Little Red Riding Hood: A Casebook*, trans. Alan Dundes (Madison, WI: University of Wisconsin Press, 1989), 98.

28. "Von der Liebe zum Vaterlande," *Völkischer Beobachter*, 23 March 1930.

29. Uwe Lars Nobbe, "Kleist und wir," *Völkischer Beobachter*, 20 November 1936.

30. Stolzing, "Dem Dichter der *Hermannschlacht*."
31. Ziegler, "Heinrich von Kleist."
32. Langenbucher, "Heinrich von Kleist."
33. "Die Kleist-Woche in Bochum," *Völkischer Beobachter*, 20 November 1936.
34. Hermann Claudius, "Bekenntnis," *Völkischer Beobachter*, 20 November 1936.
35. Indeed, in the case of Kleist, it is more surprising that the paper – with its eagle eye for such things – didn't draw on subtle indications of anti-Semitism that subsequent scholars have identified in his writings. See John Warrack, *German Opera* (Cambridge University Press, 2001), 270 and Ingo Hermann, *Hardenberg: Der Reformkanzler* (Berlin: Siedler Verlag, 2003), 306.
36. Hermann Eris Busse, "Johann Peter Hebel: Zum 175. Geburtstag," *Völkischer Beobachter*, 10 May 1935.
37. Gustav Christian Rassy, "Blumengarten der Dichtkunst: Zum 175. Geburtstag Jean Pauls," *Völkischer Beobachter*, 20 March 1938.
38. "Politisches Bekenntnis," *Völkischer Beobachter*, 20 March 1938.
39. "Politisches Bekenntnis."
40. E. T. A. Hoffmann, "Das öde Haus," *Völkischer Beobachter*, 30 August 1923. Translations from *The Lock and Key Library: German Stories* (New York: Reviews of Reviews Co., 1909).
41. Dr. Gernet-Beürle, "Vom deutschen Geist der Spätromantik: Clemens Brentano zu seinem 100. Todestag," *Völkischer Beobachter*, 29 July 1942.
42. Gernet-Beürle, "Vom deutschen Geist der Spätromantik: Clemens Brentano zu seinem 100. Todestag."
43. Gassert and Mattern (eds.), *The Hitler Library*, 66.
44. Paul Bülow, "Romantik des Volksliedes: Zum 100. Todestag Achim von Arnims," *Völkischer Beobachter*, 21 January 1931.
45. Gernet-Beürle, "Vom deutschen Geist der Spätromantik: Clemens Brentano zu seinem 100. Todestag."
46. Nearly the same poem is registered as having been written in 1840, by Heinrich Heine!
47. "Auf ünbekannte anti-Semitische Gedichte von Franz Grillparzer und Wilhelm Karl Grimm."
48. Herbert Müller, "Der letzte Ritter der Romantik," *Völkischer Beobachter*, 12 June 1926.
49. Joseph Eichendorff, "Aus dem Leben eines Taugenichts," *Völkischer Beobachter*, 13–26 April 1929.
50. Müller, "Der letzte Ritter der Romantik."
51. Rudolf Hofmüller, "Der letzte Ritter der Romantik: Zum 150. Geburtstag Eichendorffs," *Völkischer Beobachter*, 10 March 1938.
52. Konrad Karkosch, "Eichendorff und die deutsche Seele: Zu seinem Todestage am 26. November," *Völkischer Beobachter*, 21 November 1941.

53. "Wilhelm Müller: Zum 100. Todestage des Dichters der Griechenlieder," *Völkischer Beobachter*, 2 October 1927.

54. Horst Rüdiger, "Hölderlin," *Völkischer Beobachter*, 20 March 1935. For discussion of discourse on Hölderlin in Nazi culture specifically related to Heidegger's readings, see Emmanuel Faye, *Heidegger: The Introduction of Nazism into Philosophy in Light of the Unpublished Seminars of 1933–1935* (New Haven, CT: Yale University Press, 2009).

55. Rüdiger, "Hölderlin."

56. Hermann Burte, "Friedrich Hölderlin: Zu seinem 100. Todestag," *Völkischer Beobachter*, 6 June 1943.

57. L., "Im Geiste Goethes und Jean Pauls …," *Völkischer Beobachter*, 10 February 1935.

58. W. St., "Goethes *Urfaust*," *Völkischer Beobachter*, 15 November 1931.

59. Curt Hotzel, "Friedrich Nietzsches Umnachtung," *Völkischer Beobachter*, 3 January 1939.

60. Johann Wolfgang von Goethe, *Faust: A Tragedy*, ed. Cyrus Hamlin, trans. Walter Arndt (New York: W. W. Norton, 1976), 261, l. 10253.

61. Goethe, *Faust: A Tragedy*, 258, l. 10134.

62. Goethe, *Faust: A Tragedy*, 259, l. 10188.

63. Goethe, *Faust: A Tragedy*, 294, ll. 11563 ff.

64. Goethe, *Faust: A Tragedy*, 259, l. 10181.

65. Georg Schott, "Goethes Ideal vom Führer: Eine zeitgemässe Faustbetrachtung," *Völkischer Beobachter*, 9 March 1932.

9 Romantic Music as "Our Greatest Legacy"

1. Literature on *Musikpolitik* in German and National Socialist culture has evolved tremendously over the last twenty years. As representative of its findings, I cite an early contribution to the field, while acknowledging the many scholars who have been building on that start. "Noted composers, performers, educators, critics, and musicologists contributed, through statements, manifestoes, articles, and books, to the justification of totalitarian design and practice. This development played a crucial part in the legitimization of Nazi power in the cultural sphere … The musicologists in the Third Reich played an especially crucial role in matters of definition and the subsequent re-writing of the musical past. Trained in their discipline and properly primed politically, they applied Nazi categories to an evaluation of German musicians for hero-status, as possible precursors and prophets, while the words, deeds, and musical accomplishments of the same great masters were cited in confirmation of Nazi ideals … Equipped with racial and folk norms, the musicologists combed through the past and present music cultures to verify Nazi truths, to weed out alien and decadent components, and to establish the folk-related art in confirmation of the Nazi myth of 'blood and soil'":

Michael Meyer, "The Nazi Musicologist as Myth Maker in the Third Reich," *Journal of Contemporary History*, 10(4), 1975: 649–665. See, among the books on the subject, Levi, *Mozart and the Nazis*; Kater and Riethmüller, *Music and Nazism*; Karen Painter, *Symphonic Aspirations: German Music and Politics, 1900–1945* (Cambridge, MA: Harvard University Press, 2007); Nicholas Vazsonyi (ed.), *Wagner's Meistersinger: Performance, History, Representation* (University of Rochester Press, 2004); Etlin (ed.), *Art, Culture, and Media under the Third Reich*; Applegate and Potter (eds.), *Music and German National Identity*; Potter, *Most German of the Arts*; Kater, *The Twisted Muse*; Dennis, *Beethoven in German Politics*; Cuomo, *National Socialist Cultural Policy*; Steinweis, *Art, Ideology, and Economics in Nazi Germany*; Levi, *Music in the Third Reich*; Albrecht Dümling and Peter Girth, *Entartete Musik: Banned by the Nazis* (Los Angeles Philharmonic Association, 1991); Gilliam, *Music and Performance during the Weimar Republic*; Meyer, *The Politics of Music in the Third Reich*; Taylor and van der Will, *The Nazification of Art*; Heister and Klein, *Musik und Musikpolitik im faschistischen Deutschland*; Wulf, *Musik im Dritten Reich*; and Prieberg, *Musik im NS-Staat*.

2. Joseph Goebbels, Berlin, 28 May 1938, cited in Huener and Nicosia (eds.), *The Arts in Nazi Germany*, 184.
3. G. B. Mähr-Altstadt, "Franz Schuberts Abstammung," *Völkischer Beobachter*, 17 November 1928.
4. Alexander Witeschnik, "Franz Schuberts Wienertum," *Völkischer Beobachter*, 16 February 1943.
5. Mähr-Altstadt, "Franz Schuberts Abstammung."
6. Witeschnik, "Franz Schuberts Wienertum."
7. Mähr-Altstadt, "Franz Schuberts Abstammung."
8. Josef Stolzing, "Auf den Spuren Schuberts," *Völkischer Beobachter*, 17 November 1928.
9. Walter Persich, "Schubert reist nach Preussen: Eine Erzählung vom Vaterland jenseits der Gau- und Stammesgrenzen," *Völkischer Beobachter*, 29 August 1943.
10. "Die Schubert-Ehrung in Wien," *Völkischer Beobachter*, 23 July 1928.
11. Hans Buchner, "Schubert der Klassiker der Romantik," *Völkischer Beobachter*, 17 November 1928.
12. Gottrau, "Vom Wesen deutscher Musik."
13. "3. = austaltung im Residenztheater," *Völkischer Beobachter*, 31 October 1930.
14. "Die Schubertfeier in der Walhalla," *Völkischer Beobachter*, 11 November 1928.
15. "Die Schubertfeiern ein jüdischer Geschaftsrummel," *Völkischer Beobachter*, 20 April 1928.
16. "Man feiert Schubert," *Völkischer Beobachter*, 8 December 1928.
17. "Grossen Deutschen Fest-Feier," *Völkischer Beobachter*, 1 April 1922.
18. "Morgenfeier," *Völkischer Beobachter*, 19 April 1933.

19. "Die Reichs-Kultur-Kammer eröffnet: Der Führer bei der Feier in der Berliner Philharmonie," *Völkischer Beobachter*, 16 November 1933.

20. "Hausmusik- im Krieg erst recht!," *Völkischer Beobachter*, 20 November 1940. (Original emphasis.)

21. "Grosse deutsche Festfeier," *Völkischer Beobachter*, 22 February 1922.

22. "Das erste Konzert des nationalsozialistischen Symphonieorchesters," *Völkischer Beobachter*, 12 January 1932 and "Die erste Konzertreise des nat.-soz. Symphonie-Orchesters," *Völkischer Beobachter*, 12 February 1932.

23. R. Tr., "Zweites Berliner Kampfbundkonzert," *Völkischer Beobachter*, 24 September 1932.

24. Hans Buchner, "Karl Maria von Weber," *Völkischer Beobachter*, 5 June 1926.

25. Karl Grunsky, "Karl Maria von Weber: Zum 150. Geburtstag," *Völkischer Beobachter*, 18 December 1936.

26. Buchner, "Karl Maria von Weber."

27. Josef Stolzing, "Die Oper als Kunstform," *Völkischer Beobachter*, 22 May 1930.

28. "Münchner Festspiele: Oberon," *Völkischer Beobachter*, 19 September 1920.

29. Voelsing, "Die Idee einer Nationaloper." Weber quote from *Briefe an den Akademischen Musikverein in Breslau*, 1814.

30. Josef Klingenbeck, "Um Webers 'Euryanthe,'" *Völkischer Beobachter*, 19 March 1934.

31. Erwin Bauer, "Der Freischutz der Salzburger Festspiele," *Völkischer Beobachter*, 5 August 1939.

32. Heinrich Stahl, "Die Oper vom deutschen Wald," *Völkischer Beobachter*, 2 February 1942.

33. Edmund Pesch, "Karl Maria von Webers Heimkehr," *Völkischer Beobachter*, 8 December 1944. Wagner's memorial oration was also repeated in "Aus der letzten Lebenszeit Karl Maria von Webers: Zu seinem 100. Todestag, 5 Juni 1926," *Völkischer Beobachter*, 1 May 1926.

34. Josef Stolzing, "Der Kreis um Gerhart Hauptmann," *Völkischer Beobachter*, 16 November 1932.

35. Wagner, *Some Explanations Concerning Judaism in Music*, 118.

36. Gustav Christian Rassy, "Beinahe eine Tischrede: Zum 80. Todestag Robert Schumanns," *Völkischer Beobachter*, 29 July 1936.

37. A three-part story about Wagner depicts him and his family in Italy, where they confront an Italian fisherman who is about to put his dogs to sleep. Written by Gustav Renker, novelist, conductor, and composer who produced a number of *Heimat* novels as well as a novel about Wagner's last days in Venice; the story ended with the composer buying the dogs to save them and make them family pets. (Gustav Renker, "Der Tierfreund: Eine Richard-Wagner-Geschichte," *Völkischer Beobachter*, 8 February 1933.)

38. Otto Daube, "Parsifal-Bayreuth: Die deutschen Theater," *Völkischer Beobachter*, 13 May 1925. See Köhler, "Kunstanschauung und Kunstkritik," 27.

39. Köhler, "Kunstanschauung und Kunstkritik," 28.
40. Herbert H. Mueller, "Richard Wagner zum Gedächtnis zu seinem Todestage am 13. Februar," *Völkischer Beobachter*, 13 January 1927.
41. Alexander Dillmann, "Lohengrin – ein Völkisches Bekenntnis," *Völkischer Beobachter*, 3 October 1934.
42. "Richard Wagner und das Kunstempfinden unserer Zeit: Rundfunkrede von Reichsminister Dr. Goebbels."
43. Hans Joachim Moser, "'Das nenn' ich mir einen Abgesang!: Die ersten 'Meistersinger' vor siebzig Jahren," *Völkischer Beobachter*, 21 June 1938.
44. Josef Stolzing, "Der Weltkrieg im Ring des Niebelungen," *Völkischer Beobachter*, 7–8 August 1923.
45. Wagner, *What is German?*
46. Stolzing, "Der Weltkrieg im Ring des Niebelungen."
47. Julius Brittner, "Richard Wagner und wir," *Völkischer Beobachter*, 23 August 1928.
48. Josef Stolzing, "Münchener Wagner- u. Mozartfestspiele: Götterdämmerung," *Völkischer Beobachter*, 17 August 1929.
49. For instance, Frederic Spotts, *Hitler and the Power of Aesthetics*, 256–257 and Pamela Potter, "Music in the Third Reich" in Huener and Nicosia (eds.), *The Arts in Nazi Germany*, 87–88.

10 Realist Paradox and Expressionist Confusion

1. Hitler, *Mein Kampf*, 257–262.
2. "Although artistic modernism had made important inroads in Germany before 1918, it was during the Weimar Republic that it emerged in its full force in literature, painting and sculpture, architecture, music, and theater. Many of the artistic innovations attracted the wrath of cultural conservatives spanning the right side of the political spectrum. They condemned artistic modernism as overly cerebral and international. It did not conform to their notion of authentic 'Germanness'": Steinweis, "Anti-Semitism and the Arts in Nazi Ideology and Policy," 20.
3. "Modernity was rejected; 'beauty' was defined, once more, against industrial and bourgeois civilization. Man must, through such contemplation, revive the wellsprings of his being, which had been obscured by the degeneration of modern art. Beauty was 'genuine,' but it could not be chaos. A principle of order was an essential part of the beautiful: Hitler and the Nazis never objected to the use of the most modern technology, but it had to be harnessed in the service of a concept of beauty which, in Winckelmann's words … was like the still surface of the ocean, smooth as a mirror although constantly in motion": Mosse, *Nationalization of the Masses*, 191.
4. "Lessing spricht noch immer," *Völkischer Beobachter*, 28 September 1928.

5. R. W., "Henrik Ibsen: Zu seinem 100. Geburtstag am 20. März," *Völkischer Beobachter*, 18 March 1928.

6. Rudolf Erckmann, "Gerhart Hauptmann," *Völkischer Beobachter*, 16 November 1932. See Köhler, "Kunstanschauung und Kunstkritik," 27.

7. Josef Stolzing, "Gehart Hauptmanns *Die Weber*," *Völkischer Beobachter*, 1 October 1928.

8. Erckmann, "Gerhart Hauptmann."

9. Stolzing, "Gehart Hauptmanns *Die Weber*."

10. "Ein Abgesang: Auch ein Heinrich, vor dem uns graute …: Leben und Taten des Dichterakademie-Präsidenten Mann," *Völkischer Beobachter*, 19 February 1933.

11. "Ein Abgesang: Auch ein Heinrich, vor dem uns graute …"

12. Hellmuth Langenbucher, "Wilhelm Raabe, ein Dichter der Deutschen," *Völkischer Beobachter*, 8 September 1931.

13. Hellmuth Langenbucher, "'Moses Freudenstein': Ein Beitrag Raabes zur Psychologie des Judentums," *Völkischer Beobachter*, 8 September 1931.

14. Baldur von Schirach, "Theodor Storm: ein Dichter der Heimatliebe," *Völkischer Beobachter*, 29 July 1927.

15. Gustav Willibald Freytag, "Erinnerungen an Gustav Freytag," *Völkischer Beobachter*, 27 February 1927.

16. Freytag, "Erinnerungen an Gustav Freytag." For some discussion of Freytag's reception as anti-Semitic, see Larry Lee Ping, *Gustav Freytag and the Prussian Gospel: Novels, Liberalism, and History* (New York: Peter Lang, 2006), 18–19.

17. Zimmermann, "Der gefälschte Gustav Freytag!"

18. Wally P. Schultz, "Gustave Courbet: Ein Gedenkblatt zu seinem 125. Geburtstag," *Völkischer Beobachter*, 15 June 1944.

19. Rudolf Paulsen, "Ein Maler der deutschen Seele: Vom künstlerischen Schaffen Heinz Basedows," *Völkischer Beobachter*, 4 March 1931.

20. Wilhelm Rüdiger, "Der Dürer-Geist im deutschen Künstler," *Völkischer Beobachter*, 1 May 1932.

21. H. M. Soi [?], "Lyriker und Waffenhändler: Jean Arthur Rimbaud," *Völkischer Beobachter*, 27 February 1936.

22. Erhard Buschbeck, "Jean Arthur Rimbaud: Dichter und Waffenlieferant," *Völkischer Beobachter*, 12–13 October 1944.

23. Rudolf Paulsen, "Zum Tode Stefan Georges," *Völkischer Beobachter*, 6 December 1933.

24. Erwin Damian, "Rainer Maria Rilkes Weg und Wert: Zu des Dichters zehntem Todestag," *Völkischer Beobachter*, 29 December 1936.

25. Heinz Grothe, "Zwischen Chaos und Ordnung: Zur Neuausgabe von Rilkes Werken in zwei Bänden," *Völkischer Beobachter*, 3 May 1939.

26. "Hermann Bahr im Wandel der Zeiten," *Völkischer Beobachter*, 23 September 1925. On Bahr's opinions of Hitler, see Donald G. Daviau, *Hermann Bahr* (Boston, MA: Twayne Publishers, 1985), 168.

27. "Hermann Bahrs jüdisches Schönheitsideal," *Völkischer Beobachter*, 1 August 1927.

28. Josef Stolzing, "Erinnerungen an Hermann Bahr," *Völkischer Beobachter*, 17 January 1934.

29. W., "Wedekind-Gedenkfeier im Schauspielhaus," *Völkischer Beobachter*, 15 March 1928.

30. "Aus der jüdischen Stammtafel Hugo von Hofmannsthals," *Völkischer Beobachter*, 13 August 1929.

31. "Hugo von Hofmannsthal," *Völkischer Beobachter*, 18 July 1929.

32. Pidder Lüng, "Skandal um Kokoschka," *Völkischer Beobachter*, 18 February 1932.

33. "Besinnliches zu Feuerbachs 100. Geburtstag," *Völkischer Beobachter*, 12 September 1929.

34. W. Spanner, "Adolf Menzel: Zum 125. Geburtstag," *Völkischer Beobachter*, 8 December 1940.

35. Franz Hofmann, "Franz von Lenbach und seine Zeit," *Völkischer Beobachter*, 13 December 1936.

36. Georg Fuchs, "Lenbachs politisches Bekenntnis," *Völkischer Beobachter*, 13 December 1936.

37. "Die Münchener Lenbach-Feier," *Völkischer Beobachter*, 14 December 1936.

38. Wilhelm Rüdiger, "Arnold Böcklin: Zu seinem hundersten Geburtstage," *Völkischer Beobachter*, 16 October 1927. For more on Böcklin and German political culture, see Suzanne Marchand, "Arnold Böcklin and the Problem of German Modernism," in Marchand and David F. Lindenfeld (eds.), *Germany at the Fin de Siècle: Culture, Politics, and Ideas* (Baton Rouge, LA: Louisiana State University Press, 2004), 129–166.

39. "Arnold Böcklin: Zu seinem 25. Todestage am 16. Januar 1901," *Völkischer Beobachter*, 16 January 1926.

40. Maria Groener, "Böcklin und Feuerbach," *Völkischer Beobachter*, 19 October 1927.

41. Friedrich Nietzsche, *Thus Spake Zarathustra*, "The Flies in the Marketplace," trans. Thomas Common (Ware: Wordsworth Editions, 1997).

42. Thilo Schoder, "Edvard Munch: Zum 70. Geburtstag des grossen Malers," *Völkischer Beobachter*, 13 December 1933. For discussions on the contorted Nazi reception of Munch, see Stephanie Barron and Peter W. Guenther (eds.), *Degenerate Art: The Fate of the Avant-Garde in Nazi Germany* (Los Angeles County Museum of Art, 1991), 90–95 and Sue Prideaux, *Edvard Munch: Behind the Scream* (New Haven, CT: Yale University Press, 2007), 313–319.

11 Nordic Existentialists and Volkish Founders

1. Mosse, *Nazi Culture*, 57–60.

2. Hans F. K. Günther, "Sören Kierkegaard, ein Prophet aus nordischem Blute," *Völkischer Beobachter*, 23 December 1926. For more on Kierkegaard and Nazi

ideology, see A. Dirk Moses, *German Intellectuals and the Nazi Past* (Cambridge University Press, 2007), 276–280.

3. Mosse, *Nazi Culture*, xxvii, 93–96.

4. Steven E. Aschheim, *The Nietzsche Legacy in Germany, 1890–1990* (Berkeley, CA: University of California Press, 1992), 233, 235. See also Peter Fritzsche (ed.), *Nietzsche and the Death of God: Selected Writings* (Boston, MA: Bedford/St. Martin's Press, 2007), introduction; Wolin, *Seduction of Unreason*, 57–58; and Martin Schwab, "Selected Affinities: Nietzsche and the Nazis," in Rabinbach and Bialas (eds.), *Nazi Germany and the Humanities*, 140–177 for discussions of the commonalities between Nietzsche's philosophy and Nazi ideology, and the implications thereof.

5. Aschheim, *The Nietzsche Legacy in Germany*, 252.

6. Aschheim, *The Nietzsche Legacy in Germany*, 233.

7. "Nietzsches Beziehungen zum Hause Richard Wagners," *Völkischer Beobachter*, 9 September 1930.

8. "Nietzsches Beziehungen zum Hause Richard Wagners."

9. Friedrich Nietzsche, in *Nachgelassene Fragmente, Sommer 1876*, in *Nietzsche Werke IV* 2 (New York: Walter de Gruyter, 1967–) 17 [4].

10. K. Kanetsberger, "Der Philosoph und die Gemeinschaft," *Völkischer Beobachter*, 25 August 1935.

11. Ernst Nickell, "Der Einsame in Sils-Maria," *Völkischer Beobachter*, 30 July 1937.

12. Friedrich Nietzsche, *Ecce Homo* (Leipzig: Naumann, 1906), I, 3.

13. Friedrich Nietzsche, *Über die Zukunft unserer Bildungsanstalten*, in *Nietzsche Werke III* 2 (New York: Walter de Gruyter, 1967–), 241.

14. Friedrich Nietzsche, *Nachgelassene Fragmente, Sommer 1872 bis Ende 1874*, in *Nietzsche Werke III* 4 (New York: Walter de Gruyter, 1967–), 437.

15. Friedrich Nietzsche, *Nutzen und Nachteil der Historie*, in *Unzeitgemässe Betrachtungen I–III (1872–1874)*, in *Nietzsche Werke III* 1 (New York: Walter de Gruyter, 1967–), 212.

16. Kanetsberger, "Der Philosoph und die Gemeinschaft."

17. Kanetsberger, "Der Philosoph und die Gemeinschaft."

18. Friedrich Nietzsche, *Götzendämmerung*, in *Nietzsche Werke VI* 3 (New York: Walter de Gruyter, 1967–), 106.

19. Nietzsche, *Götzendämmerung*, in *Nietzsche Werke VI* 3, 106.

20. Friedrich Nietzsche, *Jenseits von Gut und Böse: Zur Genealogie der Moral*, in *Nietzsche Werke VI* 2 (New York: Walter de Gruyter, 1967–), 193.

21. Arthur Rathje, "Nietzsche und das neue Werden," *Völkischer Beobachter*, 22 January 1934.

22. Josef Stolzing, "Friedrich Nietzsche: Zu seinem 25. Todestag," *Völkischer Beobachter*, 23 August 1925.

23. "Die Propheten," *Völkischer Beobachter*, 20 April 1930.

24. Friedrich Nietzsche, *Nachgelassene Fragmente,* in *Nietzsche Werke VII 1* (New York: Walter de Gruyter, 1967–), 545.

25. Friedrich Würzbach, "Um der Zukunft willen: Eine Betrachtung zum 90. Geburtstag Friedrich Nietzsches," *Völkischer Beobachter,* 15 October 1934.

26. Eduard A. Mayr, "Der Wahrheit Freier: Zum 30. Todestage Friedrich Nietzsches," *Völkischer Beobachter,* 24 August 1930.

27. Eduard A. Mayr, "*Im Westen nichts Neues*: Eine Bemerkung (franz. *remarque*) über das berühmtgemachte Buch von Remarque," *Völkischer Beobachter,* 16 May 1929.

28. Eduard Grunertus, "Am Grabe Friedrich Nietzsches," *Völkischer Beobachter,* 24 August 1930.

29. Stolzing, "Friedrich Nietzsche: Zu seinem 25. Todestag."

30. "Die Propheten."

31. Nietzsche, *Über die Zukunft unserer Bildungsanstalten,* in *Nietzsche Werke III 2.*

32. Paul H. Kuntze, "Nietzsche: Höchster Wille zum Leben," *Völkischer Beobachter,* 7 September 1933.

33. Würzbach, "Um der Zukunft willen: Eine Betrachtung zum 90. Geburtstag Friedrich Nietzsches."

34. Hermann Stenzel, "Pathos des neuen Menschen: Zu Nietzsches 35. Todestag," *Völkischer Beobachter,* 25 August 1935.

35. Stolzing, "Friedrich Nietzsche: Zu seinem 25. Todestag."

36. Eduard Stemplinger, "Friedrich Nietzsche als Prophet," *Völkischer Beobachter,* 13 June 1937.

37. E. von Baer, "Nietzsche als Warner vor der jüdischen Gefahr: Das objektive Urteil des Philosophen," *Völkischer Beobachter,* 24 August 1930.

38. von Baer, "Nietzsche als Warner vor der jüdischen Gefahr: Das objektive Urteil des Philosophen."

39. "Die Propheten."

40. Stolzing, "Zu seinem 25. Todestag."

41. Würzbach, "Um der Zukunft willen."

42. See Stern, *The Politics of Cultural Despair* and Mosse, *The Crisis of German Ideology.*

43. Alfred Rosenberg, "Paul de Lagarde und die Banken," *Völkischer Beobachter,* 8 May 1921.

44. Adolf Hösel, "Künder deutscher Weltanschauung: Zum 45. Todestag des Politikers und Philosophen Paul de Lagarde," *Völkischer Beobachter,* 22 December 1936.

45. Hellmuth Langenbucher, "Paul de Lagarde," *Völkischer Beobachter,* 22 December 1931.

46. Langenbucher, "Paul de Lagarde."

47. Rudolf Paulsen, "Julius Langbehn: Zum 90. Geburtstag des 'Rembrandtdeutschen,'" *Völkischer Beobachter,* 26 March 1941.

48. Hellmuth Langenbucher, "Der Rembrandtdeutsche: Zum 25. Todestag Julius Langbehns am 30. April," *Völkischer Beobachter*, 1 May 1932.

49. R. V., "Der Rembrandtdeutsche Julius Langbehn: Grosse Deutsche über Grossdeutschland," *Völkischer Beobachter*, 28 March 1938.

50. "Das Leben des Rembrandtdeutschen," *Völkischer Beobachter*, 11 October 1926.

51. Christian Wilhelm Mack, "Der Rembrandtdeutsche als Rassenerzieher," *Völkischer Beobachter*, 21 December 1926.

52. Georg Schott, "Zum Gedächtnis H. St. Chamberlains," *Völkischer Beobachter*, 16 April 1929.

53. "Grosse Chamberlain-Feier in Bayreuth," *Völkischer Beobachter*, 17 September 1925.

54. Josef Stolzing, "Houston Stewart Chamberlain: Zu seinem 71. Geburtstag," *Völkischer Beobachter*, 9 September 1926.

55. Schott, "Zum Gedächtnis H. St. Chamberlains."

56. Stolzing, "Houston Stewart Chamberlain: Zu seinem 71. Geburtstag."

57. Schott, "Zum Gedächtnis H. St. Chamberlains."

58. Josef Stolzing, "Houston Stewart Chamberlain," *Völkischer Beobachter*, 18 February 1927.

59. Karl Ziesel, "Houston Stewart Chamberlain: Zum 7. Todestag des Künders und Sehers deutsches Zukunft," *Völkischer Beobachter*, 9 January 1934.

60. Ziesel, "Houston Stewart Chamberlain: Zum 7. Todestag des Künders und Sehers deutsches Zukunft."

61. "Der andere Chamberlain: H. St. Chamberlains Wendung zum Deutschtum," *Völkischer Beobachter*, 25 May 1940.

12 Music after Wagner

1. "Ein König des Walzers: Zum 125. Geburtstages von Johann Strauss-Vater," *Völkischer Beobachter*, 15 March 1929.

2. Hans Buchner, "Die Strauss-Woche," *Völkischer Beobachter*, 28 October 1925.

3. Norbert Wiltsch, "Johann Strauss: Zu seinem 100. Geburtstag," *Völkischer Beobachter*, 24 October 1925.

4. Siegfried Wagner, "An die tanzende Jugend," *Völkischer Beobachter*, 20 June 1926.

5. Hans Severus Ziegler, "Briefe vom 7. deutschen Brahmsfest," *Völkischer Beobachter*, 8 June 1929. See also Daniel Beller-McKenna, *Brahms and the German Spirit* (Cambridge, MA: Harvard University Press, 2004), 180–190 and David B. Dennis, "Brahms's *Requiem eines Unpolitischen*," in Nicholas Vazsonyi (ed.), *Searching for Common Ground: Diskurse zur deutschen Identität 1750–1871* (Vienna: Böhlau, 2000), 283–298.

6. "Johannes Brahms: Zur Münchner Brahms-Woche," *Völkischer Beobachter*, 22 October 1931.

7. Ludwig K. Mayer, "Johannes Brahms: Zu seinem hundertsten Geburtstag," *Völkischer Beobachter*, 7 May 1933.

8. Wilhelm Jensen, "Brahms als Niederdeutscher," *Völkischer Beobachter*, 27 October 1933.

9. G. A., "Ein deutsches Requiem," *Völkischer Beobachter*, 9 April 1928.

10. "Anton Brückner," *Völkischer Beobachter*, 13 September 1925.

11. Gottrau, "Vom Wesen deutscher Musik."

12. Lore Reinmoeller, "Träger einer Tradition: Zu einem neuen Buch über Johannes Brahms," *Völkischer Beobachter*, 27 October 1944.

13. "Johannes Brahms: Zur Münchner Brahms-Woche."

14. Reinmoeller, "Träger einer Tradition: Zu einem neuen Buch über Johannes Brahms."

15. Jensen, "Brahms als Niederdeutscher."

16. Hans Buchner, "Johannes Brahms," *Völkischer Beobachter*, 15 September 1923.

17. Jensen, "Brahms als Niederdeutscher."

18. "Johannes Brahms: Zur Münchner Brahms-Woche."

19. Jensen, "Brahms als Niederdeutscher."

20. Jensen, "Brahms als Niederdeutscher."

21. "Das Deutsche Requiem von Brahms," *Völkischer Beobachter*, 23 February 1940.

22. Josef Stolzing, "Meine Erinnerungen an Anton Brückner: Zu seinem dreizigsten Todestage, 12 Oktober 1896," *Völkischer Beobachter*, 13 October 1926.

23. Karl Grunsky, "Musikant aus Herzensgrund: Frühes Beginnen, Widerstände und endlicher Triumph," *Völkischer Beobachter*, 11 October 1936.

24. Stolzing, "Meine Erinnerungen an Anton Brückner: Zu seinem dreizigsten Todestage, 12 Oktober 1896."

25. Grunsky, "Musikant aus Herzensgrund: Frühes Beginnen, Widerstände und endlicher Triumph."

26. "Anton Brückner."

27. Josef Stolzing, "Anton Brückner in Audienz beim Kaiser," *Völkischer Beobachter*, 22 March 1931.

28. "Meister Anton: Kleine Geschichten aus dem Leben Brückners," *Völkischer Beobachter*, 11 October 1936.

29. "Anton Brückner."

30. Stolzing, "Meine Erinnerungen an Anton Brückner: Zu seinem dreizigsten Todestage, 12 Oktober 1896."

31. Josef Stolzing, "Wie Anton Brückner seine Dritte dem Meister widmete," *Völkischer Beobachter*, 10 January 1932.

32. Josef Stolzing, "Meine Lehrjahre bei Brückner von Friedrich Klose," *Völkischer Beobachter*, 11 December 1929.

33. "Meister Anton: Kleine Geschichten aus dem Leben Brückners."

34. R. Freiherr von Lichtenberg, "Erinnerungen an Anton Brückner," *Völkischer Beobachter*, 15 June 1927.

35. Stolzing, "Anton Brückner in Audienz beim Kaiser."

36. Erwin Bauer, "Liederfrühling der Musik," *Völkischer Beobachter*, 25 April 1943.

37. Karl Grunsky, "Das zweite Baden-Badener Anton-Brückner-Fest," *Völkischer Beobachter*, 10 October 1931.

38. "Das erste Konzert des nationalsozialistischen Symphonieorchesters."

39. "Die erste Konzertreise des nat.-soz. Symphonie-Orchesters."

40. Josef Stolzing, "Zum SS-Konzert," *Völkischer Beobachter*, 8 November 1934.

41. Max von Millenkovich-Morold, "Brückner-Feier in St. Florian," *Völkischer Beobachter*, 14 May 1932. Information on Millenkovich-Morold in Köhler, "Kunstanschauung und Kunstkritik," 24.

42. Friedrich Bayer, "Das erste grossdeutsche Brücknerfest," *Völkischer Beobachter*, 3 July 1939.

43. "Für Anton Brückner," *Völkischer Beobachter*, 7 July 1939.

44. Stolzing, "Zum SS-Konzert."

45. "Der Wagner des Liedes," *Völkischer Beobachter*, 22 February 1933.

46. Hans Buchner, "Max Reger," *Völkischer Beobachter*, 13 March 1923.

47. Hans Buchner, "Max Reger: Briefe eines deutschen Meisters," *Völkischer Beobachter*, 3 January 1929.

48. "Ein Erinnerungsbuch an Max Reger," *Völkischer Beobachter*, 4 November 1930.

49. R. Tr., "Zweites Berliner Kampfbundkonzert."

50. "Das 'Orchesters des Führers' zurückgekehrt," *Völkischer Beobachter*, 14 October 1938.

51. Fritz Wolffhuegel, "Reger-Musik in München," *Völkischer Beobachter*, 28 May 1931.

52. Buchner, "Max Reger."

53. Hans Buchner, "Max Reger," *Völkischer Beobachter*, 29 August 1923.

54. "Musik-Rundschau," *Völkischer Beobachter*, 6 March 1923. About Pfitzner and the Nazis, see Kater, *Composers of the Nazi Era*, 144–182.

55. Hermann Seeliger, "Hans Pfitzner 'Werk und Wiedergabe,'" *Völkischer Beobachter*, 27 November 1929.

56. Erwin Bauer, "Der volkstümliche Hans Pfitzner," *Völkischer Beobachter*, 24 April 1939.

57. Wolfgang Gottrau, "Kunst aus teuschem Herzen: Hans Pfitzners Musikdramen," *Völkischer Beobachter*, 12 November 1931.

58. Gottrau, "Kunst aus teuschem Herzen: Hans Pfitzners Musikdramen."

59. Erich Valentin, "Dein Erdenpensum, Palestrina," *Völkischer Beobachter*, 11 June 1937.

60. "Münchner Festspiele: Palestrina," *Völkischer Beobachter*, 30 September 1920.

61. J. F. [?], "Palestrina," *Völkischer Beobachter*, 21 August 1923.

62. Gottrau, "Kunst aus teuschem Herzen: Hans Pfitzners Musikdramen."

63. Lothar Band, "Ein kämpferischer Musiker: Zum 75. Geburtstag von Hans Pfitzner," *Völkischer Beobachter*, 6 May 1944.

64. Hans Pfitzner, *Futuristengefahr: bei Gelegenheit von Busonis Ästhetik* (Leipzig: Süddeutsche Monatshefte, 1918).

65. Hans Pfitzner, *Die neue Ästhetik der musikalischen Impotenz* (Munich: Süddeutsche Monatshefte, 1920).

66. "Hans Pfitzner: Zu seinem 65. Geburtstag," *Völkischer Beobachter*, 5 May 1934.

67. Alfred Morgenroth, "Hans Pfitzner – ein Rufer in die Zeit: Ein Musiker kämpft für Deutschland," *Völkischer Beobachter*, 15 June 1938.

68. Hermann Seeliger, "Zum 60. Geburtstag Hans Pfitzner," *Völkischer Beobachter*, 5 May 1929.

69. In *Letters of Heinrich and Thomas Mann, 1900–1949*, ed. Hans Wysling, trans. Don Reneau (Berkeley, CA: University of California Press, 1998), 367.

70. "Der Jude in der Musik," *Völkischer Beobachter*, 12 March 1936.

71. Otto Repp, "Der musikalische Kramladen," *Völkischer Beobachter*, 20 November 1938.

72. Hans Buchner, "Von zwei Welten in der Musik," *Völkischer Beobachter*, 20 February 1921.

73. Hans Buchner, "Gustav Mahler in der Akademie," *Völkischer Beobachter*, 26 January 1929.

74. Reinmoeller, "Judentum und Musik: Zu einem Buche von Karl Blessinger."

75. "Gustav Mahler in London – abgeblitzt!," *Völkischer Beobachter*, 3 May 1930.

76. "Der Jude in der Musik."

77. Hans Buchner, "Carmen neu einstudiert," *Völkischer Beobachter*, 27 January 1928.

78. Heinrich Stahl, "Musik und 'Zivilization,'" *Völkischer Beobachter*, 28 June 1940.

79. Erich Valentin, "Impressionist der Musik: Zu Claude Debussys 75. Geburtstag," *Völkischer Beobachter*, 21 August 1937.

80. Alexander Dillmann, "Giacomo Puccini: Zum 10. Todestag," *Völkischer Beobachter*, 29 November 1934.

81. Buchner, "Carmen neu einstudiert."

82. Ludwig K. Mayer, "Friedrich Smetana," *Völkischer Beobachter*, 12 May 1934.

83. Köhler, "Kunstanschauung und Kunstkritik," 27.

84. Fritz Wolffhuegel, "Ein nordisch-nationaler Musiker: Zum 30. Todestag Eduard Griegs," *Völkischer Beobachter*, 4 September 1937.

85. Erwin Bauer, "Der Russe Mussorgskij: Zum 100. Geburtstag des volksbewussten Komponisten," *Völkischer Beobachter*, 21 March 1939.

86. "Jean Sibelius 75 Jahre Alt," *Völkischer Beobachter*, 8 December 1940.

13 Heralds of the Front Experience

1. Hitler, *Mein Kampf*, 167.

2. Hitler, *Mein Kampf*, 161.

3. Hitler, *Mein Kampf*, 166.

4. "Germany, which faced defeat, emphasized in a special way that soldiers never die but, resurrected, continue to fight not only in Valhalla but in every patriot's heart. The patriots were exhorted not to give in to defeat, but to fight on until the nation itself had been resurrected": Mosse, *Toward the Final Solution*, 175.

5. Gassert and Mattern (eds.), *The Hitler Library*, 192.

6. Erich Limpach, "Neudeutsche Kriegsliteratur," *Völkischer Beobachter*, 16 February 1929.

7. Limpach, "Neudeutsche Kriegsliteratur."

8. Limpach, "Neudeutsche Kriegsliteratur."

9. Bz., "'Weltkrieg und Dichtung,'" *Völkischer Beobachter*, 4 June 1927.

10. Bz., "'Weltkrieg und Dichtung.'"

11. Philipp Witkop, "Walter Flex: ein deutscher Idealist," *Völkischer Beobachter*, 5 July 1937.

12. Hermann Böhme, "Das ewige Deutsche: Walter Flex zum Gedächtnis," *Völkischer Beobachter*, 15 October 1933.

13. J. A. Goyda, "Ernst Jünger," *Völkischer Beobachter*, 25 June 1927.

14. "Im Westen nichts Neues," *Völkischer Beobachter*, 16 February 1929.

15. "Im Westen nichts Neues."

16. Thomas R. Nevin, *Ernst Jünger and Germany: Into the Abyss, 1914–1945* (Durham, NC: Duke University Press, 1996), 81–82. For more on Jünger and Nazism, see Elliot Yale Neaman, *A Dubious Past: Ernst Jünger and the Politics of Literature after Nazism* (Berkeley, CA: University of California Press, 1999) and Allan Mitchell, *The Devil's Captain: Ernst Jünger in Nazi Paris, 1941–1944* (New York: Berghahn Books, 2011).

17. Ernst Jünger, "Revolution und Idee," *Völkischer Beobachter*, 23 September 1923.

18. "Lloyd George über Ernst Jüngers Buch *In Stahlgewittern*," *Völkischer Beobachter*, 28 December 1929.

19. "Im Westen nichts Neues."

20. "Im Westen nichts Neues."

21. "Im Westen nichts Neues."

22. "Im Westen nichts Neues."

23. "Im Westen nichts Neues."

24. Limpach, "Neudeutsche Kriegsliteratur."

25. Mayr, "*Im Westen nichts Neues*: Eine Bemerkung (franz. *remarque*) über das berühmtgemachte Buch von Remarque."

26. Nietzsche to Carl von Gersdorff, 21 June 1871, in *Selected Letters of Friedrich Nietzsche*, trans. Christopher Middleton (Indianapolis, IN: Hackett, 1996), 80.

27. "Das Urteil einer deutschen Frau über Remarques Buch," *Völkischer Beobachter*, 13 January 1931.

28. Hans Richard Mertel, "Das Filmgeschäft mit Remarque," *Völkischer Beobachter*, 11 March 1930.

29. "Remarques Kriegsroman als deutschfeindlicher Hetzfilm," *Völkischer Beobachter*, 1 April 1930.
30. Mertel, "Das Filmgeschäft mit Remarque."
31. Mertel, "Das Filmgeschäft mit Remarque."
32. "Das Verbot des Hetzfilmes," *Völkischer Beobachter*, 13 December 1930.
33. Mertel, "Das Filmgeschäft mit Remarque."
34. "Das Verbot des Hetzfilmes."
35. Mertel, "Das Filmgeschäft mit Remarque."
36. "Das Verbot des Hetzfilmes."
37. Mertel, "Das Filmgeschäft mit Remarque."
38. "Remarques Kriegsroman als deutschfeindlicher Hetzfilm."
39. "Remarques Kriegsroman als deutschfeindlicher Hetzfilm."
40. "Neue Kundgebungen gegen den Schandfilm Remarks," *Völkischer Beobachter*, 9 December 1930.
41. "Schluss mit dem Remarque-Film!," *Völkischer Beobachter*, 10 December 1930.
42. "Tut jetzt endlich auch Herr Wirth seine Pflicht und verbietet den Schandfilm?," *Völkischer Beobachter*, 11 December 1930.
43. "Remarque-Debatte im Preussischen Landtag," *Völkischer Beobachter*, 18 December 1930.
44. "Remarque-Debatte im Preussischen Landtag."
45. Robert Wohl, *The Generation of 1914* (Cambridge, MA: Harvard University Press, 1979), 55, 80. For more on First World War literature in Germany see Modris Eksteins, *Rites of Spring: The Great War and the Birth of the Modern Age* (Boston, MA: Houghton Mifflin, 1989); George L. Mosse, *Fallen Soldiers: Reshaping the Memory of the World Wars* (Oxford University Press, 1991); Jay W. Baird, *To Die for Germany: Heroes in the Nazi Pantheon* (Bloomington, IN: Indiana University Press, 1992); and Jay W. Baird, *Hitler's War Poets: Literature and Politics in the Third Reich* (Cambridge University Press, 2008).
46. See Mosse, *Fallen Soldiers*, 159–183.

14 Weimar Culture Wars 1

1. Hitler, *Mein Kampf*, 50, 254–255.
2. "Die *Münchener Post* und der Geheimrat Goethe."
3. "Die *Münchener Post* und der Geheimrat Goethe."
4. Johann Wolfgang von Goethe, in conversation with Eckermann, 4 January 1824.
5. "Die *Münchener Post* und der Geheimrat Goethe."
6. "Was hat Goethe dem heutigen Deutschland zu sagen: Zu Goethes Todestag."
7. "Was hat Goethe dem heutigen Deutschland zu sagen: Zu Goethes Todestag."
8. Johann Wolfgang von Goethe, letter to Friedrich von Müller, 12 June 1825.
9. "Was hat Goethe dem heutigen Deutschland zu sagen: Zu Goethes Todestag."

10. Goethe, *Maximen und Reflexionen – Nachlaß, Über Kunst und Kunstgeschichte.*

11. H., "Goethe: das Orakel seiner und unserer Zeit."

12. "Was hat Goethe dem heutigen Deutschland zu sagen: Zu Goethes Todestag."

13. Goethe, in conversation with Eckermann, 26 July 1826.

14. H., "Goethe: das Orakel seiner und unserer Zeit."

15. S., "Zum Goethejahr," *Völkischer Beobachter*, 1 January 1932.

16. S., "Zum Goethejahr."

17. S., "Die Goethe-Gedächtnis-Woche in Weimar und Wir," *Völkischer Beobachter*, 10 February 1932.

18. S., "Die Goethe-Gedächtnis-Woche in Weimar und Wir."

19. Hans Severus Ziegler, "Thomas Mann spricht," *Völkischer Beobachter*, 27 March 1932.

20. Johst, "Aufblick zu Goethe."

21. "Der Geist von Weimar einst und jetzt," *Völkischer Beobachter*, 10 February 1932. The latter is a reference to Mann's description of Nazism in his 1930 speech, "An Appeal to Reason." Thomas Mann, "An Appeal to Reason," in *Order of the Day*, trans. H. T. Lowe-Porter (New York: Alfred A. Knopf, 1942), 53–54.

22. Johann Wolfgang von Goethe, *Egmont*, act 5, scene 4, trans. Anna Swanwick (New York: P. F. Collier, 1909).

23. "Der Geist von Weimar einst und jetzt."

24. Dr. S., "Die eiserne Goethe-Front," *Völkischer Beobachter*, 27 March 1932.

25. Hanns Johst, "Im Anfang war die Tat," *Völkischer Beobachter*, 22 March 1932.

26. Johann Wolfgang von Goethe, *Faust*, trans. George Madison Priest (New York: Covici, Friede, 1932).

27. Alfred Rosenberg, "Goethe und Wir," *Völkischer Beobachter*, 22 March 1932. Citation from Rosenberg, *The Myth of the Twentieth Century*, Book III, ch. 2, trans. James B. Whisker (Torrence, CA: Noontide Press, 1982).

28. F. H., "Goethe und Österreich: Prof. Koch in der Münchener Goethe-Akademie," *Völkischer Beobachter*, 14 July 1932.

29. "Schiller auf der Streckfolter, oder: Die Eroberung der Poesie durch die Jugend," *Völkischer Beobachter*, 7 May 1925.

30. Hans Severus Ziegler, "Weimarer Schiller-Festspiele für die deutsche Jugend," *Völkischer Beobachter*, 5 July 1927.

31. Stolzing, "Schillers Sendung als Dramatiker: Noch heute harren seine Probleme der Lösung durch das deutsche Volk."

32. M., "Beethoven, der Musiker," *Völkischer Beobachter*, 29 January 1921.

33. W., "Beethovenfeier im Wilhelmsgymnasium," *Völkischer Beobachter*, 25 December 1920.

34. Josef Stolzing, "Der Piscator der Oper," *Völkischer Beobachter*, 24 March 1928.

35. "Die Weltheuchelei um Beethoven," *Völkischer Beobachter*, 8 April 1927.

36. Julius Nitsche, "Jonny neben Beethoven: Erinnerung an eine Jahrhundertfeier in wirrer Zeit," *Völkischer Beobachter*, 25 March 1937. See Susan Cook, *Opera for a New Republic: The Zeitopern of Krenek, Weill and Hindemith* (Ann Arbor, MI: UMI Research Press, 1988), 85–105, 206–210, for a synopsis and discussion of Krenek's operetta.
37. "Ein Heinrich Heine-Denkmal," *Völkischer Beobachter*, 11 January 1929.
38. "Ein Brief über Heinrich Heine." Baldur von Schirach repeated this anecdote in "Heinrich Heine, der 'Dolmetscher' der deutschen Seele," *Völkischer Beobachter*, 21 April 1928.
39. "Ein Brief über Heinrich Heine."
40. "Das Heinrich Heine-Denkmal in Hamburg."
41. "Das Heinrich Heine-Denkmal in Hamburg."
42. Rosenberg, "Der Fall Heine."
43. "Niemals ein Heine-Denkmal in Düsseldorf," *Völkischer Beobachter*, 23 December 1930.
44. "Heinrich Heine als Kommunistenagitator."
45. "Humbug um Heine," *Völkischer Beobachter*, 13 November 1931.
46. "Heinrich-Heine-Schandmäler in Deutschland," *Völkischer Beobachter*, 3 January 1931.
47. F. G. von M., "Parsifal-Erinnerung eines Kindes," *Völkischer Beobachter*, 22 May 1930.
48. Otto Daube, "Die Wagner-Bewegung der Gegenwart," *Völkischer Beobachter*, 13 September 1927.
49. Margarethe Strauss, "Die Richard Wagner-Stipendinstiftung: Deutsche Kunst dem deutschen Volke," *Völkischer Beobachter*, 19 June 1930.
50. B. B. R., "Neue Judenhetze gegen Richard Wagner," *Völkischer Beobachter*, 13 August 1927.
51. "Richard Wagner-Wauwau: Ein trauriges Kapitel deutscher Kulturgeschichte," *Völkischer Beobachter*, 6–7 March 1927.
52. Paul Schwers, "Richard Wagners Werke in neuer Geltung," *Völkischer Beobachter*, 16 July 1929.
53. "Richard Wagner-Wauwau: Ein trauriges Kapitel deutscher Kulturgeschichte."
54. Josef Stolzing, "Bayreuther Bühnenfestspiele 1927: Parsifal," *Völkischer Beobachter*, 24 July 1927.
55. Miss., "Alljudas Kampf gegen Richard Wagner."
56. Josef Stolzing, "Die Münchner Festspiele," *Völkischer Beobachter*, 3 August 1923.
57. Josef Stolzing, "Bayreuther Nachklänge," *Völkischer Beobachter*, 9 August 1930.
58. "Eine Meistersinger-Schändung in Berlin," *Völkischer Beobachter*, 2 May 1928.
59. "Einspruch gegen Klemperers 'Holländer,'" *Völkischer Beobachter*, 12 February 1929.
60. "Judas Kampf gegen Bayreuth," *Völkischer Beobachter*, 13 February 1927.

61. Hans Severus Ziegler, "Ein Protest gegen jüdische Wagnerinszenierung," *Völkischer Beobachter*, 30 March 1927.

62. Josef Stolzing, "Bayreuther Bühnenfestspiele 1927: Der Ring des Nibelungen," *Völkischer Beobachter*, 28 July 1927.

63. Heinrich Hespe, "Eine unerhörte 'Parsifal'-Schändung," *Völkischer Beobachter*, 18 December 1927.

64. "Wertheimer und Thomas Mann," *Völkischer Beobachter*, 13 May 1931.

65. See Dennis, "The Most German of all German Operas."

66. "Die erste Konzertreise des nat.-soz. Symphonie-Orchesters."

67. Hans Gatettner, "Auf zur Wagner-Morgenfeier!," *Völkischer Beobachter*, 24 February 1932.

68. Gatettner, "Auf zur Wagner-Morgenfeier!"

69. L. St., "Richard-Wagner-Morgenfeier des nationalsozialistischen Reichs-Symphonie-Orchesters," *Völkischer Beobachter*, 2 March 1932.

70. R. Tr., "Zweites Berliner Kampfbundkonzert."

71. Otto Daube, "Bayreuth: Geleitwort für die Festspiele, 1925," *Völkischer Beobachter*, 27 June 1925.

72. Herbert H. Mueller, "Bayreuth – des deutschen Geistes Offenbarung," *Völkischer Beobachter*, 12 August 1926.

73. Emma von Sichart, "Bayreuther Eindrücke," *Völkischer Beobachter*, 29 May 1927.

74. Herbert H. Mueller, "Bayreuths 25. Festspieljahr," *Völkischer Beobachter*, 7 July 1927.

75. Herbert H. Mueller, "Uhurufe über Bayreuth," *Völkischer Beobachter*, 29 November 1927.

76. Paul Pretzsch, "Was ist uns heute Bayreuth?," *Völkischer Beobachter*, 10 August 1928.

77. Schwers, "Richard Wagners Werke in neuer Geltung."

15 Weimar Culture Wars 2

1. Steinweis, "Anti-Semitism and the Arts in Nazi Ideology and Policy," 20.

2. As Eric Michaud pressed the point, Nazi ideologues believed that contemporary art "opened up the way for 'subhumans,' incapable of repressing their destructive instincts. Amid this chaos there developed an 'infantile predilection' for social outcasts and 'an almost perverse desire' for alien races and their way of behaving." What "justified the condemnation of contemporary art was that by allowing what was repressed by *Kultur* to resurface within it, this art was setting the repressed in the place of the ideal." This "eruption into art of what used to be repressed and its replacement of the ideal" were precisely what Hitler and Goebbels condemned: Michaud, *The Cult of Art in Nazi Germany*, 151–152.

3. "Stefan Zweig," *Völkischer Beobachter*, 28 January 1932. On Nazi treatment of Zweig, see Steinweis, *Art, Ideology, and Economics in Nazi Germany*: 52–53 and Kater, *Composers of the Nazi Era*, 223–257.

4. Aliquis, "Komposition aus Unflat: Der Bucherfolg des Jahres 1931," *Völkischer Beobachter*, 28 January 1932.

5. "Deutsche Kultur im Spiegel des Berliner Tageblatts," *Völkischer Beobachter*, 3 May 1927.

6. "Der Geist von Weimar einst und jetzt."

7. "Maximilian Harden-Witkowski," *Völkischer Beobachter*, 1 November 1927.

8. Aliquis, "Komposition aus Unflat: Der Bucherfolg des Jahres 1931."

9. "Die Dreigroschen-Oper: Ein Bankerott des Leipziger Spiessbürgertums," *Völkischer Beobachter*, 11 January 1929.

10. F. A. Hauptmann, "Vom Leipziger Musikjudentum," *Völkischer Beobachter*, 24 February 1928. On Kurt Weill in this context, see Kater, *Composers of the Nazi Era*, 57–85.

11. "Dreigroschenoper in Berlin," *Völkischer Beobachter*, 20 September 1928.

12. F. A. Hauptmann, "Verjüdung das Leipziger Musiklebens: Eine neue und eine alte Judenoper," *Völkischer Beobachter*, 8 February 1929.

13. "Dreigroschenoper in Berlin."

14. "Noch einmal Die Dreigroschenoper in Leipzig," *Völkischer Beobachter*, 15 January 1929.

15. Arno Schmieder, "Thomas Manns Appell an die Vernünft," *Völkischer Beobachter*, 24 December 1930.

16. "'Heldentum,' wie Mann es versteht," *Völkischer Beobachter*, 19 February 1933.

17. Josef Stolzing, "Thomas Mann als Nobelpreisträger," *Völkischer Beobachter*, 15 November 1929. For Mann's relations with Nazi Germany, see Saul Friedländer, *Nazi Germany and the Jews: The Years of Persecution, 1933–1939* (New York: HarperCollins, 1998), 11–14, 79, 108, 130, 300, 337.

18. Stolzing, "Thomas Mann als Nobelpreisträger," 149.

19. Stolzing, "Thomas Mann als Nobelpreisträger," 199.

20. Ludwig Brehm, "Thomas Mann: der Bekenner," *Völkischer Beobachter*, 16 January 1932.

21. T. F., "Mann über Liebermann," *Völkischer Beobachter*, 26 July 1927.

22. R., "Thomas Mann und seine Sprößlinge," *Völkischer Beobachter*, 19 August 1928.

23. Stolzing, "Thomas Mann als Nobelpreisträger."

24. Schmieder, "Thomas Manns Appell an die Vernünft."

25. According to http://en.wikipedia.org/wiki/Shechita: "*Shechita* is the ritual slaughter of animals, as prescribed for slaughter of mammals and birds according to Jewish dietary laws. The act is performed by drawing a very sharp knife across the animal's throat and allowing the blood to drain out. Islamic law requires a similar procedure. The practice is based on the Biblical law that men

must not eat the blood of animals, one of the seven Noahide Laws incumbent on all Noah's children, not only the Jews. The animal must be killed with respect by a shochet who has in mind the life of the animal as he draws the knife across its neck. The animal can be in a number of positions, for example, lying on its back – 'shechita munachas.' The aim is to sever all the major blood vessels in the neck, causing blood pressure in the brain to drop as instantaneously as the pain signal travels to the brain. With the animal rendered unconscious, the heart must continue to pump to aid the removal of blood from the rest of the carcass. For these latter reasons, prior stunning by humane bolt or other methods are not permitted. The Nazi Party banned shechita in Germany in 1933."

26. See Thomas Mann, *The Magic Mountain*, trans. H. T. Lowe-Porter (New York: Alfred A. Knopf, 1939), 556–567.

27. "Thomas Manns Verherrlichung des Schächtens," *Völkischer Beobachter*, 28 April 1927.

28. The statement appears in Thomas Mann, *Gesammelte Werke*, vol. 11 (Frankfurt am Main: S. Fischer, 1960), 625, l. 14.

29. "Thomas Manns neuer Romanheld: Joseph von Agypten," *Völkischer Beobachter*, 5 May 1928.

30. "Thomas Manns Verherrlichung des Zionismus," *Völkischer Beobachter*, 24 April 1930.

31. Dietrich Lober, "Thomas Mann auf dem Markte," *Völkischer Beobachter*, 6 March 1928.

32. http://en.wikipedia.org/wiki/Bremen_(aircraft).

33. "Thomas Mann," *Völkischer Beobachter*, 3 August 1928.

34. "Flieger-Protest gegen Thomas Mann," *Völkischer Beobachter*, 18 August 1928.

35. Sch. W., "Thomas Mann in hochachtungsvoller Ergebenheit an … den Bolschewismus!," *Völkischer Beobachter*, 1 July 1931.

36. Mann, "An Appeal to Reason," in *Order of the Day*, 53–54, 55–57.

37. Arno Schmieder, "Thomas Mann als 'Politiker,'" *Völkischer Beobachter*, 21 November 1930.

38. "Thomas Mann bei seinen Freunden in Paris: Sie feiern Ihn als den großen Europäer," *Völkischer Beobachter*, 13 May 1931.

39. "Wertheimer und Thomas Mann."

40. W., "Thomas Mann in hochachtungsvoller Ergebenheit an … den Bolschewismus!"

41. Richard von Schaukal, "Thomas Mann oder deutsche Prosa auf Zeithöhe," *Völkischer Beobachter*, 24 November 1931.

42. Lanzelot, "Thomas Mann!," *Völkischer Beobachter*, 10 December 1940.

43. Merkur, "Einstein als Naturforscher," *Völkischer Beobachter*, 7 April 1923. For general background on National Socialist rejections of Einstein's theories, see Philipp Frank, *Einstein: His Life and Times* (New York, Da Capo Press, [1947] 2002), 254 ff.

44. The 5 April 1920 letter the *Völkischer Beobachter* inaccurately paraphrased actually ran: "If I catch sight of an expression like 'German citizens of Jewish faith' I cannot help smiling a little sadly. What is there to be found in this pretty label? What is Jewish faith? Does there exist a kind of unbelief by virtue of which one ceases being a Jew? There is not. But it suggests that the right people believe two things, i.e. (1) I don't wish to have anything to do with my poor (East European) Jewish brethren, and (2) I do not want to be taken for a child of my own people, but only as a member of a Jewish community. Is this sincere? Can the 'Aryan' feel any respect for such underhanded fellows? I am neither a German citizen, nor is there in me anything that can be designated as 'Jewish faith.' But I am a Jew and am glad to belong to the Jewish people, even if I do not consider them in any way God's elect. Let us calmly leave anti-Semitism to the non-Jew and retain our love for people of our kind." Albert Einstein, quoted in Ronald W. Clark, *Einstein: The Life and Times* (New York: HarperCollins, 1984), 461.
45. Kerberus, "Einstein als Jude," *Völkischer Beobachter*, 12 June 1923.
46. "Pablo Picasso und der Probleme der Malerei," *Völkischer Beobachter*, 25 March 1928.
47. "Der Dessauer Bauhausfilm," *Völkischer Beobachter*, 16 June 1927.
48. "Kandinsky als Zeichner," *Völkischer Beobachter*, 12 March 1932.
49. "Der ärgerniserregende Freispruch im Falle George Grosz," *Völkischer Beobachter*, 16 April 1929. For more on the case, see Beth Irwin Lewis, *George Grosz: Art and Politics in the Weimar Republic* (Madison, WI: University of Wisconsin Press, 1971).
50. "'Maulhalten, weiterdienen!,'" *Völkischer Beobachter*, 6 December 1930.
51. "Niemals ein Heine-Denkmal in Düsseldorf."
52. Sela, "Schichtls musikalisches Raritätenkabinet oder Der tolle Nach-Fastnachtsspur," *Völkischer Beobachter*, 21 February 1923.
53. "Jüdischer Terror in der Musik: Neue Musik – Paul Aron," *Völkischer Beobachter*, 6 January 1929.
54. "Die Verjüdung u. Verfremdung unserer Opern Bühnen," *Völkischer Beobachter*, 1–2 July 1928.
55. Sela, "Schichtls musikalisches Raritätenkabinet oder Der tolle Nach-Fastnachtsspur."
56. "Jüdischer Terror in der Musik: Neue Musik – Paul Aron."
57. Sela, "Schichtls musikalisches Raritätenkabinet oder Der tolle Nach-Fastnachtsspur." See Joan Evans, "Stravinsky's Music in Hitler's Germany," *Journal of the American Musicological Society*, 56(3), 2003, 525 and Steinweis, *Art, Ideology, and Economics in Nazi Germany*, 22.
58. Fritz Stege, "Eine neues Musikschandwerk: Eine Strawinsky 'Welt'-Uraussführung in Berlin," *Völkischer Beobachter*, 30 October 1931.
59. Herbert Gerigk, "Die Wandlung der neuen Musik," *Völkischer Beobachter*, 27 September 1938.

60. Again, see Cook, *Opera for a New Republic*, 85–105, 206–210 for background on this operetta. For more on Nazi attacks on the work, see Kater, *Composers of the Nazi Era*, 200–208.

61. Hauptmann became a Nazi Party member in 1925 and founded the *Kulturpolitische Abteilung der NSDAP Kreis Leipzig*; he was also a leader of the *Kampfbund für deutsche Kultur* and the *NS-Kulturgemeinde Kreis Leipzig*: see Adelheid von Saldern and Lu Seegers, *Inszenierte Stolz* (Stuttgart: Franz Steiner, 2005), 120, n. 26. See also Köhler, "Kunstanschauung und Kunstkritik," 27.

62. F. A. Hauptmann, "Die erste Jazz-Oper. Von einem tschechischen Juden. Uraufführung in Leipzig," *Völkischer Beobachter*, 19 February 1927.

63. "Jonny unantastbar," *Völkischer Beobachter*, 26 June 1928.

64. Hauptmann, "Die erste Jazz-Oper. Von einem tschechischen Juden. Uraufführung in Leipzig."

65. Rud. Burock, "'Jonny spielt auf' auch in Dresden," *Völkischer Beobachter*, 19 November 1927.

66. "Der Kampf um 'Jonny,'" *Völkischer Beobachter*, 11 December 1927.

67. Hans Buchner, "Krenek's Jazzoper 'Jonny,'" *Völkischer Beobachter*, 20 December 1927.

68. Miss., "Alljudas Kampf gegen Richard Wagner."

69. "Die Wiener Nationalsozialisten gegen 'Jonny.' Stinkbomben in der Wiener Staatsoper," *Völkischer Beobachter*, 29 January 1928.

70. "'Jonny spielt auf' unter polizeilichem Schutz," *Völkischer Beobachter*, 30 January 1928.

71. "Wer ist Krenek, der Komponist von 'Jonny spielt auf'?," *Völkischer Beobachter*, 13 June 1928.

72. Alfred Rosenberg, "Jonny," *Völkischer Beobachter*, 15 June 1928.

73. J. B., "Jonny spielt auf und die Polizei tanzt," *Völkischer Beobachter*, 19 June 1928.

74. Köhler, "Kunstanschauung und Kunstkritik," 24.

75. Wilhelm Weiss, "Jonny in München," *Völkischer Beobachter*, 19 June 1928.

76. Sch. W., "Die Polizei spielt auf," *Völkischer Beobachter*, 21 June 1928.

77. Baldur von Schirach, "Ein Abend bei Jonny: Betrachtungen eines 'Pfui' – Rufers," *Völkischer Beobachter*, 24 June 1928.

78. Diogenes, "Fort mit Jonny! Jonny in Breslau," *Völkischer Beobachter*, 22 June 1928.

79. "Fort mit dem Jonny!," *Völkischer Beobachter*, 21 June 1928.

80. M. F., "Jonny, der neueste Heilige der Bayerischen Volkspartei: Die entlarvten Patentchristen," *Völkischer Beobachter*, 24 June 1928.

81. "Jonny auch in Paris ausgepfiffen," *Völkischer Beobachter*, 24 June 1928.

82. "Jonny in Neuyork durchgefallen," *Völkischer Beobachter*, 27 January 1929.

83. "Die Verjüdung u. Verfremdung unserer Opern Bühnen."

84. "Arteigene und artfremde Musik," *Völkischer Beobachter*, 10 November 1931.

85. Hans Buchner, "Bemerkungen zu den Münchner Festspielen," *Völkischer Beobachter*, 19 August 1920. For more on Schoenberg in the Nazi era, see Kater, *Composers of the Nazi Era*, 183–210.

86. Buchner, "Von zwei Welten in der Musik."

87. Sela, "Schichtls musikalisches Raritätenkabinet oder Der tolle Nach-Fastnachtsspur."

88. Hans Buchner, "Elektra," *Völkischer Beobachter*, 24 August 1923.

89. Buchner, "Elektra."

90. "Eine Italienische Ehrung Arnold Schoenbergs," *Völkischer Beobachter*, 31 January 1926.

91. F. A. Hauptmann, "Alcina von Händel: Uraufführung in Leipzig," *Völkischer Beobachter*, 24 June 1928.

92. "Musik-Auffassung von gestern: Vortrag Arnold Schoenbergs in der Gesellschaft für Neue Musik," *Völkischer Beobachter*, 24 February 1933.

93. Ludwig K. Mayer, "Musik in unserer Zeit," *Völkischer Beobachter*, 18 December 1938.

16 "Honor your German Masters"

1. Mosse, *Nationalization of the Masses*, 23, 211.

2. Hitler, *Mein Kampf*, 261.

3. Hitler, *Mein Kampf*, 259.

4. "The ideology of the Nazi revolution was based upon what were presumed to be Germanic traditions; while the revolution looked to the future, it tried to recapture a mythical past and with it the old traditions which to many people provided the only hope of overcoming the chaos of the present": Mosse, *Nationalization of the Masses*, 195.

5. "Luther und die Judenfrage."

6. "Zum 450. Geburtstag Luthers," *Völkischer Beobachter*, 10 November 1933.

7. "Luthers Persönlichkeit ist eine Weltmacht geworden."

8. "Luther-Festtage in Wittenberg," *Völkischer Beobachter*, 12 September 1933.

9. Bornhausen, "Martin Luthers deutsche Sendung."

10. "Luthers Persönlichkeit ist eine Weltmacht geworden."

11. "Luthers Persönlichkeit ist eine Weltmacht geworden."

12. Friedrich Schulze-Langendorff, "Voraussetzungen für Luthers Reformation," *Völkischer Beobachter*, 6 November 1927.

13. "Luthers Persönlichkeit ist eine Weltmacht geworden."

14. Schulze-Langendorff, "Voraussetzungen für Luthers Reformation."

15. Bornhausen, "Martin Luthers deutsche Sendung."

16. Dr. Olms, "Die deutsche Nation: Luthers Wunschbild ist unser Ziel," *Völkischer Beobachter*, 10 November 1933.

17. W. Albrecht, "Hier Spricht ein Mensch!," *Völkischer Beobachter*, 1 November 1933.

18. "Das deutsche Bachfest in Bremen," *Völkischer Beobachter*, 11 October 1934.

19. Buchner, "Joh. Sebastian Bach."

20. Grunsky, "Weg zu Johann Sebastian Bach."

21. Hans Buchner, "Musikrundschau," *Völkischer Beobachter*, 19 October 1923.

22. "Morgenfeier."

23. Cited in "Drei Altmeister der Musik: Reichsminister Dr. Joseph Goebbels über Bach, Händel und Schütz," *Völkischer Beobachter*, 31 March 1935.

24. "Grosse deutsche Festfeier."

25. Hartmann, "Georg Friedrich Händel und England: Ein Beitrag zur Geschichte nordischer Kulturverbundenheit."

26. "Wie Händels 'Fest-Oratorium' entstand," *Völkischer Beobachter*, 11 June 1936.

27. Buchner, "Zum Münchner Mozartfest."

28. Josef Klingenbeck, "Salzburgs Sendung: Eröffnungsfeier der neuen Hochschule für Musik im Mozarteum," *Völkischer Beobachter*, 14 June 1939.

29. Krause, "Schiller, ein Führer zum Neuen Reich."

30. Stauffacher, in Friedrich Schiller, *Wilhelm Tell*, act 2, scene 2, trans. William F. Wertz (Washington, DC: The Schiller Institute, 1988).

31. Rosselmann, in Schiller, *Wilhelm Tell*.

32. Friedrich Schiller, *Die Jungfrau von Orleans*, act 1, scene 5.

33. Attinghausen, in Schiller, *Wilhelm Tell*, act 4, scene 2.

34. Krause, "Schiller, ein Führer zum Neuen Reich."

35. Hans Fabricius, *Schiller als Kampfgenosse Hitlers: Nationalsozialismus in Schillers Dramen* (Bayreuth: N. S. Kultur-Verlag, 1932).

36. Hans Fabricius, "Schiller und die Volksverderber: Zum Todestage des Dichters," *Völkischer Beobachter*, 10 May 1931.

37. Krötz, "Wir Jungen und Schiller: Zu seinem 175. Geburtstag."

38. "Was hat Goethe dem heutigen Deutschland zu sagen: Zu Goethes Todestag."

39. H., "Goethe: das Orakel seiner und unserer Zeit." Citation from *Conversations with Heinrich Luden*, 13 December 1813.

40. *Conversations of Goethe, Recorded by His Friend Johann Peter Eckermann* Thursday, 2 October 1828, 287.

41. "'Höchstes hast du vollbracht, mein Volk': Grosse Deutsche über Grossdeutschland: Johann Wolfgang von Goethe."

42. Alfred Rosenberg, "Beethoven," *Völkischer Beobachter*, 26 March 1927.

43. "Die Neunte mit Havemann: Das Kampfbundorchester spielte," *Völkischer Beobachter*, 31 January 1933.

44. Heribert Schröder, "Beethoven im Dritten Reich: Eine Materialsammlung," in Helmut Loos (ed.), *Beethoven und die Nachwelt: Materialien zur Wirkungsgeschichte Beethovens* (Bonn: Beethoven-Haus, 1986), 196.

45. "Beethovens Neunte Symphonie: Das zweite Konzert des Münchener Festsommers," *Völkischer Beobachter*, 23 June 1935.

46. "Morgenfeier" and Heinrich Stahl, "Fidelio im Nationaltheater," *Völkischer Beobachter*, 22 April 1941.

47. "Die Reichs-Kultur-Kammer eröffnet: Der Führer bei der Feier in der Berliner Philharmonie."

48. "Gewaltiger Ausklang der XI. Olympischen Spiele in Anwesenheit des Führers," *Völkischer Beobachter*, 17 August 1936.

49. David B. Hinton, *The Films of Leni Riefenstahl* (London: Scarecrow, 1978), 58.

50. Herbert A. Frenzel, "Beethovens 'Neunte' unter Furtwängler: Völkerverbindende Macht der Musik," *Völkischer Beobachter*, 9 September 1937.

51. F. Bayer, "Generalfeldmarschall Göring in der Staatsoper: Fidelio, künstlerisches Symbol der Befreiung," *Völkischer Beobachter*, 28 March 1938.

52. "Das grosse Hassen: Marxistische Hetze zum Wagner-Jahr," *Völkischer Beobachter*, 1 February 1933.

53. "Der Festablauf am 21. März," *Völkischer Beobachter*, 21 March 1933.

54. Hugo Rasch, "Die Festvorstellung in der Staatsoper," *Völkischer Beobachter*, 23 March 1933.

55. "Richard Wagner zum Gedächtnis," *Völkischer Beobachter*, 15 August 1933.

56. "Die Reichs-Kultur-Kammer eröffnet: Der Führer bei der Feier in der Berliner Philharmonie."

57. "Der Führer legt den Grundstein zum Nationaldenkmal Richard Wagners," *Völkischer Beobachter*, 7 March 1934.

58. Repp, "Der musikalische Kramladen."

59. Friedrich W. Herzog, "Richard Wagners revolutionäre Tat," *Völkischer Beobachter*, 17 July 1937.

60. Hugo Rasch, "Bayreuther Festspiele 1933: Der Führer und Dr. Goebbels im Festspielhaus," *Völkischer Beobachter*, 25 July 1933.

61. Heinrich Stahl, "Der Führer und Bayreuth," *Völkischer Beobachter*, 20 April 1939.

62. "Deutsche Arbeiter erleben Bayreuth," *Völkischer Beobachter*, 8 August 1939.

63. M., "Wagner-Begeisterung in Rom," *Völkischer Beobachter*, 15 January 1934.

64. Hellmut Ludwig, "Deutscher und italienischer Opernstil," *Völkischer Beobachter*, 28 August 1938.

65. Hans Antropp, "Festlicher Auftakt in Salzburg: Die Meistersinger unter Furtwängler in Anwesenheit von Dr. Goebbels," *Völkischer Beobachter*, 25 July 1938.

17 The Nazi "Renaissance"

1. Adolf Hitler, Speech at the Nürnberg rally of 1935, cited in Frederic Spotts, *Hitler and the Power of Aesthetics*, 174.

2. Joseph Goebbels, "Die deutsche Kultur vor neuen Aufgaben," Berlin, Grosser Saal der Philharmonie, Eröffunung der Reichskulturkammer, 15 November, 1933, in *Goebbels-Reden, Band 1: 1932–1939*, 138–139.

3. See Köhler, "Kunstanschauung und Kunstkritik," 256–257 for contemporary assertion of these "common opinions." Michaud addressed the issue indirectly: "As Baldur von Schirach said, 'In Germany, there is nothing more alive than our dead.' The immense effort of realization that was sweeping a whole people toward its ideal Third Reich was certainly quite the reverse of the work of mourning. It was the work of anamnesis that asserted itself as faith in one's own power to reawaken the lost object … The aim of Nazism was to conjure into reality this defunct object, not found only in the Wunschtraum, the dream, and the desire to resuscitate what was dead": Michaud, *The Cult of Art in Nazi Germany*, 173.

4. Cited in Spotts, *Hitler and the Power of Aesthetics*, 174.

5. "Münchner Festspiele: Die Frau ohne Schatten," *Völkischer Beobachter*, 19 September 1920. On the complex issues regarding Richard Strauss and National Socialism, see Kater, *Composers of the Nazi Era*, 211–263 and Pamela Potter, "Strauss and the National Socialists: The Debate and Its Relevance," in Bryan Gilliam (ed.), *Richard Strauss: New Perspectives on the Composer and His Work* (Durham, NC: Duke University Press, 1992), 93–114.

6. Hans Buchner, "'Elektra' neu einstudiert," *Völkischer Beobachter*, 12 October 1927.

7. "Theater: Ariadne auf Naxos," *Völkischer Beobachter*, 4 September 1923.

8. Alfred Rosenberg, "Richard Strauss Judenstämmling?," *Völkischer Beobachter*, 7 February 1926.

9. Heinrich Werner, "Zum Briefwechsel Richard Strauss–Hugo Hoffmannstal," *Völkischer Beobachter*, 21 April 1926.

10. "Richard Strauss: Die ägyptische Helena," *Völkischer Beobachter*, 13 June 1928.

11. "Hugo von Hofmannsthal."

12. Hugo Rasch, "Festliche Tage in Bayreuth," *Völkischer Beobachter*, 6 August 1933.

13. "Die Reichs-Kultur-Kammer eröffnet: Der Führer bei der Feier in der Berliner Philharmonie."

14. Max Neuhaus, "Richard-Strauss-Feier der Philharmoniker," *Völkischer Beobachter*, 7 March 1934.

15. Max Neuhaus, "Richard Strauss zum 70. Geburtstag," *Völkischer Beobachter*, 11 June 1934.

16. Herbert Gerigk, "Die neue Strauss-Oper 'Daphne,'" *Völkischer Beobachter*, 18 October 1938.

17. "Richard Strauss zu Ehren," *Völkischer Beobachter*, 13 June 1939.

18. Friedrich Bayer, "Strauss' 'Friedenstag,'" *Völkischer Beobachter*, 12 June 1939.

19. "Dr. Goebbels ehrt Richard Strauss," *Völkischer Beobachter*, 12 June 1939.

20. Heinrich Stahl, "Symphonie des heiteren Lebens: Richard Strauss zum 75. Geburtstag," *Völkischer Beobachter*, 11 June 1939.

21. Friedrich Bayer, "Richard Strauss: Ein Musikerbildnis," *Völkischer Beobachter*, 28 December 1942.

22. Erwin Voelsing, "Ein Musiker von Weltrang: Zum achtzigsten Geburtstag von Richard Strauss," *Völkischer Beobachter*, 13 June 1944.

23. Hans Severus Ziegler, "Deutsche Festspiele in Weimar," *Völkischer Beobachter*, 30 July 1926. About Siegfried Wagner and the Nazis, see Kater, *Twisted Muse*, 34–38.

24. Herbert H. Mueller, "Siegfried Wagner. Zu seinem Geburtstag am 6. Juni," *Völkischer Beobachter*, 5 June 1927.

25. "Siegfried Wagners Märchen-Oper 'An allem ist Hütchen schuld' im Bayerischen Rundfunk," *Völkischer Beobachter*, 15 July 1932.

26. Emma von Sichart, "Jung-Bayreuth," *Völkischer Beobachter*, 29 June 1928.

27. Herbert H. Mueller, "Siegfried Wagner, ein Tondichter des deutschen Volkstums: Zu seinem 60. Geburtstage am 6. Juni," *Völkischer Beobachter*, 5 June 1929.

28. "Siegfried Wagners 'Heilige Linde,'" *Völkischer Beobachter*, 11 July 1929.

29. Herbert H. Mueller, "Siegfried Wagner: 'Das Flüchlein, das jeder mitbekam,'" *Völkischer Beobachter*, 20 November 1929.

30. "Neue Opern und vergessene Komponisten," *Völkischer Beobachter*, 11 January 1933.

31. Josef Stolzing, "Siegfried Wagners künstlerische Sendung," *Völkischer Beobachter*, 2 August 1930.

32. Herbert Gerigk, "Carl Orffs Carmina Burana," *Völkischer Beobachter*, 16 June 1937. On Orff in the Nazi era, see Kater, *The Twisted Muse*, 188–202 and Kater, *Composers of the Nazi Era*, 111–143.

33. Ludwig K. Mayer, "Paul Graener: Zur Erstaufführung der Oper 'Friedemann Bach,'" *Völkischer Beobachter*, 18 December 1932.

34. "Eine Rede Paul Graeners: Pflichten des deutschen Komponisten," *Völkischer Beobachter*, 3 September 1935.

35. Erich Roeder, "Max von Schillings: Zum 75. Geburtstage des Komponisten," *Völkischer Beobachter*, 18 April 1943.

36. L. Biagioni, "Max von Schillings in der Selbstkritik," *Völkischer Beobachter*, 23 July 1943.

37. Heinz Steguweit, "Letzte Begegnung mit Max von Schillings: Ein Gedenkblatt zum 70. Geburtstag des Komponisten," *Völkischer Beobachter*, 19 April 1938.

38. Hilde Fürstenberg, "Der Klassiker des hohen Nordens," *Völkischer Beobachter*, 4 August 1938. On Hamsun, see Monika Žagar, *Knut Hamsun: The Dark Side of Literary Brilliance* (Seattle, WA: University of Washington Press, 2009).

39. See Köhler, "Kunstanschauung und Kunstkritik," 26.

40. Karl Muth-Klingenbrunn, "Karl May," *Völkischer Beobachter*, 4 February 1929. For the significance of Karl May in German popular literature, see George L. Mosse, *Masses and Man: Nationalist and Fascist Perceptions of Reality* (Detroit, MI: Wayne State University Press, 1987), 52–68.

41. Friedrich Schulze-Langendorff, "Franz Wolfram Scherer: Zu seinem 60. Geburtstag," *Völkischer Beobachter*, 12 June 1927.

42. Ernst Friedrich, "Das Jüdenmadel aus Sosnowice," *Völkischer Beobachter*, 5 August 1927. The paper promoted this book as "describing in an exciting way the fate of a beautiful Jewish girl, who came from the east to Germany, where she succeeded in gaining respect and riches through cunning use of her charm and through skillful speculation on the stock exchange. As the Jew lusts after blond Aryan women, so does the Jewess lust after blond Aryan men. The Jewish girl from Sosnowice draws into her net blonds and succeeds in enticing from a German General Staff officer important military secrets, which she sells to Russia. Thrilling is the description of the whole Jewish milieu which the author succeeds in giving": *Völkischer Beobachter*, 13 July 1927, cited in Layton, "*Völkischer Beobachter*, 1925–33," 248.

43. Ludwig Thoma, "Der Klient," *Völkischer Beobachter*, 25 August 1931; Ludwig Thoma, "Unser guter, alter Herzog Karl," *Völkischer Beobachter*, 25 September 1931; Ludwig Thoma, "Der Lindermann," *Völkischer Beobachter*, 21 October 1931.

44. Hellmuth Langenbucher, "Ludwig Thomas Weg zur völkischen Weltanschauung," *Völkischer Beobachter*, 25 August 1931.

45. See Mosse, *Nazi Culture*, 94–95, for general discussion and translation of Goebbels' *Michael*.

46. M. B. [?], "*Der Wanderer* auf der Nationalsozialistischen Volksbühne," *Völkischer Beobachter*, 31 October 1929.

47. "Der Führer ehrt den Dichter der Deutschen Revolution," *Völkischer Beobachter*, 31 October 1933.

48. Dietrich Eckart, "Der erste Antisemit," *Völkischer Beobachter*, 5 May 1928.

49. "Albert Leo Schlageter occupies a place of his own in the Nazi gallery of heroes. An early Nazi, he fell in battle fighting against the French in 1923, and the afterword to an edition of his letters is a good example of the homage paid to him. Schlageter, like all Nazi heroes, symbolized the 'new man.' The conversation between his friend August and August's father shows quite clearly the exaltation of the 'new man' – the young generation. Hanns Johst, the most famous of the playwrights who wrote for the Third Reich, had dramatic power and his play *Schlageter* was often performed, especially in the early days of the regime": Mosse, *Nazi Culture*, xxviii.

50. Hans Gatettner, "Der deutsche Dichter nach dem Sieg: Die beispielgebende Persönlichkeit Hanns Johst," *Völkischer Beobachter*, 7 July 1940. On Johst, see

also Jan-Pieter Barbian, "Literary Policy in the Third Reich," in Cuomo (ed.), *National Socialist Cultural Policy*, 60–175.

51. "Hanns Johsts Flucht," *Völkischer Beobachter*, 7 April 1927.

52. Hanns Johst, "Thomas Paine," *Völkischer Beobachter*, 27 June 1928. For more on Johst's play on Thomas Paine, see Hugh Frederick Garten, *Modern German Drama* (New York: Taylor & Francis, 1964), 228 and London, *Theatre under the Nazis*, 96–110.

53. Karl Berger, "Dem völkischen Literaturhistoriker," *Völkischer Beobachter*, 14 November 1931.

54. Kurt Karl Eberlein, "Der deutsche Maler Hans Thoma: Zu seinem 10. Todestag," *Völkischer Beobachter*, 7 November 1934.

55. "Max Slevogt 60 Jahre alt: Ein weltberühmter bayerischer Meister," *Völkischer Beobachter*, 10 October 1928.

56. Wilhelm Rüdiger, "Der Bildhauer Arno Breker: Zum 40. Geburtstag des Künstlers," *Völkischer Beobachter*, 19 July 1940. On Breker and Nazism see Jonathan Petropoulos, "From Seduction to Denial: Arno Breker's Engagement with National Socialism," in Etlin (ed.), *Art, Culture, and Media under the Third Reich*, 205–229.

57. Werner Rittich, "Der Lyriker Arno Breker: Zu einer Ausstellung von neuen Werken des Künstlers," *Völkischer Beobachter*, 16 June 1944.

18 *Kultur* at War

1. Joseph Goebbels, "Das Kulturleben im Kriege," Rede zur Jahrestagung der Reichskulturkammer und der NS-Gemeinschaft "Kraft durch Freude" 27 November 1939, in Goebbels, *Die Zeit ohne Beispiel: Reden und Aufsätze aus den Jahren 1939/40/41* (Munich: Zentralverlag der NSDAP, Franz Eher Nachf., 1944), 219–223.

2. In Saul Friedländer's powerful words: "The important thing is the constant identification of Nazism and death; not real death in its everyday horror and tragic banality, but a ritualized, stylized, and aestheticized death, a death that wills itself the carrier of horror, decrepitude, and monstrosity, but which ultimately and definitely appears as a poisonous apotheosis." Nazism, he continued, was a force that: "ended in nothing, after having accumulated an extraordinary power, unleashed a war without parallel, committed crimes heretofore beyond imagination – a force that hacked the world to pieces in order to founder in nothingness": Friedländer, *Reflections of Nazism*, 43, 58.

3. "War was not an end in itself; for National Socialism, war remained, in the same way as propaganda, art, and politics, 'a means to an end.' Warfare was far more directly identified with the process that led to the 'realization of the Idea,' so that in the Nazi Weltanschauung it had the same function as all its other 'battles.' Like the 'battle for art,' 'the battle on the birth front,' and the 'battle for production,' it

was part and parcel of 'the battle for life' that was to lead to the realization of the essence of the German people": Michaud, *The Cult of Art in Nazi Germany*, 206–207.

4. Michaud reproduces Speer's explanation of the "theory of ruin value" as follows: "'By using special materials and by applying certain principles of statistics, we should be able to build structures that even in a state of decay, after hundreds or (such were our reckonings) thousands of years, would more or less resemble Roman models. To illustrate my ideas I had a romantic drawing prepared. It showed what the reviewing stand on the Zeppelin Field would look like after generations of neglect, overgrown with ivy, its columns fallen, the walls crumbling here and there, but the outlines were still clearly recognizable.' Delighted by the 'luminous logic' of this sketch, Hitler ordered that in the future the Reich's most important buildings should be constructed according to the 'law of ruins.' Speer had hit the bull's eye by responding 'to the Führer's desire' in this way and, on his behalf, anticipating the moment when 'men fell silent.' That moment would come long after the movements of the community's fighters had been frozen and immobilized in stone, and when history would at last recognize them as a people of artists and founders of culture who had constructed their own monument": Michaud, *The Cult of Art in Nazi Germany*, 212.

5. Rabinbach and Bialas (eds.), *Nazi Germany and the Humanities*, xxbc.

6. Wilhelm Rüdiger, "Albrecht Dürer und die Soldaten," *Völkischer Beobachter*, 18 August 1928.

7. Wiedermann, "Albrecht Dürers Bedeutung als Festungs-Baumeister."

8. W. Rüdiger, "Albrecht Dürer und die Soldaten."

9. W. Rüdiger, "Albrecht Dürer und die Soldaten."

10. W. Rüdiger, "Albrecht Dürer und die Soldaten" and Wiedermann, "Albrecht Dürers Bedeutung als Festungs-Baumeister."

11. Hengl Sepp, "Dürer und Lucas Cranach als Ringsportspezialisten," *Völkischer Beobachter*, 23 October 1942.

12. Friedrich Schiller, *Wallenstein's Camp*, trans. James Churchill (Boston, MA: F. A. Niccolls, 1902).

13. "Schiller-Festwoche in Weimar," *Völkischer Beobachter*, 10 November 1934.

14. Adam, "Das Faustische und das Heroische: Ein Gespräch vor 140 Jahren und der Freundschaftsbund zwischen Goethe und Schiller."

15. "Goethe und die *Sudd. Presse*," *Völkischer Beobachter*, 15 March 1922.

16. Dresler, "Goethe und der nationale Gedanke."

17. "Was hat Goethe dem heutigen Deutschland zu sagen: Zu Goethes Todestag."

18. Alfred Bäumler, "Schopenhauer und das 19. Jahrhundert: Zum 150. Geburtstag des Philosophen," *Völkischer Beobachter*, 22 February 1938.

19. Grunsky, "Ein urwüchsiger deutscher Denker: Zum 75. Todestage Arthur Schopenhauers."

20. Josef Stolzing, "Leben heisst kämpfen," *Völkischer Beobachter*, 22 February 1938.

21. Ludwig Schiedermair, "Beethoven und das 'Schicksal,'" *Völkischer Beobachter*, 21 October 1925.

22. "Goethe und Bismarck über Beethoven," *Völkischer Beobachter*, 26 March 1927.

23. "Die Macht der Musik," *Völkischer Beobachter*, 7 May 1929.

24. Friedrich Riessner, "Bismarck und die Musik," *Völkischer Beobachter*, 15 August 1935.

25. "Landsturmmann Beethoven," *Völkischer Beobachter*, 26 March 1927.

26. "Das 'Orchesters des Führers' zurückgekehrt."

27. Heinrich Stahl, "Das Kampfethos des deutschen Genius," *Völkischer Beobachter*, 30 October 1939.

28. H. B. L., "Jeanne d'Arc ein Symbol? Das unversehrte Reims unter deutschem Schutz," *Völkischer Beobachter*, 28 June 1940.

29. Richard Biedrzynski, "Rembrandt und das Reich: Notizen zu einer niederländischen Reise," *Völkischer Beobachter*, 17 December 1942.

30. Simon Schama, *Rembrandt's Eyes* (New York: Alfred A. Knopf, 1999), 482–483.

31. Friedrich W. Herzog, "Auf Goethes Spuren im Elsass," *Völkischer Beobachter*, 8 July 1940.

32. "Goethes Gartenhaus in Weimar bombardiert," *Völkischer Beobachter*, 18 August 1940.

33. Baser, "Händels Martyrium in London."

34. "Das Mozartjahr," *Völkischer Beobachter*, 27 January 1941.

35. "Kleist und Mozart im deutschen Osten," *Völkischer Beobachter*, 22 March 1941.

36. "Die 100-Jahr-Feier des Mozarteums," *Völkischer Beobachter*, 26 April 1941.

37. "Erste Vorschau auf die Reichs-Mozartwoche in Wien," *Völkischer Beobachter*, 12 May 1941.

38. Friedrich W. Herzog, "Von Bayreuth nach Salzburg," *Völkischer Beobachter*, 16 July 1941.

39. "Beginn der Salzburger Festspiele," *Völkischer Beobachter*, 4 August 1941.

40. Joseph Goebbels, "Auch Mozarts Musik verteidigt der deutsche Soldat," *Völkischer Beobachter*, 6 December 1941.

41. "Ein Kranz des Führers zum Gedenken Mozarts," *Völkischer Beobachter*, 7 December 1941.

42. "Gauleiter Dr. Scheel bei den Salzburger Mozart-Feiern," *Völkischer Beobachter*, 7 December 1941.

43. Johannes Jacobi, "Der Widerhall des Mozart-Jahrs in Europa," *Völkischer Beobachter*, 13 January 1942.

44. Köhler, "Kunstanschauung und Kunstkritik," 24–25.

45. Friedrich Didier, "Über Goethe und das Reich: Dr. Rainer Schlösser sprach auf der Reichskulturtagung der Hitler-Jugend," *Völkischer Beobachter*, 16 June 1941.

46. Meunier, "Heinrich von Kleist: Zu seinem 130. Todestag."

47. "In Dankbarkeit und Treue: Ansprache von Reichsminister Dr. Goebbels in der Feierstunde der NSDAP am Vorabend des Geburtstages Adolf Hitlers," *Völkischer Beobachter*, 20 April 1942.

48. Erwin Bauer, "Die Meistersinger von Nürnburg," *Völkischer Beobachter*, 18 November 1940.

49. *Correspondence of Wagner and Liszt*, vol. 2, trans. Francis Hueffer (London: Grevel, 1888), 78.

50. *Correspondence of Wagner and Liszt*, 84.

51. Erich Lauer, "Richard Wagner über die Engländer: Einige Zeugnisse aus seinen Briefen," *Völkischer Beobachter*, 16 June 1939.

52. Willibert Dringenberg, "Richard Wagner durchschaut die Engländer," *Völkischer Beobachter*, 21 May 1940.

53. Heinrich Stahl, "Die neue Götterdämmerung," *Völkischer Beobachter*, 1 July 1941.

54. Frederic Spotts, *Bayreuth: A History of the Wagner Festival* (New Haven, CT: Yale University Press, 1996), 189.

55. "Winifred Wagner begrüsst Soldaten und Arbeiter," *Völkischer Beobachter*, 19 July 1940.

56. "Festlicher Beginn des 'Rings' in Bayreuth," *Völkischer Beobachter*, 21 July 1940.

57. "Götterdämmerung vor Soldaten und Arbeitern Mainfrankens," *Völkischer Beobachter*, 25 July 1940.

58. Herzog, "Von Bayreuth nach Salzburg."

59. Hermann Killer, "Volkserlebnis Bayreuth," *Völkischer Beobachter*, 16 July 1941.

60. "Schau vom Festspielhügel," *Völkischer Beobachter*, 23 July 1941.

61. Friedrich W. Herzog, "Bayreuth, Hüter der Idee," *Völkischer Beobachter*, 14 August 1942.

62. "Richard Wagner und die deutsche Schule," *Völkischer Beobachter*, 13 September 1942.

63. Erwin Voelsing, "Die Meistersinger von Nürnburg," *Völkischer Beobachter*, 7 August 1943.

64. Günther M. Greif-Bayer, "Der 'Musikant-Gottes,'" *Völkischer Beobachter*, 31 January 1943.

65. "Theater und Unterhaltungsstätten bis 6. Februar geschlossen," *Völkischer Beobachter*, 4 February 1943.

66. Schulz, "Schillers Weg zur deutschen Freiheit."

67. Ludwig Thoma, "Ein Gedenkblatt für Rembrandt," *Völkischer Beobachter*, 21 June 1943.

68. Heinz Steguweit, "Goethe für 1944," *Völkischer Beobachter*, 12 January 1944.

69. Richard Biedrzynski, "Der italienische Faust: Zum 425. Todestag Leonardo da Vincis," *Völkischer Beobachter*, 30 April 1944. For further analysis of National Socialist interpretations of Leonardo as Faustian, see Michaud, *The Cult of Art in Nazi Germany*, 131.

70. Joachim Nettelbeck was a German hero in the battle of Kolberg in 1807.

71. Heinrich von Kleist, *Germania an ihre Kinder,* in *Gesammelte Schriften,* ed. Ludwig Tieck (Berlin: G. Reimer, 1826), 398.

72. "Philipp Otto Runge und Kleist: Gegenwärtiges über zwei Gemälde der Befreiungszeit," *Völkischer Beobachter,* 23 April 1944.

73. Richard Biedrzynski, "Programm der Programmlosigkeit: Zu einem Buch über die Selbstbildnisse Rembrandts," *Völkischer Beobachter,* 25 August 1944.

74. Biedrzynski, "Eroica eines Lebens: Zum 275. Todestag Rembrandts."

75. Johann Wolfgang von Goethe, "Selige Sehnsucht," in *Westöstlicher Divan* (1819).

76. Freiherr von Merck, "Mit den Augen Goyas," *Völkischer Beobachter,* 19 November 1944.

77. Friedrich Schiller, "Die Schlacht bei Lützen," *Völkischer Beobachter,* 23–24 February 1945. Citation from Friedrich Schiller, *The History of the Thirty Years' War,* trans. A. J. W. Morrison (Boston, MA: F. A. Niccolls, 1901).

78. W. B. von Pechmann, "Goethes Kriegserlebnisse," *Völkischer Beobachter,* 2 March 1945.

79. Biedrzynski, "Der Mut zum Schmerz: Deutsche Meisterwerke für unsere Zeit."

80. Hymmen, "Zurufe eines Unsterblichen: Zum 175. Geburtstag Friedrich Hölderlins."

81. Alfred Rosenberg, "Friedrich Nietzsche," *Völkischer Beobachter,* 17 October 1944.

82. Alfred Bäumler, "Friedrich Nietzsche: Zu seinem 100. Geburtstag," *Völkischer Beobachter,* 13 October 1944.

83. Gatettner, "Eine Nietzsche-Revision: Zu einem Vortrag Prof. Bäumlers."

84. Like so many others, a short time after giving this speech, Bäumler denied complicity with the regime in front of a de-Nazification tribunal: declaring his association with Nazism "an error and a madness," he said he had never been the "Philosopher of National Socialism" – though he was widely known as such in the 1930s and 1940s: see Hans D. Sluga, *Heidegger's Crisis: Philosophy and Politics in Nazi Germany* (Cambridge, MA: Harvard University Press, 1993), 241.

Conclusion

1. See Kathleen James-Chakraborty, "The Drama of Illumination: Visions of Community from Wilhelmine to Nazi Germany," in Etlin (ed.), *Art, Culture, and Media under the Third Reich,* 181, for details on the *Lichtdom* – a feature at the rallies from 1934 to 1938.

2. For discussion about the relevance of Kershaw's concept to academics and artists, see Rabinbach and Bialas (eds.), *Nazi Germany and the Humanities,* xv and Steven P. Remy "'We Are no Longer the University of the Liberal Age': The Humanities and National Socialism at Heidelberg," in Rabinbach and Bialas (eds.), *Nazi Germany and the Humanities,* 25.

3. Richard Wolin has offered the following explication of inconsistencies within Nazi cultural appropriations: "As in many other cases, in the sphere of higher education the Nazis often valued considerations of stability over absolute ideological rectitude – whose terms proved difficult to define in any event. Thus 'in lieu of a [central] institution capable of declaring certain [ideological] positions obligatory, thereby providing conformist scholars with clear guidelines, a thoroughgoing Nazification of pedagogy and scholarship was hardly conceivable.' [Quote from Michael Grüttner, 'Wissenschaft,' in *Enzyklopädie des Nationalsozialismus*, ed. W. Benz (Stuttgart: Klett-Cotta, 1997), 144.] This malleable, ideological 'gray zone' was especially characteristic of the *Geisteswissenschaften*, where 'the borders between a traditional, national-conservative orientation, with its inclination toward nationalism and its penchant for '*Deutschtümelei*,' and an unequivocal National Socialist orientation remained fluid'": Wolin, *The Seduction of Unreason*, 94.

4. Despite its significance, the *Völkischer Beobachter* is not yet available in digital form. When it finally is, scholars will be able to check for omissions I may have made. Regarding the mass of articles that I processed, I should point out that I have focused my efforts on those sections which did place a Nazi "spin" on the cultural-historical subject at hand, according to the main ideological concepts outlined above. To be sure, not every article in the *Völkischer Beobachter* involved such interpretations and not every column of each cited article was as exploitative as the passages I have discussed. It is for this reason that I will post online a full bibliography of the cultural-historical related articles I found in the *Völkischer Beobachter*: see www.luc.edu. This online resource will allow other scholars to investigate this valuable material and ask of it different questions than mine.

5. Adolf Hitler, Speech to the National Socialist Women's Congress in 1935, reported in *Völkischer Beobachter*, 15 September 1935, in Adam, *Art of the Third Reich*, 140.

6. Rudolf Hess, Meeting of the Women's Association, cited in *Völkischer Beobachter*, 27 May 1936, in Adam, *Art of the Third Reich*, 149.

7. Gerhard Köhler identified Alfred Rosenberg, Wilhelm Weiss, Josef Stolzing, F. von Leoprechting, Rainer Schlösser, and Adolf Dresler as acting editors before 1933. He listed ten of the represented authors as "Mitarbeiter" or staff writers. These included Erwin Bauer, Wolfgang Gottrau, Florentine Hamm, F. A. Hauptmann, Franz Hofmann, Otto Keller, Max von Millenkovich-Morold, Wilhelm Rüdiger, Heinrich Stahl, and Norbert Wiltsch. See Köhler, "Kunstanschauung und Kunstkritik," 23–29.

8. Köhler listed fourteen of those who wrote articles discussed here as "Gelegenheitsberichterstatter" or "occasional contributors," as indicated above (*ibid.*). But clearly, all the other authors had similar relations with the paper.

9. For important assessments of the collaboration of scholars in all disciplines, see Rabinbach and Bialas (eds.), *Nazi Germany and the Humanities*, ix–xiv;

Steinweis, *Studying the Jew*, passim; Wolin, *The Seduction of Unreason*, 90–93; and Michaud, *The Cult of Art in Nazi Germany*, 30–33, 41–45.

10. Huener and Nicosia address the "catastrophic compliance" that characterized much of the art and scholarly world in Nazi Germany, arguing that participants were "largely motivated" by "career considerations and political opportunism" that "almost always trumped moral considerations, as most possessed no more civil courage than the vast majority of ordinary German citizens." Scholars as well as artists "opted for compliance with the overall policies of the regime, adapting to circumstances in order to preserve their own interests": Huener and Nicosia (eds.), *The Arts in Nazi Germany*, 5.

11. As Mosse perceived, "National Socialism built upon the development of the national cult which had taken place for over a century before the movement was founded. This development is vital for an understanding of the Nazi political style; without it, National Socialism as a mass movement cannot be properly analyzed": Mosse, *Nationalization of the Masses*, 183.

12. In Claudia Koonz's powerful phrase: "The road to Auschwitz was paved with righteousness": Koonz, *The Nazi Conscience*, 2.

13. Adolf Hitler, *Bei der Kulturtagung des Reichsparteitages*.

14. Michaud refers to the *Meistersinger*-based slogan as "an injunction to remember its past and to construct its future on the ideal model of that past": Michaud, *Cult of Art in Nazi Germany*, 86.

15. Hitler, *Bei der Kulturtagung des Reichsparteitages*.

16. Cited in Michaud, *The Cult of Art in Nazi Germany*, 101.

INDEX